Thai Law
for Foreigners
กฎหมายไทยสำหรับชาวต่างชาติ

Benjawan Poomsan Becker
เบญจวรรณ ภูมิแสน เบคเกอร์
and
Roengsak Thongkaew
เริงศักดิ์ ทองแก้ว

Thai Law for Foreigners
กฎหมายไทยสำหรับชาวต่างชาติ

Copyright ©2008 by Paiboon Publishing
info@paiboonpublishing.com
www.paiboonpublishing.com

Printed in Thailand

The information contained in this book may change after publication, and there
may be some minor errors contained within. We advise the reader to verify in
advance the correctness of the data.

This book is not a substitute for advice from a knowledgeable lawyer, doctor,
financial adviser, or other trained professional. Paiboon Publishing and its author
accept no responsibility for any loss, injury, dispute, or inconvenience caused
by using this book.

ISBN 978-1-887521-57-4

Edited by Rich Baker

Cover Design and Typesetting by
Douglas Morton • 72 Studio, Chiang Mai, Thailand

From The Publisher

After receiving so many requests from our readers to provide a practical book that explained Thai law in simple, understandable terms, Paiboon Publishing was determined to publish *Thai Law For Foreigners*. There are few English-language books on Thai law that answer basic legal questions or explain the law in terms that laymen can understand. We have published a number of books on learning the Thai language, Thai-Western relationships, Thai culture, and various other practical aspects of living in Thailand. We publish this book believing it will prove its usefulness many times over to foreign nationals and various organizations that assist foreigners in Thailand.

Please note that the laws related to the subjects presented in this book may change after the publication date. As a result, some of the opinions, conclusions, and ideas presented here may become outdated. Before proceeding in any legal matter, the reader should verify the timely accuracy of the information provided in this book with the relevant authorities, and may very well want to consult with an appropriate professional. Each person's situation and experiences can, and usually will, differ, so you will have to adapt the information provided to your unique set of circumstances and location. Law in general is a difficult and very complicated subject to explain clearly and simply. We are limited in the depth of information we can provide on each topic in this book, so our goal is to provide you with a good overview of each subject. You certainly need to do your own research and exercise due diligence to educate yourself and prepare for any particular legal situation you may be faced with.

This book is for your reference and guidance only and is not a substitute for advice from a knowledgeable lawyer, doctor, financial adviser, or other trained professional. Paiboon Publishing and its authors accept no responsibility for any loss, injury, dispute, or inconvenience directly, indirectly, or consequentially caused by a reader's interpretation of and/or use of any materials or opinions in this book.

We are the publisher of this book providing an overview of Thai law, but we do not answer legal questions or provide legal advice. Please contact a qualified lawyer for any legal advice you may need. There are websites that provide lawyer referrals and others that allow you to post your legal questions. (Please see more information on "Suggested websites" in the Reference section.)

Although we do not provide legal advice and cannot respond to legal questions, we would appreciate your input in helping us to improve this book for the next revision and the second volume. Please send you comments and suggestions to thailaw4u@gmail.com.

We hope you find this book useful and we thank you for your continued support of our publications.

— *The Paiboon Publishing Team*

About This Book

Thai Law For Foreigners has been designed for foreigners visiting, living, and conducting business in Thailand. It is also intended for those foreigners who plan to marry or who are already married to Thai citizens. In addition, this book provides reference material for researchers, law students, lawyers, and other professionals. Although the information provided focuses on the relationship between foreigners and Thai law, it is also a handy general reference guide for Thai people to understand the basics of Thai law.

This book has been written in both English and in Thai. The first half of the book is written in English and the Thai version comprises the second half. Benjawan and Ruengsak wrote parts of the book in Thai and some parts in English, and then the material was translated into both Thai and English. Ruengsak wrote some of the Thai portion and did research on various topics. All of the English sections have been written or translated by Benjawan. Most of the book has been translated into Thai, but a few parts appear only in English. The Thai translation is not a direct or literal translation, but rather, the content has been translated into Thai to provide the overall meaning and intent. Since the book is bilingual, it will also be beneficial to Thais who live outside of Thailand or who may have changed their citizenship. It will be an ideal resource for Thais who interact with foreigners in Thailand. Thai lawyers and business people with foreign clients can benefit significantly from using this book as it provides a basic understanding of Thai law and its impacts on the individual. The book can also serve as an aid to the Thai spouse, or friends of foreign nationals, and assist them in their legal matters, since they will be equipped with the understanding of the law and be able to communicate directly in Thai with the legal staff.

The book was released only a few months after the Thai Constitution of 2007 was promulgated and is based on the laws as they pertain to that document. As the new constitution is implemented, there may be changes to the law as it affects foreigners. Additionally, some parts of the book are based on Thai law as it existed under the Constitution of 1997 as these sections were not changed by the Constitution of 2007. As Thai law evolves under the new constitution, we will reflect those changes in the next edition of the book.

The first part of the book provides an introduction to the Thai legal system and how it developed over time. It starts with the Sukhothai period and continues up to the present, with a brief history of Thailand during each major successive period, along with the resulting changes to the legal system. This initial part also explains the structure of the Thai government, the constitution, and the court system.

The second part focuses on legal procedures in Thailand. It gives practical information for those who currently need to deal with court procedures in both criminal and civil matters. It also includes important subjects such as hiring a lawyer and working with an interpreter.

The third part is particularly useful for people who have families in Thailand or are married to Thai nationals. It discusses numerous aspects of family matters from the dowry and prenuptial agreement to getting married and filing for a divorce. Information on other personal matters such as making a will, adopting children, and Thai citizenship are also explained in this part of the book.

The fourth part of the book includes practical information on living in Thailand. It discusses how the legal system applies to everyday activities. It demystifies ordinary situations such as opening a bank account, getting a driver's license, renting a house, and much more.

The final part comprises a comprehensive reference section. This has information on immigration and visa requirements, and we explain where the most up-to-date information can be found. We have given special attention to sources on the Internet and on Thai government websites. We have included suggestions on finding lawyers, a listing of the various departments of the Thai government, positions of rank for all Thai police, a directory of the law schools in Thailand, a list of all the Thai kings, suggested websites for further research, and much more. We have also included sixteen sample forms, that have been translated into English, for many common legal matters.

In writing this book, we have used various legal volumes and websites for reference. (See the list of reference materials at the end of the book.) There may be some minor discrepancies in numbers, names, or details in the book, since different sources use different descriptions. However, we used the data from the most credible sources we could find. The book presents an overview of Thai law that we believe will be useful to you. We apologize if some information is inconsistent; this will be improved in the next edition.

Now you have in your hands a book on Thai law that is user-friendly, practical, and informative.

Acknowledgements

We are grateful to the many people who have helped make this book possible. Special thanks to:

Colonel Robert S. Chester, USMC (Retired), for his many helpful suggestions and reviews of the draft of the book. His guidance and feedback on the legal issues from a foreigner's perspective have made Thai law more accessible, and this book more useful, to foreign readers.

Dr. Chawalit Nilwong, a legal consultant from Thai Inter Law Company Limited specializing in law for foreigners, who provided guidance and background information on the content of the book.

Richard Barrow from www.thaiprisonlife.com, who gave us stories on an an average day in Thai prison and a foreigner's view of the Thai courts.

Khun Govit Thatarat from www.lawyerthai.com, who has contributed information on the structure of the Thai government.

Venerable Bodhicitta from www.BuddhaNet.net for contributing the article on Buddhist Funeral Rites In Thailand And Southeast Asia.

The Director of Visa and Travel Documents Division, Department of Consular Affairs, Ministry of Foreign Affairs who has given Paiboon Publishing permission to use the information on the Ministry's website in the reference section.

Paiboon Publishing's editing and translating team Khun Salinee Pawaluksanawat, Khun Panlapa Engbunmeesakul and Khun Porntip Prommart.

Our editors Nicholas Terlecky, who organized and polished our rough drafts; our dear lawyer friend, Harry "Hari" J. DePietro, who played a critical role in improving the legal language; and last but not least, a grateful thanks to Rich Baker, our final editor, for his work in making our writing smooth and clear.

— Roengsak and Benjawan

Map Of Thailand

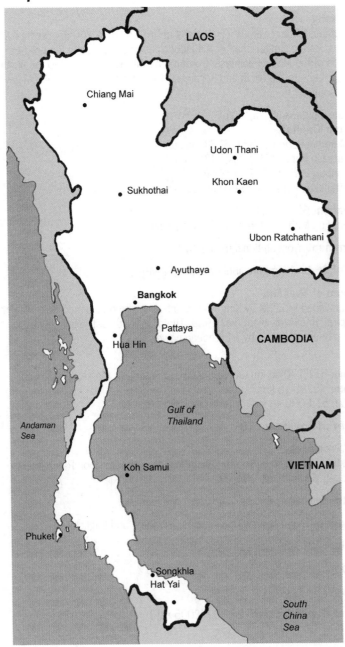

Thailand Facts

Geography-
Southeast Asia. Latitude 15 degrees north; longitude 100 degrees east. It occupies the western half of the Indochinese peninsula and the northern two-thirds of the Malay Peninsula. Bordered by Burma (Myanmar) to the north and west; Laos to the north and northeast; Cambodia to the east; and Malaysia to the south.

Capital- Bangkok (Krung Thep).

The Four Capitals-
Sukhothai Period 1238–1368 (9 kings)
Ayuthaya Period1350–1767 (34 kings)
Thonburi Period 1767– 1782 (one king)
Rattanakosin (Bangkok) Period 1782–present (9 kings)

Population- 65 million (2006).
Bangkok Metropolitan Area- 9—10 million.

Government- Constitutional monarchy.

Head of State- King Bhumibol Adulyadej (1946–).

Kingdom of Thailand-
Established in 1238 by King Khunsri Intrathit who proclaimed Sukhothai the capital. Known as Siam until 1939. The only Southeast Asian country never to have been colonized by a European power.

Area-
Land: 511,770 sq km (about the size of France or the state of Texas).
Water: 2,230 sq km.
Total: 514,000 sq km.

Number of Provinces- 76

Major Provinces-
Nakhon Ratchasima (Korat), Chiang Mai, Khon Kaen, Ubon Ratchathani, Phuket, Udon Thani, Songkhla.

Climate- Tropical monsoon, warm, hot, and humid.

Languages- Thai, regional Thai dialects, hilltribes, and English.

Ethnicity- Thai 75%, Chinese 14%, others 11%

Religion- Buddhist 94%, Muslim 5%, Christian 1%

Currency- Baht; US$1 ≈ 35 Baht

GDP Per Capita Income- $8,300 (2005 est.)

Country's Major Sources of Income-
Export of agricultural products, tourism.

Export Commodities-
Rice, tapioca, rubber, corn, jewelry, sugar cane, coconuts, soybeans, transistors, rubber, plastic, seafood.

Exports-
$105.8 billion (2005 est.): textiles and footwear, fishery products, rice, rubber, jewelry, automobiles, computers and electrical appliances.

Imports-
$107 billion (2005 est.): capital goods, intermediate goods and raw materials, consumer goods, fuel.

Industries-
Tourism, textiles and garments, agricultural processing, beverages, tobacco, cement, light manufacturing (jewelry and electric appliances, computers and parts, integrated circuits, furniture, plastics), automobiles and automotive parts; world's second-largest tungsten producer and third-largest tin producer.

Arable Land- 29%

Natural Resources-
Tin, rubber, natural gas, tungsten, tantalum, timber, lead, gypsum, lignite, fluorite, fish, arable land.

Import Commodities-
Computers, capital goods, intermediate goods and raw materials, consumer goods, fuel.

Labor Force
35.36 million; agriculture 49%, industry 14%, services 37%

Main Export Countries-
US, Japan, Singapore, China, Hong Kong, Malaysia

Main Import Countries-
Japan, US, China, Malaysia, Singapore, Taiwan.

GDP/PPP- $545.8 billion (2005 est.)

Inflation- 4.8%

Unemployment- 1.4% (2005 est.)

Life Expectancy
Male: 69 years
Female: 73 years
Average: 72.2 years.

Infant Mortality Rate- 19.5/1,000

Literacy Rate- 96%

Time- GMT + seven hours.

Difference between BE and AD- 543 years

International Dialing Code- 66

Coastline- 3,219 kilometers.

Electric Current- 220 volts, 50 cycles.

Communications-
Telephones: 6.7 million main lines (2004). Mobile cellular: 27 million (2005). Radio broadcast stations: AM, 204; FM, 334; short-wave, six (1999). Radios: 13.96 million (1997). Television broadcast stations: 111 (2006). Televisions: 15.19 million (1997). Internet hosts: 786,226 (2005). Internet users: 8.5 million (2005).

Transportation-
Railways: 4,071 km (2002). Highways: 64,600 km (paved, 62,985 km; unpaved, 1,615 km). Waterways: 4,000 km principal waterways; 3,701 km with navigable depths of 0.9 m or more throughout the year; numerous minor waterways navigable by shallow-draft native craft. Ports and harbors: Bangkok, Laem Chabang, Pattani, Phuket, Sattahip, Si Racha, Songkhla. Airports: 111 (2002).

Contents

Part 2 Legal Procedures

Part 3 Personal and Family Matters

Part 4 Living In Thailand

Part 5 Reference

Part 1
History, Government Structure, and Judicial System of Thailand

History Of Thailand And Background Of Thai Law

A brief history of Thailand will give you a good background of both the formation of the country and how its system of law developed. This includes a general history of Thailand, as well as a description of the legal system as it developed during each period of Thailand's history.

Thailand was known as Siam until 1939. The name Thailand literally means "Land of the Free." It is also affectionately referred to as the "Land of Smiles." It is the only Southeast Asian country that was never colonized by a European power. On June 24, 1932, the "People's Party" (*Khana Raat*), led a bloodless 'revolution' that transformed the country from an absolute monarchy to a constitutional monarchy. The king is regarded as the head of the state, and Thailand has a checks and balance system similar to that of Western countries.

The origin of the Thai people is not clearly known but ethnologists have many theories. One possibility is that they came from southern China and migrated to the Chao Phraya lowlands, which were then ruled by the Khmer empire.

We will start our history of Thailand during the Sukhothai period.

The Sukhothai Period (1238—1376)

The Thai leader who drove the Khmers out of Sukhothai in central Thailand was Pho Khun Sri Intharathit, who is regarded as the first king of the Thai nation. He proclaimed the city of Sukhothai as his capital. It was established in the year 1238 and is considered the first official capital of the country. The Sukhothai kingdom extended from Lampang and Vientiane in the north to Nakhon Si Thammarat in the south. During this period, Sukhothai had extensive trade and cultural relations with China.

King Ramkamhaeng the Great was the third, and the most well known, king of this period. He invented the Thai alphabet in 1283 and was well loved by his people. Thus, he became the first of the "Great" kings of Thailand.

The system of government at the time is described as "father governs children." The people brought their civil disputes directly to the king. These matters included any disagreement or quarrel they could not solve among themselves. There was a bell in front of the palace that could be rung to give notice that justice or advice was sought. The king would examine the petition, meet directly with the parties involved, and make a judgment. If the king was not available, his representative would render judgment on his behalf. This approach was possible due to the small population and nature of the society. The relationship between the people and their king was a close one. During this period, the country was blessed with an abundance of natural resources. This is best described by the old Thai saying from the time, "In the river, there are fish. In the field, there is rice."

Sukhothai was an independent kingdom until 1376, when it was overpowered by the nearby kingdom of Ayutthaya, which made a colony of Sukhothai. The Sukhothai Period had one dynasty (the Phraruang Dynasty) which had nine kings. Its monarchs still reigned in Sukhothai while it was a vassal state of Ayutthaya. But in 1438 Sukhothai was completely absorbed by its new master. The last monarch of Sukhothai was King Phra Maha Thammaracha IV.

The Ayutthaya Period (1350—1767)

The Ayutthaya period was established in 1350 by its first king, Phra Chao U-thong. During this period, a Khmer-style of government emerged, which replaced the paternalistic "father governs children" style of rule. In the new reign, the king was viewed as god-like and held absolute power and unquestioned authority to directly and personally control all aspects of the country's administration and the peoples' lives.

There were major changes in the Thai language and the various royal ceremonies. The Thai population grew, and with more people there were more problems. Lifestyles had changed dramatically from those of the Sukhothai era. There were more political, economic, and social conflicts. Therefore, new laws and more complicated legal processes emerged.

During the Ayutthaya period, a feudal system called *sakdina* was established. This system was considerably different from the feudalism of Europe. Under *sakdina* a 'status' was assigned to each person according to particular criteria. This system was used to assign power and responsibility to each individual. Correspondingly, it was used to determine the fine or punishment accessed in a court judgment; the higher the person's rank, the more their responsibility, therefore the more severe punishment they should be subjected to.

Sakdina, or individual personal status, was stated in terms of units of land measured in *rai* (one *rai* being the equivalent of 1,600 square meters). This personal status did not necessarily reflect that a person actually owned a particular amount of land – this measurement merely indicated a person's status as expressed in a value commonly appreciated by the population. We can classify the social ranks as follows:

1. The king held the highest rank and the greatest power. He was treated as a "divine" being.

2. The royal family members acquired their status by birth and could be regarded as higher or lower depending on their contribution to the country. Their *sakdina* would range from 15,000 *rai* up to 100,000 *rai*.

3. The lords and the government officials received their authority to govern the common people from the king. For lords, the *sakdina* was from 400 up to 10,000 *rai*. For government officials, the *sakdina* could be between 25 and 400 *rai*. Government officials never became lords. Government officials and lords retained their status only as long as they lived. Their status could not be inherited by their children. They could be promoted or demoted according to their performance.

4. The common people (*prai*) comprised the majority of society and were assigned the rank of 25 *rai*. Their status could also be changed up or down from as high as that of a lord to as low as that of a slave. Their duty was to serve the king and country. It was mandated that all men registered with a lord. Men with the minimum height of two and a half *sawks* (1 *sawk* is 0.5 meters) were allowed to enlist with a lord of their choice. If a man failed to register with a lord, he would have no rights in court and no legal protection. There were two kinds of *prai*: *prai-luang* and *prai-som*.

   Prai-luang, or "royal commoners," were the king's soldiers. They belonged to various departments. They could serve the king by working or by sending tribute in place of their labor. Tribute could be either tangible assets or money, and was collectively called "official money." Those who chose to serve the king would be on duty six months of the year. They served every other month.

   Prai-som, "or lord-serving commoners," were common people assigned by the king to the lords or the government officials as part of the lords' or officials' benefits. This type of commoner would stay with a lord as long as he was serving the country. After the lord died, they would be transferred to *prai-luang* status, except if the son of that lord (who also was a lord) was permitted by the king to keep those commoners in his service.

5. Slaves were naturally at the lowest level of society with five *rai* given as their rank. Slaves had no rights to determine how they spent their time

or what they did with their labour. They were traded like merchandise. A slave could become a commoner if liberated. There were seven classified types of slaves depending upon the method or reason for their indenture: slaves that were captured from a war; slaves that could not pay off their debts; slaves that were inherited from one's parents; slaves that sold themselves because of destitution or poverty; slaves that were born while their parents were slaves; slaves that were offered as gifts; slaves that were saved from being punished.

6. Monks did not belong to any of the standard social ranks because they had a special status in society. Their duty was to conserve and promote Buddhism. Monkhood was a respected position. Many men used this as a tool to change their status. Any man could become a monk whether he was of royal blood, a lord, a commoner, or a slave. When a man became a monk, he would have the opportunity to become a learned person. Monks had connections with all ranks of society.

The *sakdina* system is deeply ingrained in Thai society. It continues to exist in various forms to the present day. The workings of Thailand's class society are very subtle and it is sometimes difficult for foreigners to fully appreciate the ways Thais interact with each other according to their relative status. Learning Thai history can help you appreciate why Thai people act in certain ways. For example, a Thai may ask you how old you are or how much money you make. Don't be offended, since they are only trying to determine your social ranking and how they must relate to your relative position in their society.

Nowadays, social classes are determined according to the family root (whether royal, famous, high or common), the amount of money you have (the main criteria now), education (the higher, the more respected even with less money), being a monk (special social status, which is automatically high), age (the older you are, the higher your status is), career (certain careers such as the civil service are more prestigious than, say, being a restaurant owner).

In Thai society, people with higher social status are expected to carry out certain obligations, such as paying the bill in a restaurant, which is both a duty and an honor. According to Thai thought, a foreigner – because he can afford to travel to Thailand – is usually considered as being wealthy. Correspondingly, he will occupy a high social status. Therefore, as a "rich" foreigner, he'll be expected to pay for things when interacting with most Thais.

This may mean you will be charged more when you hire a lawyer, since your high status presumes your ability to pay more. This belief however, is not necessarily held by most sophisticated Thais, or by Thais who have traveled outside of Thailand. You will also have to accept the fact that you will always be a foreigner in Thailand – even if you've lived in Thailand a long time, can speak Thai fluently, and have been granted Thai citizenship.

The following is a brief introduction to the legal systems in place during the Ayutthaya period:

The court system was established early in the period. The king himself would receive the petition or complaint. If the king did not sit in judgment himself, an investigator or a judge would be designated to hold an inquiry between the disputing parties. Section 20 of the Public Prosecution Act of the Ayutthaya period provides that "it is necessary to have a representative to defend one in a criminal matter." We can conclude therefore, that the lawyer system started during this period. People with 400 *rai* or more in rank could have a representative in court because they were regarded as high ranking. It would amount to a loss of face and would be inappropriate to be in a situation in which they were directly interrogated. At times, an investigation included yelling and scolding. To save face, a representative would go to court and be subjected to the trial. However, representatives did not question or cross-examine witnesses as they do today. The judge would allow family members or close relatives to represent defendants. For example, a father might represent a son, or a wife might represent her husband. Representatives did not need to know the law, but they needed to know the facts of what had happened in the case. Representatives were allowed in most cases except the following circumstances in which the defendants would have to go to court to defend themselves: a doctor accused of causing death to a patient, robbery, murder, adultery, estate matters, theft, embezzlement of government assets, arson, fraud involving money, removing gold leaf from Buddha statues, and cases of children suing their parents.

There were many wars and many international interactions during the Ayutthaya period. Siam traded and communicated with many foreign countries including China, Japan, Portugal, Spain, Holland, England, France, and many Arab countries.

The capital of Ayutthaya was conquered by the Burmese on two occassions. The first was in 1569 during the reign of King Phra Mahintharathirat. At that time, the Thais lost their capital primarily due to their lack of unity. The country became a vassal state of Burma for fifteen years until King Phra Naresuan the Great defeated the Burmese and declared independence in 1584.

Ayutthaya lost its capital city for the second time in 1767 during the reign of King Phra Chao Ekkathat. This loss resulted in the complete destruction of Ayutthaya. Virtually everything of value was burned including the palace, religious artifacts, works of art, buildings, temples and monasteries. Everything was either looted or destroyed by the Burmese. Almost nothing of the Thai capital remained.

Ayutthaya was the Thai capital for 417 years and saw the reign of 33 kings of five dynasties from 1350—1767 as follows:

1. The Ou Thong Dynasty, which consists of three kings.

2. The Suphanabhumi Dynasty, of thirteen kings.

3. The Sukhothai Dynasty, of seven kings.

4. The Prasart Thong Dynasty, of four kings.

5. The Baan Phluluang Dynasty, of six kings.

The Thonburi Period (1767—1782)

The Thonburi Period lasted for only fifteen years, from 1767 to1782. King Taksin the Great was the only king during this period. He was the Thai military commander-in-chief who liberated the country from Burma only seven months after Ayutthaya was destroyed, then declared himself king.

King Taksin realized that Ayutthaya was too devastated to be rebuilt. Even if it could have been rebuilt, his army was insufficiently strong to protect it from further attack. King Taksin chose instead to build a new capital city in Thonburi, on the west bank of the Chao Phraya River, in what is now a part of modern-day Bangkok. This was a more strategic location than Ayutthaya because it was closer to the sea.

This was a period of constant warfare as Thailand fought to regain territory lost after the destruction of Ayutthaya.

But King Taksin was able to reunite the country and Siam became prosperous again in a relatively short time. The new capital was the center of the kingdom both economically and politically, but the Ayutthayan legal system continued to be used during the period.

After King Taksin's reign ended, the capital was moved to present-day Bangkok on the east bank of the Chao Phraya River.

The Rattanakosin (Bangkok) Period (1782-present)

The Rattanakosin Period, also known as the Bangkok Period, began in 1782 when Bangkok was established as the Thai capital by King Yodfa Chulaloke (King Rama I the Great of the Chakri Dynasty). The new capital, across the river from Thonburi, was in a more defensible position because the Chao Phraya River bordered it on three sides.

To date, the Chakri Dynasty has had nine kings. For ease of identification we refer to them as King Rama I-IX respectively. King Bhumibol Adulyadej the Great (or King Rama IX) is the ninth and present king of this dynasty. (See the list of all Thai kings in the reference section.)

The court system of the Ayutthaya period was carried over to the beginning of the Bangkok period.

Beginning with the reign of King Rama III, Thailand interacted with many foreign countries for trade and other official matters. The king gave power to the head of each official department, who was also a member of the royal family. However, the legal system was disorganized. There were no formal, consistent standards for the court process.

During this time, European nations were intent on extending their colonial possessions into Southeast Asia. Many Westerners came to do business in Thailand and there were numerous disputes between Thais and foreigners. The Thais were at a disadvantage because the Europeans refused to be tried in Thai courts. Westerners complained that there were no standards and that the Thai legal system was slow and complicated. Westerners further complained that the punishment administered by Thai courts was cruel and old fashioned.

Thailand soon adopted an Indian concept, *jarit nakhonbaan*, or trial by ordeal, to prove facts or the truth in criminal cases. *Jarit nakhonbaan* literally means "to torture the suspect until he confesses." The methods used included squeezing the head, hammering on the fingernails, and whipping the back. There were ways to prove one's innocence such as surviving being held under water for a long time or walking across burning charcoal. It was said that if the person was innocent, he would then be protected by a divinity. Since the Europeans (mainly the French and British) refused to be tried in the Thai courts, they established their own courts in Thailand.

Although Thailand has never been subjugated by any European power, maintaining the sovereignty of the kingdom was costly. Along with other compromises, Thailand was forced to concede territory to France and England. To preserve the country's independence, the Thai kings (King Rama IV and V) negotiated land concessions to appease the colonialists. At the beginning of the Bangkok period, the surface area of Thailand was 1,296,877 square kilometers. Land area was relinquished fourteen times – four times to England, six times to France, twice to Burma, once to Vietnam and once to Cambodia. At present, the area of Thailand is only 513,115 square kilometers. Altogether, the country lost 783,762 square kilometers.

The reign of King Rama V (also known as King Chulalongkorn) was one of the most significant in Thai history. King Rama V traveled extensively throughout the kingdom to personally investigate and understand his subjects' conditions and aspirations. He instituted many social and political changes and is considered one of the seven great kings in Thai history.

In 1873, Chulalongkorn abolished the requirement of prostration in front of the monarch, and in 1905 he put an end to slavery. The abolition of slavery was his most important contribution to the country.

King Chulalongkorn visited many foreign countries, making two grand tours to Europe, as well as journeys to Singapore, Indonesia, and India. Based partly on what he saw and learned while traveling, the king drastically changed Thailand. He upgraded the country's administrative system by establishing government ministries, and developed infrastructure such as public schools for common people, the railway system, the post office, the telegraph, hospitals, and more.

In addition to restructuring the government and modernizing Thailand's infrastructure, King Rama V also revolutionized the Thai legal system. In 1881 he proclaimed that every Thai could have a lawyer to represent them in court without condition, and in 1888 he abolished trial by ordeal in the Thai justice system.

The King sent his fourteenth son, Phra Ong Jao Rapee Pattanasak (known as Than-Rapee), to study law in England. (Than-Rapee is regarded as the father of Thai law. He died on August 7, 1920 and the Thai legal circle honors him every year on Rapee Day on that date.) In 1897, using the Ministry of Justice building, Than-Rapee established the first law school in Thailand. Thailand lacked people knowledgeable in law, and Than-Rapee personally selected the first law students and trained them himself.

At the end of 1897, for the first time in Thailand, a graduating exam for law students was given. The new Thai legal system was accepted internationally and the courts set up by the colonial powers were eliminated.

King Chulalongkorn's death on October 23, 1910 at the age of 58 was a great loss to the Thai people. He had reigned for 42 years. Every year, Thais honor this great king on "Chulalongkorn Day," the anniversary of his death, which is a national holiday. Thais from all walks of life lay wreaths at his equestrian statue at the Royal Plaza in Bangkok and at numerous statues of him in the provinces. Along with the pictures of the present King and Queen, you can see the image of King Rama V everywhere in Thailand – in houses, businesses, and on gold neck chains. He is called "Phra Piya Maharat," which means "The Great Beloved King," and many Thais believe in his ability to bring good luck and prosperity to whoever pays respect to him.

The next major reform of the legal system was made during the reign of King Rama VI, or King Vajiravudh, who decided to make Thai law consistent with other countries' legal systems. The Thai Legal Studies Council was founded during this time, as was Chulalongkorn University in 1916, the first university in Thailand.

At that time, the legal system and the law in Thai courts was based on what had been taught by Than-Rapee. This was the common law system, which Than-Rapee learned in England and which draws abstract rules from specific cases. King Rama VI decided that common law was no longer appropriate, and the legal system was changed from common law to code law in 1924. Code law, used in the majority of countries, begins with abstract rules which judges then apply to the various cases before them. The code law system has been taught in Thailand's law schools ever since.

In June 1932, during the reign of King Rama VII, a group of young intellectuals who had been educated abroad and were inspired by concepts of Western democracy, led a 'revolution' to abolish the absolute monarchy and change the kingdom into a democracy. Their movement was known as the "People's Party," or "Khana Raat," and it was led by Luang Pradit Manudharm (Pridi Panomyong). To avoid bloodshed, King Rama VII graciously agreed to end the absolute monarchy and accepted the country's first constitution. In fact, just before the 'revolution' started, the king had already made plans to turn his powers over to the people. Thailand is now a constitutional monarchy and the king serves as a ceremonial head of state. (See "The Constitution of the Kingdom of Thailand.")

The Legal Studies Council established during the reign of King Rama VI was merged with the first law school. The Faculty of Law and Politics was added to Chulalongkorn University in 1933. This faculty was then absorbed by Thammasart University.

Chulalongkorn University re-established its Faculty of Law in 1951. These two universities are prominent for their legal teachings. The largest open university in Thailand, Ramkhamhaeng University, which was established in 1971, is also well known for graduating legal professionals. At present, a faculty of law is included in many undergraduate schools in Thailand. See the list of Thailand's Faculties of Law in the reference section.

Thailand's current king, Rama IX, or King Bhumibol Adulyadej, is the world's longest reigning monarch. During his reign there have been many military coups, and new or revised charters and constitutions. Many of these occurrences have had their effect on the changing face of Thai law. In the next chapter, the present structure of the Thai government, the kingdom's constitution, and its court system will be described.

The Structure Of The Thai Government

The Constitution Of The Kingdom Of Thailand

The constitution of Thailand is the supreme law governing the kingdom. Over the years, Thailand has suffered political instability and numerous coups. After a successful coup, the military regime often abrogates the existing constitution and promulgates new laws. The constitution of Thailand has been changed and modified many times to make it reflect the changes in society. However, all the constitutions include the same important element – that the king is the head of the constitutional monarchy.

Constitution Day falls on December 10 and is a national holiday. On that day in 1932, King Rama VII relinquished his absolute powers and the first permanent constitution of the kingdom was established.

Since the system of governing the country changed in 1932, Thailand has had eighteen charters and constitutions:

1. Temporary Charter for the Administration of Siam Act 1932

2. The Constitution of the Siam Kingdom 1932

3. The Constitution of the Kingdom of Thailand 1946

4. The Constitution of the Kingdom of Thailand (Temporary) 1947

5. The Constitution of the Kingdom of Thailand 1949

6. The Constitution of the Kingdom of Thailand 1932 (Revised 1952)

7. Charter for the Administration of the Kingdom 1959

8. Constitution of the Kingdom of Thailand 1968

9. Temporary Charter for Administration of the Kingdom 1972

10. Constitution for Administration of the Kingdom 1974

11. Constitution for Administration of the Kingdom 1976

12. Charter for Administration of the Kingdom 1977

13. Constitution of the Kingdom of Thailand 1978

14. Charter for Administration of the Kingdom 1991

15. The Constitution of the Kingdom of Thailand 1991

16. The Constitution of the Kingdom of Thailand 1997

17. The Constitution of the Kingdom of Thailand (Interim) 2006

18. The Constitution of the Kingdom of Thailand 2007

Every new Thai constitution has recognized the king as the head of state, commander-in-chief and "Upholder of all Religions." He enjoys the highest status, which no one may hold in contempt. His symbolic power comes from the people of Thailand and is exercised through the three branches of government: the executive, the legislature, and the judiciary. There are five entities that have the power to enact Thai law.

The king, whose royal command symbolically results in law. He has little direct power under the constitution but is a symbol of national identity and unity. However, he has the power to approve or disapprove bills adopted by the Parliament. Bills do not become effective as laws without the approval of the king, unless later re-approved by the Parliament.

The party of a coup d'etat or revolution. These groups use force or threat of force to change the government. Their announcements are effective as law, as with the declaration of marshal law. The first coup d'etat was in 1932. Most of the coups in Thailand have been led by the military.

The parliament (or the National Assembly). Its main duty is to approve new laws. Parliament consists of the members of the House of Parliament and the Senate. Under the 2007 Constitution, there are 150 senators and 400 members of the House of Representatives.

The National Legislative Assembly. According to the Constitution of 1991, its duty is to draft the constitution.

The prime minister and the Cabinet ministers. Their duty is to propose new laws to parliament for review. Under the 2007 Constitution, there is one prime minister and no more than 35 Cabinet ministers. The prime minister needs to receive more than half of the votes from the members of parliament for election and may not hold office for more than eight years consecutively.

Under the 2007 Constitution, the Thai government is a 'checks and balance' form of government, much like seen in many Western countries. It consists of the executive, legislature, and judiciary.

The Executive Branch

The executive branch of the government is headed by the prime minister. It consists of the prime minister, the ministers of the various ministries, deputy ministers, and the permanent officials of the various ministries. The Prime Minister is selected by the House of Representatives, with the President of the House of Representatives submitting a recommendation to the King for appointment. Usually the person recommended for appointment as the Prime Minister is the leader of the political party having the largest number of elected members of parliament. Sometimes, however, a coalition government may be formed, in which a number of political parties collectively join together to represent a majority of the members of the House of Representatives. If such a coalition government is formed, the coalition may choose their own person as prime minister, and the president of the House of Representatives would then usually submit the name of the coalition's suggested prime minister to the king. The prime minister must be a member of the House of Representatives. After the recommendation of the president of the House of Representatives is submitted to the king, the king appoints the prime minister.

The Prime Minister is the head of government. He is responsible for the administration of government agencies except the courts and the legislative body. The prime minister selects the people, usually members of the House of Representatives, whom he wants appointed as ministers or deputy ministers to head each ministry of the government.

When a coalition is formed of various political parties, each party traditionally seeks a representative portion of ministerial and deputy ministerial appointees from that party's membership. Upon recommendation by the prime minister, the king reviews and appoints the ministers and deputy ministers. Under the 2007 constitution, the king will appoint the prime minister and up to 35 other ministers.

Once the prime minister and other ministers and deputy ministers are appointed, they must relinquish their position as a member of the House of Representatives, since they cannot be a member of the House and a minister simultaneously.

The prime minister and the other ministers (ministers and deputy ministers) collectively make up a body known as the Council of Ministers. The Council of Ministers, sometimes referred to as the Cabinet, administers the government and all of its activities, except those of the parliament and the courts. It sets governmental policy and goals, and the individual ministers and deputy ministers carry out those policies and goals within their own designated ministries.

Each ministry of the government has a minister as its leader. There are twenty ministries in Thailand as follows:

- Office of the Prime Minister
- Ministry of Defense
- Ministry of Finance
- Ministry of Foreign Affairs
- Ministry of Tourism and Sports
- Ministry of Social Development and Human Security
- Ministry of Agriculture and Cooperatives
- Ministry of Transport
- Ministry of Natural Resources and Environment
- Ministry of Information and Communication Technology
- Ministry of Energy
- Ministry of Commerce
- Ministry of the Interior
- Ministry of Justice
- Ministry of Labor
- Ministry of Culture
- Ministry of Science and Technology
- Ministry of Education
- Ministry of Public Health
- Ministry of Industry

In the Reference section we provide additional information regarding the various government agencies that belong to each of the twenty ministries, public enterprises that are governed under each ministry, plus information on public organizations, independent agencies, and other public agencies. We show where each agency or organization is positioned within the government structure. For example, the Department of Consular Affairs is under the Ministry of Foreign Affairs, the Royal

Thai Army is under the Ministry of Defense, and the National Intelligence Agency is under the Office of the Prime Minister.

The Legislative Branch

The Legislative Branch is the law-making section of the government, charged with the primary responsibility of promulgating and approving new laws that govern society. The full legal name of the legislative branch of government is the National Assembly, and it is also known as parliament. The National Assembly consists of the two legislative bodies, each with its own responsibilities. These bodies are the House of Representatives and the Senate.

The House of Representatives, or the 'lower house' of parliament, consists of 400 members, of which 320 are directly elected from constituencies and eighty are selected from party lists with selection determined by the percentage of votes each of the major parties received in the elections.

In Thailand, eligible voters must be at least eighteen years old, be registered in their household (residence registration) for a minimum of ninety days, and must be a Thai citizen. (Those who have changed their citizenship to Thai, must have held that status for a minimum of five years.) During an election, a voter will cast one vote for a candidate for the House of Representatives and another vote for the party of choice.

When the Senate is elected, each voter will cast one vote for the person he wants to see elected as a senator from the senatorial constituency in which the voter lives.

The Senate, or the 'upper house' of parliament, under the 2007 Constitution, consists of 150 members elected from the 76 provincial constituencies, but without any political party affiliation. In those provinces where the number of residents entitles the province to more than one elected senator (based on population), the voters in that province may still only make one selection for senator. In those provinces entitled to two or more senators, the candidate with the second highest number of votes will also be elected as a senator. Senators elected under the 2007 Constitution will serve for a term of six years.

The House of Representatives is the first legislative branch to consider most of the proposed legislation submitted by the Cabinet (prime minister, ministers and deputy ministers) or by a member of parliament. If the House approves a proposed bill, it is sent to the Senate for consideration. If the Senate approves the bill as submitted, and each house approves the bill on the third review, the bill will be submitted to the prime minister for forwarding to the king for his approval. (Each bill must be reviewed and approved on three separate occasions by both the House and Senate before being sent to the king for his approval.) If the Senate does not agree to the bill as proposed by the House of Representatives, it may amend the bill and return it, as amended, to the House of Representatives for consideration. If the House does not agree with the amendment, the two bodies appoint a committee to try to resolve their differences.

The Judicial Branch

The judicial branch is headed by the president of the Supreme Court. The judicial branch of the government consists of all the courts of Thailand. The courts are independent bodies, and also serve as a check and balance against both the executive and legislative branches of government.

The judiciary hears cases involving actual conflicts between individuals, between individuals and businesses, or between individuals or businesses and the government, and decides each case on its own merits. When a law applies to a case under consideration, the court will apply the terms of the law, but if it believes the law may be contrary to the Constitution, it has a duty to refer the case to the Constitutional Court for a determination of whether there is such a conflict.

Other than in cases of conflict with the Constitution, the courts determine the facts of the case, apply the laws as enacted to the facts, and then enter a ruling on the case. The appropriate courts also review executive actions of the government, how the executive branch carries out its functions, and can render judgments against the governmental bodies in appropriate cases.

The following is an overview of the court system. (See "Thai Court System" for a thorough explanation of the court system.)

The courts of Thailand consist of trial courts (courts of the first instance), appellate courts, and the Supreme Court. In addition, under the provisions of the 2007 Constitution, a new Constitutional Court has been established to rule on the validity of laws, regulations, and governmental decisions. The Constitutional Court also considers the applicability of a law, and whether it is applied in a manner consistent with the Constitution.

The trial courts (courts of the first instance) consist of the district courts and provincial courts, plus the central courts (Central Criminal Court and Central Civil Court located in Bangkok), labor courts, family and juvenile courts, tax courts, and the recently established International Trade and Intellectual Property Court.

Appellate courts are authorized to consider appeals from most trial courts, and the Supreme Court considers cases appealed from the appellate courts as well as from other courts from which an appeal may be taken directly to it (such as Labor Court decisions) without having to first be considered by the appellate courts. For most cases, the decision of the Supreme Court is the final authority and the decision, when announced, is not subject to further appeal or review.

The Constitutional Court was established under the provisions of the 2007 Constitution. The decisions of the Constitutional Court are deemed final and binding on the National Assembly, Council of Ministers, courts, and other State organizations. There is no appeal from the decisions of the Constitutional Court, and its rulings are absolutely final.

The scope of the Constitutional Court's powers is very broad. It decides on the legality of any law which is being considered or has been adopted by the National Assembly. The court has the power to decide whether the law complies with or is in any way contrary to the Constitution, and has the power to declare the law void, or to declare any part of the law void and unenforceable.

Judges in Thailand are highly revered and hold a high status because they work under the name of the king. They must have good ethics, be honest, have a good personal background, and have achieved a high level of education. To become a judge one has to pass a special exam besides passing the bar exam.

There are additional requirements and experience needed to become a judge. The following are some of the qualifications that would satisfy the additional requirements that judges would need to possess: being a graduate with a law degree from a law school inside or outside of Thailand; having worked in court as a court officer for a number of years, depending on the position; experience as a lawyer for at least ten years; holding an honors degree or a position as a lecturer or professor within a law faculty for at least five years.

The Balance Of Powers

Each of the three branches of government (executive, legislature, and judiciary) has a degree of control over the actions of the other branches. The power of each branch of government to have authority to place limits upon actions of the other is known as the system of checks and balances.

The executive, through the power of preparing the budget, has a degree of control over the functions of the judicial courts, such as the number of employees the courts may afford to pay. The executive also has control over legislation passed by the parliament, in that all bills must be submitted to the king through the prime minister, and if the prime minister is opposed to a particular bill, he can express those feelings to the king, who may decline to approve it in the form in which it is submitted to him. The executive also exerts extensive control over the government, as it is tasked with the execution and enforcement of those laws passed by the parliament and approve by the king.

The legislative branch can approve, amend, or reject proposed laws, and it gives thorough review to the budget submitted to it by the executive. It can make changes to the budget within limitations specified in the Constitution.

The courts have a degree of control over legislation approved by the parliament by interpreting the law and, in the case of the Constitutional Court, in determining whether the law is consistent with the 2007 Constitution. Any law found to be inconsistent with the Constitution by the Constitutional Court is rendered ineffective and cannot be followed. The courts also review governmental actions and can require changes or reconsideration in appropriate cases, such as environmental reviews.

The Thai Court System

Under the 2007 constitution, the court system of Thailand consists of four distinct courts which function in the name of His Majesty the King.

1. The Constitutional Court

2. The Administrative Courts

3. The Military Courts

4. The Courts of Justice

We will explain the first three courts briefly, since most foreigners will likely be dealing with the courts of justice, which will be explained in more detail.

The Constitutional Court

The Constitutional Court consists of one president and eight judges who are appointed by the king under the recommendation of the Senate. They are government judicial officials who may serve one nine-year term on the Constitutional Court.

The Constitutional Court has been established to rule on the validity of laws, regulations, and governmental decisions under the provisions of the 2007 Constitution. The court also considers the applicability of laws as applied, and whether they are applied in a manner consistent with the Constitution. It has a very broad scope of power. It has the power to declare a law void, or to declare any part of a law void and unenforceable.

The Administrative Courts

Administrative courts review how the government administers the law, and examine governmental policies. They have the power to try disputes between government agencies, state enterprises, local administrative organizations, or among government officials.

There are three levels of administrative courts: lower, appeals, and the higher courts. The number of judges for each level is assigned by the Administrative Court Judge Committee. The committee consists of the president of the higher court, a committee of nine qualified judges selected by other judges of this court, and two qualified committees who are selected by the Senate and one selected by the Council of Ministers. The president of the higher court is selected and approved by the Administrative Judge Committee and the Senate. The recommendation is then forwarded to the prime minister to present to the king for appointment.

The Military Courts

Military courts, for the most part, conduct criminal trials and sometimes hear other cases involving military officials who fall under the jurisdiction of military courts. The king gives the authority to the chief military commander and to the Interior minister to appoint or remove military judges. Military courts have independent power in their trials and other courts may not interfere with their procedures.

There are three levels of military courts – lower, middle, and higher – comparable to the civilian court system, which is called lower, appeals, and Supreme Court respectively. In case of "unusual circumstances," such as during a war or when martial law is enforced, there is only one court in the military court system.

The Courts of Justice

Courts of justice conduct all cases that make it to court, except for the types of cases that are handled by the three courts mentioned above.

Thailand has no jury system. In most cases, two judges decide on verdicts of guilty or innocent, liable or not. For cases that are not complicated, or with minimal penalty, only one judge presides. For cases that are complex, or with heavy penalties, there are three judges.

Courts of justice in Thailand consist of three levels: courts of first instance, and two higher courts which are the courts of appeals and the Supreme Court. Under the 2007 Constitution, the courts of first instance (lower court) consist of the following nine courts: municipal courts, provincial courts, civil courts, criminal courts, labor courts, tax courts, bankruptcy courts, juvenile and family courts, and the Intellectual Property and International Trade Court. The chart on the following page shows an overview of the court system in Thailand.

The Courts Of First Instance

The courts of first instance (lower courts, and also called trial courts) process cases in the initial or primary level for civil, criminal, and other specialized cases. The following courts of first instance are located in Bangkok.

- Civil Court
- Criminal Court
- South Bangkok Civil Court
- South Bangkok Criminal Court
- Thonburi Civil Court
- Thonburi Criminal Court
- Municipal Courts (District Courts) located in Bangkok
- Minburi Provincial Court
- Central Juvenile and Family Court
- Central Tax Court
- Labor Court
- Central International Trade and Intellectual Property Court
- Central Bankruptcy Court

Courts Of Justice In Thailand

Constitutional Court	— Constitutional Court	

| Administrative Court | — Supreme Administrative Court | |
| | — Lower Administrative Court | |

Military Court	— Higher Military Court	
	— Middle Military Court	
	— Lower Military Court	

| Courts of Justice | — Higher Court | — Supreme Court |
| | | — Courts of Appeal |

	— Lower Court	— Court of First Instance
		— Municipal Court
		— Provincial Court
		— Civil Court
		— Criminal Court
		— Labor Court
		— Tax Court
		— Bankruptcy Court
		— Juvenile and Family Court
		— Intellectual Property and International Trade Court

Courts in other provinces are general courts, which are provincial courts, municipal courts, and central juvenile and family courts. They are divided up by territorial jurisdiction.

The civil court administers cases involving conflicts between people or institutions such as businesses or corporations. The criminal court considers lawsuits brought by a prosecutor employed by the government that charges a person with the commission of a crime. The juvenile and family court has jurisdiction in criminal cases of children between seven and eighteen years of age. Children under seven years old are not considered punishable under Thai law. There is no imprisonment of children under fourteen years old. Juvenile and family courts need two professional judges and two lay judges for a trial, and at least one of the judges must be female. The court also dispenses judgments in family matters such as divorce and child support cases.

The following four courts are considered specialized courts:

The tax court hears customs duty and tax disputes. The labor court handles complaints regarding labor and employment. The International Trade and Intellectual Property Court was established to consider disputes such as trademark and copyright infringements. The bankruptcy court review cases submitted by debtors or creditors.

Court officers in courts of first instance are divided into two categories:

Judicial officers and administrative officers. In a large courthouse in Bangkok, a "chief judge" wields the most power in court. In other smaller courts in Bangkok and in the provinces, the "head judge" is the highest judicial rank.

Judges, prosecutors, and other attorneys must pass a bar exam for these positions and hold qualifications as defined by the law. The king appoints or removes them from their positions. Judges and prosecutors in the courts of justice can remain in office until the age of seventy.

The Courts Of Appeal

Courts of appeal consider appeals from the courts of first instance. When a party does not agree with the judgment or court order in the lower court, he can appeal it to a court of appeals. In a civil case, either party may appeal to a higher court. In a criminal case, only the defendant has the right to an appeal.

The procedures of the appeals courts are more like reviews rather than re-trials. There are no trials in court with the judge at the bench, and no witnesses. At least three judges are required to hear an appeal. The judges will go over the details of the initial case and determine if there were any unfair factors or discrepancies in the proceedings. If the court of appeals affirms the lower court's judgment, the case ends, unless the losing party appeals to the Supreme Court. If the judgment is reversed, usually the appellate court will send the case back to a lower court and order the lower court to take further action.

The appeals court can require various actions to take place. It may order that a new trial be held; the trial court's judgment be modified or corrected; or the trial court reconsider the facts, take additional evidence, or consider the case in light of a recent decision by the appellate court.

There are ten courts of appeal and all of them are located in Bangkok. One court hears appeal cases from the courts of first instance that are located in Bangkok. The remaining courts hear appeals from the provincial courts. They are called Court of Appeals Region 1 to Region 9. Each regional court has jurisdiction for a specific number of provinces:

Region 1 has jurisdiction in Chai Nat, Nonthaburi, Pathum Thani, Ayutthaya, Lop Buri, Samut Prakan, Saraburi, Singburi, and Ang Thong.

Region 2 has jurisdiction in Chanthaburi, Chachoengsao, Chon Buri, Trat, Nakhon Nayok, Prachin Buri, Rayong, and Sa Kaeo.

Region 3 has jurisdiction in Chaiyaphum, Nakhon Ratchasima, Buri Ram, Yasothon, Si Sa Ket, Surin, Ubon Ratchathani, and Amnat Charoen.

Region 4 has jurisdiction in Kalasin, Khon Kaen, Nakhon Phanom, Maha Sarakham, Mukdahan, Roi Et, Loei, Sakon Nakhon, Nong Khai, Nong Bua Lamphu, and Udon Thani.

Region 5 has jurisdiction in Chiang Mai, Chiang Rai, Nan, Phayao, Phrae, Mae Hong Son, Lampang, and Lamphun.

Region 6 has jurisdiction in Kamphaeng Phet, Tak, Nakhon Sawan, Phichit, Phitsanulok, Phetchabun, Sukhothai, Uttaradit, and Uthai Thani.

Region 7 has jurisdiction in Kanchanaburi, Nakhon Pathom, Prachuap Khiri Khan, Phetchaburi, Ratchaburi, Samut Songkhram, Samut Sakhon, and Suphan Buri.

Region 8 has jurisdiction in Krabi, Chumphon, Nakhon Si Thammarat, Phang Nga, Phuket, Ranong, and Surat Thani.

Region 9 has jurisdiction in Trang, Narathiwat, Pattani, Phatthalung, Yala, Songkhla, and Satun.

The Supreme Court

There is one Supreme Court and it is located in Bangkok. It has jurisdiction over all of Thailand. It receives cases from the courts of appeals and directly from specialized courts.

The president of the Supreme Court is the highest rank of the judicial system. Three judges are required in considering a case. However, if it is a very important case, the president of the Supreme Court will take it to the grand meeting, with no less than half the number of Supreme Court judges present.

The Supreme Court has ten specialized departments that can dispense absolute judgment on a case. There are about ten Supreme Court judges in each of the following departments.

- Juvenile and Family
- Labor
- Tax
- International Trade and Intellectual Property
- Bankruptcy
- Criminal Matters of Politicians
- Commerce and Economy
- Consumers
- Environment
- Administration

The Supreme Court is located at 6 Thanon Ratchadamnoen Nai, Kwang Prabarommaharachawang, Pranakorn District, Bangkok 10200.

Other Legal Institutions

Besides the courts mentioned above, there are some additional important legal institutions. They are often referred to in context with the Thai legal system.

The Alternative Dispute Resolution Office (ADRO)

The Alternative Dispute Resolution Office (ADRO), of the Office of the Judiciary, also known as the Thai Arbitration Institute, has duties and responsibilities for the promotion, co-operation, and administration of settlement proceedings for civil, criminal, and commercial disputes that can be compromised, by means of mediation, conciliation, or arbitration in accordance with the laws on arbitration.

The ADRO is also responsible for developing systems, forms, criterion, procedures, rules, processes, and standards for conciliation and settlement of civil and commercial disputes by arbitration, mediation, and other dispute settlement mechanisms both in and out of court.

The office is located at the Alternative Dispute Resolution Office, the Office of the Judiciary, 5th-6th floor. Criminal Court Building, Ratchadapisak Road, Chatuchak, Bangkok 10900. Tel: 02 541-2298

The Office Of The Attorney General

The Office of the Attorney General (OAG) has jurisdiction for all types of criminal cases and some civil cases. The OAG is considered the lawyer for the country. It can file charges in criminal cases to the courts of first instance, the courts of appeals and the Supreme Court. It also gives legal advice to the government and governmental agencies. It can file a suit for victims who are entitled to claim for property damages in criminal cases such as theft. It can order the cancellation or continuance of an investigation of a case. The attorney general or the acting attorney general is the person who decides whether or not to prosecute a murder case or to ask a judge to reward a person who cooperates in providing information that leads to the arrest of certain suspects.

One of the most important duties and responsibilities of the OAG is protecting the interests of the government. In civil cases, it can represent the government in all courts as a lawyer. The OAG has the power to ask for proof from someone who claims that he has Thai citizenship. It can revoke the Thai citizenship of a non-Thai born citizen whose father is an alien, or of someone who makes a threat to the national security, holds the nation in contempt, or acts in any way that is deemed harmful to the good order of society or the morals or morale of the people.

Another important role for the Office of the Attorney General is protecting rights and freedom, as well as assisting people in the legal process – for example, in filing a motion to a court to release a suspect when incarceration is not necessary while the case is pending, or in filing a motion to a court to release someone who has been jailed by mistake.

Some additional duties and responsibilities of the OAG are preventing money laundering; controlling drug use and trafficking; reviewing the acquisition of property for certain individuals; and bringing charges against the prime minister, ministers, members of the parliament and other government officials who have been investigated for unusual increase in their personal wealth.

The Office of the Attorney General is located on Ratchadapisek Road, Bangkhen, Bangkok 10900. (Tel: 02 541-2770-9.)

The Lawyers' Council Of Thailand

The Lawyers' Council of Thailand is an association of lawyers. Its activities include setting rules and regulations for members, issuing lawyer's permits, keeping records of registrations and records of lawyers' activities, and the maintenance of model ethical codes related to the legal profession. (See "Lawyer's Ethics" under "Legal Procedures.")

The Lawyers' Council also holds training sessions and orientations for members. As of August 2007 there were 48,197 lawyers in Thailand, 19,874 located in Bangkok and 29,323 in the provinces.

The Lawyers' Council is the national representative of the legal profession, serving the public and the profession by promoting justice, professional excellence, and respect for the law. It also provides lawyers to people who cannot afford one, including representing foreigners and finding interpreters for them. (We explain more about getting a lawyer from the Lawyers' Council in the "Legal Procedures" section.)

The Lawyers' Council provides free legal consultation on business days during business hours. Its phone numbers are 02 281-6463, 02 281-5170, and 02 281-8308. It's most likely that the staff will answer questions in Thai only, so you will need to be able to speak some Thai or have a translator call for you. You can also send your questions by e-mail to: legalaid@lawyerscouncil.or.th. There is a 24-hour hotline that you can call at 02 282-9906 to contact volunteer lawyers for consultation in criminal matters and to get help in setting up a meeting to interrogate suspects.

The Lawyers' Council of Thailand is located at: 7/89 Mansion 10, Rajadamnoen Avenue, Pranakorn District, Bangkok 10200. (Tel. 66 2 629-1430 [Automated]).

Part 2
Legal Procedures

Going To Court
People Involved With Legal Procedures
The following is a list of the various people involved in the criminal and civil process in Thailand and some of the terminology used in the court system.

1. The police and administrative officers including Immigration officers, district officers, officers of the Excise Department, officers of the Harbor Department, Customs offices, etc. These officers have the duty and power to investigate and prevent crime and arrest those who commit criminal acts.

2. Investigative officers including officers in the National Police Office, Department of Special Investigations, and the Ministry of Justice. Their duties are to investigate, question suspects, and gather information and evidence. They decide whether a case should be sent to the prosecutor and whether the suspect should be arrested.

3. Prosecutors called "lawyers of the land." After they receive a case from the police or other officer (listed in No. 1 and 2 above), they decide whether the defendant should be prosecuted and appear in court.

4. "The courts" refers to the judges, courthouses, and all courts listed in the court system.

5. Lawyers represent plaintiffs (civil matters) and defendants (criminal and civil matters) in legal proceedings. They are registered as lawyers with the Lawyers' Council and have a license to practice law.

6. Public lawyers ("volunteer lawyers") are like public defenders in other countries, such as the United States. In criminal cases, the court will ask defendants if they need a lawyer and will provide a public lawyer for a defendant who cannot afford one. Public lawyers belong to the Lawyers'

Council and are registered with the Court of Justice. When the case is resolved, they are paid from the budget of the Department of Justice.

7. Correctional officers include the jailers and officers in the Department of Corrections. They perform duties related to the custody, control, and supervision of individuals convicted of, or arrested for, a criminal offense and who are confined in a place of detention other than a place used exclusively for incarceration, such as a prison.

8. Probation officers are the officials whose main responsibility is to supervise, give advice, and control assigned inmates, probationers or parolees within institutions of the Department of Corrections, or within the community. They periodically write and submit reports to the courts regarding the inmates, probationers, or parolees they supervise.

9. The victim is a person who has suffered harm, including physical or mental injury, emotional suffering, economic loss, or substantial impairment of their fundamental rights, through criminal acts.

10. The suspect, or accused, is the individual accused of committing a crime, but who has not yet been charged and sent to court.

11. The defendant is the individual formally charged with an offense. Referred to in court as the "defendant" rather than as a "suspect".

12. Bailsman. This person can also be called a bondsman (the term refers to either gender). The bailsman posts bail to get a suspect or defendant out of custody on temporary release.

13. A witness is a person who has made a statement or agreed to give evidence in a case, or a person who testifies at a court hearing.

14. An expert witness is a person with knowledge, experience, training, or skills in a particular field who can provide the court with an assessment, opinion, or judgment within the area of his or her competence, which is not considered known or available to the general public.

15. The Lawyers' Council's primary duty is to give legal advice to people and assist them in legal matters. They also represent and defend suspects, defendants, or victims when there is a request or court order to do so.

16. Psychologists and social workers assist in investigations and questioning witnesses in certain cases.

17. A minor is a person under twenty years old.

18. An interpreter is a person who has the ability and training to translate two languages (e.g. Thai into English and English into Thai) and is able to facilitate communications in the legal process. This includes sign-language interpreters for the deaf.

What To Do And Where To Go In Court

Unless you are a court officer or work in the legal profession, you don't want to go to court in Thailand. Thais consider going to court, or having matters that require them to go to court, to be bad luck. They try to avoid it at all cost. However, there are many reasons why people go to court, not just for lawsuits or to defend themselves in criminal matters.

If you need to attend a court proceeding, we offer the following recommendations. First you need to dress neatly and respectfully, with your hair smartly combed. Men do not need to wear a tie, but should wear appropriate trousers and a suitable shirt preferably tucked inside. For women, a blouse with trousers or skirt is acceptable. Use your common sense; do not wear tank tops, revealing or scanty outfits, bright or colorful clothes, or any outfit that shows disrespect for the court. No shorts, sunglasses, flashy jewelry, hats, flip-flops, or sandals are allowed.

In Thai courts, there is a reception or public relations department (similar to an information desk) at the entrance. The public relations officer answers questions about that particular courthouse, its calendar, and where you should go, etc. They also help with writing petitions and completing request forms, complaints, or other forms. You may ask them to make copies of case documents and post bail for a defendant with the Public Relations Department. This is roughly the equivalent of the clerk of court's office in the US court system.

You submit a petition or a statement, or file a lawsuit or an allegation (งานรับฟ้อง *ngaan rap fong*) with the Claims Department. Again, it serves similar functions to the US clerk of court's office.

When you file documents with the court, a case officer will be assigned. To request the results of the submission or copies of the claims, contact the case officer.

The filing department can provide you with copies of court files or court orders, (งานเก็บสำนวนความ *ngaan gep sam-nuan-kwaam*). This is also analogous to the US clerk of court's office.

Visiting a suspect or defendant brought to court will require you to make arrangements with the court police. If you need to go to court as a witness, contact the judge's clerk office (งานหน้าบัลลังก์ *ngaan naa-ban-lang*).

If you have problems in court, contact the court's clerk or the head judge for assistance. To contact a probation officer, go to the probation office.

Going To Court As A Plaintiff

You can go to court as a plaintiff in either a criminal or civil case. For criminal matters, the prosecutor is your representative, and for civil matters, you will be represented by a private lawyer.

You should study the documents of the charges or lawsuit (equivalent to the complaint in Western courts) thoroughly beforehand and check for accuracy of all forms and statements. Sign your name where necessary on all documents and on the lawyer appointment form (known as the "power of attorney" – the form that is used to authorize a lawyer to appear on your behalf). Make sure you have enough money to pay the required fees. In civil cases, there are more court fees than in criminal matters. Thais must bring their house registration documents and Thai citizen's ID card. Foreigners may use a passport along with other identification.

Going To Court As A Defendant Or Suspect
If you have to go to court as a defendant, you need to prepare. If your statements have not been submitted, write them down and take them with you for your reference. Be sure to bring the appointment letter or the subpoena and a copy of the complaint. Thais must bring their house registration documents and Thai citizen's ID card. Foreigners may use a passport along with other identification. For criminal matters, you may need to prepare proof of assets to be used to post bail.

Going To Court As A Witness
The witness subpoena will state what date you need to appear in court. Make sure you are appropriately dressed and arrive early so you have time to verify where to go and what to do. Bring the witness subpoena and an ID with you. If you know you will be required to testify, it is a good idea to make a written record of the events you will testify about. You should do this as soon after the event as possible and use it to refresh your memory before you go to court. This will help you give statements in good order that accurately depict what happened and why.

Going To Court As A Bailsman (Bondsman)
A bail bondsman is any individual, juristic person, or entity that acts as a surety and pledges money or property as bail for the future appearance of a criminal defendant in court. When you go to court, you need to prepare documents regarding any assets that will be used as a bail bond.

Assets that can be used to post bail include real estate, cash, money in a bank, an official bank letter, government bonds, or a land deed with a letter from a government office certifying the value at which the land has been assessed. If you are married, bring a letter of approval from your spouse.

Thai government officials may use their governmental position as a bail bond. If you are one such official, bring a letter certifying salary, as well. (See more details on bail bonds in the next section.)

Criminal Matters

A criminal case is a lawsuit brought by a prosecutor employed by the local government which charges a person with the commission of a crime, or by an individual who claims to have been damaged by a criminal act. The claims are usually made to the police at a police station. In Thailand, criminal cases are divided into two categories.

1. Criminal cases that cannot be compromised or settled are initiated by government prosecutors. These are criminal cases that affect the public peace or cause harm to society, the security of the country, are a threat to life or physical well being, or to public or personal property. Included are other serious crimes such as dealing drugs, deforestation, illegal gambling, and corruption.

2. Criminal cases that can be compromised. These are criminal cases that do not affect the public peace. They are offenses that affect an individual or a group of individuals. Some of these criminal cases include trademark infringement, defamation by slandering or libel, revealing trade secrets, committing fraud, cheating a creditor, embezzlement, trespassing, rape, molestation, copyrights matters, etc. The victim must personally file a complaint within the three-month statute of limitations, which runs from the date of acknowledgment (knowing) of the crime and the recognition of the suspect.

For cases that can be compromised, a representative can file a complaint for the victim if the victim is a minor, disabled person, legal entity, or juristic person. If the victim is dead or injured, parents, children, or spouse can file a complaint on the victim's behalf.

Criminal Procedures And Court Stages
When a criminal act is reported, the following procedures normally take place:

1. Investigation Stage
The police will conduct the initial investigation, interview witnesses, collect evidence, and issue a police report. By law, the police have the power to perform the following:

- Look for suspects, compile evidence, and question witnesses.
- Upon receipt of a subpoena – search a person or a location to look for witnesses and evidence and to arrest suspects. There are some exceptions to the subpoena requirement – for example, in very serious matters or situations of life and death.
- Issue subpoenas to witnesses and suspects.
- Confiscate items that can be used as evidence.
- Place a suspect in custody for investigation.
- Allow a suspect to post bail during the investigation.

Scope Of Power For Criminal Investigators:

- For misdemeanors or lesser offenses, police officers or investigators may confine the suspect only as long as the questioning session lasts. Questions that may be asked are basic identity questions such as who they are and where they live.

- Police and investigators are prohibited from confining a suspect for more than 48 hours. The time begins when a suspect is brought to the police station. When necessary the time period may be extended to not more than three days.

- If it is necessary to confine a suspect for more than three days, the case must be sent to court for consideration. The court will do one of the following three things:

   a. If it is a criminal offense and the punishment for the crime will result in jail time of less than six months and with less than a 500 baht fine, the court will order the suspect to be held only once for no more than seven days.

   b. If it is a criminal offense and the potential sentence is more than six months in jail but less than ten years and with more than a 500 baht fine, the judge has the power to order the suspect be held on several separate occasions. Each period can be up to twelve days. These multiple confinements cannot exceed 48 days.

   c. If it is a criminal offense and the jail sentence could be longer than ten years, the judge has the power to order several periods of custody of up to twelve days each, but not more than 84 days in total.

After the investigating officer has gathered evidence and witnesses for the case, he will summarize it in a report and then do one of the following:

- Stop the investigation if there is no suspect.

- Determine that the case should not be prosecuted. If the suspect is in the custody of the investigating officer, he will be released. If the suspect is in the custody of the court, the officer will request the court release the suspect.

- Determine that the case should be prosecuted and submit the investigation report to the prosecutor for further legal procedures.

   If it is a criminal case that can be compromised in the investigative stage, such as embezzlement or fraud between individuals, the victim can withdraw the complaint and the investigating officer has the power to fine the accused for the amount provided by law.

2. Prosecution Stage

After the prosecutor receives a complaint from the police, he considers the case and will do one of the following:

- Stop the investigation if there is no suspect.
- Determine, based on evidence presented by the police, that there are insufficient grounds for prosecution and make a request to the court (in that jurisdiction) to release the suspect in custody. If the suspect has posted bail, it will be returned to him.
- If the prosecutor decides to press charges, he will submit the complaint to the court (in that jurisdiction) and arrange for the suspect (in custody or out on bail) to appear in court for further legal procedures.

3. Court Stage
Initial Court Stage
In the court of first instance, the court will do one of the following:

a. Dismiss the case.

b. Hold a trial, then make a ruling and impose punishment either by confiscating property, imposing a fine, or authorizing detention, imprisonment, or capital punishment.

c. If the defendant appeals, the case is sent to the court of appeals for further consideration. If not contested, the case is finished and the judgment is final.

The defendant must be present during the trial and examination of witnesses. A judge may order certain stages of the trial to take place outside the defendant's presence in the following cases:

- If the maximum penalty is less than three years in prison and/or the fine will be not more than 5,000 baht. (If the defendant has a lawyer and has court permission, he can be excused from being present.)
- When there are more than two defendants in a case, the court may conduct a trial and have witnesses examined outside the presence of a defendant or co-defendant(s) if the prosecutor successfully asserts that the examination of the witness will have no effect on the excluded defendant(s); or if the court otherwise deems it appropriate to do so.

Appellate Stage
The court of appeals may either affirm the lower court's judgment or reverse it. If the judgment is reversed, the appellate court sends the case back to the lower court and orders the lower court to take further action. If the court of appeals affirms the

lower court's judgment, the case ends and the defendant will begin to serve his sentence unless he appeals to the Supreme Court. If the Supreme Court does not accept the case, then the judgment of the court of appeals is deemed final. If the Supreme Court accepts the case, the judgment of the Supreme Court is final and must be followed.

4. Penalty Stage

If the court enters a judgment of guilty, a defendant may be fined, have his property confiscated, be detained, imprisoned, or executed. Some defendants may be placed on probation or ordered to do community service instead of paying a fine. If the judgment is to confiscate property and the defendant does not have money or property to pay the fine, he can be incarcerated and pay off the debt at the rate of 200 baht per day. If the fine is less than 80,000 baht and the defendant cannot pay, he may request the court to permit him to do community service at the rate of 200 baht per day instead of paying the fine.

If the defendant is sentenced to prison, he will be sent to the prison located wherever the law states he should be incarcerated and will be supervised by Corrections officers. Bang Kwang Prison in Nonthaburi and Klong Prem Prison in Bangkok hold prisoners convicted of serious crimes who have been sentenced to thirty years imprisonment or more, or to capital punishment. In Thailand, capital punishment is execution by lethal injection. The first execution by lethal injection was carried out in October 2001. Prior to lethal injection, executions were administered by a firing squad, and prior to that, beheading was the official method of execution.

On certain auspicious occasions, such as the King's birthday or when the Interior minister or the Council of Ministers makes a special proposal to the King, some prisoners may be pardoned or their sentences may be reduced.

Rights Of Suspects In Criminal Cases

The suspect or the accused has the following rights:

- To have a lawyer represent them in a criminal matter without going through the investigating and prosecuting stage. A judge will consider the case from the evidence and witness statements. If the judge decides there is a sufficient factual basis, he will stamp a seal accepting the case for prosecution. The suspect will then have to defend himself in court. (From this point on, he is referred to as the defendant.) If the judge decides there is an insufficient factual basis, he will dismiss the case.

- To meet and consult with his lawyer in private. The accused may make a written or oral request to a policeman to meet with his lawyer at a police station. The suspect will have to name the lawyer with whom he wants to meet. A suspect who cannot afford a lawyer will have a lawyer provided to him at no cost.

- If not a Thai speaker, to have an interpreter provided by the police or court to translate or explain the legal procedures.
- To have a lawyer present with them at the investigating stage.
- If incarcerated, to receive visitation during business hours or other times that are allowed by the police on duty.
- To be treated if sick. If the suspect is ill before confinement, the police must escort him to a government hospital for treatment. If the suspect is sick during confinement, the police on duty are required to make a request to the police station chief for permission to send the suspect to the hospital.
- To bail. The suspect can post bail himself or it can be done by friends, relatives, his lawyer, or a bailsman. The person requesting bail must submit a written request to the investigating officer, who will ask for particular additional documents and announce the results of the bail review within 24 hours.

Bail

Release on bail is called "temporary release." In making a request for temporary release of a suspect or defendant, a bailsman needs to bring certain necessary documents along with the particular court's request form. All necessary items are then submitted to the court. The following information on posting bail bond in criminal courts, as well as the costs listed below, is taken from information provided by the Provincial Police Bureau. Some items may vary slightly according to each court, and the minimum bail amounts may be different because the amount of bail for each case is set by the presiding judge of each jurisdiction. In Thailand, there are three categories for submitting a request for temporary release (bail):

1. Request for temporary release using assets.

2. Request for temporary release using cash.

3. Request for temporary release using one's government employment status.

Request For Temporary Release Using Assets
Items needed from the bailsman:

1. Citizen's ID card or official government ID card or state enterprise employee ID card and one photocopy thereof.

2. House registration and one photocopy thereof.

3. A married bailsman must have an original letter of consent from their spouse along with his or her ID card (as listed in No.1), a photocopy of

the consent letter plus the house registration and one photocopy thereof. (See Letter of Consent form in the Reference section.)

4. If the bailsman is divorced or widowed, the divorce or death certificate and one photocopy thereof.

5. The assets, such as a land deed, *Nor Sor 3*, *Nor Sor 3 Gor*, or government bond. (The *Nor Sor 3* is a form of land deed that is issued by a land office to certify permission for using the land.)

6. If land is used as a bail bond, a letter of the land assessment issued by a governmental agency within the last ninety days.

7. If using a bank account as a bail bond, the regular deposit bank book (bank statement) and a letter from the bank stating the amount of money in the account.

8. If the land owner cannot go to court personally, there must be a power of attorney that is certified by the district officer along with the documents in No.3. (See Power of Attorney form in the Reference section.)

9. A request letter for posting bond using a land deed or *Nor Sor 3*. The request also includes the amount of assets and the contract of the bail bond.

10. A request form for posting bond using a regular bank deposit account.

When the court grants the temporary release, the following will happen:

1. The court will issue a receipt for the assets along with an appointment letter.

2. The bailsman must promise to the court that he will bring the suspect or defendant to court on the date written on the appointment letter. If the bailsman fails to do so, the court will issue an order penalizing the bailsman as provided for in the bail contract.

After the judgment is made, the bail bond will be returned.

1. The court will order the bail bond returned on the day the judgment is read. The bailsman does not need to submit a request.

2. The bailsman needs to bring the receipt issued on the day the bail request was submitted along with his citizen's ID card three days after judgment has been entered. Contact the public relations desk.

Request For Temporary Release Using Cash

Items needed from the bailsman:

1. Citizen's ID card or official government ID card or state enterprise employee ID card and one photocopy thereof.

2. House registration and one photocopy thereof.

3. Cash equal to the amount of the bail.

4. A request letter and contract for the bail bond.

When the court grants temporary release, the following will take place:

1. The court will issue a receipt for the amount of cash along with an appointment letter.

2. The bailsman promises the court that the suspect or defendant will be brought to court on the date written on the appointment letter. If the bailsman fails to do so, the court will penalize the bailsman as provided for in the contract.

After the judgment is made, the bail bond will be returned.

1. The court will order the bail bond returned on the day judgment is read. The bailsman does not need to submit a request again.

2. The bailsman needs to bring the receipt for the amount of cash posted on the day the bail request was submitted along with his citizen's ID card on the day of judgment. Contact the financial officer on that day and the money will be returned the following day.

3. If the bailsman cannot go to receive the money in person, he may ask that the money be transferred to his account by making a request to the court's financial officer.

Request For Temporary Release Using One's Government Employment Position

Items needed from the bailsman:

1. Citizen's ID card or official government ID card or state enterprise employee ID card and one photocopy thereof.

2. House registration and one photocopy thereof.

3. A married bailsman must have an original letter of consent from his or her spouse along with his or her ID card (as listed in No.1), a photocopy of the consent letter plus the house registration and one photocopy thereof. (See Letter of Consent form in the Reference section.)

4. If the bailsman is divorced or widowed, bring the divorce or death certificate and one photocopy thereof.

5. A letter certifying the position of the bailsman, which includes details of their position, job title, and current salary. The letter must be issued by the institution that the bailsman belongs to, along with the date and location the document was issued. This letter must be addressed to a specific judge.

6. If the bailsman is a state enterprise employee, the documents listed in No.'s 1—5 plus a letter of certification that indicates the comparison of their rank with official government ranks.

7. A bailsman in this category must personally appear in court on each occasion listed in the court order. He may not use the power of attorney to send someone else.

8. A request letter and contract of the bail bond.

Bail Rates For Using One's Government Position As A Bail Bond

Government Officials:

- Level 3—5 or equivalent—the position equals an amount up to 60,000 baht.

- Level 6—8 or equivalent—the position equals an amount up to 200,000 baht.

- Level 9—10 or equivalent—the position equals an amount up to 500,000 baht.

- Level 11 or equivalent—the position equals an amount up to 800,000 baht.

Police and Military Officials:

- State in the bail bond contract which level the bondsman is equivalent to when compared to the official government ranks.

State Enterprise Employees:

- State in the bail bond contract which level the bondsman is equivalent to when compared to the official government ranks.

Members of Parliament or Political Officials:

- The position equals an amount up to 800,000 baht.

Local Political Officials:

- The position equals an amount up to 60,000 baht for both members of provincial councils and members of municipal councils.

Note: In the event that a bondsman's position does not cover the required bail, more bondsmen with government positions or other assets may be added to make up the deficit.

When the court grants the temporary release, the bondsman must enter into a contract with the court in which he promises to bring the suspect or defendant to court on the date of the appointment. If he fails to do so, the court will penalize him as provided for in the contract.

Minimum Amount Of Bail For Various Cases

Listed here are some general bail rates for various charges. This information is from the Court of Justice and the Thai Police Department websites and may be subject to change. These bail rates are those amounts used in adult criminal cases. (Juvenile and family courts have different rates, which are normally lower for the same charge.)

Cases Concerning Life and Bodily Injury:

- Murder – from 300,000 baht.
- Attempted murder – from 200,000 baht.
- Careless driving causing death – 200,000 baht when a personally owned vehicle was involved, and from 250,000 baht when a commercial vehicle was involved.
- Serious body injury harm – from 150,000 baht.

Cases Concerning Danger to the Public:

- Arson – from 100,000 baht.

- Carelessly causing fire – from 100,000 baht.
- Perjury or using or producing false documents – from 100,000 baht.

Cases Concerning Property:

- Receiving stolen property – from 100,000 baht.
- Theft – from 150,000 baht.
- Theft and use of a vehicle in the commission of a crime or use of when causing serious crime – from 200,000 baht.
- Snatching property – from 150,000 baht.
- Extortion – from 100,000 baht.
- Robbery – from 200,000 baht.
- Gang robbery – from 300,000 baht.
- Cheating and fraud, cheating a lender, or embezzlement – from 100,000 baht
- Cheating the public – from 200,000 baht.
- Trespassing or causing property damage – from 100,000 baht.

Cases Concerning Government Officials:

- Misconduct or inappropriate action – from 150,000 baht.
- Perjury or making false declarations – from 100,000 baht.

Cases Concerning the use of Firearms:

- Carrying firearms without registration – from 100,000 baht.
- Carrying firearms with registration – from 50,000 baht.

Cases Concerning Sex:

- Rape and indecent assault – from 200,000 baht.
- Obscenity or pornography – from 200,000 baht.
- Having sex with minors, molestation of women, or providing women for prostitution – from 200,000 baht.

Bail rates for charges that are against specific acts in criminal matters are as follows:

The Firearms Act:

- Firearms without registration – from 100,000 baht.
- Firearms with registration – from 100,000 baht.
- Possessing bomb materials – from 200,000 baht.

The Forestry Act (Trespassing on forest land or causing harm to animals in the forest):

- Up to 10 *rai* – from 100,000 baht.
- More than 10 *rai* – from 150,000 baht.

The Narcotic Drugs Act:

- Possession of marijuana – from 10,000 baht.
- Sale of marijuana – from 200,000 baht.
- Possession of heroin or methamphetamine – from 100,000 baht.
- Sale of heroin or methamphetamine – from 300,000 baht.

Recently, Thai law has allowed private bail bond companies to post bail for suspects. In Thailand, this service is provided by most insurance companies through what is called a "bail bond policy". With the exception of drug cases, use of a bail bond company is permitted in most cases. Bond companies generally charge a non-refundable fee equal to ten percent of the total amount of the bail before they post a bond. This fee represents the bondsman's compensation for his or her services.

The criteria used by the court in considering releasing a suspect or defendant on bail is:

- The seriousness of the charge.
- The credibility of the evidence and witnesses.
- The conditions of the case.
- The credibility of the bailsman and the assets used.
- Whether the suspect is a flight risk.
- Whether there will be any damage or danger caused by the release of the suspect.
- Whether the suspect is likely to destroy evidence or harm or threaten any witness who may be called to testify at trial.

The judge will decide whether the suspect will be released on bail. If release is ordered, either the prosecutor or police may object to the release.

In less serious cases (such as injury caused in a fight, defamation, extortion, or petty theft) the judge may release the defendant without bail. This is the equivalent to an OR ("own recognizance") release in the US and other Western countries. The judge makes a finding as to the credibility of the defendant, and the defendant must promise to appear in court.

Below is additional information regarding criminal matters:

— The suspect or defendant is presumed innocent until proven guilty beyond a responsible doubt, as in Western countries. This legal maxim was made a part of the Thai legal system long ago and the archaic notion that a defendant is guilty until proven innocent no longer exists in Thailand.

— The burden of proof is on the prosecutor. The prosecution presents witnesses and evidence in the trial first, and then the defendant presents witnesses and evidence for the defense.

— Each witness has to swear or affirm to tell the truth. Each witness answers questions from the court, the prosecutor, and the defendant (or his lawyer).

— The defendant has one month to appeal to the court of appeals or to the Supreme Court. This time begins from the day that the judgment is read. The jurisdiction of the Supreme Court is discretionary and not all appealed cases are accepted by the Supreme Court.

— If the defendant cannot afford a lawyer and the potential penalty includes imprisonment, or if the defendant is less than eighteen years old, the court may appoint volunteer lawyers for the case at no cost to the defendant.

— If a witness is a minor, an examination is usually carried out by a psychologist or a social worker and a report of the examination is provided to the judge.

— For cases that concern the secrecy and security of the country, the proceedings will be closed to the public.

— The 2002 Drug Addict Rehabilitation Act provides that suspects deemed to be drug abusers, or who possessed drugs without the intent to sell them, or both, be sent to court within 48 hours (or within 24 hours if a minor.) The charge(s) are placed on hold while the suspect attends court-ordered drug rehabilitation. The suspect can be placed in a rehabilitation program as many times as necessary for as long as three years; but each program cannot last longer than six months. If the suspect successfully rehabilitates to the judge's satisfaction, the charges will be dropped.

Civil Matters

A civil case is a lawsuit brought by two or more people against one or more parties. "People" includes individuals, businesses, or government agencies. The result is an award of money to be paid by one party to the other and/or an order to affirmatively take some action or refrain from some action. A judgment in a civil matter never includes the imposition of a criminal penalty.

Civil Procedures

A lawsuit can be filed in Thailand if any of the following circumstances or conditions exist – if both parties live in Thailand; the cause of action happened in Thailand; the defendant has property in Thailand; or the aggrieved party holds Thai citizenship. The aggrieved party, known as the plaintiff, files a complaint with the court setting forth his allegations and the purported facts relating to the case. Once the complaint is filed, the following usually occurs:

The Pre-Trial Stage

If the case is accepted by the court, the court will issue a summons to be served on the defendant(s). The plaintiff must have the summons and a copy of the complaint served on the defendant by a court officer within the number of days specified (normally seven days after the complaint is filed), otherwise the court may consider the plaintiff insincere about bringing his action. The plaintiff must pay the cost of the court official's service on the defendant. If the defendant cannot be found, the court official may effectuate service by posting the summons where it is easily seen at the defendant's residence (known as "residential service"), or by publishing the summons in a newspaper or other media (known as "service by publication"). This posting or publication process takes fifteen days from the date of posting the summons or publication.

At the conclusion of this fifteen-day period, the defendant has fifteen days to respond to the allegations by either admitting or denying them. The defendant may also file a counter-claim against the plaintiff for a related cause of action he might have against the plaintiff.

After the defendant has filed his answer to the complaint, the two parties establish a list of issues in dispute and the court sets a date for a settlement conference or pre-trial hearing. This step is required to determine which issues need to be proved in court through the presentation of evidence. After the parties agree on the issues to be presented at trial, the court sets a trial date and determines which party has the burden of proof on each issue.

If the defendant fails to reply within the time specified in the summons, the plaintiff may request a default judgment. This request for a default judgment must be filed within 15 days after the expiration of the defendant's answer time. If the plaintiff does not do so, the court will remove the case.

If the plaintiff is not a resident of Thailand, he will need to post a security (such as cash, land deed, or official letter from a bank) to cover the defendant's costs and legal fees in case the defendant wins the case.

The court fees are 2.5 percent of the amount in dispute (not to exceed 200,000 baht), which is to be deposited with the court at the time of the lawsuit's initial filing and again at the time of filing any appeal.

For small claims where the amount in dispute is less than 300,000 baht, the filing fee in the court of first instance is 200 baht.

The court may order the losing party to pay the winning party's attorney fees, service fees, and witness fees. The security deposit from the plaintiff may be held until the defendant has exhausted all their appeals.

It is required that both parties submit a list of evidence and issues to the court, and the opposing party must receive a copy of this list at least seven days before the date of the settlement conference or trial. New evidence may be brought in later on a showing of reasonable cause.

After the plaintiff and the defendant have submitted their respective cases (or if the defendant fails to appear), the court will hear the testimony of the witnesses. The witnesses must be sworn in and give their testimony to the court. They will be examined and cross-examined by the lawyers for each party.

If related documents are in languages other than Thai, they must be translated into Thai and submitted along with the originals or certified copies thereof. Written or oral testimony of witnesses must be translated or interpreted into Thai. Translation expenses are paid by the presenting party. (See more information on translation and interpretation in the next section.)

Both parties are entitled to present their final arguments after all the evidence has been presented and the witnesses have been heard. In civil matters, the burden of proof is on the plaintiff. After the parties both rest their respective cases, the judges will make a decision that will be given in writing and read aloud in court.

The Judgment Stage

The court will issue an order to the losing party (now known as the "debtor") to pay the winning party (now know as the creditor) his costs associated with the action, to deliver property, perform a certain action, or refrain from a certain action. The judgment allows the party deemed liable to the other party seven days to comply. However, the liable party may make a motion to stay the execution of judgment if there is another trial pending that might affect the case. The court may award costs and lawyers' fees no more than five percent of the amount in dispute for an action brought in the court of first instance and not more than three percent for an appeal filed in the court of appeals or the Supreme Court.

If the debtor fails to pay according to the judgment, the creditor may apply for a writ of execution to seize property of the debtor and sell the seized property to the public to satisfy the judgment. In some cases, the debtor may be jailed if he does not comply with the judgment. This process usually takes time before all debts are collected. The losing party has one month to file an appeal to the court of appeals or the Supreme Court.

Arbitration And Mediation

The parties in a dispute may elect to settle existing or future cases through mediation or arbitration.

Mediation is a process in which a neutral third person, the "mediator," encourages and facilitates the resolution of a dispute between two or more parties. It is an informal (and theoretically) non-adversarial process which has as its objective assisting the disputing parties in reaching a mutually acceptable and voluntary agreement.

Arbitration is the process by which the parties to a dispute submit their differences to the judgment of an impartial person or group appointed by mutual consent or statutory provision. Most arbitration cases in Thailand are conducted under the supervision of the International Chamber of Commerce (ICC). However, there are also two main domestic arbitration institutes in Thailand: the Alternative Dispute Resolution Office (ADRO), also known as the Thai Arbitration Institute, and the Thai Commercial Arbitration Institute of the Board of Trade. They were both established to reduce the number of cases that end up in court, and reduce the expenses that would occur during a court procedure. Both can save time in resolving a dispute.

Administrative costs and arbitrator fees in Thailand are quite reasonable and are structured based on claim amounts. These fees are considerably less than those charged by many similar bodies in other countries.

Foreign arbitrators and foreign lawyers may participate as arbitrators and act as legal advisors in arbitration proceedings conducted in Thailand where the governing law is not Thai law, or where it is not necessary to apply for enforcement of a foreign judgment from a Thai court.

Lawyers And Interpreters

In this section we provide information on lawyer and interpreter issues in the Thai legal system. By Thai law decree, foreigners are not allowed to be discriminated against in legal proceedings. To get a fair hearing in criminal matters, foreigners are entitled to a lawyer and an interpreter in all procedures (with some exceptions).

For a foreigner, it is not easy to select a competent lawyer in Thailand. There are many qualified Thai lawyers who do not charge high fees and who are willing to help you with your case. However, the main problem is the language barrier. Most Thai lawyers do not speak English well enough to explain all of the legal procedures, and this is the main disadvantage for them getting foreign clients. Those who can speak fluent English usually work for larger law firms and charge high fees.

This chapter gives you information about how to get a lawyer and how to work with an interpreter, and may help you save money when you prepare for legal matters.

To obtain an attorney, you may contact the Lawyers' Council and make a request for a lawyer. The police and the court system are required to provide an interpreter for a non-Thai speaker. For example, if you speak Burmese, a Burmese interpreter will be provided for you. You may refuse to sign documents or continue with any procedures without a full understanding of the documents or statements being made.

The Lawyers' Council will provide lawyers that are registered with the Council. Most are lawyers who do not work full time, do not have many cases, are young and want to get experience, or are retired from the law but still want to contribute to society. They are paid from a limited budget from the Ministry of Justice and they most likely will only speak Thai.

English-speaking lawyers and legal consultants are not normally listed with the Lawyers' Council. The interpreters that are listed with the court seldom speak foreign languages well. Court interpreter pay is so low that qualified interpreters do not register with the court system. Normally, the court will have to "send an invitation" to local individuals who they feel are qualified to interpret in legal proceedings. The court will arrange for payment of interpreters. For civil matters, the parties have to hire their own interpreters.

Qualifications Of A Lawyer In Thailand

There are many legal consultants in Thailand who are not native Thais (foreigners) and most of them work for law firms in larger cities. They may have a degree in law from their own country, but they are not allowed to work as a lawyer in Thailand. There are few foreign consultants that are qualified to practice law in Thailand.

To become a lawyer in Thailand, one must meet the following requirements and have the following qualifications:

- Be a Thai citizen.
- Have a bachelor's degree or junior college degree in law from an institute approved by the Lawyers' Council.
- Demonstrate good conduct, morality, integrity, and honesty.
- Not be in the process of serving a court order for imprisonment or having filed for bankruptcy.
- Not have any contagious diseases.
- A private lawyer cannot be a government employee or a local official with a position that pays a salary.
- Have passed the bar exam.

How To Select A Lawyer

Before you decide on a lawyer, you need to understand your case, know what questions to ask the prospective lawyers, and know how to prepare. If you choose an inadequate lawyer, you will most likely add to your problems. A suitable, knowledgeable lawyer will be one who is able to work with you efficiently, quickly, and is affordable. The following are tips to use when you interview a prospective lawyer:

You may ask to see the lawyer's license. A professional lawyer in Thailand must have a license issued by the Lawyers' Council. He must have passed the legal exam and have legal training. It is illegal for a lawyer to represent someone in court or claim that he is a lawyer if he does not have this license.

You will want to ask the lawyer about his past experience with cases like yours. Many attorneys specialize in particular areas and may not be familiar with your type of case. Others may be engaged in a more generalized practice and may be able to assist with cases of limited complexity or of a more common nature. You should also inquire as to their education and training. Some may have advanced training in specialized areas that may be helpful to your case.

Ask the lawyer whether he knows of or has anything to do with the opposing party. This is to avoid conflict of interests and to protect your confidence before you explain your case. In smaller provinces, this situation may not be unusual, since local people in a small town know one another and the lawyer may have worked for the opposing party or their relatives.

Ask about expenses and retainer fees. Lawyer's fees vary because each lawyer charges differently. One client may pay 40,000 baht for a divorce case and another may pay up to 150,000 baht. The reputation and skills of lawyers are the deciding factor of their fees. Some lawyers do not charge for initial consultations, but you should verify this beforehand.

Normally, a lawyer will listen to you explain your case first, in order to determine how complicated it is, how many witnesses are involved, and how long it will take. He will then decide what he can do in the legal process to help. He may quote a rate per day, per case, or per hour. Lawyers in the provinces usually give a lump-sum rate. You and the potential lawyer will need to agree on the fee in advance. You should also discuss potential expenses in addition to the attorney fees. These could include costs of experts, witnesses, or even forensic testing. This is an important stage because you have to make sure what the fees cover and whether and when there will be additional charges.

Check the prospective lawyer's reputation and whether he has a good knowledge of Thai law and how it applies to foreigners. Depending on your budget, you should determine the most appropriate lawyer for your case that you can afford. Keep in mind that if you hire a lawyer that does not speak your language, you will also have to hire an interpreter. Remember, you get what you pay for.

Sometimes, a lawyer may include in his fee the cost for translating documents into English (which are actual costs) and court costs (in civil matters). In that case, you wouldn't have to pay the court costs. In civil cases, the court charges 2.5 percent of the amount of dispute up to a maximum cost of 200,000 baht. If the lawyer includes the court costs, verify with him how much the court costs will be.

There are some cases of lawyers being investigated by the Lawyers' Council for charging clients up to five percent of the amount of dispute and for informing clients that the maximum court cost is higher than 200,000 baht. For criminal matters, there are no court costs (only some nominal fees). It is not against the lawyer's ethics code to charge high fees, but it is against the ethics code to charge expenses that are more than actual costs.

If you are involved in a criminal case, you will most likely need to have a lawyer because you may not understand the legal process and the Thai language. Almost all legal documents are written in Thai. For a misdemeanor case, such as an offense against the Traffic Act or Labor Act, for which the penalty is only a fine, you may select to proceed without a lawyer, or hire a lawyer by the hour, or at a flat rate to resolve the case.

Some cases make it to court, but some end at the police station. For misdemeanor cases, the court allows a lawyer and an interpreter to be the same person, so it is convenient to hire a lawyer who can speak your language.

For general cases or cases that can be compromised, such as embezzlement or rape, when there is fine as well as imprisonment, or fine and three-five year probation, lawyers and interpreters are needed (and can be the same person). If you hire a lawyer that can speak English, the minimum fee is usually around 30,000 baht.

For serious cases or cases that cannot be compromised, such as murder, robbery, drug trafficking, or money laundering, specialized lawyers are needed and interpreters have to be provided. Minimum fees for this type of case start at 100,000 baht.

There are no set legal fees. A lawyer can charge as he sees fit. But whatever fee your lawyer charges, the amount should be reasonable. For civil matters, the amount can be a contingency fee based on the amount involved in the case such as ten or twenty percent of the dispute amount, or what you and your lawyer agree upon. The lawyer may charge by the hour or charge a flat rate. If you choose a lawyer who speaks English, or if he is from a large law firm, don't be surprised at fees of 100—200 US dollars per hour. Some top law firms with high international standards that work for enterprises may charge up to 1,000 dollars per hour. These high-end firms usually quote their fees in US dollars. If this is the case, be aware of the monetary exchange rate and whether you are asked to pay in dollars or baht.

You may want to obtain a second or third opinion from a different lawyer or law firm. This way you can compare prices and the lawyers' experience, personality, and reputation. You might also obtain a better idea of the complexity of your case and what resolution may involve.

After you are satisfied with your lawyer and want to hire him, you will assign him to begin the legal process by signing a power of attorney form, which authorizes him to act on your behalf. Ask the lawyer for a contract that covers what you have agreed to. If you don't understand what it says in the contract, ask him to clarify the content so that there will be no misunderstandings later. Make sure you obtain a copy of all documents in Thai and English (or your native language) at the time of signing and retain them for possible later use. All parties should follow strictly what is written in the contract. Make photocopies of all documents before you give them to your lawyer. File all documents and all correspondences neatly so it will be easy for you to find and for reference.

It's your responsibility to follow your case closely. Even though you have assigned a lawyer to work on your case, you still need to pay close attention to the procedures. There may be something that you have overlooked that you may want to tell the lawyer. You should contact your lawyer immediately if you have additional information. The information may not sound important to you, but it may be important to the case. If you have any questions, ask your lawyer and work with him closely so that there will be no misunderstandings.

Your lawyer can work more efficiently if you provide the necessary information in a timely manner. Make sure you are candid with your lawyer. If you are not, it will make your situation more difficult and could seriously jeopardize the attorney's ability to assist you.

Often, people ask friends for lawyer referrals. If you live in a large city and don't have contacts, it's easy to find law offices. You can just walk in and talk to a lawyer. There are directories and advertisement for law firms in magazines, newspapers, pamphlets, and on the Internet. Those you see advertised in English are generally able to speak English, but their fees will be higher.

If you are in a small town and you want to hire a lawyer, you can ask people in the area to refer you to one. In this case, it will be harder to find a lawyer who can speak your language. Their fees are usually lower, but you will have to pay for an interpreter, which will increase the overall price.

Lawyer's Ethics

Thai legal ethics are very similar to those placed on most United States attorneys. They are issued by the Lawyers' Council and found in Section 51 of the Lawyers' Act of 1985, which provide that a lawyer shall abide by the Regulations on Professional Ethics. You should consider this when choosing a lawyer, but remember it is only an expectation. The individual lawyer may or may not follow the code.

It is against a lawyer's ethics if the lawyer:

- Does not respect or fear the power of the court, or commits any act of contempt toward the court or the judge inside or outside of court which will cause damage to the power of the court or the judge.

- Does not accept the job when a judge has assigned him to defend a defendant in a criminal case, except if he has a good excuse.

- Produces a false statement, document, or evidence, or uses tactics to deceive the court or to cause any acts in order to receive undisclosed orders or judgment.

- Conspires directly or indirectly to produce false evidence, to urge witnesses to testify falsely, to conceal any witnesses or evidence that should be presented to the court, or to promise a bribe to an official or to conspire to give a bribe to an official.
- Creates any acts that promote a lawsuit or a case in matter that has no basis.
- Uses tricks to persuade someone to give him a case to represent or defend.
- Deceives the client that he would win the case while knowing that he would lose.
- Claims that he has more knowledge than other lawyers.
- Claims that he has connections in order to get other benefits.
- Reveals the confidential information and secrets of a client, except if he has permission from the client or from the court.
- Intentionally misses appointments or abandons his case.
- Intentionally misses certain duties that should be done in processing the case for his client, or conceals information that should be disclosed to his client.
- Has been a consultant or has obtained details of the case of one party and later represents the same case for the opposing party.
- Has accepted the case and later, without good cause, seeks more benefits from the client than what was agreed upon.
- Causes any acts that amount to fraud or embezzlement, or possesses or keeps money or assets belonging to the client for longer than usual without permission from the client, unless there are good reasons.
- Tries to obtain or causes any acts in the form of bidding for a case where the party is already represented by a lawyer, except with the permission of the lawyer representing that client.
- Advertises or allows others to advertise the lawyer's fees, or advertises that there will be no fees for representing the case.
- Advertises the name, qualification, location, address, or office in a way that will persuade people with a lawsuit to seek him as a lawyer.
- Conducts legal practice or behaves in a manner contrary to good morals and defames the honor of the law profession.
- Agrees or promises to give a commission or reward to someone who finds cases or brings cases to him.

Other Ethics

During court appearances, a lawyer must dress conservatively and appropriately to the situation.

Male lawyers should wear appropriate business attire and avoid bright colors. A white shirt, black necktie, or other well-mannered colors and suit or slacks and jacket should be worn. The wearing of shoes with open heels is not appropriate. Female lawyers should dress in a courteous outfit with a skirt or trousers and a respectfully colored blouse and wear closed heel shoes.

During court appearances, a lawyer who is qualified to wear the lawyer's gown must wear it.

A lawyer must comply strictly to the orders of the chairman of the Lawyers' Council and of the Committee of Lawyers Ethics according to their power and responsibilities provided by law.

Finding A Thai Interpreter Or Translator

Here we will explain the difference between a translator and an interpreter. In Thai, a translator is called *puu-plae ek-ga-saan* ("document translator") and an interpreter is called *laam* ("one that connects"). Often, people use these terms interchangeably, even in English.

Translators

Translators deal with written text. They translate from one language (source language) to another (target language). You will need a translator to translate documents like birth certificates, divorce papers, prenuptial agreements, and other written documents or text. There are different levels of translator based on training, skills, and talent. A good translator has the ability to write well and express things clearly in the target language. Professional Thai translators almost always work in only one direction, translating only into Thai. It is more difficult to find a Thai translator who can translate into English or other languages well.

The key skills of the translator are the ability to understand the source language and the culture of the country where the text originated, and the ability and resources to use a first-rate library of dictionaries and reference materials. For translating into your language, you may find a native speaker of your language who is proficient in Thai, or a Thai translator who is experienced in your language and who has lived in your country for a while.

In Thai court proceedings and in certain institutions, foreign documents are admissible, but must be originals or certified correct copies, and must be translated into Thai. Some documents have to be notarized and authenticated by a Thai embassy or consulate. The translation can be done by Thai translators in your home country.

In Thailand, there are many translation agencies in cities such as Bangkok, Chiang Mai, Pattaya, Phuket, and Hua Hin. They are located in the tourist areas (and in Bangkok near the embassies). Translation agencies have translators experienced in many languages and they will certify a translation as true and correct. Some documents have to be certified by translation agencies that have been approved by the embassies or the court, so confirm with the translator or agency that their work is accepted by the officials you are dealing with.

The quality of translation varies from agency to agency, but for basic documents such as birth certificates, there is a standard form, so the standards are comparable. For important documents, you may want to be more selective in your choice of translator. You can ask different agencies to give you sample translations, which they may or may not charge you for. One-page document translations should cost between 500 to 1,000 baht depending on the length, number of words, and the difficulty of the subject. Some agencies charge extra to certify the translation.

Interpreters

An interpreter works with the spoken word, relaying what someone says into another language, and sometimes vice versa. An interpreter has to be able to translate, on the spot, in both directions, without the use of any dictionaries. An interpreter is needed for situations in which a client requires assistance in understanding what someone is saying, or to help someone else understand what the client is saying.

For legal proceedings in Thailand, the language used in court is complex and formal, and you will need an interpreter unless you are very fluent in Thai.

There are two types of interpreting: consecutive and simultaneous. For consecutive interpreting, the interpreter will wait until the speaker stops (usually short sentences, a paragraph, or a complete thought) before interpreting. For simultaneous interpreting, the interpreter starts interpreting as he hears the source language, with a few seconds overlap. The best way to interpret simultaneously is to work in a booth wearing a pair of headphones and speaking into a microphone. In some courtrooms, the interpreter has a headset and a microphone and the defendant listens on the receiver. If there is no equipment, the interpreter will speak to his audience (client) in a soft voice that will not interrupt the main speaker or other people he is not interpreting for. In court, if the judge, the lawyer, or the prosecutor asks the defendant or the witness a question, it is usually interpreted consecutively. Otherwise, the interpreter has to work simultaneously.

Hiring a professional interpreter in Thailand can be expensive. It can cost from 2,000—10,000 baht a day depending on the duration of the job and distance the interpreter must travel. You can hire an interpreter for important court appearances or for a meeting with your lawyer. If you don't feel the need for an interpreter when you meet with the lawyer, you may want to bring a Thai friend or Thai relative who can also speak your language. However, you need to be careful that the interpreter you use does not act as if he was a lawyer or a legal consultant himself, which is illegal. Usually they don't know the law well enough to give you legal advice, and their advice may not be consistent with your attorney's. You must ensure they are interpreting the language only, and not changing the meaning of the advice.

The interpreter you select to use in court has to be a person that the court approves to interpret for you. In addition, according to the summary of the House of Representatives on May 18, 2005 for the amendment of criminal procedures, the Minister of Justice stated that in order to raise the standards of the Thai court system to match international standards, when necessary, the court must provide interpreters for the victims, the suspects, and the defendants in criminal cases. This is sometimes a problem because interpreters provided directly by the Thai court are usually not very fluent in foreign languages. The more qualified interpreters usually work for themselves or for a translation agency. If you want to hire a skilled interpreter, you will have to pay for it yourself.

You can hire professional interpreters from translation agencies. An alternative method to finding an interpreter is to think about hiring a Thai university student. You may go to the faculty of foreign languages at a university and ask the dean (or a professor) for recommendations of students who are fluent in your language. These students are usually adept in their language skills and should be willing to work for a lower fee and for the experience. A student is eligible to help you in many legal procedures, including in court, if approved by the judge.

Requirements Of A Qualified Interpreter
A qualified interpreter should have:

- Knowledge in the specific field. A court interpreter should have a good working knowledge of the law, court procedures, and terminology used.
- Knowledge of the general subject matter of the testimony that will be interpreted.
- Intimate familiarity with Thai culture and general knowledge of the client's own culture.
- Extensive vocabulary in both languages.
- Ability to express thoughts clearly, concisely, and articulately in both languages
- Excellent note-taking technique for consecutive interpreting, or excellent short-term memory.
- At least 100 hours of booth experience for simultaneous interpreting.

A Foreigner's View Of The Thai Courts

The following story is written by our friend Richard Barrow, an English teacher in Thailand for over ten years, who has created an exclusive website about prison life in Thailand. If you want to learn more about the Thai prison system, please visit this website at www.thaiprisonlife. com.

WHEN I WAS YOUNGER, I once sat on the jury of a murder trial. It lasted for about seven days. I had always been fascinated by courtroom dramas and after watching *Twelve Angry Men* I fancied myself as head juror. Alas, I was only nineteen at the time and no one voted for me in that position. Although it was a serious case, I did enjoy my time listening to the arguments of the prosecution and defense. The evidence was overwhelming and I think we all knew quite early on what the verdict would be.

On the final day, we were sent to deliberate the verdict just before lunch. There wasn't really much to discuss and I think we could have gone back in straight away with a guilty verdict. However, out of respect for the accused, we decided we should at least put on a show of having a meaningful discussion. We were also hungry and decided to order the free lunch and give our verdict after we had rested.

In Thailand, the courts of justice don't quite work in the same way. In the criminal courts, there are always at least two judges and no jury. Although it may seem to be unfair, not being judged by a panel of your peers, I think it is probably better if amateurs, like myself, didn't have so much of a say in the lives of the accused. But then, that leaves a lot of responsibility on the shoulders of the judges.

Once, I was in court for the trial of a defendant who had been accused of attempted murder. This was a Westerner who was being put on trial in a foreign land. Everything was conducted in Thai. At the beginning of the case, there was a discussion between the judges and the defense team as to whether there should be translations for the defendant during the trial. The judge was of the opinion that it would slow the proceedings down too much and asked the lawyer to only translate what she felt was necessary. Really, the defendant was lucky to have a lawyer who spoke English. Another prisoner I spoke to said he couldn't afford his own lawyer, so the court appointed one for free, who unfortunately didn't speak any English. He said there was a court interpreter, but all he said was, "You, come here. Sit down. Stand up.

Sign here." Other than that, he had no idea what was going on or even how much time he was sentenced to. In fact, he was the last to know.

The courtroom wasn't very large. There were probably about six or so of these rooms on this floor alone. At the front was the raised platform where the judges sat. Above them was a portrait of HM the King. Below was the symbol of the court, a downward pointing dagger with scales balancing on it. In front of the bench sat the court clerk. On the judges' right was the table for the prosecution. On the left was the table for the defense. In the middle of the room, facing the judges' bench, was the chair and table for the witnesses. The room was roughly split in half by a low railing. Behind this were benches where members of the public and interested parties sat. In Thailand, courts are usually open to the public. So, in theory, if you are respectfully dressed, you could go and watch a trial. (Just remember, no cameras are allowed, and you should turn off your mobile phone.)

At about 9.35 a.m., John (not his real name) was escorted into the courtroom by a policeman. He was barefoot and chained at the ankles. A length of string was attached to the chains which enabled him to hold them off the floor as he hobbled along. The policeman told him to sit down on the front bench next to where I was sitting. I asked him whether he remembered me visiting him in prison and he said "Yes" but he didn't remember my name. While we were waiting for the judges to arrive, I tried to have a conversation with him. He wasn't looking too good.

Shortly, the two judges arrived through their private entrance at the front of the court. No-one announced their arrival, but everyone stood up anyway. They wore black robes with dark velvet edging around the neck and down the front. People didn't *wai*, but bowed instead. The public prosecutor sat on my left. The first day was reserved for the prosecution. The burden of proof rests on the prosecution and she had to prove the crime beyond a reasonable doubt. In the morning, she called three witnesses: the victim, the arresting officer, and a witness to the crime. Each was called forward and they put their hands together in a prayer-like gesture and promised to tell the truth. As in Western courts, the prosecutor asked a series of questions and then the defense was allowed to cross examine. However, there were some notable differences.

In Western courts, there would be a stenographer making a record of everything that was said. However, in Thailand, this is left up to the judge. In front of him was a tape recorder. This wasn't to record the witnesses. What happens is that after the witness has answered the question, the judge then paraphrases what he said. But, he doesn't do this for everything. Only what he deems to be relevant.

During the cross-examination, I could see the defense lawyer pausing before he asked each question so that the judge could have time to record the answer. However, sometimes the judge didn't bother to record anything, which obviously annoyed the defense. He just told them to ask the next question. The witness had said he was in hospital for four days. However, under cross examination, he said he was only in ICU for the first day. The judge didn't record that.

I also noticed that the judges participated more in the questioning of the witness. Sometimes they asked questions that they felt the prosecutor should have asked. Or a question to clarify an answer. The prosecutor sometimes left the courtroom during cross-examination. There were two judges, but only one lead judge. The other was there as support. Every now and then he would change tapes and the court clerk would then take this to type up. At the start of each tape he would record something and then quickly rewind it to see if it recorded properly. The last witness of the morning was supposed to be the doctor. However, he didn't turn up, which seemed to annoy the judges. After a few phone calls, they decided to postpone the next trial date. The prosecutors were supposed to finish on this day and then the following week the defense team would have their turn. But, as the doctor couldn't come, so the trial was put off for just over two weeks.

It was doubtful that the verdict would be read out on that day. From previous experience, I would say it would take two to three weeks before they set a date for the verdict to be read. By about 12 p.m., the court clerk had finished typing up the testimonials from the witnesses. These were then read out in court. Each witness was then asked if what had been read was a true account. Each said it was. Then each party had to sign these statements. At first John didn't want to sign this document. It was all written in Thai. He said that he was being framed and didn't want to be a part of all this. The lawyer managed to persuade him by saying that he was only signing to witness the document, not to affirm that what was written was the truth.

Part 3
Personal and Family Matters

Personal And Family Matters

Thai family law reflects the basis of Thai society and culture. In the past, the law gave more importance to the husband than the wife. As an example, the law stated that the Thai man was the leader of the family and could have multiple wives and could also sell his children or his wives. Men had rights to decide what to do with common property. There were many inequalities between the rights of men and women. The Constitution of 1974, Section 28, Paragraph 2, provides that "men and women have equal rights."

Thai family law has now been transformed to match international standards. Women have equal rights under the law. Rights for women and children have been promoted and protected by a variety of different organizations. The antiquated laws regarding family matters have been abolished. However, in practice the old Thai system still affects the way that Thais interact beyond the legal system.

This part of the book will give you general information on a number of aspects of family and personal legal matters in Thailand. The information will also help you understand the situations where you may need to adapt the concept of the law to the actual Thai culture and person you are dealing with.

Thai Citizenship

Thailand has different requirements for a person to obtain Thai citizenship or nationality based on various conditions. A person who is born with parents who both hold Thai citizenship is automatically a Thai citizen, whether or not they were born inside or outside of Thailand. A person born in Thailand does not automatically have Thai citizenship if one of the parents is an alien.

Citizenship depends on the immigration status (whether illegal or legal) and the marriage status of the parents. The criteria for a person born to a mother or father of Thai nationality, whether born inside or outside of the Thai kingdom, is listed on the following page, and is in accordance with the Thai Nationality Act of 1992.

Children Born Within The Territory Of The Kingdom of Thailand

Case	Nationality of Father	Nationality of Mother	Marital Status	Nationality of Child
1	Thai	Thai	Registered	Thai
2	Thai	Thai	No	Thai
3	Thai	Legal Alien	Registered	Thai
4	Thai	Legal Alien	No	Thai
5	Thai	Illegal Alien	Registered	Thai
6	Thai	Illegal Alien	No	Thai
7	Legal Alien	Thai	Registered	Thai
8	Legal Alien	Thai	No	Thai
9	Illegal Alien	Thai	Registered	Thai
10	Illegal Alien	Thai	No	Thai
11	Legal Alien	Legal Alien	Registered	Thai
12	Legal Alien	Legal Alien	No	Thai
13	Legal Alien	Illegal Alien	Registered	Cannot Acquire Thai Nationality
14	Legal Alien	Illegal Alien	No	Cannot Acquire Thai Nationality
15	Illegal Alien	Legal Alien	Registered	Cannot Acquire Thai Nationality
16	Illegal Alien	Legal Alien	No	Cannot Acquire Thai Nationality
17	Illegal Alien	Illegal Alien	Registered	Cannot Acquire Thai Nationality
18	Illegal Alien	Illegal Alien	No	Cannot Acquire Thai Nationality

Source: Royal Thai Consulate General

Children Born Outside The Territory Of The Kingdom of Thailand

Case	Nationality of Father	Nationality of Mother	Marital Status	Nationality of Child
1	Thai	Thai	Registered	Thai
2	Thai	Thai	No	Thai
3	Thai	Other Nationality	Registered	Thai
4	Thai	Other Nationality	No	Cannot acquire Thai Nationality
5	Other Nationality	Thai	Registered	Thai
6	Other Nationality	Thai	No	Thai

Source: *Royal Thai Consulate General*

Naturalization And Its Requirements

A foreign national who wants to obtain Thai citizenship must go through the naturalization process. The Thai Nationality law specifies the conditions which must be met to become a naturalized citizen. The application to change to Thai citizenship has to be satisfied and approved by the Interior minister. The processing fee is 5,000 baht and it may take up to three years. The applicant will have to swear to be faithful and loyal to Thailand.

For the latest details and an application form and other required documents, contact the Criminal Investigation Division Group I, Subdivision 3, Police Department, Rama I Road, Bangkok.

According to a section of the Thai Nationality Act of 1965, to apply for naturalization, one must:

1. Become of age according to the Thai law (twenty years old).

2. Have good conduct.

3. Be gainfully employed.

4. Have continually resided in Thailand for five years or more on the day of application.

5. Have a good command of the Thai language.

According to Section 11, items 4 and 5 do not apply to the following: a foreign national who has done exceptionally good deeds for the country, or a child or spouse of a person who has been naturalized or has changed back to Thai citizenship or who previously had Thai citizenship.

If the child is underage and sponsored by a mother or father having Thai nationality, there must be evidence of both sponsorship and the child's birth. The child will be exempted from items 1, 3, 4, and 5.

A person born to either a father or mother of Thai nationality, whether born within or outside Thailand, may apply for Thai nationality. A person is still considered as having Thai nationality unless:

- He or she desires to renounce Thai nationality by declaring his or her intention to the required Thai authories.
- His or her nationality is revoked by the government of the kingdom of Thailand.

If a person of Thai nationality desires to renounce his or her Thai nationality while outside of Thailand:

- He or she may file an application stating his or her intention to a Thai consulate or embassy.
- Once filed, the Thai consulate will conduct an investigation of the person and his or her witnesses, then file a report on the application.

A person of Thai nationality who has renounced his or her nationality and is living outside of Thailand may re-apply for Thai citizenship by filing an application to a Thai consulate or embassy.

If a spouse of a person of Thai nationality is a citizen of a foreign country, they can file an application for Thai nationality with a Thai consulate or embassy.

Applications for any of the above requests are submitted with relevant supporting documents. Supporting documents must comport with the following:

- Any document, including those issued by the government of a foreign country that is included in the application needs to be certified by the proper authorities.
- If the document is in a foreign language other than English, it must be translated into Thai, then examined and certified by appropriate authorities.
- If the supporting document is a copy, it will need to be certified as a true copy by designated authorities in each country.

Applying For A Thai Birth Certificate

A child born to a Thai parent outside Thailand may be entitled to acquire Thai nationality and obtain a Thai passport. (See table, Children Born Outside The Territory Of The Kingdom of Thailand). Having a Thai birth certificate makes the child eligible for a Thai passport. The child may be able to have dual citizenship until reaching adulthood, when he or she will have to choose one citizenship.

Parents may apply for a Thai birth certificate for their child at the Thai embassy or consulate in the country of birth. (Check with the local Thai embassy or consulate, since each one has slightly different requirements, or call to verify what documents are needed.) The following documents are generally required to obtain a Thai birth certificate:

1   Certificate of Birth or Notification of Birth, which has been translated into Thai.

2   Two copies of the marriage certificate of the parents.

3   Two copies of the passport of the father and the passport of the mother (either two Thai passports or one foreign and one Thai passport).

4   Two copies of the ID cards of the father and of the mother.

5   Two photos of the child.

To obtain a Thai birth certificate for a child who is born in the United States to a Thai parent, please submit the following documents:

1. Parents' passports including green card or any other US or Thai ID cards, if any, with three copies.

2. Certificate of marriage with three copies.

3. US birth certificate issued by the county's vital statistics office.

4. Completed application forms.

5. Two photographs of the child (check size requirement).

6. Fifteen-dollar fee for legalization of birth certificate, which is notarized by the US Department of State.

It takes five working days for the embassy or consulate to issue a Thai birth certificate.

Marriage In Thailand

Getting married in Thai culture usually refers to having a 'wedding ceremony' in which Buddhist monks perform the ritual of tying the bond between the bride and the groom, in which friends, neighbors, and relatives come to witness the 'wedding', and the couple is announced as husband and wife.

Although we use the term 'Buddhist wedding' in this section, it should be noted at the outset that there is no such thing as a 'Buddhist wedding.' Buddhism, as a philosophy or religion, does not recognize marriage. It has no place in the theology.

The presence of monks at a Thai 'wedding ceremony', during which they chant mantras, is purely cultural and symbolic, and is done for good luck.

To make their union valid and legal under Thai law, the couple has to register the marriage at the civil registration district office (commonly called the *amphur*), which handles most registration matters. (It is also called the district registrar and is open from 8:30 a.m. to 4 p.m.). A marriage may also be registered at a Thai consulate (for those registered outside of Thailand).

Sometimes when you ask Thais, "Are you married?" the answer will be "Yes, but we didn't register the marriage." It means they only had a wedding ceremony, but they are not legally married.

This section contains information on all the various aspects that have to do with getting married in Thailand. We explain the engagement, the dowry, a prenuptial agreement, Thai marriage, and the wedding ceremony, along with the legal requirements for each.

Engagement And Dowry

In Thai culture, it is customary to get engaged before the wedding, and for the man to give the bride and the bride's family a dowry. By law, it is not necessary to have an engagement or to give a dowry. Traditionally, the engagement ceremony is held a few months prior to the wedding at the bride's house. It takes place in the morning and includes close relatives and friends of both the bride and groom.

Engagement parties do not normally involve religious services. This is when the couple formally introduces themselves to each other's family. They also announce the terms of the dowry and the date of the wedding. At the most auspicious moment, the man places the engagement ring on his future bride's finger. Food and drink are served afterwards. The party usually does not last very long.

Nowadays, because of the tight economy and the influence of Western culture, many Thai couples just live together without getting married or even getting engaged. However, the engagement, the dowry, and Thai wedding ceremony are still very important to many Thais and they are difficult for foreigners, especially Westerners to comprehend. (To learn more about the cultural aspects of Thai-Western relationships, please read *Thailand Fever*, also published by Paiboon.)

To get engaged, the man will have to bring certain things to the woman as a promise to marry her – usually a wedding ring or a certain amount of gold. On the engagement day, or on the day that the man's family comes to ask the woman's family for permission to allow the man to marry their daughter, the woman's family may ask for a dowry and set what the dowry will be. Sometimes the engagement happens on the day of the wedding. In such cases the man has to bring both the engagement gift and the dowry at the same time. Sometimes the engagement gift and the dowry can be the same thing. In Thai, this combination of engagement gift and dowry is called *sin-sot tong-man*, which literally means "dowry-gold-to engage."

To register a marriage in Thailand, both parties must have the following qualifications:

1. The couple must each be at least seventeen years old. If one of the partners is less than twenty years old, the couple must have the consent of both parents of the underage partner (if both are still alive), one of the parents (if the other one is deceased or is in a position where consent cannot be given), or of the legal guardian or adoptive parent(s).

2. Must not be mentally incapacitated.

3. Must not be a close or direct relative, nor share a parent through marriage (half-brothers and sisters are not allowed to marry).

4. Must not have the same adoptive parents.

5. Must not be the same sex.

6. Must not be currently married elsewhere.

Now a little more background information about the dowry. The most common questions about the dowry asked by non-Thais are "What is it?" and "How much should it be?"

According to the definition in Thai law, the dowry means objects or property that the groom gives to the bride's parents or her guardians to show gratitude for allowing the woman to marry him. It is compensation to the bride's family for raising her. Sometimes the dowry is called the 'bride price.'

How much should the man pay the woman's family? There is no set amount. It is determined by the man's wealth and the value of the woman, which is based on her family background, beauty, education, whether she is a virgin, has been married before, or has children. A bride with a good family background, high education, and who has never been married, can ask for a higher amount of dowry. A beautiful bride will naturally expect to get more than a bride who is not perceived as beautiful. If you intend to take your bride away from her family home, the dowry may be higher.

In the past, the dowry was quoted by a number of cows or buffalos, amount of rice or land, and jewelry. The bride's family would receive and keep the entire dowry. Nowadays, the concept of the dowry is more fluid, and numerous items are taken into consideration. The woman's family may set the amount of the dowry, which can be in the range of 50,000 baht up to a million baht. Sometimes the family may ask for gold and other assets, as well. The groom can also make an offer if the woman's family does not know his situation and his ability to pay. Sometimes the parents of the bride-to-be just quote the bride price, but don't really expect to get the money. They quote the price so they can tell the neighbors how much the dowry will be. This is simply a way to show their status.

The groom must show that he can pay the amount that the family quotes. Then the family will either give the dowry back or just have the groom pay for the wedding ceremony. If the groom and the bride have about the same status – such as having the same level of education, are about the same age, have both never been married, and have the same family social standing – then the groom may not have to pay any dowry. In some cases the bride's family may even pay half of the wedding expenses.

After the engagement, the wedding ceremony, or the registration of marriage, if the parties decide to break up and the woman is to blame (through having an affair, for example), the man has the right to get the engagement gift or the dowry back. However, if the man is at fault, it will not be returned. If the break up is consensual, the woman may feel an obligation to return the dowry. If you were engaged and married in Thailand, by law, you can ask for the engagement gift and dowry back, even if you are a foreigner. However, it is not customary and is not expected.

Prenuptial Agreement

A prenuptial agreement is a new concept to Thais. Most don't know about it, at all. It is not common for Thai couples to enter into this type of agreement.

Thailand is what some Western societies call a community property jurisdiction. Thai law under the Civil and Commercial Code clearly states the difference between personal property and common property. Personal property might also be referred to as separate property and amounts to property owned by someone before they married. Common property might be referred to as community property and is the property acquired during the marriage. When there is a divorce, only common property will be taken into consideration when dividing the property between the two parties. However, keep in mind that after a few years, it may be difficult to remember or prove what property was owned before the marriage, so a prenuptial agreement might aid in dividing the property if the marriage ends in divorce.

A prenuptial agreement is not normally a topic of discussion for a Thai couple getting married in Thailand.

It's a different situation and a difficult one when a foreign man wants a future Thai wife to sign a prenuptial agreement. Often, foreign husbands are older than their Thai wives and usually have property that they have amassed over the years, or sources of income that will generate considerable wealth during the marriage, while the wives are younger and do not have much money or assets. The husband wants to plan for his future financial situation and to protect his interests in case there is a divorce. Some Thai wives feel miserable, hurt, and betrayed when they learn about the prenuptial agreement. They expect a husband to take care of them and love them forever. It is also considered unromantic by the Thai wife. Although it will most likely be a difficult endeavor, if you want to secure your financial future, it is a wise decision to have a prenuptial agreement, especially if there is a great imbalance between your assets and your future wife's resources.

Depending on your situation, you will decide whether to have a prenuptial agreement. You may have it composed either in Thailand or in your home country. If you live outside of Thailand and your property is mostly in your home country, you will probably want to have the agreement drafted by an experienced lawyer there. Then the document should be translated into Thai. If not, it will have to be read in Thai by an interpreter to your soon-to-be spouse, if he or she does not understand complicated legal materials in your native language. This is so your spouse clearly understands what the agreement states before signing it. This stage is vitally important to prevent your new spouse from claiming misunderstanding of the content of the prenuptial agreement.

If your main residence and some of your property is in Thailand, the prenuptial agreement can be written in Thailand, again using a trusted lawyer. In this case, Thai law will apply. Under Thai law, you may be able to specify the properties involved and categorize them as common property and personal property. You may also specify how finances will be managed during the course of your marriage.

It is recommended that the prenuptial agreement be drafted by an experienced lawyer and possibly be prepared as a bilingual agreement. You should still have documented proof that your future spouse understands the contents of the agreement before signing it, even if it is in Thai. This could mean getting witness statements attesting that the spouse read, indicated understanding, and agreed to the document before signing it. To be valid, Thai law requires two witnesses to sign the prenuptial agreement.

Marrying In Thailand

If you marry a Thai citizen, or even if both you and your spouse are foreigners, you may register your marriage in Thailand. It is a fairly simple process if you have all the required documents ready. Once registered, it will be considered a legal marriage pursuant to Thai law, and the marriage will be recognized throughout the world.

When unregistered couples have children, the children usually take the father's surname. If the parents separate, in most cases, the children stay with their mother but still use the surname of the father. This is sometimes confusing to foreigners who want to marry a Thai woman and sponsor her child but wonder why the child does not have the same family name as the mother.

You may register your marriage in any registration office within the country. The registration, which is the actual legal documentation of the marriage, usually takes place a few days before or after the wedding ceremony, and sometimes on the same day. The marriage certificate is issued shortly after the registration is submitted, and the certificate is recognized by most countries (along with a certified translation into the official language of the country).

Some foreigners prefer to have a lawyer assist in the registration process, to acquire the official documents from their embassy in Thailand, have them translated, and to expedite the process with minimal fuss. For a reasonable fee, a qualified law firm that has expertise in Thai law and the laws of your country can help reduce delays and complications. Depending on personal situations, for some it is better to register the marriage in Thailand, and for others it is better to register in their home country. You should consult with your experienced lawyer and determine which is better for you.

You and your future spouse can do the paperwork yourselves, but it can be a very time-consuming experience. If you are a foreigner, you will need to get numerous documents from your embassy (in Bangkok). Forms need to be submitted and transmitted from one Thai government office to another, and many of these government offices are located in different parts of Bangkok.

After you have gathered together all of your documents, you may want to register at the local registration office in the area where your future Thai spouse lives. As mentioned before, the marriage can be registered at any registration office in Thailand, but some people prefer to do it in their home district and close to the time of the wedding, which usually takes place in their hometown.

The procedure, requirements, and documents necessary for registering your marriage if you are a foreigner marrying a Thai are as follows:

- Appear in person with your passport at your embassy in Thailand to complete a declaration attesting that you are single and free to marry in accordance with Thai Law (blank forms are available at the embassy). This process has now been enforced and required by all Thai registration offices. In the past, there were problems when foreigners registered their marriage in Thailand while they were still married or only legally separated from their spouses in their home country. Your embassy will check your background with the proper authorities and will be able to verify your marital status and notarize your document. Of course, there will be some fees for this. If you have previously been married, which ended by divorce or death, you will also need the original certificates. In addition, a criminal background check needs to be done in your home country and a report submitted.

- The completed declaration will then have to be translated into Thai by an approved translation office.

- Take the declaration, translations, supporting documents, reports, and photocopies of your passport to the Legalization Division of the Consular Affairs Department at 123 Chaengwattana Road, Laksi, Bangkok 10210 (Tel: 66-2 575-1056-60; Fax: 575-1054; e-mail: consular04@mfa.go.th) where the consular official's signature will be authenticated. Your documents are then ready for submission to the registration office (*amphur*), which will register the marriage and issue the marriage certificate in Thai.

At the registration office, you need to bring all of the documents listed above plus the following:

- In cases where the woman is a widow or a divorcee, the dissolution of the former marriage must have taken place at least 310 days before the next marriage. This is to avoid problems in case the woman was pregnant. Pregnancy test results from a medical office are accepted if the time between the former marriage and the next marriage is less than 310 days; but this rule shall not apply if:

a. a child has been born during that period.

b. the same couple that are divorced intend to remarry.

c. there is a court order allowing the woman to marry.

- The applicants' occupation and annual income (this information may be requested by some registration offices).
- Any and all alimony payments and outstanding private debts must be fully disclosed.
- Names and addresses of two contact persons residing in the same area as the applicants need to be provided.
- Two witnesses.
- An original valid passport.
- The Thai must bring their Thai ID and house registration (plus a name-change certificate if there was a name change).

If you marry a Thai in your home county, you will register the marriage there. However, this will not have any effect on your spouse's legal status in Thailand; he or she will still be considered single. To make your marriage valid in Thailand, you have to register the marriage with the Thai embassy or consulate in your home country. If you do not register, it will only be effective in your home country. This may be an advantage for a Thai woman, since her legal rights in Thailand will remain the same. She will still have the title "Miss," as if she was not married, and she can benefit from the legal process as before. Some women choose not to register with the Thai government, so as to keep their rights as a single female Thai citizen.

For those who live outside Thailand, the following are the rules and regulations and documents for registering your marriage at a Thai embassy or consulate in your home country:

- One of the parties must be a Thai national.
- The two parties must appear in person to register.
- Thai citizen's ID card or the original valid Thai passport and original valid passport of the foreign party, with a photocopy of each.
- The original divorce certificate or court's judgment (if one person was previously married).
- Certificate of name change (if applicable) and a photocopy.
- Some embassies may ask for a pregnancy test stating that the woman is not pregnant.

If a Thai woman is married to a foreigner and the marriage is registered in Thailand, she will lose a few of her legal rights, and some privileges regarding land ownership will be restricted. Thai men do not lose any rights if they are married to a foreigner and the marriage is registered in Thailand.

The following is additional information if you are legally married to a Thai woman in Thailand. Laws regarding foreign ownership of Thai property change often, so you should check with governmental authorities and a lawyer to verify what is still current:

- Your Thai wife can keep the land she owned before getting married.
- She can inherit land and any buildings attached to it.
- She can still buy a house or land, but the foreign husband will have to sign a declaration at the land office that the money used to purchase the land is all hers. In case of a divorce or her death, the foreign husband will have no claim to the house or land. (For additional information on a foreigner's ability to buy land in Thailand, see *How To Buy Land And Build A House In Thailand*, also published by Paiboon.)

Another extremely important item to consider when you marry a Thai woman is that you and your wife should each have a legal will. There is a sample will in the back of this book, but your wills should be prepared by a lawyer. Without a will, if your wife dies before you, her relatives may be legally able to take what they think belongs to her, including your house. (More information on how to draft a will appears later in this book.)

The Wedding Ceremony

For a marriage to be legal, it is not necessary to have a wedding ceremony, it only needs to be registered. However, if you are getting married to a Thai woman, she and her family will likely want to have a wedding ceremony, and you, as a foreign husband, will be expected to pay some dowry.

If you are a foreign woman and you marry a Thai man, it will be less complicated for you. Since there are more cases of foreign men marrying Thai woman, this section will refer to the groom as a foreigner and the bride as Thai. However, the same details apply to Thai men marrying a foreigner with some slight adjustments on some aspects of the process.

Thai weddings vary according to the part of the country and the preferences and beliefs of the families. There are a variety of wedding cerenonies, such as the Lanna style (in the north), Isaan style (in the northeast), and the traditional Thai 'Buddhist wedding'. There is also a Muslim style wedding. A traditional Thai 'Buddhist wedding' ceremony is the most common and is popular when the groom is a foreigner. Since this is a law book and not a culture book, we will discuss the traditional Thai wedding style briefly.

The date of the wedding (and sometimes what time of the day the ceremony should take place) is determined by consulting with Buddhist monks or astrologers. They will refer to astrological charts and determine the most auspicious time and date for the wedding. In modern times, convenience often plays a larger role than astrology in determining the wedding day. Still, most Thais will avoid getting married on what is deemed to be an unlucky day. After the big day is decided upon, the couple will print and send out wedding invitation cards.

Traditional Thai Buddhist weddings usually start early in the morning. Often the bride will begin preparing her hair and dress as early as four o'clock in the morning. The ceremony starts with Buddhist monks chanting mantras and blessing the bride and the groom. Food is then served, with the monks eating before the guests. After the meal, the blessing period, called *rot-naam-sang*, begins. The bride and the groom sit side by side on the floor or on a small stage, each wearing a headband joined by a white cord. Behind them stand the two best men and the two bridesmaids (all four should be unmarried). The pouring of holy water comes next, and the most senior person starts first, followed by the other guests. Each person walks up and pours holy water (blessed by a monk) on to the hands of the bride and groom from a conch shell or decorative bowl, wishing them happiness, prosperity, and a long life together. The water blessing ceremony usually ends before noon, but some people decide to perform it in the afternoon or at the reception.

The reception party usually takes place in the evening and is a time for food, music, dancing, and speeches. Wedding gifts are accepted in the form of money enclosed in an envelope with the name of the giver. Guests who don't attend the evening reception bring gifts in the morning to the wedding ceremony instead, or they can put money in the invitation card and have it delivered to the bride and the groom if they cannot attend the ceremony or the reception.

A wedding ceremony costs less than the reception party. Some couples choose to do the ceremony only and have a small party afterwards. If you hold the wedding ceremony in a village, it can cost 30,000—50,000 baht. Receptions are more expensive because there will be more guests to cater for. The cost will include the location rental, drinks, food, entertainment, and other expenses, and can be as high as 100,000—300,000 baht or more. This expense may be paid for from the dowry, or both the bride and groom might share the expenses, or the groom may pay for the entire party. Each situation is different and should be discussed and agreed to long before the bill is presented.

Bringing Your Thai Spouse And Children To Your Home Country

Thais are allowed to travel freely and return to Thailand at anytime unless their Thai citizenship has been renounced or revoked. Many countries require a Thai citizen to obtain a visa prior to visiting that country. Usually, a Thai citizen will have to apply for a particular type of visa that will serve the purpose of their visit.

Thai law does not regulate the requirements for bringing your Thai spouse and children to your home country. Your home country will establish the procedures for admitting your Thai family and you will need to investigate the relevant laws and regulations. For example, the UK allows its citizens to bring a Thai spouse and any children under eighteen years old, as long as that citizen can show that he or she can financially support and accommodate the family. If you are a UK citizen married to a Thai, you will also need to show the marriage certificate and a birth certificate for each child (the originals in Thai and the certified English translations). The family will normally be given permission to stay in the UK for the same period that the sponsor does, and will probably be allowed to work if the permission to stay lasts for one year or more. Make sure your spouse has a copy of your passport when applying for entry after you –UK Immigration will need to see the page showing your name, your entry clearance sticker (if you have one) and how long your permission lasts. (See more information for UK immigration at http://www.ukvisas. gov.uk.)

US regulations are more complicated and difficult than most other countries. Some people bring their Thai spouse or spouse-to-be as a fiancé(e) instead of declaring them as a wife or husband. In some cases, this method can reduce the time required for immigration processing. The procedure also differs depending on if you are a US citizen or just a legal permanent resident.

To bring your Thai spouse and children to the US, the US Immigration Department must approve an immigrant visa petition that you file for your spouse. The State Department only grants a limited number of visa requests each year for lawful permanent residents, and the State Department visa bulletin must show that a spouse immigrant visa is available to your spouse, based on the date you filed the immigrant visa application.

If you are a US citizen, your spouse and children are entitled to immediate entry if your visa petition is approved. If your spouse is outside the US when your visa petition is approved and when an immigrant visa number (if required) becomes available, your spouse will be notified to go to the local US consulate to complete the processing for an immigrant visa. If your spouse is legally inside the US when your visa petition is approved and when an immigrant visa number (if required) becomes available, he or she may use the Form I-485 to apply to adjust his or her status to that of a lawful permanent resident. (More information on the US visa requirements is available at http://travel.state.gov/visa/visa, the official US government website.

Each country has different rules and regulations and we suggest that you seek the advice of a reputable attorney who can analyze your situation and advise you on your options, and allow you to determine the best course of action.

Before you decide to bring your Thai family to live with you in your home country, you need to consider many issues including, but not limited to, the following:

- Financial costs (of airfares, accommodation, daily expenses, childcare, education, and healthcare).
- Visa requirements and documents.
- Education or special education requirements for your spouse and children.
- Language issues.
- Culture shock.
- Limited employment opportunities for your spouse or children.
- New living arrangements.
- Costs for reoccurring visits to Thailand to visit the extended family back home.
- Your spouse sending money back to Thailand.
- Weather extremes.

Adopting Children From Thailand

If you live outside Thailand and want to adopt a Thai child, you can do so through adoption agencies, social welfare departments, or non-governmental agencies (referred to as a "competent authority") licensed in your home country by your government to handle the matter of inter-country adoptions.

The competent authority will make a report that includes details of the prospective adoptive parent's physical and mental health, family status, assets, liabilities, and financial standing, personal repute, and conditions of the place of residence. In addition, the size of the existing family and ability to give love and care for the child, motivation, and any special reasons related to the welfare and interest of the child will be considered. Parental relationships and obligations to the children of previous marriages (if applicable) and other matters pertinent to the applicants will be reviewed. (For more information, see www.adoption.org. This organization provides guidelines on how to process your adoption application.)

You can also adopt children from Thailand independently. However, you cannot adopt more than one child at a time (including twins or siblings) or in the case of the adoption of children of the applicants' Thai spouse. The process usually takes one to two years. You may want to adopt a specific child, who may be a relative, your spouse's child, or a child from an orphanage. The paperwork is tedious and difficult, so you will need a Thai lawyer to assist in the process.

We have included some general information on adopting children in Thailand from the Department of Local Administration, the Interior Ministry, and the Child Adoption Center. First, you must meet the basic qualifications before you can adopt a child from Thailand. If you meet these basic qualifications, you can then apply for adoption by presenting the appropriate documents to the Department of Public

Welfare. Once the application is approved, you must register the adoption to complete the process. These steps are discussed in detailed below.

Qualifications

1. The adoptive parent must be more than 25 years old and must be at least fifteen years older than the person being adopted.

2. The adopted person who is more than fifteen years old must give his or her consent.

3. If the adopted person is a minor, consent must be received from:

   - both parents if they are still alive;
   - the father or mother if only one is alive or if only one has custody;
   - the legal representative or the prosecutor who has made a request to the court to approve the adoption;
   - the person in charge of the hospital or other institution approved by the local governmental agency;
   - the person who has taken care of an abandoned child for more than one year.

4. The adoptive parent and adopted person (this assumes that the adopted person is an adult) must receive consent from their spouse except where:

   - the spouse is unable to provide consent;
   - the spouse has left the area and his or her whereabouts are unknown for more than one year.

5. A minor cannot be an adopted son or daughter of someone else (except if he or she has been adopted by your spouse).

A prospective foreign adoptive parent must have a legitimate spouse and be eligible to adopt a child from Thailand under the laws of their home country.

Benefits Of Registration Of Adoption

1. The adopted child has the right to use the last name and inherit the assets of the adoptive parent. However, the adoptive parent cannot inherit the assets of the adopted person.

2. From the date of registration, the adoptive parent has the authority to raise the adopted person as if the adopted person was his or her own legal child.

3. From the date of registration, biological parents no longer have power or rights over the child. However, in Thailand, they are still considered the biological parents and the adopted person will not lose rights and responsibilities as a child to their biological parents. (In Thailand it is up to the child whether to pay respect to biological parents.)

Application For Approval

An official application form is required to be filled out and returned by the applicants to the Department of Public welfare or authorized agencies. The completed form has to be submitted with the additional required documents:

- Medical certificate verifying good physical health, mental stability, or infertility of the applicants (if applicable).
- Document certifying marriage.
- Documents certifying occupation and income.
- Documents certifying financial status.
- Documents certifying assets.
- Letters of recommendation given by at least two references.
- Extract of divorce decree of the applicants (if applicable).
- Four photographs of the applicant (check size requirement), including photographs of the applicants' children (if any) and their home area.
- Document from the immigration authority of your home country permitting the immigration of a child to be adopted.
- Confirmation from a concerned authority that after the adoption is finalized under Thai law, it will also be legalized under the concerned laws of the applicants' home country.

All of the documents must be originals and be verified by the Thai embassy or consulate in the applicants' home country, or sent through diplomatic channels. Therefore, the documents in other languages have to be attached with their translation, either in Thai or English, which have to be verified by the Thai embassy or consulate. After this process is completed, you have to register the adoption.

Process Of Registration Of Adoption In Thailand

The registration process is the final step in the adoption. It is completed by submitting the request for registration. Once registered, the adoption is recognized by the Thai government, and the adoptive parents and adopted person gain the benefits of adoption. A detailed explanation of the registration process follows.

To begin the process, the adoptive parents and the adopted person must submit a request to the local registrar officer (*amphur*). If either the adoptive parents and/or the adopted person is married, they must bring their spouse with them to the registrar's office to give consent.

1. If the adoptive parents live in Bangkok (including foreigners) they must submit a request to the Child Adoption Center at the Department of Public Welfare at 255 Ratchavithi Road, Bangkok 10400. For those who live outside Bangkok, submit a request to the local registrar office or the Office of the Public Welfare Department of the province, along with the letter of consent from the person who can authorize the adoption.

2. A foreigner who lives outside Thailand must submit the request to a public welfare or social welfare department that is approved by his or her home country's government to supervise the adoption process.

3. After the adoption committee approves the adoption, the adoptive parents have to submit another request for registration of the adoption.

4. The adopted person that is married must bring their spouse to give consent.

5. If the adopted person is older than fifteen years, he or she has to provide consent in writing.

It takes about one hour for the registration of the adoption. You should bring the adopted person's birth certificate, house registration, passport (if any), and one photograph. The adoptive parents should bring their ID cards, house registration, permission letter from the Department of Public Welfare (for an adopted person who is a minor), marriage certificates (of both the adoptive parents and adopted person (if the adopted person is married), and two witnesses.

The adopted person will be eligible to hold the citizenship of the country of the adoptive parents after the adoption process is complete.

Domestic Violence

Domestic violence in Thailand is increasing every year. The One Stop Crisis Center (OSCC) reports that in 2006, children and women were victims of domestic violence at the rate of 39 incidents per day, compared to 32 in 2005 and 19 in 2004. However, the real numbers may be higher. The Ministry of Social Development and Human Security estimates that incidents of domestic violence take place in 18 million families in Thailand. The Ministry proposed the Domestic-Violence Victim Protection Bill before the Cabinet, which was passed and is now a part of Thai law.

Most domestic violence is caused by men, and the victims are usually women and children. In Thailand this type of violence used to be considered a family problem between individuals and was not viewed as criminal. Even today, when a wife is beaten by her husband, neighbors do not want to become involved because of the fear of intruding into what they consider to be other people's personal business. Historically in Thailand it has been a cultural fact that a wife is considered the property of her husband. Some people also believe in karma, and that it is the fate of the wife or children to end up in a bad domestic situation. Thai women who live with this violence are at a loss as to how to cope with their circumstances. Thai society expects couples to sort out domestic issues, including violence, on their own. Therefore, women victims often opt to suffer silently and deal with it by themselves.

Many Thais are still unaware that domestic violence is now a crime that has to be reported. Thai men no longer have the right to physically abuse their wives and children. Of course, women also don't have the right to do physical harm to their husband and children.

When Thai women seek advice, the suggestions – especially from non-family members – are often not helpful. Only when the violence exacerbates and results in injuries that require medical attention or results in a fatality do the victims or their relatives seek help from the police or medical personnel.

In Thailand, when a husband and wife end up at the police station, the police try to resolve the matter and may not even write a report. The laws in Thailand regarding domestic violence usually carry negligible penalties.

The usual causes of domestic violence by male partners are related to drinking, infidelity, gambling, financial problems, and general irresponsibility. Prostitution and HIV/AIDS are also contributing factors. Alcohol abuse is a very common problem in families all over Thailand, while historically Thai society has condoned the practice of men visiting prostitutes. The Thai wife whose husband is accustomed to visiting prostitutes will have a difficult time if she finds this behavior acceptable.

Gambling is one of the most damaging factors leading to domestic violence and family financial problems. It affects the family's standard of living in addition to spreading the seeds of domestic violence. The urge to gamble in Thai society is rampant. Thai women also display a strong desire to gamble, but their number is far fewer than men.

Another factor contributing to domestic violence is that Thai society is more forgiving of antisocial behavior, especially when men gamble, have affairs, and drink to excess. Thai women get unequal treatment even in this category and are more forcefully ostracized and chastised for their misdeeds.

Many organizations in Thailand are now working on educating people about domestic violence, women's and children's rights, and what to do when one becomes a victim. The Pavena Foundation for Children and Women at www.pavena.thai.com is a non-profit organization founded by Pavena Hongsakul, a Bangkok member of parliament. It is located at 82/12 Soi Ram Intra 39, Ram Intra Road, Bangkhen, Bangkok 10220. (Tel: 02-552-6570.)

In addition, the Friends of Women Foundation at www.friendsofwomen.net is a non-governmental organization which works to protect the rights of women and assists women in crisis situations. It can be contacted at Friends of Women Foundation, 386/61-62 Ratchadaphisek 42, (Soi Chalermsuk), Ratchadaphisek Road, Lardyao, Chatuchak, Bangkok 10900. (Tel: 02 513-1001.)

If you are a foreigner who is the victim of domestic violence, you may also seek help from your embassy, which will direct you to the right organization or arrange to help you get back home.

This section does not describe all Thai men. We want to make it clear that there are many loving Thai men who are wonderful husbands and family men who would never think of hurting their wife or children. At this point in time, some Thai women are starting to embrace the idea of marrying a foreign man as an alternative to getting married to a Thai man. This trend is particularly apparent in more educated Thai women who have already married and divorced a Thai man.

Getting Divorced

In Thai culture, getting a divorce has always been looked upon as a significant loss of face and an indication of failure. Because of certain social stigma, many Thai couples are forced to live together or stay married unhappily until they die. In the past, the divorce rate was low because couples felt obligated to continue living together, and this created many family problems.

Thailand's national statistics for 2005 show that the divorce rate has risen over the past ten years. In 2003, the average rate of divorce was 1.28 couples per 1,000 people, compared to less than one couple per 1,000 in 1994. The number of couples registered as husband and wife at governmental registration offices across the country has also dramatically declined. According to figures in 2003, the number of registered marriages was only five per 1,000 people, a fall from seven per 1,000 in 1994. The largest decline in registered marriages was in the country's northeastern region. Only five marriages per 1,000 people were registered in 2003, compared to eight per 1,000 ten years ago. The statistics may show a decline in the belief of the institution of marriage and in traditional family values.

These figures may appear low compared to other countries, but these statistics can be deceptive. One reason the numbers are low may be because many couples in the provinces only have a wedding ceremony and never register their marriage. Also there is no statistical data available on the rate of infidelity or the separation of families, which is relatively high.

These days, more Thai women are becoming autonomous economically and to a greater extent are more independent. They have additional sources of emotional support and a determination to divorce an abusive husband and live on their own. The divorce rate in Thailand has been growing steadily and women are now re-marrying more often than staying single. There is still a degree of shame attached to a woman divorcing her husband in Thailand, but in increasing numbers Thai women are becoming determined to live by themselves unmarried rather than continue to be miserable and married. There are three ways to dissolve a marriage in Thailand:

1. Either the husband or wife dies.

2. By divorce registration.

3. By court order granting the divorce.

As noted above, divorce in Thailand can take two forms: divorce with the consent of the two parties, which is finalized at a registration office; or a contested divorce obtained by a court order.

Divorce Registration With Mutual Consent

If you registered your marriage in Thailand, you may obtain an uncontested divorce in Thailand by appearing in person with your spouse at the registration office or at the embassy or consulate where you registered your marriage. It is a simple process that requires you to complete and sign several forms, and it usually takes less than one hour. Once completed, the documents are certified by the signatures of at least two witnesses.

You need to bring to the registration office your passport (if a foreigner), Thai spouse's citizen's ID card, original marriage certificate, and a divorce contract (if any). The divorce contract is the settlement agreement between you and your spouse on how property is divided, support issues, child custody, and visitation rights.

Once you get to the registration office where you registered your marriage, inform the officer that you want to register your divorce. You will be asked the terms of your settlement for your assets, your children's living arrangements, child support, alimony, and other matters. It is recommended that you decide these matters beforehand and record them in a divorce contract. This will expedite the process and help ensure there are no disagreements before you go to the registration office. After you fill out a request form and sign it, the registrar will issue a divorce certificate along with a divorce registration that contains the details of the conditions of the divorce. The process requires a minimal fee.

The wife may change her last name back to her maiden name. (Thai law now allows a woman to choose to keep her maiden name when she gets married.)

Divorce With A Court Order

If your spouse refuses to give you a divorce or you cannot agree on the terms of settlement, you may go to court and obtain a divorce. Thai law requires that you establish grounds for a divorce before the court will grant the divorce.

Grounds For Divorce

Thai law sets out the following grounds for a divorce:

- The husband has treated or honored another woman as his own wife, or the wife has committed adultery.
- One spouse has committed a criminal offence or a serious act of misconduct. (Thai law does not define misconduct, but acts that shame the other spouse or subject them to insults or ridicule will suffice.)
- One spouse has harmed the other or suffers from mental illness.
- One spouse has deserted the other for one year or more.
- Either party has lived separately for three years or more.
- One spouse has disappeared for three years or more.
- There is a lack of marital support from the other. (Thai law requires both parties to the marriage to support the other to the extent they are able to. If one party does not, it is grounds for divorce.)
- One spouse has been declared insane for more than three years and is not curable.
- One spouse has broken the bond of good behavior. (Thai law allows the parties to a marriage to enter into an agreement of good behavior and define the terms within the agreement. If one party fails to live up to this agreement, it is grounds for divorce.)
- One spouse has an incurable disease that may affect the other.
- One spouse has a permanent physical handicap that makes it impossible to cohabit as husband and wife.

The process of petitioning the court for a divorce is complicated, so you will need to hire a lawyer. A lawyer can process the divorce in court and act on your behalf if you are living outside Thailand. To do so, you will need to provide him with a power of attorney.

You will have to supply your lawyer with the facts regarding your marriage, children (if any), assets, and pertinent dates and circumstances of the marriage. If you have a prenuptial agreement, it will be reviewed and considered in the Thai court. Remember that Thailand is considered a community property jurisdiction, so property acquired during the marriage is subject to division, with half going to each spouse. If you have considerable assets in your home country, and are seeking a divorce in Thailand, division of those assets will be very complicated and involve conflicts of law and other concepts outside the scope of this book. You will need the assistance of an attorney in Thailand and your home country to resolve these issues. Also, both parties are responsible for debts incurred during the course of the marriage.

If the parties cannot decide on a settlement agreement for the division of property, child custody and support, and other such matters, the court will decide for them. This is almost never a good resolution and will significantly increase the costs for obtaining the divorce. Fees for having this process done by a lawyer for a simple case can start at approximately 30,000 baht and exceed 100,000 baht depending on how complex the case is. It takes two months or longer to get a court order for dissolution. The lawyer will represent you in the preliminary hearings, but you may have to appear in court if the court orders you to do so.

A court order dissolves the marriage and the divorcing parties do not need to register their divorce. If there are other conditions that they want to register, they can do so in the presence of a registrar officer to finalize the divorce.

If you register your marriage in your home country, your divorce will need to take place there and will be processed according to the laws of your home country. You will need to consult with a lawyer from your home county to determine the steps necessary to get your divorce.

Making A Will

A will is the instructions of a person or the testator regarding what to do with their assets or estate after they die. In Thailand, disposition of a deceased person's property and probating of their will is governed under the Civil and Commercial Code. You should have a will in order to ensure that your assets are distributed as you wish them to be, and to avoid problems and disputes among your heirs after your death.

A will may also contain instructions on how to dispose of your body when you die, what type of funeral you want, and who should be notified in the event of your death. A will may also contain directions from you as to what to do if you are seriously injured and left in a vegetative state, whether to try extraordinary methods to revive you should you suffer heart failure or some other illness, and other such instructions.

You may designate the executor and indicate who should take care of any minor children in your will. While the Thai courts are not bound by these, it is your best opportunity to inform them and your heirs of your desires and intent. Without such instructions, others will make these decisions after your death without the benefit of your intent.

Once you write a will, you should review it periodically to verify that it continues to represent your intentions. A will can be revised at any time before the testator's death. To create a will, the testator must be at least fifteen years of age and have full mental capacity. Although a will remains valid under Thai law even after marriage or divorce, it should be reviewed and modified as necessary to reflect the change in circumstances.

In most cases a will must be in writing and is valid when the testator signs it in the presence of two witnesses who are over twenty years of age and are of full mental capacity. An oral will may be made in time of war and under special circumstances.

Foreigners should definitely have a written will. It can be a simple document written in either Thai or your native language or both.

Authenticated wills that have been written outside of Thailand may be accepted in Thai courts, but must be translated into Thai. Under Thai Law, probate (the process of disposing of the deceased's estate) and trusts do not exist. You may want to make a will to distribute your material goods in each country in which you have assets. In this case, each will needs to address the assets that you own in that country only.

There is no inheritance or death tax in Thailand. However, if land or buildings and certain assets are to be transferred to beneficiaries, the Land Department will charge fees for the transfer.

Your funeral will be arranged by the person appointed as executor in your will, or a person who is specifically prearranged by you or your family.

Although making a will is a simple process, we suggest that you use a lawyer to assist you in drafting and executing your will in order to ensure that it complies with Thai law. Once a will is written, it should be kept in a safe place. This could be in your own possession, with someone you trust outside of Thailand, with a lawyer, or in a bank deposit box. You should also inform the appropriate people that you have a will and where it is located. If it is not known that you have a will, nobody will be able to execute your wishes.

Forms Of Will

A Handwritten Will.

The testator may handwrite the will and date and sign it. Fingerprints are optional. The testator's handwriting serves to authenticate this will, so attesting witnesses are not required. Although not required for a handwritten will, it is recommended that witnesses be obtained.

A Regular Will

This kind of will is written in the form of a letter that can be handwritten or typed. It needs to be dated and the testator must sign it in the presence of two witnesses. If fingerprints are used as identification by the testator the will, there must be two additional witnesses to the fingerprints.

A Civil Documented Will

The testator must go to a district office (amphur) with two witnesses and make a request to an official to write a will. The government official will record the intent of the testator then read it back to him for verification. The testator signs the will and the witnesses then sign the document attesting to its authenticity. The official then signs and dates the will and adds a stamp or seal as evidence. The testator may sign to receive the will that has been recorded, or it can be left on file at the district office.

A Secret Will

The testator can handwrite the will or can ask someone else to write it, but the will must contain the signature of the testator. The will has to be sealed in an envelope with the signature of the testator on the envelope seal. The testator must take the sealed envelope to the district office with two witnesses and confirm ownership of the will to the district officer. The district officer will record the statements and date the envelope with a government stamp. The testator and the witnesses sign their names on an appropriate place on the envelope. The will can be kept by the testator or left on file at the district office.

An Oral Will (Special Case)

This form of will is allowed in circumstances where other forms of a will cannot be made, such as when the testator is in great personal danger, is close to death, or during a war or an epidemic. The testator must declare intent in the presence of two witnesses. The two witnesses must appear in front of a district officer as soon as possible and relay the statement made by the testator to the officer with the date and location where the statement was made. The district officer will make a record of the statement made by the two witnesses and they sign their names in confirmation. If fingerprints of the two witnesses are to be recorded, there must be two additional witnesses to this process.

If you plan on making a will at a district office, you need to bring a land deed (if you have one), a Thai citizen's ID card, and house registration, or a passport if you are a foreign national. The fees for making a will at the district office are minimal.

When There Is No Will Or No Valid Will

If you die without a will or without a valid will, or if your will only disposes of part of your estate, the Civil and Commercial Code rules that your property will be distributed among your heirs. This method of distribution may differ from the laws of your home country and may not comport to your desires, which is why we recommend that you execute a will. There are two kinds of heirs: by blood and by marriage. 'Blood heirs' are:

1. Children – including adopted children and children who are born under unregistered marriage that are confirmed by the father—and grandchildren.

2. Parents

3. Brothers and sisters of the same parents (whole blood)

4. Half-brothers and -sisters (sharing one parent)

5. Grandparents

6. Uncles and aunts

The six classes of heirs listed above will not all inherit your assets. This listing shows the sequence of who has rights of inheritance (in the case that those of higher recognition do not exist). However, heirs in classes 1 and 2 are entitled to inherit assets at the same time.

An heir who is a legally married spouse – the marriage needs to be registered – is entitled to inheritance as are blood heirs in classes 1 and 2. Legally married spouses who are separated still have rights to the assets.

When there is a surviving spouse, the Civil and Commercial Code provides for the following division of assets:

- If you are survived by your spouse and children, the spouse receives fifty percent and the children receive fifty percent of the assets divided equally between the children and grandchildren (if there are no surviving children).
- If you are survived by your children and your parents, the children receive fifty percent of the estate and the parents receive fifty percent.
- If you are survived by your children but no spouse or parents, the children will receive all of your property.
- If you are survived by your spouse and your parents, the spouse receives fifty percent of the assets and your parents receive fifty percent. (This may be applied differently if your parents are not Thai and live outside of Thailand – which is another good reason to have a written will.)
- If you are survived by your spouse and siblings of whole blood, the spouse receives fifty percent of the assets and the siblings receive fifty percent.
- If you are survived by your spouse and heirs in classes, 4, 5, or 6 above, the spouse receives two thirds of the estate and the blood heirs in 4, 5, or 6 are entitled to receive the remaining one third split into equal shares.
- If blood heirs do not exist, the surviving spouse receives the entire estate.

When there is no surviving spouse, the assets are divided according to the following distribution method:

- If you die with no surviving spouse, the blood heirs are entitled to receive the entire estate divided into equal shares. For example, if you die leaving no spouse but children, the children (and/or your parents) receive the entire estate in equal shares. If you die leaving no spouse or children but have surviving parents, the parents receive the entire estate in equal shares.
- In the case that there are no heirs or anyone designated to receive the assets, the assets become the property of the State or the general public.

In Thailand, it is very common to have an executor who manages the assets of the deceased and distributes them among the heirs. In the normal course, when there is a will, it will be presented to the court for consideration. The court will make a determination as to the validity of the will and the stated intent of the deceased. It may be presented to the court by a surviving spouse or other family member, an attorney for the deceased, the individual named in the will as the executor, or anyone else with an interest in the will or possession of it. Once legally approved, the court will issue letters of testamentary authorizing the executor to take appropriate action to identify and collect the assets of the deceased and to make distribution of those assets. The court will also issue such other instructions as necessary.

An executor is either named by the testator or assigned by the court. An executor assigned in your will must have the following qualifications:

- Be over twenty years of age.
- Have full mental capacity.
- Not be declared bankrupt by a court.

An executor assigned by court order will be one of the following:

- A blood heir or a person stated in your will.
- Someone with an interest in your estate such as a spouse from an unregistered marriage.
- A prosecutor.

Because the court will consider the qualifications of the executor to manage the assets of your estate, it is not necessary for the heirs to approve the executor. However, a blood heir or a person stated in the will, someone with an interest in the estate such as a spouse who did not register the marriage; or a prosecutor may object to the appointment of an executor. To object to an assigned executor, the person who objects must send a request to the court that has jurisdiction over the death before the distribution of assets.

Dying In Thailand

You are going to die. None of us want to hear this, but it is going to happen. It's important for you to know the consequences if this should happen while you are in Thailand.

Foreigners die in Thailand through accident, illness or natural causes just like anywhere else. In this section we look at the procedures and formalities for dealing with a deceased person in Thailand.

In Thailand there are two definitions for death: 'natural death' through old age or illness; and 'unnatural death' by accident, murder, or natural disaster. In Thailand any death of a foreign national or Thai citizen must be reported to the police or the district office within 24 hours, even if it is a Sunday or a national holiday. (If the district office is closed, the death can be reported at a police station.)

If a foreigner dies in an apartment or hotel, the landlord or the hotel manager will be required to report to the district office or police station with the deceased's passport and death certificate (if available). The district office will make a record of the death in the passport.

The district office or the police will inform the embassy of the deceased foreigner within seven days and the embassy will notify the relatives as soon as possible. All forms of death – whether natural, accidental, or criminal – require a police report that in turn requires an investigation by the police at the scene, along with a forensic team to determine the cause of death. The body will be sent to a hospital or an examining office. If the person dies in a hospital, a death certificate will be issued by a doctor from that hospital and the police will file a report. If the cause of death is known to be normal or without complications, the body will be released to the family within two to three days, along with a death certificate issued by a doctor stating the cause of death. Any expenses for medical treatment or a hospital stay must be paid before the body will be released. Another death certificate called the "Civil Death Certificate" will be issued by the district office when the death is confirmed.

If the cause of death is unusual, suspicious, or the result of a suspected criminal act, an autopsy will be performed and there will be a delay in the release of the body. The death certificate may be issued with a special verification statement of death by the hospital or the examining office.

If the deceased foreigner had insurance, the insurance company will need to be contacted and given a copy of the report from the hospital, along with the Thai death certificate. The death certificate and any related documents will need to be translated into the language of the country where the insurance company is located. If the foreigner had a life insurance policy with a high amount of coverage, the insurance company may send their investigator to verify the death.

The insurance company is usually able to make the arrangements for repatriation of the body with an international funeral services company, but this should be verified. If the deceased did not have insurance, relatives should contact the appropriate embassy, which should be able to assist with recommending an international funeral service. In order to be repatriated, the body must be embalmed and placed in a zinc-lined coffin. An international funeral director can take care of these arrangements. Such companies have special caskets that are approved by Thailand Customs as well as other countries' customs departments. This procedure may take up to ten days and the following documents are required:

- Civil Death Certificate from the district office.
- Doctor's death certificate from the hospital or examining office.
- Certificate of embalming from the funeral home.

- Certificate of permission to transfer the remains from an international funeral home or the relevant embassy.
- Cover letter from the home embassy to their own customs offices (if necessary).

The Civil and the doctor's death certificates should be translated into the official language of the country the body is being sent to in order to expedite the process. Due to recent airport security measures, many airlines no longer carry coffins/ deceased persons. Check with the airline to see if it is willing to transport a coffin to your home country.

If you want convenience, it's better to use an international funeral service. These companies can arrange all the paperwork and the funeral according to the deceased's religion and final requests. The family can choose whether to cremate the body in Thailand (as is normal practice) or to return the body to the home country.

You can contact the following two international funeral services in Bangkok for detailed information. They have multi-lingual staff and also offer bereavement support. You may be able to find additional services on the Internet.

John Allison/Monkhouse
President Park Park View Tower, 99/243 (30B) Pine Tower,
Sukhumvit Road Soi 24, Klongton, Klong Toey, Bangkok, 10110
Tel: 02 382-5345; Fax: 02 262-9133; www.funeralrepatriation.com.

Kang Hay Sua Chun Foundation Funeral Services
732/2 Charoenkrung Road, Saphan Thawong, Bangkok, 10110
Tel: 02 225-9495

You will probably want to notify people about the death of your loved one. A good start is the deceased's e-mail contacts or electronic mailing lists. Also notify their work place, accountants, banks, Social Security and other governmental agencies, credit-card companies, landlord, utility providers, attorneys, doctors and dentists, clubs and associations, church or temple, schools, etc.

If you have a will, you can include instructions regarding how your funeral should take place. If it is the wish of the deceased or their family to have the funeral in Thailand, it will probably be a Buddhist ceremony in which monks come and chant at night and before cremation the next morning. A burial is not customary in Thailand; it is very expensive, and can be a lengthy process. The deceased's Thai friends can arrange a Thai funeral without much expense. Those attending the funeral usually bring money for the deceased's family to help pay for the costs.

In your will, you can also state what should be done with your remains after the cremation. Ashes can be taken by family members or kept in a chedi (a stupa) in the local temple (or a 'condo,' which is a space for placing urns rented by private cemeteries). Ashes can be scattered in Thailand or any other location that the deceased desires. They can be sent back to the deceased's home country with the help of an international funeral services company, or carried back on a plane. Your home embassy in conjunction with a local undertaker can suggest or make the necessary arrangements and process the paperwork. The article below is provided by www. buddhanet.net and it explains the Buddhist funeral rites in Thailand.

Buddhist Funeral Rites In Thailand And Southeast Asia

Funeral rites are the most elaborate of all the life-cycle ceremonies and are the ones entered into most fully by the monks. It is a basic teaching of Buddhism that existence is suffering, whether in birth, daily living, old age, or dying. This teaching is never in a stronger position than when death enters a home. Indeed, Buddhism may have won its way the more easily in Thailand because it had more to say about death and the hereafter than had animism.

The people rely upon monks to chant the sutras that will benefit the deceased, and to conduct all funeral rites and memorial services. To conduct the rites for the dead may be considered the one indispensable service rendered to the community by the monks. For this reason the crematory in each large temple has no rival in secular society.

The idea that death is suffering, relieved only by the knowledge that it is universal, gives an underlying mood of resignation to funerals. Among a choice few, there is the hope of nirvana with the extinction of personal striving. Among the vast majority there is the expectation of rebirth either in this world, in the heaven of Indra or some other, or in another plane of existence, possibly as a spirit. Over the basic mood of gloom there has grown a feeling that meritorious acts can aid the condition of the departed. Not all the teaching of anatta ('not self') can quite eradicate anxiety lest the deceased exist as pretas ('beings suffering torment'). For this reason, relatives do what they can to ameliorate their condition.

After death, a bathing ceremony takes place in which relatives and friends pour water over one hand of the deceased. The body is then placed in a coffin and surrounded with wreaths, candles, and sticks of incense. If possible, a photograph of the deceased is placed alongside, and colored lights are suspended about the coffin. Sometimes the cremation is deferred for a week to allow distant relatives to attend or to show special honor to the deceased. In this case, a chapter of monks comes to the house one or more times each day to chant from the Abhidharma, sometimes holding a broad ribbon (bhusa yong), attached to the coffin. Food is offered to the officiating monks as part of the merit-making for the deceased.

The food offered in the name of the dead is known as matakabhatta from mataka ('one who is dead'). The formula of presentation is:

"Reverend Sirs, we humbly beg to present this mataka food and these various gifts to the Sangkha (the Thai ecclesiastical body). May the Sangkha receive this food and these gifts of ours in order that benefits and happiness may come to us to the end of time."

At an ordinary funeral in northern Thailand, the cremation takes place within three days. The neighbors gather nightly to attend the services, feast, and play games with cards and dominoes. The final night is the one following the cremation. On the day of the funeral, an orchestra is employed and every effort is made to banish sorrow, loneliness, and the fear of spirits by means of music and fellowship. Before the funeral procession begins, the monks chant at the home and then precede the coffin down the steps of the house – which are sometimes carpeted with banana leaves. It is felt that the body should not leave the house by the usual route, but instead of removing the coffin through a hole in the wall or floor – which is impractical but is sometimes done – the front stairs are covered with leaves to make that route unusual.

A man carrying a white banner on a long pole often leads the procession to the crematorium ground. He is followed by elderly men carrying flowers in silver bowls, then by a group of eight to ten monks walking ahead of the coffin and holding the bhusa yong ribbon, which extends to the deceased. Often one of the monks repeats portions of the Abhidharma en route. The coffin may be carried by pall bearers or conveyed in a funeral carriage drawn by a large number of friends and relatives who feel that they are performing their last service for the deceased and are engaged in a meritorious act while doing so.

If the procession is accompanied by music, the players may ride in ox carts or in a motor truck at the rear. During the service at the cemetery the monks sit facing the coffin, on which rest the robes called pangsukula. After the chanting, the coffin is placed on a pyre made of brick. The mourners then approach with lighted torches of candles, incense, and fragrant wood, and toss them beneath the coffin so that the actual cremation takes place at once. Later the ashes may be collected and kept in an urn.

Frequently the bodies of prominent or wealthy persons are kept for a year or more in a special building at a temple. Cremations are deferred this long to show love and respect for the deceased and to perform religious rites that will benefit the departed. In such cases, a series of memorial services are held on the seventh, fiftieth, and hundredth days after the death. In one instance a wealthy merchant did not cremate the body of his daughter until he had spent all her inheritance in merit-making services for her. Another merchant spent the 10,000 baht insurance money received on the death of his small son entirely for religious ceremonies.

As along as the body is present, the spirit can benefit by the gifts presented, the sermons preached, and the chants uttered before it. This thought lies behind the use of the bhusa yong ribbon, which extends from the body within the coffin to the chanting monks before it. The dead may thus have contact with the holy sutras. When the body is cremated, the spirit is more definitely cut off from the world; it is best therefore not to force that spirit to enter the preta world finally and irrevocably until it has had the benefit of a number of religious services designed to improve its status.

At cremations it is quite common for wealthy people to have books and pamphlets printed for distribution that set forth Buddhist teachings in the form of essays, translation of the sutras, historical sketches, and explanations of ceremonies. Such books are not only a tribute to the dead and a means of making merit, but they have practical value as well.

Part 4
Living In Thailand

This part of the book provides useful information for people who are living and working in Thailand or who have retired here.

Thailand is a fun and exotic country. It is even considered a paradise by some. To live in Thailand successfully, you should research as much as possible and get to know the country, the people, the culture, and the language. Some of the topics in this section contain information about living in Thailand and may not necessarily be related directly to the legal system. But this information should provide you with ideas for your own living situation in Thailand, and hopefully will enhance your time in the Land of Smiles.

Renting An Apartment Or A House

Renting in Thailand is much cheaper and simpler than buying property, and can usually be done with minimal formality. It is the easiest way for you to provide accommodation for yourself in Thailand. To those who are interested in long-term residence, we suggest that you rent first before investing in a condominium or house. Once you have taken the time to decide that you really want to live in Thailand, you may later decide that you want to live in a different part of the city you have chosen, or even another city or province. Renting will make it easy if you decide to move.

Finding an apartment or house to rent can be done with the assistance of a real-estate agent that advertises in the newspapers or magazines. However, such agents usually focus on the more expensive properties. Advertisements are usually not very comprehensive and concentrate on large rental units in the relatively high price range of 30,000 baht plus per month. Normally, the landlord pays the real-estate agent's fee and for the advertisement. The best way to find a place to rent is to spend time looking at property in the area you prefer, with the help of a Thai friend. Here are some factors, both pros and cons, you may consider when renting an apartment.

With respect to renting in the areas where a lot of foreigners live, usually the central areas of larger cities:

- Rent will be more expensive.
- With the help of a real-estate agent, your paperwork should be easily processed.
- Usually, a longer term lease (one year) or a large deposit will be required.
- Having lots of foreigners around may mean less contact with Thai people.
- There is very little incentive, or need, to learn to speak Thai.
- Easy access to public transportation and taxis.
- You will be close to entertainment areas with exciting nightlife.
- Food from your home country can readily be found in specialty supermarkets.
- Traffic congestion will mean increased air and noise pollution.
- You will be within walking distance of banks, coffee shops, shopping malls and other amenities.
- Many of your expat friends will live nearby.
- You will be near numerous restaurants with a wide choice of food.

With respect to renting outside the downtown section of cities or in the suburbs or rural areas:

- Rental fees are usually reasonable or even cheap.
- Short term rentals are possible and common.
- You will probably need the help of a Thai friend to find an apartment. Your friend will have to help you by checking both that the paperwork actually says what has been agreed upon, and the legitimacy of the owner (i.e. whether the "landlord" renting the place is really the owner, etc.).
- Normally only a month or two of notice is required before leaving the premises.
- There are more opportunities to interact with Thai people and learn more about Thai language and culture.
- You will be further away from public transportation (except buses and minibus) and nightlife options.
- You can shop where Thai people shop and live more like Thai people live.
- There will be less traffic and therefore, better air quality.

If you come to Bangkok for a visit and don't want to rent a room in a hotel, you can rent a fully furnished apartment or condominium by the month (with a bed, television, wardrobe, a refrigerator and sometimes a fully equipped kitchen) for between 20,000—30,000 baht a month.

If you work in Bangkok, there are many good deals to be found outside the tourist areas. You can rent not just a room or apartment, but a house, for as little as 8,000—15,000 baht per month. You should look around different areas of the city to compare prices. As you go further from downtown Bangkok, you'll find many areas that are nice and quiet, just like in the provinces, but from which it takes only thirty or forty minutes to get to the downtown area by taxi or private car, and maybe only fifteen minutes to a suburban shopping mall. Most houses for rent are not furnished, so you will need to factor in the cost for your own furniture.

Renting in places where there are many foreigners such as Pattaya, Phuket, and Chiang Mai is also expensive in the tourist areas. Again, it is less expensive outside the central districts. You can rent a house from 4,000—8,000 baht in some of the smaller provinces.

Don't rush to buy a home or condominium until you are satisfied with all the criteria on your list, and that you are absolutely certain that you want to spend a long time in Thailand. If you have a Thai spouse and he or she wants to build a house on a piece of land, we suggest that you read *How To Buy Land And Build A House In Thailand*, also published by Paiboon. It has comprehensive details on how to purchase or lease land and how to get your dream house built in Thailand. A word of caution, buying a house in Thailand usually will not bring you a substantial profit but historically Thai people have a close association with land ownership and this feeling of owning land and a house overshadows thoughts of gaining profits. Over time renting is cheaper and less complicated than owning a house.

For a foreigner to rent property in Thailand, the landlord may ask for a copy of your work permit (if applicable), or a Certificate of Residence issued by Thai Immigration, or a letter of residence from your embassy certified and translated into Thai. He may also ask for a copy of your passport and proof of income, as well as a security deposit equal to two month's rent and the first month's rent paid in advance. The security deposit is refundable and should be returned when the tenant moves out.

A lease or rental agreement should be made in writing between the landlord and tenant. It is not recommend that you rent from a place where no written contract is provided. It is important to have a clear agreement that both parties will abide by.

The term of a typical agreement is usually one year, but often three-month short-stay agreements can be had. The lease or rental agreement should state the duration of the agreement or lease; how much the monthly rental fee is; that the rental fee cannot be raised during the duration of the agreement; what happens if either party does not follow the agreement; and all other terms and conditions. The tenant should keep all agreements, rent receipts, and receipts for all major household purchases as proof of payment. In addition, you should verify that the landlord actually owns the property and has the authority to rent to you. If the person is only leasing the property and sub-leases it to you, the real owner may come by one day and ask you to leave, since you have no agreement with that person. While this sounds improbable, we have heard of such cases a number of times.

Other things you need to know about renting in Thailand is that it is illegal for a foreigner to use the rental property for commercial purposes unless it is agreed to in the contract; it is not customary to sub-lease your unit, and you may have to specify how many people will be living in the apartment or the house. Some landlords are strict with the number of people and some are not. There are insurance companies that offer rental coverage to foreigners. It is neither customary nor a common practice to purchase such insurance, and it is not required by law. Property taxes are paid by the landlord.

The tenant should know that their responsibilities include paying the rent on time; paying for water, electricity and telephone bills; not causing damage to the property; and giving sufficient notice before terminating the lease or rental agreement. Also, you should make a thorough check of the property before you sign a lease or rental agreement, as if you were buying it. Check the plumbing fixtures and electrical lighting. Don't assume that anything normally included in an apartment in your home country will be included in your apartment in Thailand. When in doubt, ask, and get it written into the lease contract.

We point out something here that should be obvious: you are a foreigner in Thailand. As such, you are perceived as being wealthier than the Thai people living around you. The fact that you have a laptop computer, iPod, fancy running shoes, and a video game player 'confirms' this presumption. Be very careful not to flaunt your 'wealth' to your neighbors. Don't leave cash in your apartment, and secure your laptop and other possessions – even in your apartment. Treat your rented apartment or house as if it were a hotel room with maid service. You wouldn't leave cash lying around a hotel room and you shouldn't do it in a rental either. Again, this sounds impossible, but we've heard stories of complete possessions being taken from seemingly secure apartments.

Our friend, Chris Pirazzi, has prepared a sample lease agreement in both Thai and English for use by foreigners who want to find a place of their own. (Remember, you will need the help of a Thai friend if you can't speak Thai.) The agreement has been prepared to be fair to both the landlord and tenant. There are other rental agreements that are sold in stationary stores which are written only in Thai and the content usually favors the landlord. If there are problems such as who is responsible for fixing the broken faucets, you should be able to point to a clause in your rental or lease agreement that clarifies this and thus avoid disputes. The rental agreement prepared by Chris Pirazzi is included in the Reference section. You are welcome to use it by downloading the PDF file from http://slice-of-thai.com. Of course, you will still have to convince your landlord to agree to sign it.

Money Matters

Money is an important issue anywhere, but it is often a topic of discussion when you are in a relationship with a Thai person, whether business or personal. This section provides general information on money matters that you should be aware of.

The information provided in this book and this section in particular is based on information that was correct at the time of publication. In all cases you should check with your bank or the proper authorities to verify the procedures and amounts described in this section.

Sending Money To Thailand

Usually, after you have developed a relationship in Thailand, it will involve money. No matter what your reason, you may need to send money to somebody in Thailand, or even to yourself. Advanced technology in the banking industry has made this easy. This section is about sending a small amount of money, not for investment or retirement – less then 10,000 US dollars to Thailand. Most banks now have limits and controls on the amount of money that can be sent overseas because of money laundering and terrorism issues. Banks in Thailand do not use an International Bank Account Number (IBAN); instead, they use the SWIFT coding system for bank transactions. Here are some methods used to send money to Thailand:

- Via Western Union, the world's largest money transfer network. Many people find this convenient, cheap and fast. It takes only three simple steps and a few minutes to send and receive money worldwide. Very useful in emergency cases, it is a retail money transfer with no bank account required. The fees vary depending on the amount, the country you send from, and the country you send to. For example, the fee for sending 200 dollars to Thailand from the US is forty dollars. If you send more than 1,000 dollars, they will ask for more personal information and the reason for sending it. To send money via Western Union:

  1. Go to a Western Union agent that has a Western Union sign outside, usually at a bank, a department store, or a money mart. If you send money within Thailand, you can go to the nearest Bank of Ayudhya branch and fill out the form.

  2. Present your completed form and the amount of money to be sent. Be sure to get a receipt with a code or Money Transfer Control Number (MTCN).

  3. Inform the receiver of the transfer and the amount that you sent and the MTCN. Sometimes Western Union will give you a toll-free number you can use to call the recipient for a few minutes.

To receive money via Western Union:

  1. After the recipient is notified of the amount of the transfer and the code, they should go to the nearest Western Union service location, provide identification, and fill out the receipt form. Be sure to include the sender's name and country and the amount expected.

2. If the money has arrived, the recipient will be paid immediately. In Thailand, a recipient can receive money in the larger cities where Western Union agents are to be found in department stores, malls, or at Bank of Ayudhya branches. Recipients in the provinces can receive money from Bank of Ayudhya locations, so make sure there is a Bank of Ayudhya or a Western Union agent in the area where the recipient lives.

- Bank transfer. This is convenient if both the sender and the recipient have a bank account. The sender requests an international bank transfer at their bank. The money transfer can take one to five days depending on the bank. Not all bank branches do international money transfers. The fees are similar to Western Union, or may be less if you send larger amounts of money.

- International money order. This is inconvenient because it can be cashed only at certain bank branches, and banks in Thailand charge a high fee for cashing money orders.

- Sending a debit card to a recipient in Thailand. The sender provides a debit card such as Visa or MasterCard to the recipient, along with the pin number. The recipient can withdraw money directly from an ATM machine in Thailand. This way, the sender can control how much money to put into the account and can stop the account activities at any time. The sender's bank may charge a fee of two to five dollars per transaction, and the ATM machine in Thailand where money is withdrawn may charge a minimal fee (of about two dollars). Note: Recently, banks such as the Bank of America have added an additional one percent international exchange charge on each ATM withdrawal in Thailand. Your 300-dollar withdrawal in Thailand may end up costing you 34 dollars. Check with your bank to verify if it also includes an international exchange charge for ATM withdrawals.

- Sending cash in a letter via the postal service. Some people put small bank notes in their letters. This method used to work, but recently there have been reports that letters never reach the recipients, even if the letters were registered. Bank notes in the mail can now be detected inside the envelope, without even opening it. To deter counterfeiters, bank notes now include certain security items, such as watermarks and metal strips, which can be detected with a metal detector. Part of the new security precautions at post offices, especially concerning international airmail, is detecting metal objects in the mail. If a metal object is detected, it will be X-rayed. Therefore, any bank notes sent through the mail can be detected and removed by someone involved in the scanning process.

- By PayPal. This is the safer, easier way to make an online payment and can also be used to send money to someone. PayPal lets you send money to anyone with an e-mail address. It is free, and works with your existing credit card and current bank account. There are a few ways to do this. Go to www.paypal.com to learn more about how to sign up and other details. This is the newest way to send money and it is not yet widespread in Thailand. After you set up a PayPal account and add funds to your account from your bank with a routing number, you can then request a PayPal Visa ATM debit card and mail it to the recipient. You should make a copy of the card's front and back before mailing it. Let the recipient know the four-digit PIN number. The money you put into the PayPal account can be withdrawn in Thai baht from any ATM machine that accepts the Visa debit card for the cost of one dollar per transaction. Via the Internet, you can add funds, remove funds, change the PIN number, set the withdrawal limit, or get a new card whenever you want.

Receiving And Exchanging Money In Thailand

It is supposed to be cheaper to live and be entertained in Thailand than in your home country. But you may notice that, for many strange reasons, money seems to leave your pocket very quickly.

It is easy and convenient to exchange money when you first arrive at the airport. You should exchange just enough for a few days because you can get a better rate from banks in town or from money exchange booths. If you need to, you can also exchange money at your hotel, but change just enough until you get to a foreign exchange facility because their rates should be much higher than at your hotel.

An easy way to access your money from your home country is to use your ATM card with the PLUS, Cirrus, or STAR logo. You can also use a major credit card to get Thai currency from your account back home. Both methods provide good exchange rates. Bank debit cards will charge a fee each time you withdraw money, and may also charge an additional one percent international exchange rate fee.

Credit-card companies normally charge three or four percent of the amount, plus cash advance fees. Fees vary from bank to bank. Some machines only have displays in Thai and only take four-digit PIN numbers. You should do some investigation to determine the best method for you to receive money using debit and credit cards based on the fees charged by the banks you use. Also, you should alert your bank and credit-card company that you will be traveling in Thailand before you leave home. The bank may detect what it may think are unauthorized withdrawals and put a hold on your account, leaving you with no access to your money.

There are always unforeseen problems when you need to get cash right away. Therefore, you should have some extra cash and traveler's checks as back up. Only carry enough cash for your expenses for the day, or only an amount that you are comfortable losing. Always be careful when you carry cash, as you would in any situation. Check with your hotel about leaving your valuables in a safe if this option is available

Traveler's checks are no longer popular, but they come in handy when, for example, you can't get your money out of an ATM or you lose your credit cards. The traveler's-check companies advertise that you can get your money back if the checks are lost or stolen, but you need to follow their requirements for keeping track of your unused checks.

Thai banks open and close early – from 08:30-15:30, Monday to Friday – and they are closed on public holidays. Some branches open for half a day on Saturday. ATM machines are usually accessible 24-hours a day, since many of them are outside banks, convenience stores, and other locations.

Opening A Bank Account In Thailand

The process of opening a bank account is quite simple. You need to bring certain documents such as your passport with a valid visa, work permit, and possibly a letter of recommendation from your embassy. Some banks may require only your passport with a valid visa and an address in Thailand. You can check with different banks or different branches of the same bank to see if they will let you open an account with the documents you have. The minimum sum for opening an account in most banks is 500 baht. The bank will issue a bank pass book and an ATM card, both of which can be used to withdraw or deposit money and to make bank transfers.

The types of accounts that foreigners can open in Thailand are a savings account, fixed account, business bank account, or a current account – which will all be in Thai baht. Foreigners can also open a foreign currency deposit account in a foreign currency that the bank accepts. A checking account is not available for personal use. It is very complicated to open a checking account unless you have a legitimate business in Thailand. For business accounts, the bank needs to see a passport with a valid visa, plus all of the company paperwork. This is complicated enough that it should be prepared by an accountant.

Once a bank account is opened, the account holder will receive an ATM card that can be used for withdrawals, deposits, transferring funds, checking balance, etc. You can also request a check card (e.g. Visa Electron) or a credit card. You may qualify if you have a valid work permit, proper visa documentation, and history and proof of income and residency. You can request online banking via the Internet, as well, which is available in many banks in Thailand now.

If your ATM or credit card is lost or stolen, you should go to the nearest branch of your bank and file a report as soon as possible. Take your passport and other bank documents (if available) with you. The bank will deactivate the card and you will need to go to the bank branch where the account was opened to receive a replacement card.

Driving In Thailand

In this section you will be provided with the legal aspects of how to get a driver's license, some of the rules of the road, and what to do when you get into an accident. But first, we want to present you with an understanding of what it means to drive in Thailand – and hopefully discourage you from attempting this.

Being on the road in Thailand, as a passenger or as a driver, is a unique experience. It is similar to taking a thrill ride at an amusement park where you expect the ride to end safely. This may or may not be how your driving experience in Thailand will end. For your own safety, we recommend that you do not drive a car, motorcycle, or any other vehicle in Thailand.

First, we will discuss driving in large cities like Bangkok. People drive very fast in Bangkok. They also drive very close to each other, and the painted line on the road representing lanes is usually ignored. In addition to cars there are motorcycles, *tuk-tuks*, buses, trucks of all shapes and sizes, push-carts, and thousands of pedestrians.

Bangkok has many large roads up to ten lanes wide, which carry a huge number of vehicles, except when you get to a red light. Then you may wait up to eight minutes for the light to change. While you are idling and waiting in frustration for the light to change, scores of motorcycles will be inching their way past you up to the front of the line. When the light turns green, it's a stampede of 50cc motorcycles, cars, and *tuk-tuks* to get as far down the road until they are caught at the next eight-minute red light.

To balance out these ten-lane roads, Bangkok contains a labyrinth of tiny one-lane streets that twist and turn and weave around the massive roads. The problem is that you have to be very familiar with these shortcuts to make use of them.

An unwritten law of driving in Thailand is the hierarchy of vehicles. It is similar to the class system, in which the person with the highest social rank or class receives the most respect. On the road, the largest vehicle gets the right of way. A truck or bus has priority over a car. A motorcycle or *tuk-tuk* must allow a taxi to pass first – or suffer the consequences. And a pedestrian has absolutely no business even thinking of crossing a street. If you don't follow this primary rule of the road, you will quickly find yourself in trouble. Add to this mix the potholes, large number of one-way streets, vendors' carts, intoxicated pedestrians, and the occasional elephant, and you may start to agree that public transportation or a taxi in Bangkok and the other cities is a safer choice.

Maybe you don't intend to drive in the cities and will confine your driving to the highways in the countryside. Now that is real adventure. Larger roads in the provinces are mostly four lanes, two in each direction, separated by a median strip. These roads appear to be safe for driving, except when you come to a crossroads every few kilometers. Here, traffic will be crossing your lane while you are traveling at ninety kilometers per hour. In addition, this is also where vehicles from the other side of the median can make a U-turn into your lane. These intersections are very dangerous and you should approach each one with caution.

The other type of road is the simple two-lane paved road with a one-meter-wide shoulder. As you drive along in your lane, someone traveling in the opposite direction may want to pass a slower driver. In Thailand there is another unwritten rule that if someone is coming in the opposite direction and they want to pass a slower vehicle, they can use your lane to pass and you are expected to pull onto the side shoulder to get out of the way. To add to this, when you try to move out of the way onto the shoulder, you may find a motorcycle driving next to you. Since small motorcycles typically are not powerful enough to keep up with the traffic flow, they normally use the shoulder of the road, thus you have to time your sideways movement to avoid a head on collision and also be in between the mopeds moving alongside you so you don't bump one of them off the road.

But there is more: slow moving farm vehicles driving along the side of the road force the mopeds to pass in your lane – and now you have to judge the speed of the mopeds and the slow-moving tractors.

You say to yourself, this is too much. But wait, there is more. Finally there are the mopeds driving on your shoulder but coming at you from the opposite direction.

For most foreigners, all of the above are sufficient reasons not to drive in the countryside – or the towns. An alternative is to take public buses, which are convenient and cheap, go everywhere in the country, but are not necessarily comfortable. There are different classes of buses including air-conditioned 'luxury' types with reclining seats.

We include here a list of additional things to consider – laws or otherwise– when driving in Thailand, either in the cities or on the country roads:

- In Thailand, traffic moves on the left side of the road.
- Thais use their high beam lights to signal for passing at night.
- When oncoming cars flash their lights, this means 'I am not stopping or slowing down – get out of my way.' It's also a warning such as 'slow down' or 'there is something to watch out for ahead.'
- The legal age for driving cars and motorcycles is eighteen, but many kids younger than this drive motorcycles.
- The legal blood-alcohol limit is 0.5 milligrams of alcohol per liter of blood and 0.2 milligrams for drivers who have held their license for less than five years.
- As in all countries, drunk driving is a big problem, but the penalties are not as severe and enforcement is lax.
- The law requires the driver of a vehicle to have a valid driving license and a copy of the vehicle registration document. (An international driving license is accepted.)

- A tax sticker and at least third-party motor insurance are required for all vehicles (including motorcycles) and have to be renewed annually at the local Department of Land Transport Office.
- The driver and passengers in the front seats of vehicles are required to wear seatbelts. The driver is subject to a fine if caught by the police without seatbelts fastened.
- Speeding fines and traffic tickets can be paid at the local police station.
- Vehicles with red registration plates cannot be driven at night.
- Children's car seats are not required by law.
- Some expressways around Bangkok charge a toll, which is calculated by the distance driven.
- Motorbikes, mopeds, and other vehicles are often overloaded with passengers.
- Many trucks are overloaded beyond their carrying capacity and tend to overturn on sharp curves.
- People ride in the back of pickup trucks with no seatbelts, which causes serious injuries when they are ejected from the vehicle during an accident.
- The speed limit on the highway is usually ninety kilometers per hour, up to 100 or 120 in some areas, and fifty or sixty in urban areas.
- A motorcycle license is easy to obtain after a basic test.
- Motorcycle riders are required to wear a helmet, but this regulation is often ignored or not enforced. Police set up checkpoints periodically and fine violators.
- Thai drivers tend to ignore stop signs and often do not slow down or look for traffic in the other directions.
- In larger cities, heavy traffic usually occurs on weekdays from 7:00—9:30 a.m. and from 4:30—7:30 p.m. In smaller towns, the rush hours are shorter.
- At the start (and end) of major holidays like Songkran (Thai New Year) when a large proportion of the population of Bangkok leaves for the provinces to celebrate with their families, there are terrible traffic problems. There are also numerous accidents and many fatalities due to drunkenness and recklessness.
- Pay more attention to your driving than you would in your home country because many directional signs in English are quite small, and in some areas the road signs are in Thai only.
- Drivers in Bangkok have to go to a special orientation besides taking an exam to get their license, and they are inclined to be 'better' drivers than in the provinces.
- Don't ever get into a road-rage incident; practice your meditation instead.

- As a foreigner, you are accorded high social status, and this extends to accidents, too. In most cases, no matter who caused the accident, you will be blamed because you are a foreigner.

If you are stopped by the police, you can do what most of the locals do – offer to pay the fine on the spot and avoid going to the police station. Fines are usually between 200—400 baht. If the fine or infraction sounds outrageous, you can complain or tell the officer that you want to resolve it at the police station, or that you want to consult with someone first. If the officer issues a ticket and your license is taken, you must pay within seven days or the fine will be increased.

If you stay in Thailand for more than three months and intend to drive, you must have a Thai driver's license. An international driver's license may be accepted, but you also need to have a valid driving license from your home country along with the international license. Some insurance companies only provide full coverage for drivers with a valid Thai license. Having a Thai license also is proof that the license holder lives in Thailand and is not a tourist. Thais who have lived and driven outside of Thailand for more than a year can get a Thai license without taking an exam by showing their valid overseas driving license.

Getting A Thai Driver's License

To get a driving license you have to be in good health with no physical or mental handicaps and be of sound mind. Foreigners with an international driver's license and valid driving license from their home country, along with a Non-Immigrant visa, can apply for a Thai license. With these documents foreigners do not need to take the driving test or written exam in Thailand. You will be provided with a one-year temporary driver's license for passenger cars. (Not for commercial vehicles or motorcycles.)

In Thailand, a driver's license is obtained at the Department of Land Transport Office (Thais refer to it as *kon-song*.) In certain offices the exam is available in English. If not, the exam will be in Thai, but you may be able to use a Thai interpreter to help you during the process if you receive the permission of the examiner. Foreigners must take the Thai driving license examination if they do not have an international driving license and valid license from their home country.

If you have a work permit, you can use it as proof of residency. You also need to bring the following documents:

- Your valid passport with valid Non-Immigrant visa.
- Two copies of the passport's relevant pages for personal data and signature, the current Non-Immigrant visa, the page with the last entry stamp, and the Immigration card.
- A certified letter of address from your embassy, or from the Immigration Bureau, issued within the previous thirty days.

- A letter of certification from a doctor that you are in good health physically and mentally, issued within the previous thirty days.
- Two photos taken within the previous six months.
- A valid international driver's license and a signed photocopy or translated regular driving license from your home country certified by your embassy.

If you have your international and home-country driving licenses, you will only need to pass three simple tests: for color blindness, reflexes, and depth perception. After you have passed these tests, your documents will be checked. After paying the 105 baht fee, you will receive your one-year temporary Thai driver's license.

Parking

Parking, when you can find a space, is usually free of charge, since parking meters are not common in Thailand. Minimal parking fees are charged at certain public parking areas and garages. When parking, Thais often block other cars. This is a common occurrence and should not get you upset, because Thais usually do not set the handbrake after they are sure their car will not roll away and cause an accident. If your car is blocked by another car, you may push the 'offending' vehicle out of the way, or a local 'attendant' or security guard will help you (for a tip). Remember to leave the offending vehicle in a safe place when you unblock your car.

Parking signs are written in Thai and the police issue tickets to violators or sometimes even put a clamp on the vehicle. You need to make sure that it's legal to park, as you would back home. Ask if you can't read Thai, or try to learn enough Thai to recognize the parking signs. Sometimes it's legal to park in certain places on even-number days, but not on odd-number days.

Some roads and curbsides are painted and have the following meanings:

- Red and white stripes: no parking at any time.
- Yellow and white stripes: short-term parking, loading zone.
- White rectangle on the road: designated vehicles only.
- Diagonal white lines: motorcycle parking only.

More information on driving in Thailand and traffic signs used in Thailand can be found in manuals and books available in stores throughout the country or at stands near the Department of Land Transport Office.

Traffic Accidents

If you are involved in an accident, try to stay calm. The procedures will be slightly different from what you are used to in your home country. There are things to be aware of because foreigners will be disadvantaged through language difficulties. As we mentioned before, whether or not it's fair to you, when you (a foreigner) drive and are involved in an accident, it is usually considered your fault for not knowing how to drive the Thai way.

In Thailand it is normal for people to pay compensation at an accident scene and for the parties to resolve the matter quickly. You need to determine what is best for you in these situations and to verify beforehand with your insurance company what they recommend or require if you are involved in an accident. Therefore, you should never drive in Thailand without comprehensive insurance from a reputable and reliable insurance company.

For accidents with no injury:

- Move all vehicles involved to the side of the road to avoid blocking traffic.
- Call the emergency number 191, or 1155 for English speaking Tourist Police assistance.
- Exchange information with the other drivers: passport and ID card numbers, driver's license number, vehicle registration, insurance details, the vehicles' registration numbers, phone numbers and addresses.
- Know what your insurance company requires. Know if the company has a 24-hour assistance phone number.
- Inform your insurance company and file the necessary forms.

For accidents with injury:

- Call the emergency number 191, or 1155 for English speaking Tourist Police assistance.
- Uninjured persons should move to the side of the road.
- Call an ambulance and tend to anyone who is injured. If you are trained, apply emergency first-aid procedures.
- Do not move the vehicles involved.
- Exchange information with the other drivers: passport and ID card numbers, driver's license number, vehicle registration, insurance details, the vehicles' registration numbers, phone numbers and addresses.
- Know what your insurance company requires. Know if the company has a 24-hour assistance phone number.
- Inform your insurance company and file the necessary forms. A police report will need to be completed at the local police station.

Official organizations and government bodies dealing with roads and traffic in Thailand are the Thailand Office of Transport and Traffic Policy and Planning, the Department of Land Transport Office, and the Royal Thai Police.

Roadside assistance is sometimes provided by insurance companies, so you should check with yours. You can also contact the Royal Automobile Association of Thailand (Tel: 02 939-5770-3, 02 512-0905) in Bangkok or the Car World Club, which provides emergency roadside service 24 hours a day throughout Thailand (Tel: 02 398-0170-9).

Outside Bangkok it might be faster to get local assistance rather than wait for roadside assistance.

Working In Thailand

Thailand has become a popular destination for foreigners to live and work. Foreigners in Thailand are treated as 'guests' whether they are tourists, retirees, or workers. Unfortunately, if you are a Caucasian Westerner, have an African heritage, or other ancestry other than Asian, you will be treated as a guest forever, no matter how long you live in Thailand. That's because you stand out from the Thais. Other Asian people, especially from nearby countries, are more easily accepted into Thai society.

Although foreigners from neighboring countries look similar to the Thais, they are not necessarily provided the same social status as Thais. Thailand is more technically advanced than its neighbors, and with a growing economy comes the need for a large labor pool to draw from. In recent times, many social, political, and economic problems have occurred in Thailand due to the large number of illegal workers from Burma, Cambodia, and Laos. The government has to deal with medical costs, crimes involving foreigners, and escalating social problems. For these reasons the Thai government requires that all foreigners have a work permit if they are employed in Thailand. There are exceptions to this requirement for diplomats; foreigners who work for the United Nations or other exempt international agencies; officials in Thailand that promote education, culture, arts, or sports programs; those granted specific exemption by the Thai government; and some additional specific categories.

Your work permit is proof of your residency in Thailand and the official way for the government to keep a record of you. If you are going to be paid for your work in Thailand you must have a work permit, otherwise you are subject to a fine, imprisonment, deportation, and expulsion from the country. The government has been very strict in this regard and keeps a close eye on working foreigners. We have heard stories of foreigners being taken into custody by the police for accepting tips in a bar when playing live music for friends. Technically, in the eyes of the authorities, they were getting paid without having a work permit.

There are certain occupations and professions that are reserved for Thai nationals only such as street vending, secretarial work, architecture, garment making, shop attendance, wood carving, working in agriculture, and other jobs. You should verify that the work you are thinking of doing in Thailand is not on the list of prohibited occupations. The Thai government issues work permits for foreign workers from neighboring countries for the lower-paid jobs that would be traditionally reserved for Thais in order to alleviate the problem of labor supply. Even though there is an official minimum wage in Thailand, the actual pay these foreign workers receive is often lower than what Thais are paid. The work permit for these jobs is actually a registration to keep track of where the foreigner is working. The work permit has to be renewed every year but the Thai government has made this a simple and easy process.

On the other hand, Westerners working in Thailand usually seek jobs that are highly paid by Thai standards. Getting a work permit for these higher-paid positions is more complicated than for the lower-paid jobs.

Work Permit

To apply for a work permit in Thailand you should apply for a Non-Immigrant B (business) visa at a Thai embassy or consulate before you come to Thailand. When you arrive in the country you can then apply for a work permit. You must have the Non-Immigrant B visa to apply for a work permit. The Non-Immigrant B visa may be either for a period of three months or a multi-entry visa which allows you to leave and return to Thailand within a twelve-month period. The twelve-month multi-entry visa requires that you leave the country within each ninety-day period. You can return to Thailand using the same visa for the twelve-month period.

If you are going to be working for a company in Thailand, your work permit can be applied for in advance by your employer, and the permit will be issued in Thailand. We advise that you contact a professional with experience in obtaining visas to help you with the application process.

Securing a work permit can be a complicated and tedious ordeal because of the numerous documents you have to submit. Many law offices in cities where there is a high concentration of foreigners should be able to help you with the application.

An employer is not allowed to hire a foreigner who does not have a work permit. Also, the type of work actually done by the foreigner must match the type of work specified on the work permit. (Any violation is liable to imprisonment for a term not exceeding three years or a fine not exceeding 60,000 baht, or both). The employer must submit a notification to the government within fifteen days of the commencement of termination of the working foreigner, or a change of the location where the work is done.

If you wish to start your own business, you can obtain a work permit for yourself by setting up a company. The most comprehensive book on starting and running your own company in Thailand is *How To Establish A Successful Business In Thailand*, also by Paiboon. This book provides all the information you need to start a new business or buy an existing business or franchise.

You can enter Thailand on any type of visa and set up a company. You can then write your recommendation letter on the company letterhead using its official address. You will need to leave Thailand and apply for a Non-Immigrant B visa based on this letter plus a copy of your company's official paperwork. Remember, you must apply for the Non-Immigrant B visa outside of Thailand. You can then enter Thailand again with your Non-Immigrant B visa and apply for a work permit. It is a complicated process, so you should have a legal firm assist you in the procedure. Documents generally required when applying for a work permit are as follows:

- For non-permanent residents: passport with a Non-Immigrant B visa stamp. For permanent residents: passport, alien book, and residence permit.

- Educational qualification, resume, letter of recommendation, a reference letter, or relevant license to justify your ability to perform the job.

- Job description for the type of work, materials used, location, salary, etc.

- Letter of medical certification issued in Thailand within six months stating that the applicant is of sound mind and not suffering from alcoholism, narcotic addiction, or contagious diseases.

- Three passport photographs, preferably professional looking photos.

- Applicants married to a Thai should also provide the spouse's ID card, marriage certificate and children's birth certificate (if any).

- Documents may need to be translated into Thai, especially if they are in languages other than Thai or English.

Applications must be submitted to the Department of Employment in Bangkok or to the One-Stop Service Center, where the Department of Employment, the Immigration Bureau, and the Office of the Board of Investment jointly provide visa and work permit services within three hours at the same service point. For applications made outside Bangkok, contact a Provincial Employment Office in the province where you will be working.

The work permit expires within one year (or up to two years in some cases) starting from the date of your arrival in Thailand, and it also expires when the Non-Immigrant B Visa expires. You need to renew your work permit before the expiration date.

The work permit has the name of the employer, the activities you may be engaged in, and the location in which the duties may be performed. You have to work for the employer specified in the work permit. You are not allowed to have a work permit for one employer and work for someone else. If there are changes in your duties or you change to a different employer, you have to inform the Labor Department of these changes and they have to be approved.

You must keep the work permit with you or at your workplace during working hours to be ready to present it to an official making an inspection. If the work permit is damaged or lost, you can apply for a replacement within fifteen days from the date it is lost.

If there are any changes to your name, nationality, address, or the name of the workplace, you have to apply for the revision of such information immediately. If you resign or are terminated from your place of employment, the work permit must be returned to the registrar of the Ministry of Labor within seven days from the date of resignation or termination. In addition, you must report to the Immigration Bureau, which will then, usually, cancel the Non-Immigrant B visa and allow you seven days to leave the country. It is therefore wise to arrange to take another job and prepare your work permit changes before resigning from your current employment. The Non-Immigrant B visa can be extended within Thailand at the Immigration Bureau, but many additional documents have to be submitted by the employer. Once the visa has been extended or renewed, it is then possible to renew the work permit

It is necessary for your visa to be multi-entry if you plan to travel outside of Thailand. If you have a single-entry visa and you leave the country without a re-entry permit, you will have to apply for a new Non-Immigrant B visa and new work permit.

For the latest information on work permits, please visit the Department of Employment's official website at www.doe.go.th/service. We list here the addresses of the government agencies involved in issuing work permits and visas. Also see more information on visas and immigration in the Reference section of this book.

Department of Employment
Office of Foreign Workers Administration
Department of Employment
Mit Maitree Road, Din Daeng,
Bangkok, 10400.
Tel: 02 245-2745

One-Stop Service Center
16th Floor, 555 Rasa Tower 2,
Phaholyothin Road, Chatuchak,
Bangkok, 10900.
Tel: 02 937-1155

Immigration Bureau
507 Soi Suan Plu,
Sathorn Tai (South Sathorn) Road,
Bangkok, 10120
Tel: 02 287-3101–10

Taxes

If you are paid for work done in Thailand you have to pay taxes in Thailand. You should check with your embassy to see what the requirements are for nationals working abroad (in Thailand). Also make sure that you don't end up paying double taxes in Thailand and in your home country. The taxation issues in Thailand are very confusing, so we recommend you consult your employer or, if you have a business, hire an experienced accountant to do your taxes. There is a lot of paperwork to deal with and the documents are written in Thai.

Personal net income tax rates in Thailand (2006)	
Income in Thai Baht	Tax Rate
0–100,000	Exempted
100,001–500,000	10 percent
500,001–1,000,000	20 percent
1,000,001–4,000,000	30 percent
4,000,001+	37 percent

Source: The Revenue Department

Working With Thais

Many foreigners have a love-hate attitude toward working with Thais. The key to having an enjoyable, pleasant time working with Thai people is to try to understand and accept the Thai culture and Thai values. You have to continue to remind yourself that you are living and working in a foreign country and need to play by local rules. In this section, we will point out a few things about the nature of Thai people and the differences compared to the Western workplace. This is only a short primer on working with Thai people and you should do more research on this subject if you plan to work with or hire Thais in your company.

You should know that Thais in general are friendly – especially to foreigners. Thai people smile in most situations and that is why the country is also known as the 'Land of Smiles.' Thais use their smile to communicate instead of saying hello or thank you, when apologizing, when they don't know what to say or do, or when they are embarrassed. They try to avoid having conflicts and do not like being criticized, especially in public.

Westerners usually smile when they are happy or pleased about something. If you apply this logic, you will assume everyone around you is happy. This may be a total misunderstanding on your part since the all-purpose smile you are seeing may really be concealing something other than a happy feeling. It takes a while to understand the cultural differences in your new adopted country of Thailand. But if you wear a smile, you will receive a nice smile back. At work, try to smile enough to create a pleasant environment, even if it takes effort.

On the surface it appears that Thai people seem to get along with each other at work better than in the West. They help each other out, share food, talk about their personal situations, and avoid conflicts. However, when Thais reach the point of conflict, it's worse than in the West. Thais can be envious of one another and vindictive to those who don't treat them well.

Thais are not very good at dealing with criticism, so you have to be careful when you say something as a joke or want to give constructive criticism. Giving criticism is a delicate issue, so you have to do it with care, or just avoid giving it at all. Do not criticize or give negative opinions on Thai things. Do not allow the Thais you work with to 'lose face'. Most important of all, do not lose your temper and yell. This can be detrimental to the progress of work, will make everyone uptight and work slower, and will make you unpopular for a very long time.

Earlier in the book we talked about the class system in Thai society. You will see this manifested at work all the time. Thais will ask you questions about your age, income, education, and family background so they can determine where you should be placed within their social system. Thais use different pronouns when they address one another. In English, the pronoun for the second person is 'you', but in Thai there are uncountable pronouns that change very subtly in meaning depending on the social status. Thais have official names, nicknames, formal pronouns, and terms of endearment according to the age of the person. Try not to be offended or embarrassed when your co-workers want to find out intimate details about you. You may be asked the same questions again and again. If you don't want them to know something, you can make up a clever answer just to be polite. This will save face for everyone.

Thai people do not necessarily resent those in the upper class, but they may envy them. Some in the lower class may look up to the upper class to inspire them to reach a higher level. They also believe in karma: that people can achieve a higher station in life because of their good deeds.

The more you understand the basics of Thai society and why Thais act the way they do, the sooner you will be able to adjust to this new way of living and doing business.

Thai people try to enjoy life and have fun. They believe in *sanuk* ('fun') and like to have *sanuk* at work – which combines having fun and having a laid-back attitude. This may run contrary to the work ethic you are used to. Thais don't tend to work fast or as efficiently as in Western countries. Many conduct business on 'Thai time,' which means that they often arrive very late for appointments. Thais also tend to gossip a lot in the workplace, and foreign workers are often the target of their gossip. To work successfully within the Thai business world, you need to adjust to these traits and be patient and then be more patient. Remember, you decided to work in Thailand, so it is you that has to adjust.

Try to make friends with your neighbors and your colleagues at work. The best way to mingle well with the people around you is to be able to speak Thai with them. This will provide you with a deeper understanding of the Thai way and will impress the people you meet. Being able to speak some Thai will elevate your social status and reap many additional benefits. By being able to communicate with your Thai friends, they can keep an eye on your property when you go out of town; find a plumber or a mechanic for you when you need one; or help you understand documents written in Thai.

There are books on Thai culture that provide a vast amount of information. (See "Further Reading.") Although these books will give you some insight and enlightenment, you will need to make internal adjustments in order to accept and be at ease with the different ways in the Land of Smiles.

Crime And Punishment In Thailand

Thailand is a very popular destination for tourists and immigrants. As in any area with a lot of tourists, there are people who prey on unsuspecting or distracted visitors. The good news is that the number of serious crimes committed against foreigners is relatively low. Most foreigners feel safe walking in the tourist areas of Bangkok and other places, but you should always be alert for the kind of petty crimes like theft that occur in all major cities in the world. The more you know about the country – and in particular the types of crimes committed against (and by) foreigners – you will be better prepared to have a wonderful time, hopefully free of any unwanted misadventure. In this section we provide you with information about the usual crimes committed by Thais against foreigners, crimes committed by foreigners in Thailand, and also present you with some recent crime statistics.

Crimes Committed Against Foreigners

The most common crimes committed by Thais against foreigners are mostly petty theft, scams, cheating, and fraud. In addition, especially in Bangkok foreigners will be exposed to potential crimes involving prostitution. You need to be alert, use your common sense and judgment, and take all the precautions detailed in your tourist guidebooks – as you would anywhere else. The more you prepare yourself by being aware of the current scams and by following the safety recommendations listed on government websites, in guidebooks, and from your tour guide, you should decrease your chances of being the victim of a crime.

Serious crimes such as rape, murder and manslaughter against foreigners also happen, but they are rare. Thailand has a very high murder rate per capita. It is ranked fourteen in the world according to the United Nations Survey of Crime Trends and Operations of Criminal Justice Systems in 2000. (The top fifteen countries are Colombia, South Africa, Jamaica, Venezuela, Russia, Mexico, Lithuania, Estonia, Latvia, Belarus, Ukraine, Papua New Guinea, Kyrgyzstan, Thailand, and Zimbabwe respectively.) But the fact is that most serious crimes are committed by Thais against other Thais. When a serious crime is committed against a foreigner, it usually becomes big news nationally and even internationally. The police use all their resources to bring the perpetrator to justice quickly and are usually successful.

Thailand's tourist industry earns a lot of revenue for the country and it is everybody's desire to keep crimes against tourists to a minimum. For this reason Thais in general avoid committing crimes against foreigners, since to do so would place them in the spotlight if caught. Most serious crimes committed among Thais have nothing to do with foreigners and many are politically or business motivated or simply crimes of vengeance. Thai people know what is going on in their locality and they have a good sense of danger. If a Thai recommends that a particular place or a certain person is dangerous, you should heed the advice and avoid going there or getting involved.

The Thai government provides help to foreigners that need assistance via a 24-hour phone service. If you happen to be the victim of a crime, you can call the emergency number 191 or the Tourist Hotline or Call Center at 1155. This is a Tourist Police service provided by the Tourism Authority of Thailand. The Tourist Assistance Center, under the Office of the Permanent Secretary of the Ministry of Tourism and Sports, is responsible for tourism-related problems, handling tourists' complaints, facilitating tourists' needs, as well as coordinating with the public and private sectors regarding safety issues.

Tourist Assistance Center (The Service Center)
Ministry of Tourism and Sports,
4 Ratchadamnoen Nok Road,
Pom Prab Sattru Phai,
Bangkok, 10100.

Their branch office is located at Suvarnabhumi Airport on the second floor, Gate 3. At the Service Center, officers assist tourists, receive reports, and provide documents 24-hours a day.

They are available 24 hours a day on 1155 or 02 124-4070, or by e-mail at thai-tac@hotmail.com. Their website is www.touristassistancecenter.go.th, in Thai, English, and Chinese.

The Tourist Police

The Thai Tourist Police is a separate entity from the regular police. The Tourist Police were established to assist tourists who have problems. They are stationed in tourist areas and they do speak some English and some speak other languages too.

The Tourist Police also recruit foreign volunteers with certain qualifications to assist them in tourist areas. Volunteers are not paid and do not participate in arrests, interrogations, investigations, or inspections. If you want to donate your time to this worthy cause, please contact the Service Center and inquire about the program. In addition to providing a valuable service to the community, you will make very good contacts that may benefit you greatly. Having the Tourist Police as your friends and being known as a person who does good deeds should go a long way in a country that believes strongly in karma and in having the right connections.

The Thai Police

You can go to the local police station and fill out a report if you are the victim of a crime. The police will record your statements and do further investigation. If you deal with the Thai police or Tourist Police, as a victim of a crime, you still need to be aware of the Thai cultural traits that you know. You may be frightened, upset, or outraged, but you still need to be calm and polite. The police may not work as fast as you want or proceed the way you would expect them to, but you have to be patient.

The Thai police are increasing their effectiveness at investigating and arresting perpetrators and they have their own methods. If you do something to upset the police, you may get the opposite of what you want. There will also be language barriers if you are at a police station where everyone only speaks Thai. You should go with a Thai who can translate for you. You can call the Tourist Assistance Call Center and hopefully get assistance in the language you speak. Recently, new translation and interpreter services have been developed that provide help on the phone, or that can send a text translation to a mobile phone. These services are just starting and may not be widely available yet, and they are slow and expensive. For more serious matters, you may want to call your embassy to report an incident and ask for further advice.

Prisoner Statistics In Thailand

The following prisoner statistics are from the Department of Corrections of the Ministry of Justice for the year 2006 and provide an interesting perspective on the crimes committed in Thailand.

Number of Prisoners:
Male: 128,097 (84.5 percent)
Female: 23, 579 (15.5 percent)

Types of Prisoners:
Convicted prisoners: 108,610 (71.6 percent)
Pending appeal: 21,088 (14.0 percent)
Awaiting investigation: 11,450 (7.5 percent)
Awaiting trial: 10,060 (6.6 percent)
Others: 378 (0.3 percent)

Types of Offense:
Against narcotics law: 64,782 (59.7 percent)
Against property: 11,987 (19.3 percent)
Against life: 9,488 (8.7 percent)
Sex offense: 5,143 (4.8 percent)
Bodily harm: 3,226 (3.0 percent)
Against social security: 250 (0.2 percent)
Others: 4,734 (4.3 percent)

Sentence Terms:
Less than five years: 51,523 (47.4 percent)
Five to twenty years: 41,993 (38.7 percent)
Twenty years to fifty years: 12,131 (11.1 percent)
Life imprisonment: 2,869 (2.6 percent)
Death penalty: 94 (0.2 percent)

Age of Prisoners:
Less than twenty years old: 3,890 (3.6 percent)
Twenty – thirty years old: 41,174 (38.0 percent)
Thirty – forty years old: 35,147 (32.4 percent)
Forty – fifty years old: 21,134 (19.4 percent)
Fifty – sixty years old: 5,402 (4.9 percent)
More than sixty years old: 1,863 (1.7 percent)

Ratio of Correctional Staff to Number of Prisoners:
1:19 in 2000
1:15 in 2001
1:22 in 2002
1:20 in 2003
1:19 in 2004
1:15 in 2005
1:13 in 2006

Crimes Committed By Foreigners

Thailand is a very attractive country for tourists and foreign investors. This unfortunately also makes Thailand conspicuous for foreigners engaged in lucrative illegal businesses such as drug smuggling, human trafficking, prostitution, illegal immigration, international organized crime, firearms trading, oil smuggling, and scams targeting other foreigners. We will shed light here on a few of these crimes to increase your awareness and hopefully help you avoid any unpleasant experiences in Thailand.

Most crimes committed by foreigners in Thailand are in contravention of the narcotics laws. Many foreigners assume that the laid-back lifestyle of the Thai people extends to their attitude about drug use – and nothing could be further from the truth. Drug abuse is considered low-class, and drug smugglers are typically given very severe jail sentences in Thailand. As a foreigner, why would you want to risk potential trouble with law enforcement officials in a country where you don't even speak the language? Again, we recommend that you follow the suggestions in all the guidebooks and avoid any association with drug use or people using drugs.

Prostitution is illegal in Thailand but is found in almost every town and city in the country. From beer bars and go-go clubs to massage parlors, karaoke clubs and barber shops, prostitution exists everywhere in Thailand. You should avoid the potential legal entanglements present if you engage in activities involving prostitution. It only takes one phone call to the police to bring your exciting romantic adventure to a sudden halt and turn your dream vacation into a nightmare. And of course, there is the possibility of HIV and STD infection, which can be worse than a jail term. Prostitution involving Thai women has existed for centuries, but there is a new trend in Thailand involving foreign prostitutes both from neighboring countries and from countries of the former Soviet Union and Eastern Europe. The Thai government is cracking down on these illegal activities and is getting stricter with jail time and fines for illegal immigrants caught engaged in prostitution.

Engaging in sex with minors – anyone under the age of eighteen – is illegal whether it is consensual or not and carries very harsh legal consequences. Incidents of adults having sex with underage children have increased in Thailand in the past decade. We do not have statistics for the number of underage children working as prostitutes. Different studies give different figures, but it is estimated that there are significant number of minors working in the sex industry.

Some foreigners come to Thailand to live and work, but their actual interest is in having sexual interactions with young children. The Thai government has acted swiftly to apprehend some high-profile offenders recently and the police are diligent in their efforts to prosecute anyone having sex with minors. The penalties are both a hefty fine and imprisonment plus being blacklisted from ever entering the kingdom again.

Having sex with children – anyone under fifteen years old – is a serious crime and cannot be compromised. If convicted the penalty is from four to twenty years imprisonment and a fine of 8,000 to 40,000 baht. If the child is younger than thirteen, the penalty is from seven to twenty years and a fine of 8,000 to 40,000 baht. The penalties for convictions become more severe the younger the age of the child, with the maximum penalty being life in prison.

For women and children who have been victims of trafficking for prostitution, the Thai government and many NGOs provide counseling and support services including shelters, educational and vocational training, job placement, and financial assistance.

Recently there has been a rise in the number of cases of foreign conmen preying on other foreigners. They tend to frequent the busy tourist areas presenting hard luck stories in order to get sympathy and money. Some Western scammers present themselves as professional types pretending to be business consultants offering investments or assistance in buying property in Thailand. They may even have an office that convinces victims of their legitimacy. These people scam enough money and then close the office and open a new one or just leave the country. It's hard for the police to track them as they are very sophisticated in their methods. As you would in a similar situation at home, be very wary of anything that sounds too good to be true.

The number of organized crime syndicates in Thailand has increased gradually. The number of convicted individuals from crime organizations is still low because they work subtly and skillfully. However, the Thai police are cooperating with police departments from other countries to apprehend international criminals. Many of the criminal organizations are Asian, and they make enormous profits from gambling, drug dealing, prostitution, human trafficking, and illegal weapons.

We are only able to present a brief introduction to crime and punishment in Thailand in this book. Please refer to the "Criminal Matters" section in this book for more information on criminal procedures. And see the two articles "A Foreigner's View Of The Thai Courts" and "An Average Day In A Thai Prison" for other perspectives on the consequences of crime in Thailand.

Crime Statistics In 2006 For Foreigners In Thailand

The following statistics provide an enlightening perspective on the types of crimes committed and the county of origin of foreigners currently in prison in Thailand.

Foreign Prisoners by Gender

Gender	Number
Male	9,825
Female	2,703
Total	12,528

Foreign Prisoners by Continent

Continent	Percentage
Asia	95.8
Africa	2.3
Europe	1.5
America	0.2
Australia	0.2
Total	100 percent

Foreign Prisoners by Nationality

Rank	Country of Nationality	Number	Rank	Country of Nationality	Number	Rank	Country of Nationality	Number
1.	Burma	5,913	11	India	64	21	Philippines	28
2.	Cambodia	2,310	12	Pakistan	57	22	Korea	21
3.	Laos	2,127	13	Ghana	55	23	So. Africa	19
4.	Malaysia	431	14	Nepal	53	24	Congo	17
5.	China	292	15	Vietnam	47	25	Germany	16
6.	Minorities	245	16	Indonesia	42	26	France	16
7.	Singapore	109	17	UK	41	27	Sri Lanka	16
8.	Taiwan	109	18	Bangladesh	35	28	USA	14
9.	Nigeria	87	19	Iran	34	29	Netherlands	13
10	Hong Kong	72	20	Japan	28	30	Australia	11

Foreign Prisoners by Offense

Type of Offense	Number	Percentage
Against narcotics law	6,048	48.2
Against immigration law	3,705	29.6
Against property	768	6.1
Against life	673	5.3
Perjury, fake documents	504	4.2
Against forest law	304	2.4
Sexual assault	108	0.9
Against firearms law	60	0.5
Others	358	2.8
Total	12,528	100 percent

Western Prisoners by Offense

Type of Offense	Percentage
Against narcotics law	60.0
Perjury, fake documents	12.2
Against property	11.0
Against life	7.7
Against immigration law	2.6
Sexual assault	2.6
Others	3.9
Total	100 percent

Foreign Prisoners Increase 2005—2006.

Year	Number
2005	10,408
2006	12,528
Difference	+ 20.4 percent

Convicted Prisoners Transferred To Their Home Country

Rank	Country	Number
1	Nigeria	395
2	Hong Kong	83
3	USA	75
4	Spain	33
5	France	29
6	UK	28
7	Germany	18
8	Canada	17
9	Sweden	15
10	Italy	7
11	Switzerland	6
12	Estonia	5
13	Denmark	3
14	Australia	3
15	Israel	3
16	Austria	2
17	Norway	1
	Total	734

It is possible for a person convicted of a crime in Thailand to be transferred to their home country to serve the remainder of their sentence. Under the Legislation Procedure for Cooperation between States in the Execution of Penal Sentences Act of 1984, foreign nationals convicted of a crime in Thailand, and Thai nationals convicted of a crime in a foreign country, may apply for a prisoner transfer to their home country if a treaty providing for such transfer has been approved by Thailand and the foreign country involved. Currently, Thailand has 24 bilateral prisoner transfer treaties agreements with France, Spain, Canada, Italy, the United States of America, Sweden, the United Kingdom, Finland, Germany, Portugal, Austria, Israel, Poland, Denmark, Hong Kong, Switzerland, Norway, the Philippines, Estonia, the Czech Republic, Australia, Nigeria, the Netherlands, and Mali. Thailand is currently negotiating treaties with Vietnam, China, Belgium, and Cambodia.

The Death Penalty In Thailand

The conviction of some specific crimes in Thailand can still carry the death penalty. It is believed that the potential for sentencing of the death penalty creates a special deterrent to prevent heinous crimes, thereby fostering social safety. The methods of execution in Thailand were and are as follows:

- Prior to 1934: beheading.
- 1934 to 2001: Shooting or firing squad.
- 2001 to present: Lethal injection.

Individual Royal Pardon

The king of Thailand is a constitutional monarch and has the power to decree a royal pardon for any convicted prisoner in Thailand. Convicted prisoners, including those sentenced to death, or an interested person connected to any prisoner may submit a petition for an Individual Royal Pardon through the prison authority. After receiving the prisoner's petition, the prison authority prepares the necessary documents and then passes the petition and all supporting documentation to the Department of Corrections of the Ministry of Justice, the Office of the Prime Minister, the Office of the Privy Council, and eventually to His Majesty the King. The Individual Royal Pardon may or may not be granted.

Collective Royal Pardon

In addition to the Individual Royal Pardon, which each convicted prisoner has a right to apply for, there is also a Collective Royal Pardon, which is granted occasionally on certain important national events such as the King's or the Queen's birthdays. No petition is required, and prisoners receive benefits as indicated in the Pardon Decree, which varies for each person. The Royal Pardon for anyone sentenced to death is a commutation that reduces the death penalty to life imprisonment.

The Thai Department of Correction's website is www.correct.go.th. Here you can learn about its mission, publications, treatment programs, and other useful information. The headquarters is located at 222 Nonthaburi 1 Road, Nonthaburi Province, 11000. (Tel: 02 967-2222; Fax: 02 967-2408.)

An Average Day In A Thai Prison
— by Richard Barrow

MY FIRST IMPRESSIONS OF THAILAND, even before I came here, weren't that good. While I was traveling in Australia I saw the movie *Bangkok Hilton* starring Nicole Kidman. I don't remember much of the movie, but what stands out is Kidman going through Customs in Thailand carrying someone else's bag. She is stopped and they find drugs in the bag. It made me paranoid about ever going to Thailand. I was afraid that someone, maybe the police, would plant drugs in my bag and that I would spend the rest of my life in the notorious 'Hilton.' About two years later, I was backpacking across Asia. My itinerary included lengthy stops in many countries. However, I had only allocated a short stay in Thailand. I was still paranoid. Of course, I ended up staying much longer but that is another story.

For the past few months I have been visiting one of my former students in prison in Samut Prakan. He has been telling me about life in a prison in Thailand, which you can read at ThaiPrisonLife.com. I was at first horrified when I saw my student sentenced to three years. I didn't know how he would survive. Since I have been in Thailand, I have read a number of autobiographies written by foreigners in Thai prisons. They all talk about merciless beatings, gang rape, sadistic guards, murder, and a lot more. However, since I have been visiting my student, I have started to see a different kind of prison. I am not saying he is in a holiday resort, as it is certainly a hard life. However, the Klong Dan Central Prison seems to be a model of a modern Thai prison. There are no daily beatings. The guards aren't sadistic. There are no drugs in the prison. The food isn't even that bad.

I guess things have changed for the better over the years. It is also possible that some of the foreign prisoners who wrote books exaggerated about their harsh treatment in order to sell more books. Although I have found it a fascinating experience writing these prison-life blogs, I don't think anything I have written will propel a book to the top of the bestseller list. There are no dramatic incidents. My friend's daily life is mostly uneventful. I am not saying that those foreigners who wrote books lied about everything. They were, after all, mainly locked up in high-security prisons like Bang Kwan. I know I wouldn't survive there. But they have painted a picture that has tainted the Thai people and given the world an impression that all Thailand's prisons are hell on earth.

In the outside world we have to understand and respect the Thai culture in order to survive. From what I have heard from my student, it is much the same inside. He said that many of the foreigners don't respect the Thai way of doing things. They want everything done their way, and their demands are often unreasonable. This can lead to tension between the different nationalities and the guards that have to deal with it.

The following account is of an average day in a Thai prison. The interview was done over a period of four weeks.

My friend had been in prison for more than three months and had settled into a routine. Here he gives us an idea of what an average day is like, and how things changed for him:

"I was in that first cell for about three days. I was then moved to another cell. This one was very crowded. My old school friend, who is a trustee, suggested that I should try to transfer to his cell. To make the move, I had to bribe someone ten packets of cigarettes. In prison, cigarettes are worth more than money, and we use them to get things done. Once I arrived in the new cell, I then paid another five packets of cigarettes to the cell boss in order to have my own space on the floor. I don't really have a lot of room. It is about the width of my shoulders and the length of my body. However, I suppose I am fortunate because about thirty people in my cell have to sleep on their side on the bare floor. My mother sent me a mat to sleep on. We aren't allowed pillows, but I have a pillowcase that I stuffed with spare clothes.

"We start to wake up at about 5:30 a.m. I roll up my mat and put it in the center of the room. Others who have any bedding do the same. Some people use the toilet in the cell, but the cell boss doesn't allow anyone to make a smell. Which is understandable. So most wait until we are let out to go to the toilets on the ground floor. At first I was really too embarrassed to use the toilet in the cell for the first week or so. I couldn't go with everybody watching me. But I got used to it.

"They say prison changes you. It really does. At about 6:30 a.m. the guards come to do the head count. We have to sit in rows in the cell and then count off one by one. At the moment there are 53 prisoners in our cell which measures only four by eight meters. Once the count has finished, they let us out. Most guys then rush down the stairs for the toilet and the showers. There is always a long queue. I take my time and wait for my friends. I always do everything with my group at the same time.

"Most prisoners have to line up for the five-minute shower. However, as I am now a trustee myself, I am allowed to use the water tub to take a bath. For this I splash water all over my body, soap myself, then rinse off. I then brush my teeth. A lot of the prisoners then go to the canteen to eat the prison food. I don't usually go because it isn't always that nice. Around the prison grounds there are places where you can buy food. For breakfast I sometimes have chicken and rice, or fish cakes or fried pork with rice. A plate of this costs about 25 baht. We use a flat plastic spoon to eat. It is the kind of Chinese spoon used for noodle soup. We are not allowed forks for obvious reasons. After we finish eating, we wash our own plates and spoons and put them aside for next time.

"We are not allowed to touch money. We can buy coupons with money from our prison tab. It is like a kind of bank account inside the prison. We cannot set this up by ourselves. A relative on the outside has to do this for us and then pay money into it for us to use. If you don't have any relations or friends, then you will have a really hard life. You need money to pay for nearly everything. There are quite a few inmates without any relatives and I try to help as many as I can. These coupons are only valid for the day. Unlike outside you cannot get a refund. If I buy 100 baht of coupons, I have to use them all up, otherwise they are wasted.

"After breakfast, the new prisoners have to line up in the parade ground for the first month for the national anthem at 8:00 a.m. They also have to do exercises. I don't have to do this, as I have a job in the office. Before I forget, I should tell you how we are supposed to behave in front of the guards. In some ways it is a bit like at school. If a guard walks past us, we must move to the side and stop to allow him room. If we walk past a guard who is standing still, we must go up to him, give a short bow, and then walk on.

"This morning, I was only at work for about fifteen minutes when my name was called to go to the visitor's room. At the moment I have visitors about three or four times a week, so I keep my prison uniform at the office just in case. Inside the prison we are allowed to wear our normal clothes. However, the visitor's room is on the other side of the wall, so we have to change first. It is the same if we have to go to court. This only takes a minute, and then I head over to the control area by the front gate. There are two visitor rooms. At 8:30 a.m. we are let in for the first round of the day. There are thirteen rounds in the morning for male prisoners. You are only allowed one visitor per day. At this stage we don't know who has come to visit us. We get exactly twenty minutes to talk before the phone lines are cut. So, everyone is quick. Having visitors and receiving mail is the highlight of my day. It doesn't happen every day, so I look forward to when it does.

"During the week, I work in the records office. There is one other prisoner who works with me. My grandfather knows a guard and he got me this job. I spend most of my day writing or typing up records, either for new prisoners or for prisoners who are transferring to other prisons. After the guards found out that I am fluent in English, they made me the official translator. So, whenever a foreign inmate comes to the prison for the first time, I am called to the control area to interview them. I have to ask them certain questions and write down the answers in Thai. There are thirty prisoners from places like Singapore, Hong Kong, the Middle East, and Africa. There are also two Western prisoners. One of them used to teach English in Northern Thailand. He said he recognized me because he used to use my *Bangkok Post* column with his students. Another of the foreign prisoners also recognized me. It is funny because I have never been recognized on the street before, but as soon as I go to prison they start recognizing me. In total there are 590 foreign prisoners. However, most of these are from Burma, Laos and Cambodia.

"I spend most of my day around the office. Sometimes one of the foreign prisoners will come to me for help. Other times the guards will call for me over the loudspeakers to go and assist them with a foreign prisoner. So, I am kept busy. Now it is starting to be very hard work, as some of the foreign prisoners are becoming annoying. They demand so much and don't understand why things cannot be done straight away. They sometimes get angry with me, but there is nothing I can do. I am a prisoner, too. At the moment they get some special privileges. But I heard one of the guards say that this might stop soon, as they complain too much. We don't really get a proper lunch break. I usually eat outside the office. Sometimes I go and buy food for myself, but other times the guards give us their leftovers. I am also a bit like an office boy because the guards get me to run errands for them.

"I finish work at about 3:00 p.m. This is when we all go to take a shower. We also have our last meal for the day at that time. By 4:00 p.m. we have to line up on the second floor of our building. We line up with the others from our cell. This area is like a factory floor because some people work here during the day. We are then taken up to our cell, where we are locked in. Another head count is then done to make sure that we are all there.

"About this time they turn on the television. This is either karaoke or a movie. It is usually on until about 9:00 p.m. Sometimes they are late turning it on. The thing I don't like is that they don't wait until the end of the movie before they switch it off. Everyone in the cell has to take turns standing guard during the night for one hour. If you don't want to do it yourself, you can always bribe someone else to take your turn.

"At the moment I am reading my Harry Potter book. I have nearly finished it. Hopefully someone can send me the next one, as you cannot buy books inside prison. I also sometimes play chess. At about 9:30 p.m. our cell boss tells everyone to go to sleep. However, I cannot get to sleep until later. It wasn't easy sleeping at first because they keep the light on all night. We are locked in this cell for about fourteen hours. Our cell has a window and I can look out at the road beyond the wall. Sometimes I can see a bus driving past. During the night, I often dream of leaving the prison and catching that bus. But I know that won't happen for a long time.

"At 6:30 a.m. we are let out and the day starts again. When I was free, I always looked forward to the weekends. But not now. At the weekend there isn't much to do. We aren't allowed visitors and we don't go to work. We cannot hang around the cell. Everyone has to go down to the ground floor. In my section there are over 1,600 inmates. There isn't a lot of space. It is also very noisy at the weekend. Some play football and others play *takraw* (like foot-volleyball with a rattan ball). I sometimes play football but I often just watch. Some gamble by playing 'hi-lo' with tamarind seeds. But, this is against the rules. The other weekend a fight broke out between two of the football players. One of them nearly got killed. I guess that was the highlight of that day."

A Final Word

We trust you have found this book helpful and informative. It may not provide you with the answers to the specific questions you have, but should provide you with the background information and the resources for you to get the answers you seek regarding Thai law.

Law, in general, is a complicated and confusing subject. However, in this book we have attempted to make Thai law easier to understand, and we hope we have created a valuable and indispensable resource for our readers.

We welcome suggestions for improving this volume which we plan to update periodically. We also welcome questions and comments from our readers. Please send your e-mails to thailaw4u@gmail.com.

As we have stated previously, we do not answer legal questions or provide individual legal advice, but we will select the questions that we determine will generate information on important legal aspects or the ones that are frequently asked. Our legal team will research the suggested topics and we will provide explanations in our books, which should be beneficial to many people.

In the next volumes on Thai law, we plan to discuss certain topics in more depth and detail, give examples of specific interesting cases, and answer all those frequently asked questions.

Our website, www.ThaiLawForForeigners.com, contains updated information, useful forms that you can download, and links to many helpful and interesting related websites.

Chok dee to everyone – and stay on the right side of the law.

— Benjawan and Roengsak.

Part 5
Reference

Visas and Immigration

Information on visas and immigration is included in this reference section. These are complicated issues because Thailand has different requirements for each country. Changes are constantly being made to the immigration rules and regulations. Check the Thai government website to verify the most current information at www.mfa.go.th/web/12.php. The following is official information on visa and immigration which has been obtained with permission from the Ministry of Foreign Affairs by Paiboon Publishing, and was current at the date of publication of this book.

General Information

1. Generally, a foreign citizen who wishes to enter the Kingdom of Thailand is required to obtain a visa from a Royal Thai Embassy or a Royal Thai Consulate-General. However, nationals of certain countries do not require a visa if they meet visa exemption requirements as follows:

(1) they are nationals of countries which are exempted from visa requirements when entering Thailand for tourism purposes. Such nationals will be permitted to stay in the Kingdom for a period of not exceeding 30 days. For more information, please see Tourist Visa Exemption;

(2) they are nationals of countries which hold bilateral agreements with Thailand on the exemption of visa requirements. For more information, please see List of Countries which have Concluded Agreements with Thailand on the Exemption of Visa Requirements .

2. Nationals of certain countries may apply for visa upon arrival in Thailand. Travellers with this type of visa are permitted to enter and stay in Thailand for a period of not exceeding 15 days. For more information, please see Visa on Arrival.

3. Travellers travellling from/through countries which have been declared Yellow Fever Infected Areas must acquire an International Health Certificate verifying the receiving of a Yellow Fever vaccination. For more information, please see List of Countries which are Declared Yellow Fever Infected Areas.

4. Nationals of certain countries are required to apply for a visa only at the Royal Thai Embassy or the Royal Thai Consulate-General in the applicant's country of residence, or at the Royal Thai Embassy which has jurisdiction over his or her country of residence. Travellers are advised to enquire about authorised office for visa issuance at any Royal Thai Embassy or Royal Thai Consulate-General before departure. Contact details and locations of Royal Thai Embassies and Royal Thai Consulates-General are available at www.mfa.go.th/web/10.php.

5. To apply for a visa, a foreigner must possess a valid passport or travel document that is recognised by the Royal Thai Government and comply with the conditions set forth in the Immigration Act of Thailand B.E.2522 (1979) and its relevant regulations. In addition, the visa applicant must be outside of Thailand at the time of application. The applicant will be issued with a type of visa in accordance to his or her purpose of visit. For more information on types of visas and general requirements for each type of visa, please see Types of Visa and Issuance of Visa.

6. In general, applicants are required to apply for a visa in person. However, Royal Thai Embassies and Royal Thai Consulates-General in some countries and in some cases may also accept applications sent through representatives, authorised travel agencies or by post. Please enquire at the Royal Thai Embassy or Royal Thai Consulate-General where you intend to submit your application of acceptable ways of application.

7. Please note that the period of visa validity is different from the period of stay. Visa validity is the period during which a visa can be used to enter Thailand. In general, the validity of a visa is 3 months, but in some cases, visas may be issued to be valid for 6 months, 1 year or 3 years. The validity of a visa is granted with discretion by the Royal Thai Embassy or Royal Thai Consulate-General and is displayed on the visa sticker.

8. On the other hand, the period of stay is granted by an immigration officer upon arrival at the port of entry and in accordance with the type of visa. For example, the period of stay for a transit visa is not exceeding 30 days, for a tourist visa is not exceeding 60 days and for a non-immigrant visa is not exceeding 90 days from the arrival date. The period of stay granted by the immigration officer is displayed on the arrival stamp. Travellers who wish to stay longer than such period may apply for extension of stay at offices of the Immigration Bureau in Bangkok, located at Soi Suan Plu, South Sathorn Road, Bangkok 10120, Tel 02-2873101-10 or at an Immigration office located in the provinces. For information on application for extension of stay, see the Immigration Bureau website at www.immigration.go.th

9. Foreigners entering Thailand are not permitted to work, regardless of their types of visa, unless they are granted a work permit. Those who intend to work in Thailand must hold the correct type of visa to be eligible to apply for a work permit. Information on Work Permit applications could be obtained from the website of the Office of Foreign Workers Administration, Department of Employment, Ministry of Labour at www.doe.go.th/workpermit/index.html

10. Royal Thai Embassies and Royal Thai Consulates-General have the authority to issue visas to foreigners for travel to Thailand. The authority to permit entry and stay in Thailand, however, is with the immigration officers. In some cases, the immigration officer may not permit a foreigner holding a valid visa entry into Thailand should the immigration officer find reason to believe that he or she falls into the category of aliens prohibited from entering Thailand under the Immigration Act B.E. 2522 (1979).

11. According to the Immigration Act of Thailand B.E. 2522 (1979), foreigners who fall into any of the following categories are prohibited to enter Thailand:

(1) Having no genuine valid passport or document used in lieu of passport; or having a genuine valid passport or document used in lieu of passport without valid visa issuance by the Royal Thai Embassies, the Royal Thai Consulates-General or the Ministry of Foreign Affairs, with exception of those who meet visa exemption requirements. The terms and conditions of visa issuance and visa exemption are prescribed by the Ministerial Regulations.

(2) Having no appropriate means of living following entry into the Kingdom.

(3) Having entered the Kingdom to be employed as an unskilled or untrained labourer, or to work in violation of the Alien Work Permit Law.

(4) Being mentally unstable or having any of the diseases stated in the Ministerial Regulations.

(5) Having not yet been vaccinated against smallpox; or inoculated, or undergone any other medical treatment for protection against disease; and having refused to have such vaccinations administered by the Immigration Doctor.

(6) Having been imprisoned by judgment of the Thai Court; or by lawful injunction or judgment of the Court of a foreign country, except for when the penalty is for a petty offence, or negligence, or is provided for as an exception by the Ministerial Regulations.

(7) Having behaviour which could cause possible danger to the public; or having the likelihood of being a nuisance or constituting any violence to the

peace, safety and security of the public or to the security of the nation; or being under warrant of arrest by competent officials of foreign governments.

(8) Reason to believe that entry into Kingdom is for the purpose of being involved in prostitution, the trafficking of women or children, drug smuggling, or other types of smuggling which are against public morality.

(9) Having no money or bond as prescribed by the Minister under Section 14 of the Immigration Act B.E. 2522 (1979).

(10) Being a person prohibited by the Minister under Section 16 of the Immigration Act B.E. 2522 (1979).

(11) Being deported by either the Government of Thailand or that of other foreign countries; or having been revoked the right of stay in the Kingdom or in foreign countries; or having been expelled from the Kingdom by competent officials at the expense of the Government of Thailand unless exemption is provided by the Minister on an individual basis.

Royal Thai Embassies and Royal Thai Consulates-General may issue the following types of visas:

— Transit Visa
— Tourist Visa
— Non-Immigrant Visa
— Diplomatic Visa
— Official Visa
— Courtesy Visa

Issuance Of Visa

Transit Visa

This type of visa is issued to applicants who wish to enter the Kingdom for the following purposes :

— to travel in transit through the Kingdom in order to proceed to the country of destination or to re-enter his/her own country (category "TS")

— to participate in sports activities (sportsmen, sportswomen, etc.)(category "S")*

For those who are scheduled to stay in the Kingdom longer than one month, a Non-Immigrant Visa category "O" can be issued to them

— the person in charge or crew of a conveyance coming to a port, station or area in the Kingdom (category "C")

Documents Required

- Passport or travel document with validity not less than 6 months
- Visa application form completely filled out
- Recent(4 x 6 cm.) photograph of the applicant
- Evidence of travel from Thailand (confirmed air ticket paid in full)
- Evidence of adequate finance (20,000 Baht per person and 40,000 Baht per family)
- Visa of a third country in a passport or travel document
- Letter of invitation stating the application's participation in sports activities in the Kingdom
- Consular officers reserve the rights to request additional documents as deemed necessary

Visa Fee
800 Baht per entry (Visa fee may be changed without prior notice)

Validity of a Visa
The validity of a visa is three months.

Period of Stay
Travellers coming to Thailand with this type of visa will be permitted to stay in the Kingdom for a period not exceeding 30 days.

Extension of Stay
Those who wish to stay longer or may wish to change their type of visa must file an application for permission at the Office of Immigration Bureau located on Soi Suan Plu, off South Sathorn Road, Bangkok 10120 , Tel 02 287-3101-10 (or at http://www.immigration.go.th). The extension of stay as well as the change of certain type of visa is solely at the discretion of the Immigration officer.

Additional Requirements
Nationals of certain countries are required to apply for a visa only at the Thai Embassy or Consulate-General in their home/residence country or at the designated Thai Embassy. Therefore, travellers are advised to contact the nearest Thai Embassy or Consulate-General to find out where they may apply for a visa to Thailand before departure.

Tourist Visa

This type of visa is issued to applicants who wish to enter the Kingdom for tourism purposes.

Documents Required

- Passport or travel document with validity not less than 6 months
- Visa application form completely filled out
- Recent(4 x 6 cm.) photograph of the applicant
- Evidence of travel from Thailand (air ticket paid in full)
- Evidence of adequate finance (20,000 Baht per person and 40,000 Baht per family)
- Consular officers reserve the rights to request additional documents as deemed necessary

Visa Fee

1,000 Baht per entry (Visa fee may be changed without prior notice)

Validity of a Visa

The validity of a visa is 3 months or 6 months.

Period of Stay

Upon arrival, travellers with this type of visa will be permitted to stay in Thailand for a period of not exceeding 30 days or 60 days.

Nationals of countries which are on Thailand's Tourist Visa Exemption list or have bilateral agreements on visa exemption with Thailand will be permitted to stay for a period of not exceeding 60 days. Nationals from other countries who hold a tourist visa will be permitted to stay in Thailand for a period of not exceeding 30 days.

Extension of Stay

Those who wish to stay longer or may wish to change their type of visa must file an application for permission at the Office of Immigration Bureau located on Soi Suan Plu, off South Sathorn Road, Bangkok 10120 , Tel 02 287-3101-10 (or at http:// www.immigration.go.th). The extension of stay as well as the change of certain type of visa is solely at the discretion of the Immigration officer.

Additional Requirements

Nationals of certain countries are required to apply for a visa only at the Thai Embassy or Consulate-General in their home/residence country or at the designated Thai Embassy. Therefore, travellers are adivised to contact the nearest Thai Embassy or Consulate-General to find out where they may apply for a visa to Thailand before departure.

Non-immigrant Visa

This type of visa is issued to applicants who wish to enter the Kingdom for the following purposes:

— to perform official duties (Category "F")
— to conduct business / to work (Category "B")
— to invest with the concurrence of the Thai Ministries and Government Departments concerned (Category "IM")
— to invest or perform other activities relating to investment, subject to the provision of the established laws on investment promotion (Category "IB")
— to study, to come on a work study tour or observation tour , to participate in projects or seminars , to attend a conference or training course , to study as a foreign Buddhist monk (Category "ED")
— to work as a film-producer, journalist or reporter (Category "M")
— to perform missionary work or other religious activities with the concurrence of the Thai Ministries or Government Departments concerned (Category "R")
— to conduct scientific research or training or teaching in a research institute (Category "RS")
— to undertake skilled work or to work as an expert or specialist (Category "EX")
— other activities (Category "O") as follows:

to stay with the family, to perfrom duties for the state enterprise or social welfare organizations, to stay after retirement for the elderly, to receive medical treatment, to be a sport coach as required by Thai Government, to be a contestant or witness for the judicial process.

Documents Required

The applicants must submit the following relevant documents depending on the purpose of their visit.

— Visa application form completely filled out
— Passport or travel document with validity not less than 6 months. The validity of 18 months is required for one year visa application.
— (4 x 6 cm) photograph of the applicant, taken within the past six months
— Evidence of adequate finance (20,000 Baht per person and 40,000 Baht per family)
— Birth Certificate ("O")

- Certifcate of Marriage or its equivalents ("O")
- Transcript / Letter of acceptance from the concerned schools/ universities or institutes ("ED")
- Letter from Thailand's Board of Investment. ("IB")
- Official Note certifying the purpose of travel from the Government Agencies /Embassies and Consulates / International Organizations / State Enterprises inThailand. ("F" / "B" / "ED" / "M" / "R") Letter of approval from the Ministry of Labour (To obtain this letter, the prospective employer in Thailand is required to submit Form WP3 at the Office of Foreign Workers Administration, Department of Employment, Ministry of Labour Tel 02-2452745, 02-2453209 or at a Provincial Employment Office in the respective province. (Further information is available at www.doe.go.th/workpermit/index.html) ("B")
- Letter from a company stating the objective of the visit to Thailand ("B")
- Document showing correspondence with trading partners in Thailand. ("B")
- Letter of invitation from companies qualified to employ foreigners. ("B")
- Employment contract indicating rationale for employing the applicant as well as his/her salary, position and qualifications (document must be signed by authorized managing director and affixed the seal of the company) ("B")
- Copy of Work Permit issued by the Ministry of Labour (only in case the applicant has previously worked in the Kingdom) ("B")
- Copy of corporate documents; namely 1) list of shareholders 2) business registration and business license 3) company profile 4) details of business operation 5) list of foreign workers stating names, nationalities and positions 6) map indicating the location of the company 7) Balance sheet, statement of Income Tax and Business Tax (Por Ngor Dor 50 and Por Ngor Dor 30) of the latest year 8) Alien income tax return (Por Ngor Dor 91) and 9) Value-added tax registration (Por Ngor Dor 20) , etc.("B")
- Copy of educational records of the applicant and letters of recommendation from the prior employers, identifying job description and length of service time. ("B")
- Document indicating the number of foreign tourists (for tourism business only) ,or document indicating export transactions issued by banks (for export business only)("B")

The document(s) to be submitted for non-immigrant visa application is contingent upon necessities and appropriateness of purposes stated in the application form.

Consular officers reserve the rights to request additional documents as deemed necessary.

Copies of company documents must be signed by Board of Directors and affixed the seal of the company.

In the absence of a required document, a letter explaining the unavailability of such document must be provided.

The applicant must sign on each page of the copy.

Documents in foreign languages must be translated into Thai. If translated into English, it should be notarized by notary organs or the applicant's diplomatic/ consular mission.

3. Visa Fee
2,000 Baht for single entry and 5,000 Baht for multiple entries.

Validity of a Visa
Single-entry and multiple-entry visas are valid for three months. Multiple-entry visas could also be valid for one year.

Period of Stay
The holders of this type of visa are initially granted a period of stay in the Kingdom not exceeding 90 days unless otherwise instructed by the Office of Immigration Bureau.

Extension of Stay
Those qualified persons can obtain an additional one year stay permit counting from the date of entry in the Kingdom pertaining to the Office of the Immigration Bureau's regulations on extension of stay. The extension of stay is at the discretion of the Immigration officer.

Applicants wishing to stay in the Kingdom longer than 90 days have to file their application either at the Thai consular mission aboard or at the Office of Immigration Bureau in Bangkok located on Soi Suan Plu, off South Sathorn Road,Bangkok 10120 , Tel 02 287-3101-10 (or website at (http://www.immgration.go.th) . The consular officer must refer the case to the Office of Immigration Bureau for approval. Upon receiving approval, the consular officer may issue the visa as instructed by the Bureau.

Additional Requirements
Nationals of certain countries are required to apply for a visa only at the Thai Embassy or Consulate-General in their home/residence country or at the designated Thai Embassy. Therefore, travellers are advised to contact the nearest Thai

Embassy or Consulate-General to find out where they may apply for a visa to Thailand before departure.

Information on location and contact number of Thai Embassies and Consulates-General is available at /web/10.php

Diplomatic / Official Visa

— Upon official request, Thai Embassies and Consulates-General may grant visas to diplomatic or official passport-holders who wish to assume duties at a foreign Diplomatic Mission or Consulate or International Organization in the Kingdom and to their family members.

— Supporting documents are Note Verbal and/or documents issued by the foreign government or international organization, certifying the identity of the person concerned and his/her purposes while residing in the Kingdom.

Courtesy Visa

— Upon official request, Thai Embassies and Consulates-General may grant courtesy visas to diplomatic/official/ordinary passport-holders who wish to enter the Kingdom on official duty and/or other purposes.

— Supporting documents are documents issued by the governmental agency, foreign government or international organization, certifying the identity of the person concerned and his/her purposes while visiting the Kingdom.

Tourist Visa Exemptions

— According to the Interior Ministerial Announcements dated 1 October B.E. 2545 (2002), 20 December B.E. 2545 (2002), 18 October B.E. 2547 (2004) and 6 May B.E. 2548 (2005), passport holders from 40 countries and 1 special administrative region – Hong Kong SAR – are not required to obtain a visa when entering Thailand for tourism purposes and will be permitted to stay in the Kingdom for a period of not exceeding 30 days on each visit. Foreigners who enter the Kingdom under the Tourist Visa Exemption category may re-enter and stay in Thailand for a cumulative duration of stay of not exceeding 90 days within any 6-month period from the date of first entry.

— Please note that Tourist Visa Exemption does not apply to foreigners holding Travel Document for Aliens issued by these 40 countries.

- Foreigners entering Thailand under the Tourist Visa Exemption category must possess adequate finances for the duration of stay in Thailand (i.e., cash 10,000 Baht per person and 20,000 Baht per family).

Australia	Austria	Belgium
Brazil	Bahrain	Brunei
Canada	Denmark	Finland
France	Germany	Greece
Hong Kong S. A. R.	Iceland	Indonesia
Ireland	Israel	Italy
Japan	Republic of Korea*	Kuwait
Luxembourg	Malaysia	Monaco
Netherlands	New Zealand	Norway
Oman	Peru*	Philippines
Portugal	Qatar	Singapore
Spain	South Africa	Sweden
Switzerland	Turkey	United Arab Emirates
United Kingdom	United States of America	Vietnam

*Thailand holds bilateral agreements on visa exemption for holders of diplomatic, official and ordinary passports for a visit of not exceeding 90 days with Brazil, the Republic of Korea and Peru. Therefore, nationals of these 3 countries are exempted from visa requirements and are permitted to enter and stay in Thailand for a period of not exceeding 90 days.

For more infor.mation on countries that have bilateral agreements on visa exemption with Thailand, please see List of countries which have concluded agreements on the exemption of visa requirements with Thailand.

Visa on arrival

- According to the Interior Ministerial Announcements, passport holders from 20 countries may apply for visas at the immigration checkpoints for the purpose of tourism for the period of not exceeding 15 days.
- The applicant must possess means of living expenses at the amount of 10,000 Baht per person and 20,000 Baht per family accordingly.
- The applicant must present full paid ticket which is usable within 15 days since the date of entry
- Visa on arrival is provided at 32 designated international checkpoints and applicants should submit the application form duly filled out and to which his/her recent photograph (4 x 6 cm) is attached. The application fee is 1,000 Baht.
- Visitors who enter the Kingdom with Visa on Arrival generally cannot file an application for extension of stay except in special cases such as illness which prevents them from travelling, etc. They

can submit an application at the Office of Immigration Bureau , Immigration Division 1, Soi Suan Plu, South Sathorn Road, Bangkok 10120. Tel. 02 287-3127 or 02 287-3101(-10) ext. 2264-5 or at website http://www.immigration.go.th

List of 20 countries is as follows:
1. Bhutan : Kingdom of Bhutan
2. China : People's Republic of China (including Taiwan)
3. Cyprus : Republic of Cyprus
4. Czech : Czech Republic
5. Estonia : Republic of Estonia
6. Hungary : Republic of Hungary
7. India : Republic of India
8. Kazakhstan : Republic of Kazakhstan
9. Latvia : Republic of Latvia
10. Liechtenstein : Principality of Liechtenstein
11. Lithuania : Republic of Lithuania
12. Maldives : Republic of Maldives
13. Mauritius : Republic of Mauritius
14. Oman : Sultanate of Oman
15. Poland : Republic of Poland
16. Russian Federation
17. Saudi Arabia : Kingdom of Saudi Arabia
18. Slovakia : Slovak Republic
19. Slovenia : Republic of Slovenia
20. Ukraine

List of Thailand's Immigration Checkpoints which provide facilities for issuance of visa on arrival :
1. Suvarnabhumi International Airport
2. Don Muang International Airport , Bangkok
3. Chiangmai International Airport , Chiangmai
4. Phuket International Airport , Phuket
5. Hatyai International Airport , Songkhla
6. U Tapao Airport , Rayong
7. Mae Sai Immigration Checkpoint , Chiengrai
8. Chieng Saen Immigration Checkpoint , Chiengrai
9. Chieng Khong Immigration Checkpoint , Chiengrai
10. Betong Immigration Checkpoint , Yala
11. Sadoa Immigration Checkpoint , Songkhla
12. Samui Airport , Surat Thani
13. Sukhothai International Airport, Tak Immigration Checkpoint
14. Bangkok Harbour Immigration Checkpoint, Bangkok

15. Sri Racha Immigration Checkpoint , Chonburi
16. Mabtaput Immigration Checkpoint , Rayong
17. Nong Khai Immigration Checkpoint, Nong Khai
18. Samui Immigration Checkpoint , Surat Thani
19. Phuket Immigration Checkpoint , Phuket
20. Satun Immigration Checkpoint , Satun
21. Krabi Immigration Checkpoint , Krabi
22. Songkhla Harbour Immigraion Checkpoint , Songkhla
23. Chiangrai Airport Immigration Checkpoint, Chiangrai
24. Surat Thani Airport Immigration Checkpoint , Surat Thani

Non-Immigrant Visa "B" (Business and Work)

Foreigners who wish to work, conduct business or undertake investment activities in Thailand must apply for a Non-Immigrant Visa at the Royal Thai Embassies or Royal Thai Consulates-General. Various categories of the Non-Immigrant Visa are currently provided to meet the needs and qualifications of individual business persons. These include business visa Category "B", business-approved visa Category "B-A" and investment and business visa Category "IB". Holder of this type of visa wishing to work in Thailand must be granted a work permit before starting work. The visa fee is 2,000 Baht for single-entry with three-month validity and 5,000 Baht for multiple entries with one-year validity.

Nationals of certain countries are required to apply for a visa only at the Royal Thai Embassy or Royal Thai Consulate-General in their home/residence country or at the designated Royal Thai Embassy or Royal Thai Consulate-General. Travellers are advised to contact the nearest Royal Thai Embassy or Consulate-General to find out where they may apply for a visa to Thailand before departure. For more information on contact details and locations of the Royal Thai Embassies and Royal Thai Consulates-General, see www.mfa.go.th/web/10.php.

Application for Visa

Non-Immigrant Visa Category "B" (Business Visa) is issued to applicants who wish to enter the Kingdom to work or to conduct business. Foreigners who wish to work in Thailand must provide the following documents:

— Passport or travel document with validity of not less than 6 months.
— Completed visa application form.
— Recent passport-sized photograph (4 x 6 cm) of the applicant taken within the past 6 months.
— Evidence of adequate finance (20,000 Baht per person and 40,000 Baht per family).

— Letter of approval from the Ministry of Labour. To obtain this letter, the applicant's prospective employer in Thailand is required to submit Form WP3 at the Office of Foreign Workers Administration, Department of Employment, Ministry of Labour Tel. 02-2452745, or at the Provincial Employment Office in his or her respective province. More information is available at www.doe.go.th/workpermit/index.html

— Copy of Work Permit issued by the Ministry of Labour and alien income tax or Por Ngor Dor 91 (only in the case where applicant has previously worked in Thailand).

— Corporate documents of hiring company in Thailand such as:
  1) business registration and business license
  2) list of shareholders
  3) company profile
  4) details of business operation
  5) list of foreign workers stating names, nationalities and positions
  6) map indicating location of the company
  7) balance sheet, statement of Income Tax and Business Tax (Por Ngor Dor 50 and Por Ngor Dor 30 of the latest year)
  8) value-added tax registration (Por Por 20)

— Document indicating the number of foreign tourists (for tourism business only), or document indicating export transactions issued by banks (for export business only).

> *An alien who receives a Non-Immigrant visa can work in Thailand once he or she is being granted a work permit. An alien in violation of the Immigration Act B.E. 2522 (1979) concerning taking up employment without work permit or the Royal Decree B.E. 2522 (1979) concerning holding employment in certain restricted occupations and professions shall be prosecuted and imprisoned or fined, or shall face both penalties.*

— It is recommended that the applicant should apply for visa at the Thai Embassy/ Consulate in the country where he/she has the residence

Foreigners who wish to conduct business in Thailand must provide the following documents:

— Passport or travel document with a validity of not less than 6 months.

— Completed application form.

— Recent passport-sized photograph (4 x 6 cm) photograph of the applicant taken within the past 6 months.

— Evidence of adequate finance (20,000 Baht per person and 40,000 Baht per family) for the duration of stay in Thailand

- Letter from the applicant's company indicating the applicant's position, length of employment, salary and purpose of visit(s) to Thailand.
- Documents showing correspondence with business partners in Thailand.
- Evidence of financial status in the case where the applicant is self-employed.
- Letter of invitation from trading or associated partners/companies in Thailand.
- Corporate documents of associated partners/companies in Thailand such as:
    1) business registration and business license
    2) list of shareholders
    3) company profile
    4) details of business operation
    5) map indicating location of the company
    6) balance sheet, statement of Income Tax and Business Tax (Por Ngor Dor 50 and Por Ngor Dor 30) of the latest year
    7) value-added tax registration (Por Por 20)

Copies of company documents must be signed by the Board of Directors or authorised managing director and affix seal of company.

Additional documents may be requested as and when necessary. In the absence of a required document, applicant must provide a letter explaining the unavailability of such document. Applicant must endorse on each and every page of the submitted copies of documentation. Documents in foreign languages must be translated into Thai and should be notorised by notary organs or by the applicant's diplomatic or consular mission.

Holder of this type of visa is entitled to stay in Thailand for a maximum period of 90 days. He or she may apply for an extension of stay at the Office of the Immigration Bureau and may be granted such extension for a period of one year from the date of first entry into Thailand.

Non-Immigrant Visa category "B-A" (Business Approved Visa)

The granting of such visa to qualified applicants is under the jurisdiction of the Office of the Immigration Bureau in Bangkok. The applicant's associated company in which he or she will invest in or conduct business with may apply for this type of visa on behalf of the applicant at the Office of the Immigration Bureau. Once the application is approved, the Immigration Bureau will advise the concerned Royal Thai Embassy or Royal Consulate-General via the Ministry of Foreign Affairs to issue the visa to the applicant. The holder of this category "B-A" visa will be permitted to stay for a period of one year from the date of first entry into the Kingdom.

Non-Immigrant Visa Category "IB" (Investment and Business Visa) is issued to foreign citizens employed to work on investment projects which are under the auspices of the Board of Investment of Thailand (BOI). Such projects must be involved in or bring benefit to Thailand in the following ways:

— Export-promotion
— Increasing employment
— Utilising local raw materials
— Projects engaging the provinces
— Encouraging technology transfer to Thai nationals
— Not hindering existing domestic businesses

Non-Immigrant Visa Category "B" (Teaching)

Foreigners who intend to take up employment as school teachers at the levels below university level in Thailand must submit the following required documents:

— Passport or travel document with validity of not less than 6 months
— Completed visa application form
— Recent passport-sized photograph (4 x 6 cm) of the applicant taken within the past 6 months.
— Letter of acceptance from employing institute or school in Thailand.
— Letter of approval from government agencies such as the Office of the Private Education Commission, the Office of the Basic Education Commission.
— Evidence of educational qualification such as diplomas or teaching certificates.
— School license or business registration, list of shareholders and school profile.
— Applicant's resume.
— Police certificate verifying that applicant has no criminal record or equivalents or letter issued by authorised agencies in applicant's country. (The requirement of the submission of such police certificate is optional. The applicant must submit it if consular officer requests he/she to do so. This requirement is effective as from May 2007)

Additional Information

Upon entry into the Kingdom, applicant or his or her appointed representatives must apply for a work permit at the Office of Foreign Workers Administration, Department of Employment, Ministry of Labour in which the applicant will be obligated to pay income tax accordingly. If the applicant's associated company is located in the provinces, the applicant must apply at the Employment Office of that province.

Applicant's family members (i.e., spouse, parents and children who are unmarried and under 20 years old) are eligible to apply for a Non-Immigrant Visa (category "O") and will be allowed to stay for a period of 90 days but no longer than 1 year.

Foreign citizens who hold a Transit Visa ("TS") or Tourist Visa ("TR") and wish to engage in business activities in Thailand may apply for a change of type of visa (e.g., from Tourist Visa to Non-Immigrant Visa) at the Office of the Immigration Bureau Office located at Soi Suan Plu, South Sathorn Road, Bangkok 10120, Tel 02 2873101-10, www.immigration.go.th. The granting of change of type of visa and extension of stay is at the discretion of the immigration officer.

One Stop Service Centre for Visas and Work Permits

The One Stop Service Centre for Visas and Work Permits was established on 1 July 1997 by authority of the Regulations of the Office of Prime Minister promulgated on 30 June 1997. The objective of this centre is to simplify visa extension and permit issuance procedures to create a good investment environment. It aims to facilitate applications of visa extension and work permits (e.g., stay permission, re-entry permit, work permit). The Centre is located on 207 Rachadapisek Road, Krisda Plaza, Dindaeng, Bangkok 10310, Tel 02 693-9333

Foreigners who are eligible to apply for visa extension and work permits at the One Stop Service Centre are:

Foreigner who is an executive or expert with privileges accorded to them by the following laws:

— Investment Promotion Act B.E. 2520 (1977)
— Petroleum Act B.E. 2514 (1971)
— Industrial Estate Authority of Thailand Act B.E. 2522 (1979)

Foreigner who is an investor.

— If investing not less than 2 million Baht, he or she will be granted a 1 year permit.
— If investing not less than 10 million Baht, he or she will be granted a 2 year permit.

Foreigner who is an executive or expert.

— Foreigner's associated company should be registered with capital or possess asset of not less than 30 million Baht.

Foreigner who is member of the foreign press must present a letter from the Ministry of Foreign Affairs and a copy of an ID Press Card issued by the Department of Public Relations.

Foreigner who is a researcher or developer on science and technology.

Foreigner who is employed in a branch office of an overseas bank, foreign banking office of an overseas bank, provincial foreign banking office of an overseas bank or a representative office of foreign bank in which all offices are certified by the Bank of Thailand.

Foreigner who works on the necessary and urgent basis for a period of no longer than 15 days.

Foreigner who is an official of the representative office for foreign juristic persons concerning the International Trading Business and Regional Office of Transnational Corporation in accordance to the Foreign Business Act B.E. 2542 (1999).

Foreigner who is an expert on information technology.

Foreigner who works at regional operating headquarters.

Three-Year Non-Immigrant Visa "B" (Business only)

Foreign citizen who wishes to visit Thailand for business purpose may apply for a three-year Non-Immigrant Visa "B". This type of visa may be issued to businessmen for multiple-entries and is valid for 3 years. It allows holder to visit Thailand as often as required for as long as the visa remains valid and allows holder to stay in Thailand for a period of not exceeding 90 days during each visit.

Place of application

Application is to be submitted at the Royal Thai Embassy or the Royal Thai Consulate-General in the applicant's country of residence, or at the Royal Thai Embassy which has jurisdiction over his or her country of residence. However, Royal Thai Consulate-General headed by Honorary Consul-General is not authorized to issue this type of visa. Applicant may enquire about authorized office for visa issuance at any Royal Thai Embassy or Royal Thai Consulate-General. Information on contact details and locations of Royal Thai Embassies and Royal Thai Consulates-General is also available at www.mfa.go.th/web/10.php

Required Documentation

Applicant for a three-year Non-Immigrant Visa "B" must submit the following:

Basic documents

1. An application form completed in full and signed by applicant.

2. A passport valid for travelling to Thailand with sufficient remaining validity.

3. Two passport-sized photographs (4x6cm) taken within the previous 6 months.

Additional documents which may be requested

4. National Identity Card, Residence documentation or valid proof of identity.

5. A letter from the employer giving details of the applicant's position, length of employment, salary and purpose of the visit(s) to Thailand. If the applicant is self-employed, he or she must provide documentation of his or her business undertaking such as business registration and details of business operation.

6. Copies of correspondence with business partners in Thailand.

7. A letter of invitation from trading or associated partners/companies in Thailand.

8. Corporate documents of associated partners/companies in Thailand such as:
   — business registration and business license
   — list of shareholders
   — company profile
   — details of business operation
   — map indicating location of the company
   — balance sheet, statement of Income Tax and Business Tax (Por Ngor Dor 50 and Por Ngor Dor 30) of the latest year
   — value-added tax registration (Por Por 20)

9. A letter of recommendation from previous employer or business associations of which the applicant is a member.

Visa fee

   — The fee is 10,000 Baht.

Remarks

   — The required additional documents (4 —9) may be submitted upon request.

Supplementary documents may be requested as and when necessary.

   — The issuance of visa is at discretion of the consular officer.

   — Visa fee is non-refundable.

Non-Immigrant Visa "O-A" (Long Stay)

This type of visa may be issued to applicants aged 50 years and over who wish to stay in Thailand for a period of not exceeding 1 year without the intention of working.

Holders of this type of visa are allowed to stay in Thailand for 1 year. Employment of any kind is strictly prohibited.

Eligibility

— Applicant must be aged 50 years and over (on the day of submitting application).

— Applicant not prohibited from entering the Kingdom as provided by the Immigration Act B.E. 2522 (1979).

— Having no criminal record in Thailand and the country of the applicant's nationality or residence.

— Having the nationality of or residence in the country where applicant's application is submitted.

— Not having prohibitive diseases (Leprosy, Tuberculosis, drug addiction, Elephantiasis, third phase of Syphilis) as indicated in the Ministerial Regulation No. 14 B.E. 2535.

Required Documents

— Passport with validity of not less than 18 months.

— 3 copies of completed visa application forms.

— 3 passport-sized photos (4 x 6 cm) of the applicant taken within the past six months.

— A personal data form.

— A copy of bank statement showing a deposit of the amount equal to and not less than 800,000 Baht or an income certificate (an original copy) with a monthly income of not less than 65,000 Baht, or a deposit account plus a monthly income totalling not less than 800,000 Baht.

— In the case of submitting a bank statement, a letter of guarantee from the bank (an original copy) is required.

— A letter of verification issued from the country of his or her nationality or residence stating that the applicant has no criminal record (verification shall be valid for not more than three months and should be notarised by notary organs or the applicant's diplomatic or consular mission).

— A medical certificate issued from the country where the application is submitted, showing no prohibitive diseases as indicated in the Ministerial Regulation No.14 (B.E. 2535) (certificate shall be valid for not more than three months and should be notarised by notary organs or the applicant's diplomatic or consular mission).

— In the case where the accompanying spouse is not eligible to apply for the Category 'O-A' (Long Stay) visa, he or she will be considered for temporary stay under Category 'O' visa. A marriage certificate must be provided as evidence and should be notarised by notary organs or by the applicant's diplomatic or consular mission.

Channels to submit application

Applicant may submit their application at the Royal Thai embassy or Royal Thai Consulate-General in their home/residence country or at the Office of the Immigration Bureau in Thailand located on Soi Suan Plu, South Sathorn Road, Sathorn District, Bangkok 10120. Tel 0-2287-4948 (direct) or 0-2287-3101/10 ext. 2236.

4. Visa fee: 2,000 Baht for single entry; 5,000 Baht for multiple entries

Recommendations for foreigners with Non-Immigrant Visa "O-A" (Long Stay) while staying in the Kingdom

Upon arrival, holder of this type of visa will be permitted to stay in Thailand for 1 year from the date of first entry. During the one-year period, if he or she wishes to leave and re-enter the country, he or she is required to apply at the Immigration office for re-entry permit (single or multiple) before departure. In the case of leaving the country without a re-entry permit, the permit to stay for 1 year shall be considered void.

At the end of the 90-day stay , the foreigner must report to the immigration officer in his or her residence area and report again every 90 days during his or her stay in Thailand. The foreigner may report to the police station if there is no immigration office in his or her residence area.

Foreigner may report to the competent authority by post and should provide the following:

— A report form (Tor Mor 47).

— A copy of passport pages showing the foreigner's photo, personal details, and the latest arrival visa stamp.

— A copy of the previous receipt of acknowledgement.

— A self-addressed envelope with postage affixed.

Such documents must be sent to the Office of the Immigration Bureau, Soi Suan Plu, South Sathorn Road, Sathorn District, Bangkok 10120, and must be submitted 7 days before the end of every 90-day period. A receipt of acknowledgement will be given and should be used for future correspondence.

Foreigner who wishes to extend his or her stay shall submit a request for extension of stay at the Office of the Immigration Bureau with documented evidence of money transfer or a deposit account in Thailand or an income certificate showing an amount of not less than 800,000 Baht or an income certificate plus a deposit account showing a total amount of not less than 800,000 Baht. A one-year extension of stay shall be granted at the discretion of the immigration officer to the foreigner as long as he or she meets the above requirements.

List Of Countries Which Are Declared Yellow Fever Infected Areas

The Ministry of Public Health has issued regulations that applicants who have travelled from or through the countries which have been declared Yellow Fever Infected Areas must provide an International Health Certificate proving that they have received a Yellow Fever vaccination.

The International Health Certificate must be submitted together with the visa application form. The traveller will also have to present the said certificate to the Immigration Officer upon arrival at the port of entry in the Kingdom. As for those nationals of the countries listed below but who have not travelled from/through those countries, such a certificate is not required. However, they should possess concrete evidence showing that their domicile is not in an infected area so as to prevent unnecessary inconvenience.

Declared Yellow Fever Infected Areas

Republic of Angola	Republic of Benin
Republic of Bolivia	Federative Republic of Brazil
Burkina Faso	Republic of Burundi
Federal Republic of Cameroon	Central African Republic
Republic of Chad	Republic of Colombia
Congo Republic:Republic of Cote d' Ivoire	Republic of Ecuador
Republic of Equatorial Guinea	Federal Democratic Republic of Ethiopia
Gabonese Republic	Republic of the Gambia
Republic of Ghana	Republic of Guinea Bissau
Republic of Guinea	Cooperative Republic of Guyana
Republic of Kenya	Republic of Liberia
Republic of Mali	Islamic Republic of Mauritania

Republic of Niger

Republic of Panama

Republic of Rwanda

Republic of Senegal

Somali Democratic Republic

Republic of Suriname

Republic of Togo

Republic of Uganda

Federal Republic of Nigeria

Republic of Peru

Democratic Republic of Sao Tome & Principe

Republic of Sierra Leone

Republic of the Sudan

United Republic of Tanzania

Republic of Trinidad and Togago

Republic of Venezuela

Exemption Of Visa Requirements

Countries which have concluded agreements on the exemption of visa requirements for holders of diplomatic or official or service/special passports with Thailand and permitted to stay for a period of not exceeding 30 and 90 days.

List Of Countries Which Have Concluded Agreements On The Exemption Of Visa Requirements With Thailand

30 Days	
Cambodia	China
Laos	Mongolia
Myanmar	Oman
Vietnam	

90 DAYS	
Argentina	Luxembourg
Austria	Malaysia
Belgium	Mexico
Bhutan	The Netherlands
Brazil	Nepal
Chile	Peru
Costa Rica	The Philippines
Croatia	Poland
Czech Republic	Romania
Germany	Russian Federation
Hungary	Singapore
India	Slovak Republic
Israel	South Africa
Italy	Switzerland
Japan	Tunisia
Republic of Korea	Turkey
Liechtenstein	

List of countries which have concluded agreements on the exemption of visa requirements for holders of ordinary passports with Thailand and permitted to stay for a period of not exceeding 30 and 90 days

30 DAYS	
Laos	Russia
Vietnam	Hong Kong SAR*
Macau SAR*	

According to the Agreements on Exemption of Visa Requirements between Thailand and Hong Kong SAR and between Thailand and Macau SAR, all types of Thai passports including diplomatic and offcial passports shall be exempted from visa requirements for a visit of not exceeding 30 days to Hong Kong SAR and Macau SAR.

90 DAYS	
Argentina	Brazil
Chile	Republic of Korea
Peru	

Nationals of countries which hold Agreements on Visa Exemption Requirements with Thailand intending to work or stay in Thailand beyond the agreed bilateral arrangement must apply for an appropriate visa before entry into Thailand in order to submit the application for work or stay permit.

Q: I would like to go to Thailand for vacation for 2 weeks. I hold American passport. Do I need a visa?

A: Nationals of the United States of America and 40 other countries are eligible to travel to Thailand, for tourism purpose, with the exemption of visa and are permitted to stay in the Kingdom for a period of not exceeding 30 days. You do not need a visa, however, please make sure that you are in possession of a passport valid for at least 6 months, a round-trip air ticket, and adequate finances equivalent to at least 10,000 Baht per person or 20,000 Baht per family. Otherwise, you may be inconvenienced upon entry into the country. Furthermore, foreigners who enter the Kingdom under this Tourist Visa Exemption Scheme may re-enter and stay in Thailand for a cumulative duration of stay of not exceeding 90 days within any 6-month period from the date of first entry.

Q: As an Australian businessman, I need to travel a lot. I have to go to Thailand very frequently on business. Is there any facility for frequent business travelers like me?

A: You can apply for a 1-year or 3-year multiple-entry business visa which would allow you to travel to Thailand as frequently as you want while the visa remains valid, and you would be permitted to stay for a period of not exceeding 90 days on each visit. To ensure that your application will be conveniently processed, kindly check with the Royal Thai Embassy or Consulate-General at which you are to submit the application for more details. Since Thailand and Australia are both members of APEC and participating in APEC Business Travel Card (ABTC) scheme, you may be eligible to apply for an ABTC which serves as a multiple-entry business visa allowing entry into 17 APEC economies in one card. For more information, you may contact the Department of Immigration and Multicultural Affairs of Australia which is Australia's focal authority for this scheme.

Q: I want to work in Thailand. I am a Malaysian, living in K.L. How should I go about getting necessary visa?

A: In order to work in Thailand, there are 2 important elements: a Non-Immigrant "B" Visa and a Work Permit. First of all, you need to have a prospective employer in Thailand. Then you may apply for a Non-Immigrant Visa category "B" (business)at the Royal Thai Embassy in K.L. using the basic required documents and recommendation letter from your employer along with your company's business certifications as suggested in the website (www.mfa.go.th). Once you have obtained such visa, you can enter the Kingdom and therefore apply for a Work Permit from the Department of Employment, Ministry of Labour. In order to expedite visa issuance, your employer may, on your behalf, apply for the Work Permit in advance (with the form called Tor Thor 3). The Department of Employment will then issue a pre-approved certificate to be used in your visa application. In such case, please make sure to obtain the Work Permit (Tor Thor 2) once you arrive in Thailand.

Q: I am a Lithuanian. I want to go to Thailand for sightseeing for just a week. I understand that Lithuanian nationals have to apply for visa before entering Thailand. But there is no Thai Embassy in my country. Can you please give me some advice?

A: You have three options:

(1) Lithuanian nationals are eligible to apply for visa on arrival (VOA) at any of 24 designated checkpoints in Thailand, including, of course, all international airports. Currently nationals of 20 countries are eligible under this scheme. You can see the list of such countries in the website (www.mfa.go.th). With the Visa on Arrival, you would be granted a stay of a period of not exceeding 15 days. But you must have a passport valid for at least 6 months, a round-trip air ticket where date of departure from Thailand is within 15 days of the date of entry, and adequate finances equivalent to at least 10,000 Baht per person.

(2) There is a Royal Thai Honorary Consulate-General in Vilnius, the capital of Lithuania. You may apply for a Thai tourist visa there. In such case, you would be permitted to stay in Thailand for 30 days.

(3) You may also apply for Thai tourist visa at the Royal Thai Embassy in Moscow or at the nearest Royal Thai Embassy which would also permit you to stay for 30 days.

Q: I am an Indonesian national currently working for a company in London. My company has assigned me to attend a training course in Thailand for 6 weeks. Should I apply for visa, and where can I do that?

A: You need to obtain a Non-Immigrant Visa before entering the Kingdom. You may apply for such visa at the Royal Thai Embassy in London. Basic documents include a recommendation letter from your company verifying your status and the assignment. You will also need documents certifying that you are legally employed in Britain and confirming that you will be able to re-enter Britain without any problems.

Q: I have obtained a tourist visa from the Honorary Thai Consulate-General in Rio de Janeiro. They forgot to include a date of expiry in the visa. I had trouble at the airport but fortunately the Immigration officer allowed me to enter. Now I want to extend my stay but the Immigration Office insisted that they cannot permit the extension unless the visa is fixed. What should I do?

A: In this case, please bring your passport to the Visa Division, Department of Consular Affairs, Ministry of Foreign Affairs on Chaengwattana Road in Bangkok. If the visa is genuine, you can obtain any corrections or amendments of visa there.

Q: I am an Italian national currently staying in Koh Samui on my vacation. I entered Thailand with a tourist visa and was granted permission to stay for 60 days until the end of this month. However, I wish to stay longer. What should I do?

A: You may apply for an extension of stay at any Immigration Office in Thailand where you may be permitted to stay for another 30-day period. You must do so before your stay permits expires, otherwise you will be fined 500 Baht for each day you overstay in Thailand.

Q: I am an Indian and I just finished my study in Bangkok. Now I want to work with a company in Chiang Mai.Do I need to do anything?

A: You need to apply for a change of visa status, and apply for a Work Permit. You are therefore recommended to consult with the Immigration Office and the Department of Employment accordingly.

Q: An NGO in Thailand has invited me to go there and work for them as a volunteer for 45 days during my school break. I will not earn any money in Thailand. I am a Belgian college student in Brussels. I understand that I do not need a visa, do I?

A: Although you will work as a volunteer, you do need a Non-Immigrant visa as well as the Work Permit. The NGO must be legally registered with the Thai authority, and that you need a recommendation letter from the NGO for your visa application and the Work Permit.

Q: Please give me some advice. I am a bit confused. I am a Moroccan and going to visit Thailand for pleasure with my family. I already got a Thai tourist visa from the Honorary Consulate-General in Casablanca. I understand from what is written in the visa stamp that the visa is valid for 3 months. Does it mean that I can stay in Thailand for 3 months?

A: That is not a correct understanding. The validity of visa and the duration of stay are not the same. The 3-month validity of the visa means that you must use the visa within 3 months from the date of issue. The duration of stay is the period in which you are permitted to stay in the Kingdom granted by the Immigration Officer once you arrive in Thailand, that is, 30 days from the date of entry.

Q: I came to Thailand with a single-entry business visa, and I have been permitted to stay for 90 days until the end of next month. I was just asked by my boss to attend an urgent meeting in Singapore for several days starting from the day after tomorrow. I still have business to do in Thailand after that though. Do I need to get another visa?

A: Before you leave Thailand for Singapore, you may apply for a re-entry permit from the Immigration Office. You are able to do that at any International Airport too. The re-entry permit will allow you to enter the Kingdom again before the end of next month. The permit will also enable you to stay until the end of next month, unless you get an extension of stay from the Immigration Office.

Q: I heard that Thailand is a nice place to stay after retirement. Is there any special kind of visa for retirees?

A: Yes, there is special visa called Non-immigrant "O-A" (Long Stay). Foreigners who are 50 years of age or older who wish to stay in Thailand for a long period and do not have any intention to work in the Kingdom may apply for such visa at the Royal Thai Embassy or Royal Thai Consulate-General in their respective country. The holder of "O-A" visa is allowed to stay in Thailand for 1 year from the date of first entry, and is also able to apply for an extension of stay afterwards. Please see the qualifications and requirements for application and relevant information in the website (www.mfa.go.th).

Q: I have been in Thailand since last week with a multiple-entry business visa. I happened to lose my passport yesterday. What should I do?

A: First, you need to go to a police station for a report of the loss. Then you need to go to your Embassy in Bangkok for an issuance of new passport or temporary travel document. Finally, you need to bring the new passport or travel document to the Immigration Office for an endorsement. In case that your country does not have an Embassy in Bangkok, please go to the Visa and Travel Documents Division, Department of Consular Affairs, Ministry of Foreign Affairs, on Chaengwattana Road in Bangkok, to apply for the Emergency Certificate (EC). You then need to bring the EC to the Immigration Office for endorsement before leaving the Kingdom. You need to apply for a new visa on your new passport before coming to Thailand next time.

Issuance Of Travel Document For Aliens (TD)

Aliens as listed below are eligible to apply for Travel Document (TD) at the Ministry of Foreign Affairs, Department of Consular Affairs, Visa and Travel Documents Division located on Chaengwattana Road, Bangkok 10210 , Tel. 0-2981-7171 ext. 3201 or 3202, direct line 0-2575-1062-3

- Aliens who are granted permanent residence in Thailand or those who have been denied by their own government in issuing passport or travel document
- Stateless persons
- Aliens who are granted permanent residence in Thailand under a special ten-million investment programme

Documents Required

- A Residence Certificate with its copy
- A House Registration with its copy
- A Certificate of Alien with its copy
- 3 photographs (2 1/2 inches) taken within the past six months
- An application form completely filled out

Application Fee
500 Baht for issuing or renewal

Validity Of Document
T.D. is valid for 1 year

Issuance Of Emergency Certificate (EC)

Aliens as listed below are eligible to apply for Emergency Certificate (EC) at the Ministry of Foreign Affairs, Department of Consular Affairs, Visa and Travel Documents Division located on Chaengwattana Road, Bangkok 10210 , Tel. 0-2981-7171 ext. 3201 or 3202 / direct line 0-2575-1062-3

- Political refugees
- Stateless children under the patronage of the Department of Public Welfare
- Foreigners whose passport or travel document is lost and no consular missions of that national available in the Kingdom
- Alien's infant whose consular mission of that national is not available in Thailand

Documents Required

- An application form completely filled out
- 3 photographs (2 1/2 inches) taken within the past six months
- Daily Report on Lost Documents from Royal Thai Police with its two copies
- confirmed ticket identifying the departure date with its copy
- Letter from the Ministry of Interior (Political refugees) with its two copies
- A Certificate of Birth with its its two copies (Alien's infant)
- Letter from Department of Public Welfare with its two copies

Application Fee 300 Baht

กระทรวง ทบวง กรม ตามพ. ร. บ. ปรับปรุงกระทรวง ทบวง กรม

The 20 Ministries, Their Government Bureaus and Departments

1. **สำนักนายกรัฐมนตรี (Office the Prime Minister)**
   - สำนักงานปลัดสำนักนายกรัฐมนตรี (Office of the Permanent Secretary)
   - กรมประชาสัมพันธ์ (Public Relations Department)
   - สำนักงานคณะกรรมการคุ้มครองผู้บริโภค (The Office of the Consumer Protection Board)
   - ส่วนราชการที่รายงานตรงต่อนายกรัฐมนตรี (Offices Directly Accountable to the Minister)

- สำนักเลขาธิการนายกรัฐมนตรี (The Secretariat of the Prime Minister)
- สำนักเลขาธิการคณะรัฐมนตรี (The Secretariat of the Cabinet)
- สำนักข่าวกรองแห่งชาติ (National Intelligence Agency)
- สำนักงบประมาณ (The Bureau of the Budget)
- สำนักงานสภาความมั่นคงแห่งชาติ (Office the National Security Council)
- สำนักงานคณะกรรมการกฤษฎีกา (Office of the Council of State)
- สำนักงานคณะกรรมการข้าราชการพลเรือน (Office of the Civil Service Commission)
- สำนักงานคณะกรรมการพัฒนาการเศรษฐกิจและสังคมแห่งชาติ (Office of the National Economic and Social Development Board)
- สำนักงานคณะกรรมการพัฒนาระบบราชการ (Office of Public Sector Development Commission)

2. กระทรวงกลาโหม (Ministry of Defense)

- สำนักงานรัฐมนตรี (Office of the Ministry)
- กรมราชองครักษ์ (Royal Aide de Camp Department)
- สำนักงานปลัดกระทรวงกลาโหม (Office of the Permanent Secretary for Defense)
- กองบัญชาการทหารสูงสุด (Supreme Command Headquarters)
- กองทัพบก (Royal Thai Army)
- กองทัพเรือ (Royal Thai Navy)
- กองทัพอากาศ (Royal Thai Air Force)

3. กระทรวงการคลัง (Ministry of Finance)

- สำนักงานรัฐมนตรี (Office of the Minister)
- สำนักงานปลัดกระทรวงการคลัง (Office of the Permanent Secretary)
- กรมธนารักษ์ (The Treasury Department)
- กรมบัญชีกลาง (The Comptroller General's Department)
- กรมศุลกากร (The Customs Department)
- กรมสรรพสามิต (The Excise Department)
- กรมสรรพากร (The Revenue Department)
- สำนักงานคณะกรรมการนโยบายรัฐวิสาหกิจ (State Enterprise Policy Office)
- สำนักงานบริหารหนี้สาธารณะ (Public Debt Management Office)
- สำนักงานเศรษฐกิจการคลัง (The Fiscal Policy Office)

4. กระทรวงการต่างประเทศ (Ministry of Foreign Affairs)
- สำนักงานรัฐมนตรี (Office of the Minister)

- สำนักงานปลัดกระทรวงการต่างประเทศ
  (Office of the Permanent Secretary)
- กรมการกงสุล (Department of Consular Affairs)
- กรมพิธีการทูต (Department of Protocol)
- สำนักงานความร่วมมือเพื่อการพัฒนาระหว่างประเทศ
  (International Development Cooperation Agency)
- กรมเศรษฐกิจระหว่างประเทศ (Department of Economic Affairs)
- กรมสนธิสัญญาและกฎหมาย (Department of Treaties and Legal Affairs)
- กรมสารนิเทศ (Department of Information)
- กรมองค์การระหว่างประเทศ
  (Department of International Organizations)
- กรมยุโรป (Department of European Affairs)
- กรมอเมริกาและแปซิฟิกใต้
  (Department of American and South Pacific Affairs)
- กรมอาเซียน (Department of ASEAN Affairs)
- กรมเอเชียตะวันออก (Department of East Asian Affairs)
- กรมเอเชียใต้ ตะวันออกกลางและแอฟริกา
  (Department of South Asian, Middle East and African Affairs)

5. **กระทรวงท่องเที่ยวและการกีฬา (Ministry of Tourism and Sports)**
   - สำนักงานรัฐมนตรี (Office of the Minister)
   - สำนักงานปลัดกระทรวงการท่องเที่ยวและกีฬา
     (Office of the Permanent Secretary)
   - สำนักพัฒนาการกีฬาและนันทนาการ
     (Office of Sports and Recreation Development)
   - สำนักงานพัฒนาการท่องเที่ยว (Office of Tourism Development)

6. **กระทรวงการพัฒนาสังคมและความมั่นคงของมนุษย์
   (Ministry of Social Development and Human Security)**
   - สำนักงานรัฐมนตรี (Office of the Minister)
   - สำนักงานปลัดกระทรวงพัฒนาสังคมและความมั่นคงของมนุษย์ (Office of the Permanent Secretary)
   - สำนักงานกิจการสตรีและสถาบันครอบครัว
     (Office for Women and Families)
   - สำนักงานส่งเสริมสวัสดิภาพ และพิทักษ์เด็ก เยาวชน ผู้ด้อยโอกาส คนพิการ และผู้สูงอายุ
     (Office for the Protection of children, the Elderly and the Disadvantaged)

- กรมพัฒนาสังคมและสวัสดิการ
  (Department of Social Development and Welfare)

7. **กระทรวงเกษตรและสหกรณ์ (Ministry of Agriculture and Cooperatives)**
   - สำนักงานรัฐมนตรี (Office of the Minister)
   - สำนักงานปลัดกระทรวงเกษตรและสหกรณ์
     (Office of the Permanent Secretary)
   - กรมชลประทาน (Royal Irrigation Department)
   - กรมตรวจบัญชีสหกรณ์ (Department of Cooperative Auditing)
   - กรมประมง (Department of Fisheries)
   - กรมปศุสัตว์ (Department of Livestock Development)
   - กรมป่าไม้ (Royal Forest Department)
   - กรมพัฒนาที่ดิน (Land Development Department)
   - กรมวิชาการเกษตร (Department of Agriculture)
   - กรมส่งเสริมการเกษตร (Department of Agriculture Extension)
   - กรมส่งเสริมสหกรณ์ (The Cooperative Promotion Department)
   - สำนักงานการปฏิรูปที่ดินเพื่อเกษตรกรรม
     (Agricultural Land Reform Office)
   - สำนักงานมาตรฐานสินค้าเกษตร และอาหารแห่งชาติ
     (Office of Agricultural Products and National Food Standard)
   - สำนักงานเศรษฐกิจการเกษตร (Office of Agricultural Economics)

8. **กระทรวงคมนาคม (Ministry of Transport)**
   - สำนักงานรัฐมนตรี (Office of the Minister)
   - สำนักงานปลัดกระทรวงคมนาคม (Office of the Permanent Secretary)
   - กรมการขนส่งทางน้ำและพาณิชยนาวา
     (Department of Maritime Transport and Commerce
   - กรมขนส่งทางบก (Department of Land Transport)
   - กรมทางหลวง (Department of Highways)
   - กรมทางหลวงชนบท (Department of Rural Roads)
   - สำนักงานนโยบายและแผนการขนส่งจราจร
     (Office of Transport and Traffic Policy and Planning)

9. **กระทรวงทรัพยากรธรรมชาติและสิ่งแวดล้อม**
   (Ministry of Natural Resources and Environment)
   - สำนักงานรัฐมนตรี (Office of the Minister)
   - สำนักงานปลัดกระทรวงทรัพยากรธรรมชาติและสิ่งแวดล้อม
     (Office of the Permanent Secretary)

- กรมควบคุมมลพิษ (Pollution Control Department)
- กรมทรัพยากรทางทะเลและชายฝั่ง
  (Department of Marine and Coastal Resources)
- กรมทรัพยากรธรณี (Department of Mineral Resources)
- กรมทรัพยากรน้ำ (Department of Water Resources)
- กรมทรัพยากรน้ำบาดาล (Department of Groundwater Resources)
- กรมอุทยานแห่งชาติสัตว์ป่า และพันธุ์พืช
  (National Park, Wildlife and Plant Conservation Department)
- กรมส่งเสริมคุณภาพสิ่งแวดล้อม
  (Department of Environmental Quality Promotion)
- สำนักงานนโยบายและแผนทรัพยากรธรรมชาติ และสิ่งแวดล้อม
  (Office of Environmental Policy and Planning)

10. **กระทรวงเทคโนโลยีสารสนเทศและการสื่อสาร**
    (Ministry of Information and Communication Technology)
    - สำนักงานรัฐมนตรี (Office of the Minister)
    - สำนักงานปลัดกระทรวงเทคโนโลยีสารสนเทศและการสื่อสาร
      (Office of the Permanent Secretary)
    - กรมอุตุนิยมวิทยา (The Meteorological Department)
    - สำนักงานสถิติแห่งชาติ (National Statistical Office)

11. **กระทรวงพลังงาน (Ministry of Energy)**
    - สำนักงานรัฐมนตรี (Office of the Minister)
    - สำนักงานปลัดกระทรวงพลังงาน (Office of the Permanent Secretary)
    - กรมเชื้อเพลิงธรรมชาติ (Department of Mineral Fuels)
    - กรมธุรกิจพลังงาน (Department of Energy Business)
    - กรมพัฒนาพลังงานทดแทน และอนุรักษ์พลังงาน
      (Department of Alternative Energy Development and Efficiency)
    - สำนักนโยบายและแผนพลังงาน (Energy Policy and Planning Office)

12. **กระทรวงพาณิชย์ (Ministry of Commerce)**
    - สำนักงานรัฐมนตรี (Office of the Minister)
    - สำนักงานปลัดกระทรวงพาณิชย์ (Office of the Permanent Secretary)
    - กรมเจรจาการค้าระหว่างประเทศ (Department of Trade Negotiations)
    - กรมการค้าภายใน (Department of Internal Trade)
    - กรมการประกันภัย (Department of Insurance)
    - กรมทรัพย์สินทางปัญญา (Department of Intellectual Property)
    - กรมพัฒนาธุรกิจการค้า (Department of Business Development)

- กรมส่งเสริมการส่งออก (Department of Export Promotion)

13. กระทรวงมหาดไทย (Ministry of Interior)
- สำนักงานรัฐมนตรี (Office of the Minister)
- สำนักงานปลัดกระทรวงมหาดไทย
  (Office of the Permanent Secretary)
- กรมการปกครอง
  (Department of Provincial Administration)
- กรมการพัฒนาชุมชน
  (The Community Development Department)
- กรมที่ดิน (Department of Lands)
- กรมป้องกันและบรรเทาสาธารณภัย
  (Department of Public Disaster Prevention and Relief)
- กรมโยธาธิการและผังเมือง
  (Department of Public Works and Town Planning)
- กรมส่งเสริมการปกครองท้องถิ่น
  (Department of Local Administration Promotion)

14. กระทรวงยุติธรรม (Ministry of Justice)
- สำนักงานรัฐมนตรี (Office of the Minister)
- สำนักงานปลัดกระทรวงยุติธรรม (Office of the Permanent Secretary)
- กรมคุมประพฤติ (Department of Probation)
- กรมคุ้มครองสิทธิและเสรีภาพ
  (Department of Rights Protection and Liberties)
- กรมบังคับคดี (Legal Execution Department)
- กรมพินิจและคุ้มครองเด็กและเยาวชน
  (Department of Youth Observation and Protection)
- กรมราชทัณฑ์ (Department of Corrections)
- กรมสอบสวนคดีพิเศษ (Special Investigation Department)
- สำนักงานกิจการยุติธรรม (Office of the Justice Affairs)
- สถาบันนิติวิทยาศาสตร์ (Institute of Forensic Science)
- หน่วยงานที่รายงานตรงต่อรัฐมนตรี สำนักงานคณะกรรมการป้องกันและ
  ปราบปรามยาเสพติด (Office of the Narcotics Control Board)

15. กระทรวงแรงงาน (Minsitry of Labor)
- สำนักงานรัฐมนตรี (Office of the Minister)
- สำนักงานปลัดกระทรวงแรงงาน (Office of the Permanent Secretary)
- กรมการจัดหางาน (Department of Employment)
- กรมพัฒนาฝีมือแรงงาน (Department of Skill Development)

- กรมสวัสดิการและคุ้มครองแรงงาน
  (Department of Labor Protection and Welfare)
- สำนักงานประกันสังคม (Social Security Office)

16. กระทรวงวัฒนธรรม (Ministry of Culture)
- สำนักงานรัฐมนตรี (Office of the Minister)
- สำนักงานปลัดกระทรวงวัฒนธรรม (Office of the Permanent Secretary)
- สำนักงานศิลปวัฒนธรรมร่วมสมัย (Office of Contemporary Arts)
- กรมการศาสนา (The Religious Affairs Department)
- กรมศิลปากร (The Fine Arts Department)
- สำนักงานคณะกรรมการวัฒนธรรมแห่งชาติ
  (Office of the National Culture Commission)

17. กระทรวงวิทยาศาสตร์และเทคโนโลยี
(Ministry of Science and Technology)
- สำนักงานรัฐมนตรี (Office of the Minister)
- สำนักงานปลัดกระทรวงวิทยาศาสตร์ และเทคโนโลยี
  (Office of the Permanent Secretary)
- กรมวิทยาศาสตร์บริการ (Department of Science Service)
- สำนักงานปรมาณูเพื่อสันติ (Office of Atomic Energy for Peace)

18. กระทรวงศึกษาธิการ (Ministry of Education)
- สำนักงานรัฐมนตรี (Office of the Minister)
- สำนักงานปลัดกระทรวงศึกษาธิการ
  (Office of the Permanent Secretary)
- สำนักงานเลขาธิการสภาการศึกษา (Office of Education Council)
- สำนักงานคณะกรรมการการศึกษาขั้นพื้นฐาน
  (Office of Basic Education Commission)
- สำนักงานคณะกรรมการการการอาชีวศึกษา
  (Office of Vocational Education Commission)
- สำนักงานคณะกรรมการการอุดมศึกษา
  (Office of Higher Education Commission)

19. กระทรวงสาธารณสุข (Ministry of Public Health)
- สำนักงานรัฐมนตรี (Office of the Minister)
- สำนักงานปลัดกระทรวงสาธารณสุข (Office of the Permanent Secretary)
- กรมการแพทย์ (Department of Medical Services)
- กรมควบคุมโรค (Department of Disease Control)

- กรมพัฒนาการแพทย์แผนไทย และการแพทย์ทางเลือก
  (Department of Traditional and Alternative Medicine Development)
- กรมวิทยาศาสตร์การแพทย์ (Department of Medical Sciences)
- กรมสนับสนุนบริการสุขภาพ
  (Department of Health Service Support)
- กรมสุขภาพจิต (Department of Mental Health)
- กรมอนามัย (Department of Health)
- สำนักงานคณะกรรมการอาหารและยา
  (The Food and Drug Administration)

20. กระทรวงอุตสาหกรรม (Ministry of Industry)

- สำนักงานรัฐมนตรี (Office of the Minister)
- สำนักงานปลัดกระทรวงอุตสาหกรรม
  (Office of the Permanent Secretary)
- กรมโรงงานอุตสาหกรรม (Department of Industrial Works)
- กรมส่งเสริมอุตสาหกรรม (Department of Industrial Promotion)
- กรมอุตสาหกรรมพื้นฐานและการเหมืองแร่
  (Department of Basic Industries and Mines)
- สำนักงานคณะกรรมการอ้อยและน้ำตาลทราย
  (Office of Sugarcane and Sugar Commission)
- สำนักงานมาตรฐานผลิตภัณฑ์อุตสาหกรรม
  (Thai Industrial Standards Institute)
- สำนักงานเศรษฐกิจอุตสาหกรรม
  (Office of Industrial Economic)
- หน่วยงานที่รายงานตรงต่อรัฐมนตรี
  (Directly Accountable to the Minister)
- สำนักงานคณะกรรมการส่งเสริมการลงทุน
  (Office of The Board of Investment)

รัฐวิสาหกิจ (State Enterprises)

รัฐวิสาหกิจ คือ ธุรกิจที่รัฐเป็นเจ้าของและเป็นของส่วนรวม
State Enterprises are public-owned state businesses.

สำนักนายกรัฐมนตรี (Office of the Prime Minister)

- องค์การสื่อสารมวลชนแห่งประเทศไทย
  (Mass Communication Organization of Thailand)

กระทรวงกลาโหม (Ministry of Defense)

- องค์การสงเคราะห์ทหารผ่านศึก (The War Veterans Organization)
- องค์การแบตเตอรี่ (Battery Organization)
- องค์การฟอกหนัง (The Tanning Organization)

กระทรวงการคลัง (Ministry of Finance)

- สำนักงานสลากกินแบ่งรัฐบาล (The Government Lottery Office)
- โรงงานยาสูบ (Thailand Tobacco Monopoly)
- ธนาคารออมสิน (Government Savings Bank)
- ธนาคารอาคารสงเคราะห์ (Government Housing Bank)
- ธนาคารกรุงไทย จำกัด (มหาชน)
  (Krung Thai Bank Public Company Limited)
- ธนาคารเพื่อการเกษตรและสหกรณ์การเกษตร
  (Bank for Agriculture and Agricultural Cooperatives)
- ธนาคารเพื่อการส่งออกและนำเข้าแห่งประเทศไทย
  (Export-Import Bank of Thailand)
- บรรษัทตลาดรองสินเชื่อที่อยู่อาศัย (Secondary Mortgage Corporation)
- ธนาคารพัฒนาวิสาหกิจขนาดกลางและขนาดย่อม
  (Small and Medium Enterprise Development Bank of Thailand)
- บรรษัทประกันสินเชื่ออุตสาหกรรมขนาดย่อม
  (Small Industry Credit Guarantee Corporation)
- องค์การสุรา (Liquor Distillery Organization Excise Department)
- โรงงานไพ่ (Playing Cards Factory)

กระทรวงการท่องเที่ยวและกีฬา (Ministry of Tourism and Sports)

- การท่องเที่ยวแห่งประเทศไทย (Tourism Authority of Thailand)
- การกีฬาแห่งประเทศไทย (Sports Authority of Thailand)

กระทรวงการพัฒนาสังคมและความมั่นคงของมนุษย์
(Ministry of Social Development and Human Security)

- การเคหะแห่งชาติ (National Housing Authority)
- สำนักงานธนานุเคราะห์ (Public Pawnshop Office)

กระทรวงเกษตรและสหกรณ์ (Ministry of Agriculture and Cooperatives)

- องค์การอุตสาหกรรมป่าไม้ (The Forest Industry Organization)
- องค์การสวนยาง (Rubber Estate Organization)
- องค์การสะพานปลา (Fish Marketing Organization)

- องค์การส่งเสริมกิจการโคนมแห่งประเทศไทย
  (Dairy Farming Promotion Organization of Thailand)
- บริษัท ไม้อัด จำกัด (Thai Plywood Company Ltd.)
- องค์การตลาดเพื่อเกษตรกร
  (The Marketing Organization for Farmers)

กระทรวงคมนาคม (Ministry of Transport)

- การท่าเรือแห่งประเทศไทย (Port Authority of Thailand)
- การรถไฟแห่งประเทศไทย (The State Railway of Thailand)
- องค์การรับส่งสินค้าและพัสดุภัณฑ์
  (The Express Transportation Organization of Thailand)
- องค์การขนส่งมวลชนกรุงเทพฯ (Bangkok Mass Transit Authority)
- บริษัท การบินไทย จำกัด (มหาชน)
  (The Thai Airways International Public Company Ltd.)
- บริษัท ท่าอากาศยานไทย จำกัด (มหาชน)
  (Airports of Thailand Public Company Ltd.)
- บริษัท วิทยุการบินแห่งประเทศไทย จำกัด
  (Aeronautical Radio of Thailand Ltd.)
- บริษัท ขนส่ง จำกัด (The Transport Company Ltd.)
- บริษัท ไทยเดินเรือทะเล จำกัด
  (Thai Maritime Navigation Company Ltd.)
- สถาบันการบินพลเรือน (Civil Aviation Institute)
- บริษัท ท่าอากาศยานสากลกรุงเทพแห่งใหม่ จำกัด
  (New Bangkok International Airport Company Limited)
- การทางพิเศษแห่งประเทศไทย
  (Expressway & Rapid Transit Authority Thailand)
- การรถไฟฟ้าขนส่งมวลชนแห่งประเทศไทย
  (Mass Rapid Transit Authority of Thailand)

กระทรวงทรัพยากรธรรมชาติและสิ่งแวดล้อม
(Ministry of Natural Resources and Environment)

- องค์การสวนพฤกษศาสตร์ (Queen Sirikit Botanic Garden)
- องค์การจัดการน้ำเสีย (Wastewater Management Authority)
- องค์การสวนสัตว์ (Zoological Park Organization)

กระทรวงเทคโนโลยีสารสนเทศและการสื่อสาร
(Ministry of Information and Communication Technology)

- บริษัท กสท โทรคมนาคม จำกัด (มหาชน)
  (CAT Telecom Public Company Ltd.)

- บริษัท ไปรษณีย์ไทย จำกัด (Thailand Post)
- บริษัท ทศท คอร์เปอร์เรชั่น จำกัด (มหาชน)
  (TOT Corporation Public Company Ltd.)

กระทรวงพลังงาน (Ministry of Energy)
- การไฟฟ้าฝ่ายผลิตแห่งประเทศไทย
  (Electricity Generating Authority of Thailand)
- การปิโตรเลียมแห่งประเทศไทย (PTT Public Company Ltd.)
- บริษัท บางจากปิโตรเลียม จำกัด (มหาชน)
  (Bangchak Petroleum Public Company Ltd., BCP)

กระทรวงพาณิชย์ (Ministry of Commerce)
- องค์การคลังสินค้า กระทรวงมหาดไทย (Ministry of Interior)
- การไฟฟ้านครหลวง (The Metropolitan Electricity Authority)
- การไฟฟ้าส่วนภูมิภาค (Provincial Electricity Authority)
- การประปานครหลวง (The Metropolitan Waterworks Authority)
- การประปาส่วนภูมิภาค (The Provincial Waterworks Authority)
- องค์การตลาด (The Marketing Organization)

กระทรวงวิทยาศาสตร์และเทคโนโลยี (Ministry of Science and Technology)
- สถาบันวิจัยวิทยาศาสตร์และเทคโนโลยีแห่งประเทศไทย
  (Thailand Institute Scientific and Technological Research)
- องค์การพิพิธภัณฑ์วิทยาศาสตร์แห่งชาติ (National Science Museum)

กระทรวงสาธารณสุข (Ministry of Public Health)
- องค์การเภสัชกรรม
  (The Government Pharmaceutical Organization)

กระทรวงอุตสาหกรรม (Ministry of Industry)
- การนิคมอุตสาหกรรมแห่งประเทศไทย
  (The Industrial Estate Authority of Thailand)

หน่วยงานอิสระ (Independent Agencies)
- ศาลรัฐธรรมนูญ (The Constitutional Court)
- ศาลยุติธรรม (The Court of Justice)
- ศาลปกครอง (The Administrative Court)
- คณะกรรมการการเลือกตั้ง (The Election Commission)
- คณะกรรมการสิทธิมนุษยชนแห่งชาติ
  (National Human Rights Commission)

- คณะกรรมการป้องกันและปราบปรามการทุจริตแห่งชาติ
  (National Counter Corruption Commission)
- สำนักงานการตรวจเงินแผ่นดิน (Office of the Auditor General)
- สำนักงานผู้ตรวจการแผ่นดินของรัฐสภา
  (The Ombudsman of Thailand)
- สำนักงานคณะกรรมการกิจการโทรคมนาคมแห่งชาติ
  (The National Telecommunications Commission)
- สภาที่ปรึกษาเศรษฐกิจและสังคมแห่งชาติ
  (National Economic and Social Advisory Board)
- คณะกรรมการกิจการกระจายเสียงและกิจการโทรทัศน์แห่งชาติ
  (National Broadcasting and Television Commission)

ลำดับยศทหารบก ทหารเรือ ทหารอากาศ และยศตำรวจ
Army, Air Force, Navy and Police Ranks

ยศทหารบก
Thai Army Ranks

ชื่อยศ Thai	คำย่อ Abbreviation	ชื่อยศ English
จอมพล	จอมพล	Field Marshal
พลเอก	พล.อ.— Gen.	General
พลโท	พล.ท.— Lt.Gen.	Lieutenant-General
พลตรี	พล.ต.— Maj.Gen.	Major General
พลจัตวา	พล.จ.— Bri.Gen.	Brigadier General
พันเอก (พิเศษ)	พ.อ.(พิเศษ)	Special Colonel
พันเอก	พ.อ.— Col.	Colonel
พันโท	พ.ท.— Lt.Col.	Lieutenant Colonel
พันตรี	พ.ต.— Maj.	Major
ร้อยเอก	ร.อ.— Capt.	Captain
ร้อยโท	ร.ท.— Lt.	Lieutenant (First Lieutenant)
ร้อยตรี	ร.ต.— Sub.Lt.	Sub-Lieutenant (Second Lieutenant)
จ่าสิบเอก	จ.ส.อ.— 1MSGT	Master Sergeant First Class
จ่าสิบโท	จ.ส.ท.— 2MSGT	Master Sergeant Second Class
จ่าสิบตรี	จ.ส.ต.— 3MSGT	Master Sergeant Third Class
สิบเอก	ส.อ.— Sgt.	Sergeant
สิบโท	ส.ท.— Cpl.	Corporal
สิบตรี	ส.ต.— Pfc.	Lance Corporal (Private First Class)
สิบตรีกองประจำการ	ส.ต.ฯ— Pfc.	Private First Class

ยศทหารอากาศ
Thai Air Force Ranks

ชื่อยศ Thai	คำย่อ Abbreviation	ชื่อยศ English
จอมพลอากาศ	จอมพลอากาศ	Marshal of the Royal Air Force
พลอากาศเอก	พล.อ.อ.— ACM.	Air Chief Marshal
พลอากาศโท	พล.อ.ท.— AM.	Air Marshal
พลอากาศตรี	พล.อ.ต.— AVM.	Air Vice Marshal
พลอากาศจัตวา	พล.อ.จ.— AC.	Air Commodore
นาวาอากาศเอก (พิเศษ)	น.อ.(พิเศษ)— Gp.Capt.	Special Group Captain
นาวาอากาศเอก	น.อ.— Gp.Capt.	Group Captain
นาวาอากาศโท	น.ท.— Wg.Cdr.	Wing Commander
นาวาอากาศตรี	น.ต.— Sqn.Ldr.	Squadron Leader
เรืออากาศเอก	ร.อ.— Flt.Lt.	Flight Lieutenant
เรืออากาศโท	ร.ท.— Flg.Off.	Flying Officer
เรืออากาศตรี	ร.ต.— Plt.Off.	Pilot Officer
พันจ่าอากาศเอก	พ.อ.อ.— FS 1	Flight Sergeant First Class
พันจ่าอากาศโท	พ.อ.ท.— FS 2	Flight Sergeant Second Class)
พันจ่าอากาศตรี	พ.อ.ต.— FS 3	Flight Sergeant Third Class
จ่าอากาศเอก	จ.อ.— Sgt.	Sergeant
จ่าอากาศโท	จ.ท.— Cpl.	Corporal
จ่าอากาศตรี	จ.ต.— LAC.	Leading Aircraftman
พลทหารอากาศ	พลฯ— Amn.	Aircraftman, Airman

ยศทหารเรือ
Thai Navy Ranks

ชื่อยศ Thai	คำย่อ Abbreviation	ชื่อยศ English
จอมพลเรือ	จอมพลเรือ/ร.น.—Admf.	Admiral of the Fleet
พลเรือเอก	พล.ร.อ./ร.น.— Adm.	Admiral
พลเรือโท	พล.ร.ท./ร.น.— VAdm.	Vice Admiral
พลเรือตรี	พล.ร.ต./ร.น.— RAdm.	Rear Admiral
พลเรือจัตวา	พล.ร.จ./ร.น.— CAdm.	Commodore
นาวาเอก (พิเศษ)	น.อ.(พิเศษ)/ร.น — Spec. Capt.	Special Captain
นาวาเอก	น.อ./ร.น.— Capt.	Captain
นาวาโท	น.ท./ร.น.— Cdr.	Commander
นาวาตรี	น.ต./ร.น.— LCdr.	Lieutenant Commander
เรือเอก	ร.อ./ร.น.— Lt.	Lieutenant
เรือโท	ร.ท./ร.น.— Lt.JG.	Junior Lieutenant
เรือตรี	ร.ต./ร.น.— Sub.Lt.	Sub-Lieutenant
พันจ่าเอก	พ.จ.อ.— CPO.1	Chief Petty Officer First Class
พันจ่าโท	พ.จ.ท.— CPO.2	Chief Petty Officer Second Class
พันจ่าตรี	พ.จ.ต.— CPO.3	Chief Petty Officer Third Class
จ่าเอก	จ.อ.— PO.1	Petty Officer First Class
จ่าโท	จ.ท.— PO.2	Petty Officer Second Class
จ่าตรี	จ.ต.— PO.3	Petty Officer Third Class
พลทหารเรือ	พลฯ	Seaman, Sailor

ยศตำรวจ
Thai Police Ranks

ชื่อยศ Thai	คำย่อ Abbreviation	ชื่อยศ English
พลตำรวจเอก	พล.ต.อ.— Pol.Gen.	Police General
พลตำรวจโท	พล.ต.ท.— Pol.Lt.Gen.	Police Lieutenant-General
พลตำรวจตรี	พล.ต.ต.— Pol.Maj.Gen.	Police Major General
พลตำรวจจัตวา	พล.ต.จ.— Pol.Bri.Gen.	Police Brigadier General
พันตำรวจเอก (พิเศษ)	พ.ต.อ. (พิเศษ)— Pol.Col.	Police Special Colonel
พันตำรวจเอก	พ.ต.อ.— Pol.Col.	Police Colonel
พันตำรวจโท	พ.ต.ท.— Pol.Lt.Col.	Police Lieutenant Colonel
พันตำรวจตรี	พ.ต.ต.— Pol.Maj.	Police Major
ร้อยตำรวจเอก	ร.ต.อ.— Pol.Capt.	Police Captain
ร้อยตำรวจโท	ร.ต.ท.— Pol.Lt.	Police Lieutenant
ร้อยตำรวจตรี	ร.ต.ต.— Pol.Sub.Lt.	Police Sub-Lieutenant
ดาบตำรวจ	ด.ต.— Pol.Sen.Sgt.Maj.	Police Senior Sergeant Major
จ่าสิบตำรวจ	จ.ส.ต.— Pol.Sgt.Maj.	Police Sergeant Major
สิบตำรวจเอก	ส.ต.อ.— Pol.Sgt.	Police Sergeant
สิบตำรวจโท	ส.ต.ท.— Pol.Cpl.	Police Corporal
สิบตำรวจตรี	ส.ต.ต.— Pol.L/C.	Police Lance Corporal
พลตำรวจ	พลฯ— Pol.Const.	Police Constable, Police Private

Kings of Thailand

The Sukhothai Period (1238—1376)   สมัยสุโขทัย
The Ayutthaya Period (1350—1767)   สมัยอยุธยา
The Thonburi Period (1767—1782)   สมัยกรุงธนบุรี
The Rattanakosin Period (1782......)   สมัยรัตนโกสินทร์

The Sukhothai Period   *สมัยสุโขทัย*

Phraruang Dynasty 1238—1368   ราชวงศ์พระร่วง

1. Pho Khun Si Intharathit 1238—1257   พ่อขุนศรีอินทราทิตย์
2. Pho Khun Ban Mueang 1257—1278   พ่อขุนบาลเมือง
3. Khun Ramkhamhaeng,the Great 1278—1298
   พ่อขุนรามคำแหงมหาราช
4. Phaya Lerthai 1298—1347   พญาเลอไท
5. Phaya Nguanamthom 1347   พญางั่วนำถม
6. Phaya Luethai (Thammaracha I) 1347—1368/1374
   พญาลือไท (พระมหาธรรมราชาที่ 1)

Under the Ayutthaya Kingdom

7. Thammaracha II 1368/1374—1399   พระมหาธรรมราชาที่ 2
8. Thammaracha III (Phaya Sai Luthai) 1399—1419
   พระมหาธรรมราชาที่ 3 (ไสยลือไท)
9. Thammaracha IV (Borommapan) 1419—1438
   พระมหาธรรมราชาที่ 4 (บรมปาล)

The Ayutthaya Period   *สมัยอยุธยา*
Uthong Dynasty, First Reign 1350—1370   ราชวงศ์อู่ทอง

1. Ramathibodi I (Prince U Thong) 1350—1369
   สมเด็จพระรามาธิบดีที่ 1 (พระเจ้าอู่ทอง)
2. Ramesuan 1369—1370 First Rule   สมเด็จพระราเมศวร

Suphannaphum Dynasty, First Reign 1370—1388
ราชวงศ์สุพรรณภูมิ

3. Borommaracha Thirat I (Pha Ngua) 1370—1388
   สมเด็จพระบรมราชาธิราชที่ 1 (ขุนหลวงพะงั่ว)
4. Thong Lan 1388   พระเจ้าทองลัน

Uthong Dynasty, Second Reign 1388—1409 ราชวงศ์อู่ทอง

5. Ramesuan 1388—1395 Second Rule   สมเด็จพระราเมศวร
6. Ramracha Thirat 1395—1409   สมเด็จพระรามราชาธิราช

Suphannaphum Dynasty, Second Reign 1409—1569
ราชวงศ์สุพรรณภูมิ

7. Intha Racha(Nakharinthara Thirat) 1409—1424
   สมเด็จพระอินทราชา (นครินทราธิราช)
8. Borommaracha Thirat II (Sam Phraya) 1424—1448
   สมเด็จพระบรมราชาธิราชที่ 2 (เจ้าสามพระยา)
9. Borommatrailokkanat 1448—1488
   สมเด็จพระบรมฯไตรโลกนาถ
10. Borommaracha Thirat III 1488—1491
    สมเด็จพระบรมราชาธิราชที่ 3
11. Ramathibodi II (Chettha Thirat) 1491—1529
    สมเด็จพระรามาธิบดีที่ 2 (พระเชษฐาธิราช)
12. Borommaracha Thirat IV (Nor Phutthangkun) 1529—1533
    สมเด็จพระบรมราชาธิราชที่ 4 (หน่อพุทธางกูร)
13. Ratsadathiratcha Kuman Child King 1533   พระรัษฎาธิราชกุมาร
14. Chaiya Racha Thirat 1534—1546   สมเด็จพระฯไชยราชาธิราช
15. Kaeo Fa (Yot Fa) 1546—1548   พระแก้วฟ้า (พระยอดฟ้า)
16. Phra Maha Chakkraphat 1548—1568 & Queen Suriyothai
    สมเด็จพระมหาจักรพรรดิ และ สมเด็จพระศรีสุริโยทัย
17. Mahinthara T hirat 1568—1569   สมเด็จพระมหินทราธิราช

Sukhothai Dynasty 1569—1629   ราชวงศ์สุโขทัย

18. Maha Thammaracha Thirat 1569—1590
    สมเด็จพระมหาธรรมราชาธิราช
19. Naresuan, the Great 1590—1605   สมเด็จพระนเรศวรมหาราช
20. Eka Thotsarot 1605—1610   สมเด็จพระเอกาทศรถ
21. Si Saowaphak 1610—1611   พระศรีเสาวภาคย์
22. Songtham (Intha Racha) 1611—1628
    สมเด็จพระเจ้าทรงธรรม (พระอินทราชา)
23. Chetthathirat 1628—1629   สมเด็จพระเชษฐาธิราช
24. Athittayawong (1629)   สมเด็จพระอาทิตยวงศ์

Prasat Thong Dynasty 1630—1688 ราชวงศ์ปราสาททอง

25. Prasat Thong 1629 —1656   สมเด็จพระเจ้าปราสาททอง
26. Chaofa Chai 1656   สมเด็จเจ้าฟ้าไชย
27. Sisuthammaracha 1656   สมเด็จพระศรีสุธรรมราชา
28. Narai the Great 1656—1688   สมเด็จพระนารายณ์มหาราช

Ban Phlu Luang Dynasty 1688—1767 ราชวงศ์บ้านพลูหลวง

29. Phetracha 1688—1703   สมเด็จพระเพทราชา
30. Luang Sorasak (Phrachao Sua) 1703—1708
    (หลวงสรศักดิ์ - พระเจ้าเสือ)
31. Thaisa 1708—1732   พระเจ้าท้ายสระ
32. Borommakot 1732—1758   สมเด็จพระเจ้าอยู่หัวบรมโกศ
33. Uthumphon 1758   สมเด็จพระเจ้าอุทุมพร
34. Ekkathat 1758—1767   พระเจ้าเอกทัศน์

The Thonburi Period   *สมัยธนบุรี*

1. Tak Sin the Great 1767 – 1782   สมเด็จพระเจ้าตากสินมหาราช

The Rattanakosin Period   *สมัยรัตนโกสินทร์*

1. Phraphutthayotfa Chulalok the Great (Rama I) 1782—1809
   พระบาทสมเด็จพระพุทธยอดฟ้าจุฬาโลกมหาราช
2. Phraphutthaloetla Naphalai (Rama II) 1809—1824
   พระบาทสมเด็จพระพุทธเลิศหล้านภาลัย
3. Phranangklao (Rama III) 1824—1851
   พระบาทสมเด็จพระนั่งเกล้าเจ้าอยู่หัว
4. Phrachomklao (Mongkut or Rama IV) 1851—1868
   พระบาทสมเด็จพระจอมเกล้าเจ้าอยู่หัว
5. Phrachunlachomklao: (Chulalongkorn the Great or Rama V) 1868—
   1910   พระบาทสมเด็จพระจุลจอมเกล้าเจ้าอยู่หัว "พระปิยมหาราช"
6. Phramongkutklao (Vajiravudh or Rama VI) 1910—1925
   พระบาทสมเด็จพระมงกุฎเกล้าเจ้าอยู่หัว
7. Phrapokklao (Prajadhipok or Rama VII) 1925—1935
   พระบาทสมเด็จพระปกเกล้าเจ้าอยู่หัว
8. Ananda Mahidol (Rama VIII) 1935—1946
   พระบาทสมเด็จพระเจ้าอยู่หัวอานันทมหิดล
9. Bhumibol Adulyadej the Great: (Rama IX) 1946—Present
   พระบาทสมเด็จพระเจ้าอยู่หัวภูมิพลอดุลยเดชมหาราช

At present, there are 8 dynasties with 49 kings.
There are 7 kings with "The Great" title.

1. Ramkhamhaeng the Great of Sukhothai Period (1279—1298)

2. King Naresuan the Great (1590—1605) of Ayutthaya Period

3. King Narai the Great (1656—1688) of Ayutthaya Period

4. King Taksin the Great (1767—1782) of Thonburi Period

5. King Phraphutthayotfa Chulalok the Great
   or King Rama I (1782—1809) of Rattanakosin Period

6. King Chulalongkorn the Great
   or King Rama V (1868—1910)

7. King Bhumibol Adulyadej the Great
   or King Rama IX (1946—Present).

List of Prime Ministers of Thailand

There have been 24 prime ministers from 1932 to present. Some of them were in office more than once.

1. Phraya Manopakorn Nititada, 10 December 1932—24 June 1933
   พระยามโนปกรณ์นิติธาดา

2. General Phraya Phahol Pholphayuhasena, 24 June 1933—26 December 1938   พระยาพหลพลพยุหเสนา

3. Field Marshal Plaek Phibunsongkhram, 26 December 1938—1 August 1944 (First time)   จอมพลแปลก พิบูลสงคราม

4. Major Khuang Abhaiwongse, 1 August 1944—17 July 1945 (First time)   พันตรีควง อภัยวงศ์

5. Tawee Boonyaket, 31 August—17 September 1945
   นายทวี บุณยเกตุ

6. Mom Rajawongse Seni Pramoj, (17 September 1945—13 January 1946) (First time)   ม.ร.ว.เสนีย์ ปราโมช

7. Major Khuang Abhaiwongse, 13 January—18 March 1946 (Second time)   พันตรีควง อภัยวงศ์

8. Luang Praditmanutham or Preedee Panomyong, 24 March—21 August 1946   นายปรีดี พนมยงค์

9. Rear Admiral Thawal Thamrong Navaswadhi, 26 August 1946—8 November 1947   พลเรือตรี ถวัลย์ ธำรงนาวาสวัสดิ์

10. Major Khuang Abhaiwongse, 12 November 1947—8 April 1948 (Third time, acting)   พันตรีควง อภัยวงศ์

11. Field Marshal Plaek Phibunsongkhram, 8 April 1948—17 September 1957 (Second time)   จอมพลแปลก พิบูลสงคราม

12. Pote Sarasin, 21 September—24 December 1957
    นายพจน์ สารสิน

13. Field Marshal Thanom Kittikachorn, 1 January—20 October 1958 (First time)   จอมพลถนอม กิตติขจร

14. Field Marshal Sarit Dhanarajata, 20 October 1958—8 December 1963 (acting to 10 February 1959)   จอมพลสฤษดิ์ ธนะรัชต์

15. Field Marshal Thanom Kittikachorn, 9 December 1963—14 October 1973 (Second time)   จอมพลถนอม กิตติขจร

16. Sanya Dharmasakti, 14 October 1973—26 February 1975
    นายสัญญา ธรรมศักดิ์

17. Mom Rajawongse Seni Pramoj, 26 February—14 March 1975 (Second time) ม.ร.ว.เสนีย์ ปราโมช

18. Mom Rajawongse Kukrit Pramoj, 14 March 1975—20 April 1976
    ม.ร.ว.คึกฤทธิ์ ปราโมช

19. Mom Rajawongse Seni Pramoj, 20 April—6 October 1976
(Third time)   ม.ร.ว.เสนีย์ ปราโมช

20. Tanin Kraivichien, 8 October 1976—20 October 1977
นายธานินทร์ กรัยวิเชียร

21. General Kriangsak Chamanan, 12 November 1977—3 March 1980
พลเอกเกรียงศักดิ์ ชมะนันทน์

22. General Prem Tinsulanonda, 3 March 1980—4 August 1988
พลเอกเปรม ติณสูลานนท์

23. General Chatichai Choonhavan, 4 August 1988—23 February 1991
พลเอกชาติชาย ชุนหะวัณ

24. Anand Panyarachun, 7 March 1991—7 April 1992 (First time)
นายอานันท์ ปันยารชุน

25. General Suchinda Kraprayoon, 7 April—24 May 1992
พลเอกสุจินดา คราประยูร

26. Anand Panyarachun, 10 June—23 September 1992 (Second time)
นายอานันท์ ปันยารชุน

27. Chuan Leekpai, 23 September 1992—13 July 1995 (First time)
นายชวน หลีกภัย

28. Banharn Silpa—Archa, 13 July 1995—1 December 1996
นายบรรหาร ศิลปอาชา

29. General Chavalit Yongchaiyudh, 1 December 1996—9 November
1997   พลเอกชวลิต ยงใจยุทธ

30. Chuan Leekpai, (9 November 1997—9 February 2001)
(Second time)   นายชวน หลีกภัย

31. Thaksin Shinawatra, 9 February 2001—19 September 2006
พ.ต.ท. ทักษิณ ชินวัตร

32. General Surayud Chulanont, 1 October 2006 – Publication date
พลเอกสุรยุทธ์ จุลานนท์

คณะนิติศาสตร์ ณ มหาวิทยาลัยต่างๆ
Law Schools in Thailand

คณะนิติศาสตร์	Faculty of Law
จุฬาลงกรณ์มหาวิทยาลัย	Chulalongkorn University
มหาวิทยาลัยธรรมศาสตร์	Thammasat University
มหาวิทยาลัยรามคำแหง	Ramkhamhaeng University
มหาวิทยาลัยกรุงเทพ	Bangkok University
มหาวิทยาลัยเกษมบัณฑิต	Kaem Bundit University
มหาวิทยาลัยรังสิต	Rangsit University
มหาวิทยาลัยขอนแก่น	Khon Kaen University
มหาวิทยาลัยเซนต์จอห์น	Saint John University
มหาวิทยาลัยทักษิณ	Thaksin University
มหาวิทยาลัยธุรกิจบัณฑิต	Dhurakij Pundit University
มหาวิทยาลัยนเรศวร	Naresuan University
มหาวิทยาลัยพายัพ	Payap University
มหาวิทยาลัยศรีปทุม	Sripatum University
มหาวิทยาลัยสงขลานครินทร์	Prince of Songkla University
มหาวิทยาลัยสยาม	Siam University
มหาวิทยาลัยสุโขทัยธรรมาธิราช	Sukhothaithammathirat University
มหาวิทยาลัยหอการค้าไทย	University of the Thai Chamber of Commerce
มหาวิทยาลัยหัวเฉียวเฉลิมพระเกียรติ	Huachiew Chalermprakiatiat University
มหาวิทยาลัยโยนก	Yonok University
มหาวิทยาลัยวงษ์ชวลิตกุล	Vongchavalitkul University
มหาวิทยาลัยอุบลราชธานี	Ubon Ratchathani University
มหาวิทยาลัยเกริก	Krirk University
มหาวิทยาลัยนอร์ทเชียงใหม่	North Chiang Mai University
มหาวิทยาลัยแม่ฟ้าหลวง	Mae Fah Luang University

Provinces of Thailand by Location

In this section we have grouped the 76 provinces of Thailand by location and also ranked then in size of population. The first number is the ranking of the province according to population size.

Central Thailand:
Because of the influence of the Chao Phraya River the central region is relatively flat and very fertile for growing rice crops. This area contains many historical sites and also Thailand's capital city Bangkok.

Central Provinces:
Bangkok Metropolitan Area - 9,988,400 (as of April, 2007) registered population in six provices: Bangkok, Nonthaburi, Samut Prakan, Pathum Thani, Samut Sakhon and Nakhon Pathom. It has a population density of 1,286.92 per km².

1	Bangkok	5,800,000
18	Samut Prakan	1,115,000
22	Nonthaburi	1,007,000
26	Suphanburi	860,000
27	Ratchaburi	840,000
28	Kanchanaburi	830,000
29	Nakhon Pathom	824,000
31	Pathum Thani	872,000
32	Lop Buri	770,000
34	Ayutthaya	760,000
37	Chachoengsao	650,000
39	Saraburi	630,000
46	Sa Kaeo	540,000
58	Phetchaburi	460,000
59	Prachin Buri	450,000
60	Samut Sakhon	465,000
64	Chai Nat	340,000
67	Ang Thong	290,000
70	Nakhon Nayok	250,000
74	Sing Buri	220,000
75	Samut Songkhram	204,000

Eastern Thailand:

The four provinces of eastern Thailand extend along the Gulf of Thailand coast. This area of Thailand is famous for its beaches, gem trading, tropical fruits and rice noodles.

Eastern Provinces:

14	Chon Buri	1,200,000
44	Rayong	560,000
48	Chanthaburi	510,000
73	Trat	220,000

Northern Thailand:

Bordered by the countries of Laos and Burma this vicinity of the country is distinguished by forested mountains and luxuriant river valleys. The north encompasses working elephants, hill tribes, ancient cities, colorful celebrations, superb northern Thai and Burmese-style temples and the legendary Golden Triangle area.

Northern Provinces

5	Chiang Mai	1,650,000
13	Chiang Rai	1,230,000
16	Nakhon Sawan	1,130,000
19	Phetchabun	1,040,000
25	Phitsanulok	860,000
30	Lampang	790,000
33	Kamphaeng Phet	760,000
41	Sukhothai	620,000
43	Phichit	580,000
47	Tak	520,000
51	Phayao	490,000
54	Nan	482,000
55	Uttaradit	480,000
56	Phrae	479,000
61	Lamphun	410,000
66	Uthai Thani	330,000
71	Mae Hong Son	240,000

Northeastern Thailand:

The part of Thailand known as Issan comprises a large area which traditionally has been the poorest region of the country due to a thin layer of topsoil and being historically prone to droughts. Farming is the main occupation but the region contains some of the largest cities in the country. Bordered by the Mekong River and the countries of Laos and Cambodia this area receives the least amount of visiting tourists.

Northeastern Provinces:

2	Nakhon Ratchasima	2,610,000
3	Ubon Ratchathani	1,800,000
4	Khon Kaen	1,770,000
6	Udon Thani	1,540,000
7	Buri Ram	1,550,000
9	Si Sa Ket	1,460,000
10	Surin	1,400,000
11	Roi Et	1,320,000
15	Chaiyaphum	1,140,000
17	Sakon Nakhon	1,120,000
20	Kalasin	997,000
23	Maha Sarakham	946,000
24	Nong Khai	913,000
36	Nakhon Phanom	702,000
40	Loei	627,000
45	Yasothon	551,000
50	Nong Bua Lam Phu	500,000
63	Amnat Charoen	371,000
65	Mukdahan	338,000

Southern Thailand:

Consisting of hilly terrain, rain forests, lush tropical islands and rich mineral deposits the south receives the most annual rainfall of any place in Thailand. World famous islands of Phuket and Koh Samui attract hordes of tourists ready to enjoy the sea, sand and nighttime entertainment. The most southern provinces attract less western tourists and are not as affluent.

Southern Provinces:

8	Nakhon Si Thammarat	1,530,000
12	Songkhla	1,300,000
21	Surat Thani	950,000
35	Narathiwat	710,000
38	Pattani	630,000

```
42  Trang . . . . . . . . . . . . . . .610,000
49  Phattalung . . . . . . . . . . . .505,000
52  Prachuap Khiri Khan  . . . . . .497,000
53  Chumphon . . . . . . . . . . . .480,000
57  Yala . . . . . . . . . . . . . . .470,000
62  Krabi . . . . . . . . . . . . . .390,000
68  Phuket . . . . . . . . . . . . . .280,000
69  Satun . . . . . . . . . . . . . .277,000
72  Phang Nga . . . . . . . . . . . .240,000
76  Ranong . . . . . . . . . . . . . .179,000
```

Useful Phone Numbers in Bangkok

Phone numbers and addresses were current at the time of publication of this book and may have changed.

Emergency Calls
Police -191, Fire-199, Tourist Police -1699
Tourist Service Center 1155
Bangkok Metropolitan Administration Hotline 1555
Missing Persons Bureau 02-282-1815
Ambulance (Bangkok) 02-255-1133-6

Telephone Services:
Bangkok directory inquiries: 1133
Provincial directory inquiries: 183
Local/International directory assistance: 100
IDD: 001 + Country code + area code + phone number
AT&T direct service: 001-999-1111-1

Useful contact information:
Immigration Office
Soi Suanphlu, Sathorn Tai Road, Bangkok 10120, Tel. 02-287-3101

Revenue Department
Chakkapong Road, Bangkok 10200, Tel. 02-282-9899

Tourist Information Counter
372 Bamrung Muang Road, Bangkok 10100, Tel. 02-226 0060, 226-0072

Tourist Assistance Center
4 Ratchadamnoen Nok Road, Bangkok, Tel. 02-281-5051

Tourism Authority of Thailand Head Office
Le Concorde Building
202 Ratchadapisek Road, Tel. 02-694-1222 Fax 02-694-1220

Tourist Police, Unico House,
Soi Lang Suan, Ploenchit Road, Bangkok, Tel. 1699 or 02-652-1721

Bangkok International Airport
Phahonyothin Road, Bangkok, Tel. 02-535-1111
Departure Info 02-535-1254, 02-535-1386
Arrival Info 02-535-1310, 02-535-1305, 02-535-1149

Bangkok Domestic Airport
Phahonyothin Road, Bangkok, Tel. 02-535-2081
Departure Info 02-535-1192, 02-535-1277
Arrival Info 02-535-1253, 02-535-1305, 02-535-1149

Thai Airways International Plc.
89 Vibhavadi Rangsit Road, Bangkok, Tel. 02-513-0121

Bangkok Railway Station (Hua Lamphong)
Rama IV Road, Bangkok 10500, Tel. 02-223 7010, 223-7020, 233-7461

Northern & Northeastern Bus Terminal
Phahonyothin Road, Bangkok, Tel. 02-272 0299

Southern Bus Terminal
Boromrat Chonnani Road, Bangkok 10700, Tel. 02-435-1199, 02-434 5558

Eastern Bus Terminal
Sukhumvit Road (Ekamai), Bangkok 10110 Tel. 02-391-2504, 02392-2521

Bangkok Local Bus Services: 184

Credit Cards
American Express: 02-235-0990, 02-236-0276
Lost cards: 02-273-0044
Diner's Club: 02-233-0313, 02-233-5775
Lost cards: 02-233-5644-5
MasterCard and Visa: 02-270-1122, 02-270-1259
Lost cards: 02-252-2712

Celebrations in Thailand

Here are some of the major celebrations in Thailand. The ones that are marked with an asterisk (*) are observed as public holidays.

New Year's Day*
(January 1)
Thailand celebrates the traditional New Year's Day in grand style. Most Thai people head to their villages to take an extended holiday vacation. Exciting events take place in Bangkok and the other major cities in Thailand.

Magha Puja Day*
(Religious holiday)
(On the full-moon day of the 3rd Thai lunar month, usually in February)
A holy Buddhist Holiday which marks the occasion when 1,250 disciples of the Lord Buddha spontaneously gathered to hear his preaching.

Chiang Mai Flower Festival
(First weekend in February)
Three day festival to celebrate the beautiful flowers and decorative plants of the north. Beauty contests and a parade is held featuring colorful floats decorated with live flowers, marching bands and thousands of people in traditional Thai costumes.

Chinese New Year
(Later January or early February)
Lion dancing and firecrackers make a festive event in the Chinatown area of Bangkok. The fun loving Thais use this celebration as another excuse to party and take an extended time off to visit the relatives.

Songkran Festival*
(13 – 15 April)
The traditional Thai New Year exuberantly celebrated all over the Kingdom. Acts of merit making and paying honor to elders is now overshadowed by the riotous water splashing that keeps everyone cool in this the hottest month in Thailand. Notable celebrations in Bangkok and Chiang Mai where the party continues for 5 days.

Coronation Day*
(5 May)
The date that King Bhumibol was crowned the 9th king of the Chakri Dynasty in 1946.

Ploughing Ceremony*
(11 May)
This date marks the start of the planting season and is celebrated in Sanam Luang in Bangkok with prayers for the blessing of the upcoming rice crop. The King or a member of the royal family presides over this Bramanic ritual.

Rocket Festival
(12 – 14 May)
This festival celebrated uniquely in the Northeast and most wildly in Yasothon province consists of launching rockets made of bamboo to insure the much needed rain for the rainy season. Beauty contests, a parade and rocket contests makes this the most exciting event in the Issan area of Thailand.

Visakha Puja Day*
(Religious holiday)
(On the full-moon day of the 6th Thai lunar month, usually in May)
On this day but in different years the Buddha was born, attained Enlightenment and entered Nirvana.

Asalha Puja Day*
(Religious holiday)
(On the full-moon day of the 8th Thai lunar month, usually in July)
Thais honor this date because it marks when the Buddha gave his first sermon to his first five disciples after his Enlightenment.

Khao Phansa Day*
(Religious holiday)
(1st day of 8th waning moon, usually in July)
The day that marks the beginning of the Buddhist lent. Three months during the rainy season when it is customary for Thai men to be ordained as monks. Monks are required to remain at their resident temples during this period.

Her Majesty the Queen's Birthday*
(12 August)
This date commemorates the Queen's birthday and Mother's Day in Thailand. Elaborate celebrations are held in Bangkok in front of the Grand Palace and the Thais pay tribute to their Queen with concerts and entertainment events all over the country.

Vegetarian Festival
(Late September or early October)
Mainly celebrated by people of Chinese decent in the Phuket area who make merit by not eating meat to honor an event in 1825 when an entire Chinese Opera company overcame extreme illness by eating only vegetarian food. The culmination of the celebration is a parade where participants perform self-tortures to invoke supernatural powers.

Chulalongkorn Day*
(23 October)
This day commemorates the death of King Rama V. Thai people from all walks of life lay wreaths at his statue at the Royal Plaza in Bangkok and in the provinces.

Loi Krathong
(On the full-moon day of the 12th Thai lunar month, usually in November)
This festival of light honors the water Goddess in the evening when the Thais float their Krathongs, lotus-shaped vessels decorated with flowers, a coin and a lit candle, on the rivers all over the Kingdom. The most spectacular celebrations are held in Sukhothai and Chiang Mai.

His Majesty the King's Birthday*
(5 December)
Father's day is also celebrated on this date. The King is honored with celebrations at Sanam Luang in Bangkok and many music and singing contests are held around the country to pay tribute to the musical talents of His Majesty.

Constitution Day*
(10 December)
This date honors the day that Thailand's first Constitution was declared by King Rama VII in 1932.

New Year's Eve*
(31 December)
Elaborate celebrations are held all over Thailand counting down to the stroke of midnight.

Foreign Embassies in Thailand

Please verify the contact information listed here. Contact information and embassy locations may have changed since the printing of this book.

Embassy of Argentina
16th Fl., Suite 1601, 1 Sukhumvit 25
Ban Chang Glas Haus Building
Klongton Wattana
Bangkok 10110
Phone: (+66-2) 259-0401/ 2 279-9198
Fax: (+66-2) 259 0402
Email: embtail@mozart.inet.co.th
Office Hours: 8:30 AM—4 PM

Australian Embassy
37 South Sathorn Road
Bangkok 10120
Phone: (+66-2) 344 6300
Fax: (+66-2) 344 6593
Web Site: http://www.thailand.embassy.gov.au
Email: austembassy.bangkok@dfat.gov.au
Office Hours: Monday—Friday 8:00 AM—12:30 PM, 1:30 PM—4:30 PM

Embassy of Austria
14, Soi Nandha, off Soi 1, Sathorn Tai Road
Bangkok 10120
P.O.Box 1155 Suan Plu
Bangkok 10121
Phone: (+66-2) 303-6057-9
Fax: (+66-2) 287-3925
Email: bangkok@wko.at,bangkok-ob@bmaa.gv.at
Office Hours: Monday—Friday, 7:30 AM—3:30 PM
Visa Section: Monday—Friday, 9:00 AM—12 PM

Embassy of Belgium
Sathorn City Tower - 17th floor
175 South Sathorn Road
Tungmahamek, Bangkok 10120
Phone: (+66-2)-679-5454
Fax: (+66-2)-679-5467/65
Web Site: http://www.diplomatie.be/bangkok
Email: Bangkok@diplobel.org
Office Hours: Monday—Friday, 8 AM—4 PM
8:15 AM—11:30 AM (visa and administration)

Embassy of Brazil
34th Floor Lumpini Tower
1168/101 Rama IV Road
Thungmahamek, Sathorn
Bangkok 10120
Phone: (+66-2) 679-8567/8
Fax: (+66-2) 679-8569
Web Site: http://www.brazilembassy.or.th
Email: embrasbkk@inet.co.th
Office Hours: Monday—Friday, 9 AM—5 PM

Embassy of Brunei
No. 132 Sukhumvit Soi 23
Sukhumvit Road
Klongtoey, Vadhana
Bangkok 10110
Phone: (+66-2) 204-1476/9
Fax: (+66-2) 204-1486
Office Hours: 8:30 AM—12 PM, 1 PM—4 PM

Embassy of Cambodia
No. 185 Rajddamri Road
Lumpini Patumwan, 10330
Phone: (+66-2) 254-6630
Fax: (+66-2) 253-9859
Email: recbkk@cscoms.com

Canadian Embassy
15th Floor, Abdulrahim Place
990 Ra IV Road
Bangrak, 10500
Phone: (+66-2) 636-0540
Fax: (+66-2) 636-0565
Web Site: http://www.dfait-maeci.gc.ca/bangkok/
Email: bngkk@dfait-maeci.gc.ca
Office Hours: Monday—Thursday, 7 AM—4:15 PM, Friday: 7 AM—1 PM

Embassy of Chile
15 Sukhumvit Road Soi 61
Phone: (+66-2) 391-4858, 391-8443
Fax: (+66-2) 391-8380
Web Site: http://www.chile-thai.com/
Email: embajada@chile-thai.com

Embassy of China
57 Rachadapisake Road
Dindaeng, 10310
Phone: (+66-2) 245-7043 or(+66-2) 245-7044
Fax: (+66-2) 246-8247
Web Site: http://www.chinaembassy.or.th/chn/index.html
Email: chinaemb_th@mfa.gov.cn
Office Hours: 8:30 AM—12 PM, 1 PM—3 PM (Monday—Friday)

Embassy of Czech Republic
71/6 Ru Rudee Soi 2
Ploenchit Rd., 10330
Phone: (+66-2) 255-3027 or 255-5060
Fax: (+66-2) 253-7637
Web Site: http://www.mfa.cz/bangkok
Email: bangkok@embassy.mzv.cz

Royal Danish Embassy
10, Sathorn Soi 1
South Sathorn Road, 10120
Phone: (+66-2) 343-1100
Fax: (+66-2) 213-1752
Email: bangkok@um.dk

Embassy of Finland
16th Fl, Amarin Plaza
500 Ploenchit Rd, 10501
G.P.O. Box 295, 10330
Phone: (+66-2) 256-9306/9
Fax: (+66-2) 256-9310

Embassy of France
35 Soi Rong Phasi Kao
Charoenkrung 36 Road
Bangkok 10500
Phone: (+66-2) 266-8250/56
Fax: (+66-2) 236-7973
Web Site: http://www.bafrance-th.org
Email: bassade@bafrance-th.org

Embassy of Germany
9 South Sathorn Road
Bangkok 10120
Phone: (+66-2) 287 90 00
Fax: (+66-2) 287 17 76
Web Site: http://www.german-embassy.or.th/
Email: info@german-embassy.or.th
Office Hours: Montag bis Freitag, 9 AM— 11.30 AM

Embassy of Greece
21/159 South Sathorn Road
30th floor,Thai Wah Tower II
Bangkok 10120
Phone: (+66-2) 679-1462
Fax: (+66-2) 679-1463
Office Hours: Embassy: 9 AM—3.30 PM, Consular: 10 AM—1 PM

Embassy of Hungary
20th Floor, Oak Tower, Prakanon
President Park Condominium,
99 Sukhumvit Soi 24
Prakanong, Bangkok 10110
Phone: (+66-2) 661-1150/2
Fax: (+66-2) 661-1153
Email: huembbgk@mozart.inet.co.th
Office Hours: 8 AM—2 PM

Embassy of India
46,Soi 23 (Prasarn Mitr)
Sukhumvit Road, 10110
Phone: (+66-2) 258 0300
Fax: (+66-2) 258 4627
Email: indiaemb@indiaemb.or.th
Office Hours: Monday—Friday, 9.00 AM—12 PM

Italian Embassy
399, Nang Linchee Road
Thungmahek, Yannawa
Bangkok
Phone: (+66-2) 285-4090
Fax: (+66-2) 285-4793
Email: bitbkk@loxinfo.co.th

Embassy of Japan
1674 New Petchaburi Road
Bangkok 10320,
Phone: (+66-2) 252-6151
Fax: (+66-2) 253-4153
Office Hours: Monday—Friday, 8:30 AM—12 PM; 2 PM—4 PM

Embassy of Laos
502,502/1-3 Soi Sahakarnproon
Pracha-Uthit Road
Wangthonglang
Bangkok 10310
Phone: (+66-2) 539-66679-8
Fax: (+66-2) 539-6678
Web Site: http://www.bkklaoembassy.com
Email: embalao@bkklaoembassy.com
Office Hours: 8 AM—12 PM; 1 PM—4 PM

Embassy of Malaysia
33-35 South Sathorn Road
Tungmahek
Sathorn, Bangkok 10120
Phone: 90-312-4463547/4463548
Fax: 90-312-446 4130
Email: mwbngkok@sart.co.th

Embassy of Myanmar
132, Sathorn Nua Road,
Bangkok 10500
Phone: (+66-2) 233-2237, 234-4698, 233-7250, 234-0320, 637-9406
Fax: (+66-2) 236-6898
Email: mebkk@asianet.co.th

Embassy of Netherlands
15 Soi Tonson, Ploenchit Road
Lumpini, Pathurmwan
Bangkok 10300
P.O. Box 404
Bangkok 10500
Phone: (+66-2) 309-5200
Fax: (+66-2) 309-5205
Web Site: http://www.netherlandsembassy.in.th
Email: ban@minbuza.nl
Office Hours: Monday—Thursday, 8 AM—4 PM, Friday 8 AM—12 PM
Monday—Friday, 9 AM—12 PM (Consular)

Embassy of Norway
UBC II Building, 18th floor
591 Sukhumvit Road, Soi 33
Bangkok 10110
Phone: (+66-2) 204-6500
Fax: (+66-2) 262-0218
Web Site: http://www.emb-norway.or.th
Email: emb.bangkok@mfa.no
Office Hours: Monday—Friday 9:00 AM—12 PM, 1:00 PM—4:00 PM

Embassy of the Sultanate of Oman
82 Swng Thong Thani Tower
32 Floor, North Sathorn Rd.
Bangkok 10500
Phone: (+66-2) 639-9380/3
Fax: (+66-2) 639-9390
Office Hours: 9 AM—4 PM

Embassy of Peru
Glas Haus Bldg.
16th. Flr.
No. 1 Soi Sukhumvit 25 Rd.
Bangkok 10110
Phone: (66-2) 260-6243
Fax: (+66-2) 260-6244
Email: peru@peruthai.or.th
Office Hours: Monday—Friday, 9 AM—5 PM

Embassy of the Philippines
760 Sukhumvit Road, Soi 30/1
Bangkok 10110
Phone: (+66-2) 259-0139/014 or 258-5401
Fax: (+66-2) 259-2809
Web Site: http://www.philembassy-bangkok.net
Email: bangkokpe@dfa.gov.ph
        inquiry@philembassy-bangkok.net

Embassy of Portugal
26, Bush Lane, Bangkok 10500
Phone: (+66-2) 234-2123
Fax: (+66-2) 238-4275, (+66-2) 236-1954

Embassy of Romania
20/1, Soi Rajakhru, Phaholyothin Soi 5
Phaholyothin Road, Phayathai
Bangkok 10400
Phone: (+66-2) 6171551
Fax: (+66-2) 6171113
Email: romembkk@ksc.th.com

Embassy of Singapore
129 South Sathorn Road, 10120
Phone: (+66-2) 86 2111, (+66-2) 86 1434
Fax: (+66-2) 86 6966, (+66-2) 87 2578
Web Site: http://www.mfa.gov.sg/bangkok/
Email: singemb_bkk@sgmfa.gov.sg
Office Hours: Monday—Friday, 9.00 AM—12 pm— PM; 1.00 PM—5.00 PM

South African Embassy
Floor 12A, M-Thai Tower
All Seasons Place
87 Wireless Road, Pathumwan, Lumpini
Bangkok, 10330
Phone: (+66-2) 250-9012/14
Fax: (+66-2) 685-3500
Web Site: http://www.saembbangkok.com
Email: saembbkk_admin@csloxinfo.com

Embassy of The Republic of Korea
23 Thi-Rumit Road
Ratchadapisek, Huay Kwang
Bangkok 10320
Phone: (+66-2) 247-7537/9
Fax: (+66-2) 247-7535
Email: korembas@kormail.net
Office Hours: 8 AM—12 PM; 1 PM—4:30 PM

Embassy of Spain
Lake Rajada Office Complex
23rd Floor,Suites No.98-99,
193, Ratchadapisek Road, Klongtoey,
Bangkok 10110
Phone: (+66-2) 661-8284/6
Fax: (+66-2) 661-9220
Email: embespth@mail.mae.es
Office Hours: Monday—Thursday, 8 AM—3:30 PM; Friday 8 AM—1 PM
Visa Section: Monday—Friday, 9 AM—12 PM

Embassy of Sweden
20th floor, First Pacific Place
140 Sukhumvit Road
P.O. Box 1324, Nana Post Office
Bangkok 10112
Phone: (+66-2) 263-7200
Fax: (+66-2) 263-7260
Web Site: http://www.swedenabroad.se/bangkok
Email: bassaden.bangkok@foreign.ministry.se
Office Hours: Monday—Thursday, 7:30am—4.15 pm;
Friday, 7:30 am—1 pm

Embassy of Switzerland
35 North Wireless Road
Bangkok 10330
P.O Box 821
Bangkok 10501
Phone: (+66-2) 253-0156
Fax: (+66-2) 255-4481
Email: ban.vertretung@eda.admin.ch, ban.visa@eda.admin.ch
Office Hours: Monday—Friday, 9 AM—11.30 AM

Representative Office of Taiwan
20th Floor, Empire Tower
195 South Sathorn Road
Yannawa
Bangkok 10120
Phone: (+66-2) 670-0200/9
Fax: (+66-2) 670-0220
Email: tecoinfo@ji-net.com,tecocomu@ji-net.com

British Embassy
1031 Wireless Road
Lumpini Pathumwan
Bangkok 10330
Phone: (+66-2) 305 8333
Office Hours: Monday—Thursday, 8 AM—11 AM; 1 PM—3:30 PM
Friday, 8 AM—12 PM

U.S. Embassy
95 Wireless road 10330
Phone: (+66-2) 205-4049
Web Site: http://www.usa.or.th/
Email: acsbkk@state.gov
Office Hours: Monday—Friday, 8 AM—11 AM; 1 PM—3 PM.

Royal Thai Embassies and Consulates General (by Country)

Please verify the contact information listed here. Phone numbers and embassy locations may have changed since the printing of this book.

Argentina
Virrey del Pino 2458-6 Piso, 1426 Buenos Aires
Tel: +541 785 6504, 6521, 6532 Fax: +541 785 6548

Australia
111 Empire Circuit
Yarralumla, A.C.T. 2600, Canberra
Tel: +06 273 1149, 273 2937 Fax: +06 273 1518

Level 8 131 Macquarie Street, Sydney, NSW 2000
Tel (02) 9241-2542, 9241-2543 Fax (02) 9247-8312
Email: thaicon-sydney@diplomats.com

87 Annerley Road
South Brisbane Qld 4102
Tel (07) 3846-7771 Fax (07)3846-7772
Email:consulofthailand@hotmail.com
Level 1, 72 Flinders Street, Adelaide SA 5000
Tel (08) 8232-7474 Fax (08) 8232-7474
Suite 301 566 St Kilda Road Melbourne Victoria 3004
Tel (03) 9533-9100 Fax (03) 9533-9200

Austria
Weimarer Strasse 68, A-1180
Vienna
Tel: 310 3423, 310 1630, 310 8988
www.mfa.go.th/web/1277.php?depid=181

Arensbergstrasse 2, Salzburg
Tel: +0662 646 5660

Bangladesh
House No. NW(E) 12, Road No.59
Gulshan Model Town, Dhaka
Tel: +880 2 601 634, 601 475 Fax: +880 2 883 588

Belgium
Square du Val de la Cambre 2, 1050 Brussels
Tel: +322 640 6810, 640 1986 Fax: +322 648 3066
www.thaiembassy.be/portal

Brazil

Lote 10-Setor de Embaixadas Norte, Avenida das Nacoes Norte
P.O. Box 10-2460, 70.433 Brasilia, DF.
Tel: +061 224 6943, 224 7943, 223 5105
Fax: +061 321 2994, 223 7502

Brunei

No.1 Simpang 52-86-16, Kampong Mata-Mata
Gadong 3280 Bandar Seri Begawan
Tel: 429 653 4, 440 360, 448 331 Fax: 421 775

Canada

The Royal Thai Embassy, 180 Island Park Drive, Ottawa Ontario, K1Y 0A2
Tel: (613) 722-4444 Fax: (613) 722-6624

1040 Burrard Street, Vancouver, British Columbia
Tel: (1-604) 687-1143, 687-8848, 687-1661 Fax (1-604) 687-4434
Email: info@thaicongenvancover.org
http://www.thaicongenvancouver.org

China

40 Guang Hua Lu, Beijing 100600
Tel: (8610) 6532-1749, 6532-1848, 6532-2151 Fax: (8610) 6532-1748
http://203.150.20.55/beijing

White Swan Hotel
Southern Street, Shamian Island, Guangzhou
Tel: (8620) 8188-6986 ext. 3301 - 3303,- 3307 Fax: (8620) 8187-9451
Email: gzthaicg@public1.guangzhou.gd.cn

145,1st Floor, South Building—Kunming Hotel, Dong Feng Dong Road,
Kunming. Tel: (86871) 3168916, 3149296 Fax: (86871) 3166891
Email: thaikmg@public.km.yn.cn
www.mfa.go.th/web/2165.php?depid=193

China (Taiwan)

www.mfa.go.th/web/1157.php?depid=195
Finland
www.thaiembassy.fi

France

Embassy of Thailand
8, rue Greuze, 75016 Paris, France
Tel: 01.56.26.50.50 ,Fax: 01.56.26.04.46
http://203.150.20.55/paris

Hong Kong

Fairmont House—8th Floor, 8 Cotton Tree Drive
Central, Hong Kong. Tel: (852) 25216481 - 5 Fax: (852) 25218629
Email: thai-cg@hongkong.super.net
www.thai-consulate.org.hk

Germany

Ubierstrasse 65, D-53173 Bonn Tel: (0228) 956860 Fax: (0228) 363702
www.thaiembassy.de

Greece

23 Taigetou Street, P.O. Box 65215
Paleo Psychico 15452, Athens
Tel: (301) 6717969, 6710155 Fax: (301) 6479508

Hungary

Verecke ut.79, 025 Budapest
Tel: (36-1) 1689421, 1689422 Fax: (36-1) 2501580, 1882347

India

56-N, Nyaya Marg,, Chanakyapuri, New Delhi-110021
Tel: 611 8103, 611 8104 Fax: 687 2029
www.thaiemb.org.in
Indonesia
74, Jalan Imam Bonjol, Jakarta Pusat
Tel: 390 4225, 390 4055 Fax: 310 7469

Israel

21 Shaul Hamelech Blvd, Tel Aviv Israel
Tel: (972-3) 695-8980, 695-8984, Fax: (972-3) 695-8991
Email: thaisr@netvision.co.il
http://www.mfa.go.th/web/1315.php?depid=210

Iran

Baharestan Avenue, Park Amin-ed-Dowleh No. 4, P.O. Box 11495-111, Tehran.
Tel: +9821 753 1433, 753 7708

Italy

Via Bertoloni 26B, I-00197 Rome
Tel: +0039 6 8078379, 8081381 Fax: +0039 6 8078693

Japan

3-14-6, Kami-Osaki, Shinagawa-ku, Tokyo 141
Tel: +03 3441 1386, 1387 Fax: +03 3442 6750, 3442 6828
www.thaiembassy.jp

Bangkok Bank Building, 4th Floor, 1-9-16 Kyutaro-Machi, Oska
Tel: (81-6) 6262-9226 to 7 Fax (81-6) 6262-9228
Email: rtcg-osk@jupiter.plala.or.jp
http://www.thai-kansai.net

Kenya

Rose Avenue, off Denis Pritt Rd., P.O. Box 58349, Nairobi
Tel: +254 2 714276, 715800, Fax: +254 2 715801

Korea (South)

653-7, Hannam-dong, Yongsan-ku, Seoul
Tel: +82 2 795 3098, 795 0095 Fax: +82 2 798 3448
www.thaiembassy.or.kr

Kuwait

Surra, Area No.3, Block No.49, Ali Bin Abi-Taleb Street, Building No. 28., P.O.
Box 66647 Bayan, 43757
Tel: 531 4870, 531 7530-1, 533 9243 Fax: 531 7532

Laos

Route Phonekheng, P.O. Box 128, Vientiane
Tel: 214 5813, 214 5856 Fax: +66 1 411 0017

Malaysia

206 Jalan Ampang
50450 Kuala Lumpur
Tel: +03 248 8222, 248 8350 Fax: +03 248 6527
Malaysia

No. 1, Jalan Tunku Abdul Rahman 10350 Penang
Tel. (60-4) 2268029, 2269484 Fax:(60-4) 2263121
Email: thaipg@tm.net.my

Mexico

Sierra Vertientes 1030, Lomas de Chapultepec, 11000 Mexico, D.F.
Tel: +525 596 1290, 596 8446 Fax: +525 596 8236

Morocco

11 Rue de Tiddes, Rabat, B.P. 4436
Tel: +212 7 763 365, 763 328 Fax: +212 7 763 920

Myanmar (Burma)
45, Pyay Road, Yangon
Tel: +951 35 670, 33 082, 21 567 Fax: +951 22 784

Nepal
Jyoti Kendra, Thapathali, Kathmandu
Tel: +977 1 213 910, 213 912 Fax: +977 1 226599

Netherlands
1 Buitenrustweg, 2517 KD, The Hague
Tel: +070 345 2088, 345 9703 Fax:+ 070 345 1929
www.mfa.go.th/web/1326.php?depid=227

New Zealand
2 Cook Street, P.O. Box 17-226, Karori, Wellington
Tel: +04 476 8618, 476 8619 Fax: +04 476 3677
www.thaiembassynz.org.nz

Nigeria
1 Ruxton Road, Old Ikoyi, P.O. Box 3095, Lagos
Tel: 269 0334 Fax: 269 2855

Norway
Munkedamsveien 59 B, 0270 Oslo
Tel: +47 22832517, 22832518 Fax: 22830384

Oman
Villa 33-34 Road "O", Madinat Qaboos East, Muscat
P.O. Box 60, M.Q., Postal Code 115, Muscat,
P.O. Box 3367 Ruwi, Postal Code 112, Muscat.
Tel: +09 68 602 683, 602 684
Fax: +09 68 605 714

Pakistan
4, Street No.8, Shalimar F-8/3, Islamabad
Tel: 859 130, 859 131, 859 195 | Fax: +92-51 256 730

Philippines
107 Rada Street, Legaspi Village, Makati, Metro Manila, P.O. Box 1228, Makati
Central Post Office, 1252 Makati, Metro Manila
Tel: 815 4220, 816 0696 7, 815 4219 Fax: 815 4221

Poland
ul. Staroscinska 1B m. 2-3, 02-516. Warsaw
Tel: +48 22 492 655,496 414, 494 730 Fax: +48 22 492 630

Portugal
Rua de Alcolena 12, Restelo, 1400 Lisbon
Tel: +35 11 301 4848,301 5051 Fax: +35 11 301 8181
www.mfa.go.th/web/1332.php?depid=235

Romania
44-48 Strada Mihai Eminescu, Etaj 2, Apartamentul 5, Bucharest
Tel: +40 1 210 1338, 210 3447 Fax: +40 1 210 2600

Russia
Eropkinsky Pereulok 3, Moscow 119034
Tel: +095 201 4893, 201 3989 Fax: +095 230 2004, 210 2853
www.thaiembassymoscow.com

Saudi Arabia
Diplomatic Quarter, Ibnu Banna Road, P.O. Box 94359, Riyadh 11693
Tel: +966-1) 488 1174, 488 0797 Fax: +966-1) 488 1179
http://203.150.20.55/riyadh

Senegal
10 Rue Leon G. Damas, Angle F. Fann Residence, B.P. 3721, Dakkar
Tel: +221) 243076, 243801 Fax: +221) 256360

Singapore
370 Orchard Road, Singapore 0923
Tel: +65 235 4175, 737 2158 Fax: +65 732 0778
www.thaiembsingapore.org

South Africa
840 Church Street, Eastwood, Arcadia 0083, Pretoria
Tel: +012 342 5470, 342 4516 Fax: +012 342 4805

Spain
Calle Del Segra, 29-2 A, 28002 Madrid
Tel: +91 5632903, 5637959 Fax: +91 5640033

Sri Lanka
43, Dr. C.W.W. Kannangara Mawatha, Colombo 7
Tel: 697 406, 689 045, 689 037 Fax: 697 516
www.mfa.go.th/web/1340.php?depid=244

Sweden
Floragatan 3, 114 31 Stockholm
Box 26220, 100 40 Stockholm
Tel: +08 791 73 40 Fax: +08 791 73 51

Switzerland
Kirchstrasse 56, CH-3097 Bern-Lieberfeld
Tel: +41 31 970 30 30 Fax: +41 31 970 30 35
www.thaiembassy.se

Turkey
Cankaya Cad. Kader Sok. 45/3-4 06700 Gaziosmanpasa, Ankara
Tel: +90 312 4673409, 4673059 Fax: +90 312 438 6474

United Arab Emirates
Villa No.1, Plot No. 341, West 14/1 Al Rowdah
P.O. Box 47466 Abu Dhabi
Tel: +97 12 453 991, 431 279, 432 554 Fax: +97 12 458 687

United Kingdom
29-30 Queen's Gate, London, SW7 5JB
Tel: +07 1 5890173, 5892944 Fax: +07 1 8239695
www.thaiembassyuk.org.uk

United States of America
1024 Wisconsin Avenue, N.W., Suite 401, Washington, D.C. 20007,
Tel: +202 944 3600
www.thaiembdc.org/index.htm

611 North Larchmont Boulevard, 2nd Floor, Los Angeles, CA USA
Tel: (+1-323) 9629574, 9629577 Fax (+1-323) 9622128
Email: thai-la@mindspring.com
http://www.thai-la.net

700 North Rush Street, Chicago, Illinois USA
Tel: (+1-312) 6643129 Fax (+1-312) 6643230
Email: thaichicago@ameritech.net
http://www.thaichicago.net

Vietnam
63-65 Hoang Dieu Street, Hanoi
Tel: +84 4 235 092 94 Fax: +84 4 235 088
www.mfa.go.th/web/1488.php?depid=258

United Nations (Switzerland)
28B Chemin du Pefit-Saconnex, 1209 Geneva
Tel: (4122) 734-2010, 734-2018, 734-2020 Fax: (4122) 733-3678
E-Mail: thai.gva@itu.ch

Complaint - Thai

คำฟ้อง

คดีหมายเลขดำที่ .... /๒๕ ....

ศาล ....

วันที่ .... เดือน .... พุทธศักราช ๒๕ ....

ความ ....

.... โจทก์

ระหว่าง

.... จำเลย

ข้อหาหรือฐานความผิด ....

จำนวนทุนทรัพย์ .... บาท .... - .... สตางค์

ข้าพเจ้า ....

.... โจทก์

เชื้อชาติ .... สัญชาติ .... อาชีพ ....

เกิดวันที่ .... เดือน .... พ.ศ. .... อายุ .... ปี อยู่บ้านเลขที่ ....

หมู่ที่ .... ถนน .... ตรอก/ซอย ....

ใกล้เคียง .... ตำบล/แขวง .... อำเภอ/เขต ....

จังหวัด .... โทรศัพท์ ....

ขอยื่นฟ้อง ....

.... จำเลย

เชื้อชาติ .... สัญชาติ .... อาชีพ ....

อยู่บ้านเลขที่ .... หมู่ที่ .... ถนน ....

ตรอก/ซอย .... ใกล้เคียง .... ตำบล/แขวง ....

อำเภอ/เขต .... จังหวัด .... โทรศัพท์ ....

มีข้อความตามที่จะกล่าวต่อไปนี้

....

....

....

....

หมายเหตุ ในช่องสำหรับลงชื่อโจทก์จำเลย ถ้าเป็นราษฎรให้ลงชื่อตัวและชื่อสกุล
ถ้าพนักงานอัยการเป็นโจทก์ให้แสดงตำแหน่ง

Complaint - English

Complaint

Pending Case No. ..../Year......

Court of ....

Date............Month..................B.E. Year..................

(Criminal or Civil) Matter

Between {
.... Plaintiff

.... Defendant
}

The nature of complaint/charge..

The amount of assets in dispute....................baht........-........satang

I ....

The Plaintiff

Race ....Nationality..................Occupation..................

Date of Birth..................Month..........B.E. Year..................Age..........

Residing at..................Village No...................Street..................

Alley/Soi..................Close to..................Sub-district..................

District..................Province..................Tel:..................

Would like to submit a complaint/charge against..................

The defendant

Race..................Nationality..................Occupation..................

Residing at House No...................Village No...................

Street..........Alley/Soi..................Close to..................Sub-dist

District..................Province..................

Tel:..................

With the following detailed statement:

_____

Note: In the box above, if the plaintiff and the defendant is a civilian,

put down the first and last name. If the plaintiff is a prosecutor,

put down the position.

Petition - Thai

(๗)
คำร้อง

คดีหมายเลขดำที่_____/๒๕____
คดีหมายเลขแดงที่_____/๒๕____

ศาล_____
วันที่_____เดือน_____พุทธศักราช ๒๕_____
ความ_____

ระหว่าง

_____ โจทก์

_____ จำเลย

ข้าพเจ้า_____

เชื้อชาติ_____สัญชาติ_____อาชีพ_____เกิดวันที่_____
เดือน_____พ.ศ._____อายุ_____ปี อยู่บ้านเลขที่_____หมู่ที่_____
ถนน_____ตรอก/ซอย_____ใกล้เคียง_____ตำบล/แขวง_____
อำเภอ/เขต_____จังหวัด_____โทรศัพท์_____
ขอยื่นคำร้องมีข้อความตามที่จะกล่าวต่อไปนี้

_____

_____

_____

_____

_____

_____

หมายเหตุ ข้าพเจ้ารอฟังคำสั่งอยู่ ถ้าไม่รอให้ถือว่าทราบแล้ว
_____/ผู้ร้อง

Petition - English

(7)

Petition

Pending Case No. ..../Year ......
Judgment Case No. ..../Year ....

Court of ....
Date .... Month .... B.E. Year ....
(Criminal or Civil) Matter

Between

.... Plaintiff

.... Defendant

I ....

Race .... Nationality .... Occupation .... Date of Birth ....

Month .... B.E. Year ...... Age .... Residing at .... Village No. ......

Street .... Alley/Soi .... Close to .... Sub-district ....

District .... Province .... Tel ....

Would like to submit a petition with the following detailed statement:

....

....

....

....

....

....

Note: I am waiting for the order. If not, I have already acknowledged it.

.... Petitioner

Subpoena (Criminal) -Thai

◯ **(๑๔)**
หมายเรียก
คดีอาญา

สำหรับศาลใช้

คดีหมายเลขดำที่ ..../๒๕ ....

ในพระปรมาภิไธยพระมหากษัตริย์

ศาล ....

วันที่ .... เดือน .... พุทธศักราช ๒๕ ....

ความ อาญา

.... โจทก์

ระหว่าง {

.... จำเลย

หมายถึง ....

.... จำเลย

.............ตามที่โจทก์ได้ยื่นฟ้องกล่าวโทษจำเลยต่อศาลนี้หาว่ากระทำผิดเป็นความอาญา
มีข้อความตามสำเนาคำฟ้องซึ่งได้ส่งมาให้ทราบพร้อมกับหมายนัดไต่สวนมูลฟ้องแล้วนั้น

.............บัดนี้ ศาลได้มีคำสั่งประทับฟ้องในกระทงความผิด ....

....

....

....

และนัดจำเลยให้การแก้ข้อหาแห่งคดีพร้อมกับนัดสืบพยานโจทก์ ณ วันที่ ....

เดือน .... พ.ศ. ๒๕ .... เวลา .... นาฬิกา

.............เพราะฉะนั้น จำเลยไปศาลตามกำหนดนี้

.... ผู้พิพากษา

ศาล ....

โทรศัพท์ ....

(พลิก)

จำเลยอยู่บ้านเลขที่ .... หมู่ที่ .... ถนน ....
ตรอก/ซอย .... ใกล้เคียง .... ตำบล/แขวง ....
อำเภอ/เขต .... จังหวัด .... โทรศัพท์ ....

<u>คำเตือน</u>

ระวังให้ที่อยู่ของจำเลยตรงกับในคำฟ้อง

Subpoena (Criminal) - English

○
Subpoena
Criminal Case

For Court Use

Pending Case Number ....
B.E. Year ....

In the Name of the King

Court ....
Date .... Month .... B.E. Year ....

Criminal Matter

	.... Plaintiff
Between {	
	.... Defendant

Refers to ....
.... The

defendant

       According to the complaint to this court accusing the defendant of committing a criminal act as written in the attached copy of the complaint, to inform the defendant of the date to appear

       Now the court has accepted the charge of ....
....

....

and is submitting this subpoena to the defendant for his appearance in court to defend himself and to make an appointment to examine the plaintiff's witness on Date .... Month .... B.E. Year ....

Time ....

       Therefore, the defendant is ordered to appear by the court.

.... Judge

Court of ....
Tel: ....

(Turn over)

The defendant resides at house number............Village No..

Street...Alley/Soi........Close to..

Sub-district............District....................Province................Tel..............................

Caution

Make sure that the address of the defendant is the same as in the complaint.

Subpoena (Civil) - Thai

<u>สำหรับศาลใช้</u>

(๑๓)
หมายเรียก
คดีแพ่งสามัญ

คดีหมายเลขดำที่_____/๒๕_____

ในพระปรมาภิไธยพระมหากษัตริย์

ศาล...
วันที่.............เดือน......................พุทธศักราช ๒๕..............
ความ แพ่ง

.... โจทก์

ระหว่าง

.... จำเลย

หมายถึง...
.... จำเลย
    ด้วยโจทก์ได้ยื่นฟ้องจำเลยต่อศาลนี้มีข้อความตามสำเนาคำฟ้องและ
เอกสาร รวม......................ฉบับ ซึ่งได้ส่งมาให้ทราบพร้อมกับหมายนี้แล้ว
    เพราะฉะนั้น ให้ท่านทำคำให้การแก้คดียื่นต่อศาลภายใน ๑๕ วัน นับแต่วันที่
ได้รับหมายหรือถือว่าได้รับหมายนี้

....ผู้พิพากษา

(พลิก)

จำเลยอยู่บ้านเลขที่................................หมู่ที่......................ถนน..
ตรอก/ซอย..............................ใกล้เคียง......................ตำบล/แขวง...
อำเภอ/เขต...............................จังหวัด......................โทรศัพท์...

Subpoena (Civil) - English

<u>For Court Use</u>

Subpoena/Summons
Civil Case

Pending Case Number................

B.E. Year ....

In the Name of the King

Court...

Date............ Month................ B.E. Year.................

Civil Matter

Between { .... Plaintiff

.... Defendant

Refers to...

....The

defendant

        The plaintiff has submitted a complaint to this court claiming the defendant as described in a copy of the complaint and other documents in the total of .... documents which are attached to this subpoena.

        Therefore, you need to make a response to this court within 15 days after receiving this subpoena.

....Judge

(Turn over)

The defendant resides at house number..........Village No..

Street..Alley/Soi..........Close to..

Sub-district............District....................Province..............Tel..............................

Testimony of Defendant - Thai

◯ (๑๑ ก.)
คำให้การจำเลย

คดีหมายเลขดำที่ _____ /๒๕ _____

ศาล _____

วันที่ _____ เดือน _____ พุทธศักราช ๒๕ _____

ความ _____

_____ โจทก์

ระหว่าง {

_____ จำเลย

ข้าพเจ้า _____

_____ จำเลย

เชื้อชาติ _____ สัญชาติ _____ อาชีพ _____

เกิดวันที่ _____ เดือน _____ พ.ศ. _____ อายุ _____ ปี อยู่บ้านเลขที่ _____

หมู่ที่ _____ ถนน _____ ตรอก/ซอย _____

ใกล้เคียง _____ ตำบล/แขวง _____ อำเภอ/เขต _____

จังหวัด _____ โทรศัพท์ _____

ได้ทราบคำฟ้องตลอดแล้ว ขอให้การตามที่จะกล่าวต่อไปนี้

_____

_____

_____

_____

_____

_____

หมายเหตุ ข้าพเจ้ารอฟังคำสั่งอยู่ ถ้าไม่รอให้ถือว่าทราบแล้ว

_____ จำเลย

Testimony of Defendant - English

◯ (11 Gor)

Defendant's

Testimony

Pending Case No. ..../Year........

Court of ....

Date .... Month .... B.E. Year ....

(Criminal or Civil) Matter

.... Plaintiff

Between

.... Defendant

I ....

Race .... Nationality .... Occupation .... Date of Birth ....

Month .... B.E. Year .... Age .... Residing at .... Village No. ......

Street .... Alley/Soi .... Close to .... Sub-district ....

District .... Province .... Tel ....

Have been fully acknowledged of the complaint. I would like to give the following testimony.

....

....

....

....

....

....

....

Note: I am waiting for the order. If not, I have already acknowledged it.

.... Defendant

Witness List - Thai

Testimony of Defendant - English

◯ (๑๕ ก.)
บัญชีพยาน

คดีหมายเลขดำที่ .... /๒๕ ....

ศาล ....

วันที่ .... เดือน .... พุทธศักราช ๒๕ ....

ความ ....

.... โจทก์

ระหว่าง {

.... จำเลย

ข้าพเจ้า ....

ขอระบุพยานของข้าพเจ้ารวม .... อันดับ ตามบัญชีตารางข้างล่างนี้

อันดับ	ชื่อพยาน	บ้านเลขที่ หมู่ที่ ถนน ตรอก/ซอย	ใกล้เคียง	ตำบล/แขวง	อำเภอ/เขต	จังหวัด	หมายเหตุ

.... ผู้ระบุ

Witness List - English

○ (15 Gor)

Witness List

Pending Case No............/Year..........

Court of...

Date.............Month.....................B.E. Year...................

(Criminal or Civil) Matter

Between {

.... Plaintiff

.... Defendant

I..

Would like to specify that I have .... witnesses as in the table below.

No.	Name of Witness	(Address) House No. Village No. Street Alley/Soi	Close to	Sub-district	District	Province	Note

....The Specifier

Lawyer Appointment - Thai

◯ (๙)

ใบแต่งทนายความ

คดีหมายเลขดำที่ ..../๒๕ ....

ศาล ....

วันที่ .... เดือน .... พ.ศ. ๒๕ ....

ความ ....

ระหว่าง { .... โจทก์

.... จำเลย

ข้าพเจ้า ....

ขอแต่งให้ ....

เป็นทนายความของข้าพเจ้าในคดีเรื่องนี้ และให้มีอำนาจ* ดำเนินกระบวนพิจารณาใดๆไป
ในทางจำหน่ายสิทธิของข้าพเจ้า เช่น การยอมรับตามที่คู่ความอีกฝ่ายหนึ่งเรียกร้อง การถอนฟ้อง
การประนีประนอมยอมความ การสละสิทธิ์ หรือการใช้สิทธิในการอุทธรณ์ หรือฎีกา หรือการขอให้
พิจารณาคดีใหม่ ....

....

ข้าพเจ้ายอมรับผิดชอบตามที่ ....
ทนายความจะได้ดำเนินกระบวนพิจารณาต่อไปตามกฎหมาย
ขอรับรองว่าเป็นลายมือชื่อของผู้แต่งทนายความจริง

ลงชื่อ .... ทนายความ .... ผู้แต่งทนายความ

( )

หมายเหตุ* ตามประมวลกฎหมายวิธีพิจารณาความแพ่งมาตรา ๖๒ ทนายความไม่มีอำนาจ
ดำเนินกระบวนพิจารณาใดไปในทางจำหน่ายสิทธิของคู่ความนั้น เช่นการ
ยอมรับ ตามที่คู่ความอีกฝ่ายหนึ่งเรียกร้อง การถอนฟ้อง การประนีประนอมยอม
ความการสละสิทธิ์หรือใช้สิทธิในการอุทธรณ์หรือฎีกา หรือในการขอให้
พิจารณาคดีใหม่ ถ้าจะมอบให้มีอำนาจดังกล่าวประการใดบ้าง ให้กรอกลงใน
ช่องที่ว่างไว้โดยระบุ ให้แจ้งชัด (คำที่ไม่ใช้และช่องว่างที่เหลือให้ขีดเสีย)

คำรับเป็นทนายความ

ข้าพเจ้า..

_____

ทนายความชั้นที่.....................ใบอนุญาตที่..................................ได้รับอนุญาตให้ว่าความ
สำนักงานอยู่บ้านเลขที่..หมู่ที่..........ถนน.............................
ตรอก/ซอย..................ใกล้เคียง..................ตำบล/แขวง..
อำเภอ/เขต..........................จังหวัด...........................โทร...
ขอเข้ารับเป็นทนายความของ...
เพื่อดำเนินกระบวนพิจารณาต่อไปตามหน้าที่ในกฎหมาย

....ทนายความ
(   )

คำสั่ง

....

....

....

....ผู้พิพากษา

Lawyer Appointment - English

◯ (9)

Lawyer
Appointment Form

Pending Case No. .... / Year ....

Court of ....

Date .... Month .... B.E. Year ....

(Criminal or Civil) Matter

Between {

.... Plaintiff

.... Defendant

I ....

....

Appoint ....

....

To be my lawyer in this case and to have power to do any process that I am entitled to do such as accepting statements from the other party, case withdrawal, compromising the matter, waiving of rights or using my rights in the Court of Appeal or the Supreme Court or requesting for a new trial. ....

....

....

I am responsible for ....

So that the lawyer can proceed in all procedures according to the law

I certify that the signature of the person appointing the lawyer is true.

Signature........................Lawyer ....Person Appointing the Lawyer

(   )   (   )

Note   According to the Civil Code Section 62 regarding methods in the trial, a lawyer doen not have power to exercise the rights of the parties, such as accepting statements from the other party, case withdrawal, compromising of the matter, waiving of rights or using the rights in the Court of Appeal or the Supreme Court or requesting for a new trial. The appointer should clearly specify which power he is giving to the lawyer in the space provided (and cross out the items that are not applicable).

Acception of Lawyer Appointment

I..

....

Lawyer Level..............................License Number...........................have permission to be
a lawyer.

Location of Office at House No.................................Village No............Street................

Alley/Soi.........................Close to.....................Sub-district..

District..Province...............................Tel...............................

Accept to be the lawyer for ....

To proceed in legal procedures according to the law.

....Lawyer

(   )

Court Order

....

....

....

....Judge

Authorization Form - Thai

◯ (๑๐)

ใบมอบฉันทะ

คดีหมายเลขดำที่ _____ /๒๕ _____

คดีหมายเลขแดงที่ _____ /๒๕ _____

ศาล _____

วันที่ _____ เดือน _____ พุทธศักราช ๒๕ _____

ความ _____

ระหว่าง

{

_____ โจทก์

_____ จำเลย

ข้าพเจ้า _____

ขอมอบฉันทะให้ _____

อยู่บ้านเลขที่ _____ หมู่ที่ _____ ถนน _____

ตรอก/ซอย _____ ใกล้เคียง _____ ตำบล/แขวง _____

อำเภอ/เขต _____ จังหวัด _____ โทรศัพท์ _____

ทำการแทน โดยข้าพเจ้ายอมรับผิดชอบในการที่ผู้รับมอบฉันทะของข้าพเจ้าได้ทำไปนั้น ทุกประการ ในกิจการดังจะกล่าวต่อไปนี้

_____

_____

_____

_____

ลงชื่อ _____ ผู้มอบฉันทะ

ลงชื่อ _____ ผู้รับมอบฉันทะ

ลงชื่อ _____ พยาน

ลงชื่อ _____ พยาน

Authorization Form - English

◯ (10)

Authorization Form

Pending Case No.........../Year

Judgment Case No.........../Year.........

Court of...

Date.........Month..................B.E. Year..................

(Criminal or Civil) Matter

Between ⎧ .... Plaintiff

⎩ .... Defendant

I ....

....

authorize...

....

Residing at...........................Village No................Street.................

Alley/Soi...........................Close to.............................Sub-district ....

District..........Province.......Tel.................

To do all the process for me. I am responsible for all the actions made for the authorized person. I am authorizing him/her to do the following matters.

....

....

....

....

Signature...Authorizing Person

Signature...Authorized Person

Signature...Witness

Signature...Witness

Power of Attorney - Thai and English

Power of Attorney
หนังสือมอบอำนาจ

Duty Stamp
10 Bath
อากรแสตมป์
๑๐ บาท

Written at
ทำที่ ....

Date .... Month .... B.E. ....
วันที่ .... เดือน .... พ.ศ. ....

I.   Mr./Mrs./Miss.
ข้าพเจ้า นาย/นาง/นางสาว ....
hereby authorize and appoint Mr./Mrs./Miss.   at present working
ขอมอบอำนาจให้ นาย/นาง/นางสาว .... ปัจจุบันทำงานใน

In the position of   at the office of
ตำแหน่ง .... ตั้งอยู่ที่สำนักงานชื่อ ....

Tel.   Located on   Soi/Lane
โทร. .... ตั้งอยู่เลขที่ .... ซอย ....

Rd.   Sub-District   District
ถนน .... แขวง .... เขต ....

Province   to be lawful and legal attorney for the purpose concerning with work permit,
จังหวัด .... มีอำนาจดำเนินการเกี่ยวกับการขออนุญาตทำงาน ลงนามในเอกสารประกอบการ

sign any documents on behalf of myself including changing words on the related documents.
ขออนุญาตแทนข้าพเจ้าได้ทุกฉบับ รวมทั้งเปลี่ยนแปลงแก้ไขข้อความในเอกสารดังกล่าวด้วย

What has been done by   will remain in full force
การใดที่นาย/นาง/นางสาว .... ได้กระทำไปให้ถือเสมือนว่า

and effect as it has been done by myself.
ข้าพเจ้าได้กระทำเองทุกประการ

Signed   Grantor
ลงชื่อ .... ผู้มอบอำนาจ
       (....................................)

Signed   Grantee
ลงชื่อ .... ผู้รับมอบอำนาจ
       (....................................)

Signed   Witness
ลงชื่อ .... พยาน
       (....................................)

Signed   Witness
ลงชื่อ .... พยาน
       (....................................)

หมายเหตุ หากผู้มอบอำนาจจะระสงค์จะจำกัดขอบการมอบอำนาจเป็นอย่างอื่น ย่อมกระทำได้ โดยไม่ต้องใช้เนื้อความตามนี้
Remark   In case grantor perfer to limit the authorization giving to the grantee it could be done by using the other
         forms of power of attorney.

Being Single Certification - Thai

บันทึกรับรองการเป็นโสด

วันที่..........เดือน..................พ.ศ...........

ข้าพเจ้า..อยู่บ้านเลขที่.............หมู่ที่..............

ซอย.....................ถนน.......................................แขวง/ตำบล......................................

เขต/อำเภอ............................จังหวัด...............................ขอให้ถ้อยคำต่อหน้า...............

..............................ตำแหน่ง.................................... เขต.............

ว่าขณะนี้ข้าพเจ้ายังเป็นโสดไม่มีคู่สมรสแต่อย่างใด จึงขอรับรองและยืนยันมาเพื่อขอทำนิติกรรมด้วยตนเอง

หากเกิดการเสียหายหรือเป็นเท็จเนื่องจากการนี้ ข้าพเจ้าขอรับผิดชอบเองทั้งสิ้น

อ่านให้ฟังแล้วรับรองว่าถูกต้อง จึงลงชื่อไว้เป็นหลักฐาน

ลงชื่อ...................................ผู้ให้ถ้อยคำ

ลงชื่อ...................................ผู้สอบสวน

ลงชื่อ...................................ผู้จด/อ่าน

Being Single Certification - English

Record Certifying One's Single Status

Date...........Month..................B.E. Year............

I ....Residing at House No............Village No............

Soi.........................Street.....................................Sub-district......................................

District..............................Province...............................give a statement in the presence of

........................Position............................... District.............. that at the moment

I am still single and am not married to anyone. I would like to certify and affirm this in order to proceed

with a legal act by myself without a spouse. If there is damage or if this is a false statement, I am to be

responsible for all the consequences.

I have read this and certify that this is true and correct. Therefore, I am signing this document as evidence.

Signature...........................Person giving statement

Signature ....Person verifying

Signature ....Person taking note/reading

Spouse Consent - Thai

หนังสือยินยอมของคู่สมรส

ทำที่...

วันที่............เดือน........................พ.ศ............

โดยหนังสือฉบับนี้ ข้าพเจ้า...

อยู่บ้านเลขที่....................ตรอก/ซอย.......................ตำบล.................................

อำเภอ..จังหวัด.................................

ซึ่งเป็น (สามี/ภริยา) โดยชอบด้วยกฎหมายของ...

ขอทำหนังสือฉบับนี้ขึ้นไว้เพื่อเป็นหลักฐานว่าข้าพเจ้าได้รับทราบและยินยอมให้.................

....สามี/ภริยา ของข้าพเจ้าเป็นผู้มีอำนาจในการทำนิติกรรม/สัญญา............

....

กิจการที่...สามี / ภริยา

ของข้าพเจ้าได้กระทำไปภายในขอบเขตอำนาจหนังสือยินยอมฉบับนี้

ให้มีผลผูกพันข้าพเจ้าเสมือนข้าพเจ้าได้กระทำร่วมกัน

เพื่อเป็นหลักฐานในการนี้ จึงได้ลงลายมือไว้เป็นสำคัญต่อหน้าพยาน

ลงชื่อ.................................ผู้ให้ความยินยอม

(.................................)

ลงชื่อ.................................พยาน

(.................................)

ลงชื่อ.................................พยาน

(.................................)

Spouse Consent - English

Spouse Consent Form

Written At...

Date............Month..............B.E. Year............

With this letter, I..

Residing at House No...................Alley/Soi...................Sub-district................................

District...Province..

the legal husband/wife of...

Would like to issue this letter as evidence that I have acknowledged and given consent to

....my husband/wife with the power to proceed in the legal

act/contract of ....

The matter(s) that ....my husband/wife has performed

has limitation as stated in this consent form. It has an effect as if we performed the matter together.

For the record, I have signed my name in the presence of the witnesses.

Signature......................................Person giving consent

(......................................)

Signature ....Witness

(......................................)

Signature ....Witness

(......................................)

Divorce Agreement - Thai

หนังสือข้อตกลงหย่า

เขียนที่...

วันที่..........เดือน.......................พ.ศ. ....

ข้าพเจ้า...ทั้งสองฝ่าย

ได้เป็นสามี-ภริยากันโดยถูกต้องตามกฎหมาย จดทะเบียนสมรส ณ.................................

จังหวัด...........................เลขทะเบียนที่.......................ลงวันที่.....................

บัดนี้ทั้งสองฝ่ายมีเหตุผลบางประการ ไม่สามารถอยู่กินกันฉันท์สามีภรรยากันได้อีกต่อไป จึงขอทำ
หนังสือการหย่าขาดจากกันเป็นสามีภริยากัน โดยมีเงื่อนไขดังต่อไปนี้

ข้อ 1. เรื่องบุตร (ชื่อบุตรพร้อมค่าอุปการะเลี้ยงดูบุตรให้ละเอียด).................................

....

....

....

ข้อ 2. ค่าเลี้ยงดู (กรณีฝ่ายหญิงเรียกร้องค่าเลี้ยงดู)...

....

....

ข้อ 3. เรื่องทรัพย์สิน...

....

....

ข้อ 4. เรื่องอื่น ๆ ....

....

....

ข้าพเจ้าทั้งสองฝ่ายได้เข้าใจในข้อความที่บันทึกไว้ถูกต้อง จึงลงลายมือชื่อไว้เป็นหลักฐาน

ลงชื่อ...............................ฝ่ายชาย   ลงชื่อ...............................ฝ่ายหญิง

(   )   (   )

ลงชื่อ...............................พยาน   ลงชื่อ...............................พยาน

(   )   (   )

Divorce Agreement - English

Divorce Agreement

Written At...

Date..........Month................B.E. Year..........

We.., the two of us,

have lived as husband and wife legally and have our registration of marriage at ....

Province.............................Registration No............................Dated...........................

Now the two of us have certain reasons that we can no longer live as husband and wife. Therefore, we

would like to dissolve our marriage with the following conditions.

Item 1 Regarding the Children (List all children and amount for child support)......................

....

....

....

Item 2 Regarding the Alimony (In the case that the female is requesting alimony)................

....

....

Item 3 Regarding the Assets..

....

....

Item 4 Regarding other Matters...

....

....

We both understand the recorded statements above. Therefore, we have signed our names below

as evidence.

Signature..................................The Male   Signature ....The Female

(   )   (   )

Signature...................................Witness   Signature ....Witness

(   )   (   )

Last Will and Testament - Thai

พินัยกรรมแบบธรรมดา

(กรณีมีการตั้งผู้จัดการมรดก)

ทำที่..

วันที่..................เดือน.........................พ.ศ. ....

ข้าพเจ้า...อายุ.........ปี อยู่บ้านเลขที่...........

ตรอก/ซอย...........................ถนน...................ตำบล/แขวง........................

อำเภอ/เขต...........................จังหวัด...........................ขอทำพินัยกรรมไว้ว่าเมื่อข้าพเจ้า

ถึงแก่ความตายแล้ว ให้ทรัพย์สินของข้าพเจ้าทั้งหมดที่มีอยู่ในปัจจุบันและที่จะมีต่อไปในอนาคตนั้นตกได้

แก่บุคคลดังต่อไปนี้ คือ

(1) ....

(2) ....

(3) ....

....

....

และขอตั้งให้...เป็นผู้จัดการมรดกของข้าพเจ้า เพื่อจัดการ

แบ่งปันทรัพย์สินอันเป็นมรดกให้เป็นไปตามเจตนาของข้าพเจ้า

เพื่อเป็นหลักฐานข้าพเจ้าได้ลงลายมือชื่อไว้เป็นสำคัญ

ลงชื่อ...ผู้ทำพินัยกรรม

(...)

ข้าพเจ้าผู้มีรายนามข้างท้ายนี้ ขอรับรองว่า...ผู้ทำพินัยกรรม

ได้ทำพินัยกรรมต่อหน้าข้าพเจ้า และได้กระทำลงในขณะที่มีสติสัมปชัญญะบริบูรณ์ทุกประการ ข้าพเจ้าจึง

ลงลายมือชื่อไว้เป็นพยานในพินัยกรรม

ลงชื่อ...พยาน

(...)

ลงชื่อ...พยานและผู้เขียน

(...)

Last Will and Testament - English

Last Will and Testament

(General and basic form in the case that there is an executor)

Written At...

Date................Month.................B.E. Year...................

I...Age..............Residing at House No. ....

Alley/Soi.....................................Street.....................................Sub-district...................................

District...Province...I would like to state the following

in this will. After I die, all of the assets that I currently have and that I will acquire in the future be

devolved upon the following persons:

(1) ....

(2) ....

(3) ....

....

....

And I appoint..to be the executor of my estate and to

divide my assets as inheritance according to my wish.

For the record, I am putting down my signature as evidence.

Signature...Person making the will

(...)

I, the undersigned, certify that ....the Will Maker has made this will

in my presence and he/she has done it while he is fully sane and rational. Therefore, I am signing this

document as the witness of this will.

Signature...Witness

(...)

Signature...Witness and Recorder

(...)

Loan Contract - Thai

สัญญากู้ยืมเงิน (ทั่วไป)

สัญญาฉบับนี้ทำขึ้นเมื่อวันที่....................เดือน.................................พ.ศ.....................

ณ

เลขที่............ถนน........................ตรอก/ซอย................ตำบล/แขวง.......................อำ

ภอ/เขต....................จังหวัด...

ระหว่างข้าพเจ้า..

อยู่บ้านเลขที่..

....

ซึ่งต่อไปในสัญญานี้เรียกว่า ผู้กู้ ฝ่ายหนึ่ง

กับข้าพเจ้า...

อยู่บ้านเลขที่..

....

ซึ่งต่อไปในสัญญานี้เรียกว่า ผู้ให้กู้ อีกฝ่ายหนึ่ง

ทั้งสองฝ่ายตกลงกันทำสัญญาดังต่อไปนี้

ข้อ 1. ผู้กู้ได้กู้ยืมเงินจากผู้ให้กู้เป็นเงิน...................บาท (....................................)

โดยในวันทำสัญญานี้ผู้กู้ได้รับเงินไปเรียบร้อยแล้ว และตกลงว่าจะชำระคืนเงินให้กับผู้ให้กู้ภายในวันที่.......

เดือน...............................พ.ศ..............

ข้อ 2. ผู้กู้ตกลงจะให้ดอกเบี้ยแก่ผู้ให้กู้ในอัตราร้อยละ .... ต่อปี และตกลงจะชำระดอกเบี้ยให้ทุก

.......เดือน

ข้อ 3. เงื่อนไขตกลงอื่น ๆ (หากมี)

....

ข้อ 4. ในการกู้ยืมตามสัญญานี้ผู้กู้ได้นำหลักทรัพย์เป็นประกันให้ผู้ให้กู้ยึดถือไว้คือ

....

....

....

หลักทรัพย์ดังกล่าวผู้กู้เป็นเจ้าของกรรมสิทธิ์ ไม่มีภาระติดพันใด ๆ

ในวันทำสัญญานี้ผู้ให้กู้ได้ยึดถือหลักประกันที่ผู้ส่งมอบให้แล้ว

และผู้ให้กู้จะคืนให้เมื่อผู้กู้ได้ชำระหนี้ครบถ้วนตามสัญญาแล้ว

ข้อ 5. หากคู่สัญญาฝ่ายหนึ่งฝ่ายใดผิดสัญญาข้อหนึ่งข้อใด
ยินยอมให้คู่สัญญาอีกฝ่ายหนึ่งฟ้องร้องศาลบังคับคดี
และยอมชดใช้ค่าใช้จ่ายที่เสียไปในการดำเนินคดีและบังคับคดีได้อีกด้วย

เพื่อเป็นหลักฐานคู่สัญญาทั้งสองฝ่ายได้อ่านข้อความของสัญญานี้ดีโดยตลอดแล้วตรงตามความประ
สงค์ของคู่สัญญา ทั้งสองฝ่ายจึงได้ลงลายมือไว้เป็นสำคัญต่อหน้าพยาน

ลงชื่อ......................................ผู้กู้

ลงชื่อ......................................ผู้ให้กู้

ลงชื่อ......................................พยาน

ลงชื่อ......................................พยาน / ผู้พิมพ์

Loan Contract - English

Loan Contract (General)

This contract was made on (date).............. Month........................B.E. Year.....................

At House No.....................Street..Alley/Soi................................

Sub-district...........................District...........................Province..

Between (name)...

Residing at...

....

Hereafter referred to as the BORROWER

And (name)..

Residing at..

....

Hereafter referred to as the LENDER

The two parties agree to enter the contract as follows:

1. The BORROWER has borrowed money from the lender in the amount of ....baht

(...)

The BORROWER has received money in good order on the day of the contract and agrees to pay back the

lender by (date)............... Month......................Year...................

2. The BORROWER agrees to pay interest to the LENDER at the rate of ....% per year and

agree to pay the interest every ...... month.

3. Other conditions (if any)

....

4. For this loan, the BORROWER has brought an asset(s) as collateral to the LENDER to keep

which is (are)

....

....

....

The above asset belongs to the BORROWER solely and there is no burden attached to it.

On the date of entering this contract, the LENDER has kept the asset(s) used as collateral and will

return it (them) to the BORROWER when the BORROWER has paid off the debt as stated in this

contract.

5. If one of the parties does not follow one or more conditions in this contract, he/she will allow the other party submit a claim to court to execute the case and will compensate the expenses used in the court procedures and court order.

For the record, both parties have read the content of this contract carefully and it has been written as the two parties wish. Therefore, the two parties are putting down their signatures in the presence of the witnesses.

Signature.......................................THE BORROWER

Signature ....THE LENDER

Signature ....Witness

Signature ....Witness/ Recorder

Rental Contract

หนังสือสัญญาเช่าบ้าน/เช่าตึกแถว

Housing/Shop Rental Contract

เมื่อวันที่ On this day _____ เดือนที่ month _____ ค.ศ. year _____

สัญญาทำที่ this contract was signed at (place) _____

ระหว่าง between _____,

ซึ่งต่อไปนี้เรียกว่า **ผู้เช่า**ฝ่ายหนึ่ง a party referred to as the **tenant,**

กับ and _____,

ซึ่งต่อไปนี้เรียกว่า **เจ้าของบ้าน**อีกฝ่ายหนึ่ง a party referred to as the **landlord.**

ได้ทำสัญญากันดังต่อไปนี้ The parties agree to the following:

ข้อ 1 สถานที่เช่า | Clause 1. Rental Place

เจ้าของบ้านตกลงให้เช่าและผู้เช่าตกลงรับเช่า (เลือกข้อเดียว):

The landlord agrees to rent to the tenant, and the tenant agrees to rent from the landlord (check only one, on the left):

- ☐ บ้าน หรือ ตึกแถว — • a house or shop
- ☐ ห้องชุดที่ _____ — • apartment, flat, or room number _____
- ☐ อื่นๆ _____ — • other _____

เลขที่ located at street number _____ หมู่ที่ moo number _____

ถนน street _____ ตรอก/ซอย soi _____

ตำบล/แขวง tambon/kwaeng _____

อำเภอ/เขต amphoe/ket _____ จังหวัด province _____.

ซึ่งต่อไปนี้เรียกว่า **สถานที่เช่า** referred to as the **rental place,**

เพื่อ (เลือกกี่ข้อก็ได้): | for the purposes of (check all that apply):

- ☐ อยู่อาศัย — • residence
- ☐ ค้าขาย — • business

This is an easy-to-understand, Thai-English house/apartment/shop house rental contract which will help both the tenant and the landlord confidently complete a clear and trouble-free deal. This contract includes the enforceable terms from "standard" (stationary store) contracts, plus we've added more details to help bridge the language and culture barriers that often cause problems between Thai landlords and foreign tenants.

This is an easy-to-understand, Thai-English house/apartment/shop house rental contract which will help both the tenant and the landlord confidently complete a clear and trouble-free deal. This contract includes the enforceable terms from "standard" (stationary store) contracts, plus we've added more details to help bridge the language and culture barriers that often cause problems between Thai landlords and foreign tenants.

Download free from http://slice-of-thai.com

ข้อ 2 ค่าเช่า	**Clause 2. Rent**
ค่าเช่านับตั้งแต่	Tenant starts paying rent on:
วันที่ day _____ เดือนที่ month _____ ค.ศ. year _____ เป็นต้นไป	
ผู้เช่ายอมเสียค่าเช่าให้แก่เจ้าของบ้าน	The tenant agrees to pay the landlord rent of:
_____ บาท baht ทุก every _____ เดือน month(s)	
ผู้เช่ายอมชำระค่าเช่าแก่เจ้าของบ้านภายในวันเดียวกันของทุกๆ เดือนที่ต้องจ่าย	For each month in which rent is due, the tenant agrees to pay rent to the landlord on the same day of the month as the first payment.
ผู้เช่าตกลงจะเช่าอยู่เป็นเวลาอย่างน้อย	The tenant promises to rent for at least:
_____ เดือน months	
อาจให้มีการจ่ายค่าเช่าเรื่อยไปโดยไม่ต้องต่อสัญญาใหม่ จนกว่าผู้เช่า หรือเจ้าของบ้านต้องการยกเลิกสัญญา โดยต้องปฏิบัติตามข้อตกลงดังต่อไปนี้	Rent payments may continue indefinitely, with no need to renew this contract, until tenant or landlord wish to cease renting by following the procedure below.

ข้อ 3 ถ้าผู้เช่าจะย้ายออก	**Clause 3. If Tenant Wants to Leave**
กรณีที่ผู้เช่าต้องการย้ายออกเนื่องด้วยสาเหตุใดก็ตาม ผู้เช่าจะต้องแจ้งให้เจ้าของบ้านทราบล่วงหน้าอย่างน้อย	If the tenant wants to leave the rental place for any reason, the tenant must give the landlord advance notice of at least:
_____ อาทิตย์ weeks.	
ระหว่างนั้นผู้เช่าจะต้องยังคงจ่ายค่าเช่า	The tenant must continue to pay rent during this notice period.
เมื่อผู้เช่าแจ้งให้เจ้าของบ้านทราบแล้ว เจ้าของบ้านไม่จำเป็นต้องคืนค่าเช่าที่จ่ายไว้	When the tenant notifies the landlord, the landlord does not have to return any rent payments the tenant has already made.
อย่างไรก็ตาม ระหว่างที่รอย้ายออกนี้ หากระยะเวลาเลยกำหนดจ่ายค่าเช่าของเดือนใหม่ เจ้าของบ้านจะต้องคิดค่าเช่าตามอัตราเดิม โดยคิดตามระยะเวลาที่อาศัยอยู่จริง มิใช่คิดเต็มเดือน	However, if the notice period extends into a new rent cycle (as defined in Clause 2 above), the landlord must charge only for the percent of time that the tenant will use, not charge the full amount for that cycle.

Rental Contract (continued)

ข้อ 4 ถ้าเจ้าของบ้านจะเลิกเช่า

หากเจ้าของบ้านต้องการยกเลิกสัญญา ไม่ว่าด้วย
สาเหตุใดก็ตาม (รวมถึงหากเจ้าของบ้านต้องการ
ขายที่นั้น) เจ้าของบ้านจะต้องแจ้งให้ผู้เช่าทราบ
ล่วงหน้า อย่างน้อย

_____ อาทิตย์ weeks.

เจ้าของบ้านจะต้องอนุญาตให้ผู้เช่าอาศัยอยู่ใน
ระหว่างรอย้ายออกนี้ และหากผู้เช่ายังอาศัยอยู่
จะต้องจ่ายค่าเช่า

เจ้าของบ้านจะต้องคิดค่าเช่าตามอัตราเดิม โดยคิด
ตามระยะเวลาที่อาศัยอยู่จริง มิใช่คิดเต็มเดือน
ดังที่กล่าวไว้ในข้อสอง

ข้อ 5 ใบเสร็จ

ทุกครั้งที่มีการจ่ายค่าเช่า ทั้งเจ้าของบ้าน และผู้
เช่าตกลงเซ็นชื่อในใบเสร็จ เพื่อเป็นหลักฐานการ
จ่ายเงิน โปรดดูเอกสารเพิ่มเติมฉบับ 1 "ใบเสร็จ
ชำระค่าเช่า"

Clause 4. If Landlord Wants to Terminate

If the landlord wants to stop renting the rental place to the tenant for any reason (including sale of the rental place), then the landlord must give the tenant advance notice of at least:

_____ อาทิตย์ weeks.

The landlord must allow the tenant to stay in the rental place during this notice period, and, if and only if the tenant stays, the tenant must pay rent during this notice period. The landlord must return, to the tenant, any portion of rent that the tenant has already paid but cannot use. If the tenant must make a new rent payment during the notice period, the landlord must charge only for the percent of time that the tenant will be able to use, not charge the full amount for that cycle.

Clause 5. Receipts

Each time the tenant pays rent, both landlord and tenant agree to sign a written receipt as proof of payment. See attached Form 1, "Rent Payment Receipt."

ข้อ 6 ค่าสาธารณูปโภค และภาษี	Clause 6. Utilities and Taxes	
(คิดเป็นเปอร์เซ็นต์ 0-100)	(0%-100% for landlord and tenant):	

	เจ้าของบ้านจ่าย landlord pays	ผู้เช่าจ่าย tenant pays
ค่าไฟฟ้า electricity	_____ %	_____ %
ค่าน้ำประปา tap water	_____ %	_____ %
ค่าน้ำดื่ม drinking water	_____ %	_____ %
ค่าแก๊ส stove/heater gas	_____ %	_____ %
ค่าเคเบิ้ล cable TV	_____ %	_____ %
ค่าโทรศัพท์ telephone	_____ %	_____ %
ค่าอินเตอร์เน็ต internet	_____ %	_____ %
ค่าเก็บขยะ trash disposal	_____ %	_____ %
ค่าทำสวน yard maintenance	_____ %	_____ %
ค่าภาษีที่ดิน land tax	_____ %	_____ %
ค่าภาษีโรงเรือน property tax	_____ %	_____ %
อื่นๆ other _____	_____ %	_____ %
อื่นๆ other _____	_____ %	_____ %

ข้อ 7 ค่ามัดจำ

เจ้าของบ้านได้รับเงินล่วงหน้าไว้เป็นประกันการ
เช่าจากผู้เช่าเป็นจำนวนเงิน

_____ บาท baht.

ทั้งผู้เช่า และเจ้าของบ้านได้สำรวจสถานที่เช่า
และเห็นพร้อมกันว่า ความสึกกร่อนเสียหายที่มีอยู่
ก่อนที่ผู้เช่าจะย้ายเข้ามีดังต่อไปนี้

_____

_____

_____

_____

_____

Clause 7. Security Deposit

The landlord has already received a security
deposit from the tenant in the amount of:

_____ บาท baht.

Tenant and landlord have both inspected the
rental place and agree that the following
wear and damage existed before the tenant
moved in:

_____

_____

_____

_____

_____

Rental Contract (continued)

ข้อ 8 ความเสียหาย	**Clause 8. Damage**
หากเกิดความเสียหายขึ้นในระหว่างที่ผู้เช่าอาศัยอยู่ ซึ่งเป็นผลจากการกระทำ หรือความประมาทเลินเล่อของผู้เช่า นอกเหนือจากความเสื่อมสภาพที่เป็นธรรมดานั้น ผู้เช่าจะต้องรับผิดชอบค่าซ่อมทั้งหมด	If any damage to the rental place occurs as the result of the tenant's action or inaction, aside from reasonable wear and tear, the tenant must pay all repair costs.
ข้อ 9.การคืนค่ามัดจำ	**Clause 9. Return of Security Deposit**
เมื่อผู้เช่าย้ายออกจากสถานที่เช่า เจ้าของบ้านตกลงจะคืนเงินค่ามัดจำเต็มจำนวน ยกเว้นกรณีต่อไปนี้ เจ้าของบ้านสามารถหักค่าใช้จ่าย:	If the tenant leaves the rental place, the landlord agrees to return the full security deposit, except that the landlord may subtract:
ก) ค่าซ่อมแซมส่วนที่เสียหายที่เกิดจากผู้เช่า (ยกเว้นความเสื่อมสภาพตามปกติ) และผู้เช่ายังไม่ได้จ่าย	a) any repair costs for damage (other than reasonable wear and tear) which the tenant has caused but not yet repaired,
ข) ค่าเช่าที่ผู้เช่ายังค้างชำระ	b) any rent which is due but which the tenant has not paid, and
ค) เจ้าของบ้านสามารถยึดเงินมัดจำเต็มจำนวน ในกรณีที่ผู้เช่าย้ายออกก่อนระยะเวลาเช่าขั้นต่ำที่ได้ตกลงกันไว้ตามข้อสอง เจ้าของบ้านไม่อาจยึดค่ามัดจำ ในกรณีอื่นใด นอกเหนือจากนี้	c) the full security deposit amount, if the tenant leaves the rental place before the promised minimum period from Clause 2. The landlord shall not withhold the security deposit money for any other reason.
ข้อ 10 ความวอดวายของสถานที่เช่า	**Clause 10. Destruction of Rental Place**
ในกรณีที่เกิดความวอดวายกับสถานที่เช่า (ตัวอย่างเช่น ไฟไหม้ หรือ น้ำท่วม) ซึ่งมิได้เป็นความผิดของเจ้าของบ้าน เจ้าของบ้านไม่จำเป็นต้องคืนค่าเช่าที่ผู้เช่าได้จ่ายมาแล้ว และไม่ต้องชดใช้ค่าเสียหายต่อทรัพย์สินของผู้เช่า และผู้เช่าไม่ต้องจ่ายค่าเช่าต่อ	In the event of the destruction of the rental place (such as by fire or flood) which is not the fault of the landlord, the landlord is not required to return any rent which the tenant has already paid or compensate the tenant for any property losses, and the tenant is not required to make any further rent payments.

ข้อ 11 การดัดแปลง

หากผู้เช่าต้องการปรับปรุงเปลี่ยนแปลงสถานที่เช่า
ที่ไม่สามารถทำให้กลับคืนสภาพเดิมได้
(ตัวอย่างเช่น ต่อเติมห้อง, เปลี่ยนหน้าต่าง) ผู้เช่า
จะต้องได้รับการอนุญาตเป็นลายลักษณ์อักษรจาก
เจ้าของบ้าน (โปรดดูเอกสารเพิ่มเติมฉบับ 2
"ใบอนุญาต") ส่วนที่ปรับปรุงเพิ่มเติมนั้นจะตก
เป็นสมบัติของเจ้าของบ้าน โดยเจ้าของบ้านไม่
ต้องจ่ายเงินชดเชยใด ๆ

หากผู้เช่าต้องการแก้ไขปรับปรุงสถานที่เช่า โดย
สามารถเคลื่อนย้าย หรือถอดออกได้โดยง่าย โดย
ไม่ก่อให้เกิดความเสียหายแก่สถานที่
(ตัวอย่างเช่น ติดเครื่องทำน้ำร้อน
เครื่องปรับอากาศ หรือเครื่องเรือน) ผู้เช่าสามารถ
กระทำได้โดยไม่ต้องรับหนังสืออนุญาตเป็นลาย
ลักษณ์อักษร โดยอุปกรณ์เหล่านี้ยังเป็นสมบัติของ
ผู้เช่า โดยผู้เช่าจะต้องรับผิดชอบให้สถานที่เช่า
กลับสู่สภาพเดิม (ตัวอย่างเช่น ปิดรอยโหว่)

ในกรณีที่ไม่ชัดเจน หรือยากที่จะจำได้ว่า
ทรัพย์สินใดเป็นของผู้ใด เจ้าของบ้าน และผู้เช่า
ตกลงระบุเป็นลายลักษณ์อักษรให้ชัดเจน (โปรดดู
เอกสารเพิ่มเติมฉบับ 3 "ความเป็นเจ้าของใน
ทรัพย์สิน")

Clause 11. Improvements

If the tenant wishes to make any kind of improvement that cannot be removed without causing damage to the rental place (e.g. adding a new building or room, replacing a window), the tenant must first secure written permission from the landlord (see attached Form 2, "Written Permission Form"), and any items repaired or installed become the property of the landlord without any need for the landlord to compensate the tenant for expenses.

If the tenant wishes to make any kind of improvement to the rental place which can be removed without causing damage to the rental place (e.g. new hot water heater, new air conditioner, new furniture), the tenant does not need to secure the permission of the landlord, the repaired or installed items remain the property of the tenant, and the tenant is responsible for returning the rental place to its original state (e.g. sealing holes) if the tenant leaves the rental place.

In any case where it may be unclear or difficult to remember who owns any given structure or item, tenant and landlord agree to clarify ownership in writing (see attached Form 3, "Property Ownership Agreement").

Rental Contract (continued)

<u>ข้อ 12 พฤติกรรมของผู้เช่า</u> ผู้เช่าต้องจัดการในบริเวณสถานที่เช่าอย่าให้มีสิ่ง สกปรกและมีกลิ่นเหม็น และไม่กระทำการอึกทึก จนคนอื่นได้รับความรำคาญปราศจากความปกติ สุข และไม่กระทำสิ่งใดๆ ที่น่าหวาดเสียวน่าจะเป็น อันตรายแก่ผู้อยู่ใกล้เคียง	<u>Clause 12. Tenant Behavior</u> The tenant must take proper care of the rental place and its surroundings, and not allow them to become messy, dirty or smelly. The tenant must not make noise that annoys anyone else. The tenant must not do anything which is offensive or dangerous to those nearby.
<u>ข้อ 13 การเช่าต่อ</u> ผู้เช่ารับว่าจะไม่ให้ผู้อื่นเช่าช่วงต่อไปอีกทอดหนึ่ง เว้นแต่จะได้รับอนุญาตจากเจ้าของบ้านเป็นลาย ลักษณ์อักษร (โปรดดูเอกสารเพิ่มเติมฉบับ 2 "ใบอนุญาต")	<u>Clause 13. Subletting</u> The tenant agrees not to sublet the rental place to any other person unless the tenant obtains written permission from the landlord (see attached Form 2, "Written Permission Form")
<u>ข้อ 14 กิจการค้าขาย</u> หากผู้เช่าต้องการใช้สถานที่เช่าด้วยจุดประสงค์ที่ ต่างไปจากตกลงไว้ในสัญญา (ตัวอย่างเช่น เปลี่ยนประเภทธุรกิจ) ผู้เช่าจะต้องได้รับอนุญาต จากเจ้าของบ้านเป็นลายลักษณ์อักษร (โปรดดู เอกสารเพิ่มเติมฉบับ 2 "ใบอนุญาต")	<u>Clause 14. Change of Purpose</u> If the tenant wishes to start using the rental place for a different purpose than the one written above in this contract (e.g. change of business type, moving into the rental place as a residence), the tenant must obtain written permission from the landlord (see attached Form 2, "Written Permission Form")
<u>ข้อ 15 การตรวจ</u> ผู้เช่ายินยอมให้เจ้าของบ้าน(หรือตัวแทน) เข้า สำรวจสถานที่เช่า ภายใน 48 ชั่วโมงหลังจาก เจ้าของบ้านได้แจ้งให้ทราบ	<u>Clause 15. Inspection</u> The tenant must allow the landlord (or a representative of the landlord) to enter and inspect the rental place and its premises within 48 hours of any request from the landlord (or representative).

<u>ข้อ 16 การผิดสัญญาของผู้เช่า</u> หากผู้เช่าทำผิดสัญญาไม่ว่าข้อใด ผู้เช่ายินยอมให้ เจ้าของบ้านยึดสถานที่คืน และยกเลิกสัญญาทันที	**Clause 16. Tenant Breach of Contract** If the tenant violates any clause of this contract, the tenant agrees that the landlord has the right to seize back the rental place and any rented items immediately, and the right to terminate the contract immediately.
<u>ข้อ 17 การผิดสัญญาของเจ้าของบ้าน</u> หากเจ้าของบ้านทำผิดสัญญาไม่ว่าข้อใด เจ้าของ บ้านยินยอมให้ผู้เช่าย้ายออก พร้อมทรัพย์สินของ ผู้เช่า โดยไม่ต้องจ่ายค่าเช่าเพิ่ม และผู้เช่ามีสิทธิ์ ยกเลิกสัญญาทันที	**Clause 17. Landlord Breach of Contract** If the landlord violates any clause of this contract, the landlord agrees that the tenant has the right to leave immediately with all the tenant's belongings, without making any more rent payments, and that the tenant has the right to terminate the contract immediately.
<u>ข้อ 18 การแปล</u> หากมีข้อขัดแย้งระหว่างสัญญาภาษาไทย และ ฉบับแปลภาษาอังกฤษ ให้ยึดฉบับภาษาไทยเป็น หลัก	**Clause 18. Translation** In the event of any dispute over differences in the English or Thai clauses of this contract, the Thai language clauses shall be authoritative.

Rental Contract (continued)

ข้อ 19 อื่นๆ	Clause 19. Other

ข้อ 20 การเซ็นชื่อ

ทั้งสองฝ่ายมีความเข้าใจในข้อสัญญานี้โดยตลอด
แล้ว จึงได้ลงลายมือไว้เป็นหลักฐาน

Clause 20. Signatures

Both parties have read and understood all
clauses of this contract and have signed
below as evidence of this.

เจ้าของบ้าน Landlord

    ลายเซ็น Signature _____

    (เขียนตัวบรรจง Print Name _____)

พยานของเจ้าของบ้าน Landlord's Witness

    ลายเซ็น Signature _____

    (เขียนตัวบรรจง Print Name _____)

ผู้เช่า Tenant

    ลายเซ็น Signature _____

    (เขียนตัวบรรจง Print Name _____)

พยานของผู้เช่า Tenant's Witness

    ลายเซ็น Signature _____

    (เขียนตัวบรรจง Print Name _____)

Rental Contract (continued)

ฟอร์ม 1 ใบเสร็จชำระค่าเช่า
ใช้ใบเสร็จนี้เป็นบันทึกหลักฐานการจ่ายค่าเช่า

Form 1. Rent Payment Receipts
Use these receipts to keep a written record of all rent payments.

เมื่อวันที่ On this day _____ เดือนที่ month _____ ค.ศ. year _____,

ผู้เช่า the tenant _____

ชำระค่าเช่าเป็นเงิน paid rent in the amount of _____ บาท baht

แก่เจ้าของบ้าน to the landlord _____.

     ลงชื่อผู้เช่า Tenant Signature _____

     ลงชื่อเจ้าของบ้าน Landlord Signature _____

เมื่อวันที่ On this day _____ เดือนที่ month _____ ค.ศ. year _____,

ผู้เช่า the tenant _____

ชำระค่าเช่าเป็นเงิน paid rent in the amount of _____ บาท baht

แก่เจ้าของบ้าน to the landlord _____.

     ลงชื่อผู้เช่า Tenant Signature _____

     ลงชื่อเจ้าของบ้าน Landlord Signature _____

เมื่อวันที่ On this day _____ เดือนที่ month _____ ค.ศ. year _____,

ผู้เช่า the tenant _____

ชำระค่าเช่าเป็นเงิน paid rent in the amount of _____ บาท baht

แก่เจ้าของบ้าน to the landlord _____.

     ลงชื่อผู้เช่า Tenant Signature _____

     ลงชื่อเจ้าของบ้าน Landlord Signature _____

เมื่อวันที่ On this day _____ เดือนที่ month _____ ค.ศ. year _____,

ผู้เช่า the tenant _____

ชำระค่าเช่าเป็นเงิน paid rent in the amount of _____ บาท baht

แก่เจ้าของบ้าน to the landlord _____.

     ลงชื่อผู้เช่า Tenant Signature _____

     ลงชื่อเจ้าของบ้าน Landlord Signature _____

ฟอร์ม 2 ใบอนุญาตเป็นลายลักษณ์อักษร **Form 2. Written Permission Form**

เจ้าของบ้านอนุญาตให้ผู้เช่าทำการต่อไปนี้ (เลือกกี่ข้อก็ได้)

☐ ปรับปรุงเปลี่ยนแปลงหรือซ่อมแซมสถานที่เช่า
☐ ให้ผู้อื่นเช่าต่อ
☐ ให้ผู้เช่าใช้สถานที่เช่าเพื่อวัตถุประสงค์ที่ต่างออกไป(ตัวอย่างเช่น เช่าเพื่อธุรกิจ)
ดังรายละเอียดต่อไปนี้

The landlord hereby gives written permission to the tenant to do the following in the rental place (check all that apply, on the left):

* make a permanent repair or improvement
* sublet the place to others
* use the rental place for a new purpose (e.g. business)

with the following specific details:

_____   _____
_____   _____
_____   _____
_____   _____
_____   _____
_____   _____
_____   _____
_____   _____
_____   _____
_____   _____

เจ้าของบ้าน Landlord
     ลายเซ็น Signature _____
     (เขียนตัวบรรจง Print Name _____)
พยานของเจ้าของบ้าน Landlord's Witness
     ลายเซ็น Signature _____
     (เขียนตัวบรรจง Print Name _____)

ผู้เช่า Tenant
     ลายเซ็น Signature _____
     (เขียนตัวบรรจง Print Name _____)
พยานของผู้เช่า Tenant's Witness
     ลายเซ็น Signature _____
     (เขียนตัวบรรจง Print Name _____)

Rental Contract (continued)

ฟอร์ม 3 ความเป็นเจ้าของในทรัพย์สิน | Form 3. Property Ownership Agreement

ใช้แบบฟอร์มนี้เพื่อความชัดเจน ในความเป็น
เจ้าของทรัพย์สินที่ผู้เช่านำติดมาด้วย ซ่อมแซม
หรือต่อเติมในสถานที่เช่า

Use this form when you wish to make it clear
who owns a structure or item which the
tenant has brought into, installed in, or
repaired in the rental place.

รายละเอียดสิ่งของ Item Description	เป็นของ เจ้าของบ้าน Belongs to Landlord	เป็นของ ผู้เช่า Belongs to Tenant
	☐	☐
	☐	☐
	☐	☐
	☐	☐
	☐	☐
	☐	☐
	☐	☐
	☐	☐

เจ้าของบ้าน Landlord

    ลายเซ็น Signature _____

    (เขียนตัวบรรจง Print Name _____)

พยานของเจ้าของบ้าน Landlord's Witness

    ลายเซ็น Signature _____

    (เขียนตัวบรรจง Print Name _____)

ผู้เช่า Tenant

    ลายเซ็น Signature _____

    (เขียนตัวบรรจง Print Name _____)

พยานของผู้เช่า Tenant's Witness

    ลายเซ็น Signature _____

    (เขียนตัวบรรจง Print Name _____)

Visa Application Form

<table>
<tr><td>

Please attach
2 photographs
taken within
the last 6 months
(3.5 x 4.5 cm)

</td><td>

APPLICATION FOR VISA
Ministry of Foreign Affairs of Thailand

</td><td>

Please Indicate Type of Visa Requested

☐ Diplomatic Visa
☐ Official Visa
☐ Courtesy Visa
☐ Non-Immigrant Visa
☐ Tourist Visa
☐ Transit Visa

Number of Entries Requested _____

</td></tr>
</table>

☐ Mr. ☐ Mrs. ☐ Miss _____

      First Name   Middle Name   Family Name (in BLOCK letters)

Former Name *(if any)*_____

Nationality_____

Nationality at Birth _____

Birth Place_____ Marital Status_____

Date of Birth _____

Type of Travel Document _____

No. _____ Issued at _____

Date of Issue _____ Expiry Date_____

Occupation *(specify present position and name of employer)*

_____

_____

Current Address _____

_____

Tel. _____ E-mail _____

Permanent Address *(if different from above)* _____

_____

_____

Tel. _____

Names, dates and places of birth of minor children *(if accompanying)*

_____

_____

Date of Arrival in Thailand _____

Traveling by _____

      Flight No. or Vessel's name _____

Duration of Proposed Stay _____

Date of Previous Visit to Thailand _____

Purpose of Visit: ☐ Tourism ☐ Transit
      ☐ Business ☐ Diplomatic/Official
      ☐ Other *(please specify)* _____

mfavisaform10093007

Countries for which travel document is valid
_____

Proposed Address in Thailand _____

_____

_____

Name and Address of Local Guarantor
_____

_____

Tel./Fax._____

Name and Address of Guarantor in Thailand
_____

_____

Tel./Fax._____

I hereby declare that I will not request any refund from my paid visa fee even if my application has been declined.

Signature _____ Date _____

Attention for Tourist and Transit Visas Applicants
I hereby declare that the purpose of my visit to Thailand is for pleasure or transit only and that in no case shall I engage myself in any profession or occupation while in the country.

Signature _____ **Date** _____

FOR OFFICIAL USE

Application/Reference No._____

Visa No. _____

Type of Visa:
☐ Diplomatic Visa   ☐ Official Visa   ☐ Courtesy Visa
☐ Non-Immigrant Visa ☐ Tourist Visa ☐ Transit Visa

Category of Visa: _____

Number of Entries:
☐ Single ☐ Double ☐ Multiple ☐ ___ Entries

Date of Issue _____ Fee _____

Expiry Date _____

Documents Submitted _____

_____

Authorized Signature and Seal _____

Suggested Websites

The following are websites that we suggest for further information and where to get help. Most of them are either in English or in both Thai and English. Please note that we do not endorse any of these sites and have not received any benefits by listing them here.

www.thailandtips.com – Expat tips and resources on successful living, working and retiring in Thailand.

www.ethailand.com – Tips for living in Thailand and forum discussions.

www.ajarn.com – A web guide to teaching English and living in Thailand and forum discussions.

www.lawyerthai.com – A popular blog site for Thai lawyers. There are forums in English as well. Various legal forms in Thai can be downloaded.

www.lawyerscouncil.or.th – The site for Lawyers Council of Thailand. Legal questions can be emailed in Thai to legalaid@lawyerscouncil.or.th.

www.thailandqa.com – There are different forums that you can post questions about Thailand and get responses from forum members some of whom have experience in specific subjects.

www.thaivisa.com – Contains information you need to know about visas, work permits and other useful information. There are also forums where you can post your questions.

www.farangthai.com.au – A forum website based in Australia which has various forums for members.

www.thaifoodandstuff.com – A website that sells books on Thailand and other stuff. The site is based in Australia.

www.bangkokbag.com – Budget apartment guide for property rental in Bangkok from 5,000 baht to 30,000 baht. Email: info@bangkokbag.com

www.bangkok.angloinfo.com – The local business directory of English-speaking businesses and services in Bangkok.

www.stickmanbangkok.com – A guide for living and working in Bangkok.

www.uscis.gov – U.S. government website for citizenship and immigration services and official forms.

www.immigration.go.th – The Thai Immigration Bureau's official website.

www.royalthaipolice.go.th – The Royal Thai Police official government website.

www.thaiembdc.org – The official website of the Royal Thai Embassy in Washington D.C.

www.thai-la.net – The official website of the Royal Thai Consulate General in Los Angeles where you can find out about visas for Thailand and services for Thai citizens overseas.

www.eppo.go.th/index_thaigov-T.html – A listing with links to royal Thai embassies and consulates worldwide.

www.bangkwang.net – Information on Bangkwang, Thailand's central, high-security prison for men.

www.thaiprisonlife.com – The most informative website on the Thai prison system written in English.

www.childprotection.or.th – Child Protection Foundation website.

www.pavena.thai.com – The website for a non-profit foundation for children and women.

www.lawamendment.go.th – A collection of the major legal websites in Thai.

www.buddhanet.net – A non-profit organization committed to the Buddha's teachings and lifestyle.

www.airportthai.co.th – Airport of Thailand's official website with information on arrival and departure times and important airport phone numbers.

www.mots.go.th – The official website for the Ministry of Tourism and Sports.

www.touristassistancecenter.go.th – The official website for assisting tourists, available in Thai, English and Chinese.

www.correct.go.th – The website of the Department of Corrections, Ministry of Justice.

www.translation-academy.com – Specializing in legal document translation for Thai, English, French, Chinese, Japanese, German and Spanish languages.

www.touristpolice.net – Links to many useful travel advice websites.

www.tourismthailand.org – The official website for tourism in Thailand.

www.hg.org/firms-thailand.html – Listing of law firms in Thailand.

Reference Books and Websites

Reference Books **หนังสืออ้างอิง**

1. Dr. Jiranit Hawanon, *Legal Profession*, Eighth Printing 2006, Ramkhamhaeng University Press.

ดร. จิรนิติ หะวานนท์, หลักวิชาชีพนักกฎหมาย, พิมพ์ครั้งที่ 8 พ.ศ. 2549, สำนักพิมพ์มหาวิทยาลัยรามคำแหง.

2. Surachai Suwannapricha, *Lawyer Practice*, Third Printing 2006, Ramkhamhaeng University Press.

สุรชัย สุวรรณปริชา, การว่าความ, พิมพ์ครั้งที่ 3 พ.ศ. 2549, สำนักพิมพ์มหาวิทยาลัยรามคำแหง.

3. Dr. Somchai Kasitpradit, *Civil and Commercial Code: Family*, Second Printing 2005, Ramkhamhaeng University Press.

รศ. ดร. สมชาย กษิติประดิษฐ์, กฎหมายแพ่งและพาณิชย์ว่าด้วยครอบครัว, พิมพ์ครั้งที่ 2 พ.ศ. 2548, สำนักพิมพ์มหาวิทยาลัยรามคำแหง.

4. Uthai Suppanit, *How to Be a Lawyer Manual*, Fourth Printing 1990, Ramkhamhaeng University Press.

อุทัย ศุภนิตย์, คู่มือการเป็นทนายว่าความ, พิมพ์ครั้งที่ 4 พ.ศ. 2533, สำนักพิมพ์มหาวิทยาลัยรามคำแหง.

5. Uthai Suppanit, *A Miscellany of Criminal Law*, Second Printing 2006, Buddit Aksorn Publishing.

สมศักดิ์ เอี่ยมพลับใหญ่, เกร็ดกฎหมายอาญา, พิมพ์ครั้งที่ 2 พ.ศ. 2549, สำนักพิมพ์บัณฑิตอักษร.

6. Steven H. Gifis, *Law Dictionary*, Third Edition 1991, Barron's Educational Series, Inc.

สตีเว่น เอช กิฟิส, พจนานุกรมกฎหมาย, แก้ไขปรับปรุงครั้งที่ 3 พ.ศ. 2534, บริษัทบาร์รอน เอดูเคชั่น ซีรีส์.

7. Assist. Prof. Kamthorn Kamprasert and Assist. Prof. Sumate Jarnpradap, *Thai Legal History and Major Legal System*, 1990, Ramkhamhaeng University Press.

รศ.กำธร กำประเสริฐ และ รศ.สุเมธ จานประดับ, ประวัติศาสตร์กฎหมายไทยและระบบกฎหมายหลัก, พ.ศ. 2533, สำนักพิมพ์มหาวิทยาลัยรามคำแหง.

Reference Websites เว็บไซท์อ้างอิง

www.royalthaipolice.go.th   www.immigration.go.th

www.bangkwang.net   www.pavena.thai.com

www.buddhanet.net   www.mots.go.th

www.thaiprisonlife.com   www.lawyerthai.com

www.lawyerscouncil.or.th   www.mfa.go.th

www.wikipedia.org

Further Reading

Baker, Chris and Phongpaichit, Pasuk. *A History of Thailand*
Cambridge University Press, 2005.

Becker, Benjawan Poomsan. *Speak Like a Thai: Volumes 1—5*
Bangkok: Paiboon Publishing, 2007.

Bryce, Philip. *How to Buy Land and Build a House in Thailand*
Bangkok: Paiboon Publishing, 2006.

Clift, Elayne. *Achan: A Year of Teaching in Thailand*. Bangkok
Bangkok Book House, 2007.

Cooper, Robert and Nanthapa. *Culture Shock! Thailand*
Singapore: Times Books International, 2005.

Cooper, Robert. *Thais Mean Business: The Expat's Guide to Doing
Business in Thailand*
Singapore: Marshall Cavendish, 2004.

Pirazzi, Chris and Vasant, Vitida. *Thailand Fever: A Road Map for
Thai-Western Relationships*
Bangkok: Paiboon Publishing, 2004.

The Thai Red Cross Society. *Healthy Living in Thailand*
Bangkok: Asia Books, 2001.

Wylie, Philip. *How to Establish a Successful Business in Thailand*
Bangkok: Paiboon Publishing, 2007.

Glossary

ประมวลคำศัพท์

absolute monarchy	สมบูรณาญาสิทธิราชย์	sŏm-buu-ra-naa-yaa-sĭt-tí-râat
accident	อุบัติเหตุ	ù-bàt-dti-hèet
act (n.)	การกระทำ, พระราชบัญญัติ	gaan-grà-tam, prá-râat-chá-ban-yàt
adoption	การรับบุตรบุญธรรม	gaan-ráp-bùt-bun-tam
afford (v.)	สามารถว่าจ้างได้	săa-mâat-wâa-jâang-dâai
agreement	ข้อตกลง	kɔ̂ɔ-dtòk-long
rental agreement	สัญญาเช่า	săn-yaa-châo
alimony	ค่าเลี้ยงดู	kâa-líang-duu
allegation	ข้อกล่าวหา	kɔ̂ɔ-glàao-hăa
appeal (v.)	อุทธรณ์	ù-tɔɔn
appearance	การปรากฏตัว	gaan-bpraa-gòt-dtua
appointment	การนัดหมาย, การแต่งตั้ง	gaam-nát-măai, gaan-dtɛ̀ng-dtâng
apprehend	จับกุม	jàp-gum
approval	การอนุมัติ	gaan-à-nú-mát
arbitration	การอนุญาโตตุลาการ	gaan-à-nú-yaa-dtoo-dtù-laa-gaan
arbitrator	อนุญาโตตุลาการ	à-nú-yaa-dtoo-dtù-laa-gaan
arrest (n.)	การจับกุม	gaan-jàp-gum
arson	การลอบวางเพลิง	gaan-lɔ̂ɔp-waang-pləəng
assault (n.)	การทำร้าย	gaan-tam-ráai
assets	ทรัพย์สิน	sáp-sĭn
assistance	ความช่วยเหลือ	kwaam-chûai-lʉ̆a
attorney	ทนายความ	tá-naai-kwaam
attorney general	อัยการสูงสุด	ai-ya-gaan-sŭung-sùt
autopsy	การชันสูตรศพ	gaan-chan-ná-sùut-sòp
bail (n.)	การประกันตัว	gaan-bprà-gan-dtua
to post bail	ประกันตัว	bprà-gan-dtua
bailiff	จ่าศาล	jàa-săan

bailsman	นายประกัน	naai-bprà-gan
balance of power	การคานอำนาจ	gaan-kaan-am-nâat
bank account	บัญชีธนาคาร	ban-chii tá-naa-kaan
bankruptcy	การล้มละลาย	gaan-lóm-lá-laai
bench (in court)	บัลลังก์	ban-lang
beyond a reasonable doubt	โดยไม่มีข้อกังขาใดๆ	dooi-mâi-mii kɔ̂ɔ-gang-kǎa dai-dai
bill	การร่างกฎหมาย	gaan-râang-gòt-mǎai
bond	ค่าประกันตัว, พันธบัตร	kâa-bprà-gan-dtua, pan-tá-bàt
branch	ฝ่าย, สาขา	fàai, sǎa-kǎa
executive branch	ฝ่ายบริหาร	fàai-bɔɔ-ri-hǎan
legislative branch	ฝ่ายนิติบัญญัติ	fàai-ní-dtì-ban-yàt
judicial branch	ฝ่ายตุลาการ	fàai-dtù-laa-gaan
bribe	สินบน	sĭn-bon
budget	งบประมาณ	ngóp-bprà-maan
case	คดี	ká-dii
civil case	คดีแพ่ง	ká-dii-pêng
criminal case	คดีอาญา	ká-dii-aa-yaa
certificate	ใบรับรอง	bai-ráp-rɔɔng
birth certificate	สูติบัตร	sŭu-dtì-bàt
death certificate	มรณบัตร	mɔɔ-rá-ná-bàt
divorce certificate	ใบหย่า	bai-yàa
marriage certificate	ใบทะเบียนสมรส	bai-tá-bian-sŏm-rót
name change certificate	ใบเปลี่ยนชื่อ	bai-bplìan-chʉ̂ʉ
cheating	การฉ้อโกง	gaan-chɔ̂ɔ-goong
child support	ค่าเลี้ยงดูบุตร	kâa-líang-duu-bùt
citizen	พลเมือง	pon-la-mʉang
citizen I.D. card	บัตรประชาชน	bàt-bprà-chaa-chon
citizenship	การเป็นพลเมือง	gaan-bpen-pon-la-mʉang
claim (n.)	การเรียกร้อง	gaan-rîak-rɔ́ɔng
claim (v.)	อ้าง, เรียกร้อง	âang, rîak-rɔ́ɔng

client	ลูกความ	lûuk-kwaam
coalition government	รัฐบาลผสม	rát-ta-baan-pà-sŏm
code	ประมวล	bprà-muan
civil code	ประมวลกฎหมายแพ่ง	bprà-muan-gòt-mǎai pêng
criminal code	ประมวลกฎหมายอาญา	bprà-muan-gòt-mǎai aa-yaa
coffin	หีบศพ	hǐip-sòp
commit a crime	ก่ออาชญากรรม	gɔ̀ɔ àat-cha-yaa-gam
committee	คณะกรรมการ	ká-ná-gam-ma-gaan
complaint	การร้องทุกข์	gaan-rɔ́ɔng-túk
compromise	ประนีประนอม, ยอมความ	bprà-nii-bprà-nɔɔm, yɔɔm-kwaam
confiscate	ยึด, ริบ	yút, ríp
confess	สารภาพ	sǎa-rá-pâap
confinement	การกักขัง, การจองจำ	gaan-gàk-kǎng, gaan-jɔɔng-jam
conflict	ความขัดแย้ง	kwaam-kàt-yɛ́ɛng
consent (n.)	ความยินยอม	kwaam-yin-yɔɔm
conspire	สมรู้ร่วมคิด	sŏm-rúu-rûam-kít
constitution	รัฐธรรมนูญ	rát-tà-tam-ma-nuun
consultant	ที่ปรึกษา	fii-bprèk-sǎa
contract	สัญญา, ข้อตกลง	sǎn-yaa, kɔ̂ɔ-dtòk-long
convict (v.)	ลงโทษ	long-tôot
convict (n.)	นักโทษ	nák-tôot
copyright	ลิขสิทธิ์	lík-kà-sìt
council	สภา	sà-paa
count (n.)	กระทง	grà-tong
counterclaim	ฟ้องกลับ	fɔ́ɔng-glàp
coup d'etat	รัฐประหาร	rát-tà-bprà-hǎan
court	ศาล	sǎan
administrative court	ศาลปกครอง	sǎan-bpòk-krɔɔng
constitution court	ศาลรัฐธรรมนูญ	sǎan-rát-tà-tam-ma-nuun
military court	ศาลทหาร	sǎan-tá-hǎan

court of justice	ศาลยุติธรรม	sǎan-yú-dtì-tam
court of first instance	ศาลชั้นต้น	sǎan-chán-dtôn
appeal court	ศาลอุทธรณ์	sǎn-ù-tɔɔn
supreme court	ศาลฎีกา	sǎan-dii-gaa
court clerk	เสมียนศาล	sà-mǐan-sǎan
courthouse	ศาล	sǎan
creditor	เจ้าหนี้	jâo-nîi
crime (n.)	อาชญากรรม	àat-chá-yaa-gam
custody	การคุมตัว, การดูแล	gaan-kum-dtua, gaan-duu-lɛɛ
in custody	ถูกคุมตัว	tùuk kum-dtua
debtor	ลูกหนี้	lûuk-nîi
declare	ประกาศ	bprà-gàat
defamation	การทำให้เสียชื่อเสียง	gaan-tam-hâi-sǐa-chûɯ-sǐang
defend (v.)	แก้ต่าง	gɛ̂ɛ-dtàang
defendant	จำเลย	jam-ləəi
co-defendant	จำเลยร่วม	jam-ləəi-rûam
democracy	ประชาธิปไตย	bprà-chaa-típ-bpà-dtai
department	กรม	grom
Department of Consular Affairs	กรมการกงสุล	grom-gaan-gong-sǔn
deportation	การส่งตัวกลับประเทศ	gaan-sòng-dtua-glàp-bprà-têet
dismiss	ยกฟ้อง	yók-fɔ́ɔng
dispute (n.)	ข้อพิพาท	kɔ̂ɔ-pí-pâat
divorce (n.)	การหย่าร้าง	gaan-yàa-ráang
document	เอกสาร	èek-gà-sǎan
domestic violence	ความรุนแรงในครอบครัว	kwaam-run-rɛɛng-nai-krɔ̂ɔp-krua
dowry	สินสอด	sǐn-sɔ̀ɔt
driver's license	ใบขับขี่	bai-kàp-kǐi
dynasty	ราชวงศ์	râat-cha-wong
engagement	การหมั้น	gaan-mân
embassy	สถานทูต	sà-tǎan-tûut

embezzlement	การยักยอก	gaan-yák-yɔ̂ɔk
ethics	จรรยาบรรณ, มารยาท	jan-yaa-ban, maan-rá-yâat
event	เหตุการณ์	hèet-gaan
evidence	หลักฐาน	làk-tăan
examination (witness)	การซักถาม (พยาน)	gaan-sák-tăam (pá-yaan)
cross-examination	การถามค้าน	gaan-tăam-káan
direct-examination	การซักถาม	gaan-sák-tăam
re-direct examination	การถามติง	gaan-tăam-dting
expulsion	การเนรเทศ	gaan-nee-rá-têet
fact	ข้อเท็จจริง	kɔ̂ɔ-tét-jing
factual basis	มูลเหตุ	muun-hèet
faculty of law	คณะนิติศาสตร์	ká-ná-ní-dtĭ-sàat
fee	ค่าธรรมเนียม	kâa-tam-niam
felony	ความผิดอาญาร้ายแรง	kwaam-pĭt-aa-yaa-ráai-rɛɛng
fine (n.)	ค่าปรับ	kâa-bpràp
fingerprint	ลายนิ้วมือ	laai-níu-mɯɯ
firearms	อาวุธปืน	aa-wút-bpɯɯn
forensic	นิติเวช	ní-dtĭ-wêet
fraud	การฉ้อโกง	gaan-chɔ̂ɔ-goong
government	รัฐบาล	rát-ta-baan
government official	ข้าราชการ	kâa-râat-cha-gaan
ground	มูลเหตุ	muun-hèet
guilty	ผิด	pĭt
handcuff (n.)	กุญแจมือ	gun-jɛɛ-mɯɯ
harm (n.)	การทำร้าย	gaan-tam-ráai
heir	ทายาท	taa-yâat
House of Representatives	สภาผู้แทนราษฎร	sà-paa-pûu-tɛɛn-râat-sa-dɔɔn
house registration	ทะเบียนบ้าน	tá-bian-bâan
I.D.	บัตรประจำตัว	bàt-bprà-jam-dtua
illegal	ผิดกฎหมาย	pĭt-gòt-măai

immigrant	คนเข้าเมือง	kon-kâo-mɯang
immigration	การเข้าเมือง	gaan-kâo-mɯang
impartial	ไม่ลำเอียง, ยุติธรรม	mâi-lam-iang, yút-dtì-tam
imprisonment	การจำคุก	gaan-jam-kúk
infringement	การฝ่าฝืนกฎ	gaan-fàa-fɯɯn-gòt
injury	การบาดเจ็บ	gaan-bàat-jèp
innocent	บริสุทธิ์	bɔɔ-rí-sùt
institution	สถาบัน	sà-tăa-ban
intent	เจตนา	jèet-dtà-naa
interpret	แปล, เป็นล่าม	bplɛɛ, bpen-lâam
interpreter	ล่าม	lâam
investigation	การสืบสวน	gaan-sɯ̀ɯp-sŭan
investigator	ผู้สืบสวน	pûu-sɯ̀ɯp-sŭan
investment	การลงทุน	gaan-long-tun
jail	คุก	kúk
jailer	พัศดี	pát-sà-dii
judge	ผู้พิพากษา	pûu-pí-pâak-săa
judgment	คำตัดสิน	kam-dtàt-sĭn
judicial	เกี่ยวกับศาลยุติธรรม	gìao-gàp-săan-yút-dtì-tam
jurisdiction	อำนาจศาล	am-nâat-săan
juristic person	นิติบุคคล	ní-dtì-bùk-kon
justice	ความยุติธรรม	kwaam-yút-dtì-tam
juvenile	เยาวชน	yao-wá-chon
labor	แรงงาน	rɛɛng-ngaan
land deed	โฉนดที่ดิน	chà-nòot-fii-din
landlord	เจ้าของที่ดิน, เจ้าของบ้าน	jâo-kɔ̆ɔng-fii-din, jâo-kɔ̆ɔng-bâan
law	กฎหมาย	gòt-măai
code law	กฎหมายประมวล	gòt-măai bprà-muan
customary law	กฎหมายจารีตประเพณี	gòt-măai jaa-rîit-bprà-pee-nii
lawsuit	คดีความ	ká-dii-kwaam

lawyer	ทนายความ	tá-naai-kwaam
Lawyers Council	สภาทนายความ	sà-paa-tá-naai-kwaam
legal	ถูกกฎหมาย	tùuk-gòt-mǎai
legal advice	คำแนะนำด้านกฎหมาย	kam-né-nam-taang-gòt-mǎai
legal process	ขั้นตอนทางกฎหมาย	kân-dtɔɔn-taang-gòt-mǎai
legal system	ระบบกฎหมาย	rá-bòp-gòt-mǎai
legitimate	ชอบด้วยกฎหมาย	chɔ̂ɔp-dûai-gòt-mǎai
lethal injection	การฉีดยาพิษ	gaan-chìit-yaa-pít
letter of certification	หนังสือรับรอง	nǎng-sǔu-ráp-rɔɔng
letter of consent	หนังสือยินยอม	nǎng-sǔu-yin-yɔɔm
liability	หนี้ตามกฎหมาย	nîi-dtaam-gòt-mǎai
manslaughter	การฆาตกรรมโดยไม่ได้ไตร่ตรอง	gaan-kâat-dta-gam dooi-mâi-dâai dtrài-dtrɔɔng
marijuana	กัญชา	gan-chaa
marriage	การสมรส	gaan-sǒm-rót
mediator	ผู้ไกล่เกลี่ย, ผู้เจรจา	pûu-glài-glìa, pûu-jee-ra-jaa
Member of Parliament	สมาชิกสภาผู้แทนราษฎร	sà-maa-chík sà-paa-pûu-tɛɛn râat-sa-dɔɔn
methamphetamine	ยาบ้า	yaa-bâa
military	การทหาร	gaan-tá-hǎan
minister	รัฐมนตรี	rát-ta-mon-dtrii
ministry	กระทรวง	grà-suang
Ministry of Justice	กระทรวงยุติธรรม	grà-suang-yút-dtì-tam
minor	ผู้เยาว์	pûu-yao
misdemeanor	ลหุโทษ	lá-hù-tôot
murder	การฆาตกรรม	gaan-kâat-dtà-gam
nationality	สัญชาติ	sǎn-châat
oath	คำสาบาน	kam-sǎa-baan
offense	การกระทำผิด	gaan-grà-tam-pìt
officer	เจ้าหน้าที่	jâo-nâa-tîi
order	คำสั่ง	kam-sàng

orphanage	สถานเลี้ยงเด็กกำพร้า	sà-tăan-líang-dèk-gam-práa
parliament	รัฐสภา	rát-ta-sà-paa
penalty	โทษ	tôot
perjury	การเบิกความเท็จ	gaan-bə̀ək-kwaam-tét
period	ระยะ	rá-yá
plaintiff	โจทก์	jòot
plead	ตอบข้อกล่าวหา	dtɔ̀ɔp-kɔ̂ɔ-glàao-hăa
police	ตำรวจ	dtam-rùat
political party	พรรคการเมือง	pák-gaan-mʉang
politician	นักการเมือง	nák-gaan-mʉang
politics	การเมือง	gaan-mʉang
pornography	ภาพลามก	pâap-laa-mók
child pornography	ภาพลามกเด็ก	pâap-laa-mók-dèk
possession	การครอบครอง	gaan-krɔ̂ɔp-krɔɔng
power	อำนาจ	am-nâat
power of attorney	การมอบอำนาจ	gaan-mɔ̂ɔp-am-nâat
prenuptial agreement	สัญญาก่อนสมรส	săn-yaa-gɔ̀ɔn-sŏm-rót
prime minister	นายกรัฐมนตรี	naa-yók-rát-ta-mon-dtrii
prison	คุก, เรือนจำ	kúk, rʉan-jam
private	ส่วนตัว, เอกชน	sùan-dtua, èek-ga-chon
probation	การภาคทัณฑ์	gaan-pâak-tan
procedure	ขั้นตอน, กระบวนการ	kân-dtɔɔn, grà-buan-gaan
process (n.)	ขั้นตอน	kân-dtɔɔn
promulgate	ประกาศใช้	bprà-gàat-chái
property	ทรัพย์สิน	sáp-sĭn
common property	ทรัพย์สินส่วนรวม	sáp-sĭn-sùan-ruam
personal property	ทรัพย์สินส่วนตัว	sáp-sĭn-sùan-dtua
prosecutor	อัยการ	ai-ya-gaan
prostitute	โสเภณี	sŏo-pee-nii
prostitution	การค้าประเวณี	gaan-káa-bprà-wee-nii

public	สาธารณะ	săa-taa-ra-ná
punishment	การลงโทษ	gaan-long-tôot
capital punishment	การลงโทษประหารชีวิต	gaan-long-tôot bprà-hăan-chii-wít
qualification	คุณสมบัติ	kun-na-sŏm-bàt
rape (n.)	การข่มขืน, การกระทำชำเรา	gaan-kòm-kŭɯn
gang rape	การโทรมหญิง	gaan-soom-yĭng
record (n., v.)	บันทึก, การบันทึก	ban-túk, gaan-ban-túk
register	จดทะเบียน, ลงทะเบียน	jòt-ta-bian, long-ta-bian
register one's marriage	จดทะเบียนสมรส	jòt-ta-bian sŏm-rót
regulation	กฎระเบียบ, ข้อบังคับ	gòt-rá-bĭap, kɔ̂ɔ-bang-káp
reign (n.)	รัชสมัย, รัชกาล	rát-cha-sà-măi, rát-cha-gaan
reign (v.)	ครองราษฎร์, ครองแผ่นดิน	krɔɔng-râat, krɔɔng-pèn-din
renounce	สละ	sà-là
rent (n.)	การเช่า, ค่าเช่า	gaan-châo, kâa-châo
resolution	ข้อยุติ, การแก้ปัญหา	kɔ̂ɔ-yú-dtì, gaan-gɛ̂ɛ-bpan-hăa
restriction	ข้อจำกัด	kɔ̂ɔ-jam-gàt
retainer fee	ค่าทนายความ	kâa-tá-naai-kwaam
revolution	การปฏิวัติ	gaan-bpà-dtì-wát
revoke (v.)	ยกเลิก, เพิกถอน	yók-lə̂ək, pə̂ək-tŏɔn
right (n.)	สิทธิ	sìt, sìt-tí
robbery	การโจรกรรม	gaan-joon-ra-gam
rule (n.)	กฎ	gòt
rule (v.)	ปกครอง	bpòk-krɔɔng
scam	กลโกง	gon-goong
senator	วุฒิสมาชิก	wút-tí-sà-maa-chík
sentencing	การตัดสินลงโทษ	gaan-dtàt-sĭn-long-tôot
social rank	ชั้นในสังคม	chán-nai-săng-kom
spouse	คู่สมรส, คู่ครอง	kûu-sŏm-rót, kûu-krɔɔng
statue of limitations	อายุความ	aa-yú-kwaam
state enterprise	รัฐวิสาหกิจ	rát-wí-săa-hà-gìt

status	สถานภาพ	sà-tǎa-ná-pâap
structure	โครงสร้าง	kroong-sâang
subpoena	หมายศาล, หมายเรียก	mǎai-sǎan, mǎai-rîak
sue	ฟ้อง	fɔ́ɔng
summons	หมายเรียก	mǎai-rîak
suspect	ผู้ต้องสงสัย	pûu-dtɔ̂ng-sǒng-sǎi
system	ระบบ	rá-bòp
tax	ภาษี	paa-sǐi
temporary release	การปล่อยตัวชั่วคราว	gaan-bplɔ̀i-dtua-chûa-kraao
tenant	ผู้เช่า	pûu-châo
testator	ผู้ทำพินัยกรรม	pûu-tam-pí-nai-gam
territory	อาณาเขต	aa-naa-kèet
testify	ให้การ, เบิกความ	hâi-gaan, bə̀ək-kwaam
testimony	คำให้การ	kam-hâi-gaan
theft	การลักทรัพย์	gaan-lák-sáp
trade (n.)	การค้า	gaan-káa
traffic	จราจร	jà-raa-jɔɔn
transfer	โอน	oon
translate	แปล	bplɛɛ
translator	ผู้แปล	pûu-bplɛɛ
trespassing	การบุกรุก	gaan-bùk-rúk
truth	ความจริง	kwaam-jing
underage	อายุต่ำกว่าเกณฑ์	aa-yú-dtàm-gwàa-geen
verdict	คำพิพากษา	kam-pí-pâak-sǎa
victim	ผู้เสียหาย, เหยื่อ	pûu-sǐa-hǎai, yùa
warrant	หมาย, หมายจับ, หมายเรียก	mǎai, mǎai-jàp, mǎai-rîak
wedding ceremony	พิธีสมรส	pí-tii-sǒm-rót
will (n.)	พินัยกรรม	pí-nai-gam
witness	พยาน	pá-yaan
work permit	ใบอนุญาตทำงาน	bai-à-nú-yáat tam-ngaan

About the Authors

©Asia Pacific Media Services

Benjawan Poomsan Becker is a renowned Thai and Lao translator and interpreter in the U.S. with the company Thai & Lao Language Services that she founded in 1996. As a registered court interpreter, she has worked with the Judicial Council of California for over ten years. Benjawan has written more than a dozen books for foreigners to learn the Thai and Lao languages. She has translated hundreds of legal documents from English to Thai and Thai to English. Benjawan splits her time during the year between Northern California and Bangkok, Thailand.

Roengsak Thongkaew is well known in Northeastern Thailand as a trial lawyer for the local people. He graduated from the Department of Law at Ramkhamhaeng University. While at University he was the president of many clubs. Before starting his own law firm, he worked in Bangkok for three years for a law firm specializing in assisting foreigners. He also had his own call-in radio show for people to ask legal questions. Roengsak is now the President of the Lawyers' Council of Yasothon Province which provides free legal advice.

สารบัญ

ส่วนที่ 2

จากทางสำนักพิมพ์

ทางสำนักพิมพ์ไพบูลย์ได้รับคำร้องและข้อเสนอแนะจากผู้อ่านของเราให้จัดพิมพ์
หนังสือเกี่ยวกับกฎหมายไทยที่เป็นประโยชน์และเข้าใจง่ายสำหรับบุคคลทั่วไป   เราจึงได้
จัดพิมพ์หนังสือกฎหมายไทยสำหรับชาวต่างชาติขึ้น   ตามร้านหนังสือทั่วไปยังไม่ค่อยมี
หนังสือภาษาอังกฤษที่อธิบายกฎหมายไทยเป็นภาษาชาวบ้านที่ตอบคำถามต่างๆเกี่ยวกับ
กฎหมายเบื้องต้น   หนังสือส่วนใหญ่ของสำนักพิมพ์ไพบูลย์เป็นหนังสือที่ให้ชาวต่างชาติ
เรียนภาษาไทยหรือไม่ก็เกี่ยวกับความสัมพันธ์ของชาวไทยและชาวตะวันตกในด้าน
วัฒนธรรมไทยและหนังสือคู่มือเกี่ยวกับการพักอาศัยในประเทศไทยในแง่มุมต่างๆ   เราได้
จัดพิมพ์กฎหมายไทยสำหรับชาวต่างชาติขึ้นด้วยความมั่นใจว่าหนังสือเล่มนี้จะให้ประโยชน์
กับชาวต่างชาติและองค์กรต่างๆที่ให้ความช่วยเหลือชาวต่างชาติในประเทศไทยเป็นอย่าง
มาก

ขอเรียนให้ทราบกฎหมายต่างๆที่นำเสนอในหนังสือเล่มนี้อาจมีการเปลี่ยนแปลง
บ้างหลังจากวันที่ตีพิมพ์   ข้อมูลความคิดเห็น   บทสรุปต่างๆที่อยู่ในหนังสืออาจไม่ทันต่อ
เหตุการณ์ปัจจุบัน ดังนั้นก่อนที่คุณผู้อ่านจะเริ่มดำเนินการทางด้านกฎหมายใดๆ   ควรจะ
ตรวจดูความถูกต้องของข้อมูลที่อยู่ในหนังสือว่าตรงกับหน่วยงานที่เกี่ยวข้องหรือไม่   คุณ
อาจจะปรึกษากับผู้ที่เชี่ยวชาญด้านนั้นๆด้วย   สถานการณ์และเรื่องราวของแต่ละคนไม่
เหมือนกัน จึงจำเป็นต้องดัดแปลงพลิกแพลงเนื้อหาให้เข้ากับกาละเทศะ เรื่องของกฎหมาย
เป็นเรื่องที่ซับซ้อนและเข้าใจยาก   เป็นสิ่งไม่ง่ายนักที่จะเขียนเป็นภาษาที่ชัดเจนและอ่าน
เข้าใจได้ง่าย เราไม่สามารถที่จะให้ข้อมูล ในแต่ละหัวข้อได้อย่างละเอียด จุดประสงค์ของเรา
คือให้ข้อมูลกว้างๆโดยทั่วไปเกี่ยวกับหัวข้อใดหัวข้อหนึ่ง   คุณผู้อ่านควรทำการวิจัยเพิ่มเติม
ด้วยตัวเองถ้าต้องการทราบเรื่องใดเรื่องหนึ่งที่คุณสนใจหรือเรื่องที่เกี่ยวกับผู้อ่านโดยตรง

หนังสือเล่มนี้เป็นหนังสืออ้างอิงและคู่มือแนะนำเท่านั้น ไม่ใช่เป็นสิ่งที่คุณผู้อ่าน
จะใช้แทนคำแนะนำจากทนายความ   แพทย์ ที่ปรึกษาด้านการเงินหรือผู้เชี่ยวชาญและผู้มี
ประสบการณ์ในระดับมืออาชีพ   สำนักพิมพ์ไพบูลย์และผู้เขียนไม่ขอรับผิดชอบต่อความ

เสียหาย   ข้อพิพาทหรือความไม่สะดวกใดๆที่เกิดขึ้นไม่ว่าทางตรงหรือทางอ้อมจากการตีความของผู้อ่านหรือจากการใช้หนังสือเล่มนี้

สำนักพิมพ์ฯเป็นผู้จัดพิมพ์หนังสือเล่มนี้เพื่อให้ความรู้ทั่วไปเกี่ยวกับกฎหมายไทยเท่านั้น เราจะไม่ให้คำปรึกษาหรือตอบคำถามทางด้านกฎหมาย ถ้าคุณต้องการคำแนะนำด้านกฎหมาย กรุณาติดต่อกับทนายความที่เชี่ยวชาญในเรื่องที่คุณต้องการทราบ ในส่วนอ้างอิงซึ่งเป็นส่วนสุดท้ายของหนังสือเล่มนี้ (ในภาคภาษาอังกฤษ) เราได้แนะนำเว็บไซท์ต่างๆที่คุณสามารถหาทนายความได้และเว็บไซท์บางหน้ามีกระดานสนทนาที่คุณสามารถโพสท์คำถามเกี่ยวกับกฎหมายได้

ถึงแม้ว่าทางสำนักพิมพ์ฯจะไม่ให้คำปรึกษาด้านกฎหมายและไม่สามารถตอบคำถามด้านกฎหมายให้กับผู้อ่านได้ เราขอให้คุณผู้อ่านช่วยเราปรับปรุงหนังสือเล่มนี้และหนังสือกฎหมายเล่มต่อไปโดยการส่งคำติชมหรือข้อเสนอแนะใดๆเป็นภาษาไทยหรือภาษาอังกฤษมาที่อีเมล์ thailaw4u@gmail.com

ทางสำนักพิมพ์ฯหวังเป็นอย่างยิ่งว่าหนังสือเล่มนี้จะเป็นประโยชน์แก่คุณผู้อ่านและขอขอบพระคุณที่ให้การสนับสนุนสำนักพิมพ์ของเรา

ทีมงานสำนักพิมพ์ไพบูลย์

เกี่ยวกับหนังสือกฎหมายไทยสำหรับชาวต่างชาติ

หนังสือเล่มนี้ได้จัดทำขึ้นสำหรับชาวต่างชาติที่มาเยี่ยมเยือน   พักอาศัยหรือ
ประกอบธุรกิจในประเทศไทยหรือสำหรับชาวต่างชาติที่มีความประสงค์จะแต่งงานกับคน
ไทย   หรือที่มีคู่สมรสเป็นคนไทยแล้ว   นอกจากนี้หนังสือเล่มนี้ยังสามารถเป็นคู่มืออ้างอิง
สำหรับผู้ทำวิจัย นักศึกษากฎหมาย ทนายความและผู้ประกอบอาชีพอื่นๆ ได้ ถึงแม้ว่าข้อมูล
ที่อยู่ในหนังสือจะเน้นไปที่ชาวต่างชาติว่าด้วยกฎหมายไทย   แต่ผู้อ่านคนไทยก็สามาร
นำไปใช้เป็นคู่มืออ้างอิงและเรียนรู้เกี่ยวกับกฎหมายไทยเบื้องต้นได้เช่นกัน

กฎหมายไทยสำหรับชาวต่างชาติได้เขียนเป็นทั้งภาษาอังกฤษและภาษาไทย ครึ่ง
แรกของหนังสือเขียนเป็นภาษาอังกฤษและครึ่งหลังเป็นภาษาไทย เบญจวรรณและเริงศักดิ์
เป็นผู้ร่วมกันแต่งหนังสือเล่มนี้ขึ้น   เริงศักดิ์เป็นผู้เขียนบางส่วนเป็นภาษาไทยและเป็นผู้ให้
ข้อมูลเกี่ยวกับกฎหมายจากการทำวิจัยในหัวข้อต่างๆ ส่วนเบญจวรรณเป็นผู้เขียนภาษาไทย
บางส่วนและเป็นผู้แปลภาษาไทยเป็นภาษาอังกฤษทั้งหมดและแปลภาษาอังกฤษเป็น
ภาษาไทยร่วมกับทีมงานแปลเอกสารของสำนักพิมพ์ไพบูลย์   เนื้อหาที่แปลจากไทยเป็น
อังกฤษหรืออังกฤษเป็นไทยนั้นเป็นการแปลเนื้อหาของแต่ละบท ไม่ใช่เป็นการแปลคำต่อคำ
แต่เนื้อหาก็ใกล้เคียงกันมากและบางส่วนก็เหมือนกันแทบทั้งหมด เนื่องจากหนังสือเล่มนี้ได้
เขียนเป็นสองภาษา คนไทยที่อยู่ในต่างประเทศที่ได้แปลงสัญชาติเป็นสัญชาติอื่นก็สามารถ
ได้ประโยชน์จากหนังสือเล่มนี้ นอกจากนี้คู่สมรสหรือเพื่อนๆของชาวต่างชาติที่เป็นคนไทย
ก็สามารถใช้หนังสือเล่มนี้เป็นคู่มืออ้างอิงด้านกฎหมายและจะสามารถช่วยชาวต่างชาติใน
เรื่องกฎหมายที่เกี่ยวข้องได้

หนังสือเล่มนี้ออกสู่ตลาดเพียงไม่กี่เดือนหลังจากการประกาศใช้รัฐธรรมนูญปี
2550 ข้อมูลที่เราได้มานั้นจะมาจากรัฐธรรมนูญใหม่ อย่างไรก็ตามอาจจะมีกฎหมายใหม่ที่มี
การเปลี่ยนแปลงอยู่เสมอที่เกี่ยวกับชาวต่างชาติและเนื้อหาบางส่วนของหนังสือยังคงขึ้นอยู่
กับรัฐธรรมนูญปี 2540 หลังจากที่กฎหมายใหม่ได้บัญญัติขึ้นอย่างชัดเจนในรัฐธรรมนูญ
ใหม่แล้ว เราจะแก้ไขข้อมูลในหนังสือให้ตรงกับข้อมูลล่าสุดที่มีอยู่ในการจัดพิมพ์ครั้งต่อไป

ส่วนแรกของหนังสือจะแนะนำให้ผู้อ่านให้รู้จักกับระบบกฎหมายของไทย
ประวัติความเป็นมานับจากสมัยสุโขทัยจนถึงปัจจุบันพร้อมกับประวัติกฎหมายไทยโดยย่อ
ในแต่ละยุคสมัยและการวิวัฒนาการของระบบกฎหมายในยุคนั้นๆ   ส่วนแรกนี้ยังอธิบาย
เกี่ยวกับโครงสร้างของรัฐบาลไทย   รัฐธรรมนูญและระบบศาลไทยซึ่งจะเป็นพื้นฐานให้
ผู้อ่านได้ความรู้เบื้องต้นก่อนที่จะเข้าสู่ส่วนต่อไปของหนังสือ

ส่วนที่สองจะเน้นไปที่กระบวนการกฎหมายในประเทศไทย เป็นส่วนที่ให้ข้อมูล
ที่เป็นประโยชน์สำหรับผู้ที่ต้องดำเนินเรื่องในศาลทั้งในคดีอาญาและคดีแพ่ง ส่วนนี้ยังได้
รวบรวมเนื้อหาที่สำคัญเกี่ยวกับการว่าจ้างทนายความและการใช้ล่ามในกระบวนการ
กฎหมาย

ส่วนที่สามเป็นส่วนที่เป็นประโยชน์อย่างยิ่งสำหรับชาวต่างชาติที่มีครอบครัวใน
ประเทศไทยหรือผู้ที่สมรสกับชาวไทย   ส่วนนี้จะบรรยายในหลายแง่มุมเกี่ยวกับเรื่องของ
ครอบครัว เช่น ค่าสินสอด สัญญาก่อนสมรส การจดทะเบียนสมรสและการหย่าร้าง ยังมี
ข้อมูลเกี่ยวกับเรื่องส่วนบุคคลอื่นๆ เช่น การทำพินัยกรรม การรับบุตรบุญธรรมและการได้
สัญชาติไทยในส่วนนี้อีกด้วย

ส่วนที่สี่เป็นส่วนที่ให้ข้อมูลเกี่ยวกับการพักอาศัยอยู่ในประเทศไทย   การนำ
กฎหมายไทยมาประยุกต์ใช้ในชีวิตประจำวัน   เป็นส่วนที่ให้คำตอบสำหรับสถานการณ์ที่มี
ขึ้นอยู่เสมอ เช่น การเปิดบัญชีธนาคาร การขอใบขับขี่ การเช่าบ้าน ฯลฯ

ส่วนสุดท้ายของหนังสือเป็นส่วนอ้างอิง (เฉพาะในส่วนภาษาอังกฤษ) มีข้อมูล
เกี่ยวกับการเข้าประเทศและกฎระเบียบของการตรวจลงตรา (วีซ่า) และเราได้ใช้แหล่งข้อมูล
ที่น่าเชื่อถือจากอินเตอร์เน็ตและจากเว็บไซท์ของทางรัฐบาลไทย   พร้อมกับการนำเสนอ
รายชื่อของกระทรวงและกรมต่างๆ ยศและตำแหน่งของตำรวจไทย สถาบันที่สอนวิชา
กฎหมายในประเทศไทย รายชื่อกษัตริย์ไทยและนายกรัฐมนตรี เว็บไซท์ที่แนะนำสำหรับ
การทำวิจัยเพิ่มเติมและอีกมากมาย เรายังมีแบบฟอร์มตัวอย่างที่เราได้แปลเป็นภาษาอังกฤษ
ให้คุณผู้อ่านใช้ในการสื่อสารกับชาวต่างชาติ

เราได้เขียนหนังสือเล่มนี้ขึ้นจากการทำวิจัยจากเว็บไซท์กฎหมายต่างๆ และเว็บ
ไซท์ของทางราชการซึ่งอาจจะมีข้อผิดพลาดเล็กน้อยที่เกิดขึ้นได้ในตัวเลข ชื่อ หรือ
รายละเอียดบางอย่างในหนังสือ อย่างไรก็ตามเราได้ใช้ข้อมูลจากแหล่งข้อมูลที่น่าเชื่อถือ
ที่สุด เราเชื่อว่าหนังสือเล่มนี้จะให้ความรู้ทั่วไปเกี่ยวกับกฎหมายไทยแก่คุณผู้อ่าน หากมี
ข้อผิดพลาดประการใด ทางสำนักพิมพ์ฯและผู้เขียนขออภัยมา ณ ที่นี้ และจะปรับปรุงให้ดี
ขึ้นในการจัดพิมพ์ครั้งต่อไป

สิ่งที่อยู่ในมือของคุณผู้อ่านในขณะนี้คือหนังสือกฎหมายไทยสำหรับชาวต่างชาติ
ที่เต็มไปด้วยข้อมูลและสาระที่เป็นประโยชน์อย่างยิ่ง

กิตติกรรมประกาศ

ผู้เขียนขอขอบพระคุณบุคคลหลายๆท่านที่ให้ความช่วยเหลือเราทั้งสองจนได้
หนังสือที่มีคุณภาพออกมาเป็นรูปเล่มโดยเฉพาะอย่างยิ่งท่านที่มีรายชื่ออยู่ข้างล่างนี้

พันเอกโรเบิร์ต เอส เชสเตอร์ ผู้พิพากษาศาลทหารแห่งสหรัฐอเมริกาที่ได้สละ
เวลาในช่วงที่ท่านจะเกษียณอายุให้คำแนะนำและความคิดเห็นเกี่ยวกับมุมมองของ
ชาวต่างชาติต่อกฎหมายไทย   เนื้อหาที่ท่านได้ชี้แนะทำให้หนังสือเล่มนี้เป็นประโยชน์ต่อ
ผู้อ่านชาวต่างชาติยิ่งขึ้น

ดร.ชวลิต นิลวงษ์ ที่ปรึกษาด้านกฎหมายจากบริษัทไทยอินเตอร์ลอว์ จำกัด ซึ่ง
เป็นผู้เชี่ยวชาญด้านกฎหมายไทยสำหรับชาวต่างชาติที่ได้ให้คำแนะนำและข้อมูลทั่วไป
สำหรับเนื้อหาในหนังสือเล่มนี้

คุณริชาร์ด บาร์โรว์ จาก www.ThaiPrisonLife.com ที่ได้มอบสองบทความ
ให้กับเราซึ่งเป็นบทความเกี่ยวกับประสบการณ์ของชาวต่างชาติในคุกและศาลไทย

คุณโกวิท ทาตะรัตน์ จาก www.LawyerThai.com ผู้ให้ข้อมูลเกี่ยวกับ
โครงสร้างเกี่ยวกับของรัฐบาลไทยจากเว็บไซท์แห่งนี้

ผู้อำนวยการกองตรวจลงตราและเอกสารเดินทางคนต่างด้าว   กรมการกงสุล
กระทรวงต่างประเทศที่อนุญาตให้ทางสำนักพิมพ์ไพบูลย์ใช้ข้อมูลในเว็บไซท์ของกระทรวง
ต่างประเทศเพื่อการอ้างอิงได้

ทีมบรรณาธิการและผู้แปลภาษาของสำนักพิมพ์ไพบูลย์ คุณสาลินี ภวลักษณาวัติ
คุณพัลลภา อิงบุญมีสกุล และคุณพรทิพย์ พรมมาฏร์

ทีมบรรณาธิการภาคภาษาอังกฤษของเราซึ่งได้แก่คุณนิโคลัส เทอร์เล็คกี้ ผู้ที่ทำ
การขัดเกลาต้นฉบับภาษาอังกฤษจนเป็นภาษาที่สละสลวย คุณแฮร์รี่ เจ ดีพิเอโทร เพื่อนของ
เราชาวสหรัฐอเมริกาที่เป็นทนายความและเป็นผู้ที่มีบทบาทสำคัญในการปรับปรุงแก้ไข
ภาษากฎหมายที่เป็นภาษาอังกฤษ และท้ายสุดคือคุณริช เบเกอร์ ผู้เป็นบรรณาธิการหลักใน
ส่วนภาษาอังกฤษที่ทำให้หนังสือเล่มนี้อ่านได้อย่างชัดเจนและเข้าใจได้ง่าย

เบญจวรรณและเริงศักดิ์
ผู้เขียน

ส่วนที่ 1

ประวัติศาสตร์ โครงสร้างรัฐบาลและระบบศาลไทย

ประวัติศาสตร์ไทยและประวัติความเป็นมาของกฎหมายไทย

ประวัติศาสตร์ไทยโดยสังเขปนี้จะทำให้ท่านสามารถเข้าใจถึงภูมิหลังการก่อตั้งประเทศและการพัฒนาระบบกฎหมายของประเทศไทยได้ดียิ่งขึ้น   รวมทั้งประวัติศาสตร์โดยทั่วไปของประเทศไทยและลักษณะของกฎหมายในแต่ละสมัย

ก่อนปี พ.ศ. 2482 ประเทศไทยเป็นที่รู้จักกันในนาม "ประเทศสยาม" ซึ่งมีความหมายตามตัวอักษรว่า "ดินแดนแห่งอิสระชน" หรือ "ดินแดนแห่งรอยยิ้ม" ประเทศไทยเป็นเพียงประเทศเดียวในภูมิภาคเอเชียตะวันออกเฉียงใต้ที่ไม่ได้ตกเป็นเมืองขึ้นของประเทศตะวันตก ในวันที่ 24 มิถุนายน พ.ศ. 2475 คณะราษฎร์ได้ทำการปฏิรูปเปลี่ยนแปลงการปกครองจากระบอบสมบูรณาญาสิทธิราชย์มาเป็นระบอบประชาธิปไตยอย่างไม่มีการเสียเลือดเนื้อ   พระมหากษัตริย์มีฐานะเป็นประมุขของประเทศ   โดยที่การปกครองภายในประเทศ จะเป็นการตรวจสอบและถ่วงดุลอำนาจซึ่งใกล้เคียงกับในประเทศตะวันตก

ต้นกำเนิดที่แท้จริงของคนไทยนั้นยังไม่สามารถสรุปได้แน่ชัด กระนั้น นักชนชาติวิทยาต่างสรุปออกมาเป็นทฤษฎีต่างๆมากมาย หนึ่งทฤษฎีที่มีความเป็นไปได้คือ ชาวไทยได้อพยพเคลื่อนย้ายมาจากทางตอนใต้ของประเทศจีน โดยมีการย้ายถิ่นฐานเข้ามาตามลุ่มแม่น้ำเจ้าพระยาซึ่งแต่เดิมปกครองโดยอาณาจักรเขมร

ทั้งนี้ ผู้เขียนจะขอเริ่มกล่าวถึงประวัติศาสตร์ไทย ตั้งแต่สมัยกรุงสุโขทัยเรื่อยไปตามลำดับจนถึงปัจจุบัน

สมัยกรุงสุโขทัย (พ.ศ. 1781 – พ.ศ. 1919)

ผู้นำชาวไทยที่ขับไล่ชาวเขมรออกจากเมืองสุโขทัยซึ่งตั้งอยู่บริเวณตอนกลางของ
ประเทศไทยในปัจจุบันนั้นมีนามว่า พ่อขุนศรีอินทราทิตย์ ผู้ซึ่งเป็นปฐมกษัตริย์ของชนชาว
ไทย ใน ปี พ.ศ. 1781 พ่อขุนศรีอินทราทิตย์ได้สถาปนากรุงสุโขทัยขึ้นเป็นเมืองหลวงและ
ถือได้ว่าเป็นเมืองหลวงแห่งแรกของราชอาณาจักรไทยที่ได้รับการสถาปนาขึ้นอย่างเป็น
ทางการ ในเวลานั้น ราชอาณาจักรสุโขทัยได้แผ่ขยายแสนยานุภาพทางการปกครองจาก
เมืองลำปางและนครเวียงจันทร์ทางตอนเหนือเรื่อยลงมายังเมืองนครศรีธรรมราชทางตอน
ใต้ของประเทศ ซึ่งในระหว่างนี้ สุโขทัยได้มีความสัมพันธ์ทางการค้าและทาง
ขนบธรรมเนียมประเพณีกับชาวจีนเป็นอย่างมาก

พ่อขุนรามคำแหงมหาราชเป็นกษัตริย์องค์ที่ 3 แห่งราชอาณาจักรสุโขทัย พระองค์
มีชื่อเสียงและเป็นที่รู้จักกันเป็นอย่างดีในประวัติศาสตร์ไทยเนื่องจากพระมหากรุณาธิคุณใน
การประดิษฐ์ตัวอักษรไทยขึ้นใช้เป็นครั้งแรกในปี พ.ศ. 1826 อีกทั้งพระองค์ยังทรงเป็นที่รัก
ใคร่ของชาวสุโขทัยเป็นอย่างยิ่ง ด้วยเหตุนี้เอง พระองค์จึงเป็นกษัตริย์พระองค์แรกได้รับการ
ขนานพระยศต่อท้ายพระนามว่า "มหาราช"

กรุงสุโขทัยปกครองด้วยระบอบปิตาธิปไตยหรือพ่อปกครองลูก ซึ่งประชาชน
สามารถร้องทุกข์ถึงความเดือดร้อนและข้อพิพาทที่ไม่สามารถจบลงได้ต่อพระมหากษัตริย์
โดยตรง ด้วยการไปตีกลองที่จัดเตรียมไว้บริเวณหน้าพระราชวังเพื่อยื่นฎีกาให้พระองค์ทรง
สินความเป็นธรรม พระมหากษัตริย์มีหน้าที่ตรวจสอบคำร้อง และจะทรงสอบสวนคู่กรณี
ด้วยพระองค์เอง ก่อนที่จะมีพระราชวินิจฉัย ในกรณีที่พระองค์ทรงมีพระราชกรณียกิจอื่น
พระองค์จะทรงมอบหมายหน้าที่ในการตัดสินความให้แก่ผู้แทนพระองค์ ระบอบพ่อ
ปกครองลูกในสมัยกรุงสุโขทัยสามารถดำเนินอยู่ได้ด้วยจำนวนประชาชนที่ยังมีจำนวนไม่
มากในราชอาณาจักร ประกอบกับลักษณะทางสังคมและวัฒนธรรมเอื้อต่อการปกครอง
ระบอบดังกล่าว ความสัมพันธ์ระหว่างพระมหากษัตริย์กับราษฎรจึงเป็นไปอย่างใกล้ชิด
ราชอาณาจักรสุโขทัยมีความอุดมสมบูรณ์ไปด้วยทรัพยากรทางธรรมชาติ ดังคำกล่าวแต่
โบราณว่า "ในน้ำมีปลา ในนามีข้าว"

ราชอาณาจักรสุโขทัยปกครองตนเองอยู่ได้ จวบจนกระทั่ง ปี พ.ศ. 1919 สุโขทัย
ได้ตกเป็นเมืองขึ้นของกรุงศรีอยุธยา เมื่อราชอาณาจักรอยุธยา ซึ่งตั้งอยู่ใกล้เคียงได้แผ่ขยาย
อำนาจและดินแดนมายังกรุงสุโขทัย ในสมัยสุโขทัย มีราชวงศ์ที่ทรงปกครองราชอาณาจักร
อยู่เพียงราชวงศ์เดียว คือ ราชวงศ์พระร่วง ซึ่งประกอบด้วยพระมหากษัตริย์จำนวน 9
พระองค์ ซึ่งยังคงปกครองอาณาจักรสุโขทัยเรื่อยมา เมื่อครั้งหลังจากตกเป็นเมืองประเทศ
ราชของอาณาจักรอยุธยา ในปี พ.ศ. 1981 อาณาจักรสุโขทัยได้กลายเป็นส่วนหนึ่งของ
อาณาจักรกรุงศรีอยุธยาอย่างแท้จริง โดยมีพระมหาธรรมราชาที่ 4 เป็นกษัตริย์องค์สุดท้าย
แห่งราชวงศ์พระร่วง

สมัยกรุงศรีอยุธยา (พ.ศ. 1893 – พ.ศ. 2310)

กรุงศรีอยุธยาได้รับการสถาปนาราชอาณาจักรขึ้นในปี พ.ศ. 1893 โดย
พระบาทสมเด็จพระเจ้าอู่ทอง ซึ่งเป็นปฐมกษัตริย์แห่งรัชสมัยกรุงศรีอยุธยา ในสมัยกรุงศรี
อยุธยา ระบอบการปกครองมีลักษณะคล้ายคลึงกับราชอาณาจักรเขมร ซึ่งเข้ามาแทนที่การ
ปกครองแบบปิตาธิปไตยในสมัยกรุงสุโขทัย ในการปกครองแบบใหม่นี้ พระมหากษัตริย์
เปรียบได้กับสมมุติเทพ มีอำนาจราชสิทธิเด็ดขาดในการปกครองบ้านเมืองและราษฎร

ในสมัยนี้ มีการเปลี่ยนแปลงของภาษาไทยและพระราชประเพณีต่างๆอย่างมาก
ราษฎรมีจำนวนมากขึ้น ในขณะเดียวกันก็ทำให้เกิดปัญหาต่างๆตามมามากมาย วิธีการ
ดำเนินชีวิตเปลี่ยนไปจากเดิมเป็นอย่างมาก มีความขัดแย้งทางการเมือง เศรษฐกิจและสังคม
เกิดขึ้น ดังนั้น จึงต้องมีการบัญญัติกฎหมายใหม่ที่มีกระบวนการที่ซับซ้อนยิ่งไปกว่าเดิม

ในสมัยกรุงศรีอยุธยา ได้มีการนำระบบศักดินา (feudal system) มาใช้ใน
ราชอาณาจักร ซึ่งระบบดังกล่าวแตกต่างจากระบบศักดินาหรือระบบฟิวดัลลิซึมในประเทศ
ตะวันตก ภายใต้ระบบศักดินา แต่ละคนจะมี "สถานภาพ" "อำนาจ" และ "ความรับผิดชอบ"
ที่แตกต่างกันไปตามแต่ละชนชั้น นอกจากนี้ ระบบศักดินายังเป็นเครื่องมือหนึ่งในการ
ดำเนินคดีทางศาลด้วย กล่าวคือ ผู้ที่มีศักดิ์สูงกว่าย่อมมีความรับผิดชอบมากกว่าผู้ที่มีศักดิ์ต่ำ
หรือด้อยกว่าตน

ศักดินา หรือ สถานภาพแห่งบุคคล จะได้รับการจัดสรรด้วยจำนวนที่ดินที่บุคคล
นั้นถือครองซึ่งมีหน่วยเป็น ไร่ (1 ไร่ เท่ากับ 1,600 ตารางเมตร) โดยที่ไม่จำเป็นที่บุคคลแต่
ละคนต้องถือครองจำนวนที่ดินตามศักดินาของตนอย่างแท้จริง การกำหนดที่ดินเป็นเพียง
เครื่องมือในการจัดลำดับขั้นของสถานภาพ อำนาจและความรับผิดชอบของแต่ละคนใน
สังคมเท่านั้น

ระบบศักดินา มีลำดับชั้นดังต่อไปนี้

1. พระมหากษัตริย์เป็นผู้มีอำนาจราชสิทธิสูงสุดในราชอาณาจักรและมีสถาน
   เปรียบดังสมมุติเทพ

2. พระบรมวงศานุวงศ์ผู้มีศักดิ์โดยกำเนิดหรือตามคุณงามความดีที่ได้ทำไว้
   ให้แก่ประเทศชาติ จะถือครองที่ดินตั้งแต่ 15,000 ไร่ – 100,000 ไร่

3. ขุนนางและข้าราชบริพารที่ได้รับพระบรมราชโองการให้ปกครองราษฎรจะ
   มีศักดินา ดังนี้ ขุนนางจะถือครองที่ดินตั้งแต่ 400 ไร่ – 10,000 ไร่ ในขณะที่
   ข้าราชบริพารทั่วไปจะถือครองที่ดินระหว่าง 25 ไร่ – 400 ไร่ ข้าราชบริพาร
   จะไม่สามารถก้าวขึ้นมาเป็นขุนนางได้ ทั้งตำแหน่งขุนนางและข้าราช
   บริพารจะตกอยู่แก่ตัวจนสิ้นอายุขัยเท่านั้น ไม่สืบทอดไปถึงทายาท ทั้งนี้ ขุน
   นางและข้าราชบริพารสามารถได้รับการเลื่อนตำแหน่งได้หากกระทำความดี
   ความชอบให้แก่บ้านเมือง

4. ไพร่ หรือราษฎรทั่วไป ซึ่งเป็นคนส่วนใหญ่ในสังคม จะมีสิทธิถือครองที่ดิน
   ไม่เกิน 25 ไร่ ไพร่สามารถได้รับการแต่งตั้งให้เป็นขุนนางได้ และใน
   ขณะเดียวกันก็สามารถเลื่อนลำดับไปเป็นทาสได้เช่นกัน หน้าที่หลักของ
   ไพร่คือการทำงานให้กับพระมหากษัตริย์และประเทศชาติ ในสมัยกรุงศรี
   อยุธยา มีการออกกฎระเบียบว่าไพร่ทุกนายต้องสังกัดอยู่ภายใต้การปกครอง
   ของมูลนาย ไพร่ที่มีความสูงขนาด 2.5 ศอก (1 ศอก เท่ากับ 0.5 เมตร) จะมี
   สิทธิเลือกมูลนายที่ตนต้องการไปสังกัดได้อย่างอิสระ ทั้งนี้ ไพร่ที่ไม่มีสังกัด
   จะไม่ได้สิทธิทางศาลและไม่ได้รับความคุ้มครองตามกฎหมาย ไพร่มี 2
   ชนิด ได้แก่ *ไพร่หลวง*และ*ไพร่สม*

ไพร่หลวง หรือ "ทหารหลวง" คือ ไพร่ที่ขึ้นตรงกับพระมหากษัตริย์
โดยตรง ปฏิบัติหน้าที่หลายกรมกองแตกต่างกันออกไป ไพร่หลวงสามารถ
รับใช้พระมหากษัตริย์ด้วยการทำงานหรือการส่งเครื่องบรรณาการมา
ทดแทนการทำงานของตนก็ได้ บรรณาการสามารถเป็นทรัพย์สินที่จับต้อง
ได้หรือเงิน ซึ่งที่ชื่อเรียกอย่างเป็นทางการว่า "ส่วย" การทำงานของไพร่
หลวงจะมีลักษณะเป็นการทำงานเดือนเว้นเดือนตลอด 1 ปี ในแต่ละปีต้อง
ทำงานทั้งสิ้น 6 เดือน

ไพร่สม หรือ "ราษฎรที่รับใช้ขุนนาง" คือ ราษฎรทั่วไปที่ได้รับ
มอบหมายจากพระมหากษัตริย์ให้รับใช้ขุนนางและข้าราชบริพารต่างๆ ไพร่
สมจะตกเป็นมูลนายจนกระทั่งมูลนายถึงแก่กรรม ซึ่งหากเป็นเช่นนั้น ไพร่
สมจะเปลี่ยนสถานะเป็นไพร่หลวงทันที เว้นเสียแต่ว่าบุตรชายของมูลนายที่
สิ้นชีวิตได้รับบรมราชานุญาตให้ปกครองไพร่สมคนนั้นต่อไปไว้ได้

5. ทาสเป็นชนชั้นล่างสุดของสังคม ซึ่งมีศักดินาเพียง 5 ไร่เท่านั้น ทาสจะไม่มี
อิสระในการตัดสินใจและการดำเนินชีวิตของตน ในสมัยอยุธยา มูลนาย
สามารถแลกเปลี่ยนทาสได้เยี่ยงสินค้า โดยทาสที่เป็นไทจะกลายเป็นไพร่
ทาสแบ่งออกเป็น 7 ประเภทด้วยกันขึ้นอยู่กับการผูกมัดของการเป็นทาส
อาทิ ทาสเชลย ทาสสินไถ่ ทาสที่รับมาด้วยมรดก ทาสที่เลี้ยงดูไว้ในยามเกิด
ทุกข์และอดอยาก ทาสในเรือนเบี้ย ทาสท่านให้ และทาสที่ช่วยไว้จากโทษ
ทัณฑ์

6. พระสงฆ์ไม่ได้อยู่ระบบศักดินาเนื่องจากมีสถานภาพพิเศษทางสังคม หน้าที่
ของพระสงฆ์คือการปฏิบัติธรรมวินัยและการเผยแพร่พระพุทธศาสนา
พระสงฆ์เป็นที่เคารพของคนในสังคม จึงมีคนจำนวนไม่น้อยที่อาศัย
พระสงฆ์เป็นเครื่องมือในการเลื่อนลำดับศักดิ์ของตนในสังคม ชายทุกคน
สามารถบวชเป็นพระสงฆ์ได้ ตั้งแต่พระบรมวงศานุวงศ์ ขุนนาง ไพร่หรือ
ทาส เมื่อบวชเป็นพระสงฆ์แล้ว บุคคลดังกล่าวก็จะมีโอกาสได้ศึกษาเล่า
เรียน อาจกล่าวได้ว่าพระสงฆ์มีความเกี่ยวข้องและความสัมพันธ์กับคนทุก
ชั้นในระบบศักดินา

ระบบศักดินาได้หยั่งรากลึกลงในสังคมไทย และสะท้อนให้เห็นได้ในหลากหลายรูปแบบในปัจจุบัน   การแบ่งชนชั้นของไทยเป็นเรื่องละเอียดอ่อน   ซึ่งบางครั้งทำให้ชาวต่างชาติจำนวนไม่น้อยไม่เข้าใจวิธีการโต้ตอบของชาวไทยในเรื่องสถานภาพและความสัมพันธ์   ดังนั้นการเรียนรู้เกี่ยวกับประวัติศาสตร์ไทยจะช่วยให้ผู้อ่านได้เข้าถึงการกระทำบางอย่างของคนไทย เช่น คนไทยมักจะถามเกี่ยวกับเรื่องอายุและเรื่องรายได้ และอย่าเพิ่งรู้สึกตะขิดตะขวงใจหากเจอสถานเช่นนี้   เนื่องจากการกระทำดังกล่าวเป็นเพียงการวิเคราะห์สถานทางสังคมและความสัมพันธ์ในเชิงสังคมที่คนผู้หนึ่งจะมีต่อคนอีกผู้หนึ่งในสังคมเท่านั้น

ปัจจุบันนี้   ฐานะทางสังคมนั้นได้รับการกำหนดจากสิ่งต่างๆต่อไปนี้   ได้แก่รากฐานของครอบครัว (ความเกี่ยวข้องกับพระมหากษัตริย์ ความมีชื่อเสียง ความสูงศักดิ์หรือความธรรมดาสามัญ) ความมั่งมี (ปัจจัยหลัก) การศึกษา (การศึกษาสูงย่อมได้รับการเคารพมากกว่าแม้ว่าจะมาจากครอบครัวที่ยากจน) พระภิกษุ (สถานภาพพิเศษทางสังคมที่ได้รับการเคารพนับถือจากคนในสังคม) วัยวุฒิ (ชาวไทยมักเคารพคนที่สูงวัยกว่า) อาชีพ (ในบางอาชีพ เช่น ข้าราชการ มักได้รับความเคารพนับถือจากคนในสังคมมากกว่าอาชีพอื่นๆ เช่น เจ้าของภัตตาคาร เป็นต้น)

ในสังคมไทย ผู้ที่มีสถานภาพทางสังคมสูงมักได้รับการคาดหวังให้ต้องรับหน้าที่บางอย่างมากกว่าคนที่มีสถานภาพทางสังคมที่ต่ำกว่า เช่น ผู้อาวุโสหรือผู้ที่มีสถานะทางสังคมสูงกว่ามักจะเป็นผู้ชำระเงินในร้านอาหารซึ่งถือเป็นหน้าที่และเกียรติ นอกเหนือจากนี้ความคิดที่ชาวไทยมีต่อชาวต่างชาติที่ว่าชาวต่างชาติมีเงินที่สามารถเดินทางมาประเทศไทยก็ย่อมที่จะมีฐานะดีกว่าตน ดังนั้น ในสายตาของชาวไทย คนต่างชาติกลับมีสถานะทางสังคมที่สูงกว่า คนไทยส่วนใหญ่จึงจำหน่ายสินค้าและบริการให้แก่ชาวต่างชาติในราคาสูงกว่าท้องตลาดทั่วไป เป็นต้น

จากที่กล่าวไป ชาวต่างชาติอาจต้องเสียเงินจ้างทนายความแพงกว่าอัตราของคนไทย เนื่องจากการที่สังคมไทยได้ตั้งข้อสมมุติฐานว่าชาวต่างชาติมีสถานะทางสังคมสูงกว่าและมีกำลังจ่ายมากกว่านั่นเอง อย่างไรก็ดี ความเชื่อนี้ไม่ได้เกิดขึ้นกับทุกคนในสังคมไทยโดยเฉพาะอย่างยิ่งชาวไทยที่เคยมีโอกาสเดินทางไปนอกประเทศ อีกประการหนึ่ง คุณต้อง

ยอมรับข้อเท็จจริงที่ว่า คุณจะเป็นชาวต่างชาติในสายตาของคนไทยเสมอ ไม่ว่าคุณจะอาศัย
อยู่ในประเทศไทยนานเพียงใด มีความสามารถในการใช้ภาษาไทยได้อย่างคล่องแคล่ว
อย่างไรและแม้ว่าคุณจะได้รับการเปลี่ยนโอนสัญชาติมาเป็นพลเมืองไทยแล้วก็ตาม

ต่อไป ผู้เขียนจะขอกล่าวถึงระบบกฎหมายในสมัยกรุงศรีอยุธยาโดยสังเขป ดังนี้

ระบบศาลได้ถือกำเนิดขึ้นในช่วงต้นของสมัยกรุงศรีอยุธยา พระมหากษัตริย์จะ
ได้รับคำร้องหรือคำร้องทุกข์ ในกรณีที่พระมหากษัตริย์มิได้ทรงเป็นผู้ตัดสินคดีด้วยพระองค์
เอง ผู้สืบสวนหรือผู้พิพากษาจะได้รับการแต่งตั้งให้เป็นผู้ดำเนินการสอบสวนคู่กรณี

มาตรา 20 แห่งพระราชบัญญัติการดำเนินคดีในสาธารณะ ในสมัยกรุงศรีอยุธยา
ได้บัญญัติว่า "คู่กรณีจำต้องแต่งตั้งทนายในการต่อสู้คดีทางอาญา" จึงสามารถสรุปได้ว่า
ระบบทนายความได้เริ่มต้นขึ้นแล้วในสมัยกรุงศรีอยุธยานี้เอง ผู้ที่มีศักดินาถือครองที่ดิน
มากกว่า 400 ไร่ขึ้นไปสามารถแต่งตั้งทนายให้ไปดำเนินคดีในศาลแทนตนได้เนื่องจาก
สถานภาพทางสังคมที่สูงกว่า การที่บุคคลเหล่านี้ต้องดำเนินคดีโดยไม่มีทนายนั้นถือเป็นการ
เสียหน้าและไม่เหมาะสมอย่างยิ่ง เนื่องจากการสอบสวนจะมีลักษณะกระโชกโฮกฮากและ
ใช้คำพูดที่รุนแรง การแต่งตั้งทนายเพื่อดำเนินคดีทางศาลแทนตน จึงเป็นวิธีในการหลีกเลี่ยง
การเสียหน้าและชื่อเสียงต่อหน้าสาธารณชน อย่างไรก็ตาม ทนายจะไม่สอบถามพยานของ
อีกฝ่ายเช่นในปัจจุบัน ผู้พิพากษาจะอนุญาตให้สมาชิกในครอบครัวหรือญาติผู้ใกล้ชิดเป็น
ตัวแทนให้กับจำเลยได้ เช่น บิดาอาจเป็นตัวแทนให้กับผู้เป็นบุตร ภรรยาอาจเป็นตัวแทน
ของสามี เป็นต้น ทนายหรือผู้แทนในสมัยกรุงศรีอยุธยานั้นไม่จำเป็นต้องมีความรู้ด้าน
กฎหมาย แต่จำเป็นต้องรู้ข้อเท็จจริงที่เกิดขึ้นในคดี โดยทั่วไปแล้ว ผู้ต้องหาสามารถแต่งตั้ง
ทนายหรือผู้แทนให้ไปดำเนินคดีแทนตนได้ ยกเว้นกรณีที่ผู้ต้องหากระทำความผิดในฐาน
ความผิดต่อไปนี้ (ซึ่งผู้ต้องหามีหน้าที่ต้องเดินทางไปศาลเพื่อดำเนินคดีด้วยตัวของตัวเอง)
เช่น แพทย์ที่ได้รับการกล่าวหาว่าทำให้คนไข้ของตนเสียชีวิต การลักทรัพย์ การปล้นการ
ฆาตกรรม การคบชู้ ความผิดเกี่ยวกับที่อยู่อาศัย การทำลายทรัพย์สินของรัฐ การลอบ
วางเพลิง การฉ้อโกง (เงินตรา) การลักลอบขูดทองจากองค์พระพุทธรูปและการฟ้องบิดา
มารดา เป็นต้น

ในสมัยกรุงศรีอยุธยามีศึกสงครามและการติดต่อค้าขายกับชาวต่างชาติมากมาย อาทิ จีน ญี่ปุ่น โปรตุเกส สเปน ฮอลแลนด์ อังกฤษ ฝรั่งเศสและประเทศอาหรับต่างๆ

กรุงศรีอยุธยาเสียกรุงให้แก่ประเทศพม่าถึงสองครั้งด้วยกัน ครั้งแรกเกิดขึ้นปี พ.ศ. 2112 ในรัชสมัยของพระมหินทราธิราช เนื่องด้วยการที่คนไทยแตกความสามัคคี กรุงศรีอยุธยาตกเป็นเป็นเมืองขึ้นของประเทศพม่าเป็นระยะเวลาถึง 15 ปี จนกระทั่งสมเด็จพระนเรศวรมหาราชได้ยกทัพเพื่อกอบกู้เอกราชจนได้ชัยชนะเหนือประเทศพม่าและประกาศตนเป็นอิสรภาพในปี พ.ศ. 2127

กรุงศรีอยุธยาได้แตกพ่ายลงอีกครั้งในปี พ.ศ. 2310 ในรัชสมัยพระเจ้าเอกทัศน์ การเสียเมืองครั้งนี้ยังผลให้กรุงศรีอยุธยาถูกทำลายอย่างประมาณค่ามิได้ ทุกสิ่งที่มีค่าถูกเผาทำลาย รวมถึง พระบรมมหาราชวัง ปูชนียวัตถุและปูชนียสถานต่างๆ งานศิลป์ และวัดวาอาราม ซึ่งชาวพม่าต่างทำลายและปล้นกลับไปยังบ้านเมืองของตน จึงถือได้ว่าในครั้งนั้นกรุงศรีอยุธยาได้แตกพ่ายอย่างสิ้นเชิงจนมิเหลือความเป็นกรุงเก่าไว้อยู่เลย

กรุงศรีอยุธยาเป็นราชธานีของไทยมายาวนานถึง 417 ปี ซึ่งมีพระมหากษัตริย์ปกครองทั้งสิ้น 33 พระองค์ นับเป็น 5 ราชวงศ์ด้วยกัน ตลอดระยะเวลาตั้งแต่ พ.ศ. 1893 – พ.ศ. 2310 ดังนี้

1. ราชวงศ์อู่ทอง ประกอบไปด้วยพระมหากษัตริย์ 3 พระองค์

2. ราชวงศ์สุพรรณภูมิ ประกอบไปด้วยพระมหากษัตริย์ 13 พระองค์

3. ราชวงศ์สุโขทัย ประกอบไปด้วยพระมหากษัตริย์ 7 พระองค์

4. ราชวงศ์ปราสาททอง ประกอบไปด้วยพระมหากษัตริย์ 4 พระองค์

5. ราชวงศ์บ้านพลูหลวง ประกอบไปด้วยพระมหากษัตริย์ 6 พระองค์

สมัยกรุงธนบุรี (พ.ศ. 2310 – พ.ศ. 2325)

ประเทศสยามมีกรุงธนบุรีเป็นราชธานีเป็นระยะเวลาเพียง 15 ปี นับแต่ พ.ศ. 2310–พ.ศ. 2325 โดยมีพระบาทสมเด็จพระเจ้าตากสินมหาราชเป็นพระมหากษัตริย์ปกครองประเทศ พระองค์ทรงเป็นแม่ทัพในการประกาศอิสรภาพให้แก่ชาวสยาม ภายในระยะเวลา 7 เดือน นับแต่วันที่กรุงศรีอยุธยาได้แตกพ่ายลงด้วยน้ำมือของชาวพม่า ซึ่งพระองค์ได้สถาปนาพระองค์เองเป็นพระมหากษัตริย์ขึ้นปกครองกรุงธนบุรีนับแต่บัดนั้น

พระบาทสมเด็จพระเจ้าตากสินมหาราชทรงตระหนักว่ากรุงศรีอยุธยานั้นเสียหายเกินกว่าที่จะปฏิสังขรเมืองเพื่อตั้งเป็นราชธานีอีกครั้ง และแม้ว่าพระองค์จะสามารถรวบรวมกำลังได้อีกหน ทว่ากองกำลังของพระองค์ก็ไม่แข็งแกร่งเพียงพอที่จะปกป้องการโจมตีของศัตรูเอาไว้ได้ ดังนั้น พระองค์จึงตัดสินพระทัยสร้างและสถาปนาราชธานีขึ้นมาใหม่ นามว่ากรุงธนบุรี ซึ่งตั้งอยู่ทางตะวันตกของแม่น้ำเจ้าพระยา ปัจจุบันกลายเป็นส่วนหนึ่งของกรุงเทพมหานคร ในครั้งนั้น กรุงธนบุรีเป็นราชธานีที่มียุทธศาสตร์เหมาะกับการรบมากกว่ากรุงศรีอยุธยา เนื่องด้วยมีภูมิประเทศที่ติดทะเล

ในสมัยนี้ ประเทศไทยตกอยู่ในภาวะสงครามและการกอบกู้บ้านเมืองเพื่อให้ได้มาซึ่งอิสรภาพหลังจากกรุงศรีอยุธยาได้แตกพ่ายลง

กระนั้น ด้วยพระปรีชาสามารถของพระบาทสมเด็จพระเจ้าตากสินมหาราช ทำให้พระองค์สามารถสร้างบ้านเมืองขึ้นมาใหม่ได้อีกครั้งและสยามได้กลับมาเจริญรุ่งเรืองอีกครั้งภายในเวลาไม่นาน ราชธานีแห่งใหม่นี้ถือเป็นศูนย์กลางทางด้านเศรษฐกิจและการเมืองของราชอาณาจักร อย่างไรก็ดี ยังมีการนำระบบกฎหมายในสมัยกรุงศรีอยุธยามาใช้อยู่เช่นเดิม

เมื่อครั้งสิ้นสมัยพระบาทสมเด็จพระเจ้าตากสินมหาราช เมืองหลวงได้ถูกเคลื่อนย้ายมากรุงเทพมหานครในปัจจุบัน ซึ่งตั้งอยู่ทางฝั่งตะวันออกของแม่น้ำเจ้าพระยา

สมัยกรุงรัตนโกสินทร์ (กรุงเทพมหานคร) (พ.ศ. 2325 – ปัจจุบัน)

สมัยกรุงรัตนโกสินทร์ หรือที่รู้จักกันในนาม กรุงเทพมหานคร ได้เริ่มขึ้นในปี พ.ศ. 2325 เมื่อมีการสถาปนากรุงเทพมหานครขึ้นเป็นราชธานีในรัชสมัยของ พระบาทสมเด็จพระพุทธยอดฟ้าจุฬาโลกมหาราช (ปฐมกษัตริย์แห่งราชวงศ์จักรี)

ยุทธภูมิของราชธานีที่ตั้งอยู่ในอีกฝั่งหนึ่งของแม่น้ำเจ้าพระยานี้ สามารถป้องกัน ราชธานีได้อย่างมีประสิทธิภาพ เนื่องด้วยราชธานีแห่งนี้ล้อมรอบไปด้วยแม่น้ำเจ้าพระยาถึง สามด้าน

ปัจจุบัน ราชวงศ์จักรีได้ปกครองประเทศสยามมายาวนานถึงรัชกาลที่ 9 ซึ่งนับแต่ นี้ไป ผู้เขียนจะขอกล่าวถึงพระมหากษัตริย์แต่ละพระองค์ด้วยการเรียกชื่อรัชกาลว่า รัชกาลที่ 1 – รัชกาลที่ 9 เพื่อมิให้ผู้อ่านเกิดความสับสน พระบาทสมเด็จพระเจ้าอยู่หัวภูมิพลอดุลยเดช มหาราช หรือ รัชกาลที่ 9 ทรงเป็นพระมหากษัตริย์พระองค์ที่ 9 แห่งราชวงศ์จักรี (ผู้อ่าน สามารถดูรายพระนามพระมหากษัตริย์ไทยได้ในภาคผนวก)

ระบบศาลในสมัยกรุงศรีอยุธยาได้มีการนำมาใช้กันในช่วงต้นของกรุง รัตนโกสินทร์

ในรัชกาลที่ 3 ประเทศไทยได้ติดต่อกับชาวต่างชาติมากมายทั้งด้านการค้าและ งานราชการ ทั้งนี้ พระมหากษัตริย์ทรงประธานพระราชอำนาจให้แก่บรมวงศานุวงศ์เพื่อ ดูแลงานราชการทั้งหลาย อย่างไรก็ตาม ในเวลาดังกล่าว กฎหมายยังไม่เป็นระบบระเบียบ ซึ่งไม่มีการรวบรวม ปรับปรุงและแก้ไขให้มีกระบวนการทางศาลที่เป็นระบบมาตรฐาน อย่างเดียวกันเลย

เมื่อครั้งนั้น ประเทศตะวันตกได้แผ่ขยายอำนาจเข้ามาเสาะแสวงหาเมืองอาณา นิคมในภูมิภาคเอเชียตะวันออกเฉียงใต้มากขึ้น หลายประเทศได้เข้ามาติดต่อค้าขายกับไทย ทำให้เกิดข้อพิพาทระหว่างไทยและประเทศตะวันตกเหล่านั้นมากขึ้น ในระบบศาล ประเทศ ไทยถือได้ว่าเสียเปรียบประเทศตะวันตกเป็นอย่างยิ่ง เนื่องจากไทยเสียสิทธิเสรีภาพนอก อาณาเขต กล่าวคือ ชาวต่างชาติปฏิเสธที่จะได้รับการพิจารณาตามระบบกฎหมายไทย ด้วย เหตุผลว่าระบบกฎหมายไทยไม่มีมาตรฐาน กินระยะเวลามากและมีความซับซ้อน อีกทั้ง บทลงโทษของไทยยังโหดร้ายและล้าสมัยอีกด้วย

ในสมัยก่อน ประเทศไทยได้นำแนวความคิดของอินเดีย ที่เรียกว่า จารีตนครบาล (trial by ordeal) มาใช้เพื่อเป็นบทพิสูจน์ข้อเท็จจริงและความจริงในคดีอาญา จารีตนครบาล มีความหมายว่า "การทรมานเพื่อเค้นความจริงออกมาจากผู้กระทำผิด จนบุคคลนั้นสารภาพ ผิด" เช่น การบีบกะโหลก การตอกเล็บและการเฆี่ยนตี หรือการพิสูจน์ความบริสุทธิ์ของ ผู้กระทำความผิดโดยการให้กลั้นหายใจใต้น้ำหรือการเดินบนกองถ่านที่ลุกไหม้อยู่ โดยเชื่อ ว่า ผู้บริสุทธิ์จะได้รับความคุ้มครองจากสิ่งศักดิ์สิทธิ์ ชาวตะวันตก (โดยส่วนใหญ่เป็นชาว ฝรั่งเศสและอังกฤษ) ปฏิเสธที่จะให้คนในประเทศของตนเข้ารับการพิจารณาคดีตามระบบ ศาลไทย ดังนั้น ชาวต่างชาติกลุ่มนี้จึงตั้งศาลพิจารณาคดีขึ้นในประเทศไทยเพื่อพิจารณาคดีที่ เกี่ยวข้องพลเมืองของประเทศตน

ถึงแม้ว่า ประเทศไทยจะไม่เคยตกเป็นเมืองขึ้นของประเทศตะวันตก กระนั้น ประเทศไทยกลับสูญเสียสิทธิเสรีภาพนอกอาณาเขตทางศาลซึ่งถือว่าเป็นสิ่งที่สำคัญมาก อย่างหนึ่ง สถานการณ์ที่รุมเร้า ทำให้ประเทศไทยต้องเสียดินแดนของตนให้แก่ประเทศ ฝรั่งเศสและประเทศอังกฤษอีกด้วย เพื่อที่จะรักษาอิสรภาพของประเทศไว้ ทำให้รัชกาลที่ 4 และรัชกาลที่ 5 ทรงเจรจาต่อรองแลกดินแดนของไทยให้แก่ประเทศผู้ล่าอาณานิคมทั้งหลาย

ในระยะแรกของกรุงรัตนโกสินทร์ ประเทศไทยมีอาณาบริเวณถึง 1,296,877 ตารางกิโลเมตร การเสียสละดินแดนไปถึง 14 ครั้ง ประกอบด้วย เสียดินแดนให้กับประเทศ อังกฤษ 4 ครั้ง ประเทศฝรั่งเศส 6 ครั้ง ประเทศพม่า 2 ครั้ง ประเทศเวียดนามและกัมพูชา ประเทศละ 1 ครั้ง ปัจจุบัน ประเทศไทยมีพื้นที่ทั้งสิ้น 513,115 ตารางกิโลเมตร ซึ่งรวมที่ดิน ที่สูญเสียไปทั้งหมดจำนวน 783,762 ตารางกิโลเมตร

ในรัชสมัยของพระบาทสมเด็จพระจุลจอมเกล้าเจ้าอยู่หัวมหาราช (รัชกาลที่ 5 หรือรู้จักกันในอีกพระนามหนึ่งว่า เจ้าฟ้ามหาจุฬาลงกรณ์) เป็นพระมหากษัตริย์ผู้มีบทบาท อย่างมากในประวัติศาสตร์ไทย พระองค์เดินทางไปทั่วพระราชอาณาจักรเพื่อศึกษาและทำ ความเข้าใจในสถานการณ์บ้านเมืองและชีวิตความเป็นอยู่ของประชาชนด้วยพระองค์เอง นอกจากนั้น พระองค์ยังทรงมีพระราชดำรัสให้มีการปรับปรุงเปลี่ยนแปลงทางด้านสังคม และการเมืองการปกครอง จึงถือได้ว่า พระบาทสมเด็จพระจุลจอมเกล้าเจ้าอยู่หัวมหาราช ทรงเป็นหนึ่งใน 7 พระมหากษัตริย์ผู้ยิ่งใหญ่ที่มีความสำคัญเป็นอย่างมากในประวัติศาสตร์ ไทย

ในปี พ.ศ. 2416 รัชกาลที่ 5 ได้ทรงล้มล้างขนบธรรมเนียมการเข้าเฝ้าแบบดั้งเดิมที่ข้าราชบริพารต้องหมอบกราบต่อหน้าพระพักตร์ และในปี พ.ศ. 2448 พระองค์ทรงประกาศการเลิกทาสทั้งหมดในประเทศ   ซึ่งการเลิกทาสนี้ถือเป็นพระมหากรุณาธิคุณอันล้นพ้นที่พระองค์ทรงมีต่อพสกนิกรชาวไทย

พระบาทสมเด็จพระจุลจอมเกล้าเจ้าอยู่หัวทรงเสด็จไปเจริญสัมพันธ์ไมตรียังประเทศต่างๆ อาทิ พระองค์ทรงเสด็จเยือนประเทศทางยุโรปครั้งใหญ่ถึง 2 ครั้ง ตลอดจนการเสด็จเยือนประเทศสิงคโปร์ อินโดนีเซียและอินเดีย ซึ่งพระองค์ได้นำสิ่งที่ทอดพระเนตรและศึกษาในขณะเสด็จเยือนประเทศต่างกลับมาพัฒนาเปลี่ยนแปลงประเทศไทยอย่างมากมาย พระองค์ทรงปรับปรุงระบบการบริหารราชการแผ่นดินให้ทันสมัย โดยการก่อตั้งกระทรวงต่างๆและพัฒนาโครงสร้างพื้นฐานต่างๆมากมาย เช่น โรงเรียนของรัฐ ระบบการขนส่งทางรถไฟ ระบบไปรษณีย์โทรเลข โรงพยาบาล ฯลฯ

นอกเหนือจากการปรับปรุงโครงสร้างของรัฐและระบบโครงสร้างพื้นฐานต่างๆในประเทศแล้ว พระองค์ยังทรงปฏิรูประบบกฎหมายไทยอีกด้วย ในปี พ.ศ. 2424 พระองค์ทรงประกาศอย่างเป็นทางการว่า คนไทยทุกคนต้องมีทนายเพื่อการดำเนินคดีในศาลในทุกๆกรณี   และพระองค์ได้ทรงล้มล้างระบบจารีตประเพณีอย่างเด็ดขาดออกไปจากระบบกฎหมายไทยในปีพ.ศ. 2431

นอกจากนี้ รัชกาลที่ 5 ยังทรงส่งพระองค์เจ้าพีพัฒนศักดิ์ (ท่านรพี) พระราชโอรสองค์ที่ 4 ไปศึกษาวิชานิติศาสตร์ในประเทศอังกฤษ (ท่านรพีได้รับการยกย่องว่าเป็นบิดาแห่งกฎหมายไทย ซึ่งพระองค์ทรงสวรรคตเมื่อวันที่ 7 สิงหาคม พ.ศ. 2463 ในแวดวงกฎหมายของไทยได้ยึดถือวันสวรรคตของพระองค์เป็นวันที่พสกพิกรชาวไทยจะได้เคารพในพระปรีชาสามารถและคุณูปการที่พระองค์ทรงมีต่อระบบกฎหมายไทย) ในปีพ.ศ. 2440 ท่านรพีได้สร้างโรงเรียนกฎหมายแห่งแรกขึ้นในประเทศไทย   โดยอาศัยอาคารของกระทรวงยุติธรรมเป็นที่ประกอบการเรียนการสอน ในเวลานั้น ประเทศไทยถือได้ว่าขาดแคลนผู้ที่มีความรู้ทางด้านกฎหมายอย่างลึกซึ้ง ซึ่งท่านรพีนั้นได้คัดเลือกนักเรียนนิติศาสตร์รุ่นแรกและทรงสอนให้นักศึกษากฎหมายเหล่านั้นโดยตรงด้วยตัวของพระองค์เอง

ในปลายปี พ.ศ. 2440 ถือเป็นครั้งแรกในประวัติศาสตร์ชาติไทยที่มีการสอบวิชากฎหมายเพื่อจบการศึกษา ระบบกฎหมายไทยแบบใหม่นี้เป็นที่ยอมรับกันอย่างกว้างขวางของนานาอารยประเทศ โดยที่การจัดตั้งศาลขึ้นมาใหม่ทำให้ประเทศไทยไม่ต้องเสียสิทธิเสรีภาพนอกอาณาเขตอีกต่อไป

พระบาทสมเด็จพระจุลจอมเกล้าเจ้าอยู่หัวทรงเสด็จสวรรคตเมื่อวันที่ 23 ตุลาคม พ.ศ. 2453 มีพระชนม์มายุเพียง 58 พรรษา ยังความสูญเสียให้แก่พสกนิกรชาวไทยอย่างใหญ่หลวง ด้วยพระองค์ทรงครองราชย์ยาวนานถึง 43 ปี พสกนิกรชาวไทยจึงยกย่องและเคารพบูชาพระองค์ในวัน "ปิยมหาราช หรือวันมหาจุฬาลงกรณ์" ซึ่งเป็นวันครบรอบวันสวรรคตและถือว่าวันดังกล่าวเป็นวันหยุดประจำปีของประเทศ โดยการถวายพวงมาลา ณ ลานพระบรมรูปทรงม้าและพระบรมรูปอื่นๆของพระองค์ทั่วประเทศ ท่านจะเห็นได้ว่าในบริเวณใกล้เคียงพระบรมฉายาลักษณ์ในพระบาทสมเด็จพระเจ้าอยู่หัวและสมเด็จพระนางเจ้าพระบรมราชินีนาถที่ประชาชนติดผนังไว้เพื่อชื่นชมในพระบารมีตามอาคารบ้านเรือนและสถานประกอบการนั้น มักจะมีพระบรมฉายาลักษณ์ในพระบาทสมเด็จพระจุลกล้าเจ้าอยู่หัวปรากฏอยู่ด้วยเสมอ ตลอดจนพระบรมฉายาลักษณ์ขนาดเล็กที่บรรจุอยู่ในล็อกเก็ตเพื่อนำมาคล้องสร้อยคอทองคำบูชาอีกด้วย พระองค์ทรงได้รับพระฉายาว่า "พระปิยมหาราช" ซึ่งมีความหมายว่า "พระมหากษัตริย์ผู้ทรงเป็นที่รักยิ่ง" อีกทั้ง คนไทยส่วนใหญ่ยังเชื่อว่าพระปรีชาสามารถของพระองค์จะอำนวยให้ผู้ที่เคารพศรัทธาประสบความสำเร็จในชีวิตได้อีกด้วย

การปฏิรูประบบกฎหมายครั้งสำคัญอีกครั้งหนึ่งของประเทศไทยเกิดขึ้นในสมัยพระบาทสมเด็จพระมงกุฎเกล้าเจ้าอยู่หัว (รัชกาลที่ 6) หรือเจ้าฟ้ามหาวชิราวุธ พระองค์ทรงตัดสินพระทัยที่จะปรับปรุงให้กฎหมายไทยสอดคล้องกับระบบกฎหมายของประเทศอื่นๆในรัชสมัยของพระองค์ มีการก่อตั้งเนติบัณฑิตยสภาแห่งประเทศไทยขึ้น และมีการสถาปนาจุฬาลงกรณ์มหาวิทยาลัย ซึ่งเป็นมหาวิทยาลัยแห่งแรกของไทยด้วยในปี พ.ศ. 2459

ในเวลาดังกล่าว ระบบกฎหมายของไทยและกฎหมายที่ใช้ดำเนินคดีในศาลจะเป็นไปตามที่ท่านพีได้วางรากฐานไว้ ซึ่งเป็นกฎหมายคอมมอนลอว์จากประเทศอังกฤษ (กฎหมายจารีตประเพณี) และเป็นหลักกฎหมายที่เกิดขึ้นจากการพิจารณาตัดสินของผู้พิพากษาในแต่ละคดี รัชกาลที่ 6 ทรงวินิจฉัยว่า กฎหมายคอมมอนลอว์นั้นไม่เหมาะสำหรับ

ประเทศไทย จึงมีการนำระบบกฎหมายระบบประมวล (Code Law) มาใช้ตั้งแต่ปี พ.ศ. 2467 เป็นต้นมา ระบบกฎหมายแบบประมวลมีการใช้ในประเทศต่างๆมากมาย ซึ่งเป็นหลัก กฎหมายที่ผู้พิพากษานำมาเป็นหลักในการพิจารณาตัดสินคดี ทั้งนี้ โรงเรียนกฎหมายของ ไทยได้เปลี่ยนมาจัดการเรียนการสอนกฎหมายจากระบบคอมมอนลอว์มาเป็นระบบ ประมวลทั้งสิ้นตั้งแต่นั้นเป็นต้นมา

ในเดือนมิถุนายน พ.ศ. 2475 ในรัชสมัยการปกครองของรัชกาลที่ 7 กลุ่มผู้มี ความรู้รุ่นใหม่ที่ได้รับการศึกษาจากต่างประเทศและได้รับแรงบันดาลใจจากระบอบการ ปกครองแบบประชาธิปไตยของประเทศตะวันตก ได้นำให้เกิดการ "ปฏิวัติ" เปลี่ยนแปลง ระบอบการปกครองจากระบอบสมบูรณาญาสิทธิราชย์เป็นระบอบประชาธิปไตย การ เคลื่อนไหวของบุคคลกลุ่มนี้เป็นที่รู้จักกันในนาม "พรรคประชาชน" หรือ "คณะราษฎร์" นำ โดย หลวงประดิษฐ์มนูธรรม (หรือ นายปรีดีย์ พนมยงค์) เพื่อมิให้มีการเสียเลือดเนื้อ รัชกาล ที่ 7 ทรงเห็นด้วยกับการยุติระบอบการปกครองแบบสมบูรณาญาสิทธิราชย์และทรงยอมรับ รัฐธรรมนูญฉบับแรกของประเทศไทย อันที่จริงแล้ว ก่อนที่จะมีการ "ปฏิรูป" การปกครอง พระองค์ทรงวางแผนที่จะคืนพระราชอำนาจกลับคืนสู่ประชาชนของพระองค์อยู่แล้ว ประเทศไทยจึงเป็นประเทศที่มีการปกครองด้วยระบอบประชาธิปไตยอันมีพระมหากษัตริย์ ทรงเป็นพระประมุข (กรุณาอ่าน "รัฐธรรมนูญแห่งราชอาณาจักรไทย")

เนติบัณฑิตยสภาที่ก่อตั้งขึ้นในสมัยรัชกาลที่ 6 นั้นได้ถูกรวมเข้ากับโรงเรียนสอน วิชากฎหมายแห่งแรกของไทย คณะรัฐศาสตร์และนิติศาสตร์จึงได้ถูกเพิ่มเข้าไว้เป็นคณะ หนึ่งในจุฬาลงกรณ์มหาวิทยาลัย ในปี พ.ศ. 2476 ซึ่งในเวลาต่อมาได้ถูกรวมเข้าเป็นส่วน หนึ่งของมหาวิทยาลัยธรรมศาสตร์

จุฬาลงกรณ์มหาวิทยาลัยได้สถาปนาคณะนิติศาสตร์ขึ้นมาอีกครั้งหนึ่งในปีพ.ศ. 2494 ทั้งจุฬาลงกรณ์มหาวิทยาลัยและมหาวิทยาลัยธรรมศาสตร์จึงเป็นสถาบันศึกษาวิชา กฎหมายที่มีชื่อเสียง ต่อมามหาวิทยาลัยรามคำแหง ซึ่งเป็นมหาวิทยาลัยเปิดที่ใหญ่ที่สุดของ ประเทศได้รับการสถาปนาขึ้นในปี พ.ศ. 2514 เป็นอีกหนึ่งมหาวิทยาลัยที่มีการเรียนการ สอนวิชากฎหมาย ในปัจจุบันมีมหาวิทยาลัยจำนวนมากในประเทศไทยที่เปิดการเรียนการ สอนเกี่ยวกับวิชากฎหมาย คุณสามารถอ่านรายชื่อคณะนิติศาสตร์ของมหาวิทยาลัยที่มีการ เปิดสอนในประเทศไทยได้ในภาคผนวก

พระบาทสมเด็จพระเจ้าอยู่หัวภูมิพลอดุลยเดช   พระมหากษัตริย์องค์ปัจจุบันของ
ไทย หรือ รัชกาลที่ 9 นั้นเป็นพระมหากษัตริย์ที่ทรงครองสิริราชสมบัติยาวนานที่สุดในโลก
ในระหว่างการครองราชย์ของพระองค์ได้เกิดรัฐประหาร   และการเปลี่ยนแปลงรัฐธรรมนูญ
ขึ้นหลายครั้ง   ซึ่งในหลายๆครั้งก่อให้เกิดการเปลี่ยนแปลงทางด้านนิติบัญญัติอย่างมากมาย
ในบทต่อไป   คุณจะได้ทราบเกี่ยวกับโครงสร้างของรัฐบาลไทย   รัฐธรรมนูญแห่ง
ราชอาณาจักรไทยและระบบศาลไทย

โครงสร้างของรัฐบาลไทย

รัฐธรรมนูญแห่งราชอาณาจักรไทย

รัฐธรรมนูญแห่งราชอาณาจักรไทยเป็นกฎหมายสูงสุดที่ใช้ในการปกครอง
ประเทศ เป็นเวลาหลายปีที่ประเทศไทยเผชิญกับปัญหาความไม่มั่นคงทางการเมืองและการ
ปฏิวัติรัฐประหารต่างๆ ภายหลังจากการปฏิวัติรัฐประหาร กองกำลังทหารได้ล้มล้าง
รัฐธรรมนูญที่บังคับใช้อยู่ ณ เวลานั้นและกำหนดประกาศคณะปฏิวัติขึ้นใช้ ทั้งนี้
รัฐธรรมนูญแห่งราชอาณาจักรไทยได้รับการเปลี่ยนแปลง แก้ไขและปรับปรุงเพื่อให้รับกับ
สภาพทางสังคมที่เปลี่ยนแปลงไปอยู่เสมอ อย่างไรก็ตาม รัฐธรรมนูญแต่ละฉบับล้วน
ประกอบไปด้วยหลักการที่สำคัญอย่างยิ่ง คือ ประเทศไทยเป็นราชอาณาจักรอันหนึ่งอันเดียว
จะแบ่งแยกมิได้ (รัฐเดี่ยว) และประเทศไทยมีการปกครองระบอบประชาธิปไตยอันมี
พระมหากษัตริย์เป็นประมุข

วันรัฐธรรมนูญในประเทศไทยตรงกับวันที่ 10 ธันวาคมของทุกปีและถือว่าเป็น
วันหยุดประจำชาติไทยด้วย เมื่อวันที่ 10 ธันวาคม พ.ศ. 2475 รัชกาลที่ 7 ทรงสละพระราช
อำนาจส่วนพระองค์ ซึ่งเป็นวันที่รัฐธรรมนูญฉบับแรกของไทยได้ถือกำเนิดขึ้น

นับตั้งแต่เกิดการเปลี่ยนแปลงระบอบการปกครองในปี พ.ศ. 2475 เป็นต้นมา
ประเทศไทยได้ประกาศบังคับใช้ธรรมนูญการปกครองและรัฐธรรมนูญ ดังต่อไปนี้

1. พระราชบัญญัติธรรมนูญการปกครองแผ่นดินสยามชั่วคราว พุทธศักราช 2475

2. รัฐธรรมนูญแห่งราชอาณาจักรสยาม พุทธศักราช 2475

3. รัฐธรรมนูญแห่งราชอาณาจักรไทย พุทธศักราช 2489

4. รัฐธรรมนูญแห่งราชอาณาจักรไทย (ฉบับชั่วคราว) พุทธศักราช 2490

5. รัฐธรรมนูญแห่งราชอาณาจักรไทย พุทธศักราช 2492

6. รัฐธรรมนูญแห่งราชอาณาจักรไทย พุทธศักราช 2475 แก้ไขเพิ่มเติม พุทธศักราช
   2495

7. ธรรมนูญการปกครองราชอาณาจักร พุทธศักราช 2502

8.   รัฐธรรมนูญแห่งราชอาณาจักรไทย พุทธศักราช 2511

9.   ธรรมนูญการปกครองราชอาณาจักร พุทธศักราช 2515

10.   รัฐธรรมนูญแห่งราชอาณาจักรไทย พุทธศักราช 2517

11.   รัฐธรรมนูญแห่งราชอาณาจักรไทย พุทธศักราช 2519

12.   ธรรมนูญการปกครองราชอาณาจักร พุทธศักราช 2520

13.   รัฐธรรมนูญแห่งราชอาณาจักรไทย พุทธศักราช 2521

14.   ธรรมนูญการปกครองราชอาณาจักร พุทธศักราช 2534

15.   รัฐธรรมนูญแห่งราชอาณาจักรไทย พุทธศักราช 2534

16.   รัฐธรรมนูญแห่งราชอาณาจักรไทย พุทธศักราช 2540

17.   รัฐธรรมนูญแห่งราชอาณาจักรไทย (ฉบับชั่วคราว) พุทธศักราช 2549

18.   รัฐธรรมนูญแห่งราชอาณาจักรไทย พุทธศักราช 2550

       รัฐธรรมนูญทุกฉบับของไทยบัญญัติว่าพระมหากษัตริย์ทรงดำรงอยู่ในฐานะอัน เป็นที่เคารพสักการะผู้ใดจะละเมิดมิได้ ทรงเป็นพุทธมามกะ เป็นอัครศาสนูปถัมภกและทรง ดำรงตำแหน่งจอมทัพไทย (แม่ทัพ) พระราชอำนาจในเชิงสัญลักษณ์ของพระมหากษัตริย์นี้ มาจากปวงชนชาวไทย โดยที่พระองค์จะทรงใช้อำนาจที่มีผ่านทางฝ่ายนิติบัญญัติ ฝ่าย บริหารและฝ่ายตุลาการ และทรงมีคณะที่ปรึกษาราชการแผ่นดินคณะหนึ่งเรียกว่าคณะ องคมนตรี ประกอบด้วยประธานองคมนตรี 1 คน และองคมนตรีอื่นอีกไม่เกิน 18 คน มี หน้าที่ถวายความเห็นต่อพระมหากษัตริย์ในพระราชกรณียกิจทั้งปวง การเลือกและการ แต่งตั้งองคมนตรีหรือให้องคมนตรีพ้นจากตำแหน่งให้เป็นไปตามพระราชอัธยาศัย

อำนาจ 5 ประการในการแก้ไขกฎหมายไทย

พระมหากษัตริย์   พระบรมราชโองการของพระองค์จะมีผลต่อกฎหมายในเชิงสัญลักษณ์
แม้พระราชอำนาจโดยตรงของพระองค์ถูกจำกัดอยู่ภายใต้รัฐธรรมนูญ   แต่พระองค์ทรงเป็น
สัญลักษณ์ของประเทศและเป็นศูนย์รวมใจของคนไทยทั้งชาติ อย่างไรก็ตาม พระองค์ทรงมี
พระราชอำนาจในการลงความเห็นชอบในกฎหมายต่างๆที่รัฐสภาได้นำขึ้นทูลเกล้าฯถวาย
เพื่อทรงมีพระบรมราชวินิจฉัย หากเห็นชอบก็จะทรงลงพระปรมาภิไธย และเมื่อประกาศใน
ราชกิจจานุเบกษาแล้วให้ใช้บังคับเป็นกฎหมายได้   หากปราศจากความเห็นชอบของ
พระมหากษัตริย์ กฎหมายนั้นจะไม่สามารถนำมาใช้บังคับได้เลย เว้นเสียแต่รัฐสภาได้ลง
ความเห็นยืนยันร่างกฎหมายอีกครั้ง หลังจากที่พระองค์ทรงมีพระบรมราชวินิจฉัยแล้วไม่
ทรงเห็นชอบและส่งร่างกฎหมายฉบับนั้นกลับคืนมายังรัฐสภา   อย่างไรก็ตามที่ผ่านมามี
กฎหมายหลายฉบับที่พระมหากษัตริย์ทรงมีพระบรมราชวินิจฉัยแล้วไม่ทรงลงพระ
ปรมาภิไธยเมื่อส่งร่างกฎหมายกลับคืนไปยังรัฐสภาแล้วฝ่ายรัฐสภาก็จะแก้ไขปรับปรุง
กฎหมายก่อนที่จะนำขึ้นทูลเกล้าทูลกระหม่อมอีกครั้งหรือกฎหมายฉบับนั้นอาจจะถูกยกเลิก
ไปเลยก็ได้

คณะปฏิวัติ คนกลุ่มนี้ใช้กำลังอำนาจเพื่อให้เกิดการเปลี่ยนแปลงในรัฐธรรมนูญ   ประกาศ
ของคณะปฏิวัติมีผลใช้บังคับเป็นกฎหมาย เช่นเดียวกับการประกาศกฎอัยการศึก การปฏิวัติ
เกิดขึ้นครั้งแรกในประเทศไทยเมื่อปี พ.ศ. 2475 โดยส่วนใหญ่แล้วการปฏิวัติของไทยมักนำ
โดยกองกำลังทหาร

รัฐสภา   รัฐสภามีหน้าที่หลักในการให้ความเห็นชอบกฎหมายใหม่ๆ   รัฐสภาประกอบไป
ด้วยสมาชิกวุฒิสภาและสมาชิกสภาผู้แทนราษฎร ภายใต้บทบัญญัติแห่งรัฐธรรมนูญ ปี 2550
รัฐสภาประกอบไปด้วยสมาชิกวุฒิสภาจำนวน   150   คนและสมาชิกสภาผู้แทนราษฎร
จำนวน 480 คน

นายกรัฐมนตรีและคณะรัฐมนตรี   มีหน้าที่ในการบริหารราชการแผ่นดินโดยมี
นายกรัฐมนตรีเป็นผู้นำรัฐบาลและมีหน้าที่เกี่ยวกับกฎหมาย คือการนำเสนอกฎหมายใหม่ๆ
เข้าสู่รัฐสภาเพื่อผ่านการพิจารณาหรือกรณีมีความจำเป็นเร่งด่วนฉุกเฉินอันมิอาจหลีกเลี่ยง
ได้ เพื่อประโยชน์ในอันที่จะรักษาความปลอดภัยของประเทศหรือป้องปัดภัยพิบัติสาธารณะ

คณะรัฐมนตรีมีอำนาจสนอกฎหมายในรูปแบบของพระราชกำหนดเพื่อใช้บังคับไปพลาง
ก่อนก็ได้ ภายใต้บทบัญญัติรัฐธรรมนูญแห่งราชอาณาจักรไทยปี 2550 ให้มีนายกรัฐมนตรี 1
คนและมีคณะรัฐมนตรีไม่เกิน 35 คน ผู้ดำรงตำแหน่งเป็นนายกรัฐมนตรีต้องได้รับการออก
เสียงมากกว่ากึ่งหนึ่งจากสมาชิกสภาผู้แทนราษฎรทั้งหมด และไม่สามารถดำรงตำแหน่ง
ติดต่อกันเกินระยะเวลา 8 ปี

      ภายใต้บทบัญญัติแห่งรัฐธรรมนูญปี 2550 ระบบบริหารราชการแผ่นดินของไทย
ตั้งอยู่บนระบบการตรวจสอบถ่วงดุลและการคานอำนาจ ซึ่งมีลักษณะคล้ายคลึงกันกับ
ประเทศทางตะวันตกอื่นๆ ที่ปกครองในระบอบประชาธิปไตย อันประกอบด้วยองค์กรที่ใช้
อำนาจรัฐ 3 ฝ่าย คือฝ่ายบริหาร ฝ่ายนิติบัญญัติ และฝ่ายตุลาการ มีอำนาจหน้าที่และที่มาของ
การเข้าสู่ตำแหน่ง ดังนี้

ฝ่ายบริหาร

      คณะรัฐมนตรีเป็นฝ่ายบริหารหรือรัฐบาล ประกอบไปด้วย นายกรัฐมนตรี
รัฐมนตรีว่าการกระทรวงต่างๆ รัฐมนตรีช่วยว่าการกระทรวง และปลัดกระทรวง โดยมี
นายกรัฐมนตรีเป็นหัวหน้าฝ่ายบริหาร นายกรัฐมนตรีมาจากการเลือกตั้งของสภา
ผู้แทนราษฎร โดยปกติแล้ว ผู้ที่จะดำรงตำแหน่งเป็นนายกรัฐมนตรีมักเป็นหัวหน้าพรรค
การเมืองที่มีสมาชิกสภาผู้แทนราษฎรในสภามากที่สุด อย่างไรก็ดี ในบางสมัยอาจมีการ
ก่อตั้งคณะรัฐบาลแบบผสมขึ้น กล่าวคือ เสียงข้างมากของสภาผู้แทนราษฎรมาจากพรรค
การเมืองที่มากกว่า 1 พรรค ดังนั้น ในรัฐบาลผสม ผู้แทนราษฎรในสภาต่อเลือกหัวหน้า
พรรคของตนขึ้นเป็นนายกรัฐมนตรี ประธานสภาเป็นผู้มีหน้าที่นำรายชื่อบุคคลดังกล่าวขึ้น
กราบบังคมทูลต่อพระมหากษัตริย์เพื่อทรงมีพระบรมราชโองการแต่งตั้งเป็นนายกรัฐมนตรี
ต่อไป อนึ่ง นายกรัฐมนตรีต้องเป็นสมาชิกสภาผู้แทนราษฎรเท่านั้น จะเป็นบุคคลอื่นไป
ไม่ได้

      นายกรัฐมนตรีดำรงตำแหน่งเป็นหัวหน้าคณะรัฐบาล มีหน้าที่ในการบริหาร
ปกครองหน่วยงานที่ขึ้นตรงต่อฝ่ายบริหาร ยกเว้นศาลและสภานิติบัญญัติ นายกรัฐมนตรีจะ
ทำหน้าที่เลือกคณะรัฐบาล โดยมากแล้วมักมาจากสมาชิกสภาผู้แทนราษฎร เพื่อแต่งตั้งให้

ดำรงตำแหน่งรัฐมนตรีว่าการกระทรวงหรือรัฐมนตรีช่วยว่าการกระทรวงเพื่อเป็นผู้นำฝ่าย
บริหารในกระทรวงต่างๆ

ในกรณีที่รัฐบาลผสมประกอบไปด้วยสมาชิกสภาผู้แทนราษฎรจากหลายพรรค
การเมือง พรรคการเมืองแต่ละพรรคจะคัดเลือกผู้แทนที่เหมาะสมจากพรรคตนเพื่อเสนอชื่อ
ในการดำรงตำแหน่งเป็นรัฐมนตรีและรัฐมนตรีช่วยว่าการกระทรวง พระมหากษัตริย์จะทรง
เป็นผู้ทบทวนภายใต้คำแนะนำของนายกรัฐมนตรี   เพื่อแต่งตั้งคณะรัฐมนตรีและรัฐมนตรี
ช่วยว่าการกระทรวงต่างๆ ภายใต้บทบัญญัติแห่งรัฐธรรมนูญปี 2550 พระมหากษัตริย์จะ
ทรงมีพระราชโองการแต่งตั้งนายกรัฐมนตรีหนึ่งคนและรัฐมนตรีอื่นๆ อีกไม่เกิน 35 คน
ประกอบเป็นคณะรัฐมนตรี   มีหน้าที่บริหารราชการแผ่นดินตามหลักความรับผิดชอบ
ร่วมกัน

เมื่อมีการแต่งตั้งนายกรัฐมนตรี รัฐมนตรีและรัฐมนตรีช่วยว่าการกระทรวงเป็นที่
เรียบร้อยแล้ว   ผู้ที่ดำรงตำแหน่งในฝ่ายบริหารต้องสละสมาชิกภาพการเป็น
สมาชิกสภาผู้แทนราษฎรของตน เนื่องด้วยผู้ที่ดำรงตำแหน่งทางการเมืองไม่สามารถดำรง
ตำแหน่งเป็นสมาชิกสภาผู้แทนราษฎรได้

นายกรัฐมนตรีและรัฐมนตรีว่าการกระทรวงต่างๆ   (รวมถึงรัฐมนตรีช่วยว่าการ
กระทรวง) รวมกันเรียกว่าคณะรัฐมนตรี คณะรัฐมนตรีนี้จะทำหน้าที่บริหารราชการแผ่นดิน
ทั้งหมด โดยการกำหนดนโยบายการบริหารและเป้าหมายการทำงาน ยกเว้นงานที่เป็นหน้าที่
ของฝ่ายนิติบัญญัติและฝ่ายตุลาการ ทั้งนี้ รัฐมนตรีว่าการกระทรวงต่างๆ ต้องนำโยบาย
และเป้าหมายในการบริหารราชการแผ่นดินไปมอบหมายให้ข้าราชการและหน่วยงานใน
สังกัดของตนดำเนินการต่อไป

ก่อนเข้ารับหน้าที่นายกรัฐมนตรีและรัฐมนตรีต้องถวายสัตย์ปฏิญาณต่อ
พระมหากษัตริย์ ว่าจะจงรักภักดีต่อพระมหากษัตริย์และจะปฏิบัติหน้าที่ด้วยความซื่อสัตย์
สุจริต เพื่อประโยชน์ของประเทศและประชาชน ทั้งจะรักษาไว้และปฏิบัติตามรัฐธรรมนูญ
แห่งราชอาณาจักรไทยทุกประการ

ในการบริหารราชการแผ่นดินของรัฐบาลประเทศไทยมีการแบ่งส่วนราชการตาม
พ.ร.บ. ปรับปรุง กระทรวง ทบวง กรม พ.ศ. 2545 โดยแบ่งออกเป็น 19 กระทรวง และส่วน

ราชการที่มีฐานะเทียบเท่ากระทรวง 1 แห่ง โดยมีรัฐมนตรีว่าการเป็นหัวหน้าบริหารฝ่าย
การเมือง และมีหัวหน้าบริหารฝ่ายข้าราชการประจำคือปลัดกระทรวง ดังนี้

- สำนักนายกรัฐมนตรี
- กระทรวงกลาโหม
- กระทรวงการคลัง
- กระทรวงการต่างประเทศ
- กระทรวงการท่องเที่ยวและกีฬา
- กระทรวงการพัฒนาสังคมและความมั่นคงของมนุษย์
- กระทรวงการเกษตรและสหกรณ์
- กระทรวงการคมนาคม
- กระทรวงทรัพยากรธรรมชาติและสิ่งแวดล้อม
- กระทรวงเทคโนโลยีสารสนเทศและการสื่อสาร
- กระทรวงพลังงาน
- กระทรวงพาณิชย์
- กระทรวงมหาดไทย
- กระทรวงยุติธรรม
- กระทรวงแรงงาน
- กระทรวงวัฒนธรรม
- กระทรวงวิทยาศาสตร์และเทคโนโลยี
- กระทรวงศึกษาธิการ
- กระทรวงสาธารณสุข

- กระทรวงอุตสาหกรรม

คุณสามารถอ่านรายละเอียดเกี่ยวกับหน่วยงานในสังกัดกระทรวงต่างๆ ตลอดจน
ข้อมูลองค์กร องค์กรอิสระและหน่วยงานสาธารณะได้ในภาคผนวก ซึ่งผู้เขียนได้ชี้แจงให้
ผู้อ่านเห็นถึงโครงสร้างของคณะรัฐบาล เช่น กรมการกงสุลเป็นหน่วยงานในสังกัดของ
กระทรวงการต่างประเทศ กองทัพไทยเป็นหน่วยงานในสังกัดของกระทรวงกลาโหม และ
สำนักข่าวกรองแห่งชาติเป็นหน่วยงานสังกัดสำนักนายกรัฐมนตรี เป็นต้น

ฝ่ายนิติบัญญัติ

ฝ่ายนิติบัญญัติมีหน้าที่ประการสำคัญในการออกกฎหมาย การปรับปรุงกฎหมาย
และการประกาศใช้กฎหมายใหม่ ฝ่ายนิติบัญญัติมีชื่ออย่างเป็นทางการว่า "สภานิติบัญญัติ
แห่งชาติ" หรือรัฐสภา ซึ่งประกอบไปด้วยคณะบุคคล 2 กลุ่มที่ทำหน้าที่ต่างกัน คือ คณะ
สมาชิกสภาผู้แทนราษฎรและคณะวุฒิสมาชิก

สมาชิกสภาผู้แทนราษฎร หรือ "สภาล่างของรัฐสภา" ประกอบไปด้วย
สมาชิกสภาผู้แทนราษฎรจำนวน 480 คน ซึ่งมาจากเลือกตั้งทั่วไปแบบแบ่งเขตจำนวน 400
คน และมาจากการเลือกตั้งแบบบัญชีรายชื่อที่พรรคการเมืองจัดตั้งขึ้น โดยมาจากพรรค
การเมืองที่ได้รับคะแนนเสียงส่วนใหญ่จากการเลือกตั้ง จำนวน 80 คน

ในประเทศไทย ผู้ที่มีสิทธิลงคะแนนเสียงเลือกตั้งได้คือพลเมืองไทยที่มีอายุครบ
18 ปีบริบูรณ์ และมีชื่อในทะเบียนบ้านของตนไม่ต่ำกว่า 90 วัน (สำหรับผู้ที่เปลี่ยนแปลง
สัญชาติมาเป็นสัญชาติไทย ต้องรอให้ระยะเวลาในการเปลี่ยนสัญชาติครบ 5 ปีบริบูรณ์ก่อน
จึงจะมีสิทธิเลือกตั้ง) ในระหว่างการเลือกตั้ง ผู้มีสิทธิออกเสียงเลือกตั้งจะลงคะแนนเสียง
ของตนในการเลือกผู้สมัครเป็นรายบุคคลจำนวน 1 คะแนนเสียง และอีกคะแนนหนึ่งในการ
เลือกเป็นรายพรรคการเมือง

ในการเลือกสมาชิกวุฒิสภา ผู้มีสิทธิออกเสียงเลือกตั้งจะเลือกผู้สมัครดำรง
ตำแหน่งเป็นวุฒิสมาชิกในเขตที่ผู้มีสิทธิเลือกตั้งอาศัยอยู่ได้ จำนวน 1 คนเท่านั้น

ภายใต้บทบัญญัติแห่งรัฐธรรมนูญ ปี 2550 วุฒิสมาชิกหรือ "สภาสูงของรัฐสภา" ประกอบไปด้วยสมาชิกวุฒิสภาจำนวน 150 คน มาจากการเลือกตั้งในแต่ละจังหวัด จังหวัด ละ 1 คนรวม 76 จังหวัดทั่วประเทศและมาจากการสรรหาเท่ากับจำนวนรวมข้างต้นหักด้วย จำนวนวุฒิที่มาจากการเลือกตั้ง คณะกรรมการสรรหาสมาชิกวุฒิสภาประกอบด้วย

- ประธานศาลรัฐธรรมนูญ

- ประธานกรรมการเลือกตั้ง

- ประธานผู้ตรวจการแผ่นดิน

- ประธานกรรมการป้องกันและปราบปรามการทุจริตแห่งชาติ

- ประธานกรรมการตรวจเงินแผ่นดิน

- ผู้พิพากษาในศาลฎีกาซึ่งดำรงตำแหน่งไม่ต่ำกว่าผู้พิพากษาศาลฎีกาที่ที่ ประชุมใหญ่มอบหมายจำนวน 1 คน

- ตุลาการในศาลปกครองสูงสุดที่ที่ประชุมใหญ่ตุลาการในศาลปกครองสูงสุด มอบหมายจำนวน 1 คนเป็นกรรมการ

โดยให้กรรมการเลือกกันเองให้กรรมการผู้หนึ่งเป็นประธานกรรมการ

รัฐธรรมนูญปี 2550 กำหนดให้สมาชิกวุฒิสภาดำรงตำแหน่งในแต่ละสมัยได้ไม่ เกินระยะเวลา 6 ปี

สภาผู้แทนราษฎรคือฝ่ายนิติบัญญัติซึ่งเป็นด่านแรกที่จะพิจารณากฎหมายที่ คณะรัฐมนตรีหรือฝ่ายบริหาร (อันประกอบไปด้วย นายกรัฐมนตรี รัฐมนตรีและรัฐมนตรี ช่วยว่าการต่างๆ) เสนอหรือกฎหมายที่เสนอโดยสมาชิกรัฐสภาด้วยกัน ในกรณีที่สภา เห็นชอบในการออกกฎหมายดังกล่าว สภาผู้แทนราษฎรจะส่งร่างกฎหมายนั้นไปยังวุฒิสภา เมื่อกฎหมายผ่านสภาทั้งสองเป็นที่เรียบร้อย โดยที่สภาทั้งสองได้ทบทวนและเห็นชอบใน ร่างกฎหมายดังกล่าวแล้วเป็นระยะเวลา 3 วาระด้วยกัน คือวาระที่ 1 ขั้นรับหลักการ วาระที่ 2 แปรญัตติ วาระที่ 3 ออกเสียงมติผ่านร่างกฎหมาย กฎหมายดังกล่าวจะถูกส่งไปยัง

นายกรัฐมนตรีเพื่อเตรียมการนำทูลเกล้าทูลกระหม่อมถวายพระมหากษัตริย์เพื่อทรงลงพระ
ปรมาภิไธยเห็นชอบต่อไป   (ในการออกกฎหมายแต่ละฉบับ   จะต้องได้รับการพิจารณา
เห็นชอบจากทั้งสภาผู้แทนราษฎร วุฒิสภาและพระมหากษัตริย์ ทั้ง 3 ส่วนเสียก่อน) ในกรณี
ที่วุฒิสภาไม่เห็นด้วยกับร่างกฎหมายดังกล่าวตามที่สภาผู้แทนราษฎรได้เสนอมา   วุฒิสภา
อาจปรับแก้และส่งกฎหมายกลับคืนไปยังสภาผู้แทนราษฎรเพื่อให้พิจารณากฎหมาย
ดังกล่าวอีกวาระหนึ่ง   ในกรณีที่สภาผู้แทนราษฎรไม่เห็นด้วยกับการแก้ไขดังกล่าวของ
วุฒิสภา ทั้งสองฝ่ายจำต้องจัดตั้งคณะกรรมาธิการเพื่อแก้ปัญหาความขัดแย้งให้เสร็จสิ้นลง

ฝ่ายตุลาการ

ฝ่ายตุลาการนำโดยประธานศาลฎีกา   ฝ่ายตุลาการประกอบไปด้วยศาลทุกศาลใน
ประเทศไทย ศาลในประเทศไทยถือเป็นองค์กรอิสระ ทำหน้าที่ตรวจสอบและถ่วงดุลอำนาจ
จากฝ่ายบริหารและฝ่ายนิติบัญญัติ

การพิจารณาคดีของฝ่ายตุลาการ   มักเกี่ยวข้องกับความขัดแย้งของเอกชนกับ
เอกชน หรือเอกชนกับองค์กรธุรกิจ หรือความขัดแย้งระหว่างเอกชนกับรัฐ ทั้งนี้ ศาลจะทำ
การตัดสินพิพากษาคดีตามดุลยพินิจของศาล

ศาลจะนำตัวบทบัญญัติแห่งกฎหมายไปใช้ในการพิจารณาคดี ในกรณีที่เชื่อว่าตัว
บทกฎหมายมีความขัดแย้งกับรัฐธรรมนูญ ซึ่งถือเป็นกฎหมายสูงสุดของประเทศ ศาลจะทำ
หน้าที่ส่งคดีดังกล่าวไปยังศาลรัฐธรรมนูญเพื่อวินิจฉัยความขัดกันแห่งกฎหมายต่อไป

นอกเหนือจากประเด็นกฎหมายที่ขัดกับรัฐธรรมนูญแล้ว   ศาลจะทำหน้าที่
พิจารณาข้อเท็จจริงแห่งคดี   โดยอาศัยตัวบทแห่งกฎหมายในการพิพากษาคดีเป็นสำคัญ
นอกจากนี้   ศาลยังมีหน้าที่ในการพิจารณาพิพากษาการกระทำความผิดของผู้ดำรงตำแหน่ง
ทางการเมืองด้วย เช่น การบริหารราชการแผ่นดินของฝ่ายบริหาร เป็นต้น

ต่อไปนี้จะเป็นภาพรวมของระบบศาลไทย   (ซึ่งท่านสามารถศึกษารายละเอียด
เกี่ยวกับระบบศาลไทยทั้งหมด เพิ่มเติมได้ในหัวข้อ "ระบบศาลไทย")

ศาลในประเทศไทยประกอบไปด้วย ศาลชั้นต้น ศาลอุทธรณ์และศาลฎีกา นอกจากนี้ ภายใต้บทบัญญัติแห่งรัฐธรรมนูญปี 2550 ศาลรัฐธรรมนูญของไทยได้รับการจัดตั้งขึ้นเพื่อพิจารณาถึงสภาพการบังคับใช้แห่งกฎหมาย กฎระเบียบและการตัดสินใจของคณะรัฐบาลตามบทบัญญัติในรัฐธรรมนูญ อีกทั้ง ศาลรัฐธรรมนูญยังมีอำนาจหน้าที่ในการวินิจฉัยกรณีที่บทบัญญัติแห่งกฎหมายอื่นมีความขัดแย้งกับรัฐธรรมนูญด้วย

ศาลชั้นต้นประกอบไปด้วยศาลแขวงและศาลจังหวัด รวมถึง ศาลอาญากลางและศาลแพ่งกลางที่ตั้งอยู่ในกรุงเทพมหานคร ศาลแรงงาน ศาลเยาวชนและครอบครัว ศาลภาษีอากร และศาลทรัพย์สินทางปัญญาและการค้าระหว่างประเทศที่เพิ่งได้รับการจัดตั้งขึ้นมาใหม่

ศาลอุทธรณ์มีอำนาจในการพิจารณาคดีที่ได้รับการอุทธรณ์จากศาลชั้นต้น ในขณะที่ศาลฎีกามีอำนาจในการพิพากษาคดีที่ได้รับการฎีกาจากศาลอุทธรณ์หรือคำอุทธรณ์อื่นๆที่ส่งมายังศาลฎีกาโดยตรง (เช่น คำอุทธรณ์ของศาลแรงงานจะส่งมายังศาลฎีกาโดยตรง) โดยมิต้องผ่านการพิจารณาของศาลอุทธรณ์ ส่วนใหญ่แล้ว ให้ถือว่าคำพิพากษาของศาลฎีกาเป็นที่สุด ไม่จำต้องมีการอุทธรณ์หรือการทบทวนใดๆ อีก

ศาลรัฐธรรมนูญได้รับการจัดตั้งขึ้นภายใต้บทบัญญัติแห่งรัฐธรรมนูญ ปี 2550 คำวินิจฉัยของผู้พิพากษาศาลรัฐธรรมนูญให้ถือเป็นที่สุดและผูกมัดสภานิติบัญญัติแห่งชาติ คณะรัฐมนตรี ศาลและหน่วยงานของรัฐทั้งหมด คำวินิจฉัยศาลรัฐธรรมนูญให้เป็นที่สุดและไม่มีการอุทธรณ์ใดๆทั้งสิ้น

ขอบเขตอำนาจของศาลรัฐธรรมนูญนั้นค่อนข้างกว้าง ศาลรัฐธรรมนูญมีหน้าที่ตัดสินบทบัญญัติแห่งกฎหมายที่สภานิติบัญญัติแห่งชาติได้พิจารณาหรือนำมาใช้ ว่าบทบัญญัติเหล่านั้นมีความขัดแย้งต่อรัฐธรรมนูญหรือไม่ อีกทั้ง ศาลรัฐธรรมนูญมีอำนาจในประกาศว่าบทบัญญัติแห่งกฎหมายส่วนใดส่วนหนึ่งหรือทั้งหมดมีความขัดแย้งกับรัฐธรรมนูญโดยมีสภาพเป็นโมฆะหรือขาดสภาพการบังคับใช้หรือไม่

ผู้พิพากษาในประเทศไทยมีสถานภาพทางสังคมที่สูงและเป็นที่เคารพของบุคคลทั่วไป เนื่องจากผู้พิพากษาปฏิบัติหน้าที่ในนามของพระมหากษัตริย์ จึงต้องมีคุณธรรม ความซื่อสัตย์และมีภูมิหลังที่ดี ตลอดจนต้องมีความรู้และความสามารถสูง การจะมาเป็นผู้

พิพากษาได้นั้น จำเป็นต้องผ่านการสอบคัดเลือกหลายระดับ อีกทั้งยังต้องผ่านการสอบเป็น
เนติบัณฑิตมาก่อนด้วย

นอกจากนี้   ยังมีข้อกำหนดเพิ่มเติมว่าผู้พิพากษาจำเป็นต้องมีประสบการณ์และ
คุณสมบัติ ดังเช่น สำเร็จการศึกษาปริญญานิติศาสตร์บัณฑิตจากมหาวิทยาลัยในประเทศ
หรือต่างประเทศ ผ่านการทำงานในศาลเป็นระยะเวลาหลายปี (ขึ้นอยู่กับตำแหน่งที่ทำ) เป็น
ทนายความมาแล้วอย่างต่ำเป็นเวลา 10 ปี สำเร็จการศึกษาระดับเกียรตินิยมหรือดำรง
ตำแหน่งเป็นผู้บรรยายหรือศาสตราจารย์ในคณะนิติศาสตร์เป็นระยะเวลาอย่างน้อย 5 ปี
เป็นต้น

การคานอำนาจ (การถ่วงดุลอำนาจ)

ฝ่ายบริหาร ฝ่ายนิติบัญญัติและฝ่ายตุลาการมีอำนาจพิเศษนอกเหนือจากอำนาจตน
ในการตรวจสอบซึ่งกันและกัน   ด้วยระบบที่แต่ละฝ่ายสามารถตรวจสอบอำนาจกันนี้เอง
เรียกกันว่า ระบบการตรวจสอบและการถ่วงดุลอำนาจ

ด้วยอำนาจที่ฝ่ายบริหารมีในการกำหนดงบประมาณในการบริหารราชการ
แผ่นดิน   ฝ่ายบริหารจึงมีอำนาจในการควบคุมการปฏิบัติหน้าที่ของฝ่ายตุลาการ   เช่น
ค่าใช้จ่ายเกี่ยวกับการว่าจ้างพนักงานของศาล ในขณะที่ ฝ่ายบริหารสามารถคานอำนาจของ
ฝ่ายนิติบัญญัติผ่านการลงความเห็นชอบหรือไม่เห็นชอบในการออกบังคับใช้กฎหมาย
ก่อนที่จะนำทูลเกล้าฯให้พระมหากษัตริย์ลงพระปรมาภิไธย   โดยที่ฝ่ายบริหารจะใช้อำนาจ
ของตนในการบริหารประเทศและบังคับใช้กฎหมายที่รัฐสภาเห็นชอบและพระมหากษัตริย์
ได้ทรงลงพระปรมาภิไธยแล้ว

ฝ่ายนิติบัญญัติสามารถให้ความเห็นชอบ   แก้ไขและปฏิเสธกฎหมายที่เสนอโดย
ฝ่ายบริหารได้   ตลอดจนสามารถทบทวนการเสนองบประมาณการบริหารราชการแผ่นดิน
ของฝ่ายบริหารได้เช่นกันและยังสามารถเปลี่ยนแปลงงบประมาณภายในกรอบที่
รัฐธรรมนูญกำหนดไว้ได้

ฝ่ายตุลาการมีอำนาจในการควบคุมการออกกฎหมายของรัฐสภา โดยการตีความกฎหมาย เช่น ศาลรัฐธรรมนูญสามารถตีความกฎหมายและวินิจฉัยได้ว่าบทบัญญัติใดที่ขัดแย้งต่อรัฐธรรมนูญ เป็นต้น บทบัญญัติที่ขัดหรือแย้งต่อรัฐธรรมนูญนั้นจะถือว่าไม่มีผลบังคับใช้ตามคำวินิจฉัยของศาลรัฐธรรมนูญ ฝ่ายตุลาการยังสามารถทบทวนพิจารณาการกระทำของรัฐบาลและขอให้รัฐบาลเปลี่ยนแปลงหรือพิจารณากรณีใดๆใหม่อีกครั้งได้ เช่น การทบทวนประเด็นเกี่ยวกับสิ่งแวดล้อมใหม่ เป็นต้น

ระบบศาลไทย

ภายใต้รัฐธรรมนูญ ปี 2550 ระบบศาลไทยประกอบไปด้วย 4 ศาลซึ่งปฏิบัติหน้าที่ในนามของพระมหากษัตริย์ ดังนี้

1. ศาลรัฐธรรมนูญ

2. ศาลปกครอง

3. ศาลทหาร

4. ศาลยุติธรรม

ผู้เขียนของอธิบายถึงศาลรัฐธรรมนูญ ศาลปกครองและศาลทหารก่อนเป็นลำดับแรก เนื่องจากชาวต่างประเทศส่วนใหญ่มีความสนใจในศาลยุติธรรมของไทยมาก ซึ่งผู้เขียนจะอธิบายในรายละเอียดต่อไปในภายหลัง

ศาลรัฐธรรมนูญ

ศาลรัฐธรรมนูญประกอบไปด้วยประธานศาลรัฐธรรมนูญและตุลาการศาล
รัฐธรรมนูญอีก 8 คน ตุลาการศาลรัฐธรรมนูญทุกคนได้รับการแต่งตั้งจากพระมหากษัตริย์
ภายใต้คำแนะนำของคณะวุฒิสมาชิก   มีสถานภาพเป็นเจ้าหน้าที่ฝ่ายตุลาการของรัฐและ
ปฏิบัติหน้าที่ได้ไม่เกิน 9 ปี

ศาลรัฐธรรมนูญได้รับการจัดตั้งขึ้นเพื่อให้มีหน้าที่วินิจฉัยถึงประเด็นสภาพการ
บังคับใช้ของกฎหมาย ระเบียบและวินิจฉัยปัญหาการตัดสินใจของรัฐบาลภายใต้บทบัญญัติ
แห่งรัฐธรรมนูญ ทั้งนี้ ศาลรัฐธรรมนูญมีหน้าที่วินิจฉัยการใช้กฎหมายและการขัดกันแห่ง
กฎหมายกับรัฐธรรมนูญ   อำนาจของศาลรัฐธรรมนูญนั้นกว้างมาก เนื่องจากตุลาการศาล
รัฐธรรมนูญมีอำนาจในการประกาศให้บทบัญญัติส่วนใดส่วนหนึ่งหรือทั้งหมดที่ขัดต่อ
รัฐธรรมนูญมีสภาพเป็นโมฆะหรือไม่มีสภาพการบังคับใช้ได้

ศาลปกครอง

ศาลปกครองมีหน้าที่ในการตรวจสอบการบังคับใช้กฎหมายและนโยบายการ
บริหารราชการแผ่นดินของฝ่ายบริหาร   ศาลปกครองมีอำนาจในการวินิจฉัยข้อพิพาท
ระหว่างรัฐ หน่วยงานของรัฐ รัฐวิสาหกิจ หน่วยงานปกครองส่วนท้องถิ่น หรือเจ้าหน้าที่
ของรัฐ

ศาลปกครองแบ่งออกเป็น 2 ศาลได้แก่ ศาลปกครองชั้นต้นและศาลปกครอง
ชั้นสูง   คณะตุลาการศาลปกครองในศาลปกครองแต่ละชั้นศาลจะได้รับการกำหนดโดย
คณะกรรมการตุลาการศาลปกครอง คณะกรรมการตุลาการศาลปกครอง ประกอบด้วย
ประธานศาลปกครองสูงสุดเป็นประธานกรรมการ กรรมการผู้ทรงคุณวุฒิจำนวน 9 คน ซึ่ง
เป็นตุลาการในศาลปกครองและได้รับเลือกจากตุลาการในศาลปกครองด้วยกันเอง
กรรมการผู้ทรงคุณวุฒิจำนวน 2 คน ซึ่งได้รับเลือกจากวุฒิสภาและจากคณะรัฐมนตรี อีก 1
คน ประธานศาลปกครองสูงสุดจะได้รับการคัดเลือกและความเห็นชอบจากคณะกรรมการ
ตุลาการศาลปกครองและวุฒิสภา โดยที่การเสนอชื่อดังกล่าวจะส่งไปยังนายกรัฐมนตรีเพื่อ
นำชื่อขึ้นทูลเกล้าฯถวายองค์พระมหากษัตริย์เพื่อทรงพิจารณาเห็นชอบต่อไป

ศาลทหาร

ศาลทหารมีอำนาจพิจารณาคดีอาญาทางทหารและข้อพิพาทที่เกี่ยวกับราชการ
ทหารและผู้ซึ่งตกอยู่ในเขตอำนาจของศาลทหาร   พระมหากษัตริย์ทรงมอบหมายพระราช
อำนาจให้ผู้บังชาการทหารสูงสุด   และรัฐมนตรีว่าการกระทรวงมหาดไทยทำหน้าที่แต่งตั้ง
หรือถอดถอนตุลาการศาลทหารได้ ทั้งนี้ อำนาจในการวินิจฉัยคดีของตุลาการศาลทหารเป็น
อิสระ ศาลอื่นไม่สามารถแทรกแซงกระบวนการพิจารณาคดีของศาลทหารได้

ศาลทหารประกอบด้วย ศาลทหารชั้นต้น ศาลทหารกลางและศาลทหารสูงสุด
คล้ายคลึงกับศาลยุติธรรม ที่เรียกว่า ศาลชั้นต้น ศาลอุทธรณ์และศาลฎีกาตามลำดับ ในกรณี
เกิด "เหตุการณ์พิเศษ" เช่น ภาวะสงครามหรือมีการประกาศใช้กฎอัยการศึก จะมีศาลเหลือ
เพียงศาลเดียวในระบบศาลทหาร

ศาลยุติธรรม

ศาลยุติธรรมมีหน้าที่พิพากษาคดีที่นำมาสู่ศาล   เว้นแต่คดีดังกล่าวอยู่ภายใต้เขต
อำนาจของศาลอื่นตามที่ได้กล่าวไปข้างต้น

ศาลไทยไม่มีระบบลูกขุน ในคดีส่วนใหญ่ จะมีผู้พิพากษา 2 คนนั่งบัลลังก์
พิจารณาคดีเพื่อพิพากษาว่าจำเลยมีความผิดหรือเป็นผู้บริสุทธิ์ หรือมีหน้าที่ความรับผิดชอบ
อย่างไรต่อโจทก์ สำหรับคดีที่ไม่มีความซับซ้อนหรือโทษไม่หนักมาก จะมีผู้พิพากษาเพียง
1 คนนั่งบัลลังก์เพื่อพิพากษาคดี แต่ในคดีที่มีความซับซ้อนและโทษที่หนัก จะมีผู้พิพากษา 3
คนนั่งเป็นองค์คณะในการพิจารณาคดี

ศาลยุติธรรมในประเทศไทยประกอบไปด้วย ศาลชั้นต้น ศาลอุทธรณ์และศาล
ฎีกา ภายใต้บทบัญญัติแห่งรัฐธรรมนูญ ปี 2550 ศาลชั้นต้นประกอบไปด้วยศาล จำนวน 9
ศาล ได้แก่ ศาลแขวง ศาลจังหวัด ศาลแพ่ง ศาลอาญา ศาลแรงงาน ศาลภาษีอากร ศาล
ล้มละลาย ศาลเยาวชนและครอบครัว และศาลทรัพย์สินทางปัญญาและการค้าระหว่าง
ประเทศ ตารางด้านล่างนี้จะแสดงให้ผู้อ่านทุกท่านเห็นถึงภาพรวมของระบบศาลไทย

ศาลรัฐธรรมนูญ		
ศาลปกครอง ---------->	ศาลปกครองสูงสุด	
	ศาลปกครองชั้นต้น	
ศาลทหาร -------------->	ศาลทหารสูงสุด	
	ศาลทหารกลาง	
	ศาลทหารชั้นต้น	
ศาลยุติธรรม ---------->	ศาลสูง ---------->	ศาลฎีกา
		ศาลอุทธรณ์
	ศาลชั้นต้น ------>	ศาลแขวง
		ศาลจังหวัด
		ศาลแพ่ง
		ศาลอาญา
		ศาลแรงงาน
		ศาลภาษีอากร
		ศาลล้มละลาย
		ศาลเยาวชนและครอบครัว
		ศาลทรัพย์สินทางปัญญาฯ

ศาลชั้นต้น

ศาลชั้นต้นหรือศาลล่างมีหน้าที่ในการดำเนินคดีในระยะเริ่มแรกให้แก่ประชาชน
ทั้งในคดีแพ่ง อาญาและคดีพิเศษอื่นๆ ศาลชั้นต้นที่ตั้งอยู่ในกรุงเทพมหานครประกอบไป
ด้วย

- ศาลแพ่ง

- ศาลอาญา

- ศาลแพ่งกรุงเทพใต้

- ศาลอาญากรุงเทพใต้

- ศาลแพ่งธนบุรี

- ศาลอาญาธนบุรี

- ศาลแขวงกรุงเทพ

- ศาลจังหวัดมีนบุรี

- ศาลเยาวชนและครอบครัวกลาง

- ศาลภาษีอากรกลาง

- ศาลแรงงาน

- ศาลทรัพย์สินทางปัญญาและการค้าระหว่างประเทศกลาง

- ศาลล้มละลายกลาง

ศาลที่ตั้งอยู่ในจังหวัดอื่นๆจะเป็นศาลทั่วไป เช่น ศาลจังหวัด ศาลแขวงและศาล
เยาวชนและครอบครัวกลาง ซึ่งถูกแบ่งโดยเขตอำนาจศาล

คดีที่ศาลแพ่งรับพิจารณาคือข้อพิพาทที่เกิดขึ้นระหว่างเอกชนหรือนิติบุคคล เช่น
องค์กรธุรกิจหรือบริษัท ศาลอาญาดำเนินคดีทางอาญาที่อัยการซึ่งเป็นเจ้าหน้าที่รัฐกล่าวหา
บุคคลว่าได้กระทำผิดทางอาญา ศาลเยาวชนและครอบครัวกลางรับพิจารณาคดีเด็กที่อายุ

ระหว่าง 7-18 ปี ในขณะที่เด็กอายุต่ำกว่า 7 ปี จะได้รับการยกเว้นโทษในกฎหมายไทย และ
จะไม่มีโทษจำคุกสำหรับเยาวชนที่มีอายุต่ำกว่า 14 ปี ศาลเยาวชนและครอบครัวประกอบไป
ด้วยผู้พิพากษาผู้ทรงคุณวุฒิ 2 คนและผู้พิพากษาสมทบอีก 2 คนเป็นองค์คณะในการ
พิจารณาคดี โดยต้องมีผู้พิพากษาหญิงร่วมพิจารณาคดีด้วยอย่างน้อย 1 คน ศาลเยาวชนและ
ครอบครัวของดเว้นการพิจารณาคดีเกี่ยวกับครอบครัว เช่น คดีหย่าและคดีการฟ้องขอเลี้ยงดู
บุตร

ศาลชำนัญพิเศษในประเทศไทย ประกอบไปด้วย 4 ศาล ดังต่อไปนี้

ศาลภาษีอากรมีหน้าที่พิจารณาดูแลข้อพิพาททางภาษีอากร ศาลแรงงานดูแล
รับผิดชอบคำร้องอันเกี่ยวกับแรงงานและการจ้างงาน ศาลทรัพย์สินทางปัญญาและการค้า
ระหว่างประเทศกลางดูแลคดีอันเกี่ยวกับเครื่องหมายการค้า ลิขสิทธิ์และการละเมิด
ทรัพย์สินทางปัญญาอื่นๆ และศาลล้มละลายดูแลกรณีพิพาทเกี่ยวกับลูกหนี้และเจ้าหนี้ ตาม
คำพิพากษาในกรณีที่ลูกหนี้มีหนี้สินล้นพ้นตัว

เจ้าหน้าที่ในศาลชั้นต้นแบ่งออกเป็น 2 กลุ่ม คือ เจ้าหน้าที่ทางศาลและเจ้าหน้าที่
ทางปกครอง ศาลแต่ละแห่งในกรุงเทพมหานครจะมี "อธิบดีศาล" เป็นผู้มีอำนาจในการดูแล
ส่วนศาลอื่นๆที่กระจายตัวอยู่ในจังหวัดต่างๆมักมี "หัวหน้าศาล" เป็นผู้ควบคุมดูแลและถือ
ว่าเป็นตำแหน่งสูงสุดในเขตอำนาจศาลนั้น

ผู้พิพากษา อัยการ และทนายความจำเป็นต้องได้สำเร็จการศึกษาและผ่านการสอบ
ในระดับต่างๆเพื่อที่จะให้ตนมีคุณสมบัติตามที่กฎหมายกำหนด ทั้งนี้ พระมหากษัตริย์ทรงมี
พระราชอำนาจในการแต่งตั้งผู้พิพากษาและทรงให้พ้นจากตำแหน่งได้เว้นแต่กรณีที่พ้นจาก
ตำแหน่งเพราะความตาย โดยที่ผู้พิพากษาและอัยการสามารถปฏิบัติหน้าที่จนอายุครบ 70 ปี

ศาลอุทธรณ์

      ศาลอุทธรณ์มีหน้าที่ในการพิจารณาคดีที่ได้รับการอุทธรณ์มาจากศาลชั้นต้น เมื่อ คู่ความฝ่ายใดฝ่ายหนึ่งไม่พอใจในคำพิพากษาหรือคำสั่งศาลชั้นต้น คู่ความฝ่ายนั้นสามารถ อุทธรณ์คำพิพากษาหรือคำสั่งมายังศาลอุทธรณ์ได้ ในปัญหาข้อเท็จจริงหรือข้อกฎหมายตาม บทบัญญัติแห่งกฎหมายว่าด้วยการอุทธรณ์ ทั้งในคดีแพ่งและคดีอาญา

      กระบวนการในการอุทธรณ์มีลักษณะเป็นการทบทวนคดีมากกว่าการพิจารณาคดี ใหม่ เนื่องจากโดยปกติในชั้นอุทธรณ์จะไม่มีการสืบพยานอีก เว้นแต่กรณีที่ศาลอุทธรณ์เห็น ว่าควรสืบพยานเพิ่มเติม มีอำนาจเรียกพยานมาสืบเองหรือสั่งให้ศาลชั้นต้นสืบให้ เมื่อศาล ชั้นต้นสืบพยานแล้วก็จะส่งสำนวนกลับมายังศาลอุทธรณ์เพื่อวินิจฉัยต่อไป และในการ พิจารณาจะต้องมีผู้พิพากษานั่งพิจารณาคดีอย่างน้อยจำนวน 3 คน ทั้งนี้ ศาลจะข้ามเรื่อง รายละเอียดเบื้องต้นและจะพิจารณาคดีว่ามีปัจจัยที่ไม่เป็นธรรมหรือมีข้อผิดพลาดใน กระบวนพิจารณาคดีหรือไม่ หากศาลอุทธรณ์ตัดสินพิพากษายืนตามศาลชั้นต้น ให้ถือว่าคดี ดังกล่าวได้ยุติลง เว้นเสียแต่ผู้ที่เป็นฝ่ายแพ้จะยื่นฎีกาต่อไปยังศาลฎีกา หากผู้พิพากษาศาล อุทธรณ์กลับคำพิพากษาศาลชั้นต้น ศาลอุทธรณ์จะส่งคดีกลับยังศาลชั้นต้นและมีคำสั่งให้ ศาลชั้นต้นดำเนินการตามคำพิพากษาหรือคำสั่งของศาลอุทธรณ์ต่อไป

      อย่างไรก็ดี ศาลอุทธรณ์สามารถมีคำพิพากษาหรือคำสั่ง ดังต่อไปนี้ คือการ พิพากษายืน ยกแก้หรือกลับคำพิพากษาศาลชั้นต้น หรือศาลอุทธรณ์อาจสั่งให้มีการพิจารณา ข้อเท็จจริงใหม่ หรือการสั่งให้มีการหาหลักฐานมาสนับสนุนเพิ่มเติม หรือถ้าศาลอุทธรณ์ เห็นเป็นการจำเป็น เนื่องจากศาลชั้นต้นมิได้ปฏิบัติให้ถูกต้องตามกระบวนการพิจารณาก็จะ พิพากษาสั่งให้ศาลชั้นต้นทำการพิจารณาและพิพากษาหรือสั่งใหม่ตามรูปคดี

      ศาลอุทธรณ์มีจำนวนทั้งสิ้น 10 แห่ง และทุกแห่งตั้งอยู่ในกรุงเทพมหานครทั้งสิ้น หนึ่งในศาลอุทธรณ์ 10 แห่งนั้นจะพิจารณาคดีอุทธรณ์จากศาลชั้นต้นที่ตั้งอยู่ใน กรุงเทพมหานคร และอีก 9 แห่งที่เหลือนั้นจะรับพิจารณาคดีอุทธรณ์จากศาลจังหวัดต่างๆ หรือเป็นที่รู้จักกันดีในนาม ศาลอุทธรณ์ ภาค 1-ภาค 9

      ศาลอุทธรณ์แต่ละภาคมีเขตอำนาจศาลครอบคลุมพื้นที่ดังต่อไปนี้

ศาลอุทธรณ์ ภาค 1 มีเขตอำนาจศาลครอบคลุมพื้นที่จังหวัดชัยนาท นนทบุรี ปทุมธานี อยุธยา ลพบุรี สมุทรปราการ สระบุรี สิงห์บุรีและอ่างทอง

ศาลอุทธรณ์ ภาค 2 มีเขตอำนาจศาลครอบคลุมพื้นที่จังหวัดจันทบุรี ฉะเชิงเทรา ชลบุรี ตราด นครนายก ปราจีนบุรี ระยองและสระแก้ว

ศาลอุทธรณ์ ภาค 3 มีเขตอำนาจศาลครอบคลุมพื้นที่จังหวัดชัยภูมิ นครราชสีมา บุรีรัมย์ ยโสธร ศรีษะเกษ สุรินทร์ อุบลราชธานีและอำนาจเจริญ

ศาลอุทธรณ์ ภาค 4 มีเขตอำนาจศาลครอบคลุมพื้นที่จังหวัดกาฬสินธุ์ ขอนแก่น นครพนม มหาสารคาม มุกดาหาร ร้อยเอ็ด สกลนคร หนองคาย หนองบัวลำภูและอุดรธานี

ศาลอุทธรณ์ ภาค 5 มีเขตอำนาจศาลครอบคลุมพื้นที่จังหวัดเชียงใหม่ เชียงราย น่าน พะเยาว์ แพร่ แม่ฮ่องสอน ลำปางและลำพูน

ศาลอุทธรณ์ ภาค 6 มีเขตอำนาจศาลครอบคลุมพื้นที่จังหวัดกำแพงเพชร ตาก นครสวรรค์ พิจิตร พิษณุโลก เพชรบูรณ์ สุโขทัย อุตรดิตถ์ และอุทัยธานี

ศาลอุทธรณ์ ภาค 7 มีเขตอำนาจศาลครอบคลุมพื้นที่จังหวัดกาญจนบุรี นครพนม ประจวบคีรีขันธ์ เพชรบุรี ราชบุรี สมุทรปราการ สมุทรสาคร และสุพรรณบุรี

ศาลอุทธรณ์ ภาค 8 มีเขตอำนาจศาลครอบคลุมพื้นที่จังหวัดกระบี่ ชุมพร นครศรีธรรมราช พังงา ภูเก็ต ระนองและสุราษฎร์ธานี

ศาลอุทธรณ์ ภาค 9 มีเขตอำนาจศาลครอบคลุมพื้นที่จังหวัดตรัง นราธิวาส ปัตตานี พัทลุง ยะลา สงขลา และสตูล

ศาลฎีกา

ศาลฎีกามีเพียงแห่งเดียวและตั้งอยู่ในกรุงเทพมหานคร เขตอำนาจศาลฎีกา
ครอบคลุมพื้นที่ทุกจังหวัดทั่วประเทศไทย ศาลฎีการับพิจารณาคดีที่ได้รับการฎีกามาจาก
ศาลอุทธรณ์หรือรับฎีกาโดยตรงขึ้นมาจากศาลชำนัญพิเศษ

ประธานศาลฎีกาเป็นตำแหน่งสูงสุดในฝ่ายตุลาการ ในการพิจารณาคดีของศาล
ฎีกาในแต่ละกรณี จะต้องมีผู้พิพากษานั่งพิจารณาคดีถึงสามคนเป็นองค์คณะ อย่างไรก็ตาม
หากคดีมีความสำคัญมาก ประธานศาลฎีกาจะจัดให้มีการประชุมใหญ่ ซึ่งประกอบไปด้วยผู้
พิพากษาศาลฎีกาเข้าร่วมการพิจารณาคดีไม่ต่ำกว่ากึ่งหนึ่งของจำนวนผู้พิพากษาศาลฎีกา
ทั้งหมด

ศาลฎีกาประกอบไปด้วยแผนกคดีพิเศษทั้งสิ้น 10 แผนกด้วยกัน ซึ่งแต่ละแผนก
สามารถตัดสินให้คดีถึงที่สุดได้เลยทันที และประธานศาลฎีกามีหน้าที่แต่งตั้งผู้พิพากษาศาล
ฎีกาจำนวน 10 คน มาประจำแต่ในละแผนก ดังนี้

- แผนกคดีเยาวชนและครอบครัว

- แผนกคดีแรงงาน

- แผนกคดีภาษีอากร

- แผนกคดีทรัพย์สินทางปัญญาและการค้าระหว่างประเทศ

- แผนกคดีล้มละลาย

- แผนกคดีอาญาของผู้ดำรงตำแหน่งทางการเมือง

- แผนกคดีพาณิชย์และเศรษฐกิจ

- แผนกคดีสิ่งแวดล้อม

- แผนกคดีผู้บริโภค

- แผนกคดีปกครอง (ภายใน)

ศาลฎีกาตั้งอยู่ที่ เลขที่ 6 ถนนราชดำเนินใน แขวงพระบรมมหาราชวัง เขตพระนคร กรุงเทพฯ 10200

หน่วยงานทางกฎหมายอื่นๆ

นอกเหนือจากศาลต่างๆที่กล่าวไป   มีหน่วยงานทางกฎหมายที่สำคัญอื่นๆซึ่งมักจะได้รับการกล่าวถึงในระบบกฎหมายไทย ดังนี้

สำนักระงับข้อพิพาท (ADRO)

สำนักงานระงับข้อพิพาท สำนักงานศาลยุติธรรม หรือที่รู้จักกันว่าเป็นสถาบันอนุญาโตตุลาการประจำประเทศไทยมีหน้าที่และความรับผิดชอบในการส่งเสริม   ให้ความร่วมมือและระงับข้อพิพาทในคดีแพ่ง   คดีอาญาและข้อพิพาททางพาณิชย์ต่างๆที่สามารถประนีประนอมยอมความกันได้   โดยอาศัยวิธีการไกล่เกลี่ย   การระงับข้อพิพาทหรืออนุญาโตตุลาการตามบทบัญญัติว่าด้วยอนุญาโตตุลาการ

สำนักระงับข้อพิพาทยังมีหน้าที่ในการพัฒนาระบบ   แบบฟอร์ม   เกณฑ์กระบวนการ ระเบียบ ขั้นตอนและมาตรฐานในการระงับข้อพิพาททางแพ่งและทางพาณิชย์โดยอนุญาโตตุลาการและวิธีการระงับข้อพิพาทอื่นๆทั้งในศาลและนอกศาล

สำนักระงับข้อพิพาท สำนักงานศาลยุติธรรมตั้งอยู่ที่ ชั้น 5-6 อาคารศาลอาญาถนนรัชดาภิเษก เขตจตุจักร กรุงเทพฯ 10900 โทรศัพท์ 02-541-2298

สำนักงานอัยการสูงสุด

สำนักงานอัยการสูงสุด (OAG) มีเขตอำนาจรับผิดชอบการฟ้องร้องที่ครอบคลุม คดีอาญาทุกประเภทและสามารถเป็นโจทก์ฟ้องในคดีแพ่งได้ในบางกรณี สำนักงานอัยการ สูงสุดทำหน้าที่เป็นทนายความของแผ่นดิน สามารถฟ้องจำเลยที่กระทำความผิดในคดีอาญา ได้ในศาลชั้นต้น ศาลอุทธรณ์และศาลฎีกา สำนักงานอัยการสูงสุดยังให้คำแนะนำด้าน กฎหมายแก่รัฐและหน่วยงานของรัฐด้วย นอกจากนี้ยังสามารถเป็นโจทก์ฟ้องแทนบุคคล ธรรมดาได้ในกรณีความผิดฐานทำให้เสียทรัพย์ในคดีอาญา เช่น การปล้น เป็นต้น และ สามารถยกเลิกคดีหรือสั่งให้ดำเนินการสอบสวนในคดีอาญาต่างๆได้ อัยการสูงสุดหรือ ผู้กระทำการแทนอัยการสูงสุดคือผู้ที่จะตัดสินใจว่าจะดำเนินการฟ้องร้องการฆาตกรรม ซึ่ง ผู้ตายถูกเจ้าพนักงานซึ่งอ้างว่าปฏิบัติราชการตามหน้าที่ฆ่าตายหรือไม่ หรือจะร้องขอให้ศาล บำเหน็จรางวัลให้แก่ผู้ที่ให้ความร่วมมือกับรัฐในการนำจับผู้ต้องหา

หน้าที่หลักของสำนักงานอัยการสูงสุดคือการปกป้องผลประโยชน์ของรัฐ ในคดี แพ่ง สำนักงานอัยการสูงสุดจะเป็นทนายของรัฐขึ้นต่อสู้คดีในศาลแทนรัฐ ซึ่งสำนักงาน อัยการสูงสุดมีอำนาจที่จะขอหลักฐานจากบุคคลที่อ้างว่าตนเป็นพลเมืองไทยได้ อีกทั้ง สำนักงานอัยการสูงสุดยังสามารถเพิกถอนความเป็นพลเมืองไทยของบุคคลผู้ที่ได้รับ สัญชาติโดยกำเนิดที่มีบิดาเป็นชาวต่างชาติ หรือบุคคลผู้ซึ่งทำให้ประเทศไทยตกอยู่ในความ เสี่ยง ความเสื่อมเสียหรือผู้ซึ่งกระทำการใดๆอันอาจทำให้เกิดความไม่สงบหรือขัดต่อ ศีลธรรมอันดีของประชาชนได้

อีกบทบาทหนึ่งที่มีความสำคัญของสำนักงานอัยการสูงสุดคือการปกป้อง คุ้มครองสิทธิเสรีภาพของประชาชนและช่วยเหลือประชาชนในกระบวนการยุติธรรมทาง กฎหมาย เช่น การยื่นคำร้องต่อศาลเพื่อให้ปล่อยตัวผู้ต้องหาเมื่อไม่จำเป็นต้องมีการคุมขังใน ขณะที่คดียังอยู่ในระหว่างการพิจารณา หรือการยื่นคำร้องต่อศาลเพื่อให้ปล่อยตัวผู้บริสุทธิ์ที่ ได้รับการพิพากษาให้จำคุกโดยความผิดพลาด

นอกเหนือจากนี้ สำนักงานอัยการสูงสุดยังมีหน้าที่ในการป้องกันและปราบปราม การฟอกเงิน ยาเสพติด และการค้ายาเสพติด ตลอดจนการสอบสวนการได้มาซึ่งทรัพย์สิน และการฟ้องนายกรัฐมนตรี คณะรัฐมนตรี สมาชิกรัฐสภาและเจ้าหน้าที่ของรัฐผู้ซึ่งมี

ทรัพย์สินเพิ่มมากขึ้นหรือร่ำรวยอย่างผิดปกติภายหลังการดำรงตำแหน่งทางการเมือง อย่างไรก็ตามในคดีอาญานั้น พนักงานอัยการจะมีอำนาจดำเนินคดีฟ้องร้องผู้กระทำผิดได้ต่อเมื่อมีการสอบสวนความผิดนั้นแล้วโดยเจ้าหน้าที่ตำรวจ หรือพนักงานสอบสวน กรมสอบสวนคดีพิเศษ หรือพนักงานสอบสวนอื่นของรัฐตามที่กฎหมายให้อำนาจทำการสอบสวน และทั้งนี้จะต้องได้ตัวผู้กระทำความผิดมาปรากฏตัวต่อศาลด้วย

สำนักงานอัยการสูงสุดตั้งอยู่ที่ถนนรัชดาภิเษก เขตบางเขน กรุงเทพฯ 10900 โทรศัพท์ 02-541-2770-9

สภาทนายความแห่งประเทศไทย

สภาทนายความแห่งประเทศไทยเป็นสมาคมทนายความ ที่มีกิจกรรมเกี่ยวกับการกำหนดระเบียบและกฎเกณฑ์ให้แก่สมาชิก เช่น การออกใบประกอบวิชาชีพทนายความ การเก็บบันทึกการลงทะเบียนและการบันทึกกิจกรรมต่างๆของทนายความ ตลอดจนการรักษาจรรยาบรรณและจริยธรรมประจำวิชาชีพทนายความ (กรุณาดูบท "มารยาทของทนายความ")

สภาทนายความยังจัดให้มีการอบรมและการฝึกงานเบื้องต้นให้แก่สมาชิก ในเดือนสิงหาคม พ.ศ. 2550 ประเทศไทยมีทนายความทั้งสิ้นรวม 48,197 คน ซึ่งอยู่ในกรุงเทพมหานครจำนวน 19,874 คนและจังหวัดอื่นๆ อีก 29,323 คน

สภาทนายความเป็นสมาคมของผู้ประกอบวิชาชีพทนายความแห่งประเทศไทยทำหน้าที่รับใช้ประชาชนและองค์กรต่างๆโดยการสนับสนุนให้เกิดความเป็นธรรมขึ้นในสังคม การประกอบวิชาชีพโดยสุจริตและการให้เคารพต่อกฎหมาย อีกทั้ง ยังมีการให้บริการจัดหาทนายความอาสาให้แก่ผู้ที่ไม่มีทุนทรัพย์ในการว่าจ้างทนายความ ตลอดจนการว่าความให้ชาวต่างชาติและการจัดหาล่ามให้ชาวต่างชาติด้วย (ผู้เขียนได้อธิบายในเรื่องการได้รับการจัดหาทนายความจากสภาทนายความไว้ในส่วนของ "กระบวนการทางกฎหมาย")

สภาทนายความยังให้คำปรึกษาเกี่ยวกับงานด้านกฎหมายในช่วงวันเวลาทำการปกติโดยไม่คิดค่าใช้จ่าย คุณสามารถติดต่อไปยังสภาทนายความได้ที่หมายเลข 0-2281-6463

0-2281-5170 และ 0-2281-8308 อนึ่ง พนักงานในสำนักงานทนายความจะใช้ภาษาไทยเป็น หลัก สำหรับชาวต่างชาติ จำเป็นที่จะต้องสามารถพูดภาษาไทยได้บ้างหรือต้องมีผู้แปลเป็นผู้ ติดต่อแทน คุณสามารถสอบถามคำถามเพิ่มเติมมาได้ที่ legalaid@lawyerscouncil.or.th หรือ บริการสายด่วน 24 ชั่วโมง หมายเลข 0-2282-9906 เพื่อติดต่อปรึกษาทนายความอาสาใน คดีอาญาและขอความช่วยเหลือเพื่อเข้าฟังการสอบปากคำผู้ต้องหา

สภาทนายความแห่งประเทศไทยตั้งอยู่ที่ เลขที่ 7/89 อาคาร 10 ถนนราชดำเนิน กลาง เขตพระนคร กรุงเทพฯ 10200 โทรศัพท์ 0-2629-1430 (อัตโนมัติ)

ส่วนที่ 2

กระบวนการทางกฎหมาย

การไปศาล

บุคคลที่เกี่ยวข้องกับกระบวนการทางกฎหมาย

ต่อไปนี้เป็นรายการของบุคคลที่เกี่ยวข้องในกระบวนการดำเนินคดีในคดีแพ่ง และคดีอาญาในประเทศไทย และบางข้อเป็นคำศัพท์ที่มักใช้กันในระบบศาลไทย

1. เจ้าหน้าที่ตำรวจและเจ้าพนักงานฝ่ายปกครอง รวมไปถึงพนักงานตรวจคนเข้าเมือง เจ้าหน้าที่เขต เจ้าหน้าที่กรมสรรพสามิต เจ้าหน้าที่กรมท่า เจ้าหน้าที่กรมศุลกากร เป็นต้น เจ้าหน้าที่เหล่านี้มีอำนาจและหน้าที่ในการรักษาความสงบเรียบร้อยและการสืบสวน ป้องกันการเกิดอาชญากรรมและสามารถจับกุมตัวผู้กระทำความผิดทางอาญาได้

2. เจ้าพนักงานสืบสวนสอบสวน รวมถึงเจ้าหน้าที่จากสำนักงานตำรวจแห่งชาติ กรมสืบสวนคดีพิเศษ (D.S.I) และเจ้าพนักงานจากกระทรวงยุติธรรม ซึ่งมีหน้าที่ในการสืบสวนสอบสวน ตั้งคำถามผู้ต้องหาและรวบรวมข้อมูลพยานหลักฐาน เพื่อใช้ประกอบการตัดสินใจในการยื่นสำนวนคดีต่ออัยการและการจับคุมผู้ต้องหา

3. อัยการ หรือ "ทนายความแผ่นดิน" จะเป็นผู้พิจารณาว่าจำเลยควรได้รับการฟ้องและดำเนินคดีในศาลหรือไม่ หลังจากที่ได้รับเรื่องจากเจ้าหน้าที่ตำรวจและเจ้าหน้าที่หรือเจ้าพนักงาน (ในข้อ 1 และ ข้อ 2)

4. "ศาล" หมายรวมถึง ผู้พิพากษา สำนักงานศาลและศาลทุกแห่งที่อยู่ในบัญชีรายชื่อระบบศาล

5. ทนายความทำหน้าที่ว่าความแทนโจทก์ (ในคดีแพ่ง) และจำเลย (ในคดีแพ่งและคดีอาญา) ในกระบวนการทางกฎหมาย โดยที่ผู้ที่จะเป็นทนายความต้องได้รับใบประกอบวิชาชีพทนายความจากสภาทนายความเสียก่อน

6. ทนายความสาธารณะ ("ทนายความอาสา") มีลักษณะคล้ายกับทนายของสาธารณะในประเทศอื่นๆ เช่น สหรัฐอเมริกาที่เรียกว่า public defender เป็นต้น ในคดีอาญา ศาลจะสอบถามจำเลยว่าต้องการทนายความหรือไม่ และศาลจะจัดหาทนายความอาสาเพื่อช่วยเหลือจำเลยที่ไม่มีทุนทรัพย์ในการว่าจ้างทนายเอกชน ทนายความอาสาเป็นทนายที่มาจากสภาทนายความแห่งประเทศไทยและได้รับการขึ้นทะเบียนกับทางศาลยุติธรรมเป็นที่เรียบร้อยแล้ว เมื่อคดียุติหรือสิ้นสุดลง ทนายความอาสานั้นจะได้รับค่าตอบแทนจากเงินงบประมาณของกระทรวงยุติธรรม

7. เจ้าพนักงานควบคุมความประพฤติ รวมถึงพัศดี และเจ้าหน้าที่ในกรมควบคุมความประพฤติ มีหน้าที่ในการคุมขัง ควบคุมและดูแลผู้ถูกกล่าวหา หรือถูกจับกุมในคดีอาญา หรือผู้ที่ได้รับการกักบริเวณพิเศษ เช่น เรือนจำ

8. เจ้าหน้าที่ทัณฑ์บนหรือเจ้าหน้าที่ผู้มีหน้าที่ในการดูแล ให้คำแนะนำ ควบคุมผู้กระทำผิดที่ถูกกักกันอยู่ในโรงพยาบาล ผู้ที่อยู่ในระหว่างการภาคทัณฑ์หรือผู้ที่ได้รับการปล่อยตัวแต่อยู่ภายใต้การควบคุมของพนักงานควบคุมความประพฤติ ด้วยการเขียนและรายงานต่อศาลเกี่ยวกับผู้กระทำผิดที่อยู่ภายใต้การดูแลของพวกตน

9. ผู้เสียหายคือผู้ซึ่งได้รับบาดเจ็บ ทั้งทางร่างกายและจิตใจ ความเจ็บปวดทางอารมณ์ การสูญเสียทรัพย์สินหรือการถูกลิดรอนสิทธิขั้นพื้นฐาน ผ่านการกระทำความผิดทางอาญาของผู้กระทำความผิด

10. ผู้ต้องหาหรือผู้ถูกกล่าวหา คือบุคคลผู้ซึ่งได้รับการกล่าวหาว่ากระทำความผิด แต่ยังมิได้ถูกจับกุมหรือส่งตัวไปดำเนินคดีทางศาล

11. จำเลยคือบุคคลซึ่งถูกจับกุมเนื่องจากได้กระทำความผิดอาญา และในศาลจะเรียกว่า "จำเลย" ไม่ใช่ "ผู้ต้องหา"

12. นายประกันคือผู้ซึ่งได้วางเงินประกันหรือหลักประกันไว้แก่เจ้าหน้าที่เพื่อให้มี
    การปล่อยตัวจำเลยหรือผู้ต้องหาชั่วคราว

13. พยานคือผู้ให้การ ผู้ที่ยินยอมที่จะให้พยานหลักฐานเพื่อประกอบการพิจารณาคดี
    หรือผู้ที่สาบานตนต่อหน้าการพิจารณาคดีของศาล

14. พยานผู้เชี่ยวชาญคือบุคคลที่มีความรู้   ประสบการณ์   ผ่านการฝึกอบรมหรือมี
    ทักษะในสาขาเฉพาะด้าน

15. สภาทนายความมีหน้าที่พื้นฐานในการให้คำปรึกษาและช่วยเหลือประชาชนใน
    ด้านกฎหมาย อีกทั้งยังเป็นผู้ดำเนินคดีให้กับผู้ต้องหา จำเลยหรือผู้เสียหายตามคำ
    ร้องขอหรือตามคำสั่งศาลด้วย

16. นักจิตวิทยาหรือนักสังคมสงเคราะห์จะช่วยในการสอบสวนหรือตั้งคำถามพยาน
    ในบางคดี ซึ่งผู้ต้องหาหรือจำเลยและพยานหรือผู้เสียหายเป็นเด็กหรือเยาวชน

17. ผู้เยาว์ คือ ผู้ที่มีอายุต่ำกว่า 20 ปีบริบูรณ์

18. ล่าม คือ ผู้ที่มีความสามารถและผ่านการฝึกอบรมในด้านการแปลภาษา 2 ภาษา
    (เช่น ภาษาไทยเป็นภาษาอังกฤษ และภาษาอังกฤษเป็นภาษาไทย) และสามารถ
    ถ่ายทอดการสื่อสารที่เกิดขึ้นในกระบวนการทางกฎหมายให้เป็นที่เข้าใจได้ ทั้งนี้
    ให้หมายรวมถึงผู้แปลภาษามือสำหรับผู้พิการทางหูด้วย

สิ่งที่ควรปฏิบัติเมื่อต้องไปศาล

หากคุณมิใช่ผู้ที่ทำงานในศาลหรือมีอาชีพในสายงานด้านกฎหมาย   คุณคงไม่
ประสงค์ที่จะเดินทางไปศาลเป็นแน่   คนไทยส่วนใหญ่คิดว่าการไปศาลหรือการที่มีเรื่องให้
ต้องขึ้นศาลนั้นเป็นเรื่องที่ไม่ดี จึงหาทางหลีกเลี่ยงสุดความสามารถ อย่างไรก็ตาม ยังมี
เหตุผลอีกหลายประการที่ทำให้คนต้องเดินทางไปศาล นอกเหนือจากการถูกดำเนินคดีหรือ
เพื่อต่อสู้คดีในคดีอาญา

เมื่อคุณจำเป็นต้องเดินทางไปศาล   คุณแสดงความเคารพต่อศาลด้วยการแต่งกาย
ให้สุภาพและจัดแต่งทรงผมให้เรียบร้อย ผู้ชายไม่จำเป็นต้องผูกเนคไท แต่ควรสวมกางเกง

ขายาวและเสื้อเชิ้ตให้เหมาะสม ผู้หญิงสามารถสวมกางเกงและเสื้อเชิ้ตได้ ทั้งนี้ กรุณาใช้ดุลยพินิจของตนในการแต่งตัวให้ถูกต้องตามกาลเทศะ การแต่งกายสำหรับไปศาลนั้นท่านไม่ควรใส่เสื้อแขนกุด เสื้อผ้าที่เปิดเผยเนื้อตัวมากเกินไป ไม่ใส่เสื้อผ้าสกปรกที่ส่งกลิ่นรบกวนหรือที่มีสีสันสดใสมากเกินควร หรือไม่ควรแต่งกายในลักษณะที่แสดงถึงความไม่เคารพต่อศาล อนึ่ง คุณจะไม่ได้รับอนุญาตให้สวมใส่กางเกงขาสั้น แว่นกันแดด เครื่องประดับแวววาว หมวก รองเท้าแตะหรือรองเท้าแตะเมื่อต้องขึ้นศาล

ศาลในประเทศไทยจะมีงานประชาสัมพันธ์ซึ่งมีหน้าที่ตอบคำถามเกี่ยวกับศาล ตารางการพิจารณาและสถานที่ภายในศาล เป็นต้น อีกทั้งเจ้าหน้าที่งานประชาสัมพันธ์จะทำหน้าที่อำนวยความสะดวกให้แก่ผู้ใช้บริการในการเขียนคำร้อง การกรอกแบบฟอร์มต่างๆ คุณสามารถขอให้พนักงานช่วยคัดถ่ายเอกสารเกี่ยวกับคดีและช่วยยื่นเรื่องขอประกันตัวจำเลยหรือผู้ต้องหา งานประชาสัมพันธ์ทำหน้าที่คล้ายคลึงกับสำนักงานเสมียนศาลของระบบศาลในสหรัฐอเมริกา

คุณสามารถยื่นคำร้องหรือคำแถลงต่างๆ หรือสามารถยื่นคำฟ้องหรือข้อกล่าวหาที่งานรับฟ้องซึ่งอยู่ในแผนกรับฟ้อง ซึ่งมีหน้าที่คล้ายคลึงกับสำนักงานเสมียนศาลของสหรัฐอเมริกา

เมื่อคุณได้ยื่นเอกสารให้กับทางศาลเรียบร้อยแล้ว ศาลจะมอบหมายให้มีเจ้าหน้าที่รับนำหมาย ซึ่งคุณสามารถติดตามขอทราบผลการส่งหมายหรือสำเนาคำฟ้องจากเจ้าหน้าที่ผู้นี้ได้

งานเก็บสำนวนความมีหน้าที่จัดหาสำเนาสำนวนความหรือคำสั่งศาลอื่นๆให้แก่คุณตามที่ได้ร้องขอ ซึ่งสามารถเปรียบเทียบได้กับสำนักงานเสมียนศาลของสหรัฐอเมริกา

การเดินทางไปเยี่ยมผู้ต้องหาหรือจำเลยที่อยู่ในระหว่างการดำเนินคดีที่ศาลนั้นคุณจะเป็นต้องนัดหมายกับเจ้าหน้าที่ตำรวจประจำศาล แต่หากท่านเดินทางไปศาลเพื่อไปเป็นพยานในคดี คุณต้องติดต่อโดยตรงกับงานหน้าบัลลังก์

ในกรณีที่มีปัญหาหรือข้อสงสัย สามารถติดต่อไปยังจ่าศาล หรือ ผู้พิพากษา หัวหน้าศาล หรือในกรณีที่ต้องการติดต่อเจ้าพนักงานคุมความประพฤติ กรุณาไปยัง สำนักงานคุมความประพฤติประจำศาลได้ในทันที

การไปศาลในฐานะโจทก์

คุณสามารถเดินทางไปศาลในฐานะโจทก์ได้ทั้งในคดีอาญาและคดีแพ่ง สำหรับ คดีอาญา อัยการจะทำหน้าที่เป็นโจทก์ แต่สำหรับในคดีแพ่ง คุณจำต้องมีทนายที่เป็นผู้ ดำเนินคดีทางกฎหมายในศาลให้

คุณควรศึกษาเอกสารของข้อกล่าวหาและสำนวนคำฟ้องก่อนเพื่อตรวจสอบความ ถูกต้องของเอกสารและคำแถลงการณ์ทั้งหมด ลงลายมือชื่อในเอกสารทุกฉบับและบน แบบฟอร์มการมอบอำนาจให้แก่ทนายความ (มักรู้จักกันในนาม "ใบมอบอำนาจ หรือใบ แต่งทนาย") ซึ่งเป็นแบบฟอร์มในการอนุญาตให้ทนายความสามารถดำเนินคดีในศาลได้ใน นามของคุณ ทั้งนี้ ขอให้ตรวจสอบว่าคุณสามารถชำระค่าธรรมเนียมต่างๆได้หรือไม่ ในคดี แพ่ง คุณต้องเสียค่าธรรมเนียมมากกว่าในคดีอาญา ผู้ที่เป็นคนไทยจะต้องนำทะเบียนบ้าน และบัตรประจำตัวประชาชนติดตัวไปด้วยเสมอเมื่อไปศาล สำหรับชาวต่างชาติขอให้นำ หนังสือเดินทางและเอกสารแสดงตนอื่นๆไปด้วย

การไปศาลในฐานะจำเลยหรือผู้ต้องหา

หากคุณไปศาลในฐานะจำเลยหรือผู้ต้องหา คุณต้องเตรียมตัวให้พร้อม หากคุณยัง ไม่ได้ส่งคำให้การของตน ให้คุณเขียนรายละเอียดลงไว้ในเอกสารและให้เอาติดตัวไปด้วย เพื่อใช้อ้างอิง กรุณาอย่าลืมหมายนัดหรือหมายเรียกและสำเนาคำร้องไปด้วย สำหรับคนไทย ให้นำทะเบียนบ้านและบัตรประจำตัวประชาชนติดตัวไปด้วยเสมอ สำหรับชาวต่างชาติ ขอให้นำหนังสือเดินทางและเอกสารแสดงตนอื่นๆไปด้วย อนึ่ง คุณอาจต้องเตรียมหลักฐาน แสดงหลักทรัพย์ที่จะใช้ในการประกันตัวในคดีอาญา

การไปศาลในฐานะพยานแห่งคดี

หมายเรียกพยานจะระบุวันที่ที่คุณต้องเดินทางไปเป็นพยานในศาล คุณควรแต่ง
กายให้เหมาะสมและเดินทางไปศาลก่อนเวลานัดเล็กน้อย   เพื่อที่จะได้สอบถามสถานที่
ภายในและขั้นตอนต่างๆก่อนที่จะเริ่มมีการพิจารณาคดี กรุณานำหมายเรียกพยานและบัตร
ประจำตัวประชาชนติดตัวไปด้วย ในกรณีที่ทราบว่าคุณจะต้องให้การเป็นพยานในเรื่องใด
คุณควรจดบันทึกไว้เพื่อจะได้ไม่ลืม เมื่อจำเป็นต้องไปให้การอีกเป็นครั้งที่สอง จะทำให้
คำให้การของคุณทั้งสองครั้งสอดคล้องกันและมีความสมเหตุสมผล

การไปศาลในฐานะนายประกัน

นายประกันหรือผู้ประกัน สามารถเป็นได้ทั้งบุคคลธรรมดา เจ้าหน้าที่ของรัฐหรือ
นิติบุคคลใดๆที่ได้วางเงินหรือทรัพย์สินเพื่อเป็นประกันว่าจำเลยหรือผู้ต้องหาจะมาปรากฏ
ในศาลตามนัด เมื่อคุณต้องเดินทางไปศาลในฐานะนายประกัน คุณต้องเตรียมเอกสารแสดง
กรรมสิทธิ์ในทรัพย์สินที่จะนำมาใช้ในการประกัน

ทรัพย์ที่สามารถนำมาใช้ในการประกัน ได้แก่ อสังหาริมทรัพย์ เงินสด เงินใน
บัญชีธนาคาร หนังสือรับรองจากเจ้าหน้าที่ของธนาคาร พันธบัตรรัฐบาลหรือโฉนดที่ดิน
พร้อมเอกสารประเมินราคาที่ดินที่ลงนามโดยเจ้าพนักงานกรมที่ดิน   ในกรณีที่มีคู่สมรส
กรุณาแนบใบแสดงความยินยอมของคู่สมรสมาด้วย

ข้าราชการสามารถใช้ตำแหน่งข้าราชการของตนเป็นหลักประกันได้เช่นกัน หาก
คุณเป็นข้าราชการ   คุณสามารถนำเอกสารรับรองเงินเดือนของติดตัวมาด้วย (กรุณาอ่าน
รายละเอียดเพิ่มเติมเกี่ยวกับหลักประกันได้ในบทต่อไป)

คดีอาญา

ในคดีอาญา   อัยการผู้เป็นเจ้าหน้าที่รัฐจะทำหน้าที่เป็นโจทก์ของแผ่นดิน
ดำเนินการฟ้องร้องผู้ต้องหาที่กระทำความผิดทางอาญา   หรือโจทก์ซึ่งอ้างว่าได้รับความ
เสียหายจากการกระทำความผิดทางอาญาของผู้ต้องหานั้น โดยทั่วไป ผู้เสียหายจะไปยื่นคำ
ร้องทุกข์ต่อเจ้าหน้าที่ตำรวจที่สถานีตำรวจ   ในประเทศไทยเพื่อให้สืบสวนดำเนินคดีกับ
ผู้กระทำความผิดอาญา คดีอาญาสามารถแบ่งออกได้เป็น 2 ประเภท ดังนี้

1. คดีอาญาอันเป็นความผิดต่อแผ่นดิน (ไม่สามารถยอมความกันได้) นั้นจะ
    ได้รับการดำเนินคดีโดยอัยการ เนื่องจาก เป็นความผิดอันส่งผลกระทบต่อ
    ความสงบเรียบร้อยในสังคม   ทำให้สังคมตกอยู่ในอันตราย   หรืออาจ
    ก่อให้เกิดอันตรายต่อชีวิตและทรัพย์สินของคนในสังคม   ซึ่งหมายรวมถึง
    การค้ายาเสพติด   การทำลายป่าไม้   การพนันที่ผิดกฎหมายและการทุจริต
    คอร์รัปชั่น

2. คดีอาญาอันเป็นความผิดต่อส่วนตัว (สามารถยอมความกันได้) เป็นการ
    กระทำที่ไม่ส่งผลกระทบต่อความสงบเรียบร้อยในสังคม การกระทำผิดของ
    จำเลยส่งผลต่อตัวบุคคลหรือกลุ่มบุคคลเท่านั้นได้แก่   การละเมิดสิทธิใน
    เครื่องหมายการค้า   การหมิ่นประมาทหรือการโฆษณาหมิ่นประมาทให้
    เสื่อมเสียชื่อเสียง การเปิดเผยข้อมูลความลับทางการค้า การฉ้อฉล การโกง
    เจ้าหนี้ การยักยอก การบุกรุก การข่มขืน การทำร้ายร่างกาย การละเมิด
    ลิขสิทธิ์ เป็นต้น ผู้เสียหายมีหน้าที่ต้องร้องทุกข์ภายในระยะเวลา 3 เดือนนับ
    แต่วันที่ผู้เสียหายรู้เรื่องความผิดและรู้ว่าใครเป็นผู้กระทำความผิด   หากคดี
    ขาดอายุความ   เจ้าหน้าที่ตำรวจหรือผู้เสียหายจะไม่สามารถดำเนินคดีแก่
    ผู้กระทำความผิดได้

คดีอาญาตาม 1 และ 2 ผู้เสียหายหรือตัวแทนจะให้ทนายความฟ้องร้องผู้กระทำ
ผิดต่อศาลเองก็ได้ในกรณีที่ผู้เสียหายเป็นผู้เยาว์ บุคคลไร้ความสามารถ องค์กรทางกฎหมาย
หรือเป็นนิติบุคคล ทั้งนี้ หากผู้เสียหายถึงแก่ความตายหรือได้รับบาดเจ็บ บิดามารดา บุตร
หรือคู่สมรสสามารถฟ้องร้องแทนในนามของผู้เสียหายได้เช่นกัน   หรือจะเลือกการ

ดำเนินคดีโดยแจ้งความร้องทุกข์ต่อเจ้าหน้าที่ตรวจ หรือเจ้าพนักงานกรมสอบสวนคดีพิเศษ
เพื่อให้ทำการสืบสวนสอบสวนดำเนินจับกุมผู้กระทำความผิดแล้วส่งเรื่องให้พนักงาน
อัยการซึ่งเป็นทนายแผ่นดินเป็นโจทก์ฟ้องคดีหรือดำเนินการแทนก็ได้

กระบวนการทางอาญาและขั้นตอนการดำเนินคดีในศาล

เมื่อมีการกระทำความผิดทางอาญาเกิดขึ้น จะมีกระบวนการและขั้นตอนในการดำเนินคดี
ทางอาญาดังต่อไปนี้

1. ขั้นพนักงานสอบสวน

เจ้าหน้าที่ตำรวจจะเป็นผู้เริ่มกระบวนการสอบสวน ดำเนินการรับแจ้งเหตุและ
สอบสวนรวบรวมพยานหลักฐานเป็นสำนวนคดี ตามกฎหมายได้ให้อำนาจแก่เจ้าหน้าที่
ตำรวจดังนี้

- สืบเสาะหาตัวผู้กระทำผิด รวบรวมหลักฐานและสอบสวนพยานรู้เห็น

- ตรวจค้นตัวบุคคลหรือสถานที่เพื่อรวบรวมพยานหลักฐานและจับกุมผู้ต้องหา
  เมื่อมีหมายศาล เช่น ในคดีร้ายแรงหรือสถานการณ์ที่รุนแรงอันส่งผลต่อชีวิต

- ออกหมายเรียกพยานและหมายเรียกตัวผู้ต้องหา

- ควบคุมตัวผู้ต้องหาไว้สอบสวน

- อนุญาตให้ประกันตัวผู้ต้องหาระหว่างสอบสวน

อำนาจการควบคุมตัวผู้ต้องหาของพนักงานสอบสวน

ตามกฎหมายวิธีพิจารณาความอาญาของประเทศไทย ห้ามมิให้ควบคุมผู้ถูกจับ
หรือผู้ต้องหาไว้เกินกว่าจำเป็นตามพฤติการณ์แห่งคดี ในความผิดที่มีอัตราโทษไม่สูงกว่า
ความผิดลหุโทษ เจ้าหน้าที่ตำรวจหรือพนักงานสอบสวนอาจคุมตัวผู้ต้องหาไว้สอบถาม

เพียงระยะเวลาหนึ่งเท่านั้น คำถามที่เจ้าหน้าที่ถามนั้นอาจเกี่ยวกับข้อมูลส่วนตัวว่าผู้ต้องหา
เป็นใครและอาศัยอยู่ที่ไหน เป็นต้น

เจ้าหน้าที่ตำรวจและพนักงานสอบสวนไม่สามารถควบคุมตัวผู้ต้องหาเกินกว่า 48
ชั่วโมง นับตั้งแต่เวลาที่ถูกจับมาถึงที่ทำการของตำรวจ เว้นแต่กรณีที่มีความจำเป็นก็สามารถ
ยืดเวลาได้แต่ไม่เกิน 3 วัน

หากมีเหตุจำเป็นต้องคุมตัวผู้ต้องหาเป็นระยะเวลามากกว่า 48 ชั่วโมงเพื่อทำการ
สอบสวนหรือการฟ้องคดี เจ้าหน้าที่ตำรวจและพนักงานสอบสวนต้องส่งให้ศาลเป็นผู้
พิจารณาออกหมายขัง ผู้ต้องหานั้นไว้ในระหว่างการสอบสวนภายใต้หลักเกณฑ์ดังนี้ คือ

ก. กรณีคดีความผิดอาญาที่มีอัตราโทษจำคุกไม่เกิน 6 เดือน ปรับไม่เกิน 500
บาท ศาลจะสั่งขังได้ครั้งเดียวไม่เกิน 7 วัน

ข. กรณีความผิดอาญาที่มีโทษจำคุกเกินกว่า 6 เดือน แต่ไม่ถึง 10 ปี หรือปรับ
เกินกว่า 500 บาท ศาลมีอำนาจสั่งขังได้หลายครั้งติดต่อกัน ครั้งละ ไม่เกิน 12
วัน รวมกันแล้วไม่เกิน 48 วัน

ค. กรณีความผิดอาญาที่มีอัตราโทษจำคุกเกินกว่า 10 ปีขึ้นไป ศาลมีอำนาจสั่ง
ขังได้หลายครั้งติดต่อกัน แต่ครั้งหนึ่งไม่เกิน 12 วัน รวมแล้วไม่เกิน 84 วัน

เมื่อพนักงานสอบสวนรวมพยานหลักฐานเสร็จแล้วก็จะสรุปสำนวนการ
สอบสวนมีความเห็นคดีได้ 3 ทางดังนี้

▪ เห็นควรให้งดการสอบสวนหรืองดสอบสวน กรณีได้สืบสวนสอบสวนแล้ว
ไม่รู้ตัวผู้กระทำความผิด

▪ เห็นควรสั่งไม่ฟ้อง จะส่งสำนวนการสอบสวนไปยังพนักงานอัยการต่อไป
ส่วนตัวผู้ต้องหา หากอยู่ในความควบคุมของพนักงานสอบสวนก็จะปล่อย
ตัวไป หากอยู่ในความควบคุมของศาล ให้ยื่นคำร้องขอปล่อยตัวผู้ต้องหาต่อ
ศาล

▪ เห็นควรสั่งฟ้อง ก็จะส่งสำนวนการสอบสวนพร้อมผู้ต้องหาไปยังพนักงาน
อัยการเพื่อดำเนินการต่อไป

สำหรับคดีอาญาที่สามารถเลิกกันได้ในชั้นพนักงานสอบสวน คือ คดีอาญาที่เป็น
ความผิดเล็กน้อยหรือความผิดลหุโทษ เช่น คดีที่มีโทษจำคุกไม่เกิน 1 เดือน หรือปรับไม่เกิน
1,000 บาท หรือทั้งจำทั้งปรับ และในคดีที่มีอัตราโทษปรับสถานเดียวไม่เกิน 10,000 บาท
เมื่อพนักงานสอบสวนได้เปรียบเทียบปรับและผู้ต้องหาได้ชำระค่าปรับตามกำหนดแล้ว

อย่างไรก็ดี สิทธิในการนำคดีอาญามาฟ้อง ย่อมระงับไปดังต่อไปนี้

1. โดยการตายของผู้กระทำผิด

2. ในคดีความผิดส่วนตัวเมื่อได้ถอนคำร้องทุกข์   ถอนฟ้องหรือยอมความกันโดย
ถูกต้องตามกฎหมาย

3. เมื่อคดีเลิกกันได้ (ชั้นพนักงานสอบสวนเปรียบปรับ)

4. มีคำพิพากษาเสร็จเด็ดขาดในความผิดซึ่งได้ฟ้อง

5. มีกฎหมายออกใช้ภายหลังยกเลิกความผิด

6. เมื่อคดีขาดอายุความ

7. มีกฎหมายยกเว้นโทษ

2. ชั้นพนักงานอัยการ

เมื่อเรื่องส่งมาถึงชั้นพนักงานอัยการ พนักงานอัยการจะพิจารณาและมีความเห็น
คดีไว้ใน 3 ทาง ดังนี้

- งดการสอบสวน กรณีได้ทำการสืบสวนสอบสวนแล้วไม่รู้ตัวผู้กระทำผิด

- มีความเห็นสั่งไม่ฟ้อง   จะยื่นคำร้องต่อศาลขอปล่อยตัวผู้ต้องหากรณีที่ถูก
ควบคุมอยู่ ถ้าผู้ต้องหามีประกันตัวก็จะปล่อยตัวและคืนหลักทรัพย์ในการ
ประกันตัวชั้นพนักงานอัยการ ให้กับนายประกันไป

- มีความเห็นสั่งฟ้อง ก็จะนำผู้ต้องหา (ที่อยู่ในความควบคุมหรือประกันตัว
  ไป) ยื่นฟ้องต่อศาล เมื่อศาลรับฟ้องก็จะให้เจ้าหน้าที่ราชทัณฑ์ควบคุมไว้
  ตามอำนาจศาล

3. ชั้นศาล

<u>การพิจารณาคดีในศาลชั้นต้น</u>

การพิจารณาคดีในศาลชั้นต้น ศาลจะปฏิบัติตามข้อใดข้อหนึ่งดังต่อไปนี้

ก. ศาลพิพากษายกฟ้อง

ข. ศาลพิพากษาลงโทษทางอาญา โดยการพิพากษาให้มีการริบทรัพย์สิน การ
   ปรับ การกักขัง การจำคุก หรือการประหารชีวิต

ค. ในกรณีที่จำเลยมีการอุทธรณ์ คดีจะถูกส่งไปยังศาลอุทธรณ์เพื่อการพิจารณา
   พิพากษาต่อไป หากไม่มีการยื่นอุทธรณ์ภายใน 1 เดือน นับแต่วันที่ศาล
   ชั้นต้นอ่านคำพิพากษาหรือคำสั่งให้คดีนั้นสิ้นสุดลงและให้ถือว่าคำพิพากษา
   ถึงที่สุด

จำเลยต้องปรากฏตัวในระหว่างที่มีการพิจารณาคดีและการสืบพยาน   ตาม
หลักการพิจารณาต้องทำต่อหน้าเลย เว้นแต่บางกรณี ผู้พิพากษาอาจมีคำสั่งให้มีการพิจารณา
คดีโดยที่จำเลยไม่ต้องมาร่วมการพิจารณาคดีได้ ในกรณีดังต่อไปนี้

- สำหรับการกระทำความผิดที่มีโทษสูงสุด คือ การจำคุกไม่เกิน 3 ปี และ/หรือปรับ
  ไม่เกิน 5,000 บาท (หากจำเลยมีทนายความและได้รับอนุญาตจากศาล จำเลย
  สามารถไม่มาปรากฏตัวในการพิจารณาคดีได้)

- ในกรณีที่มีจำเลยมากกว่า 2 คน ศาลอาจจัดให้มีการพิจารณาและสืบพยานโดยไม่
  มีจำเลยหรือจำเลยร่วมได้ ในกรณีที่อัยการยืนยันว่าการสืบพยานจะไม่มีผลใดๆ
  ต่อจำเลยที่ไม่เข้าร่วม หรือ ในกรณีที่ศาลเห็นว่าเป็นการเหมาะสมที่มิต้องให้
  จำเลยเข้าร่วมในการพิจารณาคดี

<u>การพิจารณาคดีในศาลอุทธรณ์</u>

ศาลอุทธรณ์อาจพิพากษายืนตามศาลชั้นต้น ยก แก้ หรืออาจกลับคำพิพากษาก็ได้ ในกรณีที่ศาลอุทธรณ์มีการพิจารณากลับคำพิพากษา ศาลอุทธรณ์จะส่งคดีกลับไปยังศาล ชั้นต้นและมีคำสั่งให้ศาลชั้นต้นดำเนินการต่อไป ในกรณีที่ศาลอุทธรณ์มีการพิพากษายืน ตามคำพิพากษาศาลชั้นต้น ให้ถือว่าคดีสิ้นสุดลง จำเลยต้องรับโทษตามคำพิพากษา ตราบใด ที่จำเลยไม่ได้มีการยื่นฎีกาต่อศาลฎีกา ทั้งนี้ หากศาลฎีกาพิจารณาไม่รับคดี ให้ถือว่าคำ พิพากษาของศาลอุทธรณ์เป็นที่สุด เช่นเดียวกับในกรณีที่ศาลฎีการับฎีกาของจำเลย ให้ถือว่า คำพิพากษาของศาลฎีกาเป็นที่สุดและต้องปฏิบัติตาม

อนึ่ง การอุทธรณ์ ฎีกา คำพิพากษาหรือคำสั่งของศาลนั้นสามารถอุทธรณ์หรือฎีกา ได้ทั้งในปัญหาข้อเท็จจริงและปัญหาข้อกฎหมาย แต่ต้องแสดงโดยแจ้งชัดถึงข้อคัดค้านคำ พิพากษาหรือคำสั่งของศาลว่า ไม่ถูกต้องอย่างไร เพราะเหตุใด และที่ถูกต้องเป็นอย่างไร อีก ทั้งต้องเป็นข้อที่ได้ยกขึ้นมาว่ากันแล้วแต่ในศาลชั้นต้น

4. ชั้นราชทัณฑ์

ในกรณีที่ศาลมีคำพิพากษาลงโทษ จำเลยอาจได้รับคำสั่งให้มีการปรับ ริบ ทรัพย์สิน กักขัง จำคุกหรือประหารชีวิตได้ จำเลยบางคนอาจได้รับทัณฑ์บนหรือมีหน้าที่ ต้องรับใช้งานสาธารณะแทนการชำระค่าปรับ ในกรณีที่ศาลมีคำพิพากษาให้ริบทรัพย์และ จำเลยไม่มีทรัพย์หรือทรัพย์สินในการชำระค่าปรับ จำเลยสามารถรับโทษคุมขังและผ่อน ชำระได้ในอัตรา 200 บาทต่อวัน ในกรณีที่ค่าปรับไม่เกิน 80,000 และจำเลยไม่สามารถชำระ ได้ จำเลยอาจมีคำร้องขอต่อศาลให้อนุญาตตนในการรับใช้งานสาธารณะในอัตราวันละ 200 บาทแทนการชำระค่าปรับ

ในกรณีจำเลยได้รับคำพิพากษาให้จำคุก จำเลยอาจถูกส่งตัวไปยังเรือนจำใดๆใน ราชอาณาจักร ซึ่งจำเลยจะอยู่ภายใต้การดูแลของเจ้าพนักงานควบคุมความประพฤติ เรือนจำ บางขวางในจังหวัดนนทบุรีและเรือนจำคลองเปรมในจังหวัดกรุงเทพมหานคร ซึ่งจะ ประกอบไปด้วยนักโทษที่ประกอบอาชญากรรมร้ายแรง และได้รับโทษจำคุกขั้นต่ำ เป็น เวลา 30 ปี ขึ้นไปหรือโทษประหารชีวิต ในประเทศไทย การประหารชีวิตจะกระทำโดยการ

ฉีดยาพิษเข้ากระแสเลือด ซึ่งได้มีการบังคับใช้วิธีดังกล่าวในเดือนตุลาคม พ.ศ. 2544 ก่อน
หน้านี้ ประเทศไทยใช้การยิงเป้าในการประหารชีวิตซึ่งแตกต่างจากสมัยโบราณที่ใช้การตัด
ศีรษะผู้กระทำความผิด

ในโอกาสอันเป็นศุภมงคล เช่น วันพระราชสมภพในพระบาทสมเด็จพระ
เจ้าอยู่หัว หรือ เมื่อรัฐมนตรีว่าการกระทรวงมหาดไทยหรือคณะรัฐมนตรีได้ทูลเกล้า
ทูลกระหม่อมถวายคำร้องต่อพระบาทสมเด็จพระเจ้าอยู่หัว พระบาทสมเด็จพระเจ้าอยู่หัว
อาจพระราชทานการนิรโทษกรรมให้แก่นักโทษ ซึ่งส่งผลเป็นการอภัยโทษหรือลดโทษ
ผู้กระทำความผิด

สิทธิของผู้ต้องหาในคดีอาญา

สิทธิของผู้ต้องหาในคดีอาญา มีดังต่อไปนี้

1. สิทธิในชั้นจับกุม

   ▪ ได้รับการแจ้งข้อกล่าวหา หากมีหมายจับต้องแสดงต่อผู้ถูกจับ

   ▪ ผู้ถูกจับมีสิทธิที่จะไม่ให้การหรือให้การก็ได้

   ▪ พบและปรึกษาทนายความ

   ▪ ได้รับการแจ้งให้ญาติหรือบุคคลที่ไว้วางใจทราบถึงการถูกจับและสถานที่
     ควบคุม

2. สิทธิของผู้ต้องหาในชั้นการสอบสวน

   ▪ พบและปรึกษาทนายสองต่อสอง ในการขอพบทนาย จะต้องร้องขอต่อนาย
     ตำรวจเวรประจำการสถานีตำรวจนั้น ๆ โดยเขียนคำร้องเป็นลายลักษณ์อักษร
     หรือจะใช้คำพูดก็ได้ แต่ต้องระบุชื่อทนายความกันด้วย และสำหรับผู้ต้องหาที่ไม่
     มีเงินจะจ้างทนายความได้ ศาลจะจัดทนายความบริการว่าความให้โดยไม่ต้องเสีย
     ค่าใช้จ่ายแต่อย่างใด

- ได้รับการอำนวยความสะดวกในด้านภาษาที่จัดหามาให้โดยเจ้าหน้าที่ตำรวจหรือ ศาล เพื่อแปลหรืออธิบายกระบวนการทางกฎหมาย ในกรณีที่จำเลยไม่สามารถ พูดภาษาไทยได้

- มีทนายอยู่ด้วยทุกครั้งในขั้นตอนการสอบสวน

- ได้รับการเยี่ยมตามสมควร คือในเวลาปกติตามที่ทางราชการกำหนด และเวลาอื่น ซึ่งต้องขออนุญาตจากนายตำรวจเวรประจำการผู้รับผิดชอบก่อน

- ได้รับรักษาโดยเร็วเมื่อเจ็บป่วย ถ้าเจ็บป่วยก่อนถูกควบคุม เจ้าหน้าที่ตำรวจจะนำ ผู้ต้องหาที่เจ็บป่วยไปโรงพยาบาลของทางราชการเพื่อรับการรักษา แต่ถ้าเจ็บป่วย ในระหว่างถูกควบคุมตัว ร้อยเวรประจำการจะเป็นผู้รายงานต่อสารวัตรหัวหน้า สถานีเพื่อพิจารณาอนุญาตนำตัวส่งโรงพยาบาล

- ได้รับการประกันตัว ผู้ต้องหาสามารถประกันตัวเองหรือให้เพื่อน ญาติ ทนายความหรือผู้ประกันประกันตนออกไปได้

ผู้ที่ขอประกันตัวผู้ต้องหาต้องเขียนคำร้องขอประกันต่อพนักงานสอบสวน เมื่อพนักงาน สอบสวนรับคำร้องแล้ว ให้ขอหลักฐานการรับสัญญาประกันซึ่งต้องลงเวลารับคำร้องไว้ด้วย หลังจากนั้นเจ้าพนักงานจะพิจารณาแจ้งผลการสั่งคำร้องให้เสร็จภายใน 24 ชั่วโมง

3. สิทธิของผู้ต้องหาชั้นถูกฟ้องเป็นจำเลยต่อศาลแล้ว มีสิทธิเช่นเดียวกับในชั้นการสอบสวน นอกจากนี้ยังมีสิทธิได้รับการพิจารณาคดีด้วยความรวดเร็ว ต่อเนื่อง และเป็นธรรม มี ทนายความช่วยเหลือคดี ตรวจดูพยานหลักฐานตลอดจนขอคัดสำเนาคำให้การในชั้น สอบสวน จำเลยมีโอกาสอย่างเต็มที่ในการต่อสู้คดี

การประกันตัว

การประกันตัวผู้ต้องหา เรียกอีกอย่างหนึ่งว่า "การปล่อยตัวชั่วคราว" ในการ ขอให้มีการปล่อยตัวชั่วคราวผู้ต้องหาหรือจำเลยนี้ นายประกันต้องนำเอกสารที่กำหนดไว้มา ให้ครบ เอกสารเหล่านี้จะถูกส่งไปยังศาล ข้อมูลที่เกี่ยวกับการประกันตัวในคดีอาญาที่จะ นำเสนอต่อไปนี้เป็นข้อมูลจากสำนักงานตำรวจภูธร แต่ละศาลอาจต้องการเอกสารที่

แตกต่างกันบ้างเล็กน้อย   รวมถึงค่าประกันตัวอาจมีความแตกต่างกันตามการพิจารณาของ ศาลผู้รับผิดชอบในคดี ในประเทศไทย คำร้องขอปล่อยตัวผู้ต้องหาหรือจำเลยชั่วคราวมี 3 ประเภทด้วยกันคือ

1. คำร้องขอปล่อยตัวชั่วคราวโดยใช้หลักทรัพย์ประกัน
2. คำร้องขอปล่อยตัวชั่วคราวโดยใช้เงินสดประกัน
3. คำร้องขอปล่อยตัวชั่วคราวโดยใช้ตำแหน่งประกัน

คำร้องขอปล่อยตัวชั่วคราวโดยใช้หลักทรัพย์ประกัน

เอกสารที่ผู้ขอประกันต้องเตรียมมาด้วย มีดังนี้

1. บัตรประจำตัวประชาชน   หรือบัตรข้าราชการ   หรือบัตรพนักงานรัฐวิสาหกิจ พร้อมสำเนา 1 ฉบับ

2. ทะเบียนบ้าน พร้อมสำเนา 1 ฉบับ

3. ในกรณีที่ผู้ขอประกันมีคู่สมรส ต้องแสดงหนังสือแสดงความยินยอม พร้อมบัตร ประจำตัวประชาชน(หรือเอกสารตามข้อ 1) และสำเนาทะเบียนบ้านของคู่สมรส พร้อมสำเนาอย่างละ 1 ฉบับ (กรุณาดูแบบฟอร์มหนังสือแสดงความยินยอมได้ใน ภาคผนวก)

4. ในกรณีที่ผู้ขอประกันหย่ากับคู่สมรสหรือเป็นหม้าย   ต้องแสดงใบหย่า   หรือ หนังสือมรณบัตรของคู่สมรส พร้อมสำเนาอย่างละ 1 ฉบับ

5. หลักทรัพย์ที่ใช้ในการประกัน เช่น โฉนดที่ดิน น.ส. 3 น.ส. 3 ก. หรือพันธบัตร รัฐบาล (น.ส. 3 เป็นเอกสารหนังสือแสดงการทำประโยชน์ในที่ดิน ออกโดยกรม ที่ดิน)

6. ในกรณีที่ใช้ที่ดินเป็นหลักประกัน ต้องมีหนังสือรับรองราคาประเมินที่ดินของ เจ้าหน้าที่กรมที่ดินที่ออกให้ไม่เกิน 90 วัน

7. ในกรณีที่ใช้บัญชีธนาคารเป็นหลักประกัน ต้องนำบัญชีเงินฝากธนาคาร (รายระ เอียดทางบัญชี) และหนังสือรับรองจากพนักงานของธนาคารมาแสดงเพื่อยืนยัน จำนวนเงินของผู้ประกันที่มีอยู่ในบัญชีเงินฝาก

8. ในกรณีที่เจ้าของที่ดินไม่สามารถเดินทางไปศาลด้วยตนเองได้ จะต้องมีหนังสือ มอบอำนาจที่นายอำเภอรับรอง พร้อมกับเอกสารในข้อ 3 (กรุณาดูแบบฟอร์ม หนังสือมอบอำนาจในภาคผนวก)

9. หนังสือคำร้องขอให้มีการประกันตัว โดยใช้โฉนดที่ดินหรือ น.ส. 3 เป็น หลักประกัน หนังสือดังกล่าวให้ระบุรวมถึงจำนวนหลักทรัพย์และสัญญาประกัน

10. หนังสือคำร้องขอให้มีการประกันตัวโดยใช้สมุดบัญชีเงินฝากของธนาคาร

เมื่อศาลพิจารณาให้ประกันตัวแล้ว จะมีขั้นตอนดังต่อไปนี้

ศาลจะออกใบรับหลักทรัพย์ไว้เป็นหลักฐาน พร้อมหมายนัด

ผู้ขอประกันต้องสัญญาต่อศาลว่าจะนำตัวผู้ต้องหาหรือจำเลยมายังศาลในวันที่ปรากฏ ในหมายนัด มิเช่นนั้น ศาลจะมีคำสั่งลงโทษผู้ขอประกันตามสัญญาประกัน

หลังจากที่ศาลมีคำพิพากษาแล้ว จะมีการคืนเงินประกันให้แก่ผู้ขอประกันต่อไป

ศาลจะสั่งคืนหลักประกัน ในวันที่อ่านคำพิพากษา โดยผู้ประกันไม่ต้องยื่นคำร้อง ขออีก ให้ผู้ขอประกันนำใบรับหลักทรัพย์ ที่เจ้าหน้าที่ออกไว้เป็นหลักฐานในวันยื่นประกัน และบัตรประจำตัวประชาชนมาแสดง หลังจากวันตัดสินแล้วสามวันทำการ ติดต่อขอรับได้ ที่งานประชาสัมพันธ์

คำร้องขอปล่อยตัวชั่วคราวโดยใช้เงินสดประกัน

เอกสารที่ผู้ขอประกันต้องเตรียมมาด้วย มีดังนี้

1. บัตรประจำตัวประชาชน หรือบัตรข้าราชการ หรือบัตรพนักงานรัฐวิสาหกิจ พร้อมสำเนา 1 ฉบับ

2. ทะเบียนบ้าน พร้อมสำเนา 1 ฉบับ

3. เงินสดเป็นจำนวนเท่ากับเงินประกัน

4. หนังสือคำร้องและสัญญาประกัน

เมื่อศาลพิจารณาให้ประกันตัวแล้ว จะมีขั้นตอนดังต่อไปนี้

ศาลจะออกใบรับเงินตามจำนวนเงินประกัน พร้อมหมายนัด

ผู้ขอประกันต้องให้คำสัญญาแก่ศาลว่าผู้ต้องหาหรือจำเลยจะเดินทางมาศาลตามหมายนัด มิเช่นนั้น ศาลจะลงโทษผู้ขอประกันตามสัญญาประกัน

หลังจากที่ศาลมีคำพิพากษาแล้ว จะมีการคืนเงินประกันให้แก่ผู้ประกันต่อไป

ศาลจะมีคำสั่งให้คืนประกันในวันที่ศาลอ่านคำพิพากษา ผู้ประกันไม่จำเป็นต้องยื่นคำร้องต่อศาลอีก

ให้นำใบรับเงิน, บัตรประจำตัวประชาชน ไปติดต่อขอรับเงินคืน กับเจ้าหน้าที่การเงินได้ในวันที่ศาลมีคำพิพากษา เพื่อนัดวันรับเงินต่อไป

ในกรณีที่ผู้ประกันไม่สามารถเดินทางมารับเงินประกันได้ด้วยตนเอง อาจทำคำร้องขอให้โอนเงินเข้าบัญชีธนาคารของผู้ประกันได้ โดยทำคำร้องยื่นที่เจ้าหน้าที่การเงิน

คำร้องขอปล่อยตัวชั่วคราวโดยใช้ตำแหน่งประกัน

เอกสารที่ผู้ขอประกันต้องเตรียมมาด้วย มีดังนี้

1. บัตรประจำตัวประชาชน หรือบัตรข้าราชการ หรือบัตรพนักงานรัฐวิสาหกิจ พร้อมสำเนา 1 ฉบับ

2. ทะเบียนบ้าน พร้อมสำเนา 1 ฉบับ

3. ในกรณีที่ผู้ขอประกันมีคู่สมรส ต้องแสดงหนังสือแสดงความยินยอม พร้อมบัตรประจำตัวประชาชน(หรือเอกสารตามข้อ 1) และสำเนาทะเบียนบ้านของคู่สมรส พร้อมสำเนาอย่างละ 1 ฉบับ (กรุณาดูแบบฟอร์มหนังสือแสดงความยินยอมได้ใน ภาคผนวก)

4. ในกรณีที่ผู้ขอประกันหย่ากับคู่สมรสหรือเป็นหม้าย ต้องแสดงใบหย่า หรือ หนังสือมรณบัตรของคู่สมรส พร้อมสำเนาอย่างละ 1 ฉบับ

5. หนังสือรับรองสถานภาพการทำงานของผู้ขอประกัน ซึ่งประกอบไปด้วย รายละเอียดเกี่ยวกับตำแหน่งหน้าที่และเงินเดือนในปัจจุบัน ซึ่งออกโดยต้นสังกัด ของผู้ขอประกัน พร้อมลงวันที่และสถานที่ที่ได้ออกหนังสือรับรอง หนังสือ รับรองฉบับนี้อาจจ่าหน้าถึงผู้พิพากษาที่พิจารณาคดีได้เลย

6. ในกรณีที่ผู้ขอประกันเป็นพนักงานรัฐวิสาหกิจ นอกจากหลักฐานข้อ 1-5 แล้ว ต้องมีหนังสือเทียบตำแหน่งกับข้าราชการพลเรือนสามัญมาแสดงด้วย

7. ผู้ขอประกันโดยใช้ตำแหน่ง ต้องมาศาลด้วยตนเองทุกครั้งตามที่ศาลนัด ไม่ สามารถมอบอำนาจได้

8. หนังสือคำร้องและสัญญาประกัน

อัตราการประกันตัวผู้ต้องหาหรือจำเลย โดยการใช้ตำแหน่งเป็นหลักประกัน

ข้าราชการพลเรือน

- ระดับ 3-5 หรือเทียบเท่า วงเงินไม่เกิน 60,000 บาท

- ระดับ 6-8 หรือเทียบเท่า วงเงินไม่เกิน 200,000 บาท

- ระดับ 9-10 หรือเทียบเท่า วงเงินไม่เกิน 500,000 บาท

- ระดับ 11 หรือเทียบเท่า วงเงินไม่เกิน 800,000 บาท

ข้าราชการตำรวจและทหาร

- ให้ทำสัญญาประกันตามระดับที่เทียบเท่าข้าราชการพลเรือน

พนักงานรัฐวิสาหกิจ

- ให้ทำสัญญาประกันตามระดับที่เทียบเท่าข้าราชการพลเรือน

สมาชิกรัฐสภาหรือข้าราชการทางการเมือง

- สามารถใช้ตำแหน่งประกันตัวได้ในวงเงินไม่เกิน 800,000 บาท

ข้าราชการการเมืองส่วนท้องถิ่น

- เจ้าหน้าที่สภาจังหวัดและสภาเทศบาล สามารถใช้ตำแหน่งประกันตัวได้ในวงเงิน
ไม่เกิน 60,000 บาท

ข้อสังเกต: ในกรณีที่ใช้บุคคลเป็นประกันหรือประกันตามวงเงิน   แล้วยังไม่
เพียงพอ ให้ใช้บุคคลตามตำแหน่งอื่น หรือหลักทรัพย์เป็นหลักประกันเพิ่มเติมได้

เมื่อศาลพิจารณาอนุญาตให้มีการปล่อยตัวชั่วคราว   ผู้ขอประกันต้องทำสัญญา
ประกันไว้ต่อศาลว่า จะนำตัวผู้ต้องหาหรือจำเลยมาศาลตามนัด ถ้านายประกันผิดสัญญา
ประกัน ศาลจะสั่งปรับตามที่กำหนดไว้ในสัญญาประกัน

จำนวนเงินประกันขั้นต่ำสุดในแต่ละกรณี

ข้อมูลต่อไปนี้เป็นอัตราเงินประกันสำหรับความผิดฐานต่างๆซึ่งนำมาจากเว็บไซท์ของศาลยุติธรรมและกรมตำรวจ ซึ่งอาจมีการเปลี่ยนแปลงได้ตามโอกาส

อัตราการประกันตัวนี้คืออัตราที่ใช้ในการประกันตัวจำเลยในคดีอาญาที่เป็นผู้ที่บรรลุนิติภาวะแล้วเท่านั้น (ศาลเยาวชนและครอบครัวจะมีอัตราการประกันตัวที่แตกต่างกันออกไป ซึ่งจะต่ำกว่าในบางกรณี)

ความผิดเกี่ยวกับชีวิตและร่างกาย

- ความผิดฐานฆ่าผู้อื่น – 300,000 บาทขึ้นไป

- ความผิดฐานพยายามฆ่า –200,000 บาทขึ้นไป

- ความผิดฐานขับรถโดยประมาททำให้ผู้อื่นถึงแก่ความตาย – ในกรณีที่รถยนต์ส่วนบุคคล 200,000 บาทขึ้นไป ในกรณีรถยนต์สาธารณะ 250,000 บาทขึ้นไป

- ความผิดฐานทำร้ายร่างกาย จนเป็นเหตุให้ผู้ถูกกระทำร้ายรับอันตรายสาหัส – 150,000 บาทขึ้นไป

ความผิดเกี่ยวกับการก่อให้เกิดภยันตรายต่อประชาชน

- ความผิดฐานลอบวางเพลิง –100,000 บาทขึ้นไป

- ความผิดฐานทำให้เกิดเพลิงไหม้โดยประมาท – 100,000 บาทขึ้นไป

- ความผิดฐานให้ความเท็จและปลอมแปลงเอกสาร –100,000 บาทขึ้นไป

ความผิดเกี่ยวกับทรัพย์

- ความผิดฐานรับของโจร –100,000 บาทขึ้นไป

- ความผิดฐานลักทรัพย์ –150,000 บาทขึ้นไป

- ความผิดฐานลักทรัพย์และความผิดฐานก่ออาชญากรรมโดยอาศัยยานพาหนะเป็น
  เครื่องมือหรือหรือมีเหตุฉกรรจ์ –200,000 บาทขึ้นไป

- ความผิดฐานวิ่งราวทรัพย์ –200,000 บาทขึ้นไป

- ความผิดฐานกรรโชกทรัพย์ –100,000 บาทขึ้นไป

- ความผิดฐานชิงทรัพย์ –200,000 บาทขึ้นไป

- ความผิดฐานปล้นทรัพย์ –300,000 บาทขึ้นไป

- ความผิดฐานฉ้อโกงและฉ้อฉล ความผิดฐานฉ้อโกงเจ้าหนี้ หรือความผิดฐาน
  ยักยอก –100,000 บาทขึ้นไป

- ความผิดฐานฉ้อโกงประชาชน –200,000 บาทขึ้นไป

- ความผิดฐานบุกรุกหรือความผิดฐานทำลายทรัพย์สิน –100,000 บาทขึ้นไป

ความผิดต่อหน้าที่ราชการ

- ความผิดฐาน เจ้าพนักงานปฏิบัติหน้าที่โดยมิชอบ –150,000 บาทขึ้นไป

- ความผิดฐานเบิกความเท็จ แจ้งความเท็จ –100,000 บาทขึ้นไป

ความผิดเกี่ยวกับการใช้อาวุธ

- ความผิดฐานพกพาอาวุธที่ไม่มีทะเบียน –100,000 บาทขึ้นไป

- ความผิดฐานพกพาอาวุธที่มีทะเบียน – 50,000 บาทขึ้นไป

ความผิดเกี่ยวกับเพศ

- ความผิดฐานข่มขืนและทำอนาจาร –200,000 บาทขึ้นไป

- ความผิดฐานกระทำอนาจารและมีสื่อลามกในครอบครอง –200,000 บาทขึ้นไป

- ความผิดฐานกระทำชำเราผู้เยาว์ โทรมหญิง ธุระจัดหาหญิง – 200,000 บาทขึ้นไป

อัตราการประกันตัวสำหรับความผิดซึ่งทางอาญาอื่นๆ

พระราชบัญญัติว่าด้วยการพกพาอาวุธ

- ความผิดฐานพกพาอาวุธที่ไม่มีทะเบียน –100,000 บาทขึ้นไป

- ความผิดฐานพกพาอาวุธที่มีทะเบียน –100,000 บาทขึ้นไป

- ความผิดฐานมีวัตถุระเบิดไว้ในครอบครอง –200,000 บาทขึ้นไป

พระราชบัญญัติป่าไม้ (การบุกรุกป่าไม้หรือทำร้ายสัตว์ป่า)

- ความผิดฐานการบุกรุกป่าที่มีพื้นที่ไม่ถึง 10 ไร่ –100,000 บาทขึ้นไป

- ความผิดฐานการบุกรุกป่าที่มีพื้นที่มากกว่า 10 ไร่ –150,000 บาทขึ้นไป

พระราชบัญญัติยาเสพติด

- ความผิดฐานมีกัญชาไว้ในครอบครอง –10,000 บาทขึ้นไป

- ความผิดฐานมีกัญชาไว้เพื่อจำหน่าย –200,000 บาทขึ้นไป

- ความผิดฐานมีเฮโรอีนและยาบ้าไว้ในครอบครอง –100,000 บาทขึ้นไป

- ความผิดฐานมีเฮโรอีนและยาบ้าไว้เพื่อจำหน่าย –300,000 บาทขึ้นไป

เมื่อไม่นานมานี้ กฎหมายไทยอนุญาตให้บริษัทเอกชนที่ดำเนินธุรกิจเกี่ยวกับสัญญา
ประกันสามารถประกันตัวผู้ต้องหาได้ ซึ่งส่วนใหญ่เป็นการให้บริการโดยบริษัทประกันภัย
ภายใต้กรมธรรม์ที่เรียกว่า "กรมธรรม์สัญญาประกัน" ส่วนใหญ่เป็นคดีอันเกี่ยวกับยาเสพติด
การใช้บริการบริษัทเอกชนที่ดำเนินธุรกิจเกี่ยวกับสัญญาประกันได้เป็นที่ยอมรับกันทั่วไป
บริษัทเหล่านี้มักจะคิดค่าธรรมเนียมการบริการเป็นเงินร้อยละ 10 ของวงเงินประกันทั้งหมด
ก่อนที่บริษัทจะออกกรมธรรม์ให้

เกณฑ์ที่ศาลใช้ในการพิจารณาปล่อยตัวชั่วคราวผู้ต้องหาหรือจำเลย ได้แก่

- ความร้ายแรงของความผิด
- ความน่าเชื่อถือของพยานหลักฐาน
- พฤติการณ์แห่งคดี
- ความน่าเชื่อถือของผู้ประกันหรือหลักทรัพย์ประกัน
- ความเป็นไปได้ที่ผู้ต้องหาจะหลบหนี
- โอกาสในการเกิดอันตรายหรือความเสียหายจากการปล่อยตัวชั่วคราวของ
  ผู้ต้องหา
- โอกาสในการทำลายหลักฐาน ทำร้ายหรือข่มขู่พยานแห่งคดีของผู้ต้องหา

ผู้พิพากษาจะพิจารณาว่าผู้ต้องหาควรได้รับการปล่อยตัวชั่วคราวหรือไม่   หากมี
คำสั่งปล่อยตัวชั่วคราว อัยการหรือเจ้าหน้าที่ตำรวจสามารถคัดค้านคำสั่งผู้พิพากษาได้

ในคดีที่ไม่รุนแรงนัก (เช่นคดีบาดเจ็บเล็กน้อยจากการทะเลาะเบาะแว้ง ความผิด
ฐานหมิ่นประมาท กรรโชกทรัพย์หรือลักทรัพย์เพียงเล็กน้อย) ผู้พิพากษาอาจให้มีปล่อยตัว
จำเลยโดยไม่ต้องมีการประกันตัว ซึ่งมีลักษณะคล้ายคลึงกับหลัก OR หรือ "การให้
หลักประกันด้วยตนเอง" (own recognizance) ในประเทศสหรัฐอเมริกาและประเทศ
ตะวันตกอื่นๆ   ผู้พิพากษามีคำสั่งปล่อยตัวตามความน่าเชื่อถือของจำเลยและจำเลยต้อง
สัญญาที่มาปรากฏตัวในศาลเมื่อถึงเวลานัดพิจารณาคดี

รายละเอียดต่อไปนี้เป็นข้อมูลเพิ่มเติมเกี่ยวกับคดีอาญา

- ในคดีอาญา ผู้ต้องหาหรือจำเลยจะได้รับการสันนิษฐานว่าเป็นผู้บริสุทธิ์จนกว่า
จะมีการพิสูจน์ถึงความผิดนั้นว่าผู้ต้องหาหรือจำเลยได้กระทำความผิดอย่างสิ้นข้อสงสัย
(beyond reasonable doubt) เช่นเดียวกับหลักในคดีอาญาของประเทศตะวันตก หลักปฏิบัติ
ทางกฎหมายนี้เป็นส่วนหนึ่งของระบบกฎหมายไทยมาเป็นเวลานานแล้ว   แต่ความคิด
โบราณที่ว่าจำเลยเป็นผู้กระทำความผิดจนกว่าจะมีการพิสูจน์ว่าเป็นผู้บริสุทธิ์ยังคงมีอยู่ใน
ประเทศไทย

- การพิสูจน์ว่าจำเลยผิดเป็นหน้าที่ของอัยการ อัยการมีหน้าที่ต้องเบิกพยานและหลักฐานในการพิจารณาคดีก่อน ต่อจากนั้นจำเลยจะเบิกพยานและหลักฐานของตนเพื่อต่อสู้ข้อกล่าวหา

- พยานแต่ละคนต้องสาบานตนและยืนยันว่าจะพูดความจริง ซึ่งพยานแต่ละคนต้องตอบคำถามของศาล อัยการและจำเลย (หรือทนายความของจำเลย)

- จำเลยมีเวลา 1 เดือนในการอุทธรณ์หรือฎีกาคดีไปยังศาลอุทธรณ์และศาลฎีกานับแต่วันที่ศาลมีคำพิพากษา ศาลฎีกามีดุลพินิจที่จะรับและไม่รับคดีอุทธรณ์ดังกล่าว

- ในกรณีที่จำเลยไม่มีทุนทรัพย์ในการจ้างทนายและหากความผิดที่จำเลยอาจได้รับโทษจำคุก หรือกรณีจำเลยมีอายุต่ำกว่า 18 ปี ศาลอาจแต่งตั้งทนายสาธารณะ (ทนายอาสา) ให้แก่จำเลยโดยไม่คิดค่าใช้จ่าย

- ในกรณีที่พยานเป็นเด็กหรือผู้เยาว์ การสืบพยานจะต้องมีนักจิตวิทยาหรือนักสังคมสงเคราะห์เข้าร่วมการพิจารณาคดีด้วยเสมอ และจะต้องมีการจัดทำรายงานการสืบพยานให้แก่ผู้พิพากษา

- ในคดีที่ความลับและความมั่นคงของประเทศเป็นสิ่งสำคัญ ศาลอาจให้มีการดำเนินคดีอย่างลับหรือไม่เปิดเผยต่อสาธารณะได้

- พระราชบัญญัติฟื้นฟูสมรรถภาพผู้ติดยาเสพติด พ.ศ. 2545 จัดให้ผู้ต้องหาที่ติดยาและ/หรือมียาเสพติดไว้ในครอบครองโดยมิได้มีเจตนาเพื่อจำหน่าย ต้องมารับการพิจารณาคดีที่ศาลภายในระยะเวลา 48 ชั่วโมง (หรือภายในเวลา 24 ชั่วโมงสำหรับผู้เยาว์) เพื่อขอให้ศาลมีคำสั่งให้ส่งตัวผู้ต้องหา เข้ารับการตรวจพิสูจน์ การเสพหรือติดยาเสพติด หากปรากฏว่าผู้ต้องหาเป็นผู้เสพหรือติดยาเสพติด คณะกรรมการฟื้นฟูสมรรถภาพผู้เสพหรือติดยาเสพติดจะมีคำสั่งให้ส่งตัวผู้ต้องหาไปสู่กระบวนการบำบัดฟื้นฟูในสถานที่กำหนด ทั้งนี้ ในระหว่างที่ผู้กระทำผิดได้รับการบำบัดฟื้นฟูตามคำสั่งศาล ข้อกล่าวหาทั้งหมดจะถูกระงับไว้ก่อน ซึ่งผู้กระทำผิดอาจได้รับคำสั่งให้เข้ารับการฟื้นฟูได้หลายครั้งตามความจำเป็นภายในระยะเวลา 3 ปี อย่างไรก็ดี การรักษาแต่ละครั้งจะไม่ใช้ระยะเวลานานเกิน 6 เดือน ในกรณีที่ผู้ต้องหาสามารถฟื้นฟูสมรรถภาพในระดับที่เป็นที่น่าพอใจของคณะกรรมการฟื้นฟู ข้อกล่าวหาทั้งหมดจะเป็นอันยกเลิกไป

คดีแพ่ง

คดีแพ่งเป็นคดีข้อพิพาทระหว่างเอกชนกับเอกชน เอกชนในที่นี้หมายถึง บุคคล
ธรรมดา องค์กรธุรกิจหรือหน่วยงานของรัฐ ผลลัพธ์ในคดีแพ่งจะเป็นเงินที่ฝ่ายหนึ่งชดใช้
ให้แก่อีกฝ่ายหนึ่ง หรือเป็นการเรียกร้องให้กระทำหรือละเว้นการกระทำบางอย่าง ในคดี
แพ่ง จะไม่มีโทษทางอาญาเข้ามาเกี่ยวข้อง

กระบวนพิจารณาคดีแพ่ง

คู่พิพาทสามารถฟ้องดำเนินคดีแพ่งได้ในประเทศไทยในกรณีที่เกิดข้อพิพาทขึ้น
ภายใต้เงื่อนไขและพฤติการณ์ดังต่อไปนี้ – คู่พิพาทอาศัยอยู่ในประเทศไทย มูลเหตุแห่งข้อ
พิพาทเกิดขึ้นในประเทศไทย จำเลยมีทรัพย์สินอยู่ในประเทศไทย หรือ ผู้ที่ได้รับความ
เสียหายเป็นคนไทย ผู้ที่ได้รับความเสียหาย หรือที่รู้จักกันในนาม "โจทก์" ฟ้องร้องต่อศาล
และนำเสนอข้อเท็จจริงอันเกี่ยวกับคดี เมื่อมีการฟ้องร้องแล้ว จะมีลำดับขั้นตอนในการ
พิจารณาคดีแพ่ง ดังต่อไปนี้

ขั้นตอนการรับฟ้องและการพิจารณาคดีชั้นต้น

ในกรณีที่ศาลรับฟ้อง ศาลจะออกหมายเรียกจำเลย โจทก์มีหน้าที่เก็บหมายเรียก
ดังกล่าวพร้อมสำเนาการฟ้องร้องคดีของตนที่ได้ส่งไปยังจำเลยโดยเจ้าหน้าที่ศาลภายใน
ระยะเวลาที่ได้ระบุไว้ (โดยทั่วไปมักเป็นระยะเวลา 7 วันนับแต่วันที่ศาลรับฟ้องคดี มิ
เช่นนั้นศาลอาจพิจารณาว่าโจทก์ไม่จริงจังกับการฟ้องร้องคดีของตน) ทั้งนี้ โจทก์มีหน้าที่
ต้องจ่ายค่าธรรมเนียมค่าการบริการให้เจ้าหน้าที่ศาลที่นำส่งเอกสารการฟ้องร้องไปยังจำเลย
ในกรณีที่ไม่พบจำเลย เจ้าหน้าที่ศาลอาจติดหมายเรียกจำเลยไว้ที่สถานที่อยู่ของจำเลยซึ่ง
สามารถสังเกตได้ง่าย หรือโดยการประกาศหมายเรียกจำเลยลงในหนังสือพิมพ์หรือสื่ออื่นๆ
กระบวนการส่งหมายเรียกและการตีพิมพ์หมายเรียกนี้ใช้เวลา 15 วันนับแต่วันที่เริ่มส่งหรือ
เริ่มตีพิมพ์

จำเลยมีเวลา 15 วันที่จะตอบรับหรือตอบปฏิเสธข้อกล่าวหา จำเลยสามารถฟ้อง
โจทก์กลับหรือฟ้องแย้งได้ถ้ามีเหตุที่เกี่ยวข้องกับโจทก์ในคดีเดียวกันแต่ถ้าจำเลยไม่
ดำเนินการภายในระยะเวลาดังกล่าวถือว่าจำเลยขาดนัดยื่นคำให้การ

หลังจากที่จำเลยได้ยื่นตอบโต้คำฟ้องของโจทก์แล้ว   คู่พิพาททั้งสองฝ่ายจะ
กำหนดประเด็นข้อพิพาท และศาลจะนัดวันในการชี้สองสถาน เพื่อพิจารณาคดีและเพื่อที่จะ
ระบุว่าประเด็นใดที่ต้องพิสูจน์และต้องนำสืบพยานหลักฐานในศาล   หลังจากที่คู่กรณี
เห็นชอบในประเด็นที่ต้องมาพิสูจน์กันในศาล   ศาลจะนัดวันและพิจารณาว่าแต่ละฝ่ายมี
หน้าที่ในการนับสืบประเด็นใดบ้าง

ในกรณีที่จำเลยไม่ยื่นคำให้การภายในระยะเวลาที่กำหนดไว้ในหมายเรียก โจทก์
อาจขอให้ศาลมีคำพิพากษาหรือคำสั่งชี้ขาดให้ตนเป็นฝ่ายชนะคดีโดยขาดนัด คำร้องนี้ต้อง
กระทำภายในระยะเวลา 15 วันนับจากวันที่สุดท้ายที่จำเลยมีสิทธิยื่นคำให้การได้สิ้นสุดลง
หากโจทก์ไม่ทำตามภายในระยะเวลาที่กำหนด ศาลจะจำหน่ายคดีนั้นเสีย

ในกรณีที่โจทก์มิได้อยู่ในประเทศไทย โจทก์มีหน้าที่ต้องวางประกัน (เงินสด
โฉนดที่ดินหรือจดหมายรับรองจากเจ้าหน้าที่ธนาคาร) ในจำนวนที่ครอบคลุมค่าใช้จ่ายของ
จำเลยทั้งหมด รวมทั้งค่าธรรมเนียมตามกฎหมาย สำรองไว้ในกรณีที่จำเลยชนะคดี

ค่าธรรมเนียมศาลคิดเป็นร้อยละ 2.5 ของจำนวนเงินในการพิพาท (แต่ไม่เกิน
200,000 บาท) ซึ่งจะต้องชำระในเวลาที่ศาลรับฟ้องคดี และในอีกครั้งหนึ่งเมื่อมีการยื่น
อุทธรณ์คดี

ในกรณีที่การฟ้องร้องที่มีทุนทรัพย์ต่ำกว่า 300,000 บาท ค่าธรรมเนียมการยื่นฟ้อง
ในศาลชั้นต้นจะอยู่ที่ 200 บาท

ศาลอาจมีคำสั่งให้ฝ่ายที่แพ้คดีชำระค่าทนาย   ค่าธรรมเนียมการบริการและ
ค่าธรรมเนียมพยานให้แก่ฝ่ายที่ชนะคดี   สำหรับหลักประกันของโจทก์จะได้คืนเมื่อมีคำ
พิพากษาเป็นที่สุด และจำเลยไม่อุทธรณ์

ขั้นตอนการพิจารณาคดี

คู่กรณีจำเป็นต้องส่งรายชื่อหลักฐานและประเด็นให้แก่ศาล และแต่ละฝ่ายต้อง
ได้รับสำเนารายการหลักฐานภายในระยะเวลา 7 วันก่อนวันที่ศาลนัดชี้สองสถานหรือวัน
พิจารณาคดี หลักฐานอื่นๆที่ไม่ได้ระบุไว้ในรายการอาจนำเข้าสู่การพิจารณาได้หากแสดง
ให้ศาลเห็นในระดับเป็นที่น่าพอใจว่ามีเหตุผลเพียงพอที่เกี่ยวข้องในคดีนั้น

หลังจากที่โจทก์และจำเลยได้ส่งประเด็นที่เกี่ยวข้องเป็นที่เรียบร้อยแล้ว (หรือ
จำเลยไม่มาปรากฏตัวที่ศาล) ศาลจะรับฟังคำเบิกความของพยาน ทั้งนี้พยานต้องสาบานตน
ที่จะให้ข้อเท็จจริงแก่ศาล ซึ่งจะได้รับการตรวจสอบจากทนายของทั้ง 2 ฝ่าย

ในกรณีที่เอกสารที่เกี่ยวข้องอื่นๆเป็นภาษาอื่น ไม่ใช่ภาษาไทย จะต้องมีการแปล
ให้เป็นภาษาไทยและส่งแนบมาพร้อมกับต้นฉบับและสำเนาที่มีการรับรองสำเนาถูกต้อง
คำให้การเป็นลายลักษณ์อักษรและคำให้การแบบปากเปล่าของพยานจำเป็นต้องมีการแปล
เป็นไทยด้วยเช่นกัน ค่าบริการแปลเอกสารนั้นให้ตกเป็นหน้าที่ของฝ่ายที่เบิกพยานปากนั้น
(กรุณาดูรายละเอียดเพิ่มเติมเกี่ยวกับการแปลเอกสารและล่ามในบทต่อไป)

คู่ความจะได้รับสิทธิให้นำเสนอประเด็นข้อพิพาทสุดท้ายหลังจากที่ได้มีนำสืบ
พยานหลักฐานเป็นที่เรียบร้อยแล้ว ในคดีแพ่ง ภาระการพิสูจน์จะตกเป็นหน้าที่ของคู่ความ
ฝ่ายที่กล่าวอ้าง ข้อเท็จจริงใดเพื่อสนับสนุนคำฟ้องหรือคำให้การของตนเว้นแต่กรณีกล่าว
อ้างข้อเท็จจริงที่เป็นที่รู้กันอยู่โดยทั่วไป หรือข้อเท็จจริงที่คู่ความอีกฝ่ายหนึ่งได้ยอมรับแล้ว
หรือข้อเท็จจริงซึ่งไม่อาจโต้แย้งได้หรือมีข้อกฎหมายสันนิษฐานไว้เป็นคุณแก่คู่ความฝ่ายที่
กล่าวอ้างนั้นเมื่อคู่ความต่างหยุดการนำสืบพยานหลักฐาน ผู้พิพากษาจะมีคำพิพากษาเป็น
ลายลักษณ์อักษรและอ่านคำพิพากษาดังกล่าวต่อหน้าคู่ความในศาลนั้น

ขั้นตอนการพิพากษาคดี

ศาลจะมีคำสั่งให้คู่ความฝ่ายที่แพ้คดี (ซึ่งได้กลายเป็น "ลูกหนี้") ชำระค่าเสียหาย
ทั้งหมดอันเกิดจากการกระทำของตน ด้วยการส่งมอบทรัพย์สิน กระทำหรืองดเว้นการ
กระทำบางประการแก่คู่ความฝ่ายที่ชนะคดี (ซึ่งบัดนี้เรียกว่า "เจ้าหนี้") คำพิพากษาให้เวลา

แต่ละฝ่ายในการชำระหนี้เป็นระยะเวลา 7 วัน อย่างไรก็ตาม ในกรณีที่มีการดำเนินคดีอื่นที่
อาจส่งผลต่อคดีปัจจุบันของฝ่ายที่แพ้คดี   ฝ่ายที่แพ้คดีนี้อาจยื่นคำร้องขอให้ศาลมีการทุเลา
การบังคับคดี ทั้งนี้ ศาลอาจกำหนดค่าใช้จ่ายและค่าธรรมเนียมทนายความไม่เกินกว่าร้อยละ
5 ของจำนวนเงินที่พิพาท สำหรับศาลชั้นต้น และไม่เกินว่าร้อยละ 3 สำหรับการยื่นอุทธรณ์
และการยื่นฎีกา

ในกรณีที่ลูกหนี้ไม่สามารถชำระหนี้ตามคำพิพากษาศาลได้   เจ้าหนี้อาจร้องต่อ
ศาลขอให้ศาลมีคำสั่งหรือออกหมายศาลในการยึดทรัพย์ของลูกหนี้และให้นำทรัพย์ดังกล่าว
ออกขายทอดตลาดเพื่อนำเงินมาชำระหนี้ให้แก่เจ้าหนี้ ในบางกรณี ลูกหนี้จะมีความผิดฐาน
ไม่ปฏิบัติตามคำสั่งหรือคำพิพากษาของศาล   ซึ่งจะได้รับการลงโทษด้วยการจำคุก
กระบวนการนี้ต้องอาศัยเวลาในการที่จะให้ลูกหนี้ชดใช้หนี้ทั้งหมดให้แก่เจ้าหนี้   ฝ่ายที่แพ้
คดีมีเวลา   1   เดือนนับแต่วันที่ได้อ่านคำพิพากษาหรือคำสั่งนั้นในการยื่นอุทธรณ์ต่อศาล
อุทธรณ์หรือยื่นฎีกาไปยังศาลฎีกาภายใต้หลักเกณฑ์การอุทธรณ์ ฎีกาตามที่กฎหมายกำหนด
เช่น คดีแพ่ง จะห้ามคู่ความอุทธรณ์คำพิพากษาในคดีที่ราคาทรัพย์สินหรือจำนวนทุนทรัพย์
ที่พิพาทกันในชั้นอุทธรณ์ไม่เกินห้าหมื่นบาท ส่วนการฎีกาห้ามคู่ความฎีกาคำพิพากษาหรือ
คำสั่งในคดีที่จำนวนทุนทรัพย์ที่พิพาทกันในชั้นฎีกาไม่เกินหนึ่งแสนบาท เป็นต้น

อนุญาโตตุลาการและการไกล่เกลี่ยข้อพิพาท

คู่ความสามารถเลือกวิธีระงับข้อพิพาทของตน ได้ด้วยการ ไกล่เกลี่ยข้อพิพาทหรือ
โดยอาศัยอนุญาโตตุลาการ

การไกล่เกลี่ยข้อพิพาทเป็นกระบวนการที่มีบุคคลภายนอกที่เป็นกลาง หรือ "ผู้
ไกล่เกลี่ย"   มาไกล่เกลี่ยและประนีประนอมยอมข้อพิพาทระหว่างคู่ความทั้งสองหรือ
ระหว่างคู่ความด้วยกัน   ซึ่งการไกล่เกลี่ยข้อพิพาทนี้เป็นกระบวนการระงับข้อพิพาทอย่าง
สันติที่มีลักษณะไม่เป็นทางการ   ซึ่งมีวัตถุประสงค์ในการช่วยคู่ความหาทางออกที่เป็นที่
พอใจกันทั้งสองฝ่าย โดยจะจัดทำสัญญาประนีประนอมยอมความกันด้วยความสมัครใจ

ในขณะที่อนุญาโตตุลาการเป็นกระบวนการการระงับข้อพิพาทที่คู่พิพาทจะต้อง
จัดส่งประเด็นข้อพิพาทที่มีระว่างกันไปยังบุคคลหรือกลุ่มบุคคลที่ได้รับการแต่งตั้งขึ้นมา

ด้วยความยินยอมของคู่กรณีหรือตามบทบัญญัติแห่งกฎหมาย   คดีที่อาศัยอนุญาโตตุลาการ
ส่วนใหญ่ของไทยจะได้รับการดำเนินการภายใต้ความดูแลของหอการค้าระหว่างประเทศ
(ไอซีซี) อย่างไรก็ดี ในประเทศไทยมีหน่วยงานเกี่ยวกับอนุญาโตตุลาการ 2 แห่ง ได้แก่
สำนักระงับข้อพิพาท สำนักงานศาลยุติธรรม (ADRO) ซึ่งเป็นสถาบันอนุญาโตของประเทศ
ไทย   และสถาบันอนุญาโตตุลาการของหอการค้าไทย   ซึ่งทั้งสองสถาบันได้รับการจัดตั้ง
ขึ้นมาเพื่อลดจำนวนจำนวนข้อพิพาทที่นำขึ้นสู่ศาล   ลดเวลาและลดค่าใช้จ่ายที่จะเกิดขึ้น
เนื่องจากกระบวนการทางศาล

        ค่าใช้จ่ายในการดำเนินการหรือค่าธรรมเนียมอนุญาโตตุลาการในประเทศไทย
ตั้งอยู่บนความสมเหตุสมผล   ซึ่งจะมากหรือน้อยขึ้นอยู่กับจำนวนเงินในข้อพิพาท
ค่าธรรมเนียมสถาบันอนุญาโตตุลาการของไทยคิดค่าใช้จ่ายเป็นจำนวนน้อยกว่าสถาบัน
อนุญาโตตุลาการในประเทศอื่นๆเป็นอันมาก
อนุญาโตตุลาการต่างประเทศหรือทนายความต่างประเทศอาจร่วมเป็นอนุญาโตตุลาการและ
ทำหน้าที่เป็นที่ปรึกษาทางกฎหมายในกระบวนการพิจารณาคดีอนุญาโตตุลาการที่เกิดขึ้นใน
ประเทศไทยได้ ในกรณีที่กฎหมายที่ใช้บังคับคู่พิพาทนั้นไม่ใช่กฎหมายไทย หรือเมื่อมีเหตุ
จำเป็นที่จะต้องบังคับใช้คำพิพากษาศาลต่างประเทศ

ทนายความและล่าม

ในส่วนนี้ผู้เขียนจะให้ข้อมูลเกี่ยวกับทนายความและล่ามในกระบวนการกฎหมาย
ไทย   กฎหมายไทยได้ประกาศว่าชาวต่างชาติจะต้องได้รับสิทธิเท่าเทียมกับคนไทยใน
กระบวนการกฎหมาย เช่นในการพิจารณาคดีความในคดีอาญานั้น ชาวต่างชาติมีสิทธิที่จะ
ใช้ทนายความและล่ามในทุกขั้นตอนเพื่อที่จะได้รับความยุติธรรมเช่นเดียวกับคนไทยที่ต้อง
ผ่านขั้นตอนต่างๆ (ยกเว้นในบางกรณี)

อาจจะเป็นเรื่องยากสำหรับชาวต่างชาติที่จะเลือกทนายที่เหมาะสมกับคดีของตน
มีทนายความที่มีคุณสมบัติจำนวนมากที่พร้อมจะช่วยคุณในอัตราค่าบริการที่เหมาะสม
อย่างไรก็ตามทนายความคนไทยมักมีปัญหาด้านภาษา   ทนายความไทยส่วนใหญ่ไม่รู้
ภาษาอังกฤษดีพอที่จะอธิบายขั้นตอนทางกฎหมายให้กับลูกความ   จึงทำให้เสียโอกาสที่จะ
ได้ลูกความชาวต่างชาติ   ทนายความไทยที่พูดภาษาอังกฤษได้ดีมักจะทำงานในสำนักงาน
ทนายความขนาดใหญ่ที่คิดค่าบริการสูง

ในบทนี้คุณจะได้ศึกษาข้อมูลเกี่ยวกับการว่าจ้างทนายความและล่าม   ซึ่งอาจจะ
สามารถช่วยคุณประหยัดค่าใช้จ่ายในด้านกฎหมายได้

คุณสามารถติดต่อกับสภาทนายความและขอให้สภาช่วยหาหรือแนะนำทนาย
ให้กับคุณ   ถ้าคุณไม่เข้าใจภาษาไทย คุณสามารถหาล่ามโดยบอกกับทางตำรวจหรือทางศาล
ให้จัดหาล่ามให้ เช่น   ถ้าคุณพูดภาษาพม่า   ก็ขอให้ทางการจัดหาล่ามพม่าให้ คุณสามารถ
ปฏิเสธที่จะเซ็นชื่อในเอกสารต่างๆจนกว่าคุณจะเข้าใจว่าเอกสารที่จะให้เซ็นนั้นคืออะไร
หรือจนกว่าจะเข้าใจขั้นตอนต่างๆเหล่านั้น

สภาทนายความจะจัดหาทนายความที่ได้ขึ้นทะเบียนไว้กับทางสภาฯ   ทนายความ
จากสภาทนายความ (ทนายขอแรง) ส่วนใหญ่ไม่ได้ทำงานเต็มเวลา บางท่านอาจจะ ไม่ค่อยมี
คดีจึงรับอาสา   หรือบางท่านอาจจะเป็นนักศึกษากฎหมายที่จบมาใหม่ที่ต้องการ
ประสบการณ์หรือบางท่านก็เป็นทนายความที่เกษียณอายุแล้วแต่ก็ต้องการช่วยเหลือสังคม

ทนายความขอแรงเหล่านี้ได้รับค่าตอบแทนจากงบประมาณที่จำกัดจากกระทรวงยุติธรรม และส่วนใหญ่จะพูดแต่ภาษาไทยเท่านั้น

ทนายความไทยหรือที่ปรึกษากฎหมายที่พูดภาษาอังกฤษส่วนใหญ่จะไม่ขึ้นทะเบียนกับสภาทนายความ   ส่วนล่ามที่ขึ้นทะเบียนกับศาลมักจะพูดภาษาอังกฤษไม่ดีเท่าที่ควร อัตราค่าจ้างล่ามในศาลนั้นต่ำมากจนล่ามเก่งๆ จะไม่ขึ้นทะเบียนกับทางศาล ในกรณีที่จำเป็นต้องใช้ล่ามและไม่มีล่ามที่ขึ้นทะเบียนกับ ทางศาลก็จะ "เชิญ" บุคคลที่มีความสามารถในท้องถิ่น เช่นอาจารย์ภาษาอังกฤษหรือบุคคลที่ทางศาลเห็นว่ามีคุณสมบัติเพียงพอที่จะเป็นล่ามในขั้นตอนต่างๆของศาลได้และศาลจะเป็นผู้ออกค่าใช้จ่ายให้กับล่ามส่วนในคดีแพ่ง คู่กรณีจะต้องจัดหาหรือจ้างล่ามด้วยตนเอง

คุณสมบัติของทนายความในประเทศไทย

มีที่ปรึกษากฎหมายหลายท่านในประเทศไทยที่เป็นชาวต่างชาติและเป็นผู้ให้คำปรึกษาเฉพาะแก่ชาวต่างชาติด้วยกัน   ที่ปรึกษากฎหมายเหล่านี้จะทำงานในสำนักงานทนายความในเมืองใหญ่ๆ   พวกเขาอาจจะมีปริญญาด้านกฎหมายจากประเทศของตนแต่จะไม่ได้รับอนุญาตให้ทำงานเป็นทนายความในประเทศไทย แต่จะเป็นเพียงที่ปรึกษากฎหมายได้   มีชาวต่างชาติเพียงไม่กี่ท่านเท่านั้นที่มีคุณสมบัติที่จะขึ้นศาลและทำหน้าที่เป็นทนายความในเมืองไทยได้อย่างเต็มตัว

ผู้ที่จะเป็นทนายความในเมืองไทยได้ต้องมีคุณสมบัติดังต่อไปนี้

- เป็นผู้ที่มีสัญชาติไทย
- จบปริญญาตรีหรืออนุปริญญาทางนิติศาสตร์จากสถาบันที่ได้รับการรับรองจากสภาทนายความ
- มีความประพฤติดีอยู่ในศีลธรรม และเป็นผู้มีความซื่อสัตย์สุจริต
- ไม่อยู่ระหว่างต้องโทษจำคุกหรือเป็นบุคคลล้มละลาย

- ไม่มีโรคติดต่อซึ่งเป็นที่รังเกียจต่อสังคม
- ทนายความเอกชนต้องไม่เป็นข้าราชการหรือมีตำแหน่งใดๆที่ได้รับเงินเดือนจากทางราชการ
- จะต้องสอบผ่านคุณสมบัติอื่นๆที่สภาทนายความกำหนดไว้

วิธีเลือกทนายความ

ก่อนที่คุณจะตัดสินใจว่าจะใช้ทนายความคนใด คุณควรจะเข้าใจคดีของตนให้ถ่องแท้เพื่อที่จะสอบถามคำถามต่างๆกับทนายความที่คุณสนใจจะว่าจ้าง ถ้าคุณเลือกทนายความผิดแล้วแทนที่จะเป็นการช่วยแก้ปัญหา จะกลับเป็นการเพิ่มปัญหาให้กับคุณ ทนายความที่มีความสามารถจะเป็นผู้ที่ช่วยคุณแก้ปัญหาได้อย่างรวดเร็วและมีประสิทธิภาพในราคาที่เหมาะสม

เมื่อคุณเข้าพบกับทนายความที่คุณคาดว่าจะว่าจ้าง คุณสามารถทำสิ่งต่อไปนี้ได้

คุณสามารถขอดูใบอนุญาตทนายความ ผู้ประกอบอาชีพทนายความต้องได้รับใบอนุญาตจากสภาทนายความ ต้องได้รับการทดสอบว่าเป็นผู้มีความรู้ทางด้านกฎหมายและได้รับการฝึกอบรมเกี่ยวกับมารยาทของทนายความแล้ว ผู้ที่ไม่มีใบอนุญาตทนายความหากมาว่าความในศาลหรือแต่งฟ้อง คำให้การ หรืออ้างตนว่าเป็นทนายถือว่าผิดกฎหมาย

คุณอาจจะถามทนายคนนั้นว่ามีประสบการณ์มากน้อยเพียงใดในคดีที่คล้ายคลึงกับคดีของคุณ ทนายความบางคนอาจจะเป็นผู้เชี่ยวชาญในบางคดีแต่อาจจะไม่คุ้นเคยกับคดีของคุณก็ได้ ทนายความบางคนอาจจะรับคดีทั่วไปแต่อาจจะไม่ถนัดกับคดีที่มีความยุ่งยากซับซ้อน คุณสามารถสอบถามถึงประวัติการศึกษาและประสบการณ์ของทนายความที่คุณต้องการจะว่าจ้าง ทนายความที่เป็นผู้เชี่ยวชาญเฉพาะด้านอาจจะเป็นประโยชน์ต่อคดีของคุณเพิ่มขึ้น

ถามทนายความว่ารู้จักหรือมีความสัมพันธ์ส่วนตัวกับคู่ความของคุณหรือไม่ ทนายความของคุณจะต้องเป็นผู้รักษาผลประโยชน์ของคุณ ทนายความไม่ควรมีความสัมพันธ์ส่วนตัวกับคู่ความฝ่ายตรงข้าม คุณควรจะถามคำถามนี้ก่อนที่จะอธิบายรายละเอียดของคดีของคุณ ในจังหวัดเล็กๆอาจจะเกิดขึ้นบ่อยครั้งเนื่องจากคนส่วนมากจะรู้จักกันและทนายความอาจจะเคยทำงานให้กับฝ่ายตรงข้ามมาก่อน

สอบถามเรื่องค่าใช้จ่ายในคดีและค่าทนาย ทนายความแต่ละคนเรียกค่าจ้างแตกต่างกัน ทนายความบางคนอาจเรียกค่าทนายในอัตรา 40,000 บาท ในคดีหย่าร้าง และทนายอีกคนอาจเรียกถึง150,000 บาท ทั้งนั้นอยู่กับชื่อเสียงและความสามารถของทนายความ ทนายความบางคนอาจจะคิดค่าปรึกษาในขั้นต้น ดังนั้นจึงควรคุยกันเรื่องค่าทนายให้ชัดเจน

ตามปกติทนายความจะให้คุณอธิบายคดีของคุณก่อนเพื่อที่จะดูว่าคดีนั้นซับซ้อนเพียงใด มีพยานกี่คน ต้องใช้เวลานานเพียงใด จึงค่อยตัดสินว่าตนจะต้องทำหน้าที่ใดบ้างและค่าใช้จ่ายจะอยู่ในราคาใด ทนายความอาจจะคิดเป็นอัตราต่อวัน ต่อชั่วโมงหรือเหมาจ่ายต่อคดี ทนายความในต่างจังหวัดหรือในจังหวัดเล็กๆ มักจะคิดค่าทนายในลักษณะเหมาจ่ายเป็นคดีๆไป คุณและทนายจะต้องตกลงกันก่อนล่วงหน้าว่าค่าทนายจะเป็นเท่าใด นอกจากค่าทนายแล้วยังมีค่าใช้จ่ายในคดีซึ่งแตกต่างจากค่าทนาย คุณควรจะสอบถามว่าจะมีค่าใช้จ่ายในคดีเพิ่มเติมหรือไม่ ค่าใช้จ่ายในคดีอาจจะรวมถึงค่าเดินทาง ค่าพยาน ค่าเอกสารต่างๆ

ตรวจสอบชื่อเสียงของทนายความที่คุณจะว่าจ้างเพื่อดูว่าทนายความผู้นั้นมีประสบการณ์มากน้อยเพียงใดเกี่ยวกับกฎหมายว่าด้วยชาวต่างชาติ คุณควรเลือกทนายความที่เหมาะสมกับคดีของคุณที่สุดตามกำลังที่คุณสามารถว่าจ้างได้ ถ้าเกิดคุณจ้างทนายความที่พูดภาษาของคุณไม่ได้ คุณก็จำเป็นต้องจ้างล่ามอีกต่อหนึ่ง

บางครั้งทนายความอาจจะรวมค่าแปลเอกสาร ค่าธรรมเนียมศาลอยู่ในค่าทนายแล้ว ในกรณีนี้คุณไม่จำเป็นต้องจ่ายค่าใช้จ่ายในศาลด้วยตนเอง ในคดีแพ่งต้องวางเงินค่าขึ้นศาลเป็นเงินร้อยละ 2.5 ของจำนวนทุนทรัพย์ที่พิพาทกันแต่ศาลจะเรียกไม่เกิน 200,000 บาท

ถ้าทนายความของคุณรวมค่าใช้จ่ายในศาลอยู่ในค่าทนายแล้ว คุณควรจะถามว่าค่าใช้จ่ายใน
ศาลเป็นเท่าไร

เคยมีทนายความบางคนที่สภาทนายความได้สอบมารยาทฐานเรียกค่าใช้จ่ายใน
ศาลสูงกว่าที่กำหนดไว้ เช่นเรียกสูงถึงร้อยละ 5 หรือสูงกว่าสองแสนบาทซึ่งเป็นเพดาน
สูงสุดของค่าธรรมเนียม สำหรับคดีอาญา ไม่จำเป็นต้องวางเงินค่าขึ้นศาล การเรียกค่า
ทนายความสูงไม่ผิดต่อมารยาททนายความ (ถ้าไม่สูงจนเกินไป) แต่จะถือว่าผิดมารยาท
ทนายความถ้าคิดค่าใช้จ่ายในคดีเกินความเป็นจริง

ในคดีอาญา คุณจำเป็นต้องใช้ทนายความเพราะคุณจะไม่เข้าใจขั้นตอนของ
กฎหมายและไม่เข้าใจภาษาไทย เอกสารเกือบทุกอย่างเขียนเป็นภาษาไทย สำหรับคดีลหุ
โทษ เช่น ทำผิดกฎจราจร หรือ พ.ร.บ.แรงงาน ซึ่งโทษเป็นเพียงค่าปรับ คุณสามารถดำเนิน
เรื่องได้โดยไม่ต้องใช้ทนายความ หรือคุณสามารถจ้างทนายความเป็นรายชั่วโมง หรือเหมา
จ่ายจนกว่าเรื่องจะสิ้นสุดลง

บางคดีจะต้องลงเอยที่ศาล บางคดีก็จบลงที่สถานีตำรวจ ในคดีลหุโทษศาล
อนุญาตให้ทนายความและล่ามเป็นคนๆเดียวกันได้ (ทนายความที่พูดภาษาของลูกความได้)
ดังนั้นจะเป็นการสะดวกสำหรับลูกความชาวต่างชาติถ้าสามารถว่าจ้างทนายความที่พูดภาษา
ของตนได้

สำหรับคดีทั่วไปหรือคดีที่ยอมความกันได้ เช่น คดียักยอกทรัพย์ หรือคดีข่มขืนที่
โทษมีทั้งจำและปรับและรอลงอาญาเป็นเวลา 3-5 ปี จำเป็นจะต้องมีล่ามและทนายความ (ซึ่ง
สามารถเป็นคนๆเดียวกันได้) ถ้าคุณว่าจ้างทนายความที่พูดภาษาอังกฤษได้ ค่าทนายความ
ขั้นต่ำมักจะอยู่ที่ 30,000 บาท

สำหรับคดีที่ร้ายแรงหรือคดีที่ยอมความไม่ได้ เช่น คดีฆาตกรรม ปล้นทรัพย์ ค้ายา
เสพติด หรือฟอกเงิน จำเป็นต้องใช้ทนายความผู้เชี่ยวชาญและมีประสบการณ์ในการ
ดำเนินคดี และจำเป็นต้องมีล่ามต่างหาก ค่าทนายความขั้นต่ำสำหรับคดีในลักษณะนี้มักจะ

เริ่มต้นที่ 100,000 บาท

ไม่มีการกำหนดค่าทนายที่แน่นอน ทนายความสามารถคิดค่าทนายได้ตามที่ตน
เห็นสมควร อย่างไรก็ตามจำนวนเงินค่าทนายที่ถูกเรียกมานั้นควรเป็นจำนวนที่เหมาะสม
สำหรับคดีแพ่งค่าจ้างทนายอาจจะขึ้นอยู่กับจำนวนเงินที่เกี่ยวข้องในคดี เช่นร้อยละ 10 หรือ
20 ของจำนวนเงินในข้อพิพาท หรือคุณจะตกลงกับทนายความล่วงหน้า ทนายความอาจจะ
เรียกเป็นรายชั่วโมงหรือเหมาจ่าย ถ้าคุณเลือกเอาทนายความที่พูดภาษาอังกฤษได้หรือ
ทนายความจากสำนักงานกฎหมายขนาดใหญ่ คุณอาจจะถูกเรียกค่าทนายความถึงชั่วโมงละ
100-200 เหรียญดอลลาร์สหรัฐ สำนักงานทนายความที่ให้บริการระดับนานาชาติที่มี
มาตรฐานสูงในบริษัทใหญ่ๆอาจจะคิดค่าทนายความถึงชั่วโมงละ 1,000 เหรียญดอลลาร์
บริษัททนายความระดับนานาชาติมักจะเรียกค่าทนายความเป็นเงินดอลลาร์สหรัฐ ในกรณีนี้
ขอให้คุณตรวจดูอัตราการแลกเปลี่ยน และให้แน่ใจว่าค่าทนายความที่ถูกเรียกมานั้นเป็นเงิน
บาทหรือเงินดอลลาร์

คุณอาจจะต้องการขอความคิดเห็นที่สองหรือที่สามจากทนายความอีกคนหนึ่ง
หรือจากสำนักงานกฎหมายแห่งอื่น ซึ่งจะให้โอกาสคุณได้เปรียบเทียบราคา ประสบการณ์
ลักษณะนิสัย และชื่อเสียงของทนายความ คุณยังจะได้เรียนรู้เพิ่มเติมถึงความซับซ้อนของ
คดีและวิธีการต่างๆที่จะต้องดำเนินการเพื่อสะสางคดี

หลังจากที่คุณพอใจที่จะว่าจ้างทนายความคนนั้น คุณก็จะเซ็นใบแต่งทนายเพื่อ
มอบคดีให้ทนายความเพื่อเริ่มดำเนินขั้นตอนทางกฎหมาย ให้คุณขอสำเนาของใบแต่งทนาย
(หรือข้อตกลงในการว่าจ้างทนาย) และให้ทำความเข้าใจเนื้อหาว่าทนายความและคุณได้ตก
ลงกันอย่างไรบ้าง ถ้าคุณไม่เข้าใจเนื้อความในข้อตกลงนั้น บอกทนายให้อธิบายให้คุณฟัง
จนกว่าจะเข้าใจ เพื่อหลีกเลี่ยงปัญหาที่อาจจะตามมาในภายหลัง ถ้าใบแต่งทนายและ
ข้อตกลงในการว่าจ้างทนายมีทั้งภาษาไทยและภาษาอังกฤษ (หรือภาษาอื่น) ให้คุณทำสำเนา
ของเอกสารทั้งหมดไว้ด้วยเพื่อไว้ใช้อ้างอิงในภายหลัง ทุกฝ่ายจะต้องทำตามข้อตกลงที่เขียน
ไว้อย่างเคร่งครัด

กรุณาทำสำเนาของเอกสารของคุณเองทุกฉบับก่อนมอบให้กับทนายความ เก็บเอกสารและการติดต่อสื่อสารระหว่างคุณและทนายความไว้ในแฟ้ม ใส่เอกสารให้เรียบร้อยเพื่อที่จะค้นหาและใช้อ้างอิงได้ง่าย

คุณมีหน้าที่ในการรับผิดชอบที่จะติดตามคดีของตนอย่างใกล้ชิด ถึงแม้ว่าคุณได้มอบหมายคดีให้กับทนายความแล้ว คุณควรจะเอาใจใส่ในขั้นตอนต่างๆ อาจจะมีบางอย่างที่คุณลืมที่จะแจ้งให้ทนายความทราบ ดังนั้นคุณควรติดต่อทนายทันทีที่ได้ข้อมูลเพิ่มเติม ข้อมูลบางอย่างอาจจะดูเหมือนไม่สำคัญต่อคุณ แต่มันอาจจะสำคัญต่อคดี ถ้าคุณมีคำถามใดๆให้ถามทนาย และทำงานด้วยกันเพื่อไม่ให้มีการเข้าใจผิดเกิดขึ้น

ทนายความของคุณจะสามารถทำงานได้อย่างมีประสิทธิภาพ ถ้าคุณจัดเตรียมข้อมูลและรายละเอียดต่างๆให้พร้อมและตรงต่อเวลา คุณจะต้องเปิดใจกับทนายของคุณ มิฉะนั้นแล้วทนายความของคุณอาจจะไม่สามารถช่วยเหลือคุณได้อย่างเต็มที่

มีคนหลายคนที่มักจะถามคนที่รู้จักให้แนะนำทนายความให้ ถ้าคุณอยู่ในเมืองใหญ่ คุณสามารถหาสำนักงานกฎหมายได้ง่าย คุณสามารถเดินเข้าไปยังสำนักงานและคุยกับทนายได้ นอกจากนี้ยังมีประกาศโฆษณาที่มีรายละเอียดของสำนักงานทนายความต่างๆในนิตยสาร หนังสือพิมพ์หรืออินเตอร์เน็ต สำนักงานทนายความที่โฆษณาเป็นภาษาอังกฤษโดยทั่วไปจะมีทนายความที่พูดภาษาอังกฤษได้ แต่ค่าทนายก็จะสูงกว่าจังหวัดเล็กๆ

ถ้าคุณอยู่ในเมืองเล็กๆและต้องการจ้างทนายความ คุณสามารถถามเพื่อนบ้านดูว่าจะแนะนำทนายความให้คุณได้หรือไม่ ในจังหวัดเล็กๆอาจจะยากที่จะหาทนายความที่พูดภาษาของคุณได้ ค่าจ้างทนายความมักจะต่ำกว่าทนายความในเมืองใหญ่ แต่คุณจะต้องจ้างล่ามต่างหากซึ่งจะทำให้ราคาสูงขึ้นไปด้วย

มารยาททนายความ

มารยาทของทนายความในประเทศไทยจะมีลักษณะคล้ายกับมารยาทของ
ทนายความในสหรัฐอเมริกา สภาทนายความเป็นผู้ออกข้อกำหนดเหล่านี้ให้ทนายถือปฏิบัติ
ตามพ.ร.บ.ทนายความ พ.ศ. 2528 มาตรา 51 ซึ่งบัญญัติว่า "ทนายความต้องประพฤติตนตาม
ข้อบังคับว่าด้วยมารยาททนายความ" เมื่อคุณพิจารณาเลือกทนาย คุณสามารถดูว่าทนายคน
นั้นทำตามข้อกำหนดหรือไม่ ทนายบางคนอาจจะไม่ปฏิบัติตามข้อกำหนดทุกข้อ

ถือว่าเป็นการผิดมารยาททนายความ ถ้าทนายความ..................
- ไม่เคารพยำเกรงอำนาจศาลหรือกระทำการใดอันเป็นการดูหมิ่นศาลหรือผู้
  พิพากษาในศาล หรือนอกศาลอันเป็นการทำให้เสื่อมเสียอำนาจศาลหรือผู้
  พิพากษา
- ไม่รับหน้าที่เมื่อผู้พิพากษาได้ขอแรงให้เป็นทนายความแก้ต่างคดีอาญา เว้น
  แต่มีข้อแก้ตัวโดยสมควร
- กล่าวความหรือทำเอกสารหรือหลักฐานเท็จ หรือใช้กลอุบายให้ศาลหลง
  หรือกระทำการใดเพื่อทราบคำสั่งหรือคำพิพากษาของศาลที่ยังไม่เปิดเผย
- สมรู้เป็นใจโดยทางตรงหรือทางอ้อม เพื่อทำพยานหลักฐานเท็จ หรือเสี้ยม
  สอนพยานให้เบิกความเท็จ หรือโดยปกปิดซ่อนงำอำพรางพยานหลักฐาน
  ใดๆซึ่งควรนำมายื่นต่อศาลหรือสัญญาจะให้สินบนแก่เจ้าพนักงานหรือสมรู้
  เป็นใจในการให้สินบนแก่เจ้าพนักงาน
- กระทำการใดอันเป็นการยุยงส่งเสริมให้มีการฟ้องร้องคดีกันในกรณีอันหา
  มูลมิได้
- ใช้อุบายเพื่อจูงใจให้ผู้ใดมอบคดีให้ว่าต่างหรือแก้ต่าง
- หลอกหลวงให้เขาหลงว่าคดีนั้นจะชนะ เมื่อตนรู้สึกแก่ใจว่าจะแพ้
- อวดอ้างว่าตนมีความรู้ยิ่งกว่าทนายความอื่น
- อวดอ้างว่าเกี่ยวเป็นสมัครพรรคพวกรู้จักคุ้นเคยกับผู้ใดเพื่อที่จะได้รับ
  ผลประโยชน์อื่นๆ

- เปิดเผยความลับของลูกความที่ได้รู้ในหน้าที่ของทนายความ เว้นแต่จะ ได้รับอนุญาตจากลูกความนั้นแล้ว หรือโดยอำนาจศาล
- จงใจขาดนัดหรือทอดทิ้งคดี
- จงใจละเว้นหน้าที่ที่ควรกระทำอันเกี่ยวแก่การดำเนินคดีแห่งลูกความของ ตน หรือปิดบังข้อความที่ควรแจ้งให้ลูกความทราบ
- ได้รับปรึกษาหารือ หรือได้รู้เรื่องกรณีแห่งคดีใดโดยหน้าที่อันเกี่ยวข้องกับ คู่ความฝ่ายหนึ่ง แล้วภายหลังไปรับเป็นทนายหรือใช้ความรู้ที่ได้มานั้น ช่วยเหลือคู่ความอีกฝ่ายหนึ่ง
- ได้รับเป็นทนายความแล้วภายหลังใช้อุบายด้วยประการใดๆ โดยปราศจาก เหตุผลอันสมควรเพื่อจะให้ตนได้รับประโยชน์นอกเหนือจากที่ลูกความได้ ตกลงสัญญาให้
- กระทำการใดอันเป็นการฉ้อโกง ยักยอกหรือครอบครองหรือหน่วงเหนี่ยว เงินหรือทรัพย์สินของลูกความนานเกินกว่าเหตุโดยมิได้รับความยินยอมจาก ลูกความ เว้นแต่จะมีเหตุผลอันสมควร
- แย่ง หรือกระทำการใดในลักษณะประมูลดีที่มีทนายความอื่นว่าต่าง แก้ต่าง อยู่แล้ว เว้นแต่ได้รับความยินยอมจากทนายความที่ว่าความอยู่ในเรื่องนั้น แล้ว
- ประกาศโฆษณาหรือยอมให้ผู้อื่นประกาศโฆษณาอัตราค่าจ้างว่าความหรือ แจ้งว่าไม่เรียกร้องค่าจ้างว่าความ
- ประกาศโฆษณาชื่อ คุณวุฒิ ตำแหน่ง ถิ่นที่อยู่หรือสำนักงานในทางโอ้อวด เป็นเชิงชักชวนให้ผู้มีอรรถคดีมาหาเพื่อเป็นทนายความว่าต่างหรือแก้ต่างให้ เว้นแต่การแสดงชื่อ คุณวุฒิหรืออื่นๆตามสมควรโดยสภาพ
- ประกอบอาชีพ ดำเนินธุรกิจหรือประพฤติตนอันเป็นอันเป็นการฝ่าฝืนต่อ ศีลธรรมอันดี หรือเป็นการเสื่อมเสียต่อศักดิ์ศรีและเกียรติคุณของ ทนายความ
- ยินยอมตกลงหรือให้คำมั่นสัญญาว่าจะให้ค่านายหน้าหรือบำเหน็จรางวัล ใดๆแก่ผู้ที่หาคดีความมาให้

มารยาทอื่นๆ

ในเวลาว่าความ ทนายความจะต้องแต่งกายสุภาพเรียบร้อยให้เหมาะสม

ทนายความชายแต่งกายแบบสากลนิยมเป็นชุดสีขาวหรือสีอื่นที่ไม่ฉูดฉาด เชิ้ต
ขาว ผ้าผูกคอสีดำหรือสีอื่นที่สุภาพไม่ฉูดฉาดและใส่เสื้อสูท กางเกงขายาว
รองเท้าหุ้มส้น

ทนายความหญิงแต่งตามแบบสากลนิยมเป็นชุดสีขาว กระโปรงและเสื้อสีสุภาพ
ไม่ฉูดฉาด รองเท้าหุ้มส้น

ในขณะว่าความ ทนายที่มีสิทธิสวมเสื้อครุยเนติบัณฑิต ต้องสวมเสื้อครุยนั้นด้วย

ทนายความจะต้องปฏิบัติตนอย่างเคร่งครัดเพื่อให้เป็นไปตามคำสั่งของสภานายก
พิเศษแห่งสภาทนายความและคณะกรรมการมารยาททนายความตามอำนาจ
หน้าที่ซึ่งมีอยู่ตามบทบัญญัติแห่งกฎหมาย

การหาล่ามและผู้แปลเอกสาร

ในส่วนนี้เราจะอธิบายถึงข้อแตกต่างระหว่างผู้แปลเอกสาร (translator) และล่าม
(interpreter) บางครั้งในภาษาอังกฤษมักจะใช้คำทั้งสองนี้สับเปลี่ยนกัน

ผู้แปลเอกสาร (Translator)

ผู้แปลเอกสารจะแปลสิ่งตีพิมพ์หรือข้อเขียนต่างๆจากภาษาหนึ่งไปยังอีกภาษา
หนึ่ง คุณจำเป็นต้องใช้บริการแปลเอกสารเพื่อแปลใบสูติบัตร ใบหย่า สัญญาก่อนสมรส
และเอกสารอื่นๆ ผู้แปลเอกสารมีความสามารถในระดับที่แตกต่างกันขึ้นอยู่กับการฝึกหัด
ทักษะและพรสวรรค์ นักแปลที่ดีมีความสามารถในการเขียนภาษาได้อย่างสละสลวยและ

แปลได้ถูกต้อง   นักแปลมืออาชีพส่วนใหญ่จะแปลจากภาษาต่างประเทศเป็นภาษาไทยแต่
มักจะไม่แปลจากภาษาไทยเป็นภาษาอื่นๆ

ทักษะที่เป็นกุญแจสำคัญนักแปลที่ดีคือ   ความสามารถในการเข้าใจภาษาที่ตนจะ
แปลพร้อมกับความเข้าใจด้านวัฒนธรรมของประเทศนั้นๆ   นักแปลจะรู้จักใช้แหล่งข้อมูล
แหล่งอ้างอิง พจนานุกรม ห้องสมุดและอินเตอร์เนตได้เป็นอย่างดี ถ้าคุณต้องการแปลภาษา
ไทยเป็นภาษาของคุณ   คุณอาจจะหาผู้แปลที่เป็นเจ้าของภาษาที่มีทักษะในการใช้ภาษาไทย
ระดับสูง หรือผู้แปลคนไทยที่มีประสบการณ์ในการแปลเป็นภาษาของคุณหรือที่ได้อาศัยอยู่
ในประเทศของคุณนานพอที่จะเข้าใจภาษาของคุณได้ดี

ในขั้นตอนต่างๆของศาลไทยและในบางสถาบัน   เอกสารที่เป็นภาษาต่างประเทศ
สามารถนำมาใช้ได้แต่จะต้องเป็นเอกสารตัวจริงหรือที่ได้รับรองสำเนาถูกต้องและต้องแปล
เป็นภาษาไทย เอกสารบางอย่างจะต้องได้รับการรับรองจากโนตารีพับลิกหรือจากสถานทูต
ไทยหรือกงสุลไทยว่าเป็นเอกสารตัวจริง คุณสามารถให้ผู้แปลภาษาไทยในประเทศของคุณ
แปลเอกสารเหล่านี้ได้

ในประเทศไทย มีบริษัทแปลภาษามากมายโดยเฉพาะในกรุงเทพ เชียงใหม่ พัทยา
ภูเก็ตและหัวหิน ซึ่งส่วนมากจะตั้งอยู่ในบริเวณของนักท่องเที่ยว (ในกรุงเทพจะตั้งอยู่ใกล้
กับสถานทูตต่างๆด้วย)   บริษัทแปลภาษามีนักแปลที่มีประสบการณ์ในหลายภาษาที่จะให้
การรับรองการแปลได้ เอกสารบางอย่างจะต้องได้รับการรับรองจากบริษัทแปลภาษาที่ทาง
สถานทูตหรือทางศาลอนุมัติ คุณควรจะสอบถามให้แน่ใจว่าผู้แปลหรือบริษัทแปลภาษานั้น
เป็นที่ยอมรับจากทางการหรือไม่

คุณภาพในการแปลของแต่บริษัทแตกต่างกันไป   สำหรับเอกสารที่ไม่มีความ
ซับซ้อน   เช่นใบสูติบัตรหรือแบบฟอร์มทั่วไปนั้นมักจะไม่ค่อยมีความแตกต่างกันมากใน
มาตรฐานการแปล สำหรับเอกสารที่สำคัญ คุณควรคัดเลือกเพื่อหาผู้แปลที่ดี คุณสามารถ
ขอให้บริษัทส่งตัวอย่างการแปลให้คุณดู อาจจะเป็นหนึ่งหน้าหรือสองหน้าแล้วเปรียบเทียบ
ดูว่าบริษัทใดแปลได้ดีที่สุด คุณอาจจะต้องจ่ายค่าตัวอย่างการแปลหรือไม่ก็ได้   ค่าแปล

เอกสารหนึ่งหน้าประมาณ 500 – 1,000 บาทขึ้นอยู่กับความยาว จำนวนคำ ความยากง่ายของ เนื้อหา บางบริษัทอาจจะคิดค่าบริการเพิ่มสำหรับการรับรองการแปล

ล่าม (Interpreter)

ล่ามคือผู้แปลภาษาพูดจากภาษาหนึ่งไปยังอีกภาษาหนึ่ง ล่ามที่ดีจะต้องมี ความสามารถในการแปลได้ทันทีได้ทั้งสองทิศทาง (เช่นจากอังกฤษเป็นไทยและจากไทย เป็นอังกฤษ) โดยไม่ต้องใช้พจนานุกรม มีหลายสถานการณ์ที่จำเป็นต้องใช้ล่ามเพื่อจะช่วย ให้ลูกความและทนายเข้าใจกันได้

ในกระบวนการกฎหมายไทย ภาษาที่ใช้ในศาลเป็นภาษาที่ซับซ้อนและเป็น ทางการ ถ้าคุณไม่เข้าใจภาษาไทยอย่างถ่องแท้ คุณจำเป็นที่จะต้องใช้ล่ามภาษาไทย การแปลโดยใช้ล่ามแบ่งออกเป็นสองประเภทด้วยกันคือ การแปลแบบหยุดเป็น พักๆ (consecutive) และการแปลแบบไม่หยุดในเวลาเดียวกันกับที่ได้ยิน (simultaneous) การแปลแบบหยุดเป็นพักนั้นล่ามจะรอให้ผู้พูดหยุดก่อนแล้วจึงค่อยแปล ซึ่งมักจะหยุด ระหว่างประโยค ย่อหน้าหรือวลี สำหรับการแปลแบบไม่หยุดนั้นล่ามจะแปลทันทีที่ได้ยินผู้ พูดเริ่มกล่าวและจะเหลื่อมเวลากันเพียงเล็กน้อย วิธีที่ดีที่สุดที่จะแปลในเวลาเดียวกันแบบไม่ หยุดนี้คือแปลอยู่ในห้องบูธเล็กๆ โดยมีหูฟังและไมโครโฟนช่วย ในห้องศาล (โดยเฉพาะใน ต่างประเทศ) ล่ามจะมีหูฟังและไมโครโฟน ส่วนจำเลยจะฟังจากการแปลจากเครื่องรับฟัง ถ้าไม่มีอุปกรณ์ดังกล่าว ล่ามก็จะแปลให้ผู้ฟังโดยการพูดเบาๆเพื่อไม่ให้เป็นการรบกวนหรือ ขัดจังหวะผู้พูดอื่นที่อยู่ในศาล ถ้าเป็นการสืบพยานในศาล จะเป็นการแปลแบบหยุดเป็น พักๆ เพื่อให้ทนายความและอัยการซักถามพยานได้อย่างชัดเจน

การว่าจ้างล่ามมืออาชีพในเมืองไทยค่อนข้างจะราคาสูง ราคาอาจตกถึง 2,000- 10,000 บาท ต่อวัน ขึ้นอยู่กับระยะเวลาของงานและระยะทางที่ล่ามต้องใช้ในการเดินทาง คุณสามารถจ้างล่ามเวลาขึ้นศาลหรือเมื่อพบกับทนาย คุณสามารถพาเพื่อนหรือญาติคนไทย ไปช่วยแปลให้คุณ อย่างไรก็ตาม คุณควรระวังด้วยว่าล่ามจะไม่ทำตัวเป็นทนายเสียเองเพราะ

ถือว่าผิดกฎหมาย   ล่ามไม่ได้รับการฝึกฝนทางด้านกฎหมายและ ไม่สามารถให้คำแนะนำ
ทางด้านกฎหมายได้

ล่ามที่คุณจ้างเพื่อแปลให้คุณในศาลจะต้องเป็นผู้ที่ศาลอนุมัติ   กระทรวงยุติธรรม
ได้กำหนดว่าขั้นตอนต่างๆในคดีอาญานั้น ศาลจะต้องจัดเตรียมล่ามให้กับจำเลย พยานหรือ
ผู้รับเคราะห์   ทั้งนี้เพื่อให้เป็นไปตามมาตรฐานสากล   บางครั้งก็อาจจะเป็นปัญหาบ้าง
เนื่องจากล่ามที่ศาลจัดให้อาจจะพูดภาษาของคุณไม่ได้ดีเท่าที่ควร ล่ามที่มีคุณวุฒิส่วนมากจะ
ทำงานเป็นเอกเทศ หรือทำงานให้กับบริษัทแปลภาษา ถ้าคุณต้องการล่ามที่ดีคุณจะต้องจ่าย
ค่าล่ามด้วยตัวเอง

อีกวิธีหนึ่งที่จะหาล่ามได้คือการว่าจ้างนักศึกษาตามมหาวิทยาลัย คุณสามารถให้
อาจารย์แนะนำนักศึกษาที่อยู่ในภาควิชาภาษาต่างประเทศที่พูดภาษาคุณได้มาเป็นล่ามให้
นักศึกษาเหล่านี้มักจะมีทักษะในด้านภาษาและต้องการทำงานเพื่อหาประสบการณ์ด้วย
ค่าจ้างที่ไม่สูงนัก   และจะสามารถช่วยเหลือคุณในขั้นตอนต่างๆของกฎหมายได้ถ้าได้รับ
อนุญาตจากทางศาล

คุณสมบัติของล่ามที่ดี

ล่ามที่ดีควรมีคุณสมบัติดังต่อไปนี้
- มีความรู้เฉพาะด้านในสาขาใดสาขาหนึ่ง   ล่ามของศาลควรมีความรู้ในด้าน
  กฎหมาย ขั้นตอนต่างๆของศาลและศัพท์กฎหมายเป็นอย่างดี
- มีความเข้าใจและความรู้ทั่วไปเกี่ยวกับเรื่องที่ตนจะต้องแปล
- คุ้นเคยกับวัฒนธรรมไทย หรือวัฒนธรรมของประเทศของผู้ที่ตนแปลให้
- รู้คำศัพท์สาขาอื่นๆอย่างกว้างขวางในทั้งสองภาษา
- มีความสามารถในการแสดงความคิดเห็นได้ชัดเจน   และพูดจาอย่างชัดถ้อยชัด
  คำในทั้งสองภาษา
- มีประสบการณ์แปลแบบไม่หยุดในเวลาเดียวกันในบูธอย่างน้อย 100 ชั่วโมง

ส่วนที่ 3

เรื่องส่วนบุคคลและครอบครัว

กฎหมายครอบครัวของไทยสิ่งหนึ่งที่สะท้อนถึงพื้นฐานของสังคมและ วัฒนธรรมไทย ในอดีตที่ผ่านมา กฎหมายมักจะให้ความสำคัญกับสามีมากกว่าภรรยา ตัวอย่างเช่น กฎหมายกำหนดว่า ชายไทยเป็นหัวหน้าครอบครัว สามารถมีภรรยาหลายคน และยังสามารถขายภรรยาและบุตรของตนเองได้ โดยชายไทยมีสิทธิตัดสินใจเกี่ยวกับสิ่งที่ เป็นกรรมสิทธิ์ของตนได้ ทำให้มีความไม่เท่าเทียมกันอย่างมากระหว่างชายและหญิง กระทั่งรัฐธรรมนูญปี พ.ศ. 2517 มาตรา 28 ย่อหน้า 2 กำหนดว่า "ชายและหญิงมีสิทธิเท่า เทียมกัน"

กฎหมายครอบครัวของไทยในปัจจุบันได้ถูกปรับให้เข้ากับมาตรฐานสากลซึ่ง หญิงและชายมีสิทธิเท่าเทียมกันภายใต้กฎหมาย สิทธิของผู้หญิงและเด็กได้รับการปกป้อง โดยองค์กรต่างๆ ส่วนกฎหมายฉบับโบราณที่มีเนื้อหาที่ล้าหลังเกี่ยวกับครอบครัวถูกยกเลิก อย่างไรก็ตาม ในทางปฏิบัติ ระบบแบบเดิมของไทย ยังคงมีผลต่อวิถีชีวิตที่เกี่ยวข้องกับ กฎหมายของชาวไทยอยู่

ในส่วนนี้ ผู้เขียนจะให้ข้อมูลทั่วไปในแง่มุมต่างๆของกฎหมายครอบครัวและ กฎหมายที่เกี่ยวข้องกับตัวบุคคลของไทย ข้อมูลนี้จะช่วยให้คุณเข้าใจสถานการณ์ต่างๆที่ คุณอาจจะนำมาประยุกต์ใช้ให้เข้ากับวัฒนธรรมไทยและบุคคลที่เกี่ยวข้อง

การได้สัญชาติไทย

ประเทศไทยมีข้อกำหนดที่แตกต่างกันสำหรับบุคคลจะที่ขอสัญชาติไทยขึ้นอยู่
กับสถานภาพ บุคคลที่บิดามารดาถือสัญชาติไทยทั้งคู่จะได้สัญชาติไทยโดยอัตโนมัติ ไม่ว่า
จะเกิดในประเทศไทยหรือไม่ก็ตาม ถ้าบิดาหรือมารดาฝ่ายใดฝ่ายหนึ่งเป็นคนต่างด้าว
บุคคลนั้นจะไม่ได้รับสัญชาติไทยโดยอัตโนมัติ

การได้สัญชาติไทยจะขึ้นอยู่กับสถานภาพการเข้าเมือง (ว่าถูกกฎหมายหรือไม่)
และสถานภาพสมรสของบิดามารดา (ว่าจดทะเบียนสมรสหรือไม่) กฎเกณฑ์การได้สัญชาติ
ไทยไม่ว่าจะเกิดในหรือนอกราชอาณาไทยที่กำหนดไว้ในพระราชบัญญัติสัญชาติไทย พ.ศ.
2535 มีดังนี้

บุคคลที่เกิดในราชอาณาจักรไทย

กรณีที่	สัญชาติของบิดา	สัญชาติของมารดา	สถานภาพสมรส	สัญชาติของบุตร
1	ไทย	ไทย	จดทะเบียน	ไทย
2	ไทย	ไทย	ไม่จดทะเบียน	ไทย
3	ไทย	ต่างด้าวโดยชอบด้วยกฎหมาย	จดทะเบียน	ไทย
4	ไทย	ต่างด้าวโดยชอบด้วยกฎหมาย	ไม่จดทะเบียน	ไทย
5	ไทย	ต่างด้าวโดยมิชอบ	จดทะเบียน	ไทย
6	ไทย	ต่างด้าวโดยมิชอบ	ไม่จดทะเบียน	ไทย

7	ต่างด้าวโดยชอบด้วยกฎหมาย	ไทย	จดทะเบียน	ไทย
8	ต่างด้าวโดยชอบด้วยกฎหมาย	ไทย	ไม่จดทะเบียน	ไทย
9	ต่างด้าวโดยมิชอบ	ไทย	จดทะเบียน	ไทย
10	ต่างด้าวโดยมิชอบ	ไทย	ไม่จดทะเบียน	ไทย
11	ต่างด้าวโดยชอบด้วยกฎหมาย	ต่างด้าวโดยชอบด้วยกฎหมาย	จดทะเบียน	ไทย
12	ต่างด้าวโดยชอบด้วยกฎหมาย	ต่างด้าวโดยชอบด้วยกฎหมาย	ไม่จดทะเบียน	ไทย
13	ต่างด้าวโดยชอบด้วยกฎหมาย	ต่างด้าวโดยมิชอบ	จดทะเบียน	ไม่ได้รับสัญชาติไทย
14	ต่างด้าวโดยชอบด้วยกฎหมาย	ต่างด้าวโดยมิชอบ	ไม่จดทะเบียน	ไม่ได้รับสัญชาติไทย
15	ต่างด้าวโดยมิชอบ	ต่างด้าวโดยชอบด้วยกฎหมาย	จดทะเบียน	ไม่ได้รับสัญชาติไทย
16	ต่างด้าวโดยมิชอบ	ต่างด้าวโดยชอบด้วยกฎหมาย	ไม่จดทะเบียน	ไม่ได้รับสัญชาติไทย

| 17 | ต่างด้าวโดยมิชอบ | ต่างด้าวโดยมิชอบ | จดทะเบียน | ไม่ได้รับสัญชาติไทย |
| 18 | ต่างด้าวโดยมิชอบ | ต่างด้าวโดยมิชอบ | ไม่จดทะเบียน | ไม่ได้รับสัญชาติไทย |

บุคคลที่เกิดนอกเขตราชอาณาจักรไทย

กรณีที่	สัญชาติของบิดา	สัญชาติของมารดา	สถานภาพสมรส	สัญชาติของบุตร
1	ไทย	ไทย	จดทะเบียน	ไทย
2	ไทย	ไทย	ไม่จดทะเบียน	ไทย
3	ไทย	สัญชาติอื่น	จดทะเบียน	ไทย
4	ไทย	สัญชาติอื่น	ไม่จดทะเบียน	ไม่ได้รับสัญชาติไทย
5	สัญชาติอื่น	ไทย	จดทะเบียน	ไทย
6	สัญชาติอื่น	ไทย	ไม่จดทะเบียน	ไทย

ที่มา: สถานกงสุลแห่งประเทศไทย

การได้สัญชาติไทยและข้อกำหนดต่างๆ

ชาวต่างชาติที่ต้องการได้รับสัญชาติไทยจะต้องผ่านกระบวนการการเปลี่ยน สัญชาติเสียก่อน คำร้องขอเปลี่ยนเป็นสัญชาติไทยจะต้องได้รับอนุญาตโดยรัฐมนตรี กระทรวงมหาดไทย โดยมีค่าธรรมเนียม 5,000 บาท และอาจจะต้องใช้เวลาถึง 3 ปี ผู้ร้อง ขอจะต้องสาบานว่าจะซื่อสัตย์และจงรักภักดีต่อประเทศไทย

สำหรับรายละเอียดเพิ่มเติม แบบคำร้อง และเอกสารประกอบอื่นๆ กรุณาติดต่อ แผนกสืบสวนอาชญากรรมที่ 1 กอง 3 สถานีตำรวจแห่งชาติ ถนนพระราม 1 กรุงเทพฯ

ตามพระราชบัญญัติสัญชาติไทย พ.ศ.2508 บุคคลที่ร้องขอสัญชาติจะต้อง

1.   บรรลุนิติภาวะตามกฎหมายไทย (20 ปีบริบูรณ์)
2.   มีความประพฤติดี
3.   ประกอบอาชีพที่มีรายได้
4.   อาศัยอยู่ในประเทศไทยเป็นเวลาไม่ต่ำกว่า 5 ปีนับตั้งแต่วันร้องขอ
5.   สามารถสื่อสารเป็นภาษาไทยได้

อย่างไรก็ตาม ตามมาตรา 11 นั้น ข้อ 4 และ 5 จะได้รับการยกเว้นในกรณีต่อไปนี้ ชาวต่างชาติคนนั้นได้กระทำคุณงามความดีแก่ประเทศไทย บุคคลนั้นเป็นบุตรหรือคู่สมรส ของบุคคลซึ่งมีสัญชาติไทยหรือเปลี่ยนกลับมาใช้สัญชาติไทย หรือบุคคลซึ่งเคยถือสัญชาติ ไทยมาก่อน

บุตรที่ยังไม่บรรลุนิติภาวะ และยังอยู่ในอุปการะของมารดาหรือบิดาที่มีสัญชาติ ไทยจะต้องมีหลักฐานแสดงการอุปการะและสูติบัตรของบุตรจึงจะได้รับการยกเว้นจากข้อ 1, 3, 4 และ 5

บุตรซึ่งเกิดจากบิดาหรือมารดาที่มีสัญชาติไทยไม่ว่าจะเกิดในหรือนอกประเทศ ไทยมีสิทธิขอสัญชาติไทยได้

บุคคลจะยังคงถือว่ามีสัญชาติไทย จนกว่า

- บุคคลนั้น มีความประสงค์จะสละสัญชาติไทย โดยร้องขอไปยังเจ้าพนักงานที่เกี่ยวข้อง
- สัญชาติของบุคคลนั้น ถูกเพิกถอนโดยรัฐบาลไทย

ถ้าบุคคลที่มีสัญชาติไทย มีความประสงค์จะสละสัญชาติไทย ขณะที่อยู่นอกประเทศไทย

บุคคลนั้น จะต้องยื่นคำร้องต่อสถานกงสุลหรือสถานทูตไทย

เมื่อยื่นคำร้องแล้ว กงสุลไทยจะดำเนินการสอบถามบุคคลนั้น และพยาน ต่อจากนั้นจึงรับรายงานแบบคำร้องนั้น

บุคคลสัญชาติไทยที่สละสัญชาติไทยแล้ว   และอาศัยอยู่นอกประเทศไทยอาจจะขอกลับมาใช้สัญชาติไทยใหม่ได้ โดยยื่นแบบคำร้องที่สถานกงสุลหรือสถานทูตไทย

ถ้าคู่สมรสของผู้ถือสัญชาติไทยเป็นบุคคลสัญชาติอื่น   คู่สมรสคนไทยสามารถยื่นคำร้องขอสัญชาติไทยได้กับสถานกงสุลหรือสถานทูตไทย

แบบคำร้องสำหรับทุกกรณีที่กล่าวมาข้างต้น จะต้องส่งพร้อมกับเอกสารต่างๆดังนี้

- เอกสารใดก็ตาม รวมถึงเอกสารที่ออกโดยรัฐบาลของต่างประเทศที่ประกอบอยู่ในแบบคำร้องนี้ จะต้องได้รับการรับรองจากหน่วยงานที่เกี่ยวข้อง
- ถ้าเอกสารเป็นในภาษาอื่นซึ่งไม่ใช่ภาษาอังกฤษ เอกสารนั้นจะต้องได้รับการแปลเป็นภาษาไทย ตรวจสอบและรับรองจากหน่วยงานที่เกี่ยวข้อง
- ถ้าเอกสารประกอบนั้นเป็นฉบับสำเนา เอกสารนั้นจะต้องได้รับการรับรองเช่นเดียวกับฉบับจริงจากหน่วยงานที่เกี่ยวข้องของแต่ละประเทศ

การขอสูติบัตรไทย

บุตรซึ่งเกิดจากบิดามารดาไทยนอกราชอาณาจักรไทย   มีสิทธิได้รับสัญชาติไทย
และหนังสือเดินทางไทย (ดู ตารางบุคคลที่เกิดนอกเขตราชอาณาจักรไทย) การมีสูติบัตร
ไทยนั้น จะทำให้บุตรขอรับหนังสือเดินทางไทยได้โดยชอบธรรม บุตรอาจจะมีสองสัญชาติ
ควบคู่กันได้จนกว่าจนเป็นผู้ใหญ่ซึ่งจะต้องเลือกเพียงสัญชาติเดียว

บิดามารดาสามารถยื่นคำร้องขอสูติบัตรให้บุตรได้ที่สถานกงสุลหรือสถานทูต
ไทยในประเทศที่บุตรเกิด (ควรตรวจสอบกับสถานทูตหรือสถานกงสุลก่อน เนื่องจากแต่ละ
ประเทศมีข้อกำหนดต่างกัน หรือควรจะโทรสอบถามเกี่ยวกับเอกสารที่ต้องใช้)

- เอกสารโดยทั่วไปที่จำเป็นในการขอสูติบัตร มีดังนี้
- ใบรับรองหรือยืนยันการเกิดที่แปลเป็นภาษาไทย
- สำเนาทะเบียนสมรส จำนวน 2 ชุด
- สำเนาหนังสือเดินทางของบิดาและมารดา จำนวน 2 ชุด (จะต้องเป็น
  หนังสือเดินทางไทยทั้ง 2 เล่ม หรือหนังสือเดินทางไทย 1 เล่ม หนังสือ
  เดินทางต่างชาติ 1 เล่ม)
- สำเนาบัตรประชาชนของบิดาและมารดา จำนวน 2 ชุด
- รูปถ่ายของบุตร 2 ใบ

การขอสูติบัตรไทย สำหรับบุตรที่บิดามารดาถือสัญชาติไทยที่เกิดในประเทศ
สหรัฐอเมริกา กรุณาส่งเอกสารดังนี้

- หนังสือเดินทางของบิดามารดา รวมถึงกรีนการ์ดหรือบัตรประจำตัวของชาว
  สหรัฐอเมริกาหรือบัตรประจำตัวประชาชนไทย (ถ้ามี) ทั้งตัวจริงและสำเนา 3 ชุด
- ทะเบียนสมรสตัวจริง และสำเนา 3 ชุด
- หนังสือรับรองการเกิดหรือสูติบัตรที่ออกให้โดยทางการของสหรัฐอเมริกา
- ใบยื่นคำร้อง
- รูปถ่ายของบุตร 2 ใบ (กรุณาสอบถามขนาดของภาพก่อน)

- ค่าธรรมเนียม 15 ดอลล่าร์ ในการจัดทำสูติบัตรซึ่งรับรองโดยกระทรวง
  ต่างประเทศสหรัฐอเมริกาให้ถูกต้องตามนิติกรรมไทย
- สถานกงสุลหรือสถานทูตจะใช้เวลา 5 วันทำการในการออกสูติบัตร

การสมรสในประเทศไทย

โดยปกติการแต่งงานในวัฒนธรรมไทยจะหมายถึงการเข้า "พิธีสมรส" ซึ่งจะมี
พระสงฆ์มาประกอบพิธีทางศาสนาในการพันธนาการเจ้าสาวและเจ้าบ่าวไว้ด้วยกัน โดยมี
เพื่อนสนิท เพื่อนบ้านและญาติพี่น้องมาเป็นสักขีพยานในพิธี จากนั้น คู่บ่าวสาวจะถือว่า
เป็นสามีภรรยากัน

การที่มีพระสงฆ์มาทำพิธีสวดมนต์ในพิธีสมรสของไทยนั้น เป็นเพียงวัฒนธรรม
และเป็นสัญลักษณ์ถึงความเป็นสิริมงคลเท่านั้น

ในการทำให้การสมรสเป็นทางการและชอบด้วยกฎหมายนั้น คู่สมรสจะต้องไป
จดทะเบียนสมรสที่สำนักงานเขตหรือที่ว่าการอำเภอ (เรียกสั้นๆว่า "อำเภอ") ซึ่งจะเป็น
ผู้ดำเนินการจดทะเบียนสมรสให้ สำนักงานเขตหรือที่ว่าการอำเภอเปิดทำการตั้งแต่ 8.30 น.
ถึง 16.00 น.) ผู้ที่อาศัยอยู่นอกประเทศสามารถจดทะเบียนสมรสได้ที่สถานกงสุลไทยอีก
ด้วย

ในบางครั้ง เมื่อคุณถามเพื่อนคนไทยว่า "คุณแต่งงานหรือยัง" คำตอบก็อาจจะ
เป็น "แต่งแล้ว แต่ไม่ได้จดทะเบียน" นั่นหมายความว่า ทั้งสองคนแค่ประกอบพิธีสมรส แต่
ยังไม่ได้จดทะเบียนสมรสให้ถูกต้องตามกฎหมาย

ในส่วนนี้ มีข้อมูลต่างๆในหลายแง่มุมที่เกี่ยวข้องกับการสมรสในประเทศไทย
ผู้เขียนจะอธิบายถึงเรื่องการหมั้น สินสอด สัญญาก่อนสมรส การแต่งงานแบบไทยและพิธี
สมรส รวมถึงข้อกำหนดทางกฎหมายของแต่ละหัวข้อต่อไป

การหมั้นและสินสอด

ในวัฒนธรรมไทย เป็นเรื่องปกติ ที่จะมีการหมั้นก่อนการพิธีสมรส โดยฝ่ายชาย
จะให้สินสอดแก่เจ้าสาวและครอบครัวของเจ้าสาว ตามกฎหมายแล้ว ไม่ใช่เรื่องจำเป็นที่
จะต้องมีการหมั้นหมายหรือให้สินสอด แต่ตามประเพณี พิธีหมั้นจะถูกจัดขึ้นก่อนพิธี
แต่งงานประมาณ 2-3 เดือนที่บ้านของเจ้าสาว พิธีจะจัดขึ้นในตอนเช้า โดยมีญาติสนิทและ
เพื่อนของทั้งสองฝ่ายมาร่วมงาน

พิธีหมั้น ส่วนมากจะไม่เกี่ยวข้องกับพิธีกรรมทางศาสนา เป็นเพียงการแนะนำ
ตัวอย่างเป็นทางการต่อครอบครัวของแต่ละฝ่าย และเป็นการประกาศค่าสินสอดทองหมั้น
และวันจัดพิธีสมรส เมื่อถึงเวลาฤกษ์มงคล ฝ่ายชายจะสวมแหวนหมั้นบนนิ้วของเจ้าสาวใน
อนาคต ต่อจากนั้นจะมีบริการอาหารและเครื่องดื่ม โดยปกติแล้ว พิธีหมั้นจะใช้เวลาไม่นาน
นัก

ในปัจจุบัน เนื่องจากเศรษฐกิจรัดตัวพร้อมกับอิทธิพลของวัฒนธรรมตะวันตก คู่
สามีภรรยาไทยมากมายอยู่กินด้วยกันโดยไม่ได้แต่งงานหรือแม้แต่หมั้นหมาย อย่างไรก็ตาม
การหมั้นหมาย การให้สินสอดและพิธีสมรสไทยก็ยังคงเป็นเรื่องสำคัญมากสำหรับคนไทย
ส่วนใหญ่ และเป็นเรื่องยากสำหรับชาวต่างชาติ โดยเฉพาะชาวตะวันตกในการทำความ
เข้าใจ (ศึกษาเพิ่มเติมเกี่ยววัฒนธรรมของไทย-ตะวันตกได้ในหนังสือ *Thailand Fever*
จัดพิมพ์โดยสำนักพิมพ์ไพบูลย์เช่นกัน)

ในพิธีหมั้น ฝ่ายชายจะต้องให้ของหมั้นแก่ฝ่ายหญิงเพื่อเป็นคำมั่นสัญญาที่จะ
แต่งงานด้วย ซึ่งโดยปกติแล้ว มักจะเป็นแหวนแต่งงานหรือทองคำจำนวนหนึ่ง ในวันหมั้น
หรือวันที่ครอบครัวฝ่ายชายมาสู่ขอครอบครัวฝ่ายหญิง ครอบครัวของฝ่ายหญิงก็อาจจะเรียก
ค่าสินสอดจากทางฝ่ายชาย ในบางครั้งพิธีหมั้นจะถูกจัดขึ้นในวันเดียวกับพิธีแต่งงาน ใน
กรณีนี้ ฝ่ายชายจะต้องนำทั้งของหมั้นมาพร้อมกับสินสอดมาด้วย ซึ่งของหมั้นและสินสอด
อาจเป็นสิ่งเดียวกันได้ ในภาษาไทย การรวมของหมั้นและสินสอดไว้ในคราวเดียวนี้ถูก
เรียกว่า *สินสอดทองหมั้น*

ในการจดทะเบียนสมรสในประเทศไทย ทั้งสองฝ่ายจะต้องมีคุณสมบัติ ดังนี้

- ทั้งสองฝ่ายจะต้องมีอายุไม่ต่ำกว่า 17 ปีบริบูรณ์ และถ้าฝ่ายใดฝ่ายหนึ่งอายุ
  ต่ำกว่า 20 ปี คู่สมรสจะต้องได้รับความยินยอมจากทั้งบิดาและมารดาของ
  ฝ่ายที่อายุต่ำกว่า 20 ปี (ถ้าทั้งบิดามารดายังมีชีวิตอยู่) จากบิดาหรือมารดา
  ฝ่ายใดฝ่ายหนึ่ง (ในกรณีที่อีกฝ่ายหนึ่งเสียชีวิตหรือไม่สามารถให้ความ
  ยินยอมได้) หรือจากผู้ปกครองตามกฎหมายหรือบิดามารดาบุญธรรม
  เสียก่อน
- จะต้องไม่เป็นบุคคลไร้ความสามารถ
- จะต้องไม่เกี่ยวข้องเป็นญาติสนิทหรือญาติสายตรง หรือมีบิดามารดา
  เดียวกัน (พี่น้องต่างบิดาหรือต่างมารดาก็ไม่อนุญาตให้แต่งงานกันได้)
- จะต้องไม่มีบิดามารดาบุญธรรมร่วมกัน
- จะต้องไม่มีเพศเดียวกัน
- จะต้องไม่สมรสซ้อน

ต่อไปจะเป็นข้อมูลอีกเล็กน้อยเกี่ยวกับสินสอดทองหมั้น   คำถามที่ชาวต่างชาติ
มักจะถามอยู่เป็นประจำบ่อย คือ "สินสอดคืออะไร" และ "ควรจะมีมูลค่าเท่าใด"

ตามคำจำกัดความในกฎหมายไทย   สินสอด   หมายถึงสิ่งของหรือทรัพย์สินที่
เจ้าบ่าวมอบให้กับบิดามารดาหรือผู้ปกครองของเจ้าสาว เพื่อแสดงถึงความรู้สึกในบุญคุณที่
อนุญาตให้เจ้าสาวแต่งงานกับตน   และเป็นการตอบแทนครอบครัวของเจ้าสาวที่ได้เลี้ยงดู
เจ้าสาวมา บางครั้งสินสอดจะถูกเรียกว่า "ค่าตอบแทนเจ้าสาว"

ฝ่ายชายควรให้สินสอดแก่ครอบครัวฝ่ายหญิงเท่าใด   ไม่มีมูลค่ากำหนดไว้
แน่นอน   มูลค่าของสินสอดจะขึ้นอยู่กับฐานะของฝ่ายชายและภูมิหลังของฝ่ายหญิง   ซึ่ง
มักจะดูจากครอบครัวฝ่ายหญิง ความงาม การศึกษา ความบริสุทธิ์ เคยแต่งงานหรือเคยมี
บุตรมาก่อนหรือไม่ เจ้าสาวที่มาจากครอบครัวที่ดี การศึกษาสูงและไม่เคยแต่งงานสามารถ
เรียกร้องสินสอดเป็นมูลค่าสูงได้ ส่วนเจ้าสาวที่ถือว่าเป็นคนสวยมักจะคาดหวังว่าจะได้รับ
สินสอดมากกว่าเจ้าสาวที่ถือว่าไม่ค่อยสวย นอกจากนี้ ถ้าฝ่ายชายตั้งใจจะพาเจ้าสาวไปอยู่ที่
ห่างไกลจากครอบครัวของเจ้าสาว สินสอดอาจจะมีมูลค่าสูงขึ้น

ในอดีต สินสอดจะถูกเรียกเป็นจำนวนวัวหรือควาย ข้าวหรือที่ดินและอัญมณี
ต่างๆ ครอบครัวของเจ้าสาวจะรับสินสอดไว้ทั้งหมด แต่ในปัจจุบัน คำนิยามของสินสอดมี
หลากหลายมาก และมีเรื่องมากมายที่ควรจะนำมาพิจารณา ครอบครัวฝ่ายหญิงอาจจะ
กำหนดมูลค่าของสินสอด ซึ่งมีมูลค่าตั้งแต่ 50,000 ถึง 1 ล้านบาท บางครั้ง อาจจะเรียกเป็น
ทองคำหรือทรัพย์สินอื่นด้วย เจ้าบ่าวก็สามารถเสนอค่าสินสอดเองได้ (ในกรณีที่ครอบครัว
ของฝ่ายหญิงไม่ทราบถึงสถานภาพทางการเงินของฝ่ายชาย) ในบางครั้ง บิดามารดาของ
เจ้าสาวในอนาคตอาจเพียงแค่เรียกสินสอด แต่ไม่ได้คาดหวังว่าจะได้รับเงินจากฝ่ายชาย
พวกเขาอาจจะแค่เรียกร้องมูลค่าเพื่อที่จะสามารถบอกคนอื่นๆได้ ซึ่งก็เป็นวิธีหนึ่งที่จะบ่ง
บอกถึงสถานะของตนเอง

เจ้าบ่าวจะต้องแสดงให้เห็นว่า เขาสามารถจ่ายในค่าสินสอดตามที่ครอบครัว
เจ้าสาวเรียกร้องได้ ครอบครัวเจ้าสาวอาจจะคืนสินสอดให้ทั้งหมดหรือเพียงให้เจ้าบ่าวจ่าย
ค่าจัดพิธีแต่งงาน ในกรณีที่เจ้าบ่าวและเจ้าสาวมีสถานะใกล้เคียงกัน เช่น มีระดับการศึกษา
เดียวกัน มีอายุใกล้เคียงกัน ไม่เคยแต่งงานมาก่อนเช่นกัน และมีสถานะทางครอบครัวเสมอ
กัน เจ้าบ่าวอาจจะไม่ต้องจ่ายค่าสินสอดเลย หรือในบางกรณี ครอบครัวเจ้าสาวอาจจะช่วย
จ่ายค่าใช้จ่ายในพิธีแต่งงานครึ่งหนึ่งก็ได้

หลังจากการหมั้น พิธีแต่งงานหรือการจดทะเบียนสมรส ถ้าคู่สามีภรรยา
ตัดสินใจแยกทางกัน และเป็นความผิดของฝ่ายหญิง (เช่น การนอกใจ) ฝ่ายชายมีสิทธิขอริบ
ของหมั้นหรือสินสอดคืนได้ อย่างไรก็ตาม ถ้าเป็นความผิดของฝ่ายชาย ก็จะไม่มีการคืน
ของให้ ในกรณีที่ การแยกทางเป็นความเห็นชอบของทั้งสองฝ่าย ทางฝ่ายหญิงควรคืน
สินสอดให้แก่ฝ่ายชาย โดยกฎหมายแล้ว ฝ่ายชายมีสิทธิขอของหมั้นและสินสอดคืน
ถึงแม้ว่าจะเป็นคนต่างชาติก็ตาม อย่างไรก็ตาม การขอสินสอดคืนทองหมั้นคืนจะไม่ทำกัน
เป็นปกติสามัญในหมู่คนไทย

สัญญาก่อนการสมรส

สัญญาก่อนสมรสนี้ จัดว่าเรื่องใหม่สำหรับคนไทย ซึ่งคนไทยส่วนมากจะยัง ไม่มี
ความรู้เกี่ยวกับเรื่องนี้ อีกทั้งยังไม่ใช่เรื่องปกติธรรมดาสำหรับคู่แต่งงานไทยที่จะเซ็นสัญญา
ก่อนสมรส

ประเทศไทยใช้ระบบการแบ่งสินสมรสซึ่งคล้ายกับของเหล่าประเทศตะวันตกที่เรียกว่า community property แต่ประมวลกฎหมายแพ่งและพาณิชย์ของไทยได้บัญญัติอย่างชัดเจนถึงข้อแตกต่างระหว่างสินส่วนตัวและสินสมรส โดยสินส่วนตัว หมายความถึงทรัพย์สินที่สามารถแยกเป็นของส่วนบุคคลซึ่งเป็นกรรมสิทธิ์ของบุคคลนั้นๆก่อนสมรส ส่วนสินสมรส หมายความถึง ทรัพย์ที่เป็นสมบัติร่วมกันและทรัพย์สินที่ได้มาระหว่างที่สมรส โดยเมื่อเกิดการหย่าร้างขึ้น จะมีเพียงสินสมรสเท่านั้นที่นำมาพิจารณาในการแบ่งทรัพย์สินกันระหว่างทั้งสองฝ่าย อย่างไรก็ตาม หลังจากเวลาผ่านไป อาจจะเป็นการลำบากที่จะพิสูจน์ว่า ทรัพย์สินใดเป็นสินส่วนตัว ดังนั้น การทำสัญญาก่อนสมรสอาจจะสามารถช่วยในการแบ่งทรัพย์สินได้ในกรณีที่การสมรสจบลงด้วยการหย่าร้าง

โดยปกติแล้ว สัญญาก่อนสมรสจะไม่เป็นหัวข้อที่คู่สมรสในประเทศไทยนำมากล่าวถึง

ถ้าชายต่างชาติต้องการให้ภรรยาไทยในอนาคตเซ็นสัญญาก่อนสมรส ก็คงจะเป็นสถานการณ์ที่ค่อนข้างแปลกและยุ่งยากพอสมควร บ่อยครั้งที่สามีชาวต่างชาติมีอายุมากกว่าภรรยาไทย และมักจะมีทรัพย์สินที่เก็บสะสมมาเป็นเวลาหลายปี หรือจะมีรายรับจากหลายแห่งเข้ามาในระหว่างการสมรส ในขณะที่ภรรยามีอายุน้อย ยังไม่มีเงินและทรัพย์สินมากนัก สามีจึงต้องการที่จะวางแผนสำหรับสถานการณ์การเงินในอนาคต และปกป้องผลประโยชน์ของตนเองหากมีการหย่าร้างเกิดขึ้น ภรรยาไทยบางคนอาจจะรู้สึกเสียใจ เจ็บปวด น้อยใจและรู้สึกเหมือนไม่ได้รับความไว้วางใจเมื่อพวกเธอทราบเรื่องสัญญาก่อนสมรส เนื่องจากหญิงไทยคาดหวังว่าสามีจะดูแลและรักพวกเธอตลอดไป นอกจากนั้น พวกเธอยังคิดว่า สัญญาก่อนสมรสเป็นการไม่แสดงถึงความรักอีกด้วย ถึงแม้ว่าจะเป็นการกระทำที่ค่อนข้างยากลำบาก แต่ถ้าสามีต้องการความมั่นคงในอนาคตทางการเงิน การเซ็นสัญญาก่อนสมรสจะเป็นการตัดสินใจที่ดีโดยเฉพาะในกรณีที่มีความเหลื่อมล้ำเป็นอย่างมากระหว่างทรัพย์สินของสามีและภรรยา

ทั้งนี้ ขึ้นอยู่กับสถานการณ์ของแต่ละบุคคลที่จะต้องตัดสินใจว่าจะต้องมีสัญญาก่อนสมรสหรือไม่ คุณอาจจะมีสัญญาก่อนสมรสทั้งในประเทศไทยและที่ประเทศของคุณประกอบกัน ถ้าคุณอาศัยอยู่นอกประเทศไทยและมีทรัพย์สินส่วนมากอยู่ที่ประเทศของคุณคุณควรให้ทนายความที่มีประสบการณ์เป็นผู้จัดเตรียมให้ จากนั้นจึงค่อยแปลเป็นภาษาไทยถ้าคู่สมรสในอนาคตของคุณ ไม่เข้าใจเนื้อหาทางกฎหมายที่เป็นภาษาของคุณในสัญญา

สัญญานั้นก็จะต้องมีล่ามแปลเพื่อที่คู่สมรสของคุณจะได้ทำความเข้าใจในเนื้อหาของสัญญา
ก่อนที่จะเซ็น ขั้นตอนนี้ สำคัญมากในการป้องกันไม่ให้คู่สมรสของคุณมาเรียกร้องใน
ภายหลังว่าไม่เข้าใจในเนื้อหาของสัญญาก่อนสมรส

ในกรณีที่ที่ทรัพย์สินส่วนใหญ่ของของคุณอยู่ในประเทศไทย สัญญาก่อนสมรส
สามารถจัดทำขึ้นในประเทศไทยได้โดยทนายความที่เชี่ยวชาญ ในกรณีนี้ กฎหมายไทยจะ
ถูกนำมาประยุกต์ใช้ โดยตามกฎหมายไทย คุณจะระบุถึงทรัพย์สินที่เกี่ยวข้องและแยก
ประเภททรัพย์สินนั้นออกเป็นสินสมรสและสินส่วนตัว อีกทั้งคุณจะสามารถระบุว่า
การเงินจะถูกจัดสรรอย่างไรในระหว่างการสมรส

ขอแนะนำว่า สัญญาก่อนสมรสควรจะได้รับการร่างโดยทนายความผู้มี
ประสบการณ์ และจัดทำขึ้นเป็นสองภาษา คุณควรจะมีเอกสารที่พิสูจน์ว่า คู่สมรสของคุณ
เข้าใจเนื้อหาของสัญญาก่อนที่จะเซ็น แม้ว่าสัญญาจะเป็นภาษาไทยก็ตาม คู่สมรสจะต้อง
อ่าน แสดงความเข้าใจและเห็นด้วยกับสัญญาก่อนที่จะเซ็น และเพื่อที่จะให้สัญญามีผล
บังคับใช้ตามกฎหมายไทย จะต้องมีพยาน 2 คนเซ็นรับรองในสัญญาก่อนสมรส

การแต่งงานกับคนไทย

ถ้าคุณต้องการแต่งงานกับคนไทยให้ถูกต้องตามกฎหมาย หรือถึงแม้ว่าทั้งคุณ
และคู่สมรสเป็นชาวต่างชาติ คุณก็จะต้องจดทะเบียนสมรสในประเทศไทย ขั้นตอนในการ
จดทะเบียนสมรสนั้นง่ายมาก ในกรณีที่คุณมีเอกสารครบถ้วน เมื่อจดทะเบียนสมรสแล้ว
การสมรสนี้จะมีผลบังคับใช้ตามกฎหมายไทย และเป็นที่ยอมรับทั่วโลก

ถ้าคู่สมรสที่ไม่ได้จดทะเบียนสมรสมีบุตร บุตรมักจะใช้นามสกุลของบิดา และ
ถ้าบิดามารดาแยกทางกัน บุตรมักจะอยู่กับมารดา แต่ยังคงใช้นามสกุลของบิดาต่อไป ซึ่ง
บางครั้งเรื่องนี้ทำให้เกิดความสับสนแก่ชาวต่างชาติที่ต้องการจะแต่งงานกับภรรยาไทยและ
ต้องการอุปถัมภ์บุตรของเธอ แต่ต้องรู้สึกประหลาดใจว่าทำไมบุตรจึงไม่ใช้นามสกุล
เดียวกันกับมารดา

คุณสามารถจดทะเบียนสมรสที่สำนักงานเขตหรือที่ว่าการอำเภอใดก็ได้ใน
ประเทศ การจดทะเบียนสมรสเป็นนิติกรรมซึ่งมักจะกระทำขึ้น 2-3 วันก่อนหรือหลังพิธี
สมรส หรือบางครั้งก็กระทำในวันเดียวกัน ทะเบียนสมรสจะออกให้หลังจากการจด

ทะเบียนไม่นานนัก และจะได้รับการยอมรับในทุกประเทศ (โดยควบคู่กับฉบับแปลเป็น
ภาษาทางการของประเทศนั้นๆพร้อมกับการรับรองเอกสาร)

      ชาวต่างชาติบางคนต้องการให้มีทนายความเข้าร่วมในการจดทะเบียนสมรส เพื่อ
ช่วยในการขอเอกสารรับรองจากสถานทูตของตนหรือช่วยเร่งกระบวนการต่างๆ   โดย
สำนักงานทนายความที่มีความชำนาญทั้งกฎหมายไทยและกฎหมายของประเทศของคุณซึ่ง
จะสามารถลดกระบวนการที่ล่าช้าและซับซ้อนลงได้   โดยเรียกเก็บค่าธรรมเนียมที่
สมเหตุสมผล ทั้งนี้ จะขึ้นอยู่กับสถานการณ์ของแต่ละบุคคลว่า การจดทะเบียนสมรสใน
ประเทศไทยหรือในประเทศของคุณเหมาะสมกว่ากัน นอกจากนี้ คุณควรจะปรึกษากับ
ทนายความที่มีประสบการณ์เพื่อตัดสินใจว่าควรจดทะเบียนสมรสที่ใดดี

      คุณและคู่สมรสสามารถจัดการเรื่องเอกสารด้วยตนเองได้ แต่มักจะเป็นงานที่ใช้
เวลามาก ถ้าคุณเป็นชาวต่างชาติ คุณจะต้องนำเอกสารจำนวนมากมาจากสถานทูตพร้อม
แบบคำร้องมากมายที่จะคุณต้องไปยื่นเองที่หน่วยงานราชการหนึ่งแล้วต้องวิ่งไปยังอีก
หน่วยงานหนึ่งซึ่งตั้งอยู่คนละส่วนในพื้นที่จังหวัดกรุงเทพมหานคร

      หลังจากที่คุณรวบรวมเอกสารทั้งหมดแล้ว คุณอาจจะต้องไปจดทะเบียนสมรสที่
ที่ว่าการอำเภอที่คู่สมรสของคุณอาศัยอยู่ อย่างที่กล่าวไปก่อนหน้านี้ว่า การจดทะเบียน
สมรสสามารถจดได้ที่ทุกสำนักงานเขตและที่ว่าการอำเภอทุกแห่งในประเทศไทย อย่างไรก็
ตาม ชาวไทยบางคนก็ยังต้องการจดทะเบียนในเขตภูมิลำเนาของตนเองในเวลาใกล้เคียงกับ
พิธีแต่งงาน ซึ่งมักจะจัดในภูมิลำเนาของตนอยู่แล้ว

      กระบวนการและเอกสารที่จำเป็นในการจดทะเบียนสมรส   ในกรณีที่คุณเป็น
ชาวต่างชาติที่ต้องการแต่งงานกับชาวไทย มีดังนี้

- นำหนังสือเดินทางของคุณไปที่สถานทูตของคุณในประเทศไทยเพื่อ
  สถานทูตรับรองว่า คุณมีสถานภาพโสดและสามารถแต่งงานได้ตาม
  กฎหมายไทย (สามารถขอแบบฟอร์มได้ที่สถานทูต) ปัจจุบันกระบวนการนี้
  ได้ถูกบังคับใช้ในสำนักงานเขตและที่ว่าการอำเภอทุกแห่ง ซึ่งในอดีตเคย
  เกิดปัญหาขึ้นเมื่อชาวต่างชาติจดทะเบียนสมรสในประเทศไทยทั้งที่ยังคง
  แต่งงานหรือเพียงแยกกันอยู่ตามกฎหมายกับคู่สมรสในประเทศของตน
  ทางสถานทูตจะตรวจสอบประวัติ และจะสามารถยืนยันสถานภาพสมรส

ของคุณได้เพื่อที่จะออกเอกสารรับรองต่อไป โดยจะมีค่าธรรมเนียมในการ
ตรวจสอบเล็กน้อย ถ้าคุณเคยแต่งงานมาก่อนและจบลงด้วยการหย่าร้าง
หรือคู่สมรสเสียชีวิต คุณก็จะได้เอกสารรับรอง นอกจากนี้ การทาง
สถานทูตจะต้องตรวจสอบและรายงานประวัติอาชญากรรมของคุณด้วย

■ คำรับรองที่สมบูรณ์จะแปลเป็นภาษาไทยโดยบริษัทแปลภาษาที่ได้รับ
อนุญาต

■ นำคำรับรอง เอกสารที่แปลเป็นภาษาไทย เอกสารประกอบอื่นๆ รายงาน
และสำเนาหนังสือเดินทางไปที่กรมการกงสุล ตั้งอยู่ที่ 123 ถนนแจ้งวัฒนะ
เขตหลักสี่ กรุงเทพฯ 10210 (โทรศัพท์ 66-2 575-1056-60 โทรสาร 575-
1054 อีเมล์ consular04@mfa.go.th) โดยจะได้รับลายเซ็นรับรองจาก
เจ้าหน้าที่ จากนั้นเอกสารของคุณก็พร้อมสำหรับการจดทะเบียนที่อำเภอซึ่ง
จะทำการจดทะเบียนสมรสและออกทะเบียนสมรสเป็นภาษาไทยให้กับคุณ

โดยคุณจะต้องนำเอกสารทั้งหมดข้างต้น พร้อมด้วยเอกสารต่อไปนี้ไปด้วย

■ ในกรณีที่ฝ่ายหญิงเป็นหม้ายหรือเคยหย่าร้างมาก่อน การสิ้นสุดของการ
แต่งงานครั้งก่อนจะต้องมีขึ้น ไม่น้อยกว่า 310 วัน ก่อนการแต่งงานครั้ง
ต่อไป เพื่อเป็นการป้องกันปัญหาการตั้งครรภ์ของฝ่ายหญิง ในกรณีที่
ระยะห่างระหว่างการแต่งงานครั้งก่อนและครั้งต่อไป น้อยกว่า 310 วัน
สามารถนำผลทดสอบการตั้งครรภ์จากสถาบันทางการแพทย์มายื่นได้ แต่
ไม่รวมถึงกรณีดังนี้

ก) มีการคลอดบุตรเกิดขึ้นในระหว่างเวลานั้น
ข) เป็นการสมรสกับคู่สมรสเดิม
ค) มีคำสั่งจากศาลให้ฝ่ายหญิงสมรสได้

■ หนังสือรับรองการทำงานและหนังสือรับรองเงินเดือน (อาจจะถูกร้องขอ
จากสำนักงานเขตหรือที่ว่าการอำเภอบางแห่ง)

- ค่าเลี้ยงดูคู่สมรสที่หย่าร้างกันแล้ว หรือหนี้ค้างชำระทั้งหมด ซึ่งจะต้อง นำมาเปิดเผย
- ชื่อและที่อยู่ของบุคคลอ้างอิงที่อยู่อาศัยในบริเวณเดียวกัน จำนวน 2 คน
- พยาน 2 คน
- หนังสือเดินทางตัวจริงที่ยังไม่หมดอายุ
- บัตรประชาชนและทะเบียนบ้านสำหรับชาวไทย (พร้อมใบเปลี่ยนชื่อ ถ้ามี)

ถ้าคุณแต่งงานกับชาวไทยในประเทศของคุณ คุณก็สามารถจดทะเบียนสมรสที่ นั่นได้ อย่างไรก็ตาม การจดทะเบียนในต่างประเทศจะไม่มีผลกับสถานภาพของคู่สมรส ของคุณในประเทศไทย โดยคู่สมรสของคุณจะยังคงมีสถานภาพเป็นโสดเช่นเดิม ถ้าจะทำ ให้การสมรสมีผลในประเทศไทย คุณจะต้องไปทำการจดทะเบียนสมรสที่สถานทูตหรือ สถานกงสุลไทยในประเทศของคุณ มิฉะนั้น การสมรสนี้จะมีผลก็แต่เพียงในประเทศบ้าน เกิดของคุณ นี่อาจจะเป็นผลดีกับหญิงไทย เนื่องจากสถานภาพทางกฎหมายของเธอใน ประเทศไทยจะยังคงเป็นเหมือนเดิม เธอยังคงมีคำนำหน้าว่า "นางสาว" เสมือนกับตอนยัง ไม่แต่งงาน และเธอก็ยังคงได้รับประโยชน์จากกระบวนการทางกฎหมายเหมือนก่อน ผู้หญิงบางคนก็เลือกที่จะไม่จดทะเบียนกับทางรัฐบาลไทย เพื่อที่จะรักษาสิทธิของเธอใน ฐานะหญิงโสดชาวไทย

สำหรับผู้ที่อาศัยอยู่นอกประเทศไทย กฎเกณฑ์ และเอกสารที่จำเป็นสำหรับการ จดทะเบียนสมรสที่สถานทูตหรือสถานกงสุลไทยในประเทศที่คุณอาศัยอยู่ มีดังนี้

- ฝ่ายใดฝ่ายหนึ่งจะต้องมีสัญชาติไทย
- คู่สมรสจะต้องมาจดทะเบียนสมรสด้วยตนเอง
- บัตรประชาชนไทยหรือหนังสือเดินทางไทยตัวจริง และหนังสือเดินทางต่างชาติ ตัวจริงของอีกฝ่าย พร้อมกับสำเนา
- ใบหย่าหรือทะเบียนหย่าตัวจริงหรือคำสั่งศาล (ถ้าฝ่ายหนึ่งเคยแต่งงานมาก่อน)
- ใบเปลี่ยนชื่อ (ถ้ามี) พร้อมสำเนา
- บางสถานทูตอาจจะขอผลทดสอบการตั้งครรภ์ด้วย

ในกรณีที่หญิงชาวไทยแต่งงานกับชาวต่างชาติ และจดทะเบียนสมรสในประเทศ
ไทย เธอจะเสียสิทธิทางกฎหมายและสิทธิพิเศษบางอย่างเกี่ยวกับการถือครองที่ดิน ส่วน
ชายไทยจะไม่เสียสิทธิใดๆ แม้ว่าจะแต่งงานกับชาวต่างชาติและจดทะเบียนสมรสใน
ประเทศไทยเหมือนกันก็ตาม

ต่อไปจะเป็นข้อมูลเพิ่มเติม ในกรณีที่คุณแต่งงานอย่างถูกกฎหมายกับหญิงไทย
ในประเทศไทย กฎหมายเกี่ยวกับการถือครองทรัพย์สินโดยชาวต่างชาติมีการเปลี่ยนแปลง
บ่อยครั้ง ดังนั้นควรจะมีการตรวจสอบกับหน่วยงานรัฐบาลและทนายความเพื่อยืนยันถึง
กฎหมายที่ใช้อยู่ในปัจจุบัน

- ภรรยาไทยสามารถเก็บรักษาที่ดินที่เธอถือครองก่อนแต่งงานได้
- ภรรยาไทยสามารถรับมรดกที่ดินและสิ่งปลูกสร้างที่ติดมากับที่ดินนั้นได้
- ภรรยาไทยสามารถซื้อบ้านหรือที่ดิน แต่สามีชาวต่างชาติจะต้องเซ็นคำรับรองที่
  กรมที่ดินว่า เงินที่นำมาซื้อที่ดินนี้เป็นของภรรยาไทยทั้งหมด ในกรณีที่มีการหย่า
  ร้างหรือภรรยาเสียชีวิต สามีชาวต่างชาติจะไม่มีสิทธิเรียกร้องในบ้านหรือที่ดิน
  ทั้งสิ้น (สำหรับข้อมูลเพิ่มเติมเกี่ยวกับการซื้อที่ดินของชาวต่างชาติในประเทศ
  ไทย โปรดอ่าน *How To Buy Land And Build A House In Thailand* จัดพิมพ์โดย
  สำนักพิมพ์ไพบูลย์เช่นกัน)

เรื่องที่สำคัญมากที่จะต้องพิจารณาคือ คุณและภรรยาคนไทยควรจะจัดเตรียม
พินัยกรรมที่ถูกต้องตามกฎหมาย โดยมีตัวอย่างของพินัยกรรมอยู่ในส่วนอ้างอิง อย่างไรก็
ตาม พินัยกรรมควรจะถูกจัดทำขึ้นโดยทนายความ ในกรณีที่ไม่มีพินัยกรรม ถ้าภรรยาไทย
เสียชีวิตก่อนคุณ ญาติพี่น้องของเธอจะมีอำนาจตามกฎหมายที่จะนำทรัพย์สินในส่วนที่คิด
ว่าเป็นของภรรยา รวมถึงบ้านของคุณสองคนไปได้ (ข้อมูลเพิ่มเติมเกี่ยวกับการร่าง
พินัยกรรมจะอยู่ลำดับถัดไป)

พิธีสมรส

การแต่งงานที่ถูกกฎหมายนั้น ไม่จำเป็นจะต้องมีพิธีสมรส แค่มีการจดทะเบียน
สมรสก็เพียงพอ อย่างไรก็ตาม ถ้าคุณจะแต่งงานกับหญิงไทย ฝ่ายหญิงและครอบครัวมักจะ
ต้องการให้ประกอบพิธีสมรส และคาดหวังให้สามีชาวต่างชาติให้สินสอดแก่ฝ่ายหญิง

แต่ถ้าคุณเป็นหญิงชาวต่างชาติ ซึ่งต้องการจะแต่งงานกับชายไทย เรื่องก็จะไม่
ซับซ้อนมากนัก แต่เนื่องจากมีกรณีที่ชายต่างชาติแต่งงานกับหญิงไทยเกิดขึ้นบ่อยครั้งกว่า
ในหัวข้อนี้ เราจึงจะกล่าวถึงเจ้าบ่าวที่เป็นชาวต่างชาติและเจ้าสาวชาวไทย อย่างไรก็ตาม
กระบวนการต่างๆ ก็จะคล้ายคลึงกัน ในกรณีที่ชายไทยแต่งงานกับหญิงชาวต่างชาติ มีเพียง
ความแตกต่างเพียงเล็กน้อยในบางแง่มุมของกระบวนการทั้งหมด

การแต่งงานของไทย มีความแตกต่างกันไปตามแต่ละภูมิภาคของประเทศ
รวมถึงแต่ละความชอบและความเชื่อของแต่ละครอบครัว เราจึงมีพิธีสมรสหลากหลาย เช่น
แบบล้านนา (ทางภาคเหนือ) แบบอีสานและแบบประเพณีไทยตามศาสนาพุทธ นอกจากนี้
ยังมีประเพณีแบบศาสนาอิสลามอีกด้วย แต่แบบประเพณีไทยตามศาสนาพุทธ เป็นแบบที่
นิยมมากที่สุดในกรณีที่ฝ่ายชายเป็นชาวต่างชาติ และเนื่องจากหนังสือเล่มนี้ เป็นหนังสือ
กฎหมาย ไม่ใช่หนังสือเกี่ยวกับวัฒนธรรมประเพณี เราจึงจะกล่าวถึงการแต่งงานแบบ
ประเพณีไทยตามศาสนาพุทธโดยย่อ

วันประกอบพิธีสมรสจะถูกกำหนดโดยพระสงฆ์หรือนักโหราศาสตร์ โดยอ้างอิง
ปฏิทินทางโหราศาสตร์ ซึ่งจะเป็นตัวกำหนดวันเวลาที่เป็นฤกษ์ที่ดีที่สุดในการประกอบพิธี
สมรส แต่ในปัจจุบัน ความสะดวกเข้ามามีบทบาทที่สำคัญมากกว่าโหราศาสตร์ในการ
กำหนดวันแต่งงาน อย่างไรก็ตาม ชาวไทยส่วนใหญ่ก็ยังคงหลีกเลี่ยงที่จะแต่งงานในวันที่
เชื่อว่าไม่เป็นมงคล หลังจากกำหนดวันได้แล้ว ว่าที่เจ้าบ่าวเจ้าสาวคู่แต่งงานจึงจะพิมพ์และ
ส่งบัตรเชิญ

พิธีสมรสแบบประเพณีไทยตามศาสนาพุทธ มักจะเริ่มในตอนเช้าตรู่ เจ้าสาว
ส่วนใหญ่จะเริ่มแต่งหน้าและทำผมตั้งแต่ตี 4 พิธีจะเริ่มจากพระสงฆ์สวดมนต์และให้พรแก่

คู่บ่าวสาว   พระสงฆ์จะฉันท์อาหารก่อนแล้วแขกจึงค่อยรับประทาน   จากนั้นจะมีพิธีรด
น้ำสังข์ โดยเจ้าสาวและเจ้าบ่าวนั่งเคียงข้างกันบนพื้นหรือที่โต๊ะคู่ขนาดเล็ก โดยทั้งสอง
สวมด้ายมงคลสีขาวที่เชื่อมศีรษะของทั้งสองซึ่งเป็นสัญลักษณ์ของการครองเรือนร่วมกัน
และมีเพื่อนเจ้าบ่าวและเพื่อนเจ้าสาวฝ่ายละ 2 คน ยืนอยู่ด้านหลัง (ทั้งสี่คนนี้ ควรจะยังเป็น
โสด) ต่อไปจะเป็นพิธีรดน้ำสังข์ โดยเริ่มจากผู้ที่มีอาวุโสที่สุด ตามด้วยแขกท่านอื่นๆ แขก
แต่ละคนจะเดินเข้ามาและรดน้ำสังข์ (ที่พระสงฆ์ให้พรแล้ว) ลงบนมือของเจ้าสาวและ
เจ้าบ่าวจากเปลือกหอยสังข์หรือจากชามประดับ   พร้อมกับอวยพรให้ทั้งคู่มีความสุข ความ
เจริญ และครองคู่กันจนแก่เฒ่า พิธีรดน้ำสังข์มักจะเสร็จสิ้นก่อนเที่ยง แต่บางคู่อาจจะทำ
พิธีนี้ในช่วงบ่ายหรือในช่วงพิธีเลี้ยงฉลองตอนเย็นก็ได้

พิธีเลี้ยงฉลองมักจะจัดขึ้นในช่วงเย็น ซึ่งเป็นช่วงเวลาของการรับประทานอาหาร
ฟังเพลง เต้นรำ และกล่าวสุนทรพจน์ ของขวัญแต่งงานมักเป็นในรูปของเงินสดใส่มาใน
ซองที่มีชื่อของผู้ให้ แขกที่ไม่ได้มาร่วมพิธีเลี้ยงฉลองในตอนเย็นสามารถนำของขวัญมาให้
ในวันรุ่งขึ้น หรือสามารถใส่เงินลงไปในบัตรเชิญแล้วฝากมาให้คู่บ่าวสาวก็ได้เช่นกัน

พิธีสมรสจะมีค่าใช้จ่ายน้อยกว่าพิธีเลี้ยงฉลอง บางคู่ก็จะไม่จัดงานเลี้ยงหรือเพียง
เลี้ยงฉลองเล็กๆ ถ้าคุณจัดพิธีสมรสในหมู่บ้านในต่างจังหวัด จะมีค่าใช้จ่ายประมาณ 30,000
– 50,000 บาท พิธีเลี้ยงฉลองจะมีค่าใช้จ่ายมากกว่า เนื่องจากมีจำนวนแขกมากว่าที่จะต้อง
บริการอาหารและเครื่องดื่ม โดยค่าใช้จ่ายจะรวมถึงค่าเช่าสถานที่ ค่าเครื่องดื่ม อาหาร ความ
บันเทิงต่างๆ และค่าใช้จ่ายอื่นๆ ซึ่งสามารถจะมีค่าใช้จ่ายประมาณ 100,000 – 300,000 บาท
หรือมากกว่า ค่าใช้จ่ายในส่วนนี้ อาจจะนำมาจากค่าสินสอด หรือเงินที่ทั้งฝ่ายเจ้าสาวและ
เจ้าบ่าวช่วยกันจ่าย หรือฝ่ายเจ้าบ่าวเป็นผู้รับผิดชอบทั้งหมดแล้วแต่สถานการณ์

การพาคู่สมรสและบุตรไปประเทศของตน

ชาวไทยมีสิทธิเดินทางไปทุกแห่งทั่วโลกได้อย่างเสรีและสามารถเดินทางกลับมา
ยังประเทศไทยได้ตลอดเวลา (เว้นเสียแต่ว่าถูกเพิกถอนสัญชาติไทย) ขณะที่ในบางประเทศ
ต้องการให้ชาวไทยขอวีซ่าก่อนที่เดินทางเข้าประเทศ โดยปกติแล้ว ชาวไทยจะต้องขอวีซ่า
ให้ตรงตามจุดประสงค์ในการเดินทางเข้าประเทศนั้นๆ

กฎหมายไทยไม่ได้ระบุข้อกำหนดต่างๆ ในการพาคู่สมรสและบุตรไปยังประเทศ
ของคุณ แต่ประเทศถิ่นกำเนิดของคุณจะเป็นผู้กำหนดระเบียบกฎเกณฑ์ และวิธีการปฏิบัติ
ในเรื่องการเข้าเมืองสำหรับครอบครัวชาวไทยของคุณ โดยคุณจะต้องตรวจสอบข้อกำหนด
และกฎหมายที่เกี่ยวข้องก่อน เช่น ประเทศอังกฤษกำหนดให้ชาวอังกฤษสามารถนำคู่สมรส
ชาวไทยและบุตรที่อายุต่ำกว่า 18 ปี มาอาศัยอยู่ด้วยได้ ในกรณีที่ ชาวอังกฤษนั้นสามารถ
แสดงให้เห็นว่า สามารถสนับสนุนทางการเงิน และเลี้ยงดูครอบครัวของตนเองได้ ถ้าคุณ
เป็นชาวอังกฤษที่แต่งงานกับชาวไทย คุณก็จำเป็นจะต้องแสดงทะเบียนสมรส และสูติบัตร
ของบุตร (ฉบับจริงเป็นภาษาไทย และฉบับแปลเป็นภาษาอังกฤษซึ่งได้รับรองแล้ว) จากนั้น
ทั้งครอบครัวจึงจะได้รับอนุญาตให้อาศัยอยู่ในประเทศอังกฤษ ตราบที่ผู้เลี้ยงดูครอบครัว
อาศัยอยู่ และอาจจะได้รับอนุญาตให้ทำงาน ถ้ามีใบอนุญาตให้อยู่อาศัยเป็นระยะเวลา
มากกว่า 1 ปีโดยคู่สมรสของคุณควรจะมีสำเนาหนังสือเดินทางของคุณด้วยในกรณีที่ทำ
เรื่องขออนุญาตเข้าประเทศในภายหลัง กองตรวจคนเข้าเมืองของประเทศอังกฤษต้องการ
ตรวจสอบหนังสือเดินทางหน้าที่ระบุชื่อคุณ พร้อมเอ็นทรีเคลียแรนซ์สติกเกอร์ (ถ้ามี) และ
อายุของใบอนุญาตของคุณ (กรุณาดูรายละเอียดเพิ่มเติมได้ที่ http://www.ukvisas.gov.uk)

กฎระเบียบของประเทศสหรัฐอเมริกาจะเข้มงวดและซับซ้อนกว่าประเทศอื่น คน
อเมริกันบางคนพาคู่สมรสชาวไทยเข้าประเทศโดยระบุว่าเป็นแค่คู่หมั้นแทนที่จะระบุว่า
เป็นภรรยาหรือสามี วิธีนี้จะสามารถลดระยะเวลาของกระบวนการตรวจคนเข้าเมืองได้
อย่างไรก็ตามแต่ละกระบวนการจะแตกต่างกันไปขึ้นอยู่กับว่าคุณเป็นพลเมืองอเมริกันหรือ
เป็นผู้ถือใบเขียว (ผู้อาศัยถาวร)

ในการนำคู่สมรสและบุตรมายังประเทศสหรัฐอเมริกา กองตรวจคนเข้าเมือง
จะต้องอนุมัติคำร้องที่คุณส่งยื่นแทนคู่สมรสเสียก่อน รัฐบาลอเมริกาจะออกวีซ่าให้แก่ผู้ขอ
มีใบเขียวเพียงจำนวนจำกัดในแต่ละปี โดยทางการกองตรวจคนเข้าเมืองจะแสดงวันที่ที่
อนุมัติวีซ่าให้กับคู่สมรสของคุณตามลำดับที่คุณส่งคำร้องขอวีซ่า

ในกรณีที่คุณเป็นพลเมืองอเมริกัน คู่สมรสและบุตรของคุณจะสามารถเข้า
ประเทศได้ทันทีถ้าคำร้องขอวีซ่าได้รับการอนุมัติ ถ้าคู่สมรสของคุณอยู่นอกประเทศ
สหรัฐอเมริกา ขณะที่คำร้องขอวีซ่าของคุณได้รับการอนุมัติและมีหมายเลขวีซ่าแล้ว คู่
สมรสของคุณจะได้รับการแจ้งให้ไปรายงานตัวที่สถานกงสุลสหรัฐฯในเมืองไทยเพื่อเรื่อง
ขอวีซ่าให้เสร็จสมบูรณ์ แต่ถ้าคู่สมรสของคุณอยู่ในประเทศสหรัฐอเมริกาอย่างผิดกฎหมาย
ในขณะที่คำร้องขอวีซ่าของคุณได้รับการอนุมัติและมีหมายเลขวีซ่าแล้ว คู่สมรสของคุณ
อาจจะต้องใช้แบบคำร้อง Form I-485 เพื่อขอเปลี่ยนสถานะเป็นผู้อาศัยถาวรตามกฎหมาย
(รายละเอียดเพิ่มเติมเกี่ยวกับข้อกำหนดในการขอวีซ่า กรุณาดูที่
http://travel.state.gov/visa/visa ซึ่งเป็นเว็บไซท์ทางการของรัฐบาลประเทศสหรัฐอเมริกา)

แต่ละประเทศก็จะมีกฎเกณฑ์ที่แตกต่างกัน ดังนั้นคุณควรขอคำแนะนำจาก
ทนายความผู้เชี่ยวชาญ ซึ่งสามารถวิเคราะห์และให้คำแนะนำในที่เหมาะสมในแต่ละ
สถานการณ์ซึ่งจะช่วยให้คุณตัดสินใจเลือกทางที่ดีที่สุด

ก่อนที่จะตัดสินใจพาครอบครัวของคุณมาอาศัยอยู่ที่ประเทศของคุณ ควรจะพิจารณา
ประเด็นต่างๆดังนี้

- ค่าใช้จ่ายต่างๆ (ค่าตั๋วเครื่องบิน ที่พัก ค่าใช้จ่ายประจำวัน ค่าเลี้ยงดูบุตร ค่า
  ศึกษาเล่าเรียน และค่าใช้จ่ายเกี่ยวกับสุขภาพ)
- ข้อกำหนดในการขอวีซ่า และเอกสารต่างๆ
- การศึกษาเพิ่มเติมที่จำเป็นสำหรับคู่สมรสและบุตร
- ปัญหาด้านภาษา
- ผลกระทบของการเปลี่ยนแปลงทางวัฒนธรรม หรือในสิ่งที่ไม่คุ้นเคย
- โอกาสทางการงานที่จำกัดของคู่สมรสและบุตร

- การจัดหาที่อยู่อาศัยใหม่
- ค่าใช้จ่ายในการกลับมาเยี่ยมครอบครัวและญาติพี่น้องที่เมืองไทย
- การส่งเงินกลับเมืองไทยโดยคู่สมรส
- สภาพอากาศที่แตกต่างจากเมืองไทย

การรับอุปการะบุตรบุญธรรมจากประเทศไทย

ในกรณีที่คุณอาศัยอยู่นอกประเทศไทย และต้องการรับอุปการะเด็กชาวไทย คุณจะสามารถทำได้โดยผ่านทางหน่วยงานบริการด้านการอุปการะบุตรบุญธรรม กรมสังคมสงเคราะห์ หรือหน่วยงานของภาคเอกชนที่ได้รับใบอนุญาตจากทางรัฐบาลในประเทศของคุณเพื่อประสานงานระหว่างประเทศเกี่ยวกับการรับอุปการะบุตรบุญธรรม

หน่วยงานที่จัดการเรื่องบุตรบุญธรรมจะจัดทำรายงานซึ่งครอบคลุมถึงรายละเอียดเกี่ยวกับสุขภาพร่างกายและจิตใจของผู้รับบุญธรรม สถานภาพของครอบครัว ทรัพย์สิน หนี้สิน ฐานะทางการเงิน ชื่อเสียงและการอยู่อาศัย นอกจากนี้ยังพิจารณาถึงขนาดของครอบครัวและความสามารถในการให้ความรักและความดูแล แรงดลใจและเรื่องอื่นๆที่เกี่ยวข้องกับสวัสดิการและผลประโยชน์ของบุตร นอกจากนั้น ความสัมพันธ์กับผู้ให้กำเนิดและภาระผูกพันกับบุตรในการสมรสครั้งก่อน (ถ้ามี) และประเด็นอื่นเกี่ยวกับผู้ขออุปการะบุตรก็จะนำมาพิจารณา (กรุณาดูรายละเอียดเพิ่มเติมที่ www.adoption.org หน่วยงานนี้จะเป็นผู้แนะนำกระบวนการต่างๆในการขอรับบุตรบุญธรรม)

นอกจากนี้ คุณยังสามารถรับอุปการะเด็กด้วยตนเอง อย่างไรก็ตาม คุณจะไม่สามารถรับอุปการะเด็กได้คราวละมากกว่า 1 คน (รวมถึงฝาแฝดและพี่น้องท้องเดียวกันด้วย) กระบวนการนี้ มักจะใช้เวลาประมาณ 1-2 ปี คุณอาจจะต้องการรับอุปการะเด็กที่เฉพาะเจาะจง ซึ่งอาจจะเป็นญาติ บุตรของคู่สมรส หรือเด็กจากสถานเลี้ยงเด็กกำพร้า ซึ่งงานเอกสารเป็นงานที่ยุ่งยาก ดังนั้นคุณควรจะมีทนายชาวไทยมาช่วยในกระบวนการนี้

ผู้เขียนได้รวบรวมข้อมูลทั่วไปเกี่ยวกับการรับอุปการะเด็กในประเทศไทยจากกรมการปกครอง กระทรวงมหาดไทยและหน่วยงานจดทะเบียนรับบุตรบุญธรรม โดย

เริ่มแรก คุณจะต้องผ่านเกณฑ์คุณสมบัติเบื้องต้นเสียก่อนจึงจะสามารถรับบุตรบุญธรรมจาก
ประเทศไทยได้ จากนั้นส่งคำร้องและเอกสารประกอบไปยังกรมประชาสงเคราะห์ เมื่อคำ
ร้องได้รับการอนุมัติแล้ว คุณจะต้องจดทะเบียนรับบุตรบุญธรรมเพื่อให้กระบวนการเสร็จ
สมบูรณ์

คุณสมบัติ

1. ∴ ผู้รับบุตรบุญธรรมจะต้องมีอายุมากกว่า 25 ปีขึ้นไป และมีอายุมากกว่าบุตรบุญ
   ธรรมอย่างน้อย 15 ปี
2. บุตรบุญธรรมที่มีอายุมากว่า 15 ปี จะต้องให้การยินยอมด้วยตัวเอง
3. กรณีที่บุตรบุญธรรมเป็นผู้เยาว์ จะต้องได้รับความยินยอมจาก
   - ทั้งบิดาและมารดา ถ้าทั้งสองยังมีชีวิตอยู่
   - บิดาหรือมารดา ถ้ามีเพียงฝ่ายหนึ่งมีชีวิตอยู่ หรือถ้าอยู่ในการ
     ปกครองของฝ่ายเดียว
   - ตัวแทนทางกฎหมาย หรืออัยการที่ทำเรื่องส่งคำร้องให้อนุมัติ
     การรับบุตรบุญธรรมไปยังศาล
   - ตัวแทนจากทางโรงพยาบาล หรือสถาบันอื่นซึ่งได้รับอนุญาต
     จากหน่วยงานรัฐบาล
   - บุคคลที่ดูแลเด็กที่ถูกทอดทิ้งมาเป็นระยะเวลามากกว่า 1 ปี
4. ผู้รับบุตรบุญธรรมและบุตรบุญธรรม (ในกรณีที่บุตรบุญธรรมบรรลุนิติภาวะ
   แล้ว) จะต้องได้รับคำยินยอมจากคู่สมรสของบุตรบุญธรรม ยกเว้น
   - คู่สมรสไม่สามารถให้คำยินยอมได้
   - คู่สมรสหายสาบสูญและหาที่อยู่ไม่พบเป็นระยะเวลามากกว่า 1
     ปี
5. บุตรบุญธรรมคนนั้นต้องไม่อยู่ในฐานะเป็นบุตรบุญธรรมของผู้อื่น (นอกจาก
   เป็นบุตรบุญธรรมของคู่สมรสของคุณ)

โดยผู้รับบุตรบุญธรรมชาวต่างชาติจะต้องมีคู่สมรสที่ถูกต้องตามกฎหมาย และมีสิทธิที่จะรับบุตรบุญธรรมจากประเทศไทยภายใต้กฎหมายของประเทศนั้น

ประโยชน์ของการจดทะเบียนรับบุตรบุญธรรม

1. บุตรบุญธรรมมีสิทธิที่จะใช้นามสกุล และรับมรดกของผู้รับบุตรบุญธรรม อย่างไรก็ตาม ผู้รับบุตรบุญธรรม ไม่สามารถรับมรดกของบุตรบุญธรรมได้
2. หลังจากวันที่จดทะเบียน ผู้รับบุตรบุญธรรมมีสิทธิที่จะเลี้ยงดูบุตรบุญธรรม เสมือนว่า เป็นบุตรโดยถูกต้องตามกฎหมายของตน
3. หลังจากวันที่จดทะเบียน บิดามารดาโดยกำเนิดจะ ไม่มีสิทธิ อำนาจในตัวบุตรบุญธรรมอีกต่อไป อย่างไรก็ตาม ในประเทศไทย พวกเขาก็ยังคงเป็นบิดามารดาโดยกำเนิดอยู่ และบุตรบุญธรรมจะไม่เสียสิทธิและความรับผิดชอบในฐานะบุตรต่อบิดามารดาโดยกำเนิด (ในประเทศไทยจะเป็นสิทธิของบุตรบุญธรรมที่จะเคารพบิดามารดาโดยกำเนิดต่อไปหรือไม่)

คำร้องขอ

คุณจะต้องส่งคำร้องขออย่างเป็นทางการ ไปยังกรมสังคมสงเคราะห์หรือหน่วยงานอื่นที่เกี่ยวข้อง พร้อมเอกสารดังนี้

- ใบรับรองแพทย์ ซึ่งยืนยันว่าผู้รับบุตรบุญธรรมมีสุขภาพร่างกายและจิตใจที่สมบูรณ์
- เอกสารยืนยันการสมรส
- เอกสารรับรองอาชีพและรายได้
- เอกสารรับรองสถานะทางการเงิน
- เอกสารรับรองทรัพย์สิน
- หนังสือรับรองจากบุคคลอ้างอิงอย่างน้อย 2 คน
- ใบหย่าของผู้รับบุตรบุญธรรม (ถ้ามี)

- รูปถ่าย 4 ใบ ของผู้ขอรับบุตรบุญธรรม (กรุณาตรวจสอบขนาด) รวมถึงรูปของ บุตรอื่นๆของคุณ (ถ้ามี) และบริเวณที่อยู่อาศัย
- เอกสารจากกองตรวจคนเข้าเมืองของประเทศถิ่นของคุณที่อนุญาตให้บุตรบุญ ธรรมเข้าประเทศ
- คำยืนยันจากหน่วยงานที่เกี่ยวข้องว่า หลังจากขั้นตอนการรับบุตรบุญธรรมเสร็จ สิ้นตามกฎหมายไทยแล้วจะมีผลตามกฎหมายที่เกี่ยวข้องในประเทศของผู้รับ บุตรบุญธรรมด้วย

เอกสารทั้งหมดจะต้องเป็นฉบับจริงและได้รับการรับรองโดยสถานทูตไทยหรือ สถานกงสุลไทยของประเทศของคุณหรือส่งผ่านทางการกงสุล เพราะฉะนั้นเอกสารที่เป็น ภาษาอื่นจะต้องแนบฉบับแปลที่เป็นภาษาไทยหรือภาษาอังกฤษพร้อมการรับรองโดย สถานทูตหรือสถานกงสุลไทยมาด้วย หลังจากเสร็จสิ้นกระบวนการนี้ คุณจะต้องจด ทะเบียนรับบุตรบุญธรรม

ขั้นตอนการจดทะเบียนรับบุตรบุญธรรมในประเทศไทย

การจดทะเบียนนี้ เป็นขั้นตอนสุดท้ายในการในรับบุตรบุญธรรม ซึ่งจะสมบูรณ์ โดยการส่งคำร้องขอจดทะเบียน เมื่อจดทะเบียนและการรับบุตรบุญธรรมจะได้รับการ รับรองจากรัฐบาลไทยแล้วจึงถือว่าถูกต้องงามกฎหมาย ขั้นตอนการจดทะเบียนรับบุตรบุญ ธรรม มีดังนี้

ขั้นตอนแรก ผู้ขอรับบุตรบุญธรรมและบุตรบุญธรรมจะต้องส่งคำร้องไปยัง เจ้าหน้าที่ทะเบียน ณ สำนักงานเขตหรือที่ว่าการอำเภอ กรณีที่ผู้รับบุตรบุญธรรมหรือบุตร บุญธรรมฝ่ายใดฝ่ายหนึ่งสมรสแล้ว ฝ่ายนั้นจะต้องให้คู่สมรสมายังสำนักงานเขตหรือที่ว่า การอำเภอเพื่อให้คำยินยอมด้วย

1. ถ้าผู้รับบุตรบุญธรรมอาศัยอยู่ในกรุงเทพฯ (รวมถึงชาวต่างชาติ) จะต้องส่งคำร้อง ไปยังกรมประชาสงเคราะห์ ตั้งอยู่ที่ 255 ถนนราชวิถี กทม. 10400 สำหรับผู้ที่

อาศัยอยู่ต่างจังหวัด ส่งคำร้องมาที่สำนักงานอำเภอหรือกรมประชาสงเคราะห์ของจังหวัด พร้อมทั้งหนังสือยินยอมจากผู้ที่มีอำนาจให้รับบุตรบุญธรรม

2. ชาวต่างชาติที่อาศัยอยู่นอกประเทศไทยจะต้องส่งคำร้องไปยังสำนักงานสวัสดิการสังคมที่ได้รับอนุญาตจากรัฐบาลของคุณให้การดูแลกระบวนการรับบุตรบุญธรรม

3. หลังจากที่คณะกรรมการอนุมัติการรับบุตรบุญธรรมแล้ว ผู้รับบุตรบุญธรรมจะต้องส่งคำร้องอีกชุดหนึ่งเพื่อใช้ในการจดทะเบียนรับบุตรบุญธรรม

4. บุตรบุญธรรมที่สมรสแล้วจะต้องนำคู่สมรสมาเพื่อให้คำยินยอมด้วย

5. ในกรณีที่บุตรบุญธรรมมีอายุเกิน 15 ปี จะต้องให้คำยินยอมเป็นลายลักษณ์อักษร

การจดทะเบียนรับรองบุตรบุญธรรม จะใช้เวลาประมาณ 1 ชั่วโมง คุณจะต้องนำสูติบัตรของบุตรบุญธรรม ทะเบียนบ้าน หนังสือเดินทาง (ถ้ามี) และรูปถ่าย 1 ใบไปด้วย ผู้รับบุตรบุญธรรมจะต้องนำบัตรประชาชน ทะเบียนบ้าน ใบรับอนุญาตจากกรมประชาสงเคราะห์ (ในกรณีที่บุตรบุญธรรมที่เป็นผู้เยาว์) ทะเบียนสมรส (ของทั้งผู้รับบุตรบุญธรรมและบุตรบุญธรรม) และพยาน 2 คน

บุตรบุญธรรมจะได้รับสิทธิให้ถือสัญชาติประเทศของผู้รับบุตรบุญธรรมหลังจากกระบวนการรับบุญธรรมเสร็จสิ้นแล้ว

ความรุนแรงในครอบครัว

ความรุนแรงในครอบครัวในประเทศไทยมีอัตราสูงขึ้นทุกปี ศูนย์พิทักษ์สิทธิเด็กและสตรี (OSCC) มีรายงานว่า ในปี พ.ศ. 2549 เด็กและผู้หญิงตกเป็นเหยื่อของความรุนแรงในครอบครัวในอัตราถึง 39 ครั้งต่อวัน เปรียบเทียบกับ 32 ครั้ง ใน พ.ศ. 2548 และ 19 ครั้ง ใน พ.ศ. 2547 อย่างไรก็ตาม ตัวเลขในความเป็น จริงอาจจะสูงกว่านี้มาก กระทรวงการพัฒนาสังคมและความมั่นคงของมนุษย์ ประเมินว่า เหตุการณ์ความรุนแรงในครอบครัว

เกิดขึ้นใน 18 ล้านครอบครัวในประเทศไทย โดยทางกระทรวงได้เสนอพ.ร.บ. คุ้มครอง
ผู้เสียหายจากความรุนแรงในครอบครัวต่อสภาซึ่งได้รับอนุมัติและบัญญัติเป็นกฎหมายแล้ว

ความรุนแรงในครอบครัวมักเกิดขึ้นจากการกระทำของฝ่ายชายและผู้เสียหาย
ส่วนใหญ่มักจะเป็นผู้หญิงและเด็ก ในประเทศไทย ความรุนแรงเช่นนี้เคยถือว่าเป็นปัญหา
ภายในครอบครัวและไม่ถือว่าเป็นอาชญากรรม แม้กระทั่งปัจจุบันนี้ เมื่อภรรยาถูกสามีทำ
ร้าย   เพื่อนบ้านมักจะไม่ต้องการเข้าไปเกี่ยวข้องเพราะเกรงว่าจะเป็นการรุกล้ำเรื่อง
ส่วนตัวของผู้อื่น

วัฒนธรรมเดิมของไทยถือว่าภรรยาเป็นทรัพย์สินของสามี นอกจากนั้นบางคนก็
เชื่อในเรื่องของกรรม   และเชื่อว่าเป็นโชคชะตาของภรรยาและบุตรที่ต้องเจอกับเรื่องไม่ดี
ภายในครอบครัว หญิงไทยจำนวนมากที่มีชีวิตอยู่กับความรุนแรงเช่นนี้เนื่องจากไม่ทราบว่า
จะรับมือกับสภาพนั้นอย่างไร   สังคมไทยคาดหวังให้คู่สมรสแก้ไขปัญหาภายในครอบครัว
รวมถึงความรุนแรงที่เกิดขึ้นด้วยกันเอง   ดังนั้นผู้เสียหายฝ่ายหญิงจึงมักจะเลือกที่จะอดทน
อย่างเงียบๆ และพยายามแก้ไขปัญหาด้วยตนเอง

ชาวไทยอีกเป็นจำนวนมากยังคงไม่ตระหนักว่า ความรุนแรงในครอบครัวนั้น ใน
ปัจจุบันถือว่าเป็นอาชญากรรมที่จะต้องรายงานแก่เจ้าหน้าที่ตำรวจ   ชายไทยไม่มีสิทธิ์ที่จะ
ทำร้ายร่างกายภรรยาและบุตรอีกต่อไป และแน่นอน หญิงไทยก็ไม่มีสิทธิ์ที่จะทำร้ายสามี
และบุตรเช่นกัน

เมื่อหญิงไทยพยายามจะขอคำแนะนำจากผู้อื่น คำแนะนำที่ได้ (โดยเฉพาะจาก
บุคคลภายนอกครอบครัว) มักจะไม่มีประโยชน์ จนกระทั่งความรุนแรงที่เกิดขึ้นนั้น รุนแรง
มากขึ้นและมีผลทำให้บาดเจ็บจนถึงขั้นต้องไปพบแพทย์หรือเสียชีวิต   ถึงขั้นนั้นแล้ว
ผู้เสียหายหรือญาติของผู้เสียหายจึงจะขอความช่วยเหลือจากเจ้าหน้าที่ตำรวจหรือแพทย์

ในประเทศไทย   เมื่อสามีและภรรยามีเรื่องกันมักจะจบลงที่สถานีตำรวจ
เจ้าหน้าที่ตำรวจจะพยายามไกล่เกลี่ยปัญหาให้   และอาจจะไม่ลงบันทึกประจำวันด้วยซ้ำ

กฎหมายในประเทศไทยเกี่ยวกับความรุนแรงในครอบครัวนั้นยังจะมีบทลงโทษเพียง เล็กน้อยเท่านั้นเมื่อเปรียบเทียบกับกฎหมายของเหล่าประเทศตะวันตก

สาเหตุส่วนใหญ่ของความรุนแรงในครอบครัวที่ก่อขึ้นโดยฝ่ายชาย มักจะ เกี่ยวข้องกับการดื่มสุรา การนอกใจ การพนัน ปัญหาทางการเงิน และการขาดความ รับผิดชอบในเรื่องทั่วๆไป โสเภณีและเชื้อ HIV หรือโรคเอดส์ก็เป็นอีกปัจจัยหนึ่ง การดื่ม สุราเป็นปัญหาที่เกิดขึ้นมากในครอบครัวทั่วประเทศไทย ในขณะที่สังคมไทยในอดีต มักจะ ให้อภัยในพฤติกรรมที่สามีไปเที่ยวหญิงโสเภณี ภรรยาไทยที่มีสามีที่ชอบไปเที่ยวหญิง โสเภณีก็จะต้องยอมอดทนรับพฤติกรรมนี้

การพนันก็เป็นหนึ่งในปัจจัยที่สำคัญที่ทำให้เกิดความรุนแรงและปัญหาทางการ เงินในครอบครัว โดยจะมีผลกระทบกับมาตรฐานความเป็นอยู่ของคนในครอบครัว อีกทั้ง ยังเป็นการหว่านเมล็ดความรุนแรงในครอบครัวอีกด้วย แรงกระตุ้นของการพนันนั้นรุนแรง มากในสังคมไทย หญิงไทยก็ชอบเล่นการพนันเช่นกัน แต่ยังมีจำนวนน้อยมากเมื่อเทียบกับ ชายไทย

อีกปัจจัยหนึ่งที่นำไปสู่ปัญหาความรุนแรงในครอบครัว คือ สังคมไทยค่อนข้าง จะเป็นสังคมที่ให้อภัยพฤติกรรมที่เป็นปฏิปักษ์กับสังคม อาทิเช่น เมื่อฝ่ายชายเล่นการพนัน มีชู้ และติดสุรา ส่วนหญิงไทยจะได้รับการปฏิบัติที่ไม่เท่าเทียมกันในเรื่องเช่นเดียวกันนี้ โดยอาจจะถูกสังคมลงโทษอย่างรุนแรงสำหรับการกระทำที่ไม่เหมาะสมนั้น

องค์กรจำนวนมากในประเทศไทยกำลังพยายามให้ความรู้กับประชาชนเกี่ยวกับ ความรุนแรงในครอบครัว สิทธิสตรีและเด็ก และจะทำอย่างไรถ้าตกเป็นผู้เสียหาย มูลนิธิ ปวีณาสำหรับเด็กและสตรี www.pavena.thai.com เป็นองค์กรที่ไม่หวังผลกำไรซึ่งก่อตั้งโดย คุณปวีณา หงสกุล สมาชิกสภาผู้แทนราษฎร ตั้งอยู่ที่ 82/12 ซอยรามอินทรา 39 ถนนราม อินทรา เขตบางเขน กรุงเทพฯ 10220 (โทรศัพท์ 0-2552-6570)

นอกจากนี้ มูลนิธิเพื่อนหญิง www.friendsofwomen.net ก็เป็นอีกองค์กรอิสระที่ ทำงานปกป้องสิทธิสตรีและช่วยเหลือผู้หญิงในสถานการณ์ฉุกเฉิน ตั้งอยู่ที่ 386/61-62 ซอย

รัชดาภิเษก 42 (ซอยเฉลิมศักดิ์) ถนนรัชดาภิเษก แขวงลาดยาว เขตจตุจักร กรุงเทพฯ 10900 (โทรศัพท์ 0-2513-1001))

ถ้าคุณเป็นชาวต่างชาติ ซึ่งตกเป็นเหยื่อของความรุนแรงในครอบครัว คุณสามารถขอความช่วยเหลือได้จากสถานทูตของคุณ ซึ่งจะแนะนำคุณให้ไปยังองค์กรที่เหมาะสมหรืออาจช่วยคุณเดินทางกลับประเทศ

ผู้เขียนไม่ได้หมายความว่าชายไทยทุกคนจะเป็นเช่นนี้ ยังมีชายไทยที่ดีๆอีกจำนวนมาก ซึ่งเป็นสามีที่ดีเยี่ยม และเป็นหัวหน้าครอบครัวที่ดี ไม่เคยคิดจะทำร้ายภรรยาหรือบุตร แต่ในปัจจุบัน หญิงไทยเริ่มจะมีความคิดที่จะแต่งงานกับชายชาวต่างชาติมากขึ้น ซึ่งเป็นอีกทางเลือกหนึ่งแทนการแต่งงานกับชายไทย แนวความคิดนี้ มักเกิดขึ้นกับหญิงไทยที่มีการศึกษาหรือที่ผ่านประสบการณ์การแต่งงานหรือการหย่ามาแล้ว

การหย่าร้าง

ในวัฒนธรรมไทย การหย่าร้างมักจะเป็นเรื่องที่เสียหน้าเป็นอย่างมาก และเป็นเครื่องบ่งชี้ถึงความล้มเหลว เนื่องจากมลทินทางสังคม คู่สมรสไทยจำนวนมากถูกบีบบังคับให้อยู่ด้วยกัน และมีชีวิตสมรสที่ไม่มีความสุขไปจนกว่าจะตายจากกัน ในอดีต อัตราการหย่าร้างค่อนข้างต่ำ เนื่องจากคู่สมรสรู้สึกมีพันธะที่จะต้องอดทนอยู่กินด้วยกันต่อไป ซึ่งเป็นสาเหตุของปัญหาครอบครัวมากมาย

สถิติของไทยปีพ.ศ. 2548 แสดงให้เห็นว่า อัตราการหย่าร้างเพิ่มสูงขึ้นในช่วงระยะเวลา 10 ปีที่ผ่านมา ใน ปี พ.ศ. 2546 อัตราการหย่าโดยเฉลี่ย คือ 1.28 คู่ ต่อประชากร 1,000 คนซึ่งกับน้อยกว่า 1 คู่ ต่อประชากร 1,000 คน ในปี พ.ศ. 2537 ส่วนจำนวนคู่สมรสที่จดทะเบียนสมรสก็ลดลงอย่างมากเช่นกัน โดยจากตัวเลขในปีพ.ศ. 2546 จำนวนการจดทะเบียนสมรสมีเพียง 5 ทะเบียนต่อประชากร 1,000 คน ซึ่งลดลงจาก 7 ทะเบียนต่อประชากร 1,000 คน ในปี พ.ศ. 2537 จำนวนการจดทะเบียนลดลงมากที่สุดในภาคตะวันออกเฉียงเหนือ ซึ่งมีการจดทะเบียนเพียง 5 ทะเบียนต่อประชากร 1,000 คน ในปี พ.ศ.

2546 เปรียบเทียบกับ 8 ทะเบียนต่อประชากร 1,000 คน เมื่อ 10 ปีที่ผ่านมา สถิตินี้แสดงให้เห็นถึงความเสื่อมถอยของความเชื่อมั่นในสถาบันการครอบครัว

ตัวเลขนี้อาจจะดูน้อยเมื่อเปรียบเทียบกับประเทศอื่น แต่สถิตินี้อาจจะไม่แสดงให้เห็นถึงความเป็นจริง เหตุผลข้อหนึ่งที่ตัวเลขนี้ต่ำ อาจจะเป็นเพราะคู่สมรสจำนวนมากในต่างจังหวัดเพียงแค่ประกอบพิธีสมรสกัน โดยไม่ได้จดทะเบียนสมรส อีกทั้งยังไม่มีข้อมูลทางสถิติเกี่ยวกับอัตราการนอกใจ และการแยกกันอยู่อย่างเป็นทางการซึ่งเป็นตัวเลขค่อนข้างสูงอีกด้วย

ปัจจุบัน หญิงไทยจำนวนมากขึ้น มีอิสระทางการเงิน และอิสระในการดำรงชีวิตมากขึ้น พวกเธอมีแหล่งสนับสนุนทางจิตใจมากขึ้น พวกเธอกล้าที่จะหย่ากับผู้ที่ทำร้ายตนและสามารถเลี้ยงตนเองได้ อัตราการหย่าร้างในประเทศไทยจึงสูงขึ้นเรื่อยๆ และผู้หญิงสามารถแต่งงานใหม่ได้บ่อยครั้งขึ้น ผู้หญิงไทยซึ่งหย่าร้างกับสามีอาจมีความอับอายอยู่บ้างแต่ก็มีหญิงไทยจำนวนมากขึ้นที่ตั้งใจอยู่เป็นโสดและเลี้ยงตนเองแทนที่จะแต่งงานและอยู่อย่างไม่มีความสุข

การสิ้นสุดการสมรสในประเทศไทย 3 วิธี ดังนี้

1. สามีหรือภรรยาเสียชีวิต
2. โดยการจดทะเบียนหย่า
3. โดยคำพิพากษาของศาล

อย่างที่กล่าวไว้ข้างต้น การหย่าในประเทศไทยมี 2 รูปแบบ คือ การหย่าโดยความยินยอมของทั้งสองฝ่ายซึ่งจะสิ้นสุดที่อำเภอ หรือการหย่าโดยได้รับคำพิพากษาจากศาล

การจดทะเบียนหย่าโดยที่ทั้งสองฝ่ายยินยอม

ถ้าคุณจดทะเบียนสมรสในประเทศไทย คุณก็จะสามารถหย่าในประเทศไทยได้โดยมาจดทะเบียนหย่าด้วยตนเองกับคู่สมรสที่อำเภอหรือสถานทูตหรือสถานกงสุลที่คุณจดทะเบียนสมรส กระบวนการนี้ง่ายและไม่ซับซ้อน เพียงกรอกและลงลายมือชื่อในแบบคำร้อง ซึ่งมักจะใช้เวลาไม่ถึง 1 ชั่วโมง เมื่อเสร็จเรียบร้อยแล้ว เอกสารจะได้รับการรับรองโดยพยานอย่างน้อย 2 คน

สิ่งที่คุณจะต้องนำไปสำนักงานเขตหรือที่ว่าการอำเภอด้วย คือ หนังสือเดินทาง (ถ้าเป็นชาวต่างชาติ) บัตรประชาชนไทยของคู่สมรส ทะเบียนสมรสตัวจริง และข้อตกลงหย่า (ถ้ามี) โดยข้อตกลงหย่าจะเป็นการตกลงระว่างคุณและคู่สมรสเกี่ยวกับเรื่องการแบ่งทรัพย์สิน การจ่ายค่าเลี้ยงดู การปกครองบุตรและสิทธิในการเยี่ยมเยียนบุตร

เมื่อคุณไปถึงสำนักงานที่คุณจะจดทะเบียนสมรสแล้วให้แจ้งเจ้าหน้าที่ว่าต้องการจะจดทะเบียนหย่า คุณจะถูกถามเกี่ยวกับข้อตกลงในการจัดการทรัพย์สิน การปกครองเลี้ยงดูบุตร เงินค่าเลี้ยงดูบุตร ค่าเลี้ยงดูแลภรรยาและเรื่องอื่นๆ ขอแนะนำว่าคุณควรจะตกลงเรื่องเหล่านี้ให้เรียบร้อยก่อนการบันทึกไว้ในทะเบียนการหย่า หลังจากที่กรอกคำร้องและลงลายมือชื่อแล้ว เจ้าหน้าที่ทะเบียนจะออกใบสำคัญการหย่าควบคู่กับทะเบียนหย่าโดยมีค่าธรรมเนียมเล็กน้อย

ฝ่ายหญิงอาจกลับไปใช้นามสกุลเดิมหลังจากที่หย่าแล้ว และกฎหมายไทยในปัจจุบันอนุญาตให้ฝ่ายหญิงเลือกใช้นามสกุลเดิมก่อนแต่งงานได้ แม้ว่าจะจดทะเบียนสมรสแล้ว

การหย่าโดยคำพิพากษาของศาล

ถ้าคู่สมรสไม่ยอมหย่าหรือทั้งสองฝ่ายไม่สามารถบรรลุข้อตกลงในการหย่าได้ คุณสามารถร้องขอหย่าต่อศาลโดยจะต้องมีเหตุฟ้องหย่า

เหตุฟ้องหย่า

กฎหมายไทยกำหนดเหตุฟ้องหย่าไว้ดังนี้

- สามีอุปการะเลี้ยงดูหรือยกย่องหญิงอื่นฉันภริยาหรือภริยาคบชู้
- สามีหรือภริยากระทำความผิดทางอาญาหรือประพฤติชั่ว ทำให้อีกฝ่ายได้รับความอับอายขายหน้าอย่างร้ายแรง ได้รับความดูถูกเกลียดชังหรือได้รับความเสียหายเกินควร

- สามีหรือภริยาทำร้ายหรือทรมานร่างกายหรือจิตใจหรือเหยียดหยามอีกฝ่ายหนึ่ง
- สามีหรือภริยาจงใจทอดทิ้งฝ่ายหนึ่งเป็นระยะเวลาเกินกว่า 1 ปี
- สามีหรือภริยาสมัครใจแยกกันอยู่เป็นระยะเวลาเกินกว่า 3 ปี
- สามีหรือภริยาฝ่ายหนึ่งหายสาบสูญไปเป็นระยะเวลาเกินกว่า 3 ปี
- สามีหรือภริยาไม่ให้ความช่วยเหลืออุปการะเลี้ยงดูอีกฝ่ายหนึ่งตามสมควร
- สามีหรือภริยาฝ่ายหนึ่งถูกประกาศว่าเป็นบุคคลวิกลจริตมาเป็นระยะเวลาเกินกว่า
  3 ปีและยากที่จะรักษาให้หายได้
- สามีหรือภริยาฝ่ายหนึ่งละเมิดข้อตกลงในความประพฤติที่ดี (กฎหมายไทย
  กำหนดให้ทั้งสองฝ่ายตั้งอยู่ในความประพฤติที่ดี และกำหนดคำจำกัดความใน
  ข้อตกลงนั้น ถ้าคู่สมรสฝ่ายหนึ่งไม่สามารถกระทำตามข้อตกลงนั้น ก็ถือว่าเป็น
  เหตุฟ้องหย่าได้)
- สามีหรือภริยาเป็นโรคติดต่ออย่างร้ายแรงอันอาจเป็นภัยแก่อีกฝ่ายหนึ่ง และโรค
  มีลักษณะเรื้อรังยากที่จะรักษาให้หายได้
- สามีหรือภริยามีปัญหาทางร่างกายซึ่งทำให้ไม่สามารถร่วมประเวณีได้

การฟ้องหย่าในศาลเป็นขั้นตอนที่ค่อนข้างซับซ้อน ดังนั้น คุณอาจจะต้องว่าจ้าง
ทนายความให้ดำเนินเรื่องหย่าในศาลและเป็นตัวแทนของคุณในกรณีที่คุณอาศัยอยู่นอก
ประเทศไทยได้ ในกรณีนี้ คุณจะต้องมอบอำนาจให้แก่ทนายความ

คุณจะต้องบอกความจริงกับทนายความเกี่ยวกับเรื่องการแต่งงาน บุตร (ถ้ามี)
ทรัพย์สิน วันเวลาที่เกี่ยวข้องและสถานการณ์ของการสมรส ในกรณีที่คุณมีสัญญาก่อน
สมรส สัญญานั้นจะต้องถูกตรวจสอบและพิจารณาในศาลไทย ทรัพย์สินที่ได้มาระหว่าง
การแต่งงานจะต้องถูกแบ่งครึ่งให้กับแต่ละฝ่าย ถ้าคุณมีทรัพย์สินจำนวนมากในประเทศถิ่น
ของคุณและทำเรื่องหย่าในประเทศไทย การแบ่งทรัพย์สินเหล่านั้นจะเป็นเรื่องยุ่งยากมาก
และมักจะมีข้อขัดแย้งทางกฎหมายและกฎระเบียบอื่นๆที่อยู่ภายนอกขอบเขตของหนังสือ
เล่มนี้ คุณควรขอความช่วยเหลือจากทนายความในประเทศไทยและในประเทศของคุณเพื่อ
วิเคราะห์ข้อพิพาทนี้ นอกจากนี้ ทั้งสองฝ่ายยังจะต้องรับผิดชอบหนี้สินที่เกิดขึ้นทั้งหมดใน
ระหว่างการสมรสอีกด้วย

ถ้าทั้งสองฝ่ายไม่สามารถตกลงกันได้ในเรื่องการแบ่งทรัพย์สิน การปกครองและ
เลี้ยงดูบุตรและเรื่องอื่นๆ ศาลจะเป็นผู้ตัดสินให้ การหย่านั้นต้องเสียค่าใช้จ่ายเป็นอย่างมาก
โดยทั่วไปค่าทนายความจะเริ่มต้นที่ประมาณ 30,000 บาท และอาจเกินกว่า 100,000 บาท
ขึ้นอยู่กับความยุ่งยากซับซ้อนของคดีนั้นๆ และจะใช้เวลา 2 เดือนหรือมากกว่าในการที่จะ
ได้รับคำสั่งให้หย่าจากศาล   ทนายความจะขอให้คุณมาแสดงตัวต่อศาลในการพิจารณาคดี
เบื้องต้น และคุณอาจจะต้องมาศาลอีก ถ้าศาลมีคำสั่งมา

คำสั่งศาลจะถือเป็นการสิ้นสุดการสมรส   โดยทั้งสองฝ่ายไม่จำเป็นต้องจด
ทะเบียนหย่าอีก แต่ถ้ายังมีเงื่อนไขอื่นๆที่ต้องการจะจดทะเบียนหย่าไว้เป็นหลักฐาน ทั้งสอง
ฝ่ายก็สามารถทำได้โดยมีเจ้าหน้าที่ทะเบียนเป็นผู้ดำเนินการเพื่อให้การหย่าเสร็จสมบูรณ์

ในกรณีที่คุณจดทะเบียนสมรสในประเทศของคุณ การหย่าก็จะต้องดำเนินการที่
นั่น   และกระทำการตามกฎหมายของประเทศนั้น   โดยคุณอาจจะต้องการปรึกษากับ
ทนายความในประเทศของคุณเพื่อช่วยดำเนินขั้นตอนที่จำเป็นในการหย่าร้าง

การทำพินัยกรรม

พินัยกรรม คือ คำสั่งสุดท้ายของบุคคลที่แสดงเจตนายกทรัพย์สินของตนให้แก่
ผู้อื่น หรือวางข้อกำหนดเกี่ยวกับทรัพย์สินของตนอันจะมีผลบังคับเมื่อตนได้ตายไปแล้ว ใน
ประเทศไทย การจัดการทรัพย์สินของผู้ที่เสียชีวิตไปแล้ว และการพิสูจน์พินัยกรรมในศาล
อยู่ภายใต้การควบคุมดูแลของประมวลกฎหมายแพ่งและพาณิชย์ โดยคุณควรจะมีพินัยกรรม
เพื่อให้มั่นใจว่า ทรัพย์สินของคุณถูกแบ่งสรรปันส่วนไปในแบบที่คุณต้องการ   และเพื่อ
หลีกเลี่ยงปัญหาและข้อโต้แย้งระหว่างทายาทของคุณ ภายหลังจากที่คุณเสียชีวิตไปแล้ว
พินัยกรรมอาจจะระบุว่า ควรจะดำเนินการอย่างไรกับร่างกายของคุณหลังจากที่
คุณเสียชีวิตแล้ว   คุณต้องการงานศพแบบใดและจะแจ้งข่าวการตายของคุณแก่ใครบ้าง
นอกจากนี้ พินัยกรรมอาจจะระบุว่าควรจะให้ทำอย่างไรในกรณีที่คุณบาดเจ็บสาหัสและอยู่
ในสภาพไม่รู้สึกตัวหรือเจ็บป่วย รวมถึงการระบุเจตนารมณ์อื่นๆของคุณ

คุณอาจจะระบุผู้จัดการมรดกและระบุว่าใครจะเป็นผู้ดูแลเด็กและผู้เยาว์ไว้ใน
พินัยกรรม ในขณะที่ศาลไทยไม่ได้กำหนดขอบเขตสำหรับเรื่องเหล่านี้ จึงเป็นโอกาสดีที่
จะแจ้งให้ศาลและทายาททราบถึงความต้องการและความตั้งใจของคุณ ถ้าไม่มีคำสั่งเหล่านี้
ผู้อื่นก็จะตัดสินใจแทนหลังจากการเสียชีวิตของคุณ โดยที่ความตั้งใจของคุณก็จะสูญเปล่า

เมื่อคุณทำพินัยกรรม คุณควรจะทบทวนพินัยกรรมของคุณเป็นระยะๆ เพื่อให้
แน่ใจว่า พินัยกรรมยังคงเป็นไปตามความต้องการของคุณ โดยพินัยกรรมสามารถแก้ไขใหม่
ได้ตลอดเวลาก่อนที่ผู้ทำพินัยกรรมจะเสียชีวิต คุณสมบัติของผู้ทำพินัยกรรม คือ ต้องมีอายุ
15 ปีบริบูรณ์ขึ้นไป โดยต้องไม่เป็นบุคคลที่ศาลสั่งให้เป็นผู้ไร้ความสามารถ แม้ว่า
พินัยกรรมจะยังคงมีผลตามกฎหมายไทยภายหลังการแต่งงานหรือหย่าร้าง แต่ก็ควรที่จะ
ทบทวนและแก้ไขพินัยกรรมเท่าที่จำเป็นเพื่อให้สอดคล้องกับสภาพการณ์ที่เปลี่ยนแปลงไป

โดยทั่วไป พินัยกรรมจะต้องเป็นการเขียนด้วยมือ และมีผลบังคับใช้หลังจากที่
ผู้ทำพินัยกรรมลงลายมือชื่อต่อหน้าพยาน 2 คน ซึ่งมีอายุมากกว่า 20 ปี และต้องไม่เป็น
บุคคลวิกลจริตหรือบุคคลที่ศาลได้สั่งให้เป็นผู้เสมือนไร้ความสามารถ พินัยกรรมแบบทำ
ด้วยวาจาจะสามารถทำขึ้นได้ในระหว่างสงคราม และในกรณีพิเศษเท่านั้น

ชาวต่างชาติก็สามารถจะมีพินัยกรรมที่เขียนด้วยลายมือได้เช่นกัน โดยสามารถทำ
เป็นเอกสารง่ายๆเป็นภาษาไทยหรือภาษาของคุณ หรือทั้งสองภาษาก็ได้

พินัยกรรมที่ได้รับการรับรองว่าเป็นพินัยกรรมจริงที่ทำขึ้นนอกประเทศไทย
สามารถมีผลบังคับใช้ในศาลไทยเช่นกัน แต่จะต้องแปลเป็นภาษาไทยเสียก่อน คุณอาจจะทำ
พินัยกรรมเพื่อแบ่งทรัพย์สินในแต่ละประเทศที่คุณมีทรัพย์สินอยู่ โดยพินัยกรรมแต่ละฉบับ
จะต้องระบุถึงทรัพย์สินที่คุณเป็นเจ้าของในประเทศนั้นเท่านั้น

ในประเทศไทย ไม่มีภาษีมรดกหรือภาษีมรณกรรม อย่างไรก็ตาม ถ้าที่ดินหรือสิ่ง
ปลูกสร้าง และทรัพย์สินถูกโอนไปให้ผู้รับผลประโยชน์ กรมที่ดินก็จะเป็นผู้เรียกเก็บ
ค่าธรรมเนียมในการโอน

งานศพของคุณจะถูกดำเนินการ โดยผู้ที่คุณระบุให้เป็นผู้จัดการมรดกใน
พินัยกรรมของคุณ หรือโดยผู้ที่คุณหรือครอบครัวของคุณกำหนดเอาไว้ก่อน

ถึงแม้ว่าการทำพินัยกรรมจะมีกระบวนการง่ายๆ เราก็ขอแนะนำให้คุณใช้
ทนายความเพื่อช่วยในการร่างและดำเนินการพินัยกรรมของคุณให้ถูกต้องตามกฎหมายไทย
เมื่อทำพินัยกรรมเสร็จเรียบร้อยแล้ว ควรเก็บรักษาไว้ในที่ปลอดภัยโดยคุณจะเก็บไว้เอง เก็บ

ไว้กับผู้ที่คุณไว้วางใจนอกประเทศไทย   เก็บไว้กับทนายความหรือเก็บไว้ในตู้นิรภัยของ
ธนาคาร   โดยที่คุณต้องแจ้งให้บุคคลที่เหมาะสมทราบว่าคุณมีพินัยกรรมและพินัยกรรมถูก
เก็บไว้ที่ใด ถ้าไม่มีใครทราบว่าคุณมีพินัยกรรม ก็ไม่มีผู้ใดสามารถทำตามความต้องการของ
คุณได้

แบบของพินัยกรรม

พินัยกรรมเขียนเองทั้งฉบับ

ผู้ทำพินัยกรรมต้องเขียนข้อความทั้งหมดด้วยตนเอง   ลงวัน   เดือน   ปีที่ทำ
พินัยกรรม และลงลายมือชื่อไว้ โดยจะมีลายพิมพ์นิ้วมือหรือไม่มีก็ได้พินัยกรรมเขียนเองทั้ง
ฉบับนี้ เป็นการรับรองว่าเป็นของจริงในตัวมันเอง ดังนั้น จึงไม่จำเป็นต้องมีพยานรับรอง
อย่างไรก็ตาม ก็ขอแนะนำให้มีพยานรับรองเอาไว้

พินัยกรรมแบบธรรมดา

พินัยกรรมแบบนี้ จะอยู่ในรูปของจดหมาย ผู้ทำจะใช้เขียนหรือพิมพ์เองหรือจะ
ให้คนอื่นเขียนหรือพิมพ์แทนก็ได้ โดยลงวัน เดือน ปี ในขณะที่ทำพินัยกรรมนั้น และผู้ทำ
พินัยกรรมต้องเซ็นชื่อต่อหน้าพยานอย่างน้อย 2 คนพร้อมกัน ถ้าจะพิมพ์ลายนิ้วมือต้องมี
พยานรับรองลายพิมพ์นิ้วมือเพิ่มต่างหากจากพยานเดิมอีก 2 คน

พินัยกรรมแบบเอกสารฝ่ายเมือง

ผู้ทำพินัยกรรมต้องไปติดต่อสำนักงานเขตหรือที่ว่าการอำเภอแห่งใดก็ได้   และ
ต้องแจ้งข้อความที่ประสงค์จะให้ปรากฏในพินัยกรรมให้ผู้อำนวยการเขตหรือนายอำเภอ
และต่อหน้าพยานอีกอย่างน้อย 2 คน พร้อมกัน เมื่อผู้อำนวยการเขตหรือนายอำเภอแล้วแต่
กรณีจดข้อความตามที่ผู้ทำพินัยกรรมแจ้งให้ทราบ   และอ่านให้ผู้ทำพินัยกรรมฟังแล้วผู้ทำ
พินัยกรรมและพยานต้องลงลายมือชื่อไว้ จากนั้น ผู้อำนวยการเขตหรือนายอำเภอต้องลง
ลายมือชื่อและวัน เดือน ปีที่ลงไว้ด้วยซึ่งแสดงว่า พินัยกรรมได้ทำขึ้นถูกต้องตามขั้นตอน
ดังกล่าว แล้ว ประทับตราตำแหน่งไว้เป็นสำคัญ ผู้ทำพินัยกรรมอาจจะลงลายมือชื่อขอรับ
พินัยกรรมที่ทำขึ้นนั้นในสมุดทะเบียนหรือจะมอบไว้กับผู้อำนวยการเขตหรือนายอำเภอไว้

พินัยกรรมแบบเอกสารลับ

ผู้ทำพินัยกรรมจะทำพินัยกรรมโดยเขียนเองทั้งฉบับ หรือให้ผู้อื่นเขียนให้ก็ได้ แต่ต้องลงลายมือชื่อในพินัยกรรมแล้วปิดผนึก   โดยจะต้องมีการลงลายมือชื่อผู้ทำพินัยกรรมตามรอยผนึกนั้น   จากนั้น   ผู้ทำพินัยกรรมนำพินัยกรรมที่ผนึกแล้วนั้นไปแสดงต่อผู้อำนวยการเขต ณ สำนักงานเขตหรือนายอำเภอ ณ ที่ว่า การอำเภอแห่งใดก็ได้ พร้อมด้วยพยานอย่างน้อย 2 คน และให้ถ้อยคำต่อบุคคลทั้งหมดว่าเป็นพินัยกรรมของตน ผู้อำนวยการเขตหรือนายอำเภอจะจดถ้อยคำของผู้ทำพินัยกรรม วัน เดือน ปี ที่นำมาแสดงไว้บนซองและประทับตราประจำตำแหน่งของผู้อำนวยการเขตหรือนายอำเภอ จากนั้น ผู้ทำพินัยกรรมและพยานจะต้องลงลายมือชื่อบนซองนั้น   โดยพินัยกรรมแบบนี้จะฝากไว้ที่สำนักงานเขตหรือที่ว่าการอำเภอที่ทำพินัยกรรมหรือรับไปก็ได้ เช่นเดียวกับพินัยกรรมแบบเอกสาร

พินัยกรรมแบบทำด้วยวาจา (กรณีพิเศษ)

พินัยกรรมแบบนี้สามารถทำได้ก็ต่อเมื่อมีเหตุการณ์พิเศษที่ทำให้ไม่สามารถทำพินัยกรรมแบบอื่นได้   เช่น   ตกอยู่ในอันตรายใกล้ความตายหรือเวลามีโรคระบาดหรือสงคราม โดยผู้ทำพินัยกรรมต้องแสดงเจตนากำหนดข้อพินัยกรรมต่อหน้าพยานอย่างน้อย 2 คน ซึ่งอยู่พร้อมกัน ณ ที่นั้น พยานทั้งสองคนนั้นจะต้องไปแสดงตนต่อผู้อำนวยการเขตหรือนายอำเภอโดยไม่ชักช้า   และแจ้งข้อความที่ผู้ทำพินัยกรรมได้สั่งไว้ด้วยวาจานั้นทั้งต้องแจ้งวัน เดือน ปี สถานที่ทำพินัยกรรมและเหตุการณ์พิเศษนั้นไว้ด้วย เมื่อผู้อำนวยการเขตหรือนายอำเภอจดข้อความที่พยานแจ้ง แล้วพยานทั้งสองต้องลงลายมือชื่อไว้ ถ้าพยานจะพิมพ์นิ้วมือต้องมีพยานรับรองลงลายมือพิมพ์นิ้วมือเพิ่มอีก 2 คน

ถ้าคุณวางแผนที่จะทำพินัยกรรมที่สำนักงานเขตหรือที่ว่าการอำเภอ   หลักฐานที่ต้องนำไปแสดง ได้แก่ เอกสารสิทธิต่างๆเกี่ยวกับทรัพย์สิน โฉนด (ถ้ามี) บัตรประจำตัวประชาชน ทะเบียนบ้าน หนังสือเดินทาง ในกรณีที่คุณเป็นชาวต่างชาติ โดยมีค่าธรรมเนียมในการจัดทำพินัยกรรมเล็กน้อย

เมื่อไม่มีพินัยกรรมหรือพินัยกรรมไม่มีผลตามกฎหมาย

ในกรณีที่คุณเสียชีวิตโดยไม่มีพินัยกรรม หรือไม่มีพินัยกรรมที่มีผลตามกฎหมาย หรือพินัยกรรมครอบคลุมเฉพาะทรัพย์สินบางส่วนของคุณ ประมวลกฎหมายแพ่งและ พาณิชย์ระบุไว้ว่า ทรัพย์สินจะถูกแบ่งสรรกันในหมู่ทายาทของคุณ วิธีในการแบ่งสรรนี้ อาจจะแตกต่างกันจากกฎหมายในประเทศของคุณ และอาจจะไม่ตรงตามความต้องการของ คุณ จึงเป็นเหตุผลที่เราแนะนำให้คุณทำพินัยกรรม

ทายาทสามารถแบ่งออกเป็น 2 ประเภท คือ โดยสืบสายโลหิต และโดยการสมรส

ทายาทโดยสืบสายโลหิตนี้ สามารถจำแนกออกได้เป็น 6 ลำดับ คือ

1. ผู้สืบสันดาน หมายถึง ผู้สืบสายโลหิตโดยตรงลงมาของเจ้ามรดก ได้แก่ บุตร หลาน เหลน รวมถึงบุตรนอกกฎหมายที่บิดารับรองแล้ว และบุตรบุญธรรมด้วย
2. บิดามารดา
3. พี่น้องร่วมบิดา มารดาเดียวกัน
4. พี่น้องร่วมบิดา หรือร่วมมารดาเดียวกัน
5. ปู่ ย่า ตา ยาย
6. ลุง ป้า น้า อา

ทายาททั้ง 6 ลำดับนี้ ไม่ใช่ว่าจะมีสิทธิรับมรดกพร้อมกันทั้ง 6 ลำดับ ในแต่ละ ลำดับต่างก็จะมีสิทธิในการรับมรดกก่อนและหลังกันตามลำดับที่กฎหมายระบุไว้ เว้นแต่ ทายาทลำดับที่ 1 คือผู้สืบสันดาน และทายาทลำดับที่ 2 คือ บิดา มารดา เท่านั้น ที่มีสิทธิ ได้รับมรดกด้วยกัน คือ ไม่ตัดสิทธิในการรับมรดกซึ่งกันและกัน ดังนั้นหากมีทายาทใน ลำดับต้น ทายาทในลำดับต่อไปก็ไม่มีสิทธิที่จะรับมรดก

ทายาทโดยธรรมที่เป็นคู่สมรส หมายถึง ทายาทโดยธรรมที่เป็นคู่สมรสของเจ้า มรดก ซึ่งอาจเป็นสามีหรือภรรยาของเจ้ามรดก แต่ต้องเป็นสามีภรรยากันโดยชอบด้วย กฎหมาย ถ้าเป็นสามีภรรยาที่ร้างกันหรือแยกกันอยู่โดยที่ไม่ได้มีการหย่าขาดจากกันตาม กฎหมายก็ถือว่าเป็นทายาทที่มีสิทธิรับมรดกซึ่งกันและกันอยู่ ซึ่งคู่สมรสนี้กฎหมายถือว่า สิทธิในการรับมรดกถือเสมือนเป็นทายาทลำดับต้น หรือลำดับที่ 1 และ 2

ในกรณีที่คู่สมรสยังมีชีวิตอยู่ ประมวลกฎหมายแพ่งและพาณิชย์กำหนดการแบ่ง
ทรัพย์สินไว้ดังนี้

- ถ้าคู่สมรส และบุตรยังมีชีวิตอยู่ คู่สมรสจะได้รับมรดกร้อยละ 50 และบุตร
  ได้รับร้อยละ 50 โดยแบ่งสรรให้เท่าๆ กันระหว่างบุตรหรือหลาน (ในกรณีที่
  ไม่มีบุตรที่ยังมีชีวิตอยู่)
- ถ้าบุตร และบิดามารดาของคุณยังมีชีวิตอยู่ บุตรจะได้รับมรดกร้อยละ 50
  และบิดามารดาได้รับร้อยละ 50 เช่นกัน
- ถ้ามีบุตรที่ยังมีชีวิตอยู่ แต่ไม่มีคู่สมรสหรือไม่มีบิดามารดา บุตรจะได้รับ
  ทรัพย์สินทั้งหมดของคุณ
- ถ้าคู่สมรส และบิดามารดาของคุณยังมีชีวิตอยู่ คู่สมรสจะได้รับมรดกร้อยละ
  50 และบิดามารดาได้รับร้อยละ 50 (โดยอาจจะแตกต่างไป ในกรณีที่บิดา
  มารดาของคุณไม่ใช่ชาวไทย และอาศัยอยู่ภายนอกประเทศไทย ซึ่งนี่ก็เป็น
  เหตุผลอีกข้อหนึ่งที่คุณควรจะทำพินัยกรรม)
- ถ้าคู่สมรส และพี่น้องร่วมบิดามารดาเดียวกันของคุณยังมีชีวิตอยู่ คู่สมรสจะ
  ได้รับมรดกร้อยละ 50 และพี่น้องร่วมบิดามารดาเดียวกันได้รับร้อยละ 50
- ถ้าคู่สมรส และทายาทในลำดับที่ 4, 5, หรือ 6 ข้างต้นยังมีชีวิตอยู่ คู่สมรสจะ
  ได้รับมรดก 2 ใน 3 ของทรัพย์สินทั้งหมด และทายาทในลำดับที่ 4, 5, หรือ
  6 ข้างต้น ได้รับ 1 ใน 3 ที่เหลือ โดยแบ่งสรรให้เท่าๆ กัน
- ถ้าทายาทโดยสืบสายโลหิตไม่มีชีวิตอยู่เลย คู่สมรสที่ยังมีชีวิตอยู่จะได้รับ
  มรดกทั้งหมด

ในกรณีที่ไม่มีคู่สมรสที่ยังมีชีวิตอยู่ ทรัพย์สินทั้งหมดจะถูกแบ่งสรร ดังนี้

ถ้าคุณเสียชีวิต โดยไม่มีคู่สมรสที่ยังมีชีวิตอยู่ ทายาทโดยสืบสายโลหิตจะได้รับ
มรดกทั้งหมดโดยแบ่งออกเป็นแต่ละส่วนเท่าๆ กัน ยกตัวอย่างเช่น ถ้าคุณเสียชีวิตโดยไม่มีคู่
สมรส แต่มีบุตร (และ/หรือบิดามารดา) ที่ยังมีชีวิตอยู่ จะได้รับทรัพย์สินทั้งหมดโดยแบ่ง
ออกเป็นแต่ละส่วนเท่าๆ กัน แต่ถ้าคุณเสียชีวิตโดยไม่มีคู่สมรสหรือบุตร แต่มีบิดามารดาที่
ยังมีชีวิตอยู่ บิดามารดาจะได้รับทรัพย์สินทั้งหมดโดยแบ่งเท่าๆ กัน

ในกรณีที่ไม่มีทายาท หรือไม่มีผู้ที่ถูกระบุให้ได้รับทรัพย์สิน ทรัพย์สินนั้นก็จะตก
เป็นของรัฐ หรือตกทอดแก่แผ่นดิน

ในประเทศไทย เป็นเรื่องธรรมดาที่จะมีผู้จัดการมรดก ซึ่งเป็นบุคคลที่ผู้ทำ
พินัยกรรม หรือศาลตั้งขึ้นให้มีสิทธิและหน้าที่ที่จะทำเพื่อให้เป็นไปตามพินัยกรรม และเพื่อ
จัดการมรดก รวบรวมทรัพย์มรดกและนำมาแบ่งปันแก่ทายาทผู้มีสิทธิ โดยเมื่อมีพินัยกรรม
พินัยกรรมก็จะถูกนำแสดงต่อศาลเพื่อพิจารณา ศาลก็จะตัดสินว่า พินัยกรรมมีผลบังคับใช้
และระบุความตั้งใจของผู้เสียชีวิต พินัยกรรมอาจจะถูกนำแสดงต่อศาลโดยคู่สมรสหรือ
สมาชิกในครอบครัว ทนายความของผู้เสียชีวิต ผู้ที่ถูกระบุว่าเป็นผู้จัดการมรดกใน
พินัยกรรมหรือผู้อื่นซึ่งมีผลประโยชน์ในพินัยกรรมก็ได้ เมื่อพินัยกรรมได้รับอนุญาตอย่าง
ถูกต้องตามกฎหมายโดยศาลแล้ว ศาลก็จะออกหนังสือบังคับให้เป็นไปตามพินัยกรรม มอบ
อำนาจให้แก่ผู้จัดการมรดกให้ดำเนินการระบุและรวบรวมทรัพย์สินของผู้เสียชีวิต และแบ่ง
สรรทรัพย์สินเหล่านั้น โดยศาลอาจจะออกคำสั่งอื่นๆที่จำเป็นอีก

ผู้จัดการมรดกนั้นจะได้รับการระบุโดยผู้ทำพินัยกรรมหรือแต่งตั้งโดยศาล โดย
ผู้จัดการมรดกจะต้องมีคุณสมบัติ ดังนี้

- มีอายุเกิน 20 ปี บริบูรณ์
- ไม่เป็นบุคคลวิกลจริตหรือบุคคลที่ศาลสั่งให้เป็นผู้เสมือนไร้ความสามารถ
- ไม่เป็นบุคคลซึ่งศาลสั่งให้เป็นบุคคลล้มละลาย

ผู้จัดการมรดกโดยคำสั่งศาล จะต้องเป็นบุคคลหนึ่ง ดังต่อไปนี้

1. ทายาทโดยสืบสายโลหิต และผู้รับพินัยกรรม

2. ผู้มีส่วนได้เสีย หมายถึง บุคคลผู้มีส่วนได้ส่วนเสียในทางมรดก เช่น คู่สมรสที่ไม่ได้
   จดทะเบียนสมรสกัน

3. พนักงานอัยการ

การแต่งตั้งผู้จัดการมรดกนั้น ศาลย่อมใช้ดุลยพินิจคำนึงถึงความเหมาะสมเพื่อ
ประโยชน์แก่มรดก การที่ศาลจะแต่งตั้งผู้ใดเป็นผู้จัดการมรดกนั้นจึงไม่จำต้องได้รับความยินยอม
จากทายาททุกคน อย่างไรก็ตาม ทายาทโดยสืบสายโลหิต หรือผู้ที่ถูกระบุไว้ในพินัยกรรม ผู้ที่มี
ส่วนได้เสีย เช่น คู่สมรสที่ไม่ได้จดทะเบียนสมรสกัน หรือพนักงานอัยการอาจจะคัดค้านการ
แต่งตั้งผู้จัดการมรดกได้ ในการคัดค้านคำร้องขอตั้งผู้จัดการมรดก ผู้ร้องคัดค้านต้องยื่นคำร้อง
ขอต่อศาลที่ผู้ตายมีภูมิลำเนาอยู่ในขณะที่ถึงแก่ความตาย การจะร้องขอให้ศาลสั่งถอนผู้จัดการมรดก
ต้องยื่นร้องขอก่อนที่การแบ่งปันมรดกจะเสร็จสิ้นลง

การเสียชีวิตในประเทศไทย

ทุกคนเกิดมาแล้วต้องตาย ไม่มีใครอยากได้ยินเรื่องนี้ แต่ก็เป็นเรื่องที่ทุกคนหนีไม่
พ้น จึงเป็นเรื่องสำคัญที่คุณควรจะรู้ถึงผลที่ตามมา ถ้าคุณเสียชีวิตขณะที่อยู่ในประเทศไทย

ชาวต่างชาติอาจจะเสียชีวิตในประเทศไทยไม่ว่าโดยอุบัติเหตุหรือเจ็บป่วย ซึ่งก็
ไม่แตกต่างกันกับที่อื่นๆ ในส่วนนี้ ผู้เขียนจะอธิบายกระบวนการและระเบียบแบบแผนใน
การจัดการเกี่ยวกับผู้ที่เสียชีวิตในประเทศไทย

ในประเทศไทย มี 2 คำจำกัดความเกี่ยวกับการเสียชีวิต คือ "เสียชีวิตตาม
ธรรมชาติ" จากความชราหรือความเจ็บป่วย และ "เสียชีวิตโดยผิดธรรมชาติ" โดยอุบัติเหตุ
ฆาตกรรมหรือภัยธรรมชาติ โดยในประเทศไทย การเสียชีวิตทั้งของชาวต่างชาติและชาว
ไทย จะต้องรายงานไปยังตำรวจหรือสำนักงานเขตหรือที่การอำเภอภายใน 24 ชั่วโมง ไม่
ว่าจะเป็นวันอาทิตย์หรือวันหยุดนักขัตฤกษ์ (ถ้าสำนักงานเขตหรือที่ว่าการอำเภอปิดทำการ
สามารถรายงานการเสียชีวิตได้ที่สถานีตำรวจ)

ในกรณีที่ชาวต่างชาติเสียชีวิตในห้องเช่าหรือโรงแรม เจ้าของห้องเช่าหรือ
ผู้จัดการโรงแรม จะต้องรายงานไปยังสำนักงานเขตหรือสถานีตำรวจ พร้อมกับหนังสือ
เดินทางของผู้เสียชีวิต และมรณบัตร (ถ้ามี) จากนั้น สำนักงานเขตจะบันทึกการเสียชีวิตไว้
ในหนังสือเดินทาง

เจ้าหน้าที่เขต หรือเจ้าพนักงานตำรวจจะแจ้งไปยังสถานทูตของชาวต่างชาติที่
เสียชีวิตภายใน 7 วัน และสถานทูตก็จะแจ้งไปยังเครือญาติโดยเร็วที่สุด การเสียชีวิตทุก

รูปแบบ ไม่ว่าจะเป็นตามธรรมชาติ อุบัติเหตุหรืออาชญากรรม ต้องมีรายงานบันทึกจาก
ตำรวจ ซึ่งจะต้องมาจากการสอบสวนของตำรวจในที่เกิดเหตุ พร้อมกับทีมพิสูจน์หลักฐาน
เพื่อระบุสาเหตุการเสียชีวิต และศพจะถูกส่งไปยังโรงพยาบาล หรือสำนักงานชันสูตรศพ ถ้า
บุคคลนั้นเสียชีวิตที่โรงพยาบาล แพทย์ของโรงพยาบาลนั้นจะออกมรณบัตรให้ จากนั้น
ตำรวจก็จะออกรายงานบันทึกให้ ในกรณีที่สาเหตุการเสียชีวิตเป็นไปโดยปกติ ไม่ซับซ้อน
ศพก็จะถูกส่งกลับไปยังครอบครัวภายใน 2-3 วัน พร้อมกับมรณบัตรซึ่งออกโดยแพทย์ที่
ระบุสาเหตุการเสียชีวิต ค่าใช้จ่ายทางการแพทย์จะต้องถูกชำระก่อนที่จะนำศพออกมา มรณ
บัตรอีกใบหนึ่งจะออกโดยสำนักงานเขตหรือที่ว่ากาอำเภอเมื่อมีการรับรองการเสียชีวิตแล้ว

ในกรณีที่เป็นการเสียชีวิตเป็นแบบผิดวิสัย มีเงื่อนงำหรือสงสัยว่ามาจาก
อาชญากรรม จะมีการชันสูตรศพและจะมีความล่าช้าในการส่งศพคืน มรณบัตรอาจจะถูก
ออกพร้อมกับรายงานการตรวจสอบสาเหตุการตายแบบผิดปกติจากโรงพยาบาลหรือ
หน่วยงานชันสูตรศพ

ในกรณีที่ชาวต่างชาติที่เสียชีวิตมีประกันชีวิต ญาติจะต้องติดต่อบริษัทประกัน
และมอบสำเนาของรายงานจากโรงพยาบาล พร้อมกับมรณบัตรไทย โดยมรณบัตรและ
เอกสารที่เกี่ยวข้องจะต้องแปลเป็นภาษาของประเทศที่บริษัทประกันตั้งอยู่ และถ้า
ชาวต่างชาติมีประกันชีวิตที่มีวงเงินประกันเป็นจำนวนมาก บริษัทประกันก็อาจจะส่งนักสืบ
มาตรวจสอบสาเหตุการเสียชีวิต

บริษัทประกันภัยส่วนใหญ่ จะสามารถจัดการเกี่ยวกับการส่งศพกลับประเทศโดย
ผ่านบริษัทจัดงานศพระหว่างประเทศได้ แต่ก็ควรจะตรวจสอบกับบริษัทประกันภัยเสียก่อน
ถ้าผู้เสียชีวิตไม่มีประกันชีวิต ญาติก็ควรจะติดต่อกับสถานทูตซึ่งจะสามารถช่วยให้
คำแนะนำเกี่ยวกับบริษัทจัดงานศพระหว่างประเทศได้ ในการขนย้ายศพ ศพจะต้องได้รับ
การเก็บรักษาไว้ในหีบศพพิเศษ เจ้าหน้าที่บริษัทจัดงานศพระหว่างประเทศจะเป็นผู้จัดการ
เรื่องเหล่านี้ให้ โดยบริษัทเหล่านี้จะมีหีบศพแบบพิเศษซึ่งได้รับอนุญาตจากกรมศุลกากรของ
ประเทศไทยเช่นเดียวกับกรมศุลกากรของประเทศอื่นๆ กระบวนการนี้อาจจะใช้เวลาถึง 10
วัน และจะต้องมีเอกสารประกอบ ดังนี้

- มรณบัตร จากสำนักงานเขตหรือที่ว่าการอำเภอ
- ใบรับรองการเสียชีวิตของแพทย์จากโรงพยาบาลหรือหน่วยงานชันสูตรศพ
- ใบรับรองการแต่งศพจากบริษัทจัดงานศพ
- ใบอนุญาตการเคลื่อนย้ายศพ จากบริษัทจัดงานศพระหว่างประเทศ หรือสถานทูตที่เกี่ยวข้อง
- จดหมายปะหน้าจากสถานทูตถึงกรมศุลกากร (ถ้าจำเป็น)

มรณบัตรและใบรับรองการเสียชีวิตจากแพทย์ควรจะได้รับการแปลเป็นภาษาทางการของประเทศที่ศพจะถูกส่งไป เพื่อเป็นการร่นกระบวนการให้รวดเร็วขึ้น

เนื่องจากมาตรการรักษาความปลอดภัยของสนามบินที่เข้มงวดขึ้น สายการบินหลายสายไม่อนุญาตให้นำหีบศพและศพขึ้นเครื่องบิน ดังนั้นควรจะตรวจสอบกับสายการบินก่อนว่า อนุญาตให้นำหีบศพกลับไปที่ประเทศของคุณหรือไม่

ถ้าคุณต้องการความสะดวกควรใช้บริการของบริษัทจัดงานศพระหว่างประเทศ บริษัทเหล่านี้สามารถจัดการงานเอกสารและงานศพทั้งหมด ให้เป็นไปตามศาสนาและความประสงค์ของผู้เสียชีวิตได้ โดยครอบครัวสามารถเลือกได้ว่าจะปลงศพในประเทศไทยหรือจะส่งศพกลับไปยังประเทศถิ่นกำเนิด

สำหรับรายละเอียดเพิ่มเติม คุณสามารถติดต่อบริษัทจัดงานศพระหว่างประเทศ 2 บริษัทที่ที่ตั้งอยู่ในกรุงเทพมหานคร บริษัทเหล่านี้มีเจ้าหน้าที่ที่สามารถพูดได้หลายภาษาและยังให้บริการสนับสนุนผู้ที่สูญเสียอีกด้วย คุณสามารถหารายละเอียดบริการเพิ่มเติมได้ในอินเตอร์เน็ต www.funeralrepatriation.com หรือที่

John Allison/Monkhouse
เพรสซิเด้นพาร์ค พาร์ควิวทาวเวอร์
99/243 (30B) ไพน์ทาวเวอร์ ซอยสุขุมวิท 24
คลองตัน เขตคลองเตย กรุงเทพฯ 10110
โทรศัพท์ 0-2382-5345 โทรสาร 0-2262-9133

Kang Hay Sua Chun Foundation Funeral Services
732/2 ถนนเจริญกรุง สัมพันธวงศ์ กรุงเทพฯ 10110
โทรศัพท์ 0-2225-9495

    คุณควรแจ้งการเสียชีวิตของผู้ที่คุณรักให้ผู้อื่นทราบ เช่น บุคคลในอีเมล์ของผู้เสียชีวิต จากนั้นก็แจ้งไปยังสถานที่ทำงาน ธนาคาร สำนักงานประกันสังคม หน่วยงานรัฐบาลต่างๆ บริษัทบัตรเครดิต เจ้าของที่ดิน หน่วยงานให้บริการสาธารณูปโภค ทนายความ แพทย์ ทันตแพทย์ สมาคม โบสถ์หรือวัด โรงเรียนและที่อื่นๆที่ผู้เสียชีวิตเกี่ยวข้องด้วย

    ถ้าคุณมีพินัยกรรม คุณสามารถแจ้งความประสงค์เกี่ยวกับการจัดงานศพของคุณไว้ในพินัยกรรมได้ ถ้าผู้เสียชีวิตหรือครอบครัวให้จัดงานศพในประเทศไทย ก็อาจจะเป็นงานศพตามศาสนาพุทธ ซึ่งจะมีพระสงฆ์มาสวดศพในตอนค่ำและก่อนการเผาศพในวันรุ่งขึ้น การฝังศพจะไม่ค่อยนิยมในประเทศไทย เนื่องจากมีค่าใช้จ่ายสูงและมีกระบวนการยืดยาวเพื่อนของผู้เสียชีวิตชาวต่างชาติสามารถจัดงานศพแบบไทยให้ได้โดยมีค่าใช้จ่ายไม่มากนัก และผู้ที่มาร่วมงานศพมักจะนำเงินสดมามอบให้แก่ครอบครัวผู้เสียชีวิตเพื่อช่วยเหลือค่าจัดงานศพ

    ในพินัยกรรมของคุณ คุณสามารถระบุว่าจะให้จัดการอย่างไรกับกระดูกของคุณที่เหลืออยู่หลังจากเผาศพแล้ว ครอบครัวสามารถนำอัฐิไปเก็บรักษาไว้หรือเก็บไว้ในเจดีย์ (สถูป) ที่อยู่ในวัด (หรือ "คอนโด" ซึ่งเป็นที่สำหรับเก็บโกศที่ให้เช่าโดยสุสานเอกชน) อัฐิสามารถนำไปโปรยในประเทศไทยหรือที่อื่นที่ผู้เสียชีวิตต้องการได้ หรือสามารถส่งกลับไปยังประเทศของผู้เสียชีวิตโดยความช่วยเหลือของบริษัทจัดงานศพระหว่างประเทศ หรือถือติดตัวไปบนเครื่องบินได้ สถานทูตโดยความร่วมมือกับผู้จัดการศพท้องถิ่นสามารถแนะนำหรือจัดการกระบวนการที่จำเป็นและงานเอกสารให้ได้

ส่วนที่ 4
การพักอาศัยอยู่ในประเทศไทย

ในส่วนนี้ จะแสดงถึงข้อมูลที่มีประโยชน์สำหรับผู้ที่พักอาศัยและทำงานอยู่ใน ประเทศไทย หรือผู้ที่ปลดเกษียณอายุอยู่ที่นี่

ประเทศไทยเป็นประเทศที่สนุกสนาน และเต็มไปด้วยสีสันมากมาย ถึงกับมีบาง คนกล่าวว่าเป็นแดนสวรรค์ การที่จะอาศัยอยู่ในประเทศไทยอย่างประสบความสำเร็จนั้น คุณควรจะศึกษาค้นคว้าและศึกษาเกี่ยวกับประเทศไทย ผู้คน วัฒนธรรม และภาษาให้มาก ที่สุด ในส่วนนี้ ผู้เขียนจะกล่าวถึงข้อมูลในการอาศัยอยู่ในประเทศไทยซึ่งอาจจะไม่ เกี่ยวข้องโดยตรงกับระบบกฎหมายมากนัก แต่จะเป็นข้อมูลที่ให้แนวความคิดสำหรับ สถานการณ์ต่างๆในการอาศัยอยู่ในประเทศไทย

การเช่าที่พัก

การเช่าที่พักในประเทศไทยนั้นถูกและง่ายกว่าการซื้ออสังหาริมทรัพย์มาก และมักจะสามารถทำได้โดยไม่มีพิธีรีตรองมากมาย อีกทั้งยังเป็นวิธีที่ง่ายที่สุดในการจัดหาสิ่งอำนวยความสะดวกให้ตัวคุณเองในประเทศไทย ผู้ที่สนใจจะหาที่อยู่อาศัยระยะยาวควรหาที่เช่าก่อนที่จะลงทุนซื้อคอนโดมิเนียมหรือบ้าน คุณอาจจะเปลี่ยนใจอยากไปอยู่ชานเมืองหรือเมืองอื่น หรือจังหวัดอื่น

การหาอพาร์ตเมนท์หรือบ้านเช่าสามารถทำได้โดยความช่วยเหลือของตัวแทนอสังหาริมทรัพย์ที่ลงโฆษณาในหนังสือพิมพ์หรือนิตยสาร อย่างไรก็ตาม ตัวแทนเหล่านี้มักจะเน้นไปที่อสังหาริมทรัพย์ที่มีราคาแพงที่ค่าเช่าราคาตั้งแต่ 30,000 บาทต่อเดือนขึ้นไปโดยปกติแล้ว เจ้าของอพาร์ตเมนท์จะเป็นผู้จ่ายค่าคอมมิชชั่นให้กับตัวแทนและค่าโฆษณาวิธีที่ดีที่สุดในการหาบ้านหรืออพาร์ตเมนท์ เพื่อนคนไทยช่วยหาในย่านที่คุณชอบ ผลดีและผลเสียต่างๆที่คุณจะต้องพิจารณาในการเช่าที่พักมีดังนี้

- การเช่าที่พักในพื้นที่ที่ชาวต่างชาติอาศัยอยู่มาก
- ค่าเช่าจะแพงกว่า
- ตัวแทนจะเป็นผู้ช่วยจัดการเรื่องเอกสารทั้งหมด
- มักจะมีสัญญาเช่าในระยะยาว (เช่น 1 ปี) หรือมีค่ามัดจำที่สูงกว่า
- การมีชาวต่างชาติอยู่รอบๆจะทำให้การติดต่อกับชาวไทยน้อยลง
- ความจำเป็นที่จะต้องพูดภาษาไทยน้อยลง
- การขนส่งสาธารณะและรถรับจ้างสะดวกกว่า
- อยู่ใกล้ย่านสถานบันเทิงยามราตรี
- สามารถหาอาหารจากประเทศของคุณได้ง่าย
- การจราจรแออัดกว่า มลพิษมากกว่า
- มีธนาคาร ร้านค้า ห้างสรรพสินค้า และความเจริญอื่นๆที่ไปมาได้สะดวก
- มีเพื่อนชาวต่างชาติของคุณอาศัยอยู่ใกล้ๆ
- อยู่ใกล้ร้านอาหารจำนวนมากซึ่งมีอาหารหลากหลายให้เลือก

- การเช่าที่พักนอกย่านใจกลางเมือง หรือในย่านชานเมือง
- ค่าเช่ามักจะสมเหตุสมผล หรือราคาถูกกว่า
- สามารถเช่าในระยะสั้นได้
- คุณอาจจะต้องให้เพื่อนคนไทยช่วยตรวจสอบเอกสารการเช่าว่ามีเงื่อนไขอย่างไรบ้าง
- สามารแจ้งย้ายออกก่อนที่จะย้ายเพียง 1 หรือ 2 เดือนเท่านั้น
- มีโอกาสที่จะติดต่อกับชาวไทยมากกว่า รวมถึงเรียนรู้ภาษาไทยและวัฒนธรรมไทยได้มากกว่า
- อยู่ไกลจากการขนส่งสาธารณะ (ยกเว้นรถประจำทาง) และสถานบันเทิงต่างๆ
- สามารถจับจ่ายซื้อของในสถานที่ที่คนไทยซื้อและใช้ชีวิตเหมือนกับคนไทย
- การจราจรไม่หนาแน่นเกินไป มลพิษจึงน้อยกว่า

ถ้าคุณมาถึงกรุงเทพและไม่อยากจะเช่าห้องในโรงแรม คุณสามารถเช่าอพาร์ตเมนท์พร้อมเฟอร์นิเจอร์ครบครันได้ หรือเช่าคอนโดมิเนียมเป็นรายเดือน (พร้อมกับเตียง โทรทัศน์ ตู้เสื้อผ้า ตู้เย็นและในบางครั้งก็มีครัวที่มีอุปกรณ์ครบ) ในราคา 20,000 – 30,000 บาท ต่อเดือน

ถ้าคุณทำงานในกรุงเทพ คุณสามารถจะเช่าไม่เพียงแค่อพาร์ตเมนท์ แต่จะสามารถเช่าบ้านทั้งหลังได้ในราคาเพียง 8,000 – 15,000 บาท ต่อเดือน โดยคุณควรจะมองหาในที่ต่างๆ รอบเมืองเพื่อเปรียบเทียบราคาก่อน และเมื่อคุณลองไปให้ห่างจากใจกลางเมืองกรุง คุณจะพบสถานที่หลายแห่งซึ่งน่าอยู่และเงียบสงบเหมือนกับอยู่ต่างจังหวัด แต่ก็ใช้ระยะเวลาเดินทางเพียง 30-40 นาทีเพื่อเข้าสู่ใจกลางเมืองโดยรถรับจ้างหรือรถยนต์ส่วนตัว และอาจจะเพียง 15 นาทีเพื่อเดินทางไปยังศูนย์การค้าที่ตั้งอยู่ย่านชานเมือง บ้านเช่าส่วนใหญ่จะไม่มีเฟอร์นิเจอร์ให้คุณ ดังนั้นคุณอาจจะต้องคิดค่าใช้จ่ายของเฟอร์นิเจอร์เอาไว้ด้วย

การเช่าที่พักในย่านที่เต็มไปด้วยชาวต่างชาติ เช่น พัทยา ภูเก็ต และเชียงใหม่จะมีราคาสูง อย่างที่กล่าวไปแล้วว่า ย่านที่อยู่นอกเมืองจะมีราคาถูกกว่ามาก โดยคุณสามารถเช่าบ้านได้ในราคาเพียง 4,000 – 8,000 บาท ในจังหวัดที่มีขนาดเล็กกว่า

อย่ารีบร้อนซื้อบ้านหรือคอนโดมิเนียมจนกว่าคุณจะพอใจกับเงื่อนไขและมาตรฐานต่างๆที่คุณตั้งไว้ และจนกว่าคุณจะมั่นใจว่าคุณต้องการใช้เวลาระยะยาวอยู่ในประเทศไทย ถ้าคุณมีคู่สมรสชาวไทยที่ต้องการจะสร้างบ้านบนที่ดินผืนหนึ่ง เราขอแนะนำให้คุณอ่าน How To Buy Land And Build A House In Thailand จัดพิมพ์โดยสำนักพิมพ์ไพบูลย์เช่นกัน ซึ่งจะประกอบด้วยรายละเอียดเกี่ยวกับการซื้อหรือเช่าที่ดิน รวมถึงวิธีการสร้างบ้านในฝันของคุณในเมืองไทย ถึงแม้ว่าการเช่าพักมักจะถูกกว่าการซื้อบ้านหรือที่ดินแต่คนไทยจะมีความภูมิใจที่ได้เป็นเจ้าของอสังหาริมทรัพย์

สำหรับชาวต่างชาติที่ต้องการเช่าที่พักในประเทศไทย เจ้าของบ้านอาจจะขอสำเนาใบอนุญาตทำงานของคุณ (ถ้ามี) หรือหนังสือรับรองการอยู่อาศัย ซึ่งออกโดยกองตรวจคนเข้าเมืองของไทย, หรือ letter of residence ที่สถานทูตของคุณรับรองและแปลเป็นภาษาไทยแล้ว นอกจากนั้น เจ้าของบ้านก็อาจจะขอสำเนาหนังสือเดินทาง และหนังสือรับรองเงินเดือน รวมถึงค่ามัดจำเท่ากับค่าเช่า 2 เดือนและค่าเช่าเดือนแรกที่ต้องจ่ายล่วงหน้าค่ามัดจำนี้ผู้เช่าควรจะได้รับคืนเมื่อย้ายออก

สัญญาเช่าควรจะทำขึ้นระหว่างผู้ให้เช่าและผู้เช่า ผู้เขียนไม่แนะนำให้คุณเช่าสถานที่ที่ไม่มีการทำสัญญา และเป็นเรื่องสำคัญมากที่จะต้องมีสัญญาเช่าที่ชัดเจนที่ทั้งสองฝ่ายจะต้องปฏิบัติตาม

ระยะเวลาของสัญญาทั่วๆไป มักจะเป็น 1 ปี แต่บ่อยครั้งที่อาจจะมีสัญญาเช่าระยะสั้น 3 เดือน สัญญาเช่าควรจะระบุระยะเวลาของการเช่า ค่าเช่า (โดยค่าเช่าจะต้องไม่เพิ่มขึ้นระหว่างระยะเวลาของสัญญา) สิ่งที่จะเกิดขึ้นถ้าฝ่ายหนึ่งไม่ทำตามสัญญา และเงื่อนไขอื่นๆ ผู้เช่าควรจะเก็บรักษาสัญญาเช่า ใบเสร็จค่าเช่า และใบเสร็จค่าใช้จ่ายทั้งหมดที่เกี่ยวกับสถานที่เช่า เพื่อเป็นหลักฐานในการจ่ายเงิน นอกจากนี้ คุณควรจะตรวจสอบว่า ผู้ให้เช่าเป็นผู้ที่มีกรรมสิทธิ์ในอสังหาริมทรัพย์นี้ และมีอำนาจที่จะให้คุณเช่าได้ ถ้าผู้ให้เช่าเป็นเพียงผู้เช่าที่ดินและให้คุณเช่าต่อ เจ้าของบ้านตัวจริงอาจจะปรากฏตัวในวันหนึ่งและขอให้คุณย้ายออกไป เนื่องจากคุณไม่ได้ทำสัญญาเช่ากับเจ้าของที่แท้จริง ถึงแม้ว่าเรื่องนี้อาจจะฟังดูไม่น่าจะเป็นไปได้ แต่เราก็เคยได้ยินเรื่องแบบนี้บ่อยครั้ง

เรื่องอื่นๆที่คุณควรทราบเกี่ยวกับการเช่าที่พักในประเทศไทย ห้ามชาวต่างชาติเช่าอสังหาริมทรัพย์เพื่อใช้ในเชิงพาณิชย์ ยกเว้นว่ามีการตกลงไว้ในสัญญาก่อน นอกจากนี้คุณไม่ควรจะให้ผู้อื่นเช่าช่วงต่อ และคุณอาจจะต้องระบุว่าจะมีผู้อยู่อาศัยในที่พักนั้นกี่คน

เจ้าของบ้านบางรายค่อนข้างเข้มงวดกับจำนวนคนที่เข้าพักอาศัย   แต่บางรายก็ไม่สนใจ
เท่าไรนัก   นอกจากนี้   มีบริษัทประกันภัยบางแห่งที่ออกกรมธรรม์ให้ผู้เช่า   แต่การซื้อ
ประกันภัยชนิดนี้ยังไม่เป็นที่นิยมในประเทศไทยและไม่มีกฎหมายบังคับ   ส่วนเรื่องภาษี
ที่ดิน เจ้าของที่ดินจะเป็นผู้รับผิดชอบ

ผู้เช่าควรชำระค่าเช่า ค่าน้ำประปา ค่าไฟฟ้า ค่าโทรศัพท์ ให้ตรงเวลา และไม่ทำ
ความเสียหายต่อทรัพย์สิน ควรแจ้งบอกเลิกสัญญาเช่าล่วงหน้าพอสมควร นอกจากนี้ คุณก็
ควรจะตรวจสอบทรัพย์สินให้ถี่ถ้วนก่อนที่จะเซ็นสัญญาเช่า ควรจะตรวจสอบการติดตั้งท่อ
น้ำและระบบไฟฟ้าก่อน

คุณเป็นชาวต่างชาติที่อยู่ในประเทศไทย คุณจะถูกมองว่าร่ำรวยกว่าคนไทยอื่นๆ
ที่อยู่รอบตัวคุณ คุณไม่ควรโอ้อวดฐานะของคุณกับเพื่อนบ้าน อย่าทิ้งเงินสดไว้ในอพาร์ต
เมนท์ของคุณ   และเก็บรักษาคอมพิวเตอร์แบบพกพาและทรัพย์สินอื่นๆให้แน่นหนา
ปลอดภัยถึงแม้จะอยู่ในอพาร์ตเมนท์ของคุณก็ตาม   เราก็เคยได้ยินอยู่บ่อยครั้งว่ามีทรัพย์สิน
ของชาวต่างชาติถูกขโมยไปจากอพาร์ตเมนท์ที่ดูเหมือนว่าจะมีการรักษาความปลอดภัย
อย่างดี

เพื่อนของผู้เขียนที่ชื่อคริส พิราซซี่ ได้เตรียมตัวอย่างของสัญญาเช่าเป็นภาษาไทย
และภาษาอังกฤษสำหรับชาวต่างชาติที่ต้องการเช่าที่พัก สัญญานี้ให้ยุติธรรมกับผู้ให้เช่าและ
ผู้เช่า ยังมีสัญญาเช่าอื่นๆที่ขายในร้านเครื่องเขียนซึ่งเป็นเฉพาะภาษาไทยและมักจะมีเนื้อหา
เอนเอียงให้เจ้าของบ้านได้เปรียบ สัญญานี้จะระบุว่าใครจะเป็นผู้รับผิดชอบในการซ่อมก๊อก
น้ำ คุณควรระบุเป็นข้อย่อยในสัญญาเช่าเพิ่มเติมเพื่อความชัดเจนและหลีกเลี่ยงข้อขัดแย้ง
ที่อาจจะเกิดขึ้นได้ ตัวอย่างสัญญาเช่านี้อยู่ในส่วนอ้างอิง คุณสามารถดาวน์โหลดได้จาก
http://slice-of-thai.com และแน่นอนคุณยังคงต้องโน้มน้าวผู้ให้เช่าให้เห็นด้วยกับการที่จะ
ใช้สัญญาฉบับนี้

เรื่องเงินๆ ทองๆ

เรื่องเงินทองเป็นเรื่องสำคัญ ไม่ว่าจะเป็นที่ใดในโลก แต่เรื่องนี้มักจะเป็นหัวข้อสนทนาอยู่เป็นประจำเมื่อคุณติดต่อกับคนไทย ไม่ว่าจะเป็นในแบบธุรกิจหรือแบบส่วนตัว ในส่วนนี้ ผู้เขียนจะเสนอข้อมูลเกี่ยวกับเรื่องเงินๆทองๆที่คุณควรจะทราบ

ข้อมูลในส่วนนี้เป็นข้อมูลที่ถูกต้องในเวลาที่ตีพิมพ์หนังสือเล่มนี้ ดังนั้น คุณควรจะตรวจสอบกับธนาคารหรือหน่วยงานที่เกี่ยวข้องเสียก่อนเพื่อความแน่ใจในขั้นตอนต่างๆ และจำนวนเงินที่ระบุในหนังสือเล่มนี้

การส่งเงินไปยังประเทศไทย

โดยปกติแล้ว หลังจากที่คุณมีความสัมพันธ์กับคนไทย ก็มักจะมีเรื่องเงินเข้ามาเกี่ยวข้อง ไม่ว่าด้วยเหตุผลใดก็ตาม คุณจะต้องมีความจำเป็นที่จะส่งเงินมาให้ใครคนหนึ่งในประเทศไทย (หรือบางครั้งต้องส่งมาให้ตัวคุณเอง) เทคโนโลยีที่ก้าวหน้าในธุรกิจการธนาคารทำให้เรื่องนี้กลายเป็นเรื่องง่าย ในส่วนนี้ เราจะกล่าวถึงการส่งเงินมายังประเทศไทยในจำนวนไม่เกิน 10,000 ดอลล่าร์เหรียญสหรัฐ ธนาคารส่วนใหญ่ในปัจจุบัน มีข้อจำกัดและการควบคุมจำนวนเงินที่สามารถส่งไปต่างประเทศ เนื่องจากปัญหาการฟอกเงินและการก่อการร้าย ธนาคารในประเทศไทยไม่มีการใช้ระบบ IBAN แต่ใช้ระบบรหัส SWIFT ในการโอนเงินระหว่างประเทศ

คุณสามารถโอนเงินมายังประเทศไทยได้โดยวิธีต่างๆต่อไปนี้

- **โดยผ่าน** Western Union ซึ่งเป็นเครือข่ายการโอนเงินที่ใหญ่ที่สุดในโลก วิธีนี้สะดวก ประหยัดและรวดเร็ว โดยมี 3 ขั้นตอนง่ายๆเพียงเวลาไม่กี่นาทีในการส่งและรับเงินทั่วโลก อีกทั้งยังเป็นประโยชน์มากในกรณีฉุกเฉิน เนื่องจากเป็นเพียงการโอนเงินปลีกย่อยโดยไม่ต้องใช้บัญชีธนาคาร ค่าธรรมเนียมในการโอนจะแตกต่างกันไปตามจำนวนเงินที่โอน ประเทศต้นทาง และประเทศปลายทาง เช่น ค่าธรรมเนียมในการโอนเงิน 200 ดอลล่าร์ จากอเมริกามายังประเทศไทย คือ 40 ดอลล่าร์ ถ้าคุณโอนเงิน

เกิน 1,000 ดอลล่าร์ ทางธนาคารจะถามข้อมูลส่วนตัวของคุณเพิ่มขึ้น และเหตุผลใน
การโอนเงิน

ขั้นตอนในการโอนเงินผ่านทาง Western Union

1. ไปที่ตัวแทนของ Western Union ที่มีป้าย Western Union ติดอยู่ด้านนอก ซึ่ง
มักจะอยู่ในธนาคารหรือห้างสรรพสินค้า ถ้าคุณจะทำการโอนเงินภายในประเทศ
ไทย คุณสามารถไปที่ธนาคารกรุงศรีอยุธยาสาขาที่อยู่ใกล้ที่สุด และกรอก
แบบฟอร์มได้เลย

2. นำแบบฟอร์มที่กรอกเสร็จแล้วไปยื่นที่พนักงาน แล้วตรวจสอบให้แน่ใจว่า
คุณได้รับใบเสร็จที่มีรหัสหรือ Money Transfer Control Number (MTCN)
เรียบร้อยแล้ว

3. แจ้งให้ผู้รับเงินทราบถึงการโอนเงินและจำนวนเงินที่โอน รวมถึงหมายเลข
MTCN บางครั้ง ทาง Western Union จะให้เบอร์โทรฟรีกับคุณเพื่อแจ้งให้ผู้รับ
เงินทราบ

ขั้นตอนการรับเงินผ่านทาง Western Union

1. หลังจากที่ผู้รับได้รับแจ้งจำนวนเงินและหมายเลขรหัสแล้ว ผู้รับจะต้อง
เดินทางไปยังศูนย์บริการ Western Union ที่อยู่ใกล้ที่สุด โดยนำบัตรประจำตัว
ประชาชน และกรอกแบบฟอร์มรับเงิน ตรวจสอบให้แน่ใจว่าได้กรอกชื่อผู้ส่ง
ประเทศ และจำนวนเงินครบถ้วนถูกต้อง

2. ถ้าเงินมาถึงแล้ว ผู้รับจะได้รับเงินทันที ในประเทศไทย ผู้รับสามารถรับเงินได้
ในเมืองใหญ่ที่มีตัวแทน Western Union ตั้งอยู่ในห้างสรรพสินค้า ศูนย์การค้า
หรือสาขาของธนาคารกรุงศรีอยุธยา ผู้รับที่อยู่ในต่างจังหวัดจะสามารถรับเงินได้
ที่ธนาคารกรุงศรีอยุธยา ดังนั้น ควรจะตรวจสอบว่า มีธนาคารกรุงศรีอยุธยาหรือ
ตัวแทนของ Western Union อยู่ในพื้นที่ที่ผู้รับอาศัยอยู่หรือไม่

- **การโอนเงินผ่านทางธนาคาร** วิธีนี้เป็นวิธีที่สะดวกในกรณีที่ทั้งผู้ส่งและผู้รับมี
บัญชีธนาคารอยู่แล้ว โดยผู้ส่งจะขอให้มีการโอนเงินระหว่างประเทศผ่านทาง

ธนาคารของตน การโอนเงินจะใช้เวลาประมาณ 1-5 วัน ขึ้นอยู่กับแต่ละธนาคาร
ซึ่งไม่ใช่ว่าทุกสาขาธนาคารจะมีบริการโอนเงินระหว่างประเทศ โดย
ค่าธรรมเนียมในการโอนจะใกล้เคียงกับที่ Western Union หรืออาจจะน้อยกว่า
ในกรณีที่คุณส่งเงินเป็นจำนวนมากกว่า

- ธนาณัติโอนเงินระหว่างประเทศ วิธีนี้ไม่ค่อยสะดวกเนื่องจากตัวธนาณัติจะ
นำไปขึ้นเงินได้ที่บางสาขาธนาคารเท่านั้น นอกจากนั้น ธนาคารในประเทศไทย
ยังเรียกเก็บค่าธรรมเนียมสูงในการขึ้นเงินธนาณัติ

- **การส่งบัตรเดบิตให้ผู้รับในประเทศไทย** โดยผู้ส่งจัดหาบัตรเดบิต เช่น Visa หรือ
MasterCard Debit Card ให้กับผู้รับ พร้อมกับหมายเลขรหัส และผู้รับสามารถ
ถอนเงินได้โดยตรงจากเครื่อง ATM ในประเทศไทย ซึ่งวิธีนี้ ผู้ส่งจะสามารถ
ควบคุมจำนวนเงินที่จะใส่ไว้ในบัญชีและสามารถระงับการใช้บัญชีเมื่อใดก็ได้
ธนาคารของผู้ส่งอาจจะเรียกเก็บค่าธรรมเนียม 2-5 ดอลลาร์ต่อการใช้บริการ 1
ครั้ง และเครื่อง ATM ในประเทศไทยซึ่งเงินถูกถอนออกไปก็จะเรียกเก็บ
ค่าธรรมเนียมเล็กน้อย (ประมาณ 2 ดอลลาร์) เมื่อไม่นานมานี้ บางธนาคาร เช่น
ธนาคารกรุงศรีอยุธยา ได้เพิ่มค่าธรรมเนียมในการแลกเปลี่ยนเงินระหว่าง
ประเทศอีกร้อยละ 1 ต่อการถอนเงินที่เครื่อง ATM 1 ครั้ง ดังนั้น การถอนเงิน
จำนวน 300 ดอลลาร์ ในประเทศไทย อาจจะต้องเสียค่าธรรมเนียมประมาณ 3-4
ดอลลาร์ อย่างไรก็ตาม ควรจะตรวจสอบกับทางธนาคารก่อนว่า มีการคิดธรรม
เนียมในการถอนเงินระหว่างประเทศหรือไม่

- **การส่งเงินสดทางจดหมายผ่านทางไปรษณีย์** โดยใส่ธนบัตรจำนวนหนึ่งลงใน
ซองจดหมาย วิธีนี้เคยใช้การได้ แต่ไม่นานมานี้ มีรายงานว่าจดหมายเช่นนี้ไม่เคย
ไปถึงมือผู้รับ ถึงแม้ว่าจะเป็นจดหมายลงทะเบียนก็ตาม เนื่องจากธนบัตรสามารถ
ถูกตรวจพบได้ ถึงจะอยู่ในซองจดหมายและซองไม่ได้ถูกเปิดตาม ปัจจุบัน มี
การเพิ่มมาตรการรักษาความปลอดภัยลงไปบนธนบัตรมากขึ้นเพื่อป้องกันการ
ปลอมแปลง เช่น เส้นลายน้ำ แถบโลหะ ซึ่งสามารถถูกตรวจพบได้โดยเครื่อง
ตรวจจับโลหะ ซึ่งเป็นส่วนหนึ่งของการรักษาความปลอดภัยภายในที่ทำการ
ไปรษณีย์ โดยเฉพาะในส่วนไปรษณีย์ระหว่างประเทศ ซึ่งก็คือการตรวจสอบ
โลหะวัตถุในพัสดุนั่นเอง ถ้ามีโลหะถูกตรวจพบ ก็จะถูกนำไปเอ็กซเรย์ ดังนั้น

ธนบัตรที่ถูกส่งมาในจดหมายก็สามารถถูกตรวจพบและก็จะสูญหายไปโดย
อัตโนมัติ

- **โดยทาง PayPal** วิธีนี้เป็นวิธีที่ง่ายและปลอดภัยในการจ่ายเงินหรือโอนเงิน
ออนไลน์ PayPal อนุญาตให้คุณส่งเงินทางอีเมล์โดยมีค่าธรรมเนียมเล็กน้อย คุณ
สามารถทำได้ถ้ามีบัตรเครดิตและบัญชีธนาคารอยู่แล้ว มีหลายวิธีในการโอนเงิน
ผ่านระบบนี้กรุณาไปที่ www.paypal.com เพื่อศึกษารายละเอียดเพิ่มเติม วิธีนี้เป็น
วิธีใหม่ล่าสุดในการโอนเงิน และยังไม่เป็นที่แพร่หลายเท่าใดนักในประเทศไทย
หลังจากที่คุณตั้งบัญชี PayPal และใส่เงินลงไปในบัญชีจากธนาคารของคุณ
พร้อมกับหมายเลข routing number แล้ว คุณจะสามารถขอบัตร PayPal Visa
ATM Debit Card และไปยังผู้รับได้ โดยคุณควรจะถ่ายสำเนาทั้งด้านหน้าและ
ด้านหลังของบัตรก่อนที่จะส่งบัตรไป แล้วแจ้งให้ผู้รับทราบหมายเลขรหัส 4
หลัก (PIN number) เงินที่คุณใส่ลงไปในบัญชี PayPal ก็จะสามารถถูกถอนได้
เป็นเงินบาทจากเครื่อง ATM ที่รับบัตร Visa Debit Card โดยมีค่าธรรมเนียม 1
ดอลลาร์ต่อการทำรายการ 1 ครั้ง โดยคุณสามารถเติมเงิน ถอนเงิน เปลี่ยนรหัส
ตั้งวงเงินในการถอน หรือขอบัตรใหม่ได้

การรับและแลกเปลี่ยนเงินในประเทศไทย

คนมักคิดกันว่า การอยู่อาศัยและท่องเที่ยวในประเทศไทย จะมีค่าใช้จ่ายน้อยกว่า
ในต่างประเทศ แต่ก็เป็นที่น่าสังเกตว่า เงินดูจะหายไปจากกระเป๋าคุณอย่างรวดเร็ว
เมื่อคุณมาถึงสนามบินประเทศไทย การแลกเปลี่ยนเงินจะสามารถทำได้ง่ายมาก
ซึ่งคุณควรจะแลกให้เพียงพอต่อการใช้จ่ายแค่ 2-3 วัน เนื่องจากว่าคุณสามารถแลกได้ใน
อัตราที่ถูกกว่าที่ธนาคารในเมืองหรือจากที่บูธแลกเปลี่ยนเงินตรา ถ้ามีความจำเป็น คุณก็
สามารถแลกเปลี่ยนเงินได้ที่โรงแรมเช่นกัน แต่ก็ควรจะแลกเท่าที่จำเป็น จนกว่าคุณจะ
สามารถหาที่แลกเปลี่ยนเงินตราโดยเฉพาะได้ เพราะที่โรงแรมจะให้อัตราแลกเปลี่ยนที่ไม่
ค่อยดีนัก
วิธีที่ง่ายที่สุดที่จะถอนเงินจากประเทศของคุณได้ คือ การใช้บัตร ATM ที่มี
สัญลักษณ์ PLUS, Cirrus หรือ STAR โดยคุณจะสามารถใช้บัตรเครดิตของคุณ โดยถอนเงิน

เป็นเงินบาทจากบัญชีในประเทศของคุณได้ ทั้งสองวิธีนี้ มีอัตราแลกเปลี่ยนเงินตราที่ดี บัตร
เครดิตหรือเดบิตของธนาคารจะเรียกเก็บค่าธรรมเนียมในแต่ละครั้งที่มีการถอนเงิน   และ
อาจจะเรียกเก็บเพิ่มอีกร้อยละ 1 สำหรับอัตราแลกเปลี่ยนระหว่างประเทศ

บริษัทบัตรเครดิตมักจะเรียกเก็บร้อยละ 3 หรือ 4 ของจำนวนเงินที่เบิกถอน
พร้อมกับค่าธรรมเนียมเบิกเงินล่วงหน้า โดยค่าธรรมเนียมนี้ จะแตกต่างกันไปตามธนาคาร
และเครื่อง ATM บางเครื่อง จะแสดงเฉพาะภาษาไทยและสามารถใส่หมายเลขรหัสได้แค่ 4
หลักเท่านั้น ดังนั้น คุณควรจะตรวจสอบเพื่อหาวิธีที่ดีที่สุดในการถอนเงินผ่านบัตรเครดิต
หรือเดบิตโดยเปรียบเทียบจากค่าธรรมเนียมที่ธนาคารเรียกเก็บ นอกจากนี้ คุณก็ควรจะแจ้ง
ธนาคารและบริษัทที่ออกบัตรเครดิตของคุณก่อนเดินทาง   เนื่องจากธนาคารอาจจะระงับ
บัญชีของคุณชั่วคราว   ซึ่งทำให้คุณไม่สามารถถอนเงินจากบัญชีของคุณได้ขณะที่คุณอยู่
ต่างประเทศ

บางครั้งคุณอาจต้องการเงินแบบเร่งด่วน   ดังนั้น   คุณควรจะมีเงินสดและเช็ค
เดินทางติดตัวสำรองเอาไว้   โดยคุณควรจะมีเงินสดติดตัวจำนวนแค่เพียงพอที่จะใช้จ่ายวัน
หนึ่งๆ หรือจำนวนคุณที่สามารถสูญเสียไปอย่างไม่เดือดร้อนเท่านั้น คุณควรระมัดระวังตัว
เสมอเวลาพกเงินสดในทุกสถานการณ์ และตรวจสอบกับทางโรงแรมว่ามีบริการฝากของมี
ค่าไว้ในตู้นิรภัยหรือไม่

ปัจจุบันเช็คเดินทางไม่เป็นที่นิยมอีกต่อไป แต่ก็ยังมีประโยชน์ในบางกรณี เช่น
คุณไม่สามารถถอนเงินจาก ATM ได้ หรือคุณทำบัตรเครดิตหาย บริษัทที่ออกเช็คเดินทาง
จะคืนเงินให้คุณ ในกรณีที่เช็คเดินทางหายหรือถูกขโมย แต่คุณจะต้องทำตามข้อกำหนด
ของบริษัท

ธนาคารของไทยเปิดบริการตั้งแต่ 8.30 ถึง 15.30 น. วันจันทร์ถึงวันศุกร์ และ
หยุดทำการในวันนักขัตฤกษ์ บางสาขาก็เปิดทำการครึ่งวันในวันเสาร์ แต่เครื่อง ATM
สามารถใช้งานได้ 24 ชั่วโมง เนื่องจากเครื่องส่วนใหญ่ตั้งอยู่ภายนอกธนาคาร ร้านสะดวก
ซื้อ และสถานที่อื่นๆ

การเปิดบัญชีธนาคารในประเทศไทย

ขั้นตอนในการเปิดบัญชีธนาคารค่อนข้างง่าย โดยคุณจะต้องนำเอกสารที่จำเป็น เช่น หนังสือเดินทางพร้อมกับวีซ่าที่ยังไม่หมดอายุ ใบอนุญาตทำงานและจดหมายรับรองจากสถานทูต (ในบางกรณี) บางธนาคารอาจต้องการแค่หนังสือเดินทางพร้อมกับวีซ่า และที่อยู่ในประเทศไทยเท่านั้น คุณสามารถตรวจสอบกับธนาคารต่างๆ หรือธนาคารเดียวกันแต่ต่างสาขาเพื่อดูว่า ธนาคารใด สาขาใดอนุญาตให้คุณเปิดบัญชีได้โดยใช้เอกสารที่คุณมี จำนวนเงินขั้นต่ำที่จะต้องฝากสำหรับการเปิดบัญชี โดยทั่วๆ ไปคือ 500 บาท จากนั้นธนาคารจะออกสมุดเงินฝากและบัตร ATM ให้ ซึ่งสามารถใช้ถอนหรือฝากเงิน และใช้ในการโอนเงินได้

ประเภทของบัญชีที่ชาวต่างชาติสามารถเปิดในประเทศไทยได้ คือ บัญชีออมทรัพย์ บัญชีฝากประจำ บัญชีธุรกิจ หรือบัญชีเดินสะพัด ซึ่งจะเป็นสกุลเงินบาททั้งหมด โดยชาวต่างชาติสามารถเปิดบัญชีเงินฝากสกุลต่างประเทศในสกุลเงินที่ทางธนาคารอนุมัติได้ บัญชีเดินสะพัดนั้น ไม่เหมาะที่จะใช้เป็นบัญชีส่วนตัว เนื่องจากการเปิดบัญชีเดินสะพัดจะค่อนข้างซับซ้อน ถ้าคุณไม่มีธุรกิจที่ถูกต้องตามกฎหมายในประเทศไทย สำหรับบัญชีธุรกิจ ธนาคารจะขอหนังสือเดินทางพร้อมกับวีซ่าที่ยังไม่หมดอายุ และเอกสารที่เกี่ยวข้องกับบริษัททั้งหมด ซึ่งมีความซับซ้อนพอสมควรและควรให้นักบัญชีช่วยจัดเตรียมเอกสารเหล่านี้

เมื่อเปิดบัญชีธนาคารแล้ว เจ้าของบัญชีจะได้รับบัตร ATM ซึ่งสามารถใช้ในการถอน ฝาก โอนเงิน และตรวจสอบยอดคงเหลือได้ คุณสามารถขอบัตรชนิดอื่น (เช่น Visa Electron) หรือบัตรเครดิตเพิ่มเติมได้ โดยคุณอาจจะต้องมีคุณสมบัติอื่น เช่น ใบอนุญาตทำงาน เอกสารวีซ่า ประวัติ หนังสือรับรองเงินเดือน และหนังสือรับรองที่อยู่อาศัย นอกจากนี้ คุณสามารถขอใช้บริการออนไลน์แบงค์กิ้งผ่านทางอินเตอร์เน็ต ซึ่งเริ่มเปิดให้บริการในประเทศไทยได้อีกด้วย

ในกรณีที่บัตร ATM หรือบัตรเครดิตสูญหายหรือถูกขโมย คุณควรแจ้งกับธนาคารสาขาที่ใกล้ที่สุด โดยนำหนังสือเดินทาง และเอกสารทางธนาคารอื่น (ถ้ามี) ไปด้วย ธนาคารจะทำการยกเลิกบัตร และคุณจะต้องไปที่ธนาคารสาขาที่คุณเปิดบัญชีเพื่อขอรับบัตรใบใหม่

การใช้รถใช้ถนนในประเทศไทย

ในส่วนนี้ คุณจะได้รับข้อมูลที่เกี่ยวกับการขอใบอนุญาตขับขี่รถยนต์ กฎต่างๆที่เกี่ยวกับการจราจรและสิ่งที่ควรทำเมื่อเกิดอุบัติเหตุ แต่อันดับแรกที่เราต้องการเสนอคือ การขับรถในประเทศไทยนั้นเป็นอย่างไร และก็หวังว่าคุณจะเลิกล้มความตั้งใจที่จะขับรถบนท้องถนนในประเทศนี้เสีย ไม่ว่าจะในฐานะผู้โดยสารหรือผู้ขับขี่ล้วนเป็นประสบการณ์ที่ "พิเศษ" คล้ายกับการนั่งเครื่องเล่นหวาดเสียวในสวนสนุกซึ่งคุณคาดหวังว่าจะได้กลับลงมาอย่างปลอดภัย แต่นี่อาจเหมือนหรือไม่เหมือนกับการขับรถในประเทศไทยก็ได้ เพื่อความปลอดภัยของคุณเอง เราจึงขอแนะนำไม่ให้คุณขับรถยนต์ จักรยานยนต์ หรือแม้กระทั่งจักรยานในเมืองไทย

อันดับแรกเราจะกล่าวถึงการขับรถยนต์ในเมืองใหญ่ๆ เช่น กรุงเทพ ซึ่งผู้ใช้รถใช้ถนนมักขับขี่ด้วยความเร็วสูง นอกจากนี้ยังขับขี่เบียดเสียดใกล้กันมากทั้งยังละเลยไม่ใส่ใจกับเส้นแบ่งเลน นอกจากรถยนต์แล้วก็ยังมีรถจักรยานยนต์ รถตุ๊ก ๆ รถโดยสาร รถบรรทุกหลากหลายขนาดและรูปทรง ตลอดจนคนเดินถนนอีกหลายพัน เมืองใหญ่เช่นกรุงเทพก็มีถนนหลายแบบซึ่งอาจกว้างถึง 10 เลนไว้รองรับพาหนะหลายประเภท ยกเว้นเมื่อติดไฟแดงซึ่งบังคับให้คุณต้องรอไฟเขียวราว 5-8 นาที ในขณะที่คุณกำลังรอและภาวนาให้ใจเย็นๆนั้น รถจักรยานยนต์ต่างๆ ก็จะพากันซอกแซกหาทางผ่านรถของคุณไปรออยู่ที่เส้นสตาร์ทด้านหน้า และเมื่อเปลี่ยนเป็นไฟเขียว รถจักรยานยนต์ 50 ซีซี รถยนต์ และรถตุ๊กๆ ก็จะพากันกวดวิ่งแข่งกันไปให้ได้ไกลที่สุดก่อนที่จะต้องไปติดไฟแดงอีก 8 นาที เพื่อให้เกิดความสมดุลกับความแข่งขันที่รุนแรงบนท้องถนน 10 เลนเช่นนี้ กรุงเทพยังมีเส้นทางลัดแคบๆ ที่วกไปวนมาเหมือนเขาวงกตและพาเราไปยังส่วนที่ลึกเข้าไปจากถนนใหญ่ หากคุณใช้เส้นทางลัดเหล่านี้ไปสักกิโลเมตรหรือมากกว่านั้น คุณอาจจะไปโผล่ในอีกส่วนหนึ่งของเมืองได้ไม่ยาก แต่ปัญหาคือคุณจะต้องมีความคุ้นเคยกับเส้นทางลัดเหล่านี้เสียก่อน

ยังมีกฎข้อหนึ่งเกี่ยวกับการขับรถในประเทศไทยที่ไม่ได้มีการบันทึกไว้ นั่นคือสถานะของพาหนะบนท้องถนน ซึ่งก็คล้ายคลึงกับระบบชั้นวรรณะในสังคมไทย บนท้องถนนก็เช่นเดียวกัน รถบรรทุกหรือรถโดยสารขนาดใหญ่ก็มีลำดับความสำคัญมากกว่า

รถยนต์ส่วนบุคคล ส่วนรถจักรยานยนต์หรือรถตุ๊กๆ ก็ต้องหลีกทางให้รถแท็กซี่ไปก่อน ส่วนคนเดินถนน ต้องเป็นผู้ระวังรถ หากคุณไม่รู้กฎเบื้องต้นเหล่านี้ คุณอาจมีปัญหาได้ใน พริบตา นอกจากนี้ยังมีหลุมบ่อ เส้นทางเดินรถทางเดียว นักท่องที่ยวเมาเอ๋ และช้างเดินข้าม ถนน เหล่านี้คงจะทำให้คุณได้เห็นด้วยกับเราว่า การใช้รถยนต์สาธารณะหรือแท็กซี่ใน กรุงเทพและเมืองใหญ่อื่นๆน่าจะปลอดภัยกว่าที่คุณจะขับเอง

หากคุณไม่ได้ตั้งใจที่จะขับรถในเมืองใหญ่ๆ แต่อยากจะขับรถตระเวนไปตามทาง หลวงแผ่นดินต่างๆ เราต้องขอบอกว่า นี่แหละคือการผจญภัยอย่างแท้จริง ถนนที่เป็น เส้นทางระหว่างจังหวัดต่างๆ เป็นถนนสี่เลน นั่นคือด้านละ 2 ช่องทางโดยมีเส้นแบ่งอยู่ตรง กลาง ฟังดูแล้วน่าจะปลอดภัยยกเว้นกรณีของทางแยกซึ่งจะปรากฏทุก 2 กิโลเมตร ในขณะ ที่คุณบิ่งรถมาด้วยความเร็ว 90 กิโลเมตรต่อชั่วโมงก็จะมีรถตัดเข้ามายังเลนของคุณ นอกจากนี้ยังมีรถอื่นๆ จากอีกฝั่งของถนนที่จะกลับรถมายังเลนของคุณ ทางแยกเหล่านี้ อันตรายมากและคุณต้องระมัดระวังให้ดี นอกจากนี้ยังมี ถนนเล็กๆที่มีเพียง 2 ช่องทางและมี ไหล่ทางกว้างเพียง 1 เมตรด้านข้าง เมื่อคุณขับรถในช่องของคุณ รถจากอีกเลนหนึ่งอาจจะ แซงรถที่ขับช้าๆเข้ามาในเลนของคุณได้ กฎที่ไม่ได้บันทึกไว้อีกข้อหนึ่งในการขับขี่พาหนะ ในประเทศไทยคือคุณต้องหลบเข้าไหล่ทางให้รถนั้นเข้ามาใช้เลนของคุณ ทำให้คุณต้อง ระมัดระวังอย่างยิ่งยวด ยิ่งไปกว่านั้น คุณจะพบว่า เมื่อคุณพยายามที่จะหลบบนไหล่ทาง อาจจะมีรถจักรยานยนต์วิ่งขนาบข้างมา และเนื่องจากรถจักรยานยนต์มักจะ ไม่มีแรงพอที่จะ วิ่งด้วยความเร็วเท่ากับการจราจรในอีกช่องทางหนึ่ง จึงมักจะวิ่งทางซ้ายของคุณบนไหล่ทาง คุณต้องกะเวลาในการหลบรถให้พอเหมาะพร้อมทั้งรักษาระยะ ไม่ให้ไปกระแทก รถจักรยานยนต์ที่กำลังวิ่งมาข้างๆ ให้ตกถนน แต่นี่ยังไม่หมด ยังมีรถที่ดัดแปลงจากเครื่อง ไถนาที่วิ่งอยู่บนไหล่ทางที่ผลักให้จักรยานยนต์ต้องเปลี่ยนมาใช้เลนของคุณ ถึงตอนนี้คุณ ต้องอาศัยทักษะประเมินความเร็วของพาหนะสองล้อกับรถไถที่กำลังคลานมาเอาเอง อย่าลืม ว่ายังมีรถจักรยานยนต์ที่วิ่งอยู่บนไหล่ทางอีกด้านหนึ่ง เหล่านี้คงเป็นเหตุผลที่เพียงพอ สำหรับชาวต่างชาติที่จะไม่ขับรถในต่างจังหวัด ทางเลือกอีกทางก็คือ การใช้รถยนต์โดยสาร ประจำทาง การคมนาคมโดยวิธีนี้สะดวก ราคาถูก และรถโดยสารเหล่านี้ก็ไปทุกแห่งหนใน ประเทศ คุณสามารถเลือกที่จะเลือกโดยสารตามชั้นต่างๆ ตามต้องการ ไม่ว่าจะเป็นชั้นหนึ่ง ที่มีเครื่องปรับอากาศและที่นั่งปรับเอนได้

เราได้สรุปสิ่งที่คุณควรระวังในการขับขี่รถยนต์ในประเทศไทยไม่ว่าจะเป็นเมืองใหญ่หรือเล็กไว้ดังนี้

- ในประเทศไทย รถยนต์ขับชิดซ้ายเหมือนกับในประเทศอังกฤษ
- ในเวลากลางคืน คนไทยใช้ไฟสูงในการกระพริบเพื่อเตือนรถอีกด้านหนึ่งที่อาจกำลังสวนมา
- หากรถที่กำลังสวนมาเปิดไฟกระพริบ หมายถึงการเตือนให้คุณ "ช้าลง" หรือ "มีด่านตรวจข้างหน้า"
- ตามกฎหมายผู้ที่จะขับขี่รถได้ต้องมีอายุ 18 ปีขึ้นไป แต่จริงๆ แล้วผู้ที่ขับรถจักรยานยนต์จำนวนมากอายุน้อยกว่า 18 ปี
- ปริมาณแอลกอฮอล์ในเลือดที่กฎหมายอนุญาตคือไม่เกิน 0.5 กรัมต่อเลือดหนึ่งลิตร และเพียง 0.2 กรัมต่อเลือดหนึ่งลิตรสำหรับผู้ที่ถือใบขับขี่มาน้อยว่า 5 ปี
- เช่นเดียวกับประเทศอื่นๆ คนเมาแล้วขับก็เป็นปัญหาใหญ่สำหรับประเทศไทยแต่บทลงโทษก็ไม่รุนแรงนัก และต้องมีการรณรงค์ให้มากขึ้น
- ผู้ขับขี่ต้องมีใบอนุญาตขับขี่รถยนต์ที่ยัง ไม่หมดอายุและมีสำเนาการจดทะเบียนรถยนต์ (ใบอนุญาตขับขี่รถยนต์สากลใช้ได้)
- แผ่นป้ายแสดงการภาษีรถยนต์และประกันภัยบุคคลที่สาม เป็นข้อบังคับสำหรับพาหนะทุกชนิด (รวมถึงรถจักรยานยนต์) โดยเอกสารเหล่านี้ต้องต่ออายุทุกปี ณ สำนักงานของกรมการขนส่งทางบกในทุกจังหวัด
- ผู้นั่งคู่กับคนขับด้านหน้าจะต้องรัดเข็มขัด มิฉะนั้นผู้ขับจะต้องถูกปรับหากตำรวจพบว่า คุณไม่ได้ปฏิบัติตามกฎข้อนี้
- ค่าปรับเนื่องจากขับเร็วกว่าที่กำหนดและใบสั่งต่างๆ จ่ายได้ที่สถานีตำรวจในพื้นที่
- ห้ามขับพาหนะที่มีป้ายทะเบียนสีแดงในเวลากลางคืน
- กฎหมายไม่ได้บังคับให้ใช้ที่นั่งพิเศษสำหรับเด็ก
- ทางด่วนหลายสายทั่วกรุงเทพเก็บค่าธรรมเนียม โดยคิดตามระยะทางที่ใช้
- รถจักรยานยนต์และพาหนะอื่นๆมักมีผู้โดยสารมากกว่าที่อนุญาต

- ส่วนใหญ่รถบรรทุกมักบรรทุกเกินกว่าที่กำหนดและมักประสบอุบัติเหตุบริเวณ ทางโค้ง
- คนที่นั่งด้านหลังของรถกระบะไม่มีการคาดเข็มขัด เมื่อเกิดอุบัติเหตุจะกระเด็น จากรถทำให้ได้รับบาดเจ็บ
- ป้ายกำหนดความเร็วจะปักไว้ข้างทางและมักไม่เกิน 120 กิโลเมตรต่อชั่วโมง สำหรับรถยนต์ แต่ในบางพื้นที่อาจลดลงเหลือเพียง 90 กิโลเมตรต่อชั่วโมง
- ทางหลวงแผ่นดินมักกำหนดความเร็วประมาณ 90 กิโลเมตรต่อชั่วโมงหรือ 100-120 กิโลเมตรต่อชั่วโมงในบางพื้นที่ และเหลือเพียง 50-60 กิโลเมตรต่อชั่วโมงใน แถบชานเมือง เป็นต้น
- ใบอนุญาตขับขี่รถจักรยานยนต์ขอได้ไม่ยาก
- ผู้ขับขี่รถจักรยานยนต์ต้องสวมหมวกนิรภัย แต่มักมีผู้หลีกเลี่ยงไม่ปฏิบัติตามกฎ ทำให้ตำรวจมักตั้งด่านตรวจและปรับผู้ไม่ปฏิบัติตาม
- ผู้ใช้ถนนไทยมักไม่หยุดรถตามสัญญาณและมักไม่ชะลอรถหรือมองรถที่อาจ สวนมาจากอีกทางหนึ่ง
- ในเมืองใหญ่ๆ การจราจรมักจะหนาแน่นในช่วง 07:00-9:30 และ 16:30-19:30 ส่วนเมืองเล็กเวลารถติดก็จะสั้นลง
- ในช่วงวันหยุดยาว เช่น สงกรานต์ (ปีใหม่ไทย) ปัญหาการจราจรจะเข้าขั้นวิกฤติ เนื่องจากคนกรุงเทพส่วนใหญ่ต้องการออกจากเมืองกรุงไปฉลองกับครอบครัว ในต่างจังหวัด และปรากฏการณ์เช่นเดียวกันก็จะเกิดขึ้นเมื่อคนหลั่งไหลกลับเข้า เมืองอีกครั้งหลังช่วงเทศกาล
- คุณต้องขับขี่ด้วยความระมัดระวังกว่าที่ขับขี่ในประเทศของตน เพราะป้าย สัญญาณต่างๆ ที่เป็นภาษาอังกฤษมักมีขนาดเล็กและในบางพื้นที่ก็อาจจะมีเพียง ป้ายภาษาไทยเท่านั้น
- นอกจากการเข้าสอบแล้ว ผู้ขับขี่รถยนต์ในกรุงเทพต้องเข้ารับการอบรม และนี่ เป็นเหตุผลที่ชาวกรุงขับรถได้ดีกว่าคนจากส่วนอื่นๆ ของประเทศ
- พยายามหลีกเลี่ยงความขัดแย้งต่างๆเมื่อใช้รถใช้ถนน ให้คุณใจเย็นๆ และทำ สมาธิจะดีกว่า

- ในฐานะชาวต่างชาติ คุณมีสถานะพิเศษทางสังคม รวมถึงกรณีของอุบัติเหตุด้วย นั่นคือในหลายๆกรณีคุณจะเป็นฝ่ายผิด เพราะมักจะถูกกล่าวหาว่าเป็นชาวต่างชาติและไม่ค่อยรู้เรื่อง

หากตำรวจเรียกให้คุณหยุดรถ คุณอาจทำแบบเดียวกับคนอื่นๆ คือ จ่ายค่าปรับให้ตำรวจเพื่อหลีกเลี่ยงการไปสถานีตำรวจ ค่าปรับจราจรนี้ไม่ควรสูงนัก (ระหว่าง 200-400 บาท) หากค่าปรับหรือค่าเสียหายสูงมาก คุณอาจบอกเจ้าหน้าที่ว่า อยากจะไปสถานีตำรวจ แทนหรือขอปรึกษาใครสักคนก่อน ในกรณีที่คุณได้ใบสั่งและถูกยึดใบขับขี่ คุณต้องไปจ่ายค่าปรับที่สถานีตำรวจภายใน 7 วันมิฉะนั้นจะต้องจ่ายค่าปรับเพิ่มขึ้น

หากคุณอยู่ในประเทศไทยเกิน 3 เดือน คุณจะต้องมีใบอนุญาตขับขี่รถยนต์ไทย และแม้ใบอนุญาตขับขี่รถยนต์สากลจะเป็นที่ยอมรับ คุณก็ยังต้องมีใบอนุญาตขับขี่รถยนต์ จากประเทศของคุณที่ยังไม่หมดอายุมาใช้ประกอบกับใบอนุญาตขับขี่สากลด้วย บริษัทประกันภัยบางแห่งอาจมีการประกันภัยสำหรับผู้ขับที่มีใบอนุญาตขับขี่รถยนต์ไทยเท่านั้น เนื่องจากการมีใบอนุญาตขับขี่รถยนต์ไทยเป็นการพิสูจน์ว่าบุคคลนั้นเป็นผู้อาศัยอยู่ในประเทศไทยและไม่ใช่นักท่องเที่ยว ส่วนชาวไทยที่อาศัยและขับขี่รถยนต์ในต่างประเทศมากกว่าหนึ่งปีก็สามารถจะขอใบอนุญาตได้โดยไม่ต้องเข้าสอบอีก โดยให้นำใบอนุญาตขับขี่รถยนต์สากลไปเทียบขอใบขับขี่ไทยได้เลย

การขอใบอนุญาตขับขี่รถยนต์ไทย

เงื่อนไขในการขอใบอนุญาตขับขี่รถยนต์ไทยคือ คุณต้องมีสุขภาพกายและสุขภาพจิตที่ดี ชาวต่างชาติสามารถนำใบอนุญาตขับขี่รถยนต์สากลและใบอนุญาตขับขี่รถยนต์จากประเทศของตนที่ยังไม่หมดอายุมาใช้ขอใบขับขี่ไทยได้ หากคุณมีเอกสารเหล่านี้คุณอาจไม่ต้องเข้าสอบข้อเขียนหรือทดสอบขับรถอีก โดยคุณจะได้ใบขับขี่ชั่วคราวสำหรับรถยนต์ส่วนบุคคลชั่วคราวหนึ่งปี (ไม่ใช่สำหรับรถโดยสารหรือรถจักรยานยนต์)

สำหรับประเทศไทย คุณสามารถขอใบอนุญาตขับขี่ได้ที่กรมการขนส่งทางบก คนไทยเรียกว่า "ขนส่ง" ซึ่งบางแห่งจะมีการสอบเป็นภาษาอังกฤษ ถ้าไม่มีแล้ว คุณอาจขอ

อนุญาตจากผู้คุมสอบให้ใช้ล่ามช่วย ชาวต่างชาติจะต้องเข้าสอบขอใบอนุญาตขับขี่ไทย หาก
ไม่มีใบอนุญาตขับขี่รถยนต์สากลและใบขับขี่รถยนต์จากประเทศของตน

หากคุณมีใบอนุญาตทำงาน   คุณสามารถใช้เป็นเอกสารรับรองการพำนักใน
ประเทศไทย นอกจากนี้คุณแสดงเอกสารต่อไปนี้

- หนังสือเดินทางและวีซ่าประเภท non-immigrant ที่ยังไม่หมดอายุ
- สำเนาหน้าแรกของหนังสือเดินทางจำนวน 2 ชุด พร้อมลายเซ็นรับรอง
  สำเนา สำเนาหน้าซึ่งมีประทับตราวีซ่าเข้าเมืองประเภท non-immigrant
  สำเนาหน้าที่ประทับวันที่เข้าเมืองครั้งล่าสุดและบัตรอนุญาตเข้าเมือง
- จดหมายรับรองที่อยู่จากสถานทูตหรือจากสำนักงานตรวจคนเข้าเมืองที่ออก
  ไว้ไม่เกิน 30 วัน
- ใบรับรองจากแพทย์ที่ออกไว้ไม่เกิน   30   วันว่า   มีสุขภาพร่างกายและ
  สุขภาพจิตที่แข็งแรง
- รูปถ่ายขนาด 1 x 1 นิ้ว จำนวน 2 รูป ถ่ายไว้ไม่เกิน 6 เดือน
- ใบอนุญาตขับขี่สากลที่ยังไม่หมดอายุ พร้อมรูปถ่ายและลายเซ็นรับรอง หรือ
  สำเนาแปลใบอนุญาตขับขี่รถยนต์จากประเทศของคุณที่สถานทูตรับรอง

หากคุณมีใบอนุญาตขับขี่รถยนต์สากลและใบอนุญาตจากประเทศของตนแล้ว
คุณต้องเข้าทดสอบพื้นฐาน 3 ส่วนคือ การทดสอบตาบอดสี การทดสอบปฏิกิริยาโต้ตอบ
และการรับรู้เชิง 3 มิติ เมื่อผ่านการทดสอบแล้ว ก็จะมีการตรวจเอกสาร จ่ายค่าธรรมเนียม
150 บาทแล้วหลังจากนั้นคุณก็จะได้ใบอนุญาตขับขี่รถยนต์ชั่วคราวของไทยเป็นเวลา 1 ปี

การจอดรถ

การจอดรถในสยามเมืองยิ้ม ไม่ยุ่งยาก เพียงหาที่ว่างพอเหมาะ นอกจากนี้ยังไม่
ต้องจ่ายค่าที่จอด เนื่องจากไม่มีมิเตอร์คิดค่าจอด ในกรณีที่จอดรถในที่สาธารณะหรือที่จอด
รถส่วนบุคคลบางแห่งอาจต้องเสียค่าจอดเล็กน้อย คุณอาจพบว่าคนไทยจอดรถขวางทางคัน
อื่นๆ แต่คุณไม่ต้องอารมณ์เสีย เพราะการแก้ปัญหานี้ก็คือ การจอดรถโดยไม่ต้องใส่เกียร์มือ

หลังจากที่จอดรถและมั่นใจแล้วว่ารถจะไม่ไหลไปเฉี่ยวรถคันอื่นๆ หากรถของคุณถูกขวาง คุณก็เพียงเข็นรถคันนั้นออกไปให้พ้นทาง หรือขอความช่วยเหลือจากผู้ดูแลที่จอด (โดยจ่าย ค่าตอบแทนเล็กน้อยเป็นค่าน้ำใจ) อย่าลืมว่าคุณต้องเข็นรถที่กีดขวางคุณไปไว้ในที่ปลอดภัย ด้วย

ป้ายสัญญาณการจอดรถมักเขียนเป็นภาษาไทย ตำรวจก็จะให้ใบสั่งผู้ละเมิดหรือ บางครั้งก็ล็อกกล้อไว้ ดังนั้นคุณต้องตรวจดูจุดที่ต้องการจอดเสียก่อน ดังเช่นที่คุณปฏิบัติใน ประเทศของคุณ หากคุณอ่านภาษาไทยไม่ออกหรือยังไม่เข้าใจดีพอ คุณอาจขอความ ช่วยเหลือจากคนไทยได้ การจอดรถนั้นบางแห่งจอดได้เฉพาะวันคู่แต่ห้ามจอดในวันคี่เป็น ต้น

ถนนและไหล่ทางบางแห่งจะมีการทาสีซึ่งมีความหมายต่างๆ ดังนี้

- แถบขาว-แดง – ห้ามจอดตลอดเวลา
- แถบขาว-เหลือง – ให้จอดชั่วคราวเพื่อรับส่งเท่านั้น
- รูปสี่เหลี่ยมมุมฉากสีขาว – ให้จอดเฉพาะพาหนะที่กำหนด
- เส้นขาวทแยง – ให้จอดเฉพาะรถจักรยานยนต์

หากคุณต้องการข้อมูลเพิ่มเติมเกี่ยวกับการขับขี่รถยนต์และป้ายสัญญาณต่างๆ ใน ประเทศไทย สามารถหาได้จากหนังสือคู่มือต่างๆ จากร้านหนังสือและแผงหนังสือที่ตั้งอยู่ ใกล้กับขนส่ง

เมื่อเกิดอุบัติเหตุ

หากคุณประสบอุบัติเหตุ ให้คุณพยายามสงบสติอารมณ์ ขั้นตอนในการแก้ไขจะ แตกต่างจากประเทศของคุณเล็กน้อย สิ่งที่คุณควรระลึกถึงคือคุณจะตกอยู่ในฐานะที่ เสียเปรียบเนื่องจากภาษา ดังที่ได้กล่าวไปข้างต้นว่า คุณ (ในฐานะชาวต่างชาติ) คือผู้ผิด เนื่องจากคุณไม่รู้วิธีการขับรถแบบไทย (ถึงแม้คุณจะเป็นผู้ถูกก็ตาม) เมื่อเกิดอุบัติเหตุ ผู้ขับมัก จ่ายค่าชดเชยและค่าปรับเพื่อแก้ปัญหาให้เร็วที่สุดและง่ายที่สุด คุณควรพิจารณาให้ดีว่าจะทำ

อย่างไรในสถานการณ์เช่นนั้น และควรตรวจสอบขอคำแนะนำจากบริษัทประกันภัยของคุณ ดังนั้นคุณ ไม่ควรขับรถในเมืองไทยหากไม่มีประกันภัยชั้นหนึ่งจากบริษัทที่มีชื่อเสียงและ เป็นที่ยอมรับ

ในกรณีที่ไม่มีผู้ได้รับบาดเจ็บ

- เลื่อนรถที่เกี่ยวข้องในอุบัติเหตุไปข้างทางเพื่อไม่ให้กีดขวางการจราจร
- ขอความช่วยเหลือจากตำรวจ โดยโทรหมายเลขฉุกเฉิน 191 หรือ 1155 สำหรับ ตำรวจท่องเที่ยวที่จะช่วยเหลือเป็นภาษาอังกฤษได้
- แลกเปลี่ยนข้อมูลของคุณกับคู่กรณี เช่น หมายเลขเอกสารประจำตัว หมายเลข ใบขับขี่ หมายเลขทะเบียนรถยนต์ เอกสารประกัน และหมายเลขโทรศัพท์
- หากคุณประสบอุบัติเหตุเอง   ตรวจสอบกับบริษัทประกันของคุณว่าต้องใช้ เอกสารอะไรบ้าง   อย่าลืมตรวจสอบว่าบริษัทประกันมีหมายเลขบริการฮ็อตไลน์ 24 ชั่วโมงหรือไม่
- แจ้งบริษัทประกันและกรอกเอกสารต่างๆที่จำเป็น

ในกรณีที่มีผู้ได้รับบาดเจ็บ

- ขอความช่วยเหลือจากตำรวจ โดยโทรหมายเลขฉุกเฉิน 191 หรือ 1155 สำหรับ ตำรวจท่องเที่ยวที่จะช่วยเหลือเป็นภาษาอังกฤษได้
- ควรเคลื่อนย้ายผู้ที่ไม่ได้รับบาดเจ็บ ให้อยู่ในที่ปลอดภัย
- โทรเรียกรถฉุกเฉินและขอให้ผู้ที่มีความรู้ในการปฐมพยาบาลช่วยเหลือ ผู้ได้รับบาดเจ็บ
- อย่าเคลื่อนย้ายรถที่เกี่ยวข้องในอุบัติเหตุ
- แลกเปลี่ยนข้อมูลของคุณกับคู่กรณี เช่น หมายเลขเอกสารประจำตัว หมายเลข ใบขับขี่ หมายเลขทะเบียนรถยนต์ เอกสารประกัน และหมายเลขโทรศัพท์
- หากคุณประสบอุบัติเหตุเอง   ตรวจสอบกับบริษัทประกันของคุณว่าต้องใช้ เอกสารอะไรบ้าง   อย่าลืมตรวจสอบว่าบริษัทประกันมีหมายเลขบริการฮ็อตไลน์ 24 ชั่วโมงหรือไม่

- แจ้งบริษัทประกันและกรอกเอกสารต่างๆที่จำเป็น

สำหรับประเทศไทย หมายเลขโทรฉุกเฉินคือ 191 และหมายเลขตำรวจท่องเที่ยว คือ 1155 การให้ปากคำจะต้องไปที่สถานีตำรวจในท้องที่ หน่วยงานและองค์กรของรัฐที่ เกี่ยวข้องกับการจราจรในประเทศไทย ได้แก่ สำนักงานนโยบายและแผนการขนส่งและ จราจร กรมการขนส่งทางบก และสำนักงานตำรวจแห่งชาติ

บริษัทประกันบางแห่งมีบริการให้ความช่วยเหลือระหว่างเส้นทาง คุณจึงควร สอบถามกับบริษัทประกันว่ามีบริการนี้หรือไม่ นอกจากนี้ คุณอาจติดต่อราชยานยนต์ สมาคมแห่งประเทศไทยในพระบรมราชูปถัมภ์ (RAAT) โทร 0-2939-5770-3, 0-2512-0905 สำหรับพื้นที่กรุงเทพ หรือ บริษัทคาร์เวิลด์ คลับ (Car World Club) ซึ่งให้บริการทั่วประเทศ ตลอด 24 ชั่วโมง โทร 0-2398-0170-9 กรณีที่คุณอยู่ต่างจังหวัด ควรติดต่อผู้ให้บริการใน พื้นที่ซึ่งจะสะดวกกว่ารอความช่วยเหลือจากส่วนกลาง

การทำงานในประเทศไทย

ประเทศไทยได้กลายเป็นที่นิยมของชาวต่างชาติที่จะเข้ามาทำงานและพักอาศัย โดยเฉพาะจากประเทศเพื่อนบ้านเช่น พม่า ลาวและกัมพูชา โดยทั่วไปชาวต่างชาติใน ประเทศไทยจะถือเป็น "แขก" ไม่ว่าชาวต่างชาติเหล่านี้จะเข้าประเทศมาในฐานะ นักท่องเที่ยว ผู้เกษียณอายุ หรือคนทำงาน แต่หากคุณเป็นชาวตะวันตกผิวขาว หรือมีบรรพ บุรุษเชื้อสายอาฟริกัน หรือเชื้อสายอื่นๆที่ไม่ใช่เอเชีย คุณจะถูกจัดเป็น "แขก"ตลอดไป ไม่ ว่าคุณจะอยู่ในสยามเมืองยิ้มนี้นานเท่าใดก็ตาม เหตุผลคือ คุณแตกต่างจากคนไทยทั้งสีผิว และหน้าตา ในขณะที่คนจากประเทศอื่นๆ ในทวีปเอเชียโดยเฉพาะประเทศใกล้เคียงจะ ได้รับการยอมรับมากกว่า อย่างไรก็ตามนี่ไม่ใช่เป็นการประกันว่า คนเหล่านี้จะมีสถานะ ทางสังคมเช่นเจ้าของประเทศ ประเทศไทยถือว่ามีความก้าวหน้ามากกว่าประเทศเพื่อน บ้านและการเติบโตทางเศรษฐกิจทำให้มีความต้องการแรงงานเพิ่มขึ้น ปัญหาทางสังคม การเมืองและเศรษฐกิจของไทยในปัจจุบันส่วนหนึ่งเกิดจากแรงงานหลบหนีเข้าเมือง โดย รัฐบาลต้องแบกภาระค่าใช้จ่ายทางการแพทย์ รวมทั้งอาชญากรรมที่เกิดจากชาวต่างชาติที่ รุนแรงขึ้นจนกลายเป็นปัญหาสังคม ด้วยเหตุผลเหล่านี้รัฐบาลไทยจึงกำหนดให้ ชาวต่างชาติที่ต้องการทำงานต้องมีใบอนุญาต ยกเว้นกรณีของนักการทูต ผู้ทำงานให้กับ องค์การสหประชาชาติหรือหน่วยงานระหว่างประเทศอื่นๆ เจ้าหน้าที่ด้านการศึกษา วัฒนธรรม ศิลปะ หรือการกีฬา หรืออาชีพอื่นๆที่ได้รับอนุญาตเป็นกรณีพิเศษจากรัฐ ใบอนุญาตทำงานของคุณถือเป็นเอกสารสำคัญที่รัฐใช้ยืนยันการพำนักอาศัยอยู่ในเมืองไทย และใช้เป็นบันทึกประวัติของคุณ หากคุณได้รับค่าจ้างขณะอยู่ในประเทศไทย ไม่ว่าจากงาน ในฐานะที่ปรึกษา ครูสอนภาษาอังกฤษ หรือแม้กระทั่งเป็นคนงานในโรงงานทอผ้า คุณต้อง มีใบอนุญาตทำงาน มิฉะนั้นถือว่าคุณทำผิดกฎหมาย ต้องจ่ายค่าปรับ จำคุก ถูกส่งกลับ ประเทศและขับไล่ออกจากประเทศ ซึ่งรัฐบาลไทยเข้มงวดมากในเรื่องนี้และกวดขันกับ ชาวต่างชาติที่ทำงานในเมืองไทย มีเรื่องของชาวต่างชาติมากมายที่ถูกจับเนื่องจากรับเงินทิป เพียงไม่กี่บาทขณะไปเล่นดนตรีให้เพื่อนในบาร์ เนื่องจากรับเงินค่าจ้างทำงานโดยไม่มี ใบอนุญาตทำงาน

มีงานและวิชาชีพหลายอย่างที่สงวนไว้ให้กับคนไทยเท่านั้น เช่น ค้าขายหาบเร่
แผงลอย งานเลขานุการ สถาปนิก ตัดเย็บเสื้อผ้า พนักงานประจำร้าน แกะสลักไม้ และอื่นๆ
คุณควรตรวจสอบให้แน่ชัดว่า งานที่คุณต้องการไม่เข้าอยู่ในข่ายนี้ รัฐบาลไทยได้ออก
ใบอนุญาตทำงานให้กับแรงงานต่างชาติจากประเทศเพื่อนบ้านเพื่อทำงานค่าจ้างต่ำซึ่งปกติ
จะสงวนไว้ให้คนไทยเพื่อบรรเทาปัญหาแรงงานผิดกฎหมาย และแม้ว่าจะมีการกำหนด
ค่าแรงขั้นต่ำไว้ แต่แรงงานต่างชาติจากประเทศเพื่อนบ้านอาจจะได้ค่าจ้างต่ำกว่าคนไทย
ระบบใบอนุญาตทำงานสำหรับแรงงานต่างชาติเหล่านี้เพียงเป็นการขึ้นทะเบียนว่า
ชาวต่างชาติเหล่านั้นไปทำงานที่ใด แรงงานเหล่านี้สามารถต่อใบอนุญาตเป็นรายปีโดยผ่าน
ระบบที่ไม่ซับซ้อนซึ่งรัฐบาลไทยจัดไว้ ส่วนชาวตะวันตกมักจะมองหางานที่มีรายได้สูงกว่า
มาตรฐานของคนไทย เช่น การสอนภาษาอังกฤษในโรงเรียนสอนภาษา การสอนวิชาอื่นๆ
ในโรงเรียนหรือมหาวิทยาลัย งานเขียน งานสื่อสารมวลชน วิชาชีพทางการแพทย์ หรือ
แม้กระทั่งทำธุรกิจ การขอใบอนุญาตทำงานสำหรับงานที่มีค่าแรงสูงเหล่านี้จะซับซ้อนกว่า
แรงงานต่างชาติจากประเทศเพื่อนบ้านดังที่ได้กล่าวมาแล้ว

ใบอนุญาตทำงาน

คุณควรขอวีซ่าประเภท Non-immigrant B (เพื่อประกอบธุรกิจ) จากสถานทูต
หรือสถานกงสุลไทยที่อยู่ใกล้บ้านคุณก่อนที่จะเดินทางเข้าประเทศไทย เมื่อมาถึงเมืองไทย
แล้ว จึงขอใบอนุญาตทำงาน อย่าลืมว่า คุณต้องมีวีซ่าประเภท Non-immigrant B (เพื่อ
ประกอบธุรกิจ) เพื่อขอใบอนุญาตทำงาน ทั้งนี้นายจ้างของคุณในประเทศไทยอาจสมัครขอ
ใบอนุญาตทำงานให้คุณได้ ใบวีซ่าประเภทนี้มีแบบให้เข้า-ออกประเทศได้ครั้งเดียวใน
ระยะเวลา 3 เดือนหรือหลายครั้งในระยะ 12 เดือน วีซ่าประเภทหลังนี้บังคับให้คุณต้อง
ออกนอกประเทศทุก 90 วัน หากคุณทำงานให้กับบริษัท นายจ้างอาจขอใบอนุญาตทำงาน
ให้คุณล่วงหน้าและใบอนุญาตทำงานนี้ก็จะออกให้ในประเทศไทย เราขอแนะนำให้คุณ
ติดต่อขอความช่วยเหลือจากผู้ที่มีความเชี่ยวชาญและประสบการณ์ การขอใบอนุญาตทำงาน
ในประเทศไทยเป็นกระบวนการที่ซับซ้อนและใช้เวลาเนื่องจากมีเอกสารเกี่ยวข้องมากมาย
ทั้งนี้มีสำนักงานกฎหมายหลายแห่งที่สามารถช่วยคุณได้ในขั้นตอนการสมัครนี้ นายจ้างไม่
สามารถจ้างชาวต่างชาติที่ไม่มีใบอนุญาตทำงานได้ นอกจากนี้ งานที่ชาวต่างชาติทำต้องตรง

กับที่ขออนุญาตไว้ (การไม่ปฏิบัติตาม มีโทษจำคุกไม่เกิน 3 ปี หรือปรับไม่เกิน 60,000 บาท หรือทั้งจำทั้งปรับ) ทั้งนี้นายจ้างต้องยื่นเอกสารต่อหน่วยงานของรัฐภายใน 15 วันนับแต่ ชาวต่างชาติเริ่มทำงานหรือยกเลิกสัญญาจ้างหรือการเปลี่ยนแปลงสถานที่ทำงาน

ในกรณีที่คุณต้องการตั้งธุรกิจของตนเอง คุณสามารถขอใบอนุญาตทำงานให้ ตนเองได้โดยการจดทะเบียนตั้งบริษัท คู่มือที่เป็นประโยชน์ในการประกอบธุรกิจใน ประเทศไทยคือ "วิธีก่อตั้งธุรกิจที่ประสบความสำเร็จในประเทศไทย (How to Establish a Successful Business in Thailand)" ที่จัดพิมพ์โดยสำนักพิมพ์ไพบูลย์เช่นกัน คู่มือนี้มีข้อมูลที่ เป็นประโยชน์ในการเริ่มธุรกิจหรือซื้อธุรกิจหรือแฟรนไชส์ ในกรณีที่คุณต้องการประกอบ ธุรกิจในประเทศไทยคุณสามารถเข้าประเทศด้วยวีซ่าใดก็ได้ แล้วเขียนหนังสือแนะนำ ตัวเองโดยใช้หัวกระดาษที่มีชื่อที่อยู่ของบริษัทที่ได้จดทะเบียนไว้ หลังจากนั้นคุณต้องออก จากประเทศเพื่อสมัครขอวีซ่าประเภท Non-immigrant B (เพื่อประกอบธุรกิจ) โดยใช้ จดหมายและเอกสารประกอบการจดทะเบียนบริษัทที่คุณทำไว้ที่เมืองไทย พึงระลึกว่า คุณ ต้องขอวีซ่าประเภทนี้จากสถานทูตหรือกงสุลไทยในต่างประเทศ หลังจากที่คุณได้วีซ่านี้ แล้ว คุณก็สามารถขอใบอนุญาตทำงานได้ เนื่องจากขั้นตอนการขอใบอนุญาตเหล่านี้มีความ ซับซ้อน คุณจึงควรปรึกษาบริษัทกฎหมายที่เชี่ยวชาญในด้านนี้

เอกสารที่ใช้ขอใบอนุญาตทำงานมีดังนี้

- กรณีพำนักชั่วคราว - หนังสือเดินทางต้องมีตราประทับวีซ่าประเภท Non-immigrant B (เพื่อประกอบธุรกิจ) กรณีพำนักถาวร - หนังสือเดินทาง ใบสำคัญคนต่างด้าว และใบสำคัญถิ่นที่อยู่
- วุฒิการศึกษาเช่น ใบประกาศนียบัตร ประวัติการทำงาน จดหมายแนะนำ และใบอนุญาตที่เกี่ยวข้องเพื่อแสดงว่าคุณมีคุณสมบัติที่จะประกอบอาชีพ ดังกล่าว
- เอกสารบรรยายลักษณะงาน เช่น ระบุประเภทของงาน วัสดุที่ใช้ ที่ตั้ง เงินเดือน และอื่นๆ

- ใบรับรองแพทย์ที่ออกในประเทศไทยไม่เกิน 6 เดือนซึ่งระบุว่า ผู้สมัครมี สุขภาพร่างกายและจิตใจที่สมบูรณ์ ไม่เป็นโรคพิษสุราเรื้อรัง ติดสารเสพติด หรือเป็นโรคติดต่อ
- รูปถ่ายขนาดรูปในหนังสือเดินทางหรือขนาด 5 x 6 ซม. ควรเป็นรูปที่แต่ง กายสุภาพเรียบร้อย
- ผู้สมัครที่คู่สมรสเป็นชาวไทย ควรแนบสำเนาบัตรประจำตัวของคู่สมรส ใบ ทะเบียนสมรส และใบสูติบัตรของบุตร (ถ้ามี) ไปด้วย
- ในกรณีที่เอกสารสำคัญเป็นภาษาอื่นนอกจากภาษาไทยและอังกฤษ อาจต้อง แปลเอกสารเหล่านี้เป็นภาษาไทย

เอกสารใบสมัครให้ส่งไปที่ กรมการจัดหางานในกรุงเทพหรือศูนย์บริการวีซ่า และใบอนุญาตทำงานแบบครบวงจร (One Stop Service Center) ซึ่งมีสำนักงานของ กรมการจัดหางาน สำนักงานตรวจคนเข้าเมือง และสำนักงานคณะกรรมการส่งเสริมการ ลงทุนได้ร่วมกันให้บริการ ในกรณีที่เอกสารครบถ้วนคุณสามารถดำเนินการให้เสร็จได้ใน เวลาเพียง 3 ชั่วโมงโดยไม่ต้องเดินทางไปที่อื่นอีก ถ้าสมัครในต่างจังหวัด ให้ติดต่อ สำนักงานจัดหางานประจำจังหวัดที่คุณทำงานอยู่

ใบอนุญาตทำงานจะหมดอายุภายในหนึ่งปี (และสูงสุดเป็น 2 ปีในบางกรณี) โดย เริ่มจากวันที่คุณเข้าประเทศ และจะหมดอายุลงพร้อมกับวีซ่าประเภท Non-immigrant B (เพื่อประกอบธุรกิจ) คุณต้องต่ออายุใบอนุญาตทำงานก่อนที่จะหมดอายุ โดยใบอนุญาต ทำงานต้องมีการระบุชื่อของนายจ้าง งานที่คุณทำและสถานที่ซึ่งคุณทำงาน ทั้งนี้คุณต้อง ทำงานให้กับนายจ้างที่ระบุไว้ในใบอนุญาตทำงานเท่านั้น นั่นคือคุณไม่ได้รับอนุญาตให้ ทำงานกับนายจ้างอื่นนอกเหนือจากที่ได้ระบุไว้ หากมีการเปลี่ยนงานหรือนายจ้าง คุณต้อง แจ้งและต้องรอให้ได้รับการอนุมัติก่อน คุณต้องพกใบอนุญาตหรือมีไว้แสดงระหว่างทำงาน ในกรณีที่เจ้าหน้าที่ไปตรวจ หากใบอนุญาตทำงานสูญหายหรือเสียหาย คุณสามารถขอ ใบอนุญาตได้ใหม่ภายใน 15 วันนับตั้งแต่สูญหาย ในกรณีที่คุณเปลี่ยนชื่อ สกุล สัญชาติ ที่ อยู่หรือบริษัท คุณก็สามารถยื่นขอเปลี่ยนได้ทันที ในกรณีที่คุณลาออกหรือเลิกสัญญา ให้ ส่งใบอนุญาตทำงานกลับไปที่สำนักทะเบียนของกระทรวงแรงงาน ภายใน 7 วันทำการนับ

จากวันที่คุณลาออกเหลือยกเลิกสัญญา นอกจากนี้คุณต้องรายงานต่อสำนักงานตรวจคนเข้าเมืองซึ่งจะยกเลิกวีซ่าประเภท Non-immigrant B (เพื่อประกอบธุรกิจ) และคุณจะได้รับอนุญาตให้อยู่ในประเทศได้อีกไม่เกิน 7 วัน ดังนั้นคุณควรหางานใหม่และเตรียมเปลี่ยนเอกสารให้เรียบร้อยก่อนที่จะลาออกจากงานที่ทำอยู่ปัจจุบัน วีซ่าประเภท Non-immigrant B (เพื่อประกอบธุรกิจ) นี้สามารถต่ออายุได้ที่สำนักงานตรวจคนเข้าเมืองในประเทศไทย แต่อาจต้องเตรียมเอกสารเพิ่มเติมซึ่งต้องยื่นโดยนายจ้าง เมื่อต่ออายุวีซ่างแล้ว คุณก็สามารถต่ออายุใบอนุญาตทำงานได้

หากคุณวางแผนที่จะเดินทางออกนอกประเทศ วีซ่าของคุณต้องเป็นประเภทเข้า-ออกได้หลายครั้ง หากวีซ่าเป็นประเภทเข้าออกได้ครั้งเดียวและคุณเดินทางต้องออกนอกประเทศ คุณจะต้องขอวีซ่าประเภท Non-immigrant B (เพื่อประกอบธุรกิจ) และใบอนุญาตทำงานใหม่อีกครั้ง

สำหรับข้อมูลล่าสุดเกี่ยวกับใบอนุญาตทำงาน กรุณาไปที่เว็บไซต์ของกรมการจัดหางาน (www.doe.go.th/service3_en.aspx) นอกจากนี้ ผู้เขียนได้เตรียมข้อมูลและที่อยู่ของหน่วยงานรัฐที่เกี่ยวข้องกับการขอ ใบอนุญาตทำงานและใบอนุญาตเข้าเมืองดังต่อไปนี้ หากคุณต้องการข้อมูลเกี่ยวกับใบอนุญาตเข้าเมืองและการเข้าเมือง กรุณาดูได้ส่วนอ้างอิงของหนังสือนี้

กรมการจัดหางาน
สำนักงานบริหารแรงงานต่างด้าว
ถนนมิตรไมตรี เขตดินแดง กรุงเทพฯ 10400
โทร 0-2245-2745

ศูนย์บริการเบ็ดเสร็จ
555 อาคารรสา ทาวเวอร์ 2 ชั้น 16
ถนนพหลโยธิน เขตจตุจักร กรุงเทพฯ 10900
โทร 0-2937-1155

สำนักงานตรวจคนเข้าเมือง
507 ซอยสวนพลู ถนนสาทรใต้
กรุงเทพฯ 10120
โทร 0-2287-3101 (ถึง 10)

ระบบภาษี

หากคุณมีรายได้จากการทำงานในประเทศไทย คุณต้องจ่ายภาษีในประเทศไทย
คุณควรตรวจสอบว่า ประเทศของคุณมีระเบียบการจ่ายภาษีอย่างไรสำหรับผู้ทำงานใน
ต่างประเทศ นอกจากนี้ต้องตรวจสอบว่า คุณไม่ต้องเสียภาษีซ้ำซ้อนคือ จ่ายภาษีที่
เมืองไทยและภาษีเงินได้ในประเทศของคุณ กฎระเบียบของระบบภาษีไทยมีความซับซ้อน
มาก ผู้เขียนจึงขอแนะนำให้คุณปรึกษานายจ้าง หรือจ้างนักบัญชีที่มีประสบการณ์เข้ามาดูแล
ในกรณีที่คุณมีธุรกิจเป็นของตนเอง นอกจากนี้ยังมีเอกสารมากมายที่เป็นภาษาไทยอีกด้วย

อัตราคำนวณภาษีเงินได้บุคคลธรรมดาในประเทศไทยประจำปี 2549 มีดังนี้

<u>รายรับเป็นเงินบาทต่อปี</u>   <u>อัตราภาษี</u>

0 - 100,000	ยกเว้นภาษี
100,001-500,000	10%
500,001 - 1,000,000	20%
1,000,001 - 4,000,000	30%
4,000,001+	37%

ที่มา: กรมสรรพากร

การทำงานร่วมกับคนไทย

ชาวต่างชาติจำนวนมากทำงานกับคนไทยด้วยความสัมพันธ์แบบทั้งรักทั้งชัง เคล็ด(ไม่)ลับในการทำงานร่วมกับคนไทยให้มีความสุขคือ   พยายามทำความเข้าใจและยอมรับวัฒนธรรมตลอดจนค่านิยมของคนไทยให้ได้   คุณควรเตือนตนเองว่า คุณทำงานและอาศัยอยู่ในประเทศของเขา จึงควรทำตามกฎของเขา ในส่วนนี้ ผู้เขียนจะกล่าวถึงลักษณะของคนไทยและข้อแตกต่างจากการทำงานในโลกตะวันตก   นี่เป็นเพียงข้อมูลเล็กๆน้อยๆ ในการทำงานร่วมกับคนไทยเท่านั้น คุณควรหาข้อมูลเพิ่มเติมหากคุณต้องการทำงานหรือว่าจ้างคนไทยเข้าทำงานในบริษัทของคุณ

โดยทั่วไปแล้ว   คนไทยอ่อนหวานและเป็นมิตรกับคนทั่วไป   โดยเฉพาะชาวต่างชาติ และมักยิ้มเสมอไม่ว่าสถานการณ์เป็นอย่างไร นี่จึงเป็นที่มาของสยามเมืองยิ้ม คนไทยใช้รอยยิ้มในหลายโอกาสทั้งเพื่อทักทาย ขอบคุณ ขอโทษ เมื่อไม่รู้ว่าจะพูดหรือทำอย่างไรดี หรือเมื่อรู้สึกอับอาย ไม่ชอบความขัดแย้งและไม่ชอบถูกวิจารณ์โดยเฉพาะในที่สาธารณะ   การยิ้มของคนไทยต่างจากชาวตะวันตกซึ่งยิ้มเมื่อมีความสุขหรือพอใจสิ่งใดสิ่งหนึ่งเท่านั้น หากคุณคิดเช่นนั้น คุณก็คงคิดว่า ผู้คนรอบตัวมีความสุขมาก นี่อาจเป็นความเข้าใจผิดอย่างร้ายแรง เนื่องจากรอยยิ้ม "สำเร็จรูป" ที่คุณเห็นอาจเป็นการปกปิดอะไรบางอย่างนอกจากความสุข คุณอาจต้องใช้เวลาในการทำความเข้าใจวัฒนธรรมที่แตกต่างระหว่างบ้านเกิดเมืองนอนของคุณกับวัฒนธรรมไทย   แต่หากคุณได้ยิ้มให้กับคนไทยแล้วคุณก็มักจะได้รับรอยยิ้มตอบกลับ ในกรณีที่ทำงาน คุณควรพยายามยิ้มเพื่อสร้างบรรยากาศการทำงานที่ดี

ดูผิวเผินแล้ว คนไทยทำงานร่วมกันได้ดีมากกว่าชาวตะวันตก เขาช่วยกันทำงานแบ่งอาหาร   พูดคุยเกี่ยวกับครอบครัวหรือข้อมูลส่วนตัวให้ฟัง   และพยายามหลีกเลี่ยงที่จะขัดแย้งกับเพื่อนร่วมงาน   อย่างไรก็ตามหากวันนั้นมาถึง   สถานการณ์จะร้ายแรงกว่าสถานการณ์เดียวกันในโลกการทำงานของชาวตะวันตก   คนไทยมักจะรู้สึกริษยาและจะแก้แค้นคนที่ทำไม่ดีกับตนได้เช่นกัน นอกจากนี้คนไทยยังรับการตำหนิแม้จะเป็นการติเพื่อก่อได้ไม่ดีนัก ดังนั้นคุณต้องระมัดระวังเมื่อพูดเล่นหรือเมื่อต้องการติเพื่อก่อให้ดี การติชมคนไทยเป็นสิ่งละเอียดอ่อนที่ต้องทำด้วยความระมัดระวัง หรือไม่ควรทำเลย นอกจากนี้คุณไม่ควรแสดงความคิดเห็นด้านลบกับอะไรก็ตามที่ถือเป็นของไทย ไม่ควรทำให้เพื่อนร่วมงาน

ไทยรู้สึก "เสียหน้า" เป็นอันขาด สิ่งสำคัญที่สุดคือ ห้ามหัวเสียและตะโกนใส่หน้าใครเป็น
อันขาด เพราะจะเป็นผลเสียต่องาน ทำให้เพื่อนร่วมงานทำงานด้วยความไม่สบายใจ งาน
เดินช้า และตัวคุณเองก็จะไม่เป็นที่นิยมอีกเป็นเวลานาน

ในตอนต้นของหนังสือ ผู้เขียนได้พูดถึงระบบชนชั้นในสังคมไทยไปบ้างแล้ว คุณ
ก็จะเห็นระบบนี้ในที่ทำงานเสมอ คนไทยมักจะถามคุณเรื่องอายุ เงินเดือน การศึกษา
ครอบครัว เพื่อที่ว่าจะได้ประเมินคุณว่าจะอยู่จุดใดในระบบชนชั้นนี้ เนื่องจากคนไทยใช้
สรรพนามในการเรียกต่างๆ กันไป เช่น คำว่า "you" สามารถเปลี่ยนแปลงไปได้หลากหลาย
ตามสถานะของบุคคล นอกจากนี้คนไทยยังใช้ชื่อจริง ชื่อเล่น คำนำหน้าอย่างเป็นทางการ
และแม้กระทั่งคำที่บ่งบอกอายุของคนนั้น คุณควรหลีกเลี่ยงที่จะทำให้ใครขายหน้า หาก
เพื่อนร่วมงานของคุณอยากจะรู้รายละเอียดส่วนตัวของคุณ บางครั้งอาจถามคำถามเดิมๆ
ซ้ำแล้วซ้ำอีก หากคุณไม่อยากตอบคำถาม ให้พยายามตอบคำถามแบบเลี่ยงๆ แต่สุภาพเพื่อ
รักษาหน้าผู้ถาม คนไทยไม่อยากจะ "เหยียบตาปลา" คนที่อยู่ในสถานะทางสังคมที่สูงกว่า
แต่ก็อาจจะรู้สึกอิจฉาอยู่ในใจ คนในชนชั้นที่ต่ำกว่าจะใช้คนที่อยู่ในชนชั้นที่สูงกว่าเป็น
แรงบันดาลใจที่จะทำงานหนักเพื่อที่จะได้ไปอยู่ในชนชั้นนั้นบ้าง นอกจากนี้ คนไทยยังเชื่อ
เรื่องเวรกรรม โดยเชื่อว่าคนในชนชั้นสูงทำกรรมดีมา จึงได้อยู่ในชนชั้นนั้น หากคุณเข้าใจ
พื้นฐานของสังคมไทยมากเท่าใดและเหตุผลว่าทำไมเขาจึงทำเช่นนั้นได้เร็วเท่าใด คุณก็จะ
ปรับตัวและพร้อมที่จะทำธุรกิจกับคนไทยได้เร็วเท่านั้น

คนไทยใช้ชีวิตด้วยความสุขและความสนุกก็เป็นสิ่งสำคัญที่สุดในชีวิต คนไทย
เชื่อในปรัชญาของความ "สนุก" ทำให้นำหลักการนี้มาประยุกต์เข้ากับการทำงานนั่นคือ
ต้องทำงานด้วยความสนุกและผ่อนคลาย นี่อาจขัดแย้งกับหลักการทำงานในประเทศบ้าน
เกิดของคุณอย่างรุนแรง นอกจากนี้คนไทยอาจไม่ทำงานอย่างรวดเร็วหรือมีประสิทธิภาพ
เช่นในประเทศตะวันตก หลายคนก็มาทำงานตาม "เวลาไทย" นั่นคือมาทำงานสายหรือมาช้า
กว่าเวลานัดหมาย การซุบซิบนินทาก็พบได้ในที่ทำงานและคนที่ตกเป็นเป้าหมายมักจะเป็น
ชาวต่างชาตินั่นเอง เพื่อทำงานให้ประสบความสำเร็จคุณต้องปรับตัว หาวิธีรับมือกับสิ่ง
เหล่านี้ และอดทนให้มากถึงมากที่สุด พึงระลึกว่า คุณเป็นผู้เลือกที่จะทำงานในประเทศนี้เอง
ดังนั้นคุณจึงต้องเป็นผู้ปรับตัวให้เข้ากับสภาพแวดล้อมในประเทศเจ้าบ้าน

ขอให้คุณพยายามสร้างมิตรภาพกับเพื่อนร่วมงานและเพื่อนบ้านเอาไว้ วิธีที่ดี
ที่สุดคือการเข้ากลุ่มกับคนรอบๆ ตัวและพยายามพูดภาษาไทยกับเขา วิธีนี้จะช่วยให้คุณ
เข้าใจพวกเขาดียิ่งขึ้น และยังทำให้เขาประทับใจในตัวคุณด้วย การที่คุณสามารถพูด
ภาษาไทยได้จะช่วยยกสถานะทางสังคมของคุณให้สูงขึ้นและเป็นประโยชน์ต่อคุณมากมาย
เมื่อคุณสามารถสื่อสารกับเพื่อนชาวไทยของคุณแล้ว เขาจะช่วยดูแลทรัพย์สินเวลาคุณไม่อยู่
บ้าน ช่วยหาช่างประปาหรือช่างซ่อมอื่นๆ เมื่อคุณต้องการหรือแม้กระทั่งช่วยคุณทำความ
เข้าใจเอกสารภาษาไทยด้วย

เนื่องจากหนังสือกฎหมายไทยเล่มนี้ จะกล่าวถึงสังคมไทยและการทำงานกับคน
ไทยเพียงเท่านี้ ยังมีหนังสือที่อธิบายวัฒนธรรมไทยอีกหลายเล่ม เช่น Culture Shock
Thailand, Dos and Don'ts in Thailand และ Thai Means Business ซึ่งจะเป็นประโยชน์และ
มีข้อมูลเกี่ยวกับคนไทยและวัฒนธรรมไทยอีกมากมาย อย่างไรก็ตาม แม้หนังสือเหล่านี้จะมี
ข้อมูลที่เป็นประโยชน์และทำให้คุณเข้าใจคนไทย และวัฒนธรรมไทยได้มากเพียงใด คุณก็
ต้องปรับตัว ยอมรับ และทำตัวให้เข้ากับวัฒนธรรมที่แตกต่างในดินแดนสยามเมืองยิ้ม

อาชญากรรมและการลงโทษผู้กระทำผิด

ประเทศไทยกำลังเป็นที่หมายซึ่งได้รับความนิยมจากทั้งนักท่องเที่ยวและผู้อพยพ
เข้าเมือง ที่ใดก็ตามที่มีนักท่องเที่ยวมากก็ย่อมมีผู้แสวงหาประโยชน์จากเหยื่อที่ไม่
ระมัดระวังตัวหรือไม่ได้ระแวงว่าจะเกิดอะไรขึ้นกับตนเอง อย่างไรก็ตาม ข่าวดีก็คือ จำนวน
คดีอาชญากรรมร้ายแรงที่เกิดกับชาวต่างชาติค่อนข้างน้อย การเตร็ดเตร่ในย่านนักท่องเที่ยว
ของเมืองหลวงหรือเมืองอื่นๆ ก็ยังถือว่า ปลอดภัยสำหรับชาวต่างชาติ อาชญากรรมที่ไม่
ร้ายแรงนี้เกิดขึ้นเช่นเดียวกับในเมืองใหญ่ทั่วโลก ยิ่งคุณมีข้อมูลอาชญากรรมที่เกิดขึ้นกับ
นักท่องเที่ยวมากเท่าใด คุณก็จะได้เตรียมตัวให้พร้อม เพื่อที่จะได้พักผ่อนได้อย่างมีความสุข
และปราศจากการผจญภัยที่เกินความคาดหมาย ในบทนี้ ผู้เขียนขอเสนอข้อมูลเกี่ยวกับ
อาชญากรรมที่คนไทยกระทำต่อชาวต่างชาติ อาชญากรรมที่กระทำโดยชาวต่างชาติใน
ประเทศไทย ตลอดจนข้อมูลสถิติอาชญากรรมล่าสุด

การก่ออาชญากรรมต่อชาวต่างชาติ

การก่ออาชญากรรมต่อชาวต่างชาติโดยชาวไทยส่วนใหญ่เป็นอาชญากรรมที่ไม่
รุนแรงซึ่งกระทำต่อนักท่องเที่ยวเช่น การลักขโมย การวิ่งราว การชิงทรัพย์ อาชญากรรม
โดยแท็กซี่ การหลอกขายอัญมณี และการหลอกลวงต้มตุ๋น นอกจากนี้ชาวต่างชาติในเมือง
หลวงก็อาจประสบกับการขายบริการทางเพศซึ่งยังผิดกฎหมายอยู่ สิ่งเหล่านี้ล้วนเกิดขึ้นกับ
นักท่องเที่ยวในยุโรป สหรัฐอเมริกาและละตินอเมริกา ตลอดจนเมืองใหญ่ต่างๆทั่วโลก
เช่นกัน ดังนั้นคุณจึงควรตื่นตัว ใช้สัญชาตญาณ และระมัดระวังตัวตามคำแนะนำที่หนังสือ
นำเที่ยวได้แนะนำไว้ ยิ่งคุณระมัดระวังตัวเรื่องการต้มตุ๋นมากเท่าใดและปฏิบัติตาม
คำแนะนำตามที่ปรากฏในเว็บไซต์ภาครัฐ หนังสือนำเที่ยว และจากผู้นำเที่ยวของคุณเอง
โอกาสที่จะตกเป็นเหยื่อก็จะลดน้อยลงด้วย ส่วนอาชญากรรมร้ายแรงต่างๆ เช่น การข่มขืน
การฆาตกรรม และการฆ่าอย่างโหดเหี้ยมก็เกิดขึ้นกับชาวต่างชาติเช่นเดียวกัน แต่ถือว่าน้อย
มาก แม้ประเทศไทยจะเป็นประเทศที่มีอัตราการฆาตกรรมต่อประชากรสูงเป็นอันดับที่ 14
ของโลกตามการสำรวจแนวโน้มอาชญากรรมและการปฏิบัติของกระบวนการยุติธรรมทาง

อาญาแห่งองค์การสหประชาชาติ ประจำปี 2543 (15 ประเทศแรกคือ โคลัมเบีย อาฟริกาใต้ จาไมกา เวเนซุเอลา รัสเซีย เม็กซิโก ลิทัวเนีย เอสโตเนีย ลัตเวีย เบลารุส ยูเครน ปาปัวนิวกินี เคอร์กิซสถาน **ประเทศไทย** และซิมบับเว ตามลำดับ) แต่ข้อมูลนี้ก็เป็นข้อมูลของ อาชญากรรมร้ายแรงซึ่งคนไทยกระทำต่อคนไทยด้วยกัน เมื่อมีการประกอบอาชญากรรม ร้ายแรงต่อชาวต่างชาติ ก็จะกลายเป็นข่าวใหญ่ระดับท้องที่ ระดับประเทศและระดับ นานาชาติ เจ้าหน้าที่ตำรวจก็จะใช้กำลังความหาผู้กระทำผิดมาลงโทษอย่างรวดเร็ว และ มักจะประสบความสำเร็จเป็นอย่างดี เนื่องจากประเทศไทยมีรายได้มหาศาลจาก อุตสาหกรรมท่องเที่ยว ดังนั้นทุกคนจึงไม่ต้องการให้มีการก่ออาชญากรรมต่อนักท่องเที่ยว และด้วยเหตุนี้ คนไทยส่วนใหญ่จึงหลีกเลี่ยงการกระทำผิดต่อชาวต่างชาติเพราะเสี่ยงต่อการ ตกเป็นเป้าสายตาของเจ้าหน้าที่ นอกจากนี้อาชญากรรมร้ายแรงในหมู่คนไทยก็ไม่มีความ เกี่ยวข้องกับชาวต่างชาติ และส่วนใหญ่เกี่ยวข้องกับการเมืองหรือการล้างแค้น คนไทยใน พื้นที่ย่อมรู้ดีว่า เกิดอะไรขึ้นและรู้ว่าอะไรเป็นอันตราย หากคนไทยแนะนำไม่ให้คุณไปที่ใด หรือบอกคุณว่าใครเป็นบุคคลอันตราย คุณก็ควรรับฟังและหลีกเลี่ยงสถานที่หรือบุคคลนั้น เสีย

รัฐบาลไทยได้จัดความช่วยเหลือให้กับชาวต่างชาติที่ต้องการความช่วยเหลือผ่าน ระบบโทรศัพท์ตลอด 24 ชั่วโมง หากคุณเป็นผู้เสียหาย ให้ติดต่อหมายเลขฉุกเฉิน 191 หรือ สายด่วนนักท่องเที่ยวหรือศูนย์บริการที่หมายเลข 1155 ซึ่งจะมีตำรวจท่องเที่ยวคอย ให้บริการ ศูนย์บริการเหล่านี้จัดตั้งขึ้นโดยการท่องเที่ยวแห่งประเทศไทย นอกจากนี้ยังมี ศูนย์บริการนักท่องเที่ยวภายใต้สำนักปลัดกระทรวงของกระทรวงการท่องเที่ยวและกีฬาซึ่ง มีหน้าที่ประสานงานและแก้ไขปัญหาต่างๆที่เกี่ยวกับการท่องเที่ยว รับคำร้องเรียนของ นักท่องเที่ยว อำนวยความสะดวกแก่นักท่องเที่ยว ตลอดจนประสานงานระหว่างภาครัฐและ เอกชนในด้านความปลอดภัย

ศูนย์บริการนักท่องเที่ยว (The Service Center)
กระทรวงการท่องเที่ยวและกีฬา
4 ถนนราชดำเนินนอก
ป้อมปราบศัตรูพ่าย กรุงเทพ 10100

สาขาของศูนย์นี้ตั้งอยู่ที่ ชั้นสอง ประตูสามของสนามบินสุวรรณภูมิ ซึ่ง
ศูนย์บริการนี้เปิดให้บริการนักท่องเที่ยวเพื่อรับคำร้องและเอกสารตลอด 24 ชั่วโมง

นอกจากนี้ยังมีการบริการตลอด 24 ชั่วโมง ผ่านหมายเลขโทรศัพท์ 1155 หรือ 0-
2124-4070 หรือทางอีเมลล์ที่ thai-tac@hotmail.com ส่วนเว็บไซท์ของศูนย์คือ
www.touristassistancecenter.go.th ซึ่งมีข้อมูลทั้งภาษาไทย อังกฤษ และจีน

ตำรวจท่องเที่ยว

ตำรวจท่องเที่ยวของไทยแยกเป็นเอกเทศจากตำรวจอื่นๆในประเทศไทย และมี
หน้าที่ช่วยเหลือและแก้ไขปัญหาที่อาจเกิดขึ้นกับนักท่องเที่ยว ตำรวจเหล่านี้จะทำงานใน
ย่านนักท่องเที่ยว สามารถพูดภาษาอังกฤษและภาษาอื่นๆได้ หากคุณต้องการความช่วยเหลือ
และไม่ได้อยู่ในย่านนักท่องเที่ยว คุณสามารถติดต่อหมายเลข 191 หรือขอให้คนไทยโทรติด
ต่อเมื่อแจ้งความ ทางตำรวจท่องเที่ยวไทยพยายามที่จะรับอาสาสมัครชาวต่างชาติเข้าไปช่วย
ทำงานในบริเวณที่มีนักท่องเที่ยว เช่น สนามบินสุวรรณภูมิ สนามบินดอนเมือง ถนน
ข้าวสาร ตลาดนัดจตุจักร ศูนย์บริการนักท่องเที่ยว ศูนย์สายด่วน (Call Center) อาสาสมัคร
จะไม่ได้รับค่าจ้าง และจะต้องมีคุณสมบัติที่เหมาะสม นอกจากนี้อาสาสมัครจะไม่เข้าไปยุ่ง
เกี่ยวกับงานทำงานหลายอย่าง เช่น การจับกุม การสอบปากคำ การสืบสวนและการตรวจค้น
เป็นต้น หากคุณต้องการสละเวลาอันมีค่าของคุณเพื่อประโยชน์แก่นักท่องเที่ยว กรุณา
ติดต่อศูนย์ช่วยเหลือนักท่องเที่ยวเพื่อขอข้อมูลเพิ่มเติม นอกจากจะได้ทำตัวให้เป็น
ประโยชน์แก่ชุมชนแล้ว คุณจะได้มีโอกาสสร้างสัมพันธ์ที่อาจเป็นประโยชน์ต่อคุณใน
อนาคต การมีเพื่อนเป็นตำรวจท่องเที่ยวและเป็นผู้ทำประโยชน์ต่อสังคมเป็นสิ่งที่มีคุณค่า
อย่างยิ่ง

ตำรวจไทย

หากคุณเป็นผู้เสียหาย คุณสามารถไปแจ้งความได้ที่สถานีตำรวจในท้องที่ ตำรวจ
จะลงบันทึกไว้แล้วทำการสืบสวนต่อไป หากคุณต้องติดต่อกับตำรวจหรือตำรวจท่องเที่ยว
ในฐานะผู้เสียหาย ขอให้คุณพยายามใช้หลักวัฒนธรรมไทยที่คุณเรียนรู้มาใช้ ณ วินาทีนั้น

คุณอาจรู้สึกตื่น ตระหนก ตกใจ หรือหวาดกลัว แต่คุณก็ต้องรักษาความสุภาพ ไม่หยาบคาย
หรือเกรี้ยวกราด แม้งานอาจจะไม่ดำเนินไปอย่างรวดเร็วอย่างที่คุณต้องการหรือตามที่ควร
จะเป็น แต่คุณก็ต้องอดทน ตำรวจไทยพยายามที่จะสืบสวนและจับกุมผู้กระทำผิดอย่างมี
ประสิทธิภาพที่สุด และก็มีวิธีการทำงานของตนเอง หากคุณทำให้ตำรวจไม่พอใจด้วยเหตุ
ใดๆ ก็ตาม ผลที่ได้อาจไม่ตรงกับที่คุณต้องการ นอกจากนี้ยังมีภาษาเป็นอุปสรรคสำคัญเมื่อ
คุณไปติดต่อสถานีตำรวจซึ่งทุกคนพูดภาษาไทย ดังนั้นคุณจึงควรหาคนไทยที่สามารถ
แปลภาษาไปกับคุณด้วย ทั้งนี้คุณอาจขอความช่วยเหลือจากศูนย์สายด่วนบริการ
นักท่องเที่ยว และหวังว่าจะได้รับความช่วยเหลือเป็นภาษาของคุณ ไม่นานมานี้ได้มีการ
บริการแปลภาษาและล่ามเพื่อให้ความช่วยเหลือผ่านโทรศัพท์หรือการส่งข้อความแปลผ่าน
โทรศัพท์มือถือ อย่างไรก็ดีการบริการเหล่านี้เพิ่งเริ่มต้นและอาจยังไม่สามารถให้บริการได้
ครบถ้วน นอกจากนี้ยังทำงานช้าและมีค่าบริการสูง ในกรณีที่คดีร้ายแรง คุณควรปรึกษา
สถานทูตของคุณเพื่อรายงานสิ่งที่เกิดขึ้นและขอคำแนะนำต่อไป

สถิติผู้ต้องขังในประเทศไทย

สถิติต่อไปนี้เป็นข้อมูลผู้ต้องขังในปี 2549 ซึ่งกรมราชทัณฑ์ กระทรวงยุติธรรมได้
รวมรวมไว้ ซึ่งจะให้ภาพรวมว่าอาชญากรรมในประเทศไทยเป็นอย่างไร

จำนวนของผู้ต้องขัง

    ชาย: 128,097 คน (84.5%)

    หญิง: 23, 579 คน (15.5%)

ประภทของผู้ต้องขัง

    จำคุก: 108,610 คน (71.6%)

    รอการอุธรณ์ : 21,088 คน (14.0%)

    ระหว่างการสืบสวน: 11,450 คน (7.5%)

    รอการพิจารณาคดี: 10,060 คน (6.6%)

    อื่นๆ: 378 คน (0.3%)

ประเภทของการกระทำผิด

    พ.ร.บ. ยาเสพติด: 64,782 คน (59.7%)

    ผิดต่อทรัพย์: 11,987 คน (19.3%)

    ผิดต่อชีวิต: 9,488 คน (8.7%)

    กระทำผิดต่อเพศ: 5,143 คน (4.8%)

    ทำร้ายร่างกาย: 3,226 คน (3.0%)

    เป็นภัยต่อความมั่นคงของสังคม: 250 คน (0.2%)

    อื่นๆ: 4,734 คน (4.3%)

ระยะเวลาต้องโทษ

    น้อยกว่า 5 ปี: 51,523 คน (47.4%)

    ระหว่าง 5 - 20 ปี: 41,993 คน (38.7%)

    ระหว่าง 20 ปี - 50 ปี: 12,131 คน (11.1%)

    จำคุกตลอดชีวิต: 2,869 คน (2.6%)

    ประหารชีวิต: 94 คน (0.2%)

อายุของผู้ต้องขัง

    น้อยกว่า 20 ปี: 3,890 คน (3.6%)

    ระหว่าง 20-30 ปี: 41,174 คน (38.0%)

    ระหว่าง 30-40 ปี: 35,147 คน (32.4%)

    ระหว่าง 40-50 ปี: 21,134 คน (19.4%)

    ระหว่าง 50-60 ปี: 5,402 คน (4.9%)

    มากกว่า 60 ปี: 1,863 คน (1.7%)

อัตราส่วนของเจ้าหน้าที่ราชทัณฑ์ต่อจำนวนผู้ต้องขัง

    1:19 ในปี 2543

    1:15 ในปี 2544

1:22 ในปี 2545

1:20 ในปี 2546

1:19 ในปี 2547

1:15 ในปี 2548

1:13 ในปี 2549

การกระทำผิดโดยชาวต่างชาติ

ประเทศไทยเป็นประเทศที่ดึงดูดทั้งนักท่องเที่ยวและนักลงทุนต่างชาติมากที่สุด
แห่งหนึ่ง   แต่เป็นที่น่าเสียดายที่ดินแดนแห่งนี้ยังดึงดูดกลุ่มชาวต่างชาติไม่พึงประสงค์ซึ่ง
ประกอบอาชีพไม่สุจริตทั้งหลายเช่น   การล่อลวงทางเพศ ผู้เสพและค้ายาเสพติด การค้า
มนุษย์ การขายบริการทางเพศ การนำคนเข้าเมืองอย่างผิดกฎหมาย เครือข่ายอาชญากรข้าม
ชาติ การค้าอาวุธ การค้าน้ำมันเถื่อน และแม้กระทั่งชาวต่างชาติที่คอยแสวงหาประโยชน์
ด้วยการหลอกลวงชาวต่างชาติด้วยกัน ผู้เขียนจะขอกล่าวถึงอาชญากรรมเหล่านี้สักเล็กน้อย
เพื่อให้คุณได้ระมัดระวังตัวในเรื่องนี้และหวังว่าจะช่วยให้คุณได้หลีกเลี่ยงประสบการณ์อัน
ไม่น่าพิสมัยในประเทศไทย

การกระทำผิดโดยชาวต่างชาติในประเทศไทยส่วนใหญ่เป็นการกระทำผิด
เกี่ยวกับยาเสพติด ชาวต่างชาติหลายคนคาดว่า การดำเนินชีวิตแบบสบายๆของคนไทยจะ
ครอบคลุมไปถึงการใช้ยาเสพติด แต่เรื่องยาเสพติดนี้ไม่ใช่เรื่องเล่นๆ การใช้ยาเสพติดถือ
เป็นการกระทำผิดที่มักพบในคนชั้นต่ำของสังคมและการลักลอบขนยาเสพติดก็มักจะ
ได้รับบทโทษจำคุกค่อนข้างสูงมาก เราจึงอยากจะถามคุณในฐานะชาวต่างชาติว่า เหตุใดคุณ
จึงอยากจะมีปัญหาในประเทศที่คุณไม่เข้าใจภาษาเล่า   และขอแนะนำอีกครั้งให้คุณปฏิบัติ
ตามคำแนะนำในหนังสือคู่มือนำเที่ยวประเทศไทย รวมถึงหลีกเลี่ยงการใช้ยาหรือการคบค้า
สมาคมกับผู้ใช้ยาเสพติด

การขายบริการทางเพศเป็นสิ่งที่ผิดกฎหมายในประเทศไทย   แต่ก็ยังพบได้ใน
เกือบทุกแห่งของประเทศในทุกรูปแบบ นับตั้งแต่บาร์ อะโกโก้ อาบอบนวด คาราโอเกะ

และร้านตัดผม และเนื่องจากกิจกรรมนี้ยังถือเป็นสิ่งผิดกฎหมาย คุณจึงควรหลีกเลี่ยงที่จะพา
ตนเองเข้าไปยุ่งเกี่ยวกับกิจกรรมนี้ คุณอาจเสี่ยงติดเชื้อโรคเอดส์และโรคทางเพศสัมพันธ์
อื่นๆซึ่งเลวร้ายยิ่งกว่าการติดคุกเสียอีก การขายบริการทางเพศโดยหญิงไทยปรากฏมาเป็น
เวลานาน แต่ก็มีกลุ่มผู้ขายบริการใหม่ๆ รวมถึงหญิงขายบริการจากประเทศเพื่อนบ้านและ
กลุ่มประเทศในสหภาพโซเวียตเดิม รัฐบาลไทยได้พยายามกวาดล้างการกระทำที่ผิด
กฎหมายเหล่านี้และเข้มงวดยิ่งขึ้น พร้อมทั้งเพิ่มบทลงโทษไม่ว่าจะเป็นการจำคุกหรือการ
ปรับให้สูงขึ้นสำหรับคดีการลักลอบเข้าประเทศเพื่อการขายบริการทางเพศ

การซื้อบริการทางเพศจากผู้ใหญ่ถือว่าผิดกฎหมายในประเทศไทย แต่การมี
เพศสัมพันธ์กับผู้ที่มีอายุต่ำกว่า 18 ปีถือว่าผิดกฎหมายร้ายแรงไม่ว่าผู้เยาว์จะยินยอมหรือไม่
ก็ตาม นั่นคือจะต้องได้รับโทษที่รุนแรงยิ่งขึ้น ทั้งนี้พบว่าการล่วงละเมิดผู้เยาว์ในประเทศ
ไทยมีจำนวนสูงขึ้นในช่วงทศวรรษที่ผ่านมา เราไม่อาจให้จำนวนตัวเลขของโสเภณีเด็กได้
การศึกษาวิจัยต่างๆได้ให้ตัวเลขที่แตกต่างกัน แต่ก็ชี้ให้เห็นว่า มีโสเภณีเด็กจำนวนไม่น้อย
ชาวต่างชาติส่วนหนึ่งเข้ามาอาศัยและทำงานในประเทศไทยบังหน้าเพื่อหาโอกาสมี
เพศสัมพันธ์กับผู้เยาว์ ไม่นานมานี้รัฐบาลไทยได้ตอบโต้และจับกุมผู้กระทำผิดที่เป็น
ชาวต่างชาติจนเป็นข่าวดังทั่วโลก นอกจากนี้ตำรวจยังทำงานอย่างแข็งขันที่จะลงโทษผู้ล่วง
ละเมิดผู้เยาว์เหล่านี้ สำหรับบทลงโทษนั้นอาจเป็นทั้งค่าปรับที่สูงลิ่ว การจำคุกและถูกขึ้น
บัญชีดำห้ามเข้าประเทศอีกต่อไป นอกจากนี้การมีเพศสัมพันธ์กับเด็กอายุต่ำกว่า 15 ปี ถือ
เป็นการทำผิดร้ายแรง และไม่อาจยอมความกันได้ ทั้งนี้ผู้ทำผิดต้องถูกจำคุก 4-20 ปี และ
ปรับตั้งแต่ 8,000-40,000 บาท หากเด็กอายุต่ำกว่า 13 ปี โทษจำคุกก็ยิ่งรุนแรงขึ้นเป็น 7-20 ปี
และปรับตั้งแต่ 8,000-40,000 บาท ซึ่งบทลงโทษนี้จะยิ่งรุนแรงขึ้นตามอายุของเด็กที่น้อยลง
โดยโทษสูงสุดคือจำคุกตลอดชีวิต

สตรีและเด็กที่ตกเป็นเหยื่อของการค้ามนุษย์ โดยเฉพาะกรณีการขายบริการทาง
เพศนั้น รัฐบาลไทยและองค์กรพัฒนาเอกชนหลายแห่งได้จัดบริการให้คำปรึกษาและ
ช่วยเหลือในด้านต่างๆ เช่น ที่พัก การศึกษาและการอบรมอาชีพ การหางานทำ และการ
ช่วยเหลือด้านการเงิน

เมื่อไม่นานมานี้ พบว่า มีนักต้มตุ๋นชาวต่างชาติที่ตระเวนหลอกลวงชาวต่างชาติ
ด้วยกันเพิ่มขึ้น โดยจะเตร็ดเตร่อยู่ในย่านของนักท่องเที่ยว แสดงตนว่า ตกเป็นเหยื่อ
ผู้เคราะห์ร้ายจากการลักขโมย ขอความเมตตาและเงินทองจากคุณ นักต้มตุ๋นตะวันตกบาง
คนอาจสวมบทบาทเป็นที่ปรึกษาทางธุรกิจซึ่งพยายามช่วยเหลือชาวต่างชาติที่ต้องการลงทุน
หรือซื้ออสังหาริมทรัพย์ในประเทศไทย บุคคลเหล่านี้อาจมีสำนักงานเป็นกิจจะลักษณะจน
ทำให้คุณหลงเชื่อว่าเป็นของจริง แต่เมื่อได้เงินจากคุณพอแล้วก็จะปิดสำนักงาน ย้ายไปเปิด
ที่ใหม่ หรือแม้กระทั่งล่องหนหายออกนอกประเทศไป เป็นการยากที่ตำรวจจะติดตามคน
เหล่านี้เพราะเป็นกลุ่มที่มีวิธีการและการนำเสนอที่แนบเนียน หากคุณตกอยู่ในสถานการณ์
เช่นนี้ คุณก็ต้องระมัดระวังป้องกันตนเองจากเหล่ามิจฉาชีพเช่นเดียวกับเมื่ออยู่ในประเทศ
ของคุณ

จำนวนเครือข่ายแก๊งก์อาชญากรข้ามชาติ (เช่น แก๊งก์ยากูซ่า) ในไทยได้เพิ่มขึ้น
อย่างช้าๆ โดยจำนวนผู้ต้องขังจากกลุ่มเครือข่ายเช่นนี้มีน้อยมากเนื่องจากเป็นกลุ่มที่ทำงาน
ลึกลับและมีทักษะสูง อย่างไรก็ตามสำนักงานตำรวจแห่งชาติได้ร่วมมือกับตำรวจใน
ประเทศอื่นๆ ในการจับกุมอาชญากรข้ามชาติเหล่านี้ โดยเครือข่ายอาชญากรเหล่านี้ส่วนมาก
เป็นแก๊งก์ชาวเอเชียและแก๊งก์ข้ามชาติที่ได้เงินมหาศาลจากการพนัน การค้ายาเสพติด การ
ขายบริการทางเพศ การค้ามนุษย์ และการค้าอาวุธ

หนังสือเล่มนี้เสนอภาพของอาชญากรรมและบทลงโทษประเทศไทยได้เพียง
เล็กน้อยเท่านั้น ข้อมูลและรายละเอียดของสถานการณ์และคดีที่น่าสนใจจะนำเสนอในเล่ม
ต่อไป กรุณาอ่านส่วน "คดีอาญา" ในหนังสือเล่มนี้ที่จะให้ข้อมูลเกี่ยวกับขั้นตอนการ
ดำเนินคดีมากขึ้น

สถิติการกระทำผิดโดยชาวต่างชาติในประเทศไทย ประจำปี พ.ศ. 2549

สถิติต่อไปนี้เป็นตัวเลขของผู้ต้องขังชาวต่างชาติที่ถูกจำคุกอยู่ในประเทศไทย

ผู้ต้องขังชาวต่างชาติจำแนกตามเพศ

เพศ	จำนวน (คน)
ชาย	9,825
หญิง	2,703
รวม	12,528

ผู้ต้องขังชาวต่างชาติ จำแนกตามทวีป

ทวีป	ร้อยละ
เอเชีย	95.84
อาฟริกา	2.35
ยุโรป	1.4
อเมริกา	0.26
ออสเตรเลีย	0.15
รวม	100%

จำนวนผู้ต้องขังชาวต่างชาติ จำแนกตามสัญชาติ

ที่	สัญชาติ	จำนวน	ที่	สัญชาติ	จำนวน	ที่	สัญชาติ	จำนวน
1.	พม่า	5,913	11	อินเดีย	64	21	ฟิลิปปินส์	28
2.	กัมพูชา	2,310	12	ปากีสถาน	57	22	เกาหลี	21
3.	ลาว	2,127	13	กานา	55	23	อาฟริกาใต้	19
4.	มาเลเซีย	431	14	เนปาล	53	24	คองโก	17
5.	จีน	292	15	เวียดนาม	47	25	เยอรมัน	16
6.	ชนกลุ่มน้อย	245	16	อินโดนีเซีย	42	26	ฝรั่งเศส	16
7.	สิงคโปร์	109	17	อังกฤษ	41	27	ศรีลังกา	16
8.	ไต้หวัน	109	18	บังคลาเทศ	35	28	สหรัฐอเมริกา	14
9.	ไนจีเรีย	87	19	อิหร่าน	34	29	เนเธอร์แลนด์	13
10	ฮ่องกง	72	20	ญี่ปุ่น	28	30	ออสเตรเลีย	11

สถิติผู้ต้องขัง จำแนกตามข้อหา

ข้อหา	จำนวน	ร้อยละ
พ.ร.บ. ยาเสพติด	6,048	48.2
พ.ร.บ. ตรวจคนเข้าเมือง	3,705	29.6
ผิดต่อทรัพย์	768	6.1
ผิดต่อชีวิต	673	5.3
ปลอมแปลงเอกสาร	504	4.2
พ.ร.บ. ป่าไม้	304	2.4
ประทุษร้ายทางเพศ	108	0.9
พ.ร.บ. อาวุธปืน	60	0.5
อื่นๆ	358	2.8
รวม	12,528	100%

ผู้ต้องขังชาวตะวันตกแยกตามข้อหา

ข้อหา	ร้อยละ
พ.ร.บ. ยาเสพติด	60.0
ปลอมแปลงเอกสาร	12.2
ผิดต่อทรัพย์	11.0
ผิดต่อชีวิต	7.7
พ.ร.บ. ตรวจคนเข้าเมือง	2.6
ประทุษร้ายทางเพศ	2.6
อื่นๆ	3.9
รวม	100%

สถิติผู้ต้องขังชาวต่างชาติในปี พ.ศ. 2549 เพิ่มขึ้นจากปี พ.ศ. 2548 ร้อยละ 20.4

ปี	จำนวน
2548	10,408
2549	12,528
ผลต่างร้อยละ	+ 20.4%

สถิติการโอนตัวนักโทษเด็ดขาดไปรับโทษในประเทศของตน (ตามข้อมูลดังต่อไปนี้)

ที่	ประเทศ	จำนวน (คน)
1	ไนจีเรีย	395
2	ฮ่องกง	83
3	สหรัฐอเมริกา	75
4	สเปน	33
5	ฝรั่งเศส	29
6	อังกฤษ	28
7	เยอรมันนี	18
8	แคนาดา	17
9	สวีเดน	15
10	อิตาลี	7
11	สวิสเซอร์แลนด์	6
12	เอสโตเนีย	5
13	เดนมาร์ก	3
14	ออสเตรเลีย	3
15	อิสราเอล	3
16	ออสเตรีย	2
17	นอร์เว	1
18	ประเทศไทย	8
	รวม	734

เป็นไปได้ที่ผู้ที่กระทำผิดกฎหมายในประเทศหนึ่งสามารถจะถูกส่งตัวกลับไป
จำคุกหรือรับโทษที่เหลือในประเทศของตน   ภายใต้พระราชบัญญัติการปฏิบัติเพื่อความ
ร่วมมือระหว่างประเทศในการดำเนินตามคำพิพากษาคดีอาญา พ.ศ. 2527 ชาวต่างชาติที่

กระทำผิดในประเทศไทยและชาวไทยที่กระทำผิดในต่างประเทศอาจขอโอนไปรับโทษใน
ประเทศของตนได้ หากได้มีการตกลงไว้ในสนธิสัญญาระหว่างประเทศไทยกับประเทศ
นั้นๆ ปัจจุบันประเทศไทยได้มีข้อตกลงการส่งผู้ต้องขังข้ามแดนกับ 24 ประเทศคือ ฝรั่งเศส
สเปน แคนาดา อิตาลี สหรัฐอเมริกา สวีเดน สหราชอาณาจักรและไอร์แลนด์เหนือ
ฟินแลนด์ เยอรมันนี โปรตุเกส ออสเตรีย อิสราเอล โปแลนด์ เดนมาร์ก ฮ่องกง
สวิสเซอร์แลนด์ นอร์เว ฟิลิปปินส์ เอสโตเนีย สาธารณรัฐเชค ออสเตรเลีย ไนจีเรีย
เนเธอร์แลนด์ และมาลี นอกจากนี้ประเทศไทยกำลังเจรจาทำสนธิสัญญากับประเทศ
เวียดนาม จีน เบลเยี่ยมและกัมพูชา

การตัดสินประหารชีวิตในประเทศไทย

การกระทำผิดบางข้อหาในประเทศไทยยังคงมีโทษร้ายแรงถึงขั้นประหารชีวิต
ทั้งนี้ตั้งอยู่บนพื้นฐานความเชื่อที่ว่า โทษประหารชีวิตจะทำให้คนเกรงกลัว เป็นการป้องกัน
ไม่ให้กระทำผิดที่เหี้ยมโหด ซึ่งจะส่งผลให้สังคมมีความสงบปลอดภัย

วิธีการประหารชีวิตในประเทศไทย

- ก่อนปี พ.ศ. 2477 ใช้วิธีตัดหัว
- ตั้งแต่ปี พ.ศ. 2477 และอีก 60 ปีต่อมา ใช้วิธียิงเป้า
- วันที่ 19 ตุลาคม 2544-ปัจจุบัน ใช้วิธีฉีดยาพิษ

การขอพระราชทานอภัยโทษรายบุคคล

พระมหากษัตริย์ของไทยทรงเป็นองค์ประมุขของการปกครองในระบอบ
ประชาธิปไตยอันมีพระมหากษัตริย์เป็นประมุขและทรงมีพระราชอำนาจในการ
พระราชทานอภัยโทษแก่ผู้ต้องขังในประเทศ ดังนั้นผู้ต้องขังซึ่งรวมถึงผู้ถูกตัดสินประหาร
ชีวิต หรือผู้เกี่ยวข้องกับผู้ต้องขังอาจถวายฎีกาขอพระราชทานอภัยโทษรายบุคคลผ่าน
เจ้าหน้าที่ราชทัณฑ์ หลังจากที่ได้ถวายฎีกา แล้ว เจ้าหน้าที่จะส่งเรื่องพร้อมเอกสารต่างๆที่
เกี่ยวข้องไปยังกรมราชทัณฑ์ กระทรวงยุติธรรม สำนักนายกรัฐมนตรี สำนักองคมนตรี และ

พระบาทสมเด็จพระเจ้าอยู่หัวในที่สุด   ทั้งนี้การอภัยโทษรายบุคคลนี้อาจทรงพระราชทาน
หรือไม่ก็ได้

การขอพระราชทานอภัยโทษรายกลุ่ม

นอกจากการขอพระราชทานอภัยโทษเป็นรายบุคคลซึ่งผู้ต้องขังมีสิทธิขอรับ
พระราชทานแล้ว ยังมีการขอพระราชทานอภัยโทษรายกลุ่ม ซึ่งมักจะพระราชทานให้ใน
วาระสำคัญของชาติ เช่นวันเฉลิมพระชนมพรรษาของพระบาทสมเด็จพระเจ้าอยู่หัวหรือ
ของสมเด็จพระนางเจ้าพระบรมราชินีนาถ ในกรณีนี้ไม่ต้องถวายฎีกา และผู้ต้องขังจะได้รับ
สิทธิตามที่กำหนดไว้ในพระราชกฤษฎีกาการอภัยโทษซึ่งแต่ละคนจะได้รับการลดโทษ
ต่างๆกันไป เช่น จะทำให้ผู้ถูกตัดสินประหารชีวิตได้รับโทษลดลงเป็นจำคุกตลอดชีวิต
เป็นต้น

คุณสามารถเข้าเยี่ยมชมเว็บไซท์ของกรมราชทัณฑ์ได้ที่ www.correct.go.th เพื่อ
ทำความเข้าใจถึงพันธกิจ เอกสารและกิจกรรม ตลอดจนข้อมูลที่มีประโยชน์อื่นๆ สำนักงาน
ใหญ่ของกรมราชทัณฑ์ ตั้งอยู่ ณ เลขที่ 222 ถนนนนทบุรี 1 จังหวัดนนทบุรี 11000
โทร: 0-2967-2222 โทรสาร: 0-2967-2408

ท้ายบท

ผู้เขียนเชื่อว่าคุณผู้อ่านคงได้รับข้อมูลข่าวสารที่เป็นประโยชน์จากหนังสือเล่มนี้ เราไม่สามารถที่จะให้ข้อมูลที่ตอบคำถามบางอย่างที่คุณต้องการ แต่อย่างน้อยคุณก็จะได้รับข้อมูลทั่วไปและแหล่งข้อมูลที่จะช่วยให้คุณหาคำตอบได้เกี่ยวกับกฎหมายไทย โดยทั่วไปแล้วเรื่องของกฎหมายเป็นเรื่องที่ซับซ้อนและเข้าใจยาก อย่างไรก็ตาม ผู้เขียนได้พยายามนำเสนอในรูปแบบที่อ่านแล้วเข้าใจง่ายเพื่อจะได้เป็นประโยชน์แก่ผู้อ่านมากที่สุด

ผู้เขียนยินดีที่จะได้รับคำแนะนำต่างๆเพื่อปรับปรุงหนังสือเล่มนี้ ซึ่งเราจึงมีโครงการที่จะปรับปรุงแก้ไขเมื่อเวลาผ่านไปสักระยะหนึ่ง เรายินดีที่จะได้รับคำถามและคำติชมต่างๆจากคุณผู้อ่านเพื่อนำไปประกอบกับหนังสือกฎหมายในชุดต่อๆไป กรุณาส่งข้อความไปที่ thailaw4u@gmail.com ตามที่ผู้เขียนได้แจ้งให้ทราบในตอนต้นของหนังสือ เราจะไม่ตอบคำถามส่วนบุคคลและจะไม่ให้คำแนะนำทางด้านกฎหมาย แต่เราจะเลือกเอาคำถามที่เห็นว่าเป็นประโยชน์ต่อบุคคลจำนวนมาก หรือเป็นคำถามที่ถามกันเป็นประจำ ทีมงานของเราจะทำวิจัยในหัวข้อนั้นๆ และจะเขียนอธิบายในเล่มต่อไป ซึ่งเราจะอธิบายแต่ละหัวข้อ แต่ละประเด็นให้ลึกซึ้งพร้อมยกตัวอย่างคดีที่น่าสนใจ

คุณผู้อ่านสามารถเข้าเยี่ยมชมเว็บไซท์ของเราได้ที่ www.ThaiLawForForeigners.com เพื่อดูข้อมูลที่เราได้ปรับปรุงแก้ไขเพื่อเติม นอกจากนี้ยังมีแบบฟอร์มที่คุณสามารถดาวน์โหลดและลิงค์ที่มีประโยชน์และน่าสนใจอีกด้วย

ขอให้คุณผู้อ่านโชคดีและอยู่ในกรอบของกฎหมาย

เบญจวรรณและเริงศักดิ์
ผู้เขียน

เกี่ยวกับผู้เขียน

เบญจวรรณ ภูมิแสน เบคเกอร์ เป็นที่รู้จักดีในสหรัฐอเมริกาในฐานะล่ามและผู้
แปลเอกสารภาษาไทยและภาษาลาว เบญจวรรณก่อตั้งบริษัทแปลภาษาชื่อศูนย์บริการ
ภาษาไทย-ภาษาลาวขึ้นเมื่อปี พ.ศ. 2539 เธอได้ทำงานเป็นล่ามที่ขึ้นทะเบียนกับสภา
ยุติธรรมแห่งรัฐแคลิฟอร์เนียมามากกว่า 10 ปี เธอได้เขียนหนังสือจำนวนมากให้ชาวต่างชาติ
เรียนภาษาไทยและภาษาลาว และได้แปลเอกสารทางด้านกฎหมายหลายร้อยฉบับจาก
ภาษาไทยเป็นภาษาอังกฤษและจากภาษาอังกฤษเป็นภาษาไทย เบญจวรรณใช้เวลาของเธอ
ส่วนหนึ่งอาศัยอยู่ที่รัฐแคลิฟอร์เนียภาคเหนือของสหรัฐอเมริกาและอีกส่วนหนึ่งอยู่ที่
ประเทศไทย

เริงศักดิ์ ทองแก้ว เป็นทนายความว่าความในศาลที่มีชื่อเสียงในภาค
ตะวันออกเฉียงเหนือ เริงศักดิ์จบการศึกษาจากคณะนิติศาสตร์มหาวิทยาลัยรามคำแหง
ขณะที่ศึกษาอยู่นั้น เขาได้เป็นประธานของหลายชมรม และก่อนที่จะได้เปิดสำนักงาน
กฎหมายของตนเอง เริงศักดิ์ ได้ทำงานที่กรุงเทพฯเป็นเวลาสามปีกับบริษัทแห่งหนึ่งที่
เชี่ยวชาญด้านกฎหมายสำหรับชาวต่างชาติ นอกจากนั้นยังได้เป็นผู้จัดรายการตอบปัญหา
ด้านกฎหมายให้กับชาวบ้านทางวิทยุ ขณะนี้เริงศักดิ์ ดำรงตำแหน่งเป็นประธานสภา
ทนายความจังหวัดยโสธรซึ่งเป็นองค์กรที่ให้คำปรึกษาทางด้านกฎหมายโดยไม่คิดค่าบริการ

Titles from Paiboon Publishing

Title: Thai for Beginners
Author: Benjawan Poomsan Becker ©1995
Description: Designed for either self-study or classroom use. Teaches all four language skills- speaking, listening (when used in conjunction with the cassette tapes), reading and writing. Offers clear, easy, step-by-step instruction building on what has been previously learned. Used by many Thai temples and institutes in America and Thailand. Cassettes & CD available. Paperback. 270 pages. 6" x 8.5"
Book   US$12.95   Stock # 1001B
Two CDs   US$20.00   Stock # 1001CD

Title: Thai for Travelers (Pocket Book Version)
Author: Benjawan Poomsan Becker ©2006
Description: The best Thai phrase book you can find. It contains thousands of useful words and phrases for travelers in many situations. The phrases are practical and up-to-date and can be used instantly. The CD that accompanies the book will help you improve your pronunciation and expedite your Thai language learning. You will be able to speak Thai in no time! Full version on mobile phones and PocketPC also available at www.vervata.com.
Book & CD   US$15.00   Stock # 1022BCD

Title: Thai for Intermediate Learners
Author: Benjawan Poomsan Becker ©1998
Description: The continuation of Thai for Beginners Users are expected to be able to read basic Thai language. There is transliteration when new words are introduced. Teaches reading, writing and speaking at a higher level. Keeps students interested with cultural facts about Thailand. Helps expand your Thai vocabulary in a systematic way. Paperback. 220 pages. 6" x 8.5"
Book   US$12.95   Stock # 1002B
Two CDs   US$15.00   Stock # 1002CD

Title: Thai for Advanced Readers
Author: Benjawan Poomsan Becker ©2000
Description: A book that helps students practice reading Thai at an advanced level. It contains reading exercises, short essays, newspaper articles, cultural and historical facts about Thailand and miscellaneous information about the Thai language. Students need to be able to read basic Thai. Paperback. 210 pages. 6" x 8.5"
Book   US$12.95   Stock # 1003B
Two CDs   US$15.00   Stock # 1003CD

Title: Thai-English, English-Thai Dictionary for Non-Thai Speakers
Author: Benjawan Poomsan Becker ©2002
Description: Designed to help English speakers communicate in Thai. It is equally useful for those who can read the Thai alphabet and those who can't. Most Thai-English dictionaries either use Thai script exclusively for the Thai entries (making them difficult for westerners to use) or use only phonetic transliteration (making it impossible to look up a word in Thai script). This dictionary solves these problems. You will find most of the vocabulary you are likely to need in everyday life, including basic, cultural, political and scientific terms. Paperback. 658 pages. 4.1" x 5.6"
Book   US$15.00   Stock # 1008B

Title: Improving Your Thai Pronunciation
Author: Benjawan Poomsan Becker ©2003
Description: Designed to help foreingers maximize their potential in pronouncing Thai words and enhance their Thai listening and speaking skills. Students will find that they have more confidence in speaking the language and can make themselves understood better. The book and the CDs are made to be used in combination. The course is straight forward, easy to follow and compact. Paperback. 48 pages. 5" x 7.5" + One-hour CD
Book & CD   US$15.00   Stock # 1011BCD

Title: Thai for Lovers
Author: Nit & Jack Ajee ©1999
Description: An ideal book for lovers. A short cut to romantic communication in Thailand. There are useful sentences with their Thai translations throughout the book. You won't find any Thai language book more fun and user-friendly.
Rated R! Paperback. 190 pages. 6" x 8.5"
Book   US$13.95   Stock #: 1004B
Two CDs   US$17.00   Stock #: 1004CD

Title: Thai for Gay Tourists
Author: Saksit Pakdeesiam ©2001
Description: The ultimate language guide for gay and bisexual men visiting Thailand. Lots of gay oriented language, culture, commentaries and other information. Instant sentences for convenient use by gay visitors. Fun and sexy. The best way to communicate with your Thai gay friends and partners! Rated R! Paperback. 220 pages. 6" x 8.5"
Book   US$13.95   Stock # 1007B
Two Tape Set   US$17.00   Stock # 1007T

Title: Thailand Fever
Authors: Chris Pirazzi and Vitida Vasant ©2005
Description: A road map for Thai-Western relationships. The must-have relationship guide-book which lets each of you finally express complex issues of both cultures. Thailand Fever is an astonishing, one-of-a-kind, bilingual expose of the cultural secrets that are the key to a smooth Thai-Western relationship. Paperback. 258 pages. 6" x 8.5"
Book   US$15.95   Stock # 1017B

Title: Thai-English, English-Thai Software Dictionary
for Palm OS PDAs With Search-by-Sound
Authors: Benjawan Poomsan Becker and Chris Pirazzi ©2003
Description: This software dictionary provides instant access to 21,000 English, Phonetic and Thai Palm OS PDA with large, clear fonts and everyday vocabulary. If you're not familiar with the Thai alphabet, you can also look up Thai words by their sounds. Perfect for the

casual traveller or the dedicated Thai learner. Must have a Palm OS PDA and access to the Internet in order to use this product.
Book & CD-ROM   US$39.95   Stock # 1013BCD-ROM

Title: Thai for Beginners Software
Authors: Benjawan Poomsan Becker and Dominique Mayrand ©2004
Description: Best Thai language software available in the market! Designed especially for non-romanized written Thai to help you to rapidly improve your listening and reading skills! Over 3,000 recordings of both male and female voices. The content is similar to the book Thai for Beginners, but with interactive exercises and much more instantly useful words and phrases. Multiple easy-to-read font styles and sizes. Super-crisp enhanced text with romanized transliteration which can be turned on or off for all items.
Book & CD-ROM   US$40.00   Stock # 1016BCD-ROM

Title: Lao-English, English-Lao Dictionary for Non-Lao Speakers
Authors: Benjawan Poomsan Becker & Khamphan Mingbuapha ©2003
Description: Designed to help English speakers communicate in Lao. This practical dictionary is useful both in Laos and in Northeast Thailand. Students can use it without having to learn the Lao alphabet. However, there is a comprehensive introduction to the Lao writing system and pronunciation. The transliteration system is the same as that used in Paiboon Publishing's other books. It contains most of the vocabulary used in everyday life, including basic, cultural, political and scientific terms. Paperback. 780 pages. 4.1" x 5.6"
Book   US$15.00   Stock # 1010B

Title: Lao for Beginners
Authors: Buasawan Simmala and Benjawan Poomsan Becker ©2003
Description: Designed for either self-study or classroom use. Teaches all four language skills- speaking, listening (when used in conjunction with the audio), reading and writing. Offers clear, easy, step-by-step instruction building on what has been previously learned. Paperback. 292 pages. 6" x 8.5"
Book   US$12.95   Stock # 1012B
Three CDs   US$20.00   Stock # 1012CD

Title: Cambodian for Beginners
Author: Richard K. Gilbert ©2008
Description: Designed for either self-study or classroom use. Teaches all four language skills- speaking, listening (when used in conjunction with the CDs), reading and writing. Offers clear, easy, step-by-step instruction building on what has been previously learned. Paperback. 290 pages. 6" x 8.5"
Book   US$15.00   Stock # 1015B
Three CDs   US$20.00   Stock # 1015CD

Title: Burmese for Beginners
Author: Gene Mesher ©2006
Description: Designed for either self-study or classroom use. Teaches all four language skills- speaking, listening (when used in conjunction with the CDs), reading and writing. Offers clear, easy, step-by-step instruction building on what has been previously learned. Paperback. 320 pages. 6" x 8.5"
Book   US$12.95   Stock # 1019B
Three CDs   US$20.00   Stock # 1019CD

Title: Vietnamese for Beginners
Author: Jake Catlett ©2008
Description: Designed for either self-study or classroom use. Teaches all four language skills- speaking, listening (when used in conjunction with the CDs), reading and writing. Offers clear, easy, step-by-step instruction building on what has been previously learned. Paperback. 292 pages. 6" x 8.5"
Book   US$15.00   Stock # 1020B
Three CDs   US$20.00   Stock # 1020CD

Title: Tai Go No Kiso
Author: Benjawan Poomsan Becker ©2002
Description: Thai for Japanese speakers. Japanese version of Thai for Beginners. Paperback. 262 pages. 6" x 8.5"
Book   US$12.95   Stock # 1009B
Three Tape Set   US$20.00   Stock # 1009T

Title: Thai fuer Anfaenger
Author: Benjawan Poomsan Becker ©2000
Description: Thai for German speakers. German version of Thai for Beginners. Paperback. 245 pages. 6" x 8.5"
Book   US$13.95   Stock # 1005B
Two CDs   US$20.00   Stock # 1005CD

Title: Practical Thai Conversation DVD Volume 1
Author: Benjawan Poomsan Becker ©2005
Description: This new media for learning Thai comes with a booklet and a DVD. You will enjoy watching and listening to this program and learn the Thai language in a way you have never done before. Use it on your TV, desktop or laptop. The course is straight forward, easy to follow and compact. A must-have for all Thai learners! DVD and Paperback, 65 pages 4.8" x 7.1"
Book & DVD   US$15.00   Stock # 1018BDVD

Title: Practical Thai Conversation DVD Volume 2
Author: Benjawan Poomsan Becker ©2006
Description: Designed for intermediate Thai learners! This new media for learning Thai comes with a booklet and a DVD. You will enjoy watching and listening to this program and learn the Thai language in a way you have never done before. Use it on your TV, desktop or laptop. The course is straight forward, easy to follow and compact. DVD and Paperback, 60 pages 4.8" x 7.1"
Book & DVD   US$15.00   Stock # 1021BDVD

Title: A Chameleon's Tale - True   Stories of a Global Refugee -
Author: Mohezin Tejani ©2006
Description: A heart touching real life   Story of Mo Tejani, a global refugee who spends thirty four years searching five continents for a country he could call home. Enjoy the ride through numerous countries in Asia, Africa, North and South America. His adventurous   Stories are unique – distinctly different from other travelers' tales. Recommended item from Paiboon Publishing for avid readers worldwide. Paperback. 257 pages. 5" x 7.5"
Book   US$19.95   Stock #1024B

Title: Thai Touch
Author: Richard Rubacher ©2006
Description: The good and the bad of the Land of Smiles are told with a comic touch. The book focuses on the spiritual and mystical side of the magical kingdom as well as its dark side. The good and the bad are told with a comic touch. The Sex Baron, the Naughty & Nice Massage Parlors, the "Bangkok haircut" and Bar Girls & the Pendulum are contrasted with tales of the Thai Forrest Gump, the Spiritual Banker of Thailand and the 72-year old woman whose breasts spout miracle milk. Paperback. 220 pages. 5" x 7.5"
Book   US$19.95   Stock #1024B

Title: How to Buy Land and Build a House in Thailand
Author: Philip Bryce ©2006
Description: This book contains essential information for anyone contemplating buying or leasing land and building a house in Thailand. Subjects covered: land ownership options, land titles, taxes, permits, lawyers, architects and builders. Also includes English/Thai building words and phrases and common Thai building techniques. Learn how to build your dream house in Thailand that is well made, structurally sound and nicely finished. Paperback. 6" x 8.5"
Book   US$19.95   Stock #1025B

Title: Retiring in Thailand
Authors: Philip Bryce and Sunisa Wongdee Terlecky ©2007
Description: A very useful guide for those who are interested in retiring in Thailand. It contains critical information for retirees, such as how to get a retirement visa, banking, health care, renting and buying property, everyday life issues and other important retirement factors. It also lists Thailand's top retirement locations. It's a must for anyone considering living the good life in the Land of Smiles. 6" x 8.5"
Book   US$19.95   Stock #1026B

Title: How to Establish a Successful Business in Thailand
Author: Philip Wylie ©2007
Description: This is the perfect book for anyone thinking of starting or buying a business in Thailand. This book will save readers lots of headaches, time and money. This guide is full of information on how to run a business in Thailand including practical tips by successful foreign business people from different trades, such as guest house, bar trade, e-commerce, export and restaurant. This is an essential guide for all foreigners thinking of doing business - or improving their business - in Thailand.
Book   US$19.95   Stock #1031B

Title: Speak Like A Thai Volume 1
-Contemporary Thai Expressions-
Author: Benjawan Poomsan Becker ©2007
Description: This series of books and CDs is a collection of numerous words and expressions used by modern Thai speakers. It will help you to understand colloquial Thai and to express yourself naturally. You will not find these phases in most textbooks. It's a language course that all Thai learners have been waiting for. Impress your Thai friends with the real spoken Thai. Lots of fun. Good for students of all levels.
Book & CD   US$15.00   Stock # 1028BCD

Title: Speak Like A Thai Volume 2
-Thai Slang and Idioms-
Author: Benjawan Poomsan Becker ©2007
Description: This volume continues the fun of learning the real Thai language. It can be used independently. However, you should be comfortable speaking the Thai phrases from the first volume before you use this one. You will not find these words and phases in any textbooks. It's a language course that all Thai learners have been waiting for. Impress your Thai friends even more. Lots of fun. Good for students of all levels.
Book & CD   US$15.00   Stock # 1029BCD

Title: Speak Like A Thai Volume 3
-Thai Proverbs and Sayings-
Author: Benjawan Poomsan Becker ©2007
Description: The third volume is an excellent supplementary resource for all Thai learners. Common Thai proverbs and sayings listed in the book with the literal translations will help you understand Thai ways of thinking that are differnt from yours. You can listen to these proverbs and sayings over and over on the CD. Sprinkle them here and there in your conversation. Your Thai friend will be surprised and appreciate your insight into Thai culture. Good for intermdiate and advanced students, but beginners can use it for reference.
Book & CD   US$15.00   Stock # 1030BCD

Title: Speak Like a Thai Volume 4
-Heart Words-
Author: Benjawan Poomsan Becker ©2008
Description: "Heart" Words contains 300 common contemporary "heart" words and phrases. They are recorded on the CD and explained in the booklet with a brief translation, a literal translation and used in a sample phrase or sentence. More than a hundred bonus "heart" words are included in the booklet for your reference. Listen and learn how Thai people express their feelings and thoughts. You will gain significant insight about the Thai people and their social contexts.
Book & CD   US$15.00   Stock # 1033BCD

Title: Speak Like a Thai Volume 5
-Northeastern Dialect-
Author: Benjawan Poomsan Becker ©2008
Description: Northeastern Dialect contains 500 Isaan words and phrases which have been carefully chosen from real life situations. They are recorded on the CD and explained in the booklet with a brief translation and a literal translation when needed. Throughout the book there are also lists of many Isaan words that are different from standard Thai. This is a fun program that will bring a smile to the face of your Isaan friends.
Book & CD   US$15.00   Stock # 1034BCD

Title: Thai Law for Foreigners
Author: Ruengsak Thongkaew and Benjawan Poomsan ©2008
Description: Thai law made easy for foreigners. This unique book includes information regarding immigration, family, property, civil and criminal law used in Thailand. Very useful for both visitors and those who live in Thailand. Written by an experienced Thai trial lawyer. It contains both the Thai text and full English translation.
Book $21.95   Stock #1032B